THE CAMBRIDGE COMPANION TO RAPHAEL

This companion volume provides a timely reassessment of Raphael, the rare painter who has never gone out of fashion, and addresses the interests of recent scholarship, which has changed the focus from concerns with attribution and definition of the artist's style and the High Renaissance to more practical matters. Essays in this volume examine the intellectual and cultural history of sixteenth-century Rome and Florence that have made it possible to set Raphael in the context of his patrons and his other contemporaries. They demonstrate Raphael's considerable skills as the manager of the largest workshop of his day, one that provided a model for many artists who followed him. An understanding of Raphael's working methods and workshop practice has led to a new appreciation for the premium placed on invention that developed during the course of the sixteenth century. Also considered are the diffusion of Raphael's style throughout Europe and changing tastes in the restoration of his paintings.

Marcia B. Hall is Professor of Art History at Temple University in Philadelphia. A scholar of Italian Renaissance painting, she is the author of numerous publications, including *After Raphael: Painting in Central Italy in the Sixteenth Century* and editor of *Michelangelo's "Last Judgment."*

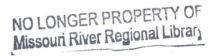

THE CAMBRIDGE COMPANION TO
Raphael

Edited by

Marcia B. Hall
Temple University

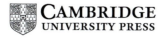

CAMBRIDGE UNIVERSITY PRESS
Cambridge, New York, Melbourne, Madrid, Cape Town, Singapore, São Paulo, Delhi

Cambridge University Press
32 Avenue of the Americas, New York, NY 10013-2473, USA

www.cambridge.org
Information on this title: www.cambridge.org/9780521003964

First published 2005
First paperback edition 2008

Printed in Hong Kong

A catalog record for this publication is available from the British Library.

Library of Congress Cataloging in Publication Data
The Cambridge companion to Raphael / edited by Marcia B. Hall.
       p. cm. – (Cambridge companions to the history of art)
       Includes bibliographical references and index.
       ISBN 0-521-80809-X
       1. Raphael, 1483-1520 – Criticism and interpretation. 2. Art, Italian – 16th century.
        3. Art, Renaissance – Italy. I. Raphael, 1483-1520. II. Hall, Marcia B. III. Series.
       N6923.R3C36   2005
       759.5 – dc22   2004051921

ISBN 978-0-521-80809-5 hardback
ISBN 978-0-521-00396-4 paperback

*Dedicated to the memory
of John Shearman,
1931–2003.*

We all learned from him.

Contents

Illustrations

FIGURES

Contributors

Costanza Barbieri is Assistant Professor of Art History at the Accademia di Belle Arti of Naples. She is the author of *Specchio di virtù. Il consorzio della Vergine e gli affreschi di Lorenzo Lotto in San Michele al Pozzo Bianco* (2000), *Notturno Sublime. Sebastiano e Michelangelo nella Pietà di Viterbo.* Exh. Cat. (2004), and coauthor of *Santa Maria in Vallicella. Chiesa Nuova* (1995). She has also published articles on Lotto, Pordenone, and Sebastiano del Piombo, on whom she is preparing a book.

Patricia Emison has taught at the University of New Hampshire for fifteen years. She is the author of *Low and High Style in Italian Renaissance Art* (1997) and of various articles on Raphael and Marcantonio. Her book *Making Michelangelo Divine* (Leiden: Brill, 2004) has appeared recently.

Carl Goldstein (Professor of Art at the University of North Carolina, Greensboro) is the author of *Visual Fact over Verbal Fiction: A Study of the Carracci and the Criticism, Theory, and Practice of Painting in Renaissance and Baroque Italy* (Cambridge University Press, 1988) and *Teaching Art: Academies and Schools from Vasari to Albers* (Cambridge University Press, 1996). Raphael's art and reputation figure prominently in both.

Marcia Hall is Professor of Art History at Temple University. She is author of *Renovation and Counter-Reformation: Vasari and Duke Cosimo in Santa Maria Novella and Santa Croce, 1565–77* (1979); *Color and Meaning: Practice and Theory in Renaissance Painting* (1992); *After Raphael: Painting in Central Italy in the Sixteenth Century* (1999), and *Michelangelo. The Frescoes of the Sistine Chapel* (2002). She has edited, among other books, *The Princeton Raphael Symposium* (with John Shearman, 1990); and *Raphael's School of Athens* (1997).

Cathleen Hoeniger (Associate Professor of Art History at Queen's University in Canada) researches the afterlife of Italian medieval and Renaissance images. Her publications include *The Renovation of Paintings in Tuscany, 1250–1500* (1995), more recent articles in the *Zeitschrift für Kunstgeschichte* and the *Journal of the American Institute for Conservation*, and a piece on Correggio for John Shearman's festschrift, *Coming About....*

Linda Pellecchia is Associate Professor at the University of Delaware. She is currently working on a book titled *Constructing Identity: Giuliano da Sangallo's Gondi Palace (1490–1870)*. Professor Pellecchia has published articles in scholarly journals and exhibition catalogues on such topics as the Renaissance interpretation of Vitruvius's *De architectura*, Bartolomeo Scala's Florentine palace, and Giuliano da Sangallo's Medici villa in via Laura. Her most recent article, "Untimely Death, Unwilling Heirs: The Early History of Giuliano da Sangallo's Unfinished Palace for Giuliano Gondi," will appear in *Mitteilungen des Kunsthistorischen Institutes in Florenz*.

Giovanna Perini is Professor in the History of Art Literature and Director of the Institute of Art History and Aesthetics at the University of Urbino, Italy. Her publications are chiefly concerned with Bolognese and northern Italian art literature and collecting, c. 1500–1800, and British art and art literature of the eighteenth century. She has published *Gli scritti dei Carracci* (Bologna, 1990); *Giovanni Ludovico Bianconi's scritti tedeschi* (Bologna, 1998), and has translated Meyer Schapiro, *Per una semiotica del linguaggio visivo* (Rome, 2002).

Sheryl E. Reiss is currently Senior Research Associate in the Office of the Vice-Provost for Research at Cornell University, where she has worked since 1993. Along with David Wilkin she was the coeditor of and a contributor to *Beyond Isabella: Secular Women Patrons of Art in Renaissance Italy* (2001). She is also the coeditor of a two-volume collection of essays, *The Pontificate of Clement VII: History, Politics, Culture* (Aldershot: Ashgate, 2005). She is currently working on a book titled *The Making of a Medici Maecenas: Giulio de' Medici (Pope Clement VII) as Patron of Art.*

Ingrid D. Rowland is Andrew W. Mellon Professor in the Humanities at the American Academy in Rome. Her books include *The Culture of the High Renaissance* (Cambridge, 1998), *Vitruvius: Ten Books on Architecture* (Cambridge, 1999, with Thomas Noble Howe), and *The Correspondence of Agostino Chigi* (Vatican Library, 2001). She also writes for *The New York Review of Books, The New Republic,* and the *London Review of Books*.

Bette Talvacchia is Professor of Art History at the University of Connecticut. Her publications, which deal primarily with Italian art of the sixteenth century with a focus on themes involving court art, patronage, and gender issues, include *Taking Positions. On the Erotic in Renaissance Culture* (1999). She has been a member of the Institute for Advanced Study at Princeton; a Senior Fellow at the Center for Advanced Study in the Visual Arts in Washington, D.C.; Andrew W. Mellon Fellow at the Metropolitan Museum of Art; and the Robert Lehman Visiting Professor at Villa I Tatti, the Harvard University Center for Italian Renaissance Studies in Florence.

Linda Wolk-Simon is an Associate Curator at the Metropolitan Museum of Art and also the reviews editor of the journal *Master Drawings.* She has published extensively on Raphael and his circle, particularly Perino del Vaga, and on Italian Old Master drawings. She is the author of *Domenico Tiepolo: Drawing, Prints and Paintings in the Metropolitan Museum of Art,* and *Sixteenth-Century Italian Drawings in New York Collections* (with William Griswold). Her articles and reviews have appeared in *Apollo, Art Bulletin, Artibus et Historiae* and *Master Drawings.*

Jeryldene M. Wood, Associate Professor of Art History at the University of Illinois, Urbana-Champaign, is the author of *Women, Art, and Spirituality: The Poor Clares of Early Modern Italy* (1996) and the editor of the *Cambridge Companion to Piero della Francesca* (2002). Her articles have appeared in *Art History, Renaissance Quarterly*, and *Konstihistorisk Tidskrift.*

Joanna Woods-Marsden is Professor of Art History at the University of California, Los Angeles. Her publications include *The Gonzaga of Mantua and Pisanello's Arthurian Frescoes* (1988) and *Renaissance Self-Portraiture: The Visual Construction of Identity and the Social Status of the Artist* (1998), as well as numerous articles, most recently on Renaissance portraiture. She is currently writing a book tentatively titled *Portrait of the Renaissance Lady: Visual Construction of Gender Difference.*

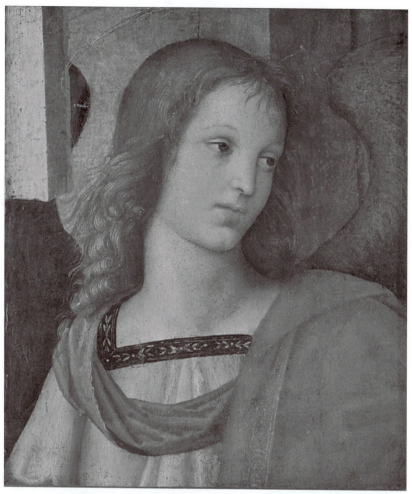

PLATE 1. Raphael, *Angel with Inscription,* from the Saint Nicholas of Tolentino Altarpiece, Paris, Louvre. Photo: Réunion des Musées Nationaux/Art Resource, NY.

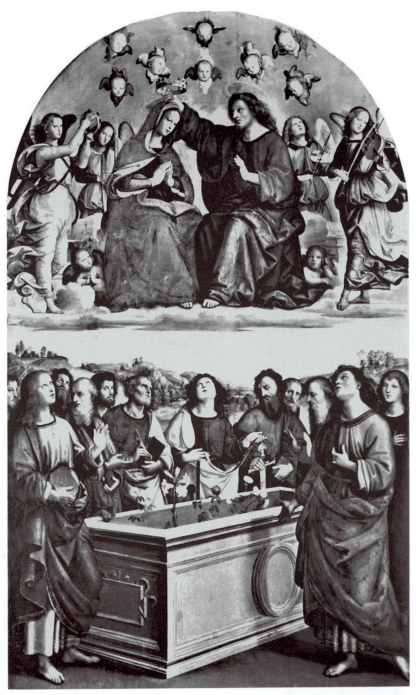

PLATE 2. Raphael, *Coronation of the Virgin*, Vatican, Pinacoteca. Photo: Alinari/Art Resource, NY.

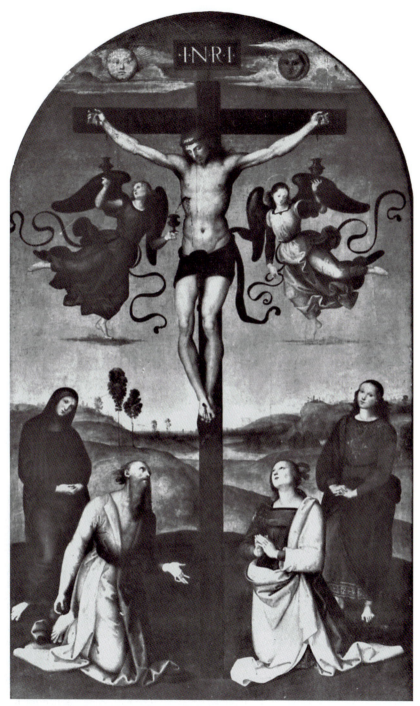

PLATE 3. Raphael, *Mond Crucifixion* (*Gavari Crucifixion*), London, National Gallery. Photo: Foto Marburg/Art Resource, NY.

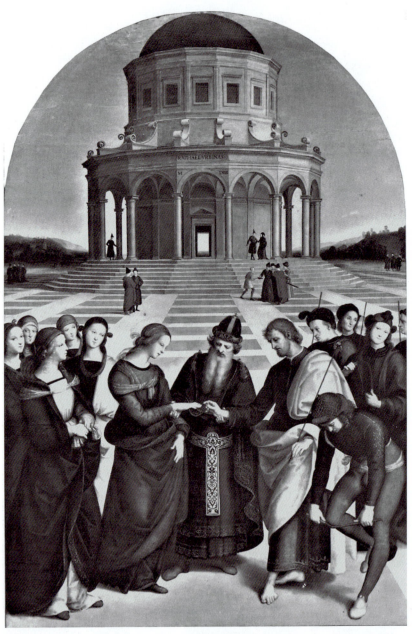

PLATE 4. Raphael, *Marriage of the Virgin*, Milan, Brera. Photo: Alinari/Art Resource, NY.

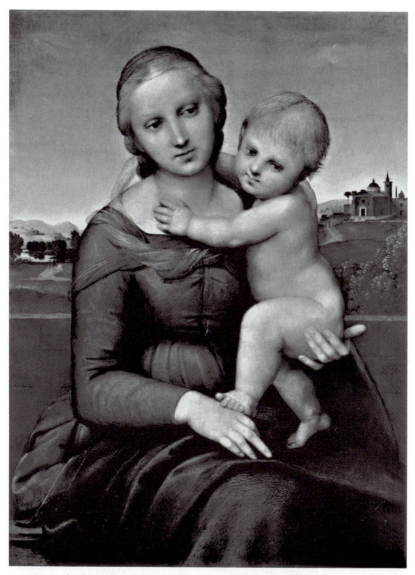

PLATE 5. Raphael, *Small Cowper Madonna*, Widener Collection. Photograph © 2002 Board of Trustees, Washington, D.C., National Gallery of Art.

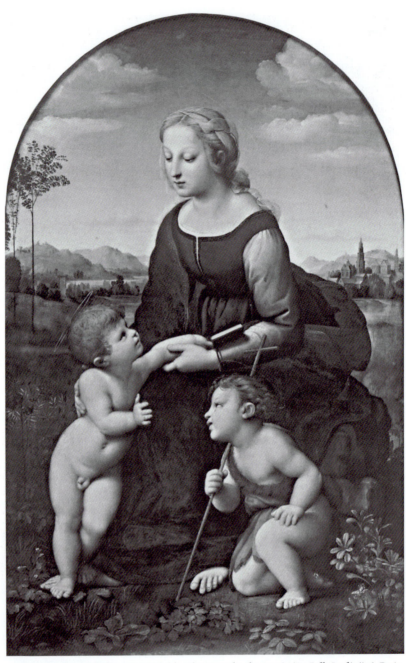

PLATE 6. Raphael, *Madonna and Child with Saint John the Baptist* (*La Belle Jardinière*), Paris, Louvre. Photo: Alinari/Art Resource, NY.

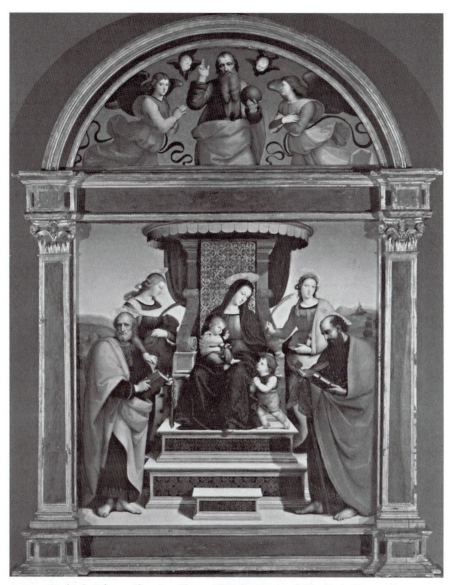

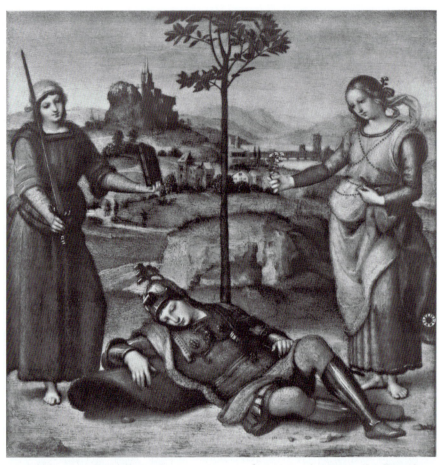

PLATE 8. Raphael, *The Knight's Dream* (*Dream of Scipio*), London, National Gallery. Photo: Alinari/Art Resource, NY.

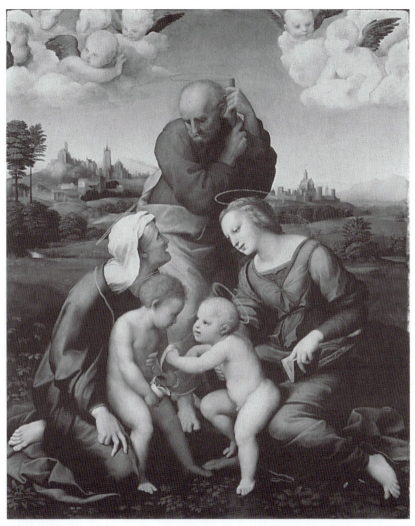

PLATE 9. Raphael, *Canigiani Holy Family*, Munich, Alte Pinakothek. Photo: Scala/Art Resource, NY.

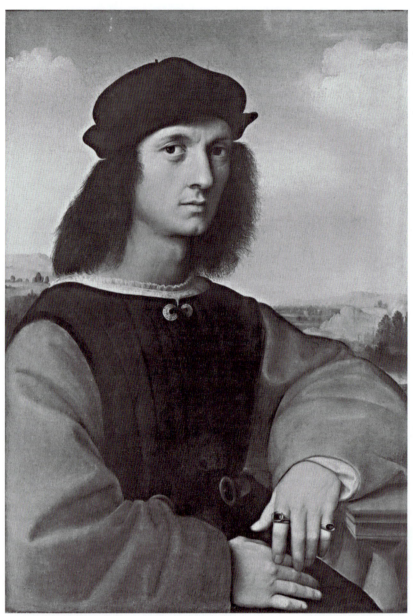

PLATE 10. Raphael, *Portrait of Angelo Doni*, Florence, Pitti Gallery. Photo: Alinari/Art Resource, NY.

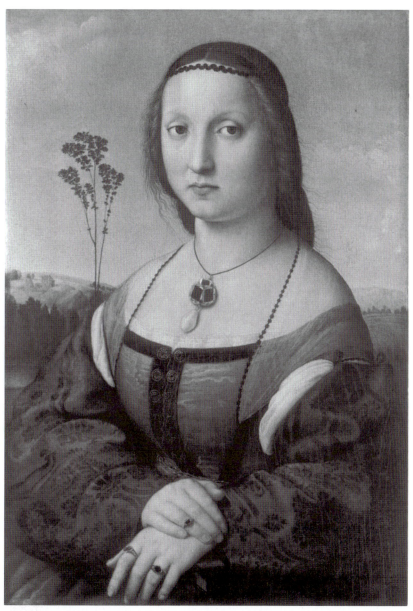

PLATE 11. Raphael, *Portrait of Maddalena Strozzi*, Florence, Pitti Gallery. Photo: Alinari/Art Resource, NY.

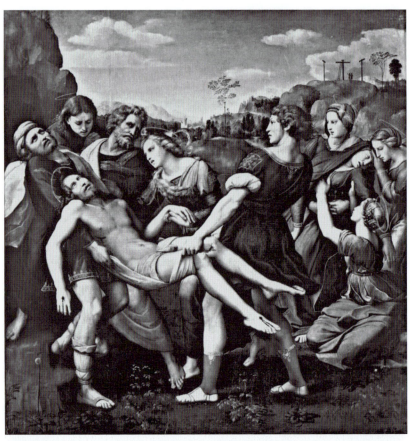

PLATE 12. Raphael, *Entombment of Christ*, Rome, Galleria Borghese. Photo: Alinari/Art Resource, NY.

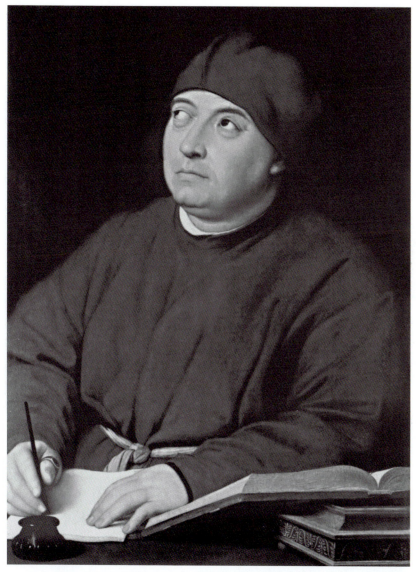

PLATE 13. Raphael, *Portrait of Tommaso Inghirami*, Florence, Pitti Gallery. Photo: Alinari/Art Resource, NY.

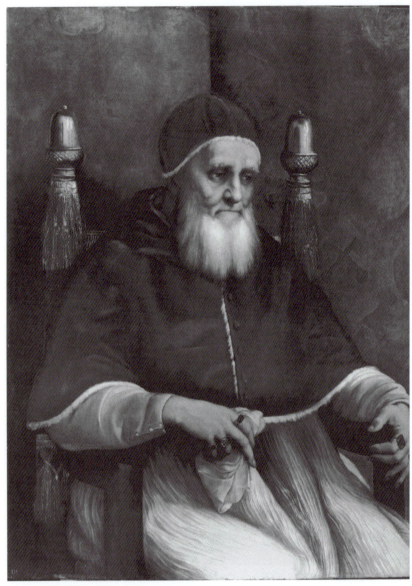

PLATE 14. Raphael, *Portrait of Pope Julius II* (Giuliano della Rovere), London, National Gallery. Photo: National Gallery, London.

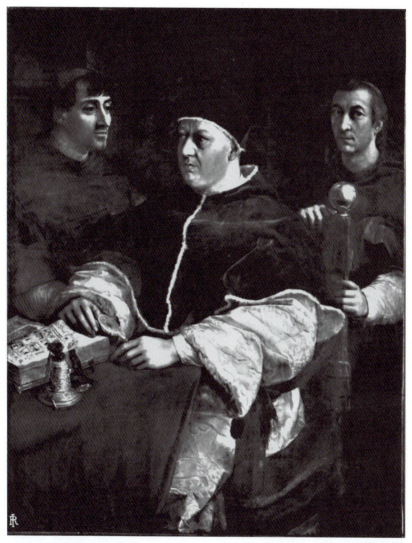

PLATE 15. Raphael, *Portrait of Pope Leo X with Two Cardinals*, Florence, Uffizi Gallery. Photo: Alinari/Art Resource, NY.

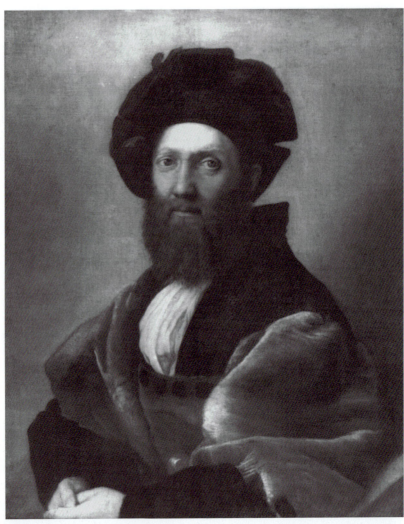

PLATE 16. Raphael, *Portrait of Baldassare Castiglione*, Paris, Louvre. Photo: Réunion des Musées Nationaux/Art Resource, NY.

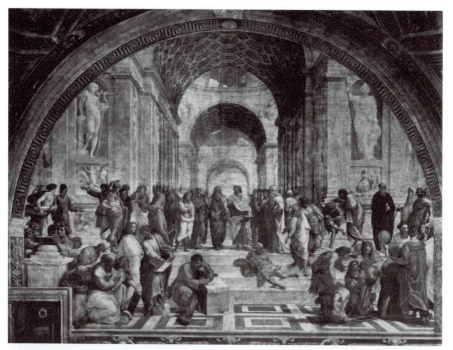

PLATE 17. Raphael, *School of Athens*, Vatican Palace, Stanza della Segnatura. Photo: Alinari/Art Resource, NY.

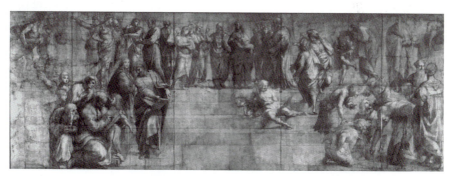

PLATE 18. Raphael, cartoon, *School of Athens*, Milan, Ambrosiana. Photo: Alinari/Art Resource, NY.

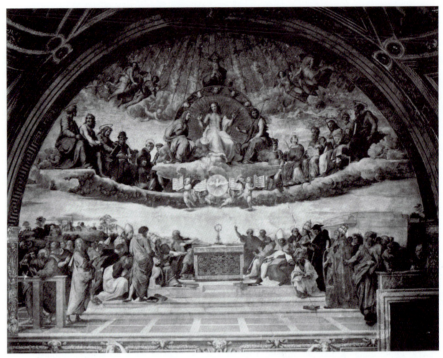

PLATE 19. Raphael, *Disputa*, Vatican Palace, Stanza della Segnatura. Photo: Alinari/Art Resource, NY.

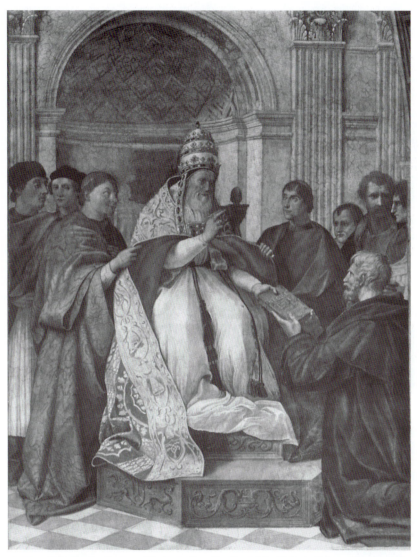

PLATE 20. Raphael, *Gregory IX Approving the Decretals*, Vatican Palace, Stanza della Segnatura. Photo: Alinari/Art Resource, NY.

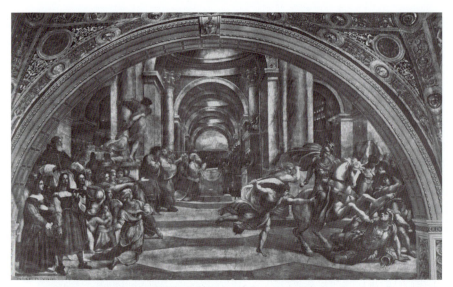

PLATE 21. Raphael, *Expulsion of Heliodorus*, Vatican Palace, Stanza d'Eliodoro. Photo: Alinari/Art Resource, NY.

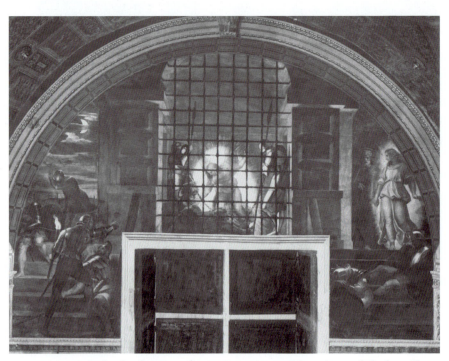

PLATE 22. Raphael, *Liberation of Saint Peter*, Vatican Palace, Stanza d'Eliodoro. Photo: Alinari/Art Resource, NY.

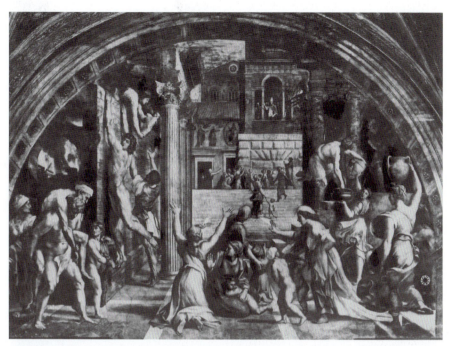

PLATE 23. Raphael, *Fire in the Borgo*, Vatican Palace, Stanza dell'Incendio. Photo: Alinari/Art Resource, NY.

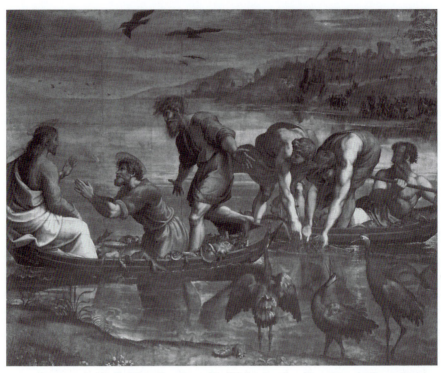

PLATE 24. Raphael, *Miraculous Draught of Fishes*, London, Victoria and Albert Museum. Photo: Art Resource, NY.

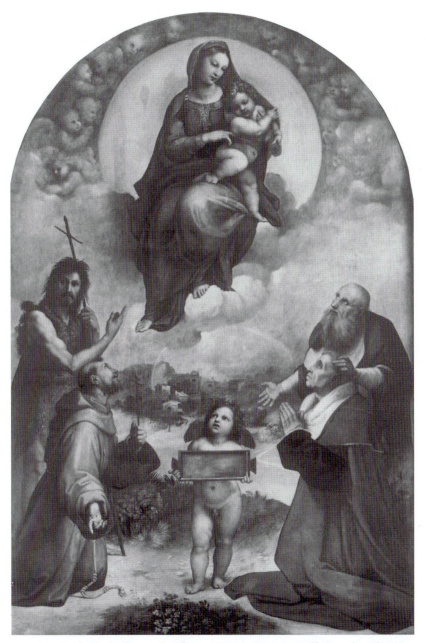

PLATE 25. Raphael, *Madonna di Foligno*, Vatican, Pinacoteca. Photo: Alinari/Art Resource, NY.

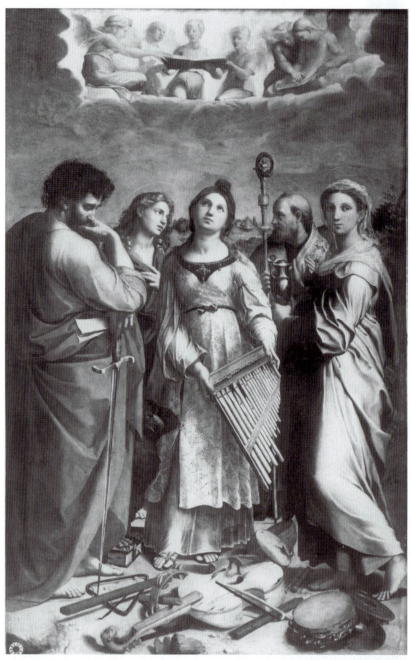

PLATE 26. Raphael, *Saint Cecilia*, Bologna, Pinacoteca Nazionale. Photo: Alinari/Art Resource, NY.

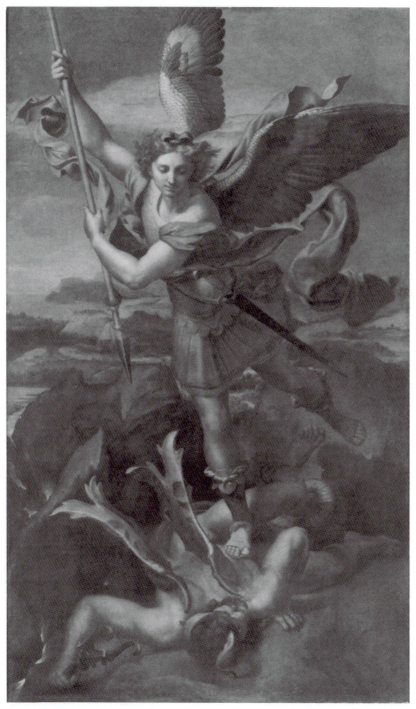

PLATE 27. Raphael, *Saint Michael*, Paris, Louvre. Photo: Réunion des Musées Nationaux/Art Resource, NY.

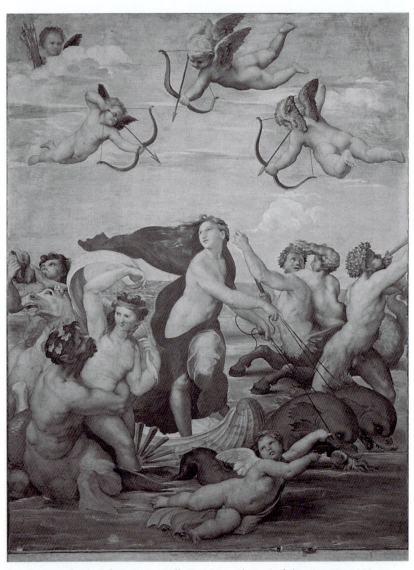

PLATE 28. Raphael, *Galatea*, Rome, Villa Farnesina. Photo: Scala/Art Resource, NY.

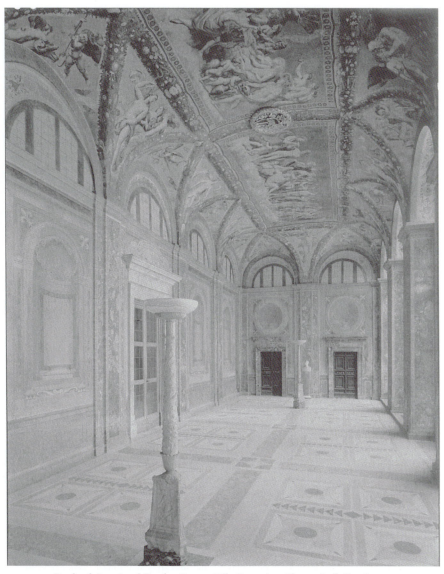

PLATE 29. Raphael, Loggia of Psyche, Rome, Villa Farnesina. Photo: Scala/Art Resource, NY.

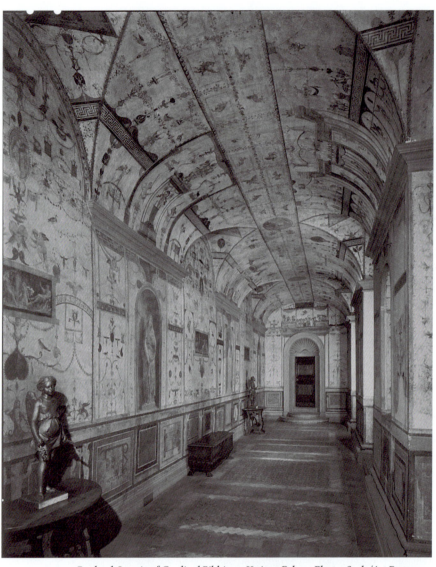

PLATE 30. Raphael, Loggia of Cardinal Bibbiena, Vatican Palace. Photo: Scala/Art Resource, NY.

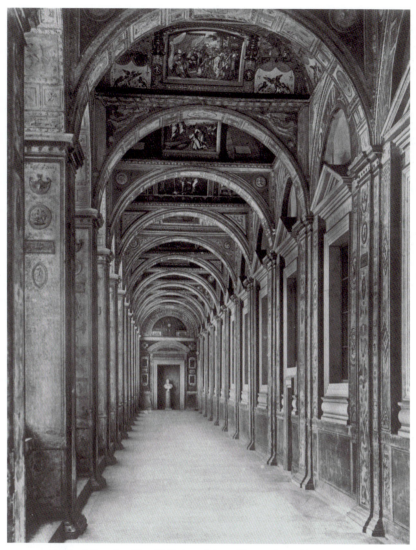

PLATE 31. Raphael, Loggia of Leo X, Vatican Palace. Photo: Alinari/Art Resource, NY.

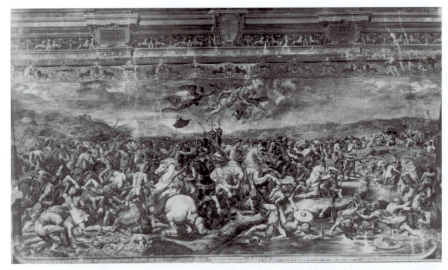

PLATE 32. Raphael, *Battle of the Milvian Bridge*, Vatican Palace, Sala di Costantino. Photo: Alinari/Art Resource, NY.

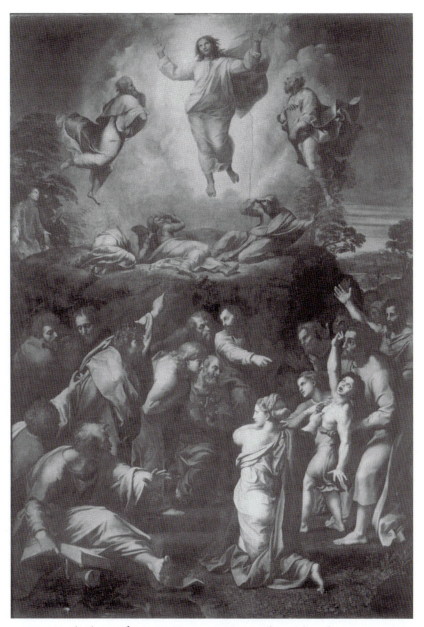

PLATE 33. Raphael, *Transfiguration*, Vatican, Pinacoteca. Photo: Alinari/Art Resource, NY.

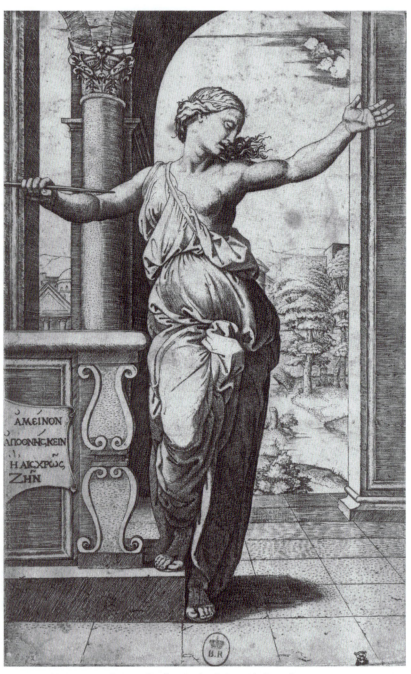

PLATE 34. Marcantonio Raimondi, after Raphael, *Lucretia* (B. 192), engraving.

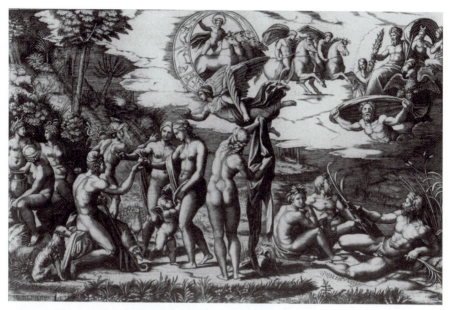

PLATE 35. Marcantonio Raimondi, after Raphael, *Judgment of Paris* (B. 245), engraving.

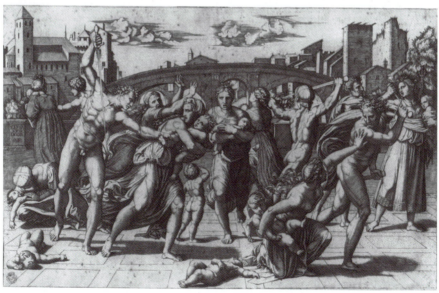

PLATE 36. Marcantonio Raimondi, after Raphael, *The Massacre of Innocents* (B. 20), engraving, Paris, Petit Palais, Musèe des Beaux Arts.

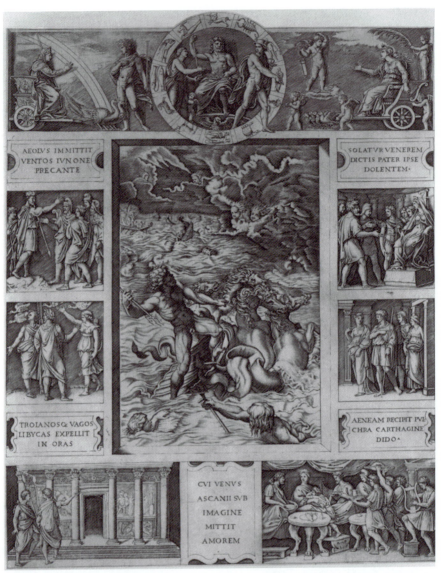

AEOLVS IMMITTIT VENTOS IVNONE PRECANTE

SOLATVR VENEREM DICTIS PATER IPSE DOLENTEM·

TROIANOSQ VAGOS LIBYCAS EXPELLIT IN ORAS

AENEAM RECIPIT PVL CHRA CARTHAGINE DIDO·

CVI VENVS ASCANII SVB IMAGINE MITTIT AMOREM

PLATE 37. Marcantonio Raimondi, after Raphael, *Quos Ego* (B. 352), engraving.

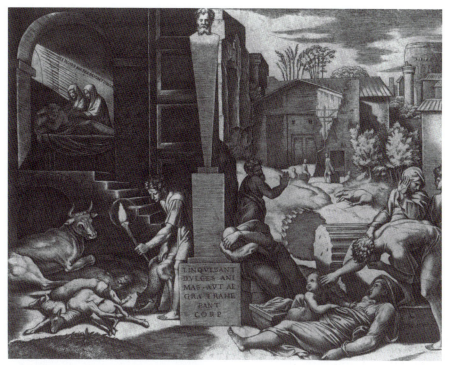

PLATE 38. Marcantonio Raimondi, after Raphael, *Il Morbetto* (B. 417), engraving, gift of W. G. Russell Allen, Washington, D.C., National Gallery of Art.

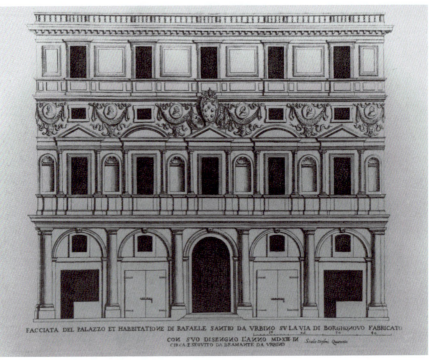

FACCIATA DEL PALAZZO ET HABBITATIONE DI RAFAELE SANTIO DA VRBINO SV LA VIA DI BORGHONOVO FABBRICATO
CON SVO DISENGNO L'ANNO MDXIII·IV Scala Dipini Quaranta
CIRCA E SEGVITO DA BRAMANTE DA VRBINO

PLATE 39. Pietro Ferrerio, Facade of Palazzo Branconio dell'Aquila by Raphael, in P. Ferrerio and G. B. Falda, *Nuovi disegni dell'architetture, e piante de palazzi di Roma.* Photo: University of Pennsylvania. Courtesy of the Anne and Jerome Fisher Fine Arts Library, University of Pennsylvania Library.

Introduction

Marcia B. Hall

Raphael is the rare painter who was never out of fashion. The closest he has ever come is the present reserved acknowledgment of his past glory. Even when he was criticized it was within the context that he was regarded as the nearly perfect paragon, as Giovanna Perini shows in her essay in this collection. Beginning early in his short life and continuing throughout the sixteenth century he continued to inspire new generations of successors. During his lifetime his generosity and geniality endeared him to patrons and pupils alike. After his death in 1520 his followers were able to learn his style, and it served as the fertile basis for their new inventions. This was in contrast to both his great contemporaries, Leonardo da Vinci and Michelangelo, who fostered slavish imitators but few, if any, followers with the freedom to develop their own art on the foundation of what they had learned from their master.

Raphael was born in Urbino, the son of Giovanni Santi, who was characterized by Vasari as a painter "of no great merit, but of good intelligence." Sometime after his father's death in 1494, Raphael went to Perugia to assist Perugino, the most renowned painter in central Italy at the time. There is debate among scholars about whether he went as an apprentice or later as a more mature assistant in the workshop. The two authors in this volume who touch on this question, Jeryldene Wood and Sheryl Reiss, disagree. How much Raphael learned from Perugino would be evident in his style for years to come. He was enlisted by another leading painter, Bernardino Pinturicchio, who must have been impressed with his skill in draftsmanship because he had Raphael draw some of the cartoons for frescoes he was executing in the Piccolomini Library in the Siena cathedral (commissioned in 1502). Raphael's first independently commissioned work was an altarpiece of *Saint Nicholas of Tolentino* (1500), which was later disassembled; parts are to be found in Capodimonte, Naples; Pinacoteca Civica, Brescia (see Fig. 30); and the Louvre, Paris (Plate 1). Among his early works he painted a *Crucifixion with Saints* (1503, Plate 3) and a *Coronation of the Virgin* (c. 1503–6, Plate 2), both very close in style to Perugino. During this period he received commissions from the court of Urbino, notably the precious *Saint George and the Dragon* (National Gallery of Art, Washington, D.C.), probably ordered when the duke was awarded the Order of the Garter in 1504, and he executed his version of the *Marriage of the Virgin* (Plate 4), which was both close to Perugino's model and a significant departure from it.

During these years Florence was suffering political upheaval in the wake of Savonarola as well as economic depression and so it would not have attracted a young and ambitious artist. In the summer of 1503, however, with the death of Cesare Borgia who had been laying siege to the city, all this changed.[1] The city government gave commissions in the next few months to Leonardo and Michelangelo to decorate the principal hall of the Palazzo Vecchio with frescoes of Florentine battles. Both artists were working on their cartoons when Raphael arrived in town the following year, no doubt eager to learn what he could from these two masters. Raphael spent the next four years based in Florence, reworking his Peruginesque style under their influence. From Leonardo he learned the blurred contours and gentle shadow of his sfumato; from Michelangelo he learned to broaden his figures and attend to the underlying anatomy, which he would continue to study from antique sculpture when he reached Rome.

It was during the Florentine period (1504–8) that Raphael worked on the series of Madonna and Child paintings for which he is famous, for example, the *Small Cowper Madonna* (Plate 5) and *La Belle Jardinière* (Plate 6). The most complex of this group is the five-figured *Canigiani Holy Family* (Plate 9); he was evidently striving for the kind of geometrical order and compositional unity that Leonardo had demonstrated in his *Madonna and Child with Saint Anne* (Paris, Louvre), on which Leonardo was working during these years. Raphael was also commissioned to paint several altarpieces and portraits, for example, the portraits of Angelo and Maddalena Doni (Plates 10 and 11). Especially in the pose of *Maddalena* one sees the influence of Leonardo's *Mona Lisa* (Louvre, Paris). In the *Colonna Altarpiece* (Plate 7) the lingering influence of Perugino is still evident, which then nearly vanishes by the time of the *Entombment* (1507, Plate 12), commissioned by Atalanta Baglione for an altar in Perugia. His assimilation of the lessons of Leonardo, Michelangelo, and even Fra Bartolomeo is apparent by the time of his *Madonna del Baldacchino*, at the end of his Florentine sojourn, his first large commission for a Florentine church (for Santo Spirito; unfinished, today in the Pitti Gallery, Florence).

According to Vasari, Donato Bramante, a distant relative of Raphael, sent Raphael word that Pope Julius II had work for him decorating the papal apartment at the Vatican Palace. Raphael abandoned what he was working on and transferred to Rome. Frescoing the Stanza della Segnatura would occupy the painter until 1511, when Pope Julius was pleased enough with his accomplishment to assign him the adjacent room, the Stanza d'Eliodoro. Julius died before its completion, but his successor, Leo X, ordered Raphael to continue and subsequently assigned him two more rooms, the Stanza dell'Incendio and the Sala di Costantino. Very quickly Raphael became popular with the Roman patrons, and he had more work of all genres than he could do. He became the city's leading portraitist, executing the portraits of both Popes Julius (Plate 14) and Leo (Plate 15), as discussed in Joanna Woods-Marsden's essay. Altarpieces include the *Madonna di Foligno*, originally for the high altar of Santa Maria in Aracoeli (Plate 25), the famous and familiar *Sistine Madonna* (1512, Gemäldegalerie, Dresden), *Saint Cecilia* (1514, Plate 26), and the *Spasimo di Sicilia* for a church in Palermo (1516–17, today in the Prado, Madrid). Occasionally patrons were fortunate enough to procure him for frescoes, but it would seem that the patron needed to be indispensable to the pope because only the super rich Sienese merchant and the Pope's banker, Agostino Chigi, received much of Raphael's attention. For Chigi Raphael decorated two chapels, one in Santa Maria della Pace (1514) and the other in Santa Maria del Popolo (where the dome was executed in the unusual medium of mosaic), and in his villa (known today as the Villa Farnesina), *Galatea* (1513, Plate 28), and the loggia of Psyche (1518, Plate 29).

The period between his arrival in Rome in 1508 and his premature death in 1520 was phenomenally productive. In his last half-decade Raphael became the architect of Saint Peter's, the Chigi Chapel (Santa Maria del Popolo), Villa Madama, Palazzo Branconio dell'Aquila (Plate 39), as well as several other palaces. Pope Leo commissioned him to design the cartoons for a set of tapestries to hang in the Sistine Chapel depicting the Acts of the Apostles (1515–16), which were sent to Flanders to be woven (cartoons are preserved in the Victoria and Albert Museum, London, Plate 24). In addition to local patrons, dukes and princes importuned him to create works for them, and Raphael was too polite ever to say no. In 1517 he promised Alfonso d'Este, duke of Ferrara, a *Triumph of Bacchus* for his *camerino*, but when its execution was repeatedly delayed, he sent cartoons of works that had been completed in an attempt to placate the duke. The *Saint Michael* (Plate 27) and the *Holy Family of Francis I* (both 1518, in the Louvre, Paris) were commissioned as gifts for the king of France, François I. Raphael's last work, completed a few days before his death, was the *Transfiguration* (Plate 33). It was installed above the bier at his funeral. He was buried in the Pantheon.

The Rome at which Raphael arrived in 1508 was already a massive construction site, especially at the Vatican. On the order of the energetic Pope Julius, Bramante had designed the statue court to display the major antique statues owned by the papacy, including the recently discovered and centrally placed *Laocoön*. The pope's architect had torn up the woods that had lain between the Villa Belvedere and the Vatican Palace to create the new Cortile del Belvedere, which required altering the slope of the hill into a three-level terrace, building loggie to enclose its flanks, and constructing an amphitheater at the lowest level, just outside the papal apartment that Raphael was to decorate.[2] On the opposite side of the palace, Bramante, nicknamed *Il ruinante* because of the vigor with which he carried out preliminary demolition, was at work rebuilding Saint Peter's. Michelangelo had been persuaded to transfer his talents from the abandoned tomb for Pope Julius to painting the Sistine vault. Elsewhere in Rome Julius had new streets cut on either side of the Tiber. On the Via Giulia he began construction of the enormous new Hall of Justice, the Palazzo dei Tribunali (never finished). Along the new Via del Lungara on the opposite side, Agostino Chigi had Baldassare Peruzzi build him a splendid villa on the Tiber (now called the Villa Farnesina), which would be frescoed by Raphael but also by Peruzzi, Sebastiano del Piombo, and Il Sodoma.

Julius had been a prominent patron of art and architecture and had amassed an important collection of antiquities while he was still a cardinal. In the 1490s Julius collected the famous *Apollo Belvedere*, which he placed in his new statue court and where it can still be seen today. Julius undertook to transform the capital of Christendom into a city that would recall and rival the grandeur of imperial Rome. The court he created at the Vatican, like that of his hated predecessor Alexander VI Borgia, would wed Christianity to classical culture. In Bramante, Michelangelo, and Raphael he found artists capable of expanding their styles under his patronage, and the influence of antique culture all around them, to fulfill his vision, and his vision inspired his artists to surpass themselves. The papal court was filled with humanists whose ardor in their study of antique texts created an ebullience that was contagious. Julius, like most popes by the time they are elected, was an old man, and he had no intention of leaving projects uninitiated. He must certainly have known that most of them could not be completed in his lifetime, but that did not deter him. Work was undertaken on a scale that would not be thinkable in cramped medieval Florence or at most centers on the Italian peninsula. The vast open areas of the city encouraged thinking on a grand scale, dotted as it was with ruins of the ancient capital that had once accommodated more than a million residents and was now populated with fewer than thirty thousand inhabitants.

It is not surprising, therefore, to see that Raphael's style changes in the new environment, with the new patronage, and with the new medium of fresco. His principal work for the next several years would be in a medium in which he had had limited experience before Rome, and the demands of fresco contributed to the changes that his style underwent. The damp plaster of fresco is unforgiving: mistakes are tedious to correct because, to do it properly, the dried plaster has to be chiseled out. The painter needs to determine with accuracy how much he can paint in a day before the plaster dries. He needs to work with broad strokes in thin layers; there is little opportunity to build up the surface, concealing or partially concealing as one can do with oil paint. The Raphael who came from Florence was well suited to this kind of large-scale project because he was very systematic in the way he prepared his composition; he was not impetuous, but he was able to improvise as needed.

The experience of working intensively on the Stanze frescoes encouraged him to broaden his style, to conceive on a large scale and in terms of the total composition. Leonardo's exploration of light and shade as the means of focusing and organizing a composition had interested Raphael in Florence, and he had emulated it in his oil paintings there. Now in the Stanza della Segnatura (Plates 17–20), facing an entire wall, he must have referred to Leonardo's cartoon for the *Battle of Anghiari* (now lost). That mural, which was to have been still larger than Raphael's – fifty-five feet in length – must have required Leonardo to think through the pattern of light and shade across the whole expanse. We have Raphael's full-scale cartoon for the figures in the *School of Athens* (Plate 18) where we see that he has done exactly that. It is a very different effect, and a far more dramatic one, than the usual quattrocento fresco in which each figure is lit separately and evenly and important figures are each granted the same degree of illumination. Raphael is not afraid to conceal parts of figures in shadow: the lower bodies of Plato and Aristotle are shaded by the adjacent figures, and Euclid, leaning over his slate, has only the top of his head in bright light. The painter makes explicit his indebtedness to Michelangelo, it would seem, by including his portrait as a postcartoon addition to the foreground in the figure of Heraclitus. The seated pose and the colossal scale have suggested to many critics that Raphael intended to imitate the Prophets of the Sistine vault on which Michelangelo was then at work, thereby acknowledging his debt not only to Michelangelo's earlier, Florentine works but also his present work in

Rome. This kind of generosity was characteristic of Raphael, according to contemporary report.

The broadening and new weightiness of Raphael's figures may well have been inspired by the Roman antiquities all around him as well. Another kind of influence of antiquity is more indirect and yet more fundamental, however. The humanists of Julius's court were reading ancient literature as never before. Especially important were the writings on rhetoric of Cicero and Quintilian in which modes of speech are divided into categories according to purpose or function. If the orator wishes to persuade he uses one kind of argument, gesture, tone; if his purpose is to praise he uses another. In the preceding century artists on the whole – with important exceptions[3] – developed one all-purpose style and did not vary it. Raphael increasingly recognized that different subject matter required different treatment: a devotional altarpiece should not be painted the same way as an episode from history. Eventually, just before his death, he discovered that even contrasting episodes in the same painting may call for different treatment (*Transfiguration*, Plate 33).[4] To accommodate these various requirements Raphael developed in the course of his Roman career modes of coloring and modes of composition, based no doubt on the categories of rhetoric. This new kind of thinking dawned slowly: in the Stanza d'Eliodoro he recognized that these historical subjects required more dramatic treatment than the contemplative scenes in the Segnatura and that he needed to heighten the contrast of his chiaroscuro. The shadows are noticeably blacker than the soft brownish tones used for shading in the preceding Stanza.[5] At the same time, he was commissioned to make an altarpiece for a major Roman church, the *Madonna di Foligno*, representing a vision of the Madonna and Child (Plate 25). For such a devotional piece, Leonardo's sfumato suited the gentle, meditative mood. On the vault of the Eliodoro, however, were to be depicted four epiphanies in which God made appearances to man – for example, *Moses and the Burning Bush* and *Jacob's Dream*. Their transcendental character needed to be apparent, so Raphael employed the color style that Michelangelo had reinvented, *cangiantismo*, in which color shifts from one hue to another in a modeling sequence. The antinaturalistic quality of this coloring is well suited to supernatural events. Thus in these four works, painted in a period of a few years, Raphael had used four different modes of coloring, matching the mode to the conditions. In the Segnatura his color mode can be called *unione* because it strives to create a flowing unity among the figures, connecting them in a melodious harmony. On the Eliodoro walls he introduced the chiaroscuro mode, which becomes most unmistakable in the *Liberation of Peter* (Plate 22). For the *Madonna di Foligno* the mode might be called *unione* again, but he has softened the contours and the shadows still more than in the Segnatura, approaching Leonardesque sfumato. On the Eliodoro vault he used *cangiantismo*, borrowed from Michelangelo's ceiling perhaps quite intentionally, again paying homage. Raphael would continue to refine and develop his use of modes for the remainder of his short career. More than any of his contemporaries he applied this kind of thinking in terms of categories of use, but his followers, often more interested in the aesthetic possibilities than in matching mode to function, would spread the idea far and wide. It is one of the most important of Raphael's contributions. We are familiar with Nicolas Poussin's adaptation, more than a century later, discussed in his famous letter to Chantelou in which he carries the idea a step further intellectually and connects the modes of painting with the Greek modes of music.[6] Poussin, of course, was a great admirer and imitator of Raphael, and I have no doubt that he derived the idea of modes from his High Renaissance mentor.

In the last half-decade of his life Raphael expanded his modal thinking to composition. Since the second quarter of the quattrocento, linear perspective had been the means by which Renaissance artists – painters and relief sculptors alike – ordered the space of their images. They had learned to manipulate the system for effect and were by no means slavishly tied to it, but it remained *the* Renaissance system.[7] Raphael demonstrated it in his early Stanze frescoes. Only in the *Parnassus* and *Repulse of Attila* was there no architecture to establish the orthogonals that measure the space and guide the eye. But his immersion in Roman antiquity showed him that there were other interesting ways to organize the space of a picture. Vasari described an excursion Raphael made with his assistant Giovanni da Udine to explore the "grottoes," what we now know were the vaults and walls of Emperor Nero's infamous Domus Aurea. Nero's Golden House was so sumptuous that it was an embarrassment to later emperors, so Trajan had it filled with rubble and built his baths on top as a gift to the residents of Rome.[8] The experience of exploring these buried rooms opened up to Raphael the world of ancient Roman wall decoration. The following year Raphael assigned Giovanni da Udine to execute Cardinal Bibbiena's loggia, in which the entire wall was covered with *grotteschi*, invented in the manner of the Domus Aurea decorations (Plate 30). No perspective system organizes the wall. There are no frames. Instead the wall is treated as a surface over which these fantastic ornaments are spread. *Grotteschi* had been the fashion in Rome since the Domus Aurea was first explored around 1480, but they had been restricted to borders or ornamental bands. Raphael's use of them in the Bibbiena's loggia and the connected *stufetta* (bathroom) constitutes a rethinking of how to decorate a wall.

The following project of Raphael and his bottega was to decorate the loggia of Leo X (Plate 31), and in it he further expanded the variation on perspective. Giovanni da Udine perfected his reinvention of ancient Roman stucco, such as he had seen in the Domus Aurea, so that relieflike elements could be incorporated into the wall, which actually protrude toward the viewer. These are combined with *grotteschi*, whereas the other parts of the decorative scheme representing biblical narratives are designed with perspectival recession.

A couple of years earlier Raphael had begun exploring another alternative to perspective, again suggested by antique example, this time relief sculpture and therefore called the relieflike style. I summarize Michelangelo's and Raphael's development of it and its culmination in Raphael's design for the *Battle of the Milvian Bridge* (Plate 32) in my essay in this volume.

Modes of composition and color gave Raphael the means to vary his style according to the commission. His successors and contemporaries quickly followed up on the implications. One finds exciting combinations of the modes of composition, for example, Francesco Salviati's midcentury decorations of the Palazzo Ricci-Sacchetti[9] or inventions of hybrid color modes, such as *unione-cangiantismo*.[10] The use of *grotteschi* and the relieflike style were carried by Perino del Vaga to Genoa, where he worked in the Palace of Andrea Doria, and by Rosso Florentino to François I's palace at Fontainebleau, to cite only two examples.

Raphael did not have a large workshop in the pre-Rome years, although he appears to have had some assistants from time to time. In Rome, as his commissions and importance grew, so did his workshop. As Bette Talvacchia shows in her essay in this volume, his workshop, and the very conception of a workshop, evolved with Raphael's career. Fresco demands a workshop: there are multiple tasks that can be carried out by pupils at all stages of experience – some menial, some requiring skill. In the early stages Raphael designed and executed everything himself, and he obviously loved the process of creating a composition. Each figure and each stage was studied in drawings of all kinds: compositional sketches; studies of light and shade, figure studies made from the model and then combined into detailed studies of groups and finally into a cartoon. Fischel counted forty-five drawings surviving for the fresco of the *Disputa* alone in the Stanza della Segnatura and estimated that four or five times that many were made.[11] The new century would no longer tolerate Perugino's system of recycling cartoons that had been made for previous commissions.[12] As his fame grew and the pressure on Raphael increased, he gathered about him more artists. Many were more collaborators than apprentices or assistants. By the middle of the second decade he had the largest workshop that had ever been assembled: Vasari reported that an entourage of fifty accompanied Raphael when he arrived daily at the Vatican. As he became busier he developed a system whereby he inserted the more experienced assistants into the preparatory stages, perhaps at first transferring and combining studies. His role in the actual execution diminished. Finding the right balance between allowing freedom to his assistants and providing the necessary oversight and intervention took some time. In the Stanza dell'Incendio scholars agree that he turned over too much to the workshop; the *Oath of Leo* is hardly ever discussed or reproduced, for example.[13] With remarkable speed he worked out a system for sharing the work, however, which constituted a major revision of workshop practice. Raphael's pupil, Giulio Romano, reported to Vasari that the master would retouch the work of his assistants until they appeared entirely his.[14] And patrons appear to have been satisfied. Reflected here is a shift in the conception of the role of artist from executant to inventor. Contracts continued to repeat the language calling for the work to be done entirely by the hand of the master, but it was expected less and less that this would actually be the case. Vasari's midcentury commission to decorate the large audience room in the Palazzo della Cancelleria is a case in point. It is known as the Sala de Cento Giorni because the patron required the painter to complete it in one hundred days.[15] Speed increasingly became a valued virtue in the cinquecento, and as the century wore on, clever invention was frequently more highly valued than refined execution.[16] Some of Raphael's followers seem hardly to have had time to take up the brush. Giulio Romano spent his time making the sketches and overseeing the operation. He was constantly under pressure from his patron, Federico Gonzaga, duke of Mantua, so that brilliant conceits like his Sala dei Giganti (Palazzo Te) was executed by the crude hand of an assistant, Rinaldo Mantovani. Raphael's innovations in workshop organization and management made possible the revolution in working practice that took place during the cinquecento.

We may imagine that euphoria fueled the achievements of the High Renaissance, but we would be mistaken to imagine this as a Garden of Eden. Envy and rivalries motivated both patrons and artists.[17] Underlying everything, of course, was the desire to surpass antiquity, but competition between equals, or would-be equals, was everywhere evident. The pope provided the example for the cardinals, the papal court, and the wealthy citizens to spend lavishly on artistic patronage. As Linda Pellecchia shows in her chapter, there resulted a boom in palace building and decoration. The opening of new streets gave access to new building sites, which were snapped up by ambitious prelates or businessmen. Coteries developed among the artists, and a rivalry between Michelangelo and Raphael was exacerbated by their respective partisans and exploited by patrons. The very size of Raphael's workshop would have created a claque of his enthusiastic allies. Michelangelo, on the other hand, it will be recalled, fired his assistants in the Sistine Chapel and sent them packing back to Florence, thereby incidentally denuding himself of supporters.[18] Michelangelo was by nature querulous, as his letters make clear.[19] He complained about Bramante, who was a distant relative of Raphael and fellow Urbinate, because he promoted his kinsman. Michelangelo blamed Bramante for Julius's decision to abandon his tomb, and for proposing him to paint the Sistine vault. He considered himself a sculptor and believed that Bramante wanted to embarrass him in the confrontation between his frescoes and those of Raphael, which were being executed at the same time in the papal apartment. When the pope ordered Bramante to build a scaffolding for Michelangelo in the Sistine, Michelangelo had it torn down, pointing out that the holes from which it was suspended could not be closed and would mar the appearance of the frescoes. As Costanza Barbieri shows in her chapter, the Venetian Sebastiano became the focus of the rivalry between the two factions and – once Michelangelo had taken up residence in Florence – his surrogate in Rome. It was principally on the issue of coloring, for which Raphael had been judged the superior and Michelangelo deficient, that Sebastiano, the pupil of Giorgione, was put forward as the champion of the Michelangelo clique. Raphael himself seems to have been aloof from these discussions and of a generous nature, but he could not have been oblivious to the antagonism and the gossip going on around him. An incident reported by Benvenuto Cellini indicates that the fervor of Raphael's supporters did not diminish after the master's death. Rosso Fiorentino received a commission to fresco a chapel in Santa Maria della Pace, where Raphael had worked. When Rosso disparaged Raphael, his followers "were quite resolved to murder him," according to Cellini, who was, admittedly, prone to exaggerate.[20]

The critical literature continued to compare Raphael and Michelangelo through much of the sixteenth century, and critics aligned themselves with one or the other. After the unveiling of the *Last Judgment* in 1541, the artists flocked to Michelangelo's standard. The chapel was always full of artists copying his fresco. Even Michelangelo himself deplored this adulation. He is reported to have remarked on passing through the chapel on business one day, "Oh, how many men this work of mine wishes to destroy."[21] The tide turned against Michelangelo and Michelangelism, however, when the Church made it clear that his kind of exaggerated anatomy did not serve its interest to present sacred images that would spur the faithful to devotion. Raphael again appears as the model for leading painters like Taddeo and Federico Zuccaro beginning around 1555. By the end of the century the Carracci had elevated Raphael to the position of the model to be copied. His hegemony in the French Academy is discussed in this volume by Carl Goldstein, and his fame in England and Germany in the eighteenth century is the subject of Giovanna Perini's essay.

Another index of Raphael's fame is the way that restorers treated his pictures. Cathleen Hoeniger examines the interventions and the discussions surrounding them from the seventeenth century on, which gives us insight into the changing technology and ideology of restoration, as well as a better understanding of the condition today of some of the artist's masterpieces. Raphael's use of prints was equally innovative. He was the first artist in Italy to use the still new medium of engraving to spread his name and fame, not only across the Italian peninsula but also across Europe. In her essay Patricia Emison asserts the centrality of these engravings in Raphael's oeuvre, making the point that we see a different Raphael in the engravings.[22] The audience was different – not commissioning patrons, but connoisseur collectors, for whom these prints were "recreational." The artist was free in this situation to explore themes and compositional problems that interested him and to demonstrate prowess to an audience that was well disposed. Some of the freedoms the modern artist enjoys were anticipated in the medium of prints.

Despite his short life the literature on Raphael is vast. This book addresses some of the interests of recent scholarship, in some cases summarizing and extending what has begun to be explored, in some cases applying new methodologies and approaches to the case of Raphael.

After many decades of neglect the intellectual and cultural history of Rome has begun to receive attention. The contributions of historians such as John O'Malley, John D'Amico, Peter Partner, Charles Stinger, and Ingrid Rowland,[23] to name a few of the most prominent, have been enormously helpful to art historians as we undertake to place Raphael and his contemporary artists in the context of their times. Before the last thirty to forty years the concerns of art historians had been with problems of attribution; with defining the classic style of the High Renaissance and Raphael's style, and distinguishing it from his pupils. Interest has now shifted to new questions of a more practical nature, such as investigation of his patronage and seeking to understand how much and what the patron stipulated. Rather than focusing on identifying hands in the workshop, we are now asking how Raphael's workshop was organized and managed, how it developed and changed in the course of his career, how it may have differed from other workshops or provided a model for them. An indication that "hand" is not the primary concern that it used to be is the way prints, executed by a second hand, are being pulled into the mainstream and treated alongside creations in other mediums. Nevertheless, it remains important to determine the authorship of drawings if we are to understand how Raphael managed his artistic establishment, and debate on these issues of attribution continues, as Linda Wolk-Simon shows in her essay.

In the concluding section of this book we examine the academic influence of Raphael in the centuries following his death, a subject that was not much studied in the wake of the collapse and discrediting of the academic tradition in the late nineteenth century. The bibliography includes some of the most useful works in today's scholarship and has been culled from the works our authors have cited.

PART I
BEFORE ROME

1   Young Raphael and the Practice of Painting in Renaissance Italy

Jeryldene M. Wood

Composed almost five centuries ago, Giorgio Vasari's description of Raphael's early career in the *Lives of the Artists* still rings surprisingly true despite its romanticized anecdotes and some well-known factual errors. Born at Urbino in 1483, he informs us, Raphael was the son of the painter Giovanni Santi, who arranged for him to apprentice with Pietro Perugino. As a young artist Raphael produced paintings in his teacher's style for patrons in Perugia and in the small town of Città di Castello. He then resided in Florence for several years, where he transformed his style after studying the art of Leonardo da Vinci and Michelangelo, before settling definitively at Rome in 1508.[1]

The sentimental stories about the blissful Santi household and the boy's tearful farewell with his parents with which Vasari enriched this biography are more than merely entertaining, for this imaginative and lightly moralizing narrative points to the importance of family and kinship for Raphael's professional fortunes.[2] Throughout the *Lives of the Artists* Vasari parallels the structure of the family and the artist's workshop so that the relationship between master and students resembles that of a father to his sons, and the shop itself becomes a clan whose network of kinship sustains its commercial and political operations. This analogy between workshop and family complements the author's fundamental conception that progress in the visual arts – both the individual maturation of artists and the historical perfection of art over time – evolves like the three stages of the human life cycle. In fact his biography of Raphael is virtually a textbook illustration of this developmental metaphor as it traces the painter from his childhood learning period at Urbino and Perugia, through an experimental phase of adolescence in the Papal States and Florence, to his mature adulthood in Rome. In addition to the idea of personal growth, the waxing and waning of the generations is equally essential to this progressive theory of the arts. Thus Raphael's achievements necessarily outshine those of Perugino, just as Giotto's reputation eclipsed Cimabue's in the trecento. Interestingly, Vasari's rising and aging generations of artists and families paradoxically underscore the continuity of traditions and the power of the status quo as well.

Vasari's "Life of Raphael" has proven a problematical legacy for modern scholars. Art historians generally follow his tripartite division of Raphael's life into Umbrian, Florentine, and Roman periods; however, in contrast to the vivid sweep of Vasari's biography, their studies largely concentrate on the details of the painter's chronological development, the attributions and dates of his paintings and drawings, and, specifically, when and by whom he was employed.[3] The fictionalized aspects of Vasari's account of Raphael's childhood, moreover, have led many to question the reliability of his information on the painter's pre-Roman years, sparking debates over the identity of his teacher, as well as the location and length of his apprenticeship.[4] Scholars have found the attribution and dating of Raphael's works especially frustrating because of his extraordinary powers of assimilation. Vasari himself recognized this problem, constantly interjecting comments about the difficulty of distinguishing the young artist's paintings from Perugino's (Plates 1 and 2; Fig. 1).[5] Although Vasari and his contemporaries clearly regarded the ability to imitate as a positive quality, today's students, who are accustomed to nineteenth- and twentieth-century equations of originality and creativity, typically consider the derivative nature of Raphael's early paintings difficult to reconcile with his reputation as the ideal Renaissance painter renowned for the inventiveness as well as the harmony of his designs. Both Renaissance workshop practices, whereby apprentices learned by imitating their teachers' styles and assisting on their projects, and Renaissance art theory, in which imitation demonstrates the artist's knowledge of and ability to compete with ancient and contemporary works of art, partially explain Raphael's reliance on older masters' works. Even so, almost a decade of assimilation suggests a steep "learning curve" to most modern viewers of his pictures.

Yet the notions of family, artistic emulation, and generational progress that shaped Vasari's "Life of Raphael," and the very derivativeness of the artist's first paintings, can serve to introduce the context in which Raphael worked – what recent sociological studies would call the "cultural field" of late fifteenth- and early-sixteenth-century Italy.[6] Accordingly, I analyze Raphael's emergence as a painter in this essay by exploring his activities before 1508 in terms of his personal agency, his fellow artists, and his patrons.

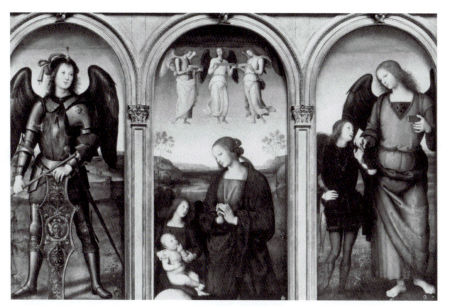

1. Perugino, *Triptych with Virgin Adoring the Christ Child, Saint Michael, and Tobias with the Archangel Raphael* (Certosa di Pavia Altarpiece), National Gallery, London. Photo: Alinari/Art Resource, NY.

In what follows, Raphael's career unfolds across time more or less geographically, beginning at Urbino with his family background and then traveling within the Papal States and to Florence for his apprenticeship and his first years as an independent painter. After returning briefly to Urbino for a discussion of his work at the Montefeltro court, the essay concludes in Perugia with some reflections on what is arguably the finest of young Raphael's paintings.

THE PAINTER'S SON

Vasari's legends about Raphael's childhood situate the painter within the social and cultural circumstances of his times. Raphael was the son of Magia di Ciarla and Giovanni Santi, a prosperous painter and courtier at Urbino, a leading cultural center of fifteenth-century Italy.[7] Like other artisans' children who displayed talent, he was expected to learn his father's trade. Even as a boy he would have started to acquire the rudiments of the craft by preparing panels, mixing colors, and copying the drawings of his father and other masters.[8] Santi's literary pursuits also suggest that he must have promoted his son's education, but whether Raphael attended school, was taught at home by his father, or was tutored by one of Santi's relatives or friends is unknown.[9] At his father's death on 1 August 1494, the eleven-year-old Raphael inherited the bulk of Santi's estate, which was administered by his guardian Bartolomeo Santi, his uncle and a local priest. Among other properties, his legacy comprised two houses in Urbino, one of which his stepmother Bernardina was to retain for her lifetime. Santi's workshop is not mentioned in the will, but its contents, such as drawings and model books, as well as his papers and writings, probably passed to his son.[10]

Raphael's patrimony also included Santi's professional affiliations and the example of his productive career as a court painter. Apparently he did cultivate his father's associates throughout his lifetime: in 1500–1 his partner on the Saint Nicholas of Tolentino altarpiece in Città di Castello (Plate 1) was Evangelista di Pian di Meleto (Santi's assistant and a witness to his will); later in Rome he hired Timoteo Viti (who finished Santi's *Muses*) to collaborate on the *Sibyls* in Santa Maria delle Pace. In addition to local painters, Santi's acquaintance had encompassed artists who came to work at the Montefeltro court such as Francesco di Giorgio, Justus of Ghent, Piero della Francesca, and the latter's assistant Luca Signorelli. Presumably he also knew Perugino, to whom, Vasari said, he entrusted his son's training.[11]

Like much late-fifteenth-century painting in the Marches, Santi's somewhat dry, methodical interpretation of Piero della Francesca's and Perugino's models verifies Vasari's assessment that he was "not a very excellent painter."[12] Nonetheless, his workshop produced altarpieces and frescoes for members of the Montefeltro court, like the *sacra conversazione* for Count Oliva at Montefiorentino. He also executed paintings for the ruling family, including the nine *Muses* in the Tempio delle Muse of the Urbino palace for Duke Guidobaldo da Montefeltro and portraits for Duchess Elisabetta Gonzaga, as well as for her sister-in-law Isabella d'Este. In fact he worked for several members of the extensive Montefeltro clan, notably for the duke's sister Giovanna da Montefeltro della Rovere, who may have ordered the *Annunciation* in Santa Maria delle Grazie at Senigallia to celebrate the birth of her son Francesco Maria in 1490.[13]

Santi's versatility as a designer of theatrical entertainments to mark such occasions as the 1474 visit of Federico d'Aragona, son of the King of Naples, and the 1488 wedding of Guidobaldo and Elisabetta, served the Montefeltro well. His *Cronaca rimata*, a verbose chronicle in *terza rima* that glorified the first duke of Urbino, Federigo da Montefeltro, ostensibly cemented his relationship with the family.[14] Dedicated to the duke's son Guidobaldo, the

Cronaca cites countless battles and jousts, and it celebrates significant rites of passage: the births, marriages, and titles bestowed on members of the clan. Although he was a writer as well as a painter, Santi promoted the prestige of the visual arts in his chronicle, contending that "letters" may bring fame to the commissioner, but painting and sculpture "will raise man to heights." Painting deserved to be counted among the liberal arts, he wrote, because it "can preserve a mortal man present before us." When he touted the magnificence of the ducal palace at Urbino and enumerated the most illustrious artists of his day, Santi was not only acclaiming Duke Federigo's patronage, but also lauding his own profession.[15]

In the absence of documents, Santi's high opinion of Perugino, praised as "a divine painter" equal to Leonardo "in fame and years" in the *Cronaca rimata*, lends credence to Vasari's contention that he placed his son in that artist's shop.[16] At the forefront of Italian painters in the 1490s, Perugino exemplified the professional fame and accomplishment to which Santi himself aspired. From Santi's vantage point, Perugino's busy workshops at Perugia and Florence must have seemed well suited to provide his son with training and experience in his craft, and his network of friends and associates, as well as a roster of affluent clients, offered opportunities for advancement. Santi was prescient, for by the turn of the sixteenth century, Perugino's approach was the prevailing mode of representation in central Italy and, as we will see, most of his son Raphael's initial commissions did indeed come from patrons connected in one way or another with Perugino's circle.[17]

THE PAINTER'S APPRENTICE

As Vasari recognized, the most compelling evidence for claiming a close relationship between the two artists is Raphael's mastery of Perugino's style. Perugino's paintings provided the younger artist with both a frame of reference and a point of departure. Seamlessly uniting the natural and the celestial, his quiet tableaux of the Madonna and Child and his introspective images of solitary saints are filled with a mellow light that models soft flesh and resplendent garments and bathes undulating meadows in pastoral vistas. His poignant, self-contained scenes in which subtle physical separations preserve a psychological distance between image and viewer are objects meant for quiet contemplation; they do not elicit strong emotions. For example, in the Certosa altarpiece, painted for the duke of Milan in 1496–1500 (Fig. 1), a trio of angels attired in light-tinged white gowns are thoroughly engrossed in their reading as they hover above the Christ Child and another angel, who glance up at the tenderly attentive Madonna. On one lateral panel a vigilant Saint Michael the Archangel gazes at the Infant Christ, while the Archangel Raphael reassures the quizzical Tobias on the other.[18]

Raphael reproduced precisely this kind of meditative spirit in the *Crucifixion* for the Gavari Chapel in San Domenico at Città di Castello (ca. 1503), duplicating Perugino's compositional structure and figural morphology so effectively that Vasari observed, "if his name were not written upon it, no one would believe it to be the work of Raffaello, but rather by Pietro" (Plate 3).[19] Raphael's emphasis on the surface plane of the composition, the layered recession of the softly rendered countryside punctuated with saplings and groves, the pale horizon that deepens the bowl-shaped landscape, and the physiognomic types and poses of the characters all follow Perugino's models. With tilted head and eyes looking heavenward as he extends one hand toward Christ, Saint Jerome particularly resembles his teacher's long-bearded hermit saints.[20] Perugino's bright, rich hues and the "shot-color" in paintings like the Certosa altarpiece were the progenitors of the brilliant yellow infusing Mary Magdalen's rose drapery in the *Crucifixion*. Yet Raphael's altarpiece is more extroverted than Perugino's. By synchronizing the poses, gestures, and gazes of the saints and angels around the crucified Christ, he generates an internal narrative as well as a dialogue with the spectator, something seldom seen in his teacher's oeuvre.

The technical correspondences between their paintings and respective workshop practices further support Vasari's assertion that Perugino was Raphael's teacher. For Raphael not only emulated Perugino's preparatory drawings and auxiliary studies in charcoal, pen, and metal point, he also adopted his procedure for transferring cartoons to panels using grids, plumb lines, and pouncing. Recent restorations of the Gavari *Crucifixion* and the Certosa altarpiece show that his oil painting technique, explicitly the method of applying ultramarine blue, conforms to the older master's practice as well. Perugino's organizational expertise, as his management of large workshops and competing projects attests, also must have been instructive to Raphael, who by 1505 was juggling orders in Florence, Perugia, and Urbino.[21] The Gavari *Crucifixion* is just one of three Peruginesque altarpieces that Raphael completed for family chapels in churches at Città di Castello from 1500 to 1504, and by about 1506 he had painted at least as many for Perugian clients.

Raphael's zealous imitation of Perugino's style in his early paintings is logical in light of his coming of age as an artist in the papal territories in ca. 1500. In the first years of the sixteenth century, the system of institutional and private art patronage in the cities of the Papal States was remarkably stable despite the devastation wrought by Cesare Borgia's military campaigns of 1502–3 and the jockeying for power among such clans as the Baglioni and Oddi of Perugia.[22] Perugino, Signorelli, and Pinturicchio had been the leading painters in the region since their collaboration on the Sistine Chapel frescoes for Pope Sixtus IV in the early 1480s.[23] We can gauge their artistic dominance in the early 1500s by the social position of their patrons, which in addition to the immediate papal circle, included churches, convents, confraternities, city councils, and a private clientele of wealthy ecclesiastics, nobles, and merchants. The quantity, expense, size, and type of projects they received similarly attest to their stature. Perugino and his workshop, for instance, completed the complex frescoes in the audience chamber of the Collegio del Cambio (the Banker's Tribunal) at Perugia in 1500 and then embarked on a series of large, lucrative altarpieces in this city; meanwhile, his Florentine workshop kept up the productive pace of the 1490s.[24] Signorelli was mainly occupied with the monumental frescoes in the San Brizio Chapel in the Cathedral at Orvieto from 1499 to 1504, but he also produced several grand altarpieces for Marchigian churches during these very years. After finishing frescoes for Bishop Baglioni in the Collegiata at Spello (1501), Pinturicchio was hired in 1502 by Cardinal Francesco Piccolomini (who became Pope Pius III) to paint the elaborate murals of the Piccolomini Library at the Siena cathedral.[25]

Novices like Raphael began their careers by assisting established masters on large projects, by executing inexpensive panels of the Madonna and Child, and by competing for ecclesiastical and domestic commissions in provincial towns.[26] The Madonnas he painted at the turn of the century imply that he followed this pattern, but Raphael's three paintings for Città di Castello confirm that he quickly carved out a place for himself as a painter capable of producing altarpieces for family funerary chapels. He established a clientele at both Città di Castello and Perugia by building on the commercial, social, and family relationships of his patrons. At Città di Castello his commissions came from influential merchants: Andrea di Tommaso Baronci ordered the Saint Nicholas of Tolentino Altarpiece on 10 December 1500 (Plate 1); Domenico Tommaso de' Gavari was the patron of the *Crucifixion* in his chapel at San Domenico (Plate 3); and the Albizzini family commissioned the *Marriage of the Virgin (Sposalizio)*, signed and dated 1504, for their chapel in San Francesco (Plate 4).[27] At Perugia his principal patrons were women connected by blood, marriage, and their affiliations with the Franciscan Order. The Colonna altarpiece (Plate 7) originally embellished the private choir of the Franciscan tertiaries at Sant'Antonio di Padova, where Ilaria Baglioni, a daughter of the city's leading citizen, was recorded in 1503.[28] In December 1505, he signed a contract for an *Assumption* with the Poor Clares of Santa Maria di Monteluce, a community that included sisters from the rival Oddi and Baglioni clans. He also made altarpieces for the mortuary chapels of these prominent families in San Francesco al Prato: the *Coronation* for the Oddi Chapel in ca. 1503–6 (Plate 2) and the *Entombment* for the Baglioni Chapel, signed and dated 1507 (Plate 12).[29]

Raphael's 1505 contract for the high altar of Santa Maria di Monteluce underscores the chasm separating sixteenth-century and modern attitudes about artistic originality.[30] On December 22 the Poor Clares of Monteluce paid him thirty gold ducats to begin painting an *Assunta* for their high altar, which was to resemble Domenico Ghirlandaio's *Coronation of the Virgin* in San Francesco at Narni (ca. 1485). References to existing paintings as models for iconography, size, and qualitative standards are plentiful in surviving Renaissance contracts, which also stipulated the division of labor since most commissions were collaborative enterprises. In the case of Monteluce, the Perugian Berto di Giovanni, who also signed the contract, was to furnish the four scenes of the predella and act as the local contact on the project. Although they wanted a magnificent altarpiece of high quality, like many monastic patrons, the Poor Clares were more anxious about the punctual completion of the work than with the nuances of individual artistic style. More important, their request for a copy of a specific painting highlights the precedence of religious doctrine over originality of design or personal creativity in ecclesiastical commissions. The Assumption, a subject associated with the Franciscan Order, was particularly significant in this instance because the church of Monteluce was not only dedicated to Maria Assunta, but it was also the site of annual civic celebrations on that Marian feast day (15 August).[31] In sum, the replication of Ghirlandaio's altarpiece guaranteed that Raphael would represent orthodox content in an approved visual form.

The challenge for an ambitious young painter like Raphael, therefore, was to make his mark within the parameters of this existing artistic system. From the available evidence we can infer that he accomplished this during his early career by creating pictures in the popular mode, maintaining a high level of quality, and fulfilling his commitments expeditiously. Ironically, the Monteluce Altarpiece, one of the few early commissions for which we have a contract, is an exceptional case of the youthful Raphael's failure to complete a project.[32]

Even without the benefit of documentation, Raphael's other altarpieces from this period offer enough visual evidence to suggest that the resemblance of his pictures to Perugino's was determined by the taste and expectations of his clients. In the Papal States the preferred mode of representation conformed above all to the serene imagery of Perugino, although its scope also extended to the somber vigor of Signorelli and the lively charm of Pinturicchio. Raphael's *Marriage of the Virgin, Sposalizio* (Plate 4), which belongs to a visual family descending from Perugino's *Delivery of the Keys* in the Sistine Chapel, bears the distinct imprint of the region's three dominant masters.[33]

The striking correspondence between Raphael's *Marriage of the Virgin*, signed and dated 1504, and Perugino's *Marriage of the Virgin*, commissioned in 1501 for the chapel containing the Virgin's ring in the Cathedral of Perugia, provides an unusually precise point for comparing the two masters' approaches.[34] As in the Sistine fresco, Perugino's angular composition balances the horizontal frieze of figures in the front and the verticality of the temple in the back. He adjusts the expansive *istoria* of the *Delivery of the Keys* to the vertical format favored in altarpieces and directs the observer's attention to the key event by halting the action at the iconic celebrant, who stands with back straight and feet planted in the center of the ceremony. Raphael employs deeper color and tonal contrasts, shifts the perspective upward, and utilizes curvilinear forms to connect the foreground and background elements in his *Sposalizio*. Eliminating the lateral porches and juxtaposing the hemispherical dome of the temple with the arched top of the panel creates a fluid, coherent design, and the open, circular configuration of the foreground characters sets up a proximate space shared with the spectator. Although their faces are cousins to Perugino's types, Raphael's characters gesture and move according to the exigencies of the story, rather than for artful effect. Thus the priest bowing forward as he guides the wedding ring and the disgruntled suitor breaking the rod at the right transform stock motifs into convincing actions.

Life studies from a model doubtless enhanced Raphael's effective portrayal of the suitor in the *Sposalizio*; nonetheless, the curled pose of this figure also resembles an archer loading his bow in the right foreground of Signorelli's *Martyrdom of Saint Sebastian*, completed for San Domenico at Città di Castello in 1498. Indeed, Raphael's extant drawing of the neighboring archer in that picture, which was located across the nave from his own

Saint Nicholas of Tolentino altarpiece, the Gavari Crucifixion, substantiates his intense study of Signorelli's art.[35] Moreover, Raphael's increasingly proficient exposition of the narrative in the *Sposalizio* had to have been honed by his drawing several *istorie* for Pinturicchio's Piccolomini frescoes in exactly this period.[36]

Yet Raphael's majestic *Coronation of the Virgin* for San Francesco al Prato pushes the limits of Perugino's pictorial paradigm (see Plate 2). This novel interpretation of the subject for Leandra (Alessandra) degli Oddi's family chapel in the most venerable Franciscan church of Perugia correlates the visual conventions of the region with an unprecedented fusion of the Coronation and the Assumption legends.[37] Raphael strengthens customary distinctions between the divine and terrestrial zones in the *Coronation* by emphasizing the flatness of the cloud bank and by largely confining the apostles to below the horizon line. Massive draperies painted in solid colors demarcate the earthly space, while lightly billowing garments shot with iridescent color, as on the gown of the angel with a viola at the far right, distinguish the celestial realm. The use of Marian roses and lilies to identify and accentuate the emptiness of Mary's tomb is a telling detail that Raphael may have borrowed from Perugino, whose slight skewing of the lid on Christ's grave in a *Resurrection* completed for the same church in 1501, carries similar connotations.[38] In contrast to Perugino's placement of the tomb parallel to the picture plane, which preserves the psychological aloofness observed in his Certosa and *Sposalizio* altarpieces, Raphael's sharply angled, cleanly lit tomb slices open the foreground, drawing observers into the scene. Dispersed around that projecting edge, Christ's disciples react to Mary's miraculous ascent in comprehensibly human fashion: looking upward, conversing, and echoing Saint Thomas's wonder at the Virgin's girdle draped across his outstretched hands. Raphael's engagement with the dramatic potential of the narrative in this altarpiece, albeit foreign to Perugino's circle, adumbrates the interests of Florentine artists such as Leonardo and Michelangelo.

THE ASPIRING ARTIST

Leonardo and Michelangelo were the celebrities of the Florentine art scene when Raphael arrived at the city in late 1504. According to Vasari, Leonardo's *Madonna and Child with Saint Anne* had caused a sensation when it was exhibited at Santissima Annunziata in 1501, Michelangelo's colossal *David* had been installed near the entrance to the Palazzo della Signoria, and both artists had been employed by the government to paint frescoes of Florentine military victories in the Great Council Chamber of the latter.[39] In truth, Leonardo and Michelangelo, who had recently returned to the city (from Milan and Rome, respectively), stood apart from their contemporaries in Florence. The painters Botticelli, Perugino, Filippino Lippi, Lorenzo di Credi, Cosimo Rosselli, and the slightly younger Piero di Cosimo, who all attended the meeting convened to determine the best location for the *David* in January 1504, actually constituted the mainstream of their profession at the time of Raphael's arrival.[40]

Born mostly in the 1440s and 1450s, this generation of painters perpetuated the idealized naturalism formulated in the workshops of the sculptor-painters Verrocchio and Pollaiuolo during the 1470s and further popularized by the prolific Ghirlandaio bottega in the 1480s and 1490s.[41] Even Perugino's mannered reveries and the highly stylized dramas of Botticelli and Filippino stem from the vividly colored, sculptural figures and rationally conceived spaces of this tradition. Notwithstanding Vasari's report about Leonardo's *Madonna and Child with Saint Anne*, few of the established painters in Florence modified their styles in light of his imaginative experiments with figural and tonal unity. Neither Perugino nor Botticelli altered their highly successful approaches, and Filippino Lippi's response was mostly confined to a deepening of color and chiaroscuro. Although Lorenzo di Credi, who had known Leonardo since their days in Verrocchio's shop, tried his friend's inventive ideas in drawings of the Madonna and Child, for the most part his conception of forms as separate entities persisted in his paintings of the 1500s.[42] Nor did Leonardo's work resonate immediately with the students of these painters, Mariotto Albertinelli, Fra Bartolommeo, and Ridolfo Ghirlandaio. Until the middle of the decade altarpieces by this younger generation owed more to Perugino's example than to Leonardo's. Albertinelli's *Visitation* of 1503, in which an architectural framework isolates Mary and Elisabeth before a landscape vista, draws on Perugino's standard format, and as late as 1507 Fra Bartolommeo's *Vision of Saint Bernard* reflects Perugino's and Filippino's versions of the theme composed in the 1480s.[43]

What at first seems a conservative preservation of the status quo or indifference to artistic innovation among the artists in Florence, however, may simply have been a practical acknowledgment of an art market in which most purchasers preferred traditional works. As elsewhere in Italy, the customary intermingling of civic and religious interests informed institutional sponsorship of the arts in early sixteenth-century Florence. The Arte della Lana (wool guild) supervised projects at the cathedral, such as Michelangelo's *David*, which initially had been commissioned for the exterior of that building. Bequests from wealthy donors allowed ecclesiastical organizations, such as parish churches, monasteries, and hospitals, as well as the lay confraternities associated with them, to finance frescoes, altarpieces, and devotional paintings. Most of the greater commissions went to established masters: in 1503 the high altarpiece for the Servite church Santissima Annunziata was awarded to Filippino Lippi, and after he died the following year, to Perugino. The Florentine government headed by Piero Soderini, the newly elected Gonfalone della Giustizia (standard bearer of justice), commissioned Leonardo's and Michelangelo's battle scenes as part of its efforts to stabilize the fractured political atmosphere in the wake of the Medici family's exile, the divisive Savonarolan years, and Cesare Borgia's recent threats to the city's sovereignty. When the Florentine heralds voiced their conviction that the optimal site for Michelangelo's *David* was in front or near the Palazzo della Signoria at the 1504 meeting, they were drawing on quattrocento precedents to resolve contemporary political issues. Not only did the *David* call to mind the city's traditional identification with the brave youth who achieved victory despite great odds, its classical style also conjured the ideal republics of antiquity, and, just as important, their revival in pre-Medicean Florence.[44]

It was only after Michelangelo and Raphael created the demand for a different artistic style among Florentine and Roman patrons that the younger Florentine painters reconsidered their approaches. In Florence Michelangelo accomplished this through public and private commissions alike, whereas Raphael toiled primarily in the domestic sector. In fact, the latter failed to receive a sizable Florentine commission until the Dei altarpiece was ordered not long before his departure for Rome in 1508 (see Fig. 4), despite a letter of introduction to Soderini from Giovanna della Rovere, an affiliation with Perugino, and solid work experience in the Papal States.[45] The artists' relative ages and social origins surely affected their status in Florence: Michelangelo, born in 1475 to a respectable Florentine family, was aligned with the class for whom he made devotional images of the Madonna and Child, whereas Raphael was eight years younger and an outsider who needed to develop a local clientele. As one would expect, the private buyers of art at this time were prominent Florentines associated with Soderini's circle, members of families such as the Strozzi and Pitti, who had returned from exile under the Medici, and the scions of wealthy clans who assumed the leadership of the major wool, silk, and banking guilds. This younger generation of affluent Florentines, like Taddeo Taddei and Angelo Doni, became the primary patrons of Raphael and Michelangelo.[46] Having reached their thirties, an age in which they were ready to marry and set up a household, these men and their brides sought to decorate their homes with works of art that honored their lineages and displayed their prosperity. Raphael answered this need, exploiting the commercial, civic, and family ties of his clients to establish his reputation as the premier Madonna painter among young mercantile families.

The *Madonna of the Meadow* for Taddeo Taddei and the *Madonna del Cardellino* for Lorenzo Nasi epitomize the domestic paintings admired by his Florentine clients in ca. 1505–6.[47] As elegant as Filippo Lippi's pictures a half century before, Raphael's graceful, fashionably blonde Madonnas lovingly attend to Christ and John the Baptist, who innocently grasp the cross and the goldfinch signifying the Passion. The images thus serve as exemplars for the Florentine mothers who were responsible for nurturing their offspring and instructing them in the tenets of the faith. Raphael retains the rich colors, clear blue skies, and spacious landscapes learned from Perugino in these pictures, yet, as so often noted, he incorporates physiognomic types and compositional motifs from Leonardo's art. The lovely facial features, softly rounded shoulders, and gently leaning postures of his Madonnas mimic the feminine beauty and the graceful movements in Leonardo's drawings for the *Madonna and Child with Saint Anne*.[48] Michelangelo's suspicion that other artists were copying his works seems justified inasmuch as the Baptist's offering of the tiny bird in the *Madonna del Cardellino* approximates the young saint on the tondo he was carving for Taddeo Taddei (ca. 1504), and the pose of the Christ Child depends on his infant in the Bruges Madonna of 1503–6.[49] Raphael's translation sweetens the sentiment of Michelangelo's ideas, however: his Christ child stands on his mother's foot, comfortably secure in her devotion, as he leans back to reach for the goldfinch.

Michelangelo's distress about copyists was anomalous in an artistic environment where appropriation was standard practice, particularly among the students and colleagues of painters like Perugino, whose workshop functioned on replication. Still, Raphael's mimetic process matured, growing more synthetic in character during his years in Florence. Perhaps taking a cue from Michelangelo's response to Leonardo's *Saint Anne* in the *Doni Tondo*, he began to shape his imagery according to the conceptual underpinnings of Leonardo's and Michelangelo's art, rather than simply grafting motifs from their works on to his existing mode. In *La Belle Jardinière* (ca. 1507–8, Plate 6), he more fully assimilates the Florentines' robust substance, compact figural arrangements, and emotionally expressive movement with the vibrant color and lucid pastoral settings of his Peruginesque approach than in previous pictures.[50] In contrast to Perugino, Raphael does not simply capitalize on an effective formula; in fact, he rarely duplicates the compositions of the many Madonnas that he painted from ca. 1504–8.

His unusually self-referential reversal of the design of the *Madonna of the Meadow* and the repetition of Christ's pose from the *Madonna del Cardellino* in *La Belle Jardinière* call to mind Vasari's distinction between Raphael's two manners: that his first pictures were virtually indistinguishable from Perugino's, but those painted in his second style had greatly improved on his *own* manner through the study of Florentine art.[51] In other words, regardless of elements borrowed from Perugino, Leonardo, or Michelangelo, the Madonnas painted in Florence record Raphael's realization of a distinctly personal style.

Whereas the newly married Angelo Doni and Maddalena Strozzi asked Michelangelo to design their household Holy Family, they hired Raphael to paint their portraits (Plates 10 and 11). As in his Marian imagery, Raphael recasts the genre by building on the traditional three-quarter view popular in Florence since the 1470s and borrowing from Perugino's 1494 *Francesco dell'Opere* and Leonardo's contemporaneous *Mona Lisa*.[52] What makes his interpretation of this couple so intriguing is his subtle conflation of the "speaking likeness" with their social status and cultural aspirations. Their accessible poses and forthright gazes, together with the tactile qualities of warm flesh and slightly mussed hair, luxurious clothing, and glistening jewels, create figures who seem, as Vasari so often put it, "to breathe and move."[53] The pair's restraint nevertheless conveys the formality and social etiquette of their times. Their calculated attitude of nonchalance, or *sprezzatura*, as Baldassare Castiglione termed the proper demeanor of noble courtiers and ladies, bespeaks their standing among the Florentine elite.[54]

The linkage of portrait and emblem in the Doni-Strozzi panels invariably calls to mind Piero della Francesca's double-sided portraits of Federigo da Montefeltro and Battista Sforza (ca. 1472–4). Indeed, as in the ducal union, it was the wife who brought the prestige of a powerful clan to the marriage; nonetheless, the Ovidian tales painted on the reverse of these pendant paintings do not directly denote the sitters' virtues as they do in the Urbino diptych, but evince the Florentines' hope for progeny to carry on the family name. Painted in grisaille to simulate classical reliefs, the stories of Deucalion and Pyrrha cleverly play on the notions of transformation and fecundity in the *istoria*. Having survived the deluge sent by Jupiter on the reverse of Angelo Doni's portrait, they then repopulate the earth by casting stones that metamorphose into children on the back of Maddalena Strozzi's likeness. Whether conceived by the artist or his patrons, the imaginative pairing of art and nature – the carved stone of the ancient myth and the vivacity of the living sitters – at once represents an appropriate marital theme and implies the education and cultural claims of their class.[55]

THE COURTIER'S SON

Vasari intersperses his description of Raphael's Florentine activities with information about his journeys to Urbino, where he supposedly went to resolve family matters after the deaths of his parents, and to Perugia, where he completed a number of works and promised to make an altarpiece for the widow Atalanta Baglioni. Although erring in some of the details (Raphael's mother and father had been dead for more than a decade), his report is essentially correct because Raphael was at Urbino several times from 1504 to 1508 to resolve the perennial quarrel with his stepmother over Giovanni Santi's estate, and he must have received the Baglioni commission by at least 1506 to have finished it in 1507.[56] On one level, this part of Vasari's biography calls attention to the chronological overlapping of Raphael's pictures for patrons in Florence, Urbino, and Perugia; on another, the gradually unfolding story of family troubles enriches his explanation of the painter's last Perugian altarpiece, the poignant Baglioni *Entombment* (Plate 12).

During the trips to his *patria*, Raphael surely saw his mother's family, especially his uncle Simone di Ciarla with whom he corresponded and his paternal uncle Don Bartolomeo, who was implicated in the dispute over Santi's will. He apparently also used these occasions to enhance his standing with the rulers, Duke Guidobaldo da Montefeltro (1472–1508) and his consort Elisabetta Gonzaga (1471–1526). The duke had recently returned from an exile forced on him by the loss of Urbino to Cesare Borgia in 1502, suffered from poor health, and was childless. In 1504 he secured his succession by designating as legal heir his nephew Francesco Maria della Rovere (1490–1538), son of Giovanna da Montefeltro della Rovere (d. 1514), who wrote the artist's letter of introduction to Soderini in 1504. The adolescent's paternal uncle, Pope Julius II, who was by no means a disinterested party, approved the Montefeltro–delle Rovere alliance, as did the French and English monarchs, who awarded offices and honors to Guidobaldo and Francesco Maria.[57] In 1505 the betrothal of the adopted heir to Eleanora Gonzaga, the niece of Guidobaldo's wife, not only ensured the survival of the lineage, but also the perpetuation of the duchy's bonds with Mantua.[58]

The great fame of Federigo da Montefeltro and the renown of literary figures such as Baldassare Castiglione and Pietro Bembo, who resided at the Urbino court, have diverted attention from the visual arts of early sixteenth-century Urbino.[59] Like Raphael, Guidobaldo was a youngster when his father died in 1482, but he inherited a state celebrated for its refined culture, with an exceptional library lodged in one of the most splendid palaces of Italy. Duke Federigo had employed a wide array of artists, including the

architects Luciano Laurana and Francesco di Giorgio, the painters Piero
della Francesca and Justus of Ghent, and the superb artisans who crafted
the illusionistic *intarsia* of the *studiolo*; he also was acquainted with Leon
Battista Alberti, the art and architectural theorist. The activities of artists
at Guidobaldo's court have yet to be sorted out, although it is clear that
he did not employ a resident court painter or import a substantial number
of outsiders, seeming to rely instead on locals such as Giovanni Santi and
Timoteo Viti for projects like the pictures of the Muses.[60]

From the mid-fifteenth-century rule of Duke Federigo and Marchese
Ludovico Gonzaga through the mid-sixteenth-century della Rovere–
Gonzaga marriage, the political and familial interests that bound Urbino
and Mantua promoted artistic exchanges and shared aesthetic sensibilities
between the two courts. In the 1490s Giovanni Santi had worked for the
Gonzaga family at Mantua, whose court artist, Andrea Mantegna, a painter
"of knightly rank," he placed above all others in the *Cronaca rimata* for his
complete mastery of the principles of painting – from drawing, invention,
grace, and movement to foreshortening, perspective, and relief.[61] In addition
to works by Mantegna, who was active until his death in 1506, the paintings
of his brother-in-law, the Venetian Giovanni Bellini, and those by Francesco
Francia of Bologna and Lorenzo Costa of Ferrara (who succeeded Mantegna
at Mantua) were admired at both courts.[62]

After returning from exile in 1503, Duke Guidobaldo had to restore his
political and cultural authority at Urbino. Raphael, a citizen, a "local" artist,
and the son of a courtier-painter well known to the court was well positioned
for success with the ruling house. Although there is consensus about which
pictures by Raphael were made for patrons at Urbino, their actual owners
have not been identified, and the works themselves cannot be dated more
precisely than ca. 1504–8.[63] According to Vasari, Raphael painted "two small
but very beautiful Madonnas (in his second manner)" and an *Agony in the
Garden* for Duke Guidobaldo "that is so finely finished that it is like an
exquisite miniature."[64] The latter, which is lost, was more likely painted for
Elisabetta Gonzaga, and several Madonnas have been advanced as ducal
commissions. The *Small Cowper Madonna*, dated by style to ca. 1504–5,
is a case in point (Plate 5).[65] Its view of San Bernardino (as seen from the
painter's childhood home) in the background, its provenance going back
to seventeenth-century Urbino, its stylistic derivations from Perugino and
Leonardo typical of the artist's "second manner," and its beauty and high
quality make the *Small Cowper Madonna* a reasonable candidate but also
exemplify the complications of pinpointing ownership. The evidence supports equally credible alternatives; for instance, Raphael's inclusion of the

church where Duke Federigo was buried may imply a patron in the ducal family, yet he could have painted this Madonna for the duke's daughter, Giovanna della Rovere, instead of his son. For that matter, that he could have designed it for a member of his own family, such as Don Bartolomeo, who was a priest at San Bernardino, is not outside the range of possibilities.

When grouped together, Raphael's modest religious images, portraits, and intimately scaled narratives and allegories for Urbino patrons accord with the genres and themes customarily desired by the Montefeltro and their extended clan. Here, Raphael apparently adjusted his approach to suit the priorities of the Montefeltro court, just as he had assimilated the regional preferences and customs of Perugia and Florence. Visually, his Urbino pictures combine a Tuscan compositional structure (perspective and *disegno*) with the precious refinement and colorism of Netherlandish painting. In the *Small Cowper Madonna*, the pensive Leonardesque Virgin comforts her wriggling child as a soft light warms the tranquil hills, shines across the still waters, and colors the diminutive figures who meander toward the distant church. So, too, the small panel of *Saint George and the Dragon* and the paired *Saints Michael and George* – perhaps ordered to commemorate the English and French knighthoods received by Guidobaldo and Francesco Maria in 1503 and 1504 – transform the ferocity of Leonardo's soldiers and rearing steeds in the *Battle of Anghiari* into warrior angels whose graceful movements seem to adhere to a chivalric code as they slay monsters in naturalistic, Netherlandish-inspired settings.[66]

Although he may have observed the conjoining of likeness and landscape in Flemish portraits at Urbino, Raphael also knew Italian versions of this type, including Piero della Francesca's diptych of Federigo da Montefeltro and Battista Sforza and Perugino's *Francesco dell'Opere* of 1494. His *Portrait of a Youth with an Apple* (ca. 1505) takes its resonant color and softly modulated lighting, clear composition, the placement of the hands, and the tree-dotted panorama from the *Francesco dell'Opere*.[67] The sitters' poised assurance is palpable in both portraits, although Raphael enlivens his young man, whose sideward glance implies that someone has interrupted the session. The quick brushstrokes on the sleeves of his red, fur-trimmed coat and the thick paint on the gold-patterned cloth, as well as the cropping of the figure at the right, heighten the spontaneous effect.

Today most scholars accept the *Youth with an Apple* as a portrayal of Francesco Maria delle Rovere, who also has been proposed as the patron of Raphael's earliest allegories, the *Three Graces* and *The Knight's Dream* or the *Dream of Scipio* (Plate 8).[68] The golden apples added to the Graces complement the fruit held in this presumed portrait, and the metaphorical themes of both panels are highly appropriate for the adolescent heir.[69] The balance of chastity, beauty, and pleasure embodied by the *Three Graces* was singled out by Alberti as an exemplary *istoria* in his treatise *De pictura* (*On Painting*) and the trio appeared on the emblematic reverses of medals exchanged among Renaissance patricians. Even in this early attempt at a classical theme, Raphael captures the essence of the antique type without directly imitating a specific source. His lovely maidens – physically linked yet psychologically distinct – are at once chaste and voluptuous, innocent and knowing. Although he probably looked to a sculptural prototype, he softens the edges of the women's bodies and subtly adjusts the *contrapposto* of their movements to harmonize with the limpid waters and low hills.[70]

The Knight's Dream encompasses the taste for chivalric legends of knights and ladies, the tales of ancient heroes, and the allegories of love and virtue that preoccupied Italian aristocrats of this era. Pietro Bembo had published *Gli Asolani*, a discourse on love, in 1505, the year before he took up residence at Urbino, and Castiglione's *Book of the Courtier* abounds with references to Roman worthies like Scipio Africanus and Julius Caesar.[71] Even Giovanni Santi introduced his rhymed chronicle with the fable of a lovestruck young poet who dreams about a strange land where Plutarch (an obvious counterpart to Virgil in Dante's *Divine Comedy*) guides him through encounters with innumerable historical and mythological characters. When the poet sees Fame, flanked by Minerva and Apollo, crowning Federigo da Montefeltro, he is compelled to write the duke's biography.[72]

In *The Knight's Dream* Raphael adapts this sort of literary conceit to painting. Loosely based on the popular *Dream of Scipio Africanus*, the brilliantly attired young knight, propped up by his shield, envisions two maidens who present him with contradictory options. The young woman at the left extends a sword and book signifying the duties of virtue, while the other offers a floral bouquet alluding to pleasure and beauty. At the center, a slender laurel tree, whose leaves are awarded to military victors and poets alike, visibly reinforces the youth's dilemma, although the equestrians traveling toward a hamlet behind Virtue hint at the direction he will select. The rustic dwellings and lakeside port, the monastery perched on the crest of a steep hill, and the blue-tinged mountains in the distance call to mind the Netherlandish and Italian pastoral paintings avidly collected in the courts.[73]

Although satisfying Albertian criteria for variety, grace, and decorum, these tiny allegories clearly did not comply with the large size recommended for the ideal *istoria* in *De pictura*. It was a Perugian patron, Atalanta Baglioni, who offered Raphael the opportunity to put all of Alberti's standards into practice. His monumental *Entombment* (Plate 12) for her mortuary chapel in San Francesco al Prato, despite a conventional format that originally included God the Father blessing in the lunette and personifications of the theological virtues in the predella, was even more iconographically and stylistically innovative than the Oddi *Coronation of the Virgin* (Plate 2) located directly across the nave of the church. Scenes of lamentation for the dead Savior were relatively common for altarpieces, but the carrying of Christ's body to the tomb was rare in Italian paintings of the period; moreover, Raphael's quotations from antique portrayals of a pagan legend, the death of Meleager, were novel in the Perugia of his day.

The profound sorrow of Christ's followers is appropriate imagery for a funerary chapel, yet the absence of a cogent connection between the *Entombment* and the dedication of the Baglioni Chapel to Saint Matthew suggests the significance of a recent family tragedy for the invention of Raphael's *istoria*.[74] In July of 1500 Grifonetto, Atalanta Baglioni's beloved son, was executed for his participation in the brutal murder of four prominent members of his family, who had gathered to celebrate a wedding.[75] Like Meleager's mother Althaea, Atalanta elected to support the welfare of her clan and to protect the stability of the state; hence she refused to forgive or give sanctuary to Grifonetto after the crime. Mother and son were reconciled, however, as he lay dying in the main piazza of Perugia. Atalanta extracted Grifonetto's forgiveness of his executioners (the men of Gian Carlo Baglioni, who had survived the attack but declined to bloody his own hands in vengeance), thereby ensuring divine mercy for his soul. An account written soon after the events attributed to Francesco Matarazzo, a humanist employed by the Baglioni, tempers the heinous affair for posterity. Indeed, his allusions to Christ's betrayal and death, which transform the bloody atrocity into a parable of reconciliation and mercy, seem a convincing source for the subject matter of Raphael's painting. Although memories of the homicides must have resonated with the Baglioni and most viewers of the *Entombment*, Vasari, who loved a good story and judged narrative effectiveness according to its emotional impact on observers, curiously ignores the notorious family history. His description of the *istoria* may obliquely refer to it, as several historians have argued; still, within the context of Raphael's biography, his sensitive passage on the *Entombment* stands out as the sole ekphrasis composed for one of the artist's early paintings.

In this inspired painting there is a dead Christ being carried to the sepulchre, executed with such loving care and so fresh that it appears to have been only just finished. In composing this work Raphael imagined to himself the grief as they lay him to rest felt by the nearest and dearest relations of some much loved person, who had sustained the happiness, dignity and well-being of a whole family. One sees the swooning figure of Our Lady and the graceful heads of other weeping figures, notably Saint John who, with his hands clasped, drops his head in a way that would move the hardest heart to pity. The diligence, the skill, the devotion, and the grace expressed in this work are really marvelous, and everyone who sees it is amazed at the attitudes of its figures, the beauty of the draperies and, in brief, the perfection of its every detail.[76]

A remarkable cache of preparatory drawings and cartoons for the *Entombment* reveals the extraordinary range of sources underlying Raphael's "inspired" invention. The drawings chart his creative process as he struggled to capture the epic dimensions of the story and suggest that his task was further complicated by the unexplained alteration of the subject from a Lamentation to an Entombment.[77] Raphael chose the best elements from other artists' works to compose the most beautiful design possible, just as the ancient Greek painter Zeuxis had selected the most beautiful features of the Crotonian maidens to fashion the ideal woman.[78] Like a great painted relief, the *Entombment* mirrors its genesis in the art of Mantegna, Michelangelo, and ancient Rome; only its verdant landscape preserves the soft brushwork of his Madonnas and courtly allegories. Espousing spiritual fervor through the expressive movements of idealized, heroic figures, and dramatically binding the Christian, the classical, and the contemporary, Raphael's *Entombment* crowns his early career and forecasts his monumental Roman paintings for Pope Julius II.

The particular circumstances surrounding the commission of the *Entombment*, the creative process of its design, and its final visual form exemplify young Raphael's versatile and resourceful practice of his art. Like most of his Perugian pictures, the altarpiece was ordered by a patrician woman for a funerary chapel in a Franciscan church. The patron Atalanta Baglioni was the sister-in-law of Leandra Baglioni Oddi, for whom Raphael recently had painted the *Coronation of the Virgin*, so that the successful completion of an earlier work and family connections once again probably prompted his employment. Raphael's versatility allowed him to satisfy the multiple demands of the Baglioni project, whether entailing compositional adjustments to suit a change in the subject matter or finding new sources of inspiration to complete the work. While the three-part visual format of the altarpiece conformed to local preferences, as we have seen, the imagery of the central panel was boldly unique in its emotional range and monumental design. In the *Entombment* Raphael begins to wed the versatility, freshness, and audacity of youth with the depth and virtuosity of the mature artist.

Conceived in Florence and executed in Perugia, the *Entombment* confirms Vasari's claim that the maturation of Raphael's style was stimulated by Florentine principles of design and invention. Toward the end of his "Life of Raphael" Vasari reiterates the notion that after a prolonged period of imitation Raphael was able to surpass the manner of his teacher Perugino through the diligent and disciplined study of works by superior artists.[79] Although he would not attain "that sublime groundwork of conceptions and that grandeur of art of which few have been the peers of Leonardo," or reach "the perfection" of Michelangelo's extraordinary nudes, Raphael eventually mastered a "wider field," representing "historical inventions well and with facility" and thereby achieving "a catholic excellence" in his art."[80]

2 Raphael and His Patrons: From the Court of Urbino to the Curia and Rome

Sheryl E. Reiss

On 14 April 1520, a Volterran then residing in Rome wrote home with news from the papal city: "Here in four days two very great men have died, each at the summit of his respective calling; Messer Agostino Chigi, in commerce, and Raphael of Urbino, in painting. They were buried with utmost pomp, the one and the other."[1] Confirming Giorgio Vasari's later account, the writer of the missive, Paolo Riccobaldi, tells us that Raphael was accompanied to his grave by other painters, and he is said to have left 1,500 ducats for his tomb.[2] Chigi is described as having left "an incredible estate."[3]

Artist and patron, virtuoso and financier; associated in life through commissions such as the frescoes of the Villa Farnesina and the decoration of the Chigi chapels in Santa Maria della Pace and Santa Maria del Popolo, linked in death in the mind and words of an astute contemporary observer.[4] The magnificent Agostino Chigi was, of course, one of Raphael's most exalted patrons during the final decade of the artist's life, when he worked for two popes, an array of humanists, high churchmen, and cardinals, not to mention princes and lords in Italy and abroad. That Raphael's passing was noted in the same breath as that of Rome's wealthiest man speaks volumes about the status the artist had achieved by the time of his untimely death at the age of thirty-seven.

From Raphael's early years in Umbria and the Marches, to the end of his career in Rome, the artist received commissions from an exceptionally diverse group of patrons.[5] This essay provides a broad and synthetic overview of the patronage support that contributed to his becoming a man who, in Vasari's words, "lived not as a painter, but as a prince."[6] Just before and after the fifth centenary of Raphael's birth in 1983, an array of publications in Italy, Europe, and the United States shed light on the topic of the artist and his patrons – particularly important were studies such as those of Alison Luchs on Raphael's female patrons in Perugia, Alessandro Cecchi on the

Doni in Florence, Gabriella Zarri on the Beata Elena Duglioli Dall'Olio in Bologna, and Claudia Conforti on Baldassari Turini da Pescia, one of the excecutors of Raphael's will.[7] This essay can be seen as an updating and as a more in-depth expansion of L. D. Ettlinger's survey of Raphael's early patrons (which was published in 1986) and could alternatively be titled "Raphael: Patronage and the Road to Rome."[8] A coda at the end of the essay will consider how the patronage that helped to shape Raphael's spectacular career changed once he was established in Rome.

In the two decades since the Raphael year, we have come to understand much more about the processes of art patronage in early modern Italy and have come to ask new questions, in particular about the relationship between what would be called in Italian *clientelismo* (political and social patronage) and *mecenatismo* (cultural patronage).[9] Borrowing approaches from an array of disciplines including social history, anthropology, economics, and psychology, the study of patronage in recent years has come to emphasize kinship bonds, self-fashioning, the signaling of social status, and the promotion of collective family agendas.[10] In her recent book on Cosimo de' Medici as patron, historian Dale Kent has proposed that patrons, like artists, can and should be studied in terms of a complete body of work, an oeuvre, for which the patron can be seen – in part, at least – as *auctor*.[11] This concept implies self-consciousness on the part of patrons who wished to express *their* priorities, concerns, and ambitions through visual means.[12] At the same time, the monolithic characterization of the individual "hero-patron" is being modified as we understand more about collaboration not only among artists, but also among patrons working together to realize commissions.[13] Also receiving greater attention is the important role played by agents and intermediaries in the implementation of art patronage.[14] The commissioning, display, and gifting of art and architecture – especially of images and buildings with public or diplomatic functions like many of Raphael's works – remind us too of the critical importance of taking into account audience and response when examining patronage strategies in the early modern period.[15] And in the past decade or so, the widespread patronage activities of women (and this is highly significant in considering Raphael's career) have become increasingly better known.[16] In Raphael's early career, networks of female patrons – both secular and religious (and related by both blood and marriage) – played a crucial role in furthering the young artist's career.

In this essay I consider Raphael's early patrons in terms of their social, political, and economic status and their relationships to one another. I also consider the spread of his fame, the increasing prices his works commanded, and how the artist privileged some patrons above others. I am particularly interested in how Raphael, so to speak, "played the patronage game," so that by the end of his all-too-brief career, illustrious patrons were vying for his time and talents. The questions I pose here are equally relevant for the artist's early career and for his years in the Eternal City. In contrast to the rich documentation of Michelangelo's interactions with Pope Clement VII (or Titian's with Federico II Gonzaga), direct information concerning Raphael's dealings with his patrons is lamentably sparse.[17] Recently, there have been additional studies with new material on Raphael's patrons – such as articles on patrons in Perugia and Città di Castello by Donal Cooper and Tom Henry – but there still is no comprehensive study on this most important topic.[18] The recent publication of John Shearman's monumental *Raphael in Early Modern Sources* (1483–1602) will surely necessitate a reconsideration of the patronage that supported the artist.[19]

EARLY PATRONS IN CITTÀ DI CASTELLO: RAPHAEL'S FIRST ALTARPIECES

As the son of Urbino's court painter Giovanni Santi, who died in 1494, Raphael would undoubtedly have been exposed to a courtly ambience as a child.[20] Raphael's training as a young artist is still a matter of dispute, as is the location of his workshop (or workshops).[21] In terms of patronage, his earliest works seem not to have been due to the munificence of Urbino's refined Montefeltro court, which was in exile for much of 1502–3 (just as Raphael was making his name), but instead to the sort of small town corporate patrons and wealthy individuals who supported the lion's share of painters active in Umbria, the Marches, and Tuscany outside Florence.[22] The commissions for several of Raphael's first works came from Città di Castello in Umbria, near the Tuscan border, which was in this period dominated by the powerful Vitelli family. Raphel's commissions for Città di Castello include a double-sided processional standard of ca.1500 representing the *Trinity with Saints Sebastian and Roch* and *The Creation of Eve*, usually said to have been commissioned by a confraternity associated with the church of the Santissima Trinità (although it may have been an ex-voto related to a recent outbreak of plague).[23] For the town Raphael also painted three major altarpieces: the now-destroyed Saint Nicholas of Tolentino Altarpiece, fragments of which survive in Paris, Brescia (Plate 1), and Naples; the so-called *Mond Crucifixion* in London (Plate 3 and Figure 2, copy in situ); and

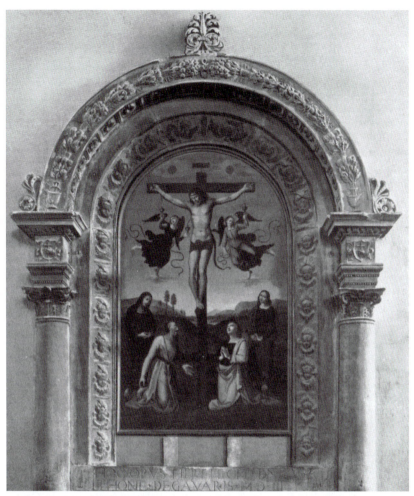

2. Copy of the *Mond Crucifixion* in its original frame. Photo courtesy of the National Gallery Archives, National Gallery, London.

the *Marriage of the Virgin* (Plate 4), signed and dated 1504, now in the Brera, Milan.[24]

These large altarpieces were each painted for private family chapels in three of Città di Castello's major churches and, as has recently been stressed, formed part of a program of altar refurbishing between approximately 1485 and 1505.[25] The contract usually associated with the San Nicola Altarpiece for Sant'Agostino, dated 10 December 1500, calls the seventeen-year-old

Raphael *"magister"* and specifies the collaboration of the much older
Evangelista di Pian di Meleto, a member of the Giovanni Santi shop.[26] It
tells us that the figures were to be painted according to the specifications
of the patron, Andrea di Tomaso Baronci, "with good painting and colors
and in the manner of a good painter and master."[27] Until recently, little was
known of this patron, a wool merchant first documented in 1466, who acted
as an intermediary for several commissions in Città di Castello's ecclesiastic
foundations.[28] The archival research of Enrico Mercati, and, more recently,
of Tom Henry, has placed Andrea Baronci within the civic, economic, and
religious life of late-quattrocento and early-cinquecento Città di Castello;
importantly, this work has also associated Baronci with the patrons of the
two other Raphael altarpieces once there.[29]

The patron of the London *Crucifixion*, Domenico Gavari, was also a wool
merchant and a prominent political figure in the town, who served on various civic and juridical bodies with Baronci.[30] The wives of the two men
interacted on property transactions, and in 1512, Clara Baronci's recently
discovered will – drawn up before the altar on which Raphael's *Crucifixion*
stood – made Gavari her universal heir.[31] Gavari's name and donation
are recorded on the stone altar frame, dated 1503 and still in situ at
San Domenico (Fig. 2); the inscription reads: "HOC OPVS FIERI FECIT
D[OMEN]NICVS/THOME DE GAVARIS MDIII."[32] The patron's stemma,
which displays a disembodied hand holding a cross, appears on the *pietra
serena* frame and underscores the relation between patron and image. The
chapel was dedicated to Saint Jerome, who appears prominently in Raphael's
panel and whose life is depicted in the predella.[33]

The Brera *Sposalizio* (Plate 4) was painted for the chapel of the Albizzini
family in San Francesco, which had been purchased in 1501 and was dedicated to Saint Joseph and the Holy Name.[34] Raphael's altarpiece was surely
intended to emulate Perugino's version of the theme (1484, now in Caen),
painted for the chapel of Saint Joseph in the duomo of Perugia that housed
the precious relic of the Virgin's Holy Ring, which had been stolen from
Chiusi in 1473.[35] A letter of 4 October 1571 tells us that the patron was Ser
Filippo di Ludovico Albizzini, a notary and wool merchant.[36] Like Gavari,
Ser Filippo and other members of the Albizzini family served on a number
of civic committees.[37] What we see here, then, in the very first years of
Raphael's career, is that as his reputation with small-town, merchant-class
patrons grew, they must have emulated their friends and fellow townspeople
in selecting the young man whose work came to be prized for its uncanny
adaptation and synthesis of elements of the styles of then far-better-known
painters such as Perugino, Pinturicchio, and Signorelli (who had enjoyed

widespread patronage in Città di Castello in the decade before Raphael's activity there).

PATRONAGE IN PERUGIA: WORKS COMMISSIONED BY WOMEN AND RAPHAEL'S FIRST FRESCO

During his early years Raphael also worked for several known patrons in Perugia, a number of them women. These works include the Vatican *Coronation of the Virgin* (or *Pala Oddi*, Plate 2), which in a Perugino contract of 1512 is described as the property of Leandra (called Alessandra in the document) Baglioni degli Oddi, widow of Simone di Guido, a scion of the Oddi family, the male members of which had been exiled in 1489 because of their violent disputes with the rival Baglioni clan.[38] The two families, who, despite their fierce rivalry, often intermarried, were both members of Perugia's magnate class.[39] Alison Luchs, and more recently Donal Cooper, have emphasized the cooperative relationships and patronage activities of Leandra, her sister-in-law Maddalena, and other women in the family, who oversaw the patronage rights of the family chapel in San Francesco al Prato, dedicated to the Assumption of the Virgin and ceded to the family in 1461.[40] Recent scholarship has demonstrated that networks of cooperative female patronage were commonplace in early modern Italy.[41] Such models for women's art patronage may mean that it is futile to separate the precise contributions of the Oddi women at San Francesco. Another sister-in-law of Leandra degli Oddi's was Atalanta Baglioni, patron of one of Raphael's best-known altarpieces, the *Entombment*, signed and dated 1507 (Plate 12). Also painted for San Francesco al Prato in Perugia, the main panel is now in the Galleria Borghese in Rome.[42] Vasari's attribution of the patronage to Atalanta is confirmed by Raphael's own notation on the back of a drawing in Lille.[43] The subject of the altarpiece has often been related (first by Jacob Burckhardt) to the life of the patron, whose estranged son Grifonetto died tragically in her arms in the summer of 1500, the victim of internecine bloodshed.[44] The previous year, the chapel of Saint Matthew in San Francesco had been ceded to Atalanta and Grifonetto for the burial of her recently deceased mother Angela and, eventually, for themselves and their descendants.[45] In her own will of 17 December 1509, Atalanta expressed her wish to be buried in the chapel, the rights of which she had assumed in 1499; thus, the Raphael altarpiece clearly formed part of a family program to ensure her salvation and that of her mother and murdered son.[46]

Raphael was also commissioned to paint altarpieces for two Franciscan convents in Perugia, which, typically, housed daughters of the town's leading families. For the nuns of Sant'Antonio of Padua, he painted the Colonna Altarpiece, datable to ca. 1505, now in the Metropolitan Museum of Art, New York (Plate 7).[47] In an interesting observation about female patronage and gendered reception, Vasari tells us that the infant Jesus was fully dressed in order to please "quelle semplici e venerende donne (those simple and venerable women)."[48] Francesco Mancini has recently identified the female saint at the right (usually identified as Cecilia) as Margaret of Cortona and has suggested that the commission was offered to Raphael by Ilaria Baglioni (ca. 1438/40–1503), born Margherita di Braccio Baglioni, elder sister of Leandra degli Oddi and sister-in-law of Atalanta Baglioni.[49] No documents confirm this hypothesis, which, if correct, would suggest once again the importance of networks of female patrons.[50]

Also commissioned for a convent just outside Perugia, that of the Poor Clares of Monteluce, was a large Coronation of the Virgin intended for the high altar of the outer, public part of the church.[51] The painting, finished by Raphael's heirs Giulio Romano and Giovanfrancesco Penni, was delivered only in the summer of 1525.[52] The *badessa* responsible, Suor Battista (1452–1523, born Antonia), was a member of the Alfani family of Perugia, and her nephew may have been the patron of Raphael's *Conestabile Madonna*; she herself was a noted poet and patron.[53] A notation in the *Memoriale* of the convent from December 1505 says that the nuns chose Raphael because of his reputation "among many citizens" and the convent's male advisors, "who had seen his works."[54] The price specified in the contract of 12 December 1505 was 177 ducats; this was more than five times the 33 ducats allocated but four years earlier for the San Nicola Altarpiece (although considerably less than the 855 ducats eventually paid for the *Transfiguration*) and suggests the rapid expansion of the young painter's reputation.[55] The "*cona*" (or *tavola*) was to be based on one by Domenico Ghirlandaio in Narni and the figures were to be by Raphael's own hand, indicating the premium already put on his work by the time he had reached the age of twenty-two.[56] The funds were to come from the bequest of a widow who had died in 1494, Suor Illuminata de Perinello.[57] Raphael continually avoided fulfilling the contract, and in June 1516, a new agreement concerning the main panel, based on an existing drawing, was signed in Rome; as was customary, a male procurator signed for the cloistered women.[58] Raphael was given one year to complete his portion in Rome (which was to arrive at Monteluce in time for Ferragosto of 1517), and the rest was to be painted in Perugia by Berto di Giovanni.[59] It is unclear whether any work had been done at that point, and little tangible came of the commission in

Raphael's lifetime. This raises the question of *why* Raphael repeatedly put this commission "on the back burner" for some fifteen years. The obvious answer, of course, is that he had simply become too "important" for the Clarisse by the time he was working for patrons like Leo X and Agostino Chigi. I suspect, however, that this is too easy an explanation – after all, at about this time he took on the commission for the *Spasimo di Sicilia*, intended for an Olivetan monastery in remote Palermo.[60] It is worth asking, I think, whether the nuns' tastes were simply too conservative and he no longer wished to accommodate them, as he had done previously for the *suore* of Sant'Antonio. Raphael also worked for male patrons in Perugia, both secular and religious. For San Severo, a Camaldolite foundation, Raphael frescoed a lunette representing the Holy Trinity with saints and angels in a small chapel. An inscription at the left of the lower part of the fresco (completed in 1521 by Perugino) reads as follows: RAFAEL DEVRBINO.DOMINO.OCTAVI/ANO.STEPHANI.VOLAT[ER]ANO. PRIO/RE.SANCTAM.TRINITATEM.ANGE/LOS.ASTANTES.SANCTOSQ'/ PINXIT/A D [M] D V. Some scholars have questioned the date provided in this inscription, which seems not to accord with the more mature style of the figures (much indebted to Fra Bartolomeo), although the naming of Stefano di Ottaviano of Volterra as prior of the monastery at that time is correct, and it may well be that the date recorded many years later was simply in error.[61] It is to be hoped that further research will clarify the circumstances surrounding the commission for Raphael's first monumental wall painting, which would shape his thinking in the *Disputa* for the Stanza della Segnatura (Plate 19).

Bernardino Ansidei, a member of a family of wealthy merchants (which originated in the Umbrian village of Catrano), is usually said to be the patron of an enthroned Madonna with saints John the Baptist and Nicholas of Bari for the Cappella di San Nicola in the Servite church of San Fiorenzo (National Gallery, London), but this is unlikely.[62] As in the case of the Oddi and Baglioni at San Francesco al Prato, the commissioning of the painting itself was part of collective family patronage of the chapel and its altar, provided in 1483 by Filippo di Ansideo di Simone, who bequeathed 100 florins for the chapel's maintenance in 1490.[63]

PATRONS IN URBINO, 1504–8: SMALL-SCALE WORKS AND PAINTINGS AS GIFTS

In the years 1504–8, customarily called Raphael's "Florentine period," he is also documented in Urbino and was almost certainly there on more than one occasion.[64] During these years he produced a number works for the court of Guidobaldo da Montefeltro and his wife Elisabetta Gonzaga, familiar to readers from Baldassare Castiglione's *Book of the Courtier*, which is set in March 1507 (when Raphael may well have been in Urbino).[65] These works include now-lost paintings, silver basins designed for the duchess, portraits (although a number of these attributions are disputed), and a number of small-scale, secular subjects such as the *Three Graces* in Chantilly and *The Knight's Dream* in London (Plate 8).[66] Whereas Vasari says that the duke commissioned a lost Agony in the Garden, a letter of Pietro Bembo's tells us, instead, that Duchess Elisabetta was the patron of the work, described as "sottile e minuto," which was requested to be given to a Camaldolite monk, Michele Fiorentino.[67] In 1540, Sebastiano Serlio credited the duchess with elevating Raphael as a youth, setting the stage for the patronage of Julius II and Leo X.[68] Famed humanists associated with Urbino, such as Castiglione and Bembo, were also patrons of Raphael or acted as agents for the court. Raphael painted a now-lost portrait of the latter, and the late John Shearman recently suggested that the Uffizi portrait of the Duchess Elisabetta was painted for Castiglione (who was her secret lover) to take to London in 1506.[69]

The small-scale works produced for Urbino – precious and refined, with evocations of northern art – appealed to tastes quite different from those of the patrons of the large (and for the most part conservative) altarpieces in Città di Castello and Perugia. This raises the question of Raphael developing different styles for different audiences.[70] Despite his work for the Montefeltro court, it is important to underscore that Raphael was not a court artist in the sense his father had been.[71]

Another patron associated with Urbino was Giovanna Feltria della Rovere, Duke Guidobaldo's sister and a daughter of Federico da Montefeltro.[72] The widow of Pope Julius II's brother Giovanni, the prefect of Rome, she was known as the Prefetessa. She was the mother of Francesco Maria della Rovere, who was adopted by the childless Guidobaldo and became duke of Urbino in 1508. Giovanna was a patron of architecture and supported Giovanni Santi in the early 1490s.[73] A letter of 21 April 1508 (Fig. 3), which Raphael wrote from Florence to his uncle in Urbino expressing condolences for the death of Duke Guidobaldo, mentions the cover of a *tavoletta* of the Virgin, apparently for the Prefetessa (sometimes identified with the *Small Cowper Madonna* in Washington, Plate 5).[74] Other paintings, such as the Louvre *Saint Michael* and *Saint George*, have been associated with her patronage and collecting as well.[75]

Most accounts of Raphael's so-called Florentine period begin with a letter, first published in the eighteenth century and lost since 1856, which is said

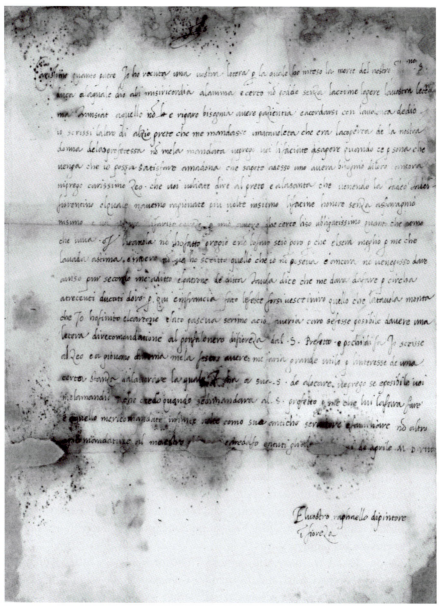

3. Letter, Biblioteca Apostolica Vaticana, Borg. Lat. 800, Photo: Copyright © Biblioteca Apostolica Vaticana.

to have been written by the Prefetessa to Piero Soderini, Gonfaloniere of the Florentine Republic, on 1 October 1504.[76] The authenticity of the letter, which says that Raphael wanted to spend some time in Florence "in order to learn," has often been questioned – most recently by Shearman, who believed it to be an eighteenth-century forgery.[77] Yet even without the letter to her credit, this woman deserves greater attention as a patron than she has been accorded thus far.

DEVOTIONAL IMAGES AND AN ALTARPIECE FOR FLORENTINE PATRONS 1504–8

Raphael's own letter of April 1508, mentioned earlier (Fig. 3), is of signal importance for our purposes, because it mentions two of his Florentine patrons, one of them by name.[78] It also tells us that at that date he was seeking a recommendation to Piero Soderini (recipient of the letter ascribed to Giovanna Feltria della Rovere) and that he hoped to work in "una certa stanza," customarily identified as in the Palazzo della Signoria.[79] The patron named in the letter is Taddeo Taddei, a friend of Pietro Bembo with close ties to Urbino, who was a patron of Michelangelo as well.[80] According to Vasari, Raphael was even invited to Taddeo's table and the letter, in which the artist says that he was "as indebted to him as to any man alive," makes clear the young painter's great affection for his patron.[81] Vasari says that in turn, Raphael, not to be outdone in courtesy, "made him two *quadri.*"[82] One of the works executed for Taddei has been identified as the *Madonna del Prato* (or *Belvedere Madonna*) in Vienna, which Filippo Baldinucci described as in the Casa Taddei in the seicento.[83] The other, described with rather less enthusiasm by Vasari as being "nella prima maniera di Pietro [Perugino]," has not been identified securely.[84] Like all of Raphael's documented patrons in Florence – in a period during which the Medici were in exile – Taddeo Taddei came from a wealthy Florentine mercantile family with aspirations to elevate his family's status.[85]

From Vasari we have the names of two of Raphael's other Florentine patrons, Lorenzo Nasi and Domenico Canigiani.[86] As we might expect, they had intimate connections to each other – indeed, their relationships, brought to light in the 1980s by Alessandro Cecchi – sound like what we might call "six degrees of separation." In this tightly knit circle, Taddeo Taddei's brother was married to Lorenzo Nasi's sister; Nasi himself was married to Sandra, one of Domenico Canigiani's sisters, and Nasi's brother was wed to yet another of Domenico's sisters.[87] For Nasi, Raphael painted the *Madonna del Cardellino* in the Uffizi and for Canigiani, who was himself married in 1507, the large *Holy Family*, now in Munich (Plate 9).[88] Vasari says that Raphael painted Nasi's Madonna around the time he took a wife and Alessandro Cecchi has associated the Canigiani picture with its patron's nuptials.[89] Although not necessarily marriage pictures per se, these devotional images would likely have been commissioned in the first years of the couples' unions and probably formed part of the *arredamento* of their homes; some may also have celebrated childbirths.[90] Surely the patrons – and their young wives – knew well the Raphael Madonnas in the palazzi of their various in-laws.[91] Other Madonnas from this period once belonged to prominent Florentine families such as the Niccolini and the Salviati, but most of the others have no secure patronage context.[92] Given the similarity of many of these paintings, it might well be asked if Raphael, in the first years of his career, produced some smaller works on spec, rather than in response to specific commissions.[93] Vasari also names among Raphael's Florentine patrons Agnolo Doni, a textile merchant and, like Taddei, a patron of Michelangelo's, who married the fifteen-year-old Maddalena Strozzi in 1504.[94] The portraits (Plates 10 and 11), discussed elsewhere in this collection, date not from the time of the wedding, but probably from a few years later.[95] In his life of Michelangelo, Vasari suggests that Doni was a parsimonious patron, who attempted to underpay the artist and ended up spending double what Michelangelo initially asked for the *Doni Tondo*.[96]

Although Raphael worked on several altarpieces for patrons outside Florence between 1504 and 1508, among them the Ansidei Altarpiece and the Borghese *Entombment* discussed earlier, as far as we know, he was commissioned to do only one altarpiece for a Florentine patron. This is the unfinished *Madonna del Baldacchino* (Fig. 4), which never reached its intended destination, the Dei family chapel in the church of Santo Spirito, which was dedicated to Saint Bernard.[97] The Dei were goldsmiths, and silk and wool merchants, with the seat of their business in Lyons.[98] The second will of Rinieri di Bernardo Dei, of 20 July 1506, left a bequest instructing his heirs to have made "unam tabulam pictam pro hornamento dicti altaris et cappelle" along with vestments and liturgical objects for the chapel.[99] Rinieri di Bernardo was also the patron responsible for the impressive Dei palazzo in Piazza Santo Spirito (now known as Palazzo Guadagni).[100] As in the case of other family chapels for which Raphael painted altarpieces, responsibility for the upkeep and ornamentation of the *cappella* and the provision of masses were shared family endeavors.[101] In Raphael's letter of April 1508, the painter mentions an individual identified only as "el patrone," who is presumably one of Rinieri's Dei's inheritors, most likely his bastard son Pietro, whom Rinieri made his universal heir.[102] This would explain the presence of Pietro's onomastic saint in the altarpiece, along with Saint Bernard, alluding to Bernardo Dei, the probable founder of the chapel.[103] Raphael tells his uncle that he has not fixed the price for this patron's *tavola*, preferring instead to have a *stima* or valuation of its worth by a third party.[104] Raphael says that once he has finished the cartoon after the holiday (Easter), he might then write with a price for the painting.[105] He also says that he expected other commissions in Florence and France from the same individual, totaling some three hundred ducats, suggesting that he already had expectations of establishing an international reputation.[106]

By the end of the same year, however, Raphael was seemingly in Rome, apparently called to the Vatican to work on the decoration of the private library of Pope Julius II, now called the Stanza della Segnatura.[107] The unfinished Dei Altarpiece came into the possession of one of the executors of Raphael's will, Baldassare Turini, and the Dei turned to Rosso Fiorentino for a substitute.[108] Although Vasari tells us that Raphael was asked to Rome through the intervention of Bramante, a distant kinsman, it is just as likely, I think, that Julius (who would have seen the *Oddi Coronation* during a visit to Perugia in 1506) relied on the advice of his own Della Rovere *parenti* at the court of Urbino when inviting the twenty-five-year-old artist to Rome and the Curia, where a new world of unimagined opportunity awaited him.[109]

CODA

Patronage in Raphael's Roman Years

Despite Raphael's apparent hopes for large-scale public commissions in Florence, his patronage base there was relatively limited and quite homogeneous, and, with one exception, he received no commissions for large, public works. Why is it, we might ask, that he seems to have been unable to break into the Florentine art world with ease? Did local artists try to impede the young man's rise? Was it because he was perceived as "foreign" or because his art was, at least initially, too "provincial" in style? Raphael's letter of April 1508, which requests a recommendation to the Gonfaloniere Piero Soderini and which indicates the young painter's desire to work in "una certa stanza" (perhaps in Florence, perhaps even in Rome) shows that he was well aware of the need to expand his repertoire to include working on major frescoes carried out for patrons of the highest order.

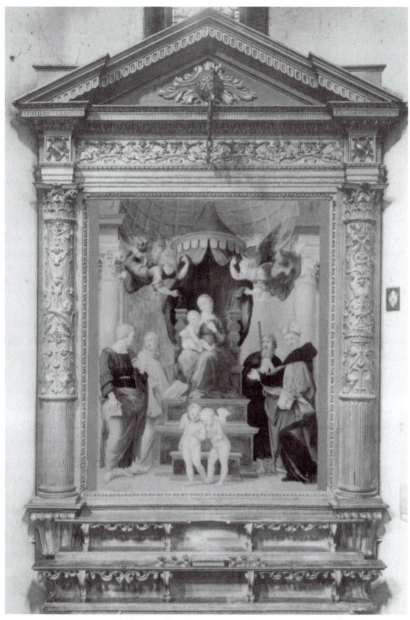

4. Photomontage of the *Madonna del Baldacchino* in its intended frame. Photo: author, with permission of the Ministero dei Beni e le Attività Culturali, Soprintendenza speciale per il Polo Museale fiorentino.

The call to Rome provided just the opportunity denied him in Florence, and the conditions of patronage for Raphael changed dramatically. The first change was one of ambience: much of Raphael's new world – the world of the early-cinquecento papal curia – was an exclusively male and ostensibly celibate culture in which women held no official position.[110] This was very different from the patronage circumstances he experienced in Florence, which involved primarily young couples seeking works for their homes or in Umbria, where he provided altarpieces for family chapels, several of these commissioned by women. The situation differed, too, from Urbino's Montefeltro court, where, as we have seen, women played an important role and commissioned Raphael often. One common thread with patronage from Urbino was the demand for paintings as diplomatic gifts. The second change was that rather than actively seeking out commissions, Raphael would soon have to deal with ever-increasing demands for his talent that he could not possibly meet. Rather than searching for commissions from powerful elites, patrons soon competed for his talent.

With this change in the conditions of patronage came a dramatic expansion of Raphael's workshop, which in a few years brought together an *équipe* of gifted young artists including Giulio Romano, Giovanni da Udine, and Perino del Vaga, without whom the master never could have accomplished even a fraction of what he was commissioned to do.[111] Eventually, the extent of the workshop's participation led to criticism of Raphael and the "bad press" concerning the vault of the loggia of the Farnesina (along with, I suspect, pressure from the patron) must have led him to work on the *Transfiguration*, his artistic "last testament," with his own hand.

Once in the Eternal City, Raphael was quickly able to realize his seemingly limitless potential with support from two extraordinary papal patrons, Julius II (r. 1503–13) and Leo X (r. 1513–21).[112] For Julius, Raphael painted the frescoes of the Stanza della Segnatura (Plates 17–20) and the Stanza d'Eliodoro (Plates 21–22), as well as the great *Sistine Madonna* in Dresden, commissioned toward the end of the pontiff's life for the church of San Sisto in Piacenza, the Emilian city that had recently become part of the Papal States.[113] Raphael figured significantly in the warrior-pope's plans to create an "imperial" papacy in early cinquecento Rome.

Leo X, the highly educated second son of Lorenzo the Magnificent de' Medici and a patron of great discernment, commissioned Raphael and his shop to execute an astonishing array of projects. These include the completion of the Stanza d'Eliodoro, the Stanza dell'Incendio, the cartoons for the Sistine Chapel tapestries (Plate 24), the pope's own loggia (Plate 31), and the commission for the Sala di Costantino (Plate 32), which Paolo Giovio called

"Raphael's last work."[114] Under Leo, Raphael was appointed architect of Saint Peter's in 1514 and Maestro delle Strade, probably in 1519. The Medici pontiff's memorable, if corpulent, features are familiar from Raphael's magnificent portrait of 1518 (Plate 15), in which the pope is flanked by two cardinals: Luigi de' Rossi and Leo's first cousin and trusted "right-hand man," Cardinal Giulio de' Medici, the future Clement VII (r. 1523–34).[115]

Raphael also worked for an array of private patrons in Rome, including churchmen, humanists, and wealthy merchants, most of whom were associated in one way or another with the papal court. First among them were the cardinals from whom he received commissions. Cardinal Giulio was the patron of the *Transfiguration* (Plate 33, intended for the cathedral of Narbonne in southern France) and primary patron of the Villa Madama on Monte Mario.[116] Giulio was a privileged "palatine cardinal," with an apartment in the Vatican Palace, as was Bernardo Dovizi da Bibbiena (1470–1520), a humanist secretary and close friend of Leo X's for whom Raphael and his workshop painted the *all'antica* loggetta (Plate 30) and *stufetta* that formed part of his quarters.[117] Raphael captured the features of another cardinal (Prado, Madrid), who has not been securely identified but who may be the depraved Francesco Alidosi, assassinated in 1511 by Francesco Maria della Rovere.[118]

Under both Julius and Leo, Raphael executed works for a number of curial humanists. These include the aged historian and secretary to Julius II, Sigismondo dei Conti (1432–1512), seen at the lower right of the visionary *Madonna di Foligno* (Vatican Pinacoteca, Plate 25).[119] For the Luxembourg-born apostolic notary Johannes Goritz (d. 1527), Raphael painted the prophet Isaiah on a nave pier of Sant'Agostino in Rome, which stood above the family's floor tomb.[120] The patronage of the *Alba Madonna* (usually dated ca. 1510–11), now in the National Gallery of Art, Washington, D.C., has often been ascribed to Paolo Giovio, the humanist physician who was Raphael's first biographer, but Giovio arrived in Rome only in 1512 (as he himself noted in his writings) and his patronage of the painting (as opposed to possible ownership later) is unlikely.[121]

During his Roman years Raphael portrayed a number of humanist friends, among them the Volterran Tommaso Inghirami, called "Fedra," (1470–1516; Plate 13), who was a canon of the Lateran and of Saint Peter's, and who served as papal librarian under Julius II.[122] During Leo's pontificate Raphael captured the likenesses of Baldassare Castiglione (Louvre, Paris, Plate 16), whom he had known many years before at Urbino, and the Ferrarese poet Antonio Tebaldi, called Tebaldeo, in a now-lost portrait praised lavishly to Bibbiena by Pietro Bembo.[123] Raphael also painted a double portrait (Galleria

Doria Pamphilj, Rome) generally thought to be of the *literati* Andrea Navagero and Antonio Beazzano (with whom Raphael, Bembo, and Castiglione visited Tivoli in April 1516).[124] These portraits of humanist friends may well have been gifts, rather than commissioned works per se.

The identity of the figure accompanying Raphael in the enigmatic double portrait in the Louvre has not been firmly established, and proposals ranging from Giulio Romano to Giovanni Battista Branconio dell'Aquila – *camerarius* to Leo, apostolic protonotary, and one of the executors of Raphael's will – have been put forth.[125] Branconio dell'Aquila certainly commissioned Raphael's tomb for the elephant Hanno (who was in the care of the papal chamberlain) and for him the artist designed the cartoon of a Visitation (now in the Prado, executed with extensive workshop participation), which was placed by Branconio's father Marino in the family's chapel in San Silvestro in Aquila.[126] For Branconio dell'Aquila, Raphael designed the richly ornamented and highly influential Palazzo dell'Aquila (also in the Borgo), which was destroyed in the seventeenth century.

Other curialists extended commissions to Raphael for domestic architecture in Rome, an area of endeavor in which he had not worked (as far as we know) prior to settling in the papal city. He designed a palazzo in the Via Alessandrina (now moved) for Leo X's doctor Jacopo da Brescia (begun ca. 1515), the end façade of which once carried the Medici pontiff's arms and an inscription referring to his munificence. By far the most important domestic architectural project Raphael undertook was the villa on Monte Mario, now known as the Villa Madama, which was designed for Giulio de' Medici, by 1517 vice-chancellor of the church. After Raphael's death, Giulio Romano and Giovanni da Udine squabbled over who was to carry out which part of the decoration of the villa's great garden loggia, clearly annoying, but also amusing the patron.[127]

In addition to Cardinal Giulio, Raphael also received commissions from other Medici relatives and favorites, who sometimes acted as agents for the pope. Leo's young and fiercely ambitious nephew Lorenzo di Piero (1492–1519), who in 1518 married a niece of the French king, Francis I, was involved in the commission for the *Holy Family of Francis I*, which was actually intended as a gift for the queen.[128] Along with the Louvre *Saint Michael* (Plate 27), which was a present for the French monarch himself, Leo stood ultimately behind the commission for the paintings, which were sent to France in 1518.[129] It is worth asking here whether Raphael's late "*maniera oscura*" was intended to appeal to the French audience for these works at a time when Leonardo da Vinci resided in France.[130]

The other major class of patrons for whom Raphael worked in Rome is that of wealthy merchant bankers, such as Bindo Altoviti (Roman-born to a Florentine family, 1491–1557), whose strikingly sensual visage was captured in the portrait now in the National Gallery of Art in Washington, D.C.[131] The ruthless Bindo was also the owner of Raphael's *Madonna dell'Impannata* of ca. 1514, now in the Palazzo Pitti, which Vasari says he had sent to Florence.

Raphael's greatest secular patron in Rome was the Sienese-born banker Agostino Chigi, whose death in April of 1520 was noted at the outset of this essay.[132] Chigi's fabulous wealth and his great appreciation for Raphael led to the creation of some of Rome's most memorable frescoes – both religious and secular – outside the Vatican palace, among them the Michelangelesque but graceful Sibyls from the outer wall of the Chigi Chapel in Santa Maria della Pace. In Chigi's *villa suburbana*, now called the Villa Farnesina, Raphael created and designed works that embodied the very essence of antiquity: the *Galatea* of ca. 1511 (Plate 28) and, some years later, prior to Chigi's marriage, the bowerlike Psyche Loggia (ca. 1517–19, Plate 29), painted almost entirely by members of the shop. Raphael was also responsible for the design of the patron's opulent mortuary chapel in Santa Maria del Popolo, outfitted with paintings, sculptures, and precious materials including shimmering mosaics and richly polychromed marbles.

A number of Raphael's works were intended for export, either to elsewhere on the Italian peninsula or to more distant locales, particularly France, as noted earlier – indeed, the *Madonna di Foligno* was his only altarpiece intended initially for a Roman site. A particularly interesting question is how patrons outside Rome were able to obtain works from Raphael. We know, for example, that the Florentine canon Antonio Pucci, nephew of Cardinal Lorenzo Pucci and future bishop of Pistoia, served as an agent for the Beata Elena Duglioli Dall'Olio in Bologna, who desired an altarpiece (Plate 26) for the newly built chapel dedicated to Santa Cecilia that she had founded in the monastery church of San Giovanni in Monte.[133]

The mechanisms that secured the commission for the large and highly dramatic *Spasimo di Sicilia* (ca. 1517) for the church of Santa Maria dello Spasimo, attached to the Olivetan monastery in Palermo, remain obscure, and, in some ways, the commission for this altarpiece is among the most puzzling from Raphael's Roman years. Although Vasari attributes the commission to the monks, the patron was, in fact, the donor of the church and monastery (authorized in a bull of June 1509), a wealthy Palermitano *doctor juris*, Giacomo Basilicò, who was devoted to the suffering of the Virgin during the Passion.[134] At the time Raphael would have been working on this picture, he continued to avoid fulfilling the commission for the *Monteluce Coronation* (dating back more than a decade), and he ignored the pleas of other would-be patrons as well.[135] This raises the question of how and why Basilicò was able to obtain a major altarpiece designed (if not entirely executed) and signed by Raphael when the artist was working for so many other patrons of seemingly much greater status, not to mention that the destination would have been seen as an exceptionally remote artistic backwater.

It was, however, not only lesser figures whom Raphael put off. Indeed, we know that for a number of years Alfonso I d'Este of Ferrara and his agents attempted tirelessly and in vain to get Raphael to work on a painting (first of an Indian Triumph of Bacchus and then of a Hunt of Meleager) he had promised to execute for the duke's *camerino*.[136] Although Raphael had received a preliminary payment of fifty ducats in 1517 and repeatedly promised his devotion to the duke, he seems constantly to have "brushed off" Alfonso's agents, finding a range of excuses.[137] There can be no question that the futility of Alfonso's efforts stemmed in part from his political weakness vis-à-vis Leo and his cousin Cardinal Giulio.[138] In an attempt to mollify the duke, Raphael sent to him two cartoons in 1518 and 1519, but this barely stemmed the torrent of fruitless entreaties.[139] At one point in 1520 the exasperated Alfonso wrote to his agent that the artist should consider what it meant to tell repeated lies to someone of his stature, respecting him "no more than a low plebian."[140] Shortly thereafter, Raphael died, and needless to say, the duke of Ferrara never received the painting by him for his *camerino* to hang by those of Giovanni Bellini, Titian, and Dosso Dossi.

An interesting incident from 1518–19 tells us much about how Raphael juggled his obligations to patrons in the last years of his all-too-short life. At some point that year, the artist's friend Cardinal Bernardo da Bibbiena (who became papal legate to France in March), had commissioned Raphael to paint the vice-regina of Naples as a diplomatic gift to Francis I, who was a legendary connoisseur of feminine beauty. Presumably because of his overwhelming obligations – among them the mostly autograph pictures intended for the French royal family – Raphael sent a *garzone* (Giulio Romano) to Naples to record the features of the famous beauty, recently identified as Doña Isabel de Requesens (rather than Giovanna of Aragona, as had long been assumed).[141] Alfonso d'Este, who was in Paris in December of 1518, expressed a wish to have the cartoon for this portrait, which Raphael sent, offering, in February 1519, to make a replica in oil.[142] Raphael subsequently indicated, however, that the execution of the cartoon was by a *garzone* and not "de sua mano," the master's hand being precisely what patrons had desired since nearly the outset of his career.[143]

ACKNOWLEDGMENTS

It is my pleasure to acknowledge my indebtedness to a number of colleagues who have discussed Raphael and his patrons with me and who have helped with various aspects of this paper, both intellectual and practical. These scholars include Alfred Acres, Alessandro Cecchi, Donal Cooper, Tracy Cooper, David Franklin, Bob Grove,Tom Henry, Alison Luchs, Nicholas Penny, Eike Schmidt, Louis Waldman, Jeryldene Wood, and Joanna Woods-Marsden. I am particularly grateful to Caroline Elam, Alexander Nagel, and Linda Wolk-Simon, who read and commented on drafts of the essay, which has profited greatly from their insight and expertise. Special thanks are due to Barbara Pezzini of the National Gallery, London. My deepest gratitude is to Marcia Hall for her patience and wisdom as an editor and as a friend. This essay is dedicated to the memory of John Shearman, who answered countless questions during its preparation and whose teaching and scholarship have been, and will continue to be, unparalleled sources of inspiration.

PART II
ROME

3 The Contested City
Urban Form in Early Sixteenth-Century Rome

Linda Pellecchia

A citizen of the vast, densely populated, imperial city that was ancient Rome
would scarcely have recognized the Eternal City at the beginning of the Renaissance. The city that had held a million and a half inhabitants at her
peak counted only 35,000 in the early thirteenth century. As Brentano remarked, "If this estimate is even close to correct, all the Romans of Rome
could have sat down in the Colosseum."[1] Years of papal absence during the
Babylonian captivity when the popes moved to Avignon had left the city
decimated. When Martin V returned the papal seat to Rome in 1420, the
abitato (the inhabited area) was essentially limited to the Campus Martius
(roughly the land enclosed by the bend of the river), the Vatican Borgo, and
part of Trastevere. The rest of the Roman city – the *disabitato* – was unoccu-
pied terrain enclosed within the Aurelian walls, punctuated by uncultivated
fields, scattered *vigne*, and a few (albeit important) religious centers.

In addition to her reduced size, the city was a contested polity. The power
politics of the papacy, the landed nobility (the barons), and the urban patriciate (called civic nobles or the Popolo Romano), not to mention the occasional display of popular resentment, is the background against which the
urban development of Rome must be seen.[2] Displays of social dominance,
from festive processions, to the creation of new streets, to the rituals of punishment incised patterns on the urban landscape. Above all, the struggle of
the sacred city (the Vatican) to control the secular one is the leitmotif of
urban transformation in Renaissance Rome.[3]

QUATTROCENTO PRECEDENTS: NICHOLAS V AND SIXTUS IV

From the perspective of the early sixteenth-century papacy, two fifteenth-century pontiffs laid the essential groundwork for grand urban

transformation by the popes. The theoretical underpinnings were articulated, according to his hagiographic biographer Giannozzo Manetti, by Pope Nicholas V in his "deathbed testament." Nicholas who early in his reign had experimented with an urban model that addressed local concerns and sought to share power with the Popolo Romano, turned to grand, utopian schemes at the end of his life, providing the spiritual justification for papal involvement in civic affairs. Formulating a vision of the ideal *polis* that would broadcast the glory and spiritual power of the Church, Nicholas set the ideological stage for the radical urban transformations of later popes. Rather like the modernist visions of Le Corbusier who would have replaced the medieval core of Paris with an ideal system of roads and airways, Manetti's Nicholas endorsed the creation of new broad, straight streets that would excise undesirable areas of the city and reformulate preexisting patterns. In this model, social reform achieved through urban design became a papal prerogative.[4]

The second quattrocento pope relevant to this discussion, who bequeathed more practical tools for urban transformation to his cinquecento successors, was Sixtus IV. A man of action rather than words, he was an ascetic Franciscan of humble origins who ruled with such ruthlessness that at his death, the Roman diarist Paolo dello Mastro said, "he was a bad pope; in all the time that he lived, 13 years, he maintained us constantly at war and in famine and without any justice."[5] Needless to say, Sixtus viewed his own pontificate differently. Immured into a house façade near Campo dei Fiori, is a plaque with the inscription:

Campo Marzio, up to a little while ago damp, filthy with smelly mud, full of disorder, now, under the pontificate of Sixtus, you are shedding this sordid aspect and all things appear splendid in their places. Just praise is owed to Sixtus, bringer of health! O how much Rome owes to his rule![6]

The pope was the restorer of Rome; everything he touched was branded *Sixtus PP IIII Urbis Renovator.*[7]

As *urbis renovator,* Sixtus laid down the basic regulations that would lead to the embellishment of the city and permit its orderly growth under pontifical control. In a papal bull of 1475, he allowed churchmen to pass some buildings to their heirs even if financed by church funds. Cardinals who had previously refrained from constructing in Rome began sumptuous palaces that decorated the city like so many jewels in a papal tiara. A second decree of 1480 permitted urban landowners to expropriate adjacent buildings to improve their personal residences and empowered the *maestri di strade* (magistrates of streets and buildings) to destroy obstructions in public streets. In a significant change, then, the concept of the public good (i.e., the right of citizens to unobstructed streets) displaced the idea of private control inherent in the structures and organization of medieval Rome. The obvious challenge to the authority of both barons and Popolo Romano inherent in Sixtus's decrees and actions did not pass unnoticed.[8]

POLITICS AND URBAN FORM: THE CITY UNDER JULIUS II

Renovatio Imperii: Actions and Imagery

If Sixtus IV was resented for meddling in the secular affairs of the city, his nephew Cardinal Giuliano della Rovere was detested for his hostile treatment of the Romans when he became Pope Julius II in 1503 (Plate 14). Even more disturbing, especially to those outside the Papal States, was Julius's belief that the papacy should rule Italy. The Italian peninsula had become the battered plaything of the opposing forces of France, Spain, and the Holy Roman Empire. In assuming the name Julius (in reference to Julius Caesar), the new pope declared his intention to rid Italy of foreign invaders. Justified by Christ's command that Saint Peter nurture both the body and soul of Christians, Julius saw no conflict between his temporal and spiritual roles.

Others were less convinced. The vision of the spiritual head of the Church acting like a power-crazed tyrant inspired Erasmus in *Julius exclusus* to prevent Julius's entrance into heaven. Written in the form of a dialogue between the guardian of the pearly gates and the newly defunct pope, Erasmus skewers the pope for his bellicose nature. At one point, the pope erupts:

JULIUS: By my triple crown I swear, and by my most renowned triumphs, if you make me angry, you – even you – will feel the might of Julius.
PETER: Madman! Up to this moment all I hear about is a leader not of the Church but of this world.... Your boasts are that you were supreme in rupturing alliances, in igniting wars, in being responsible for the slaughter of human beings. That is the power of satan, not of a pope.[9]

If his ultramontane critics imagined him as a satanic figure, Julius and his panegyrists preferred the image of a beneficent emperor. An eyewitness account of his coronation procession reveals the triumphal imagery of his reign.

On 5th December [1503] the pope arrived at San Giovanni [in Laterano] to have himself crowned...from Castel Sant'Angelo to Campo dei Fiori seven triumphal arches, the most beautiful that had ever been made in Rome, were constructed...and there was a "gran macchina" with a man inside; when the pope passed, it opened up; it was one of the most beautiful things ever made in Rome....Many old timers exclaimed that never before had so many triumphal arches been created for the pope.[10]

Julius's *renovatio imperii* was given tangible form by a triumvirate of extraordinary artists, Raphael, Michelangelo, and Bramante. Just as he pit state against state in an attempt to dominate them, Julius set a level of competition between his artists that was rarely equaled. The result was not artistic self-immolation but works of art, such as Michelangelo's Sistine ceiling, that still today inspire awe. As a patron, he created images of a divinely inspired synthesis of present and past, Christian and pagan, inspiration and knowledge, where reason and order rule (Plate 17).

Bramante's contribution to Julius's *renovatio* is more difficult to envision since his buildings, left incomplete at his death, were transformed beyond recognition in later periods. Using an imperial scale coupled with individual motifs from the latest archeological and antiquarian research, Bramante's buildings were calculated to create a heroic urban image equal to Julius's megalomaniacal dream.[11] The extraordinary new papal recreational space, the Belvedere court, illustrates the magnitude of pope's and architect's vision. Part outdoor theater, paradisiacal garden, nymphaeum, and sculpture museum, it recast the rough terrain separating the Vatican palace from the villa of Innocent VIII into a *delizia* of Neronian size. Spanning the astonishing length of 984 feet with terraced levels connected by stairs and elegant horse ramps, the Belvedere matched the scale of imperial villas. A fresco by Raphael's student Perino del Vaga romantically depicts it as a ruined ancient villa in which a *naumachia* (mock naval battle) in the foreground occupies the very site where it was believed Nero held his naval games.[12] Like his ancient predecessors, Julius used the open space for similar games, including equestrian tournaments and bloody bullfights.

The most important and certainly most controversial Vatican project was the new Saint Peter's.[13] Meant to symbolize the triumph of Julius and the Church, it was born of the destruction of the Early Christian basilica and built with the sale of indulgences that would enrage Luther. Bramante's Pantheon-styled dome and huge coffered vaults imitating those of a famous ruin (the Basilica of Maxentius) thought in the Renaissance to have been the Temple of Peace convey the message that the new Christian Temple would eclipse the old temples of the Caesars. Albertini's guide book, *A Short Work on the Marvels of New and Old Rome*, dedicated to Julius himself, is indicative of the new trend.[14] No longer content, as earlier writers had been, to dwell only on the memory of lost imperial greatness, Albertini glorifies the achievements of the new priestly city as worthy of comparison to those of the ancient *Urbs*.

For many, however, the destruction of the venerable church filled with papal tombs was a sacrilege worthy only of scorn. In Guarna da Salerno's satire, *Simia* (*The Ape*), Bramante fares no better than Erasmus's Julius.

SAINT PETER: Why did you destroy my Temple in Rome, that with its singular antiquity seemed to call the souls of the most irreligious to God?
BRAMANTE: It's not true that I destroyed it. It was the workers on the command of pope Julius.
SAINT PETER: You were the trap. On your advice and through your misdeeds Julius was persuaded; on your direction and orders the workers pulled it down.
BRAMANTE: You have found me out. I confess the fact.
SAINT PETER: Why did you risk doing it?
BRAMANTE: To lighten the pope's purse a bit since it was splitting – so swollen and large it was.[15]

Later in the text, after Bramante threatens to punch Saint Peter in the nose, the architect recovers his poise, laying down the conditions under which he will consent to enter heaven. He wants to redo the narrow and difficult climb to heaven and entirely rebuild paradise with new and more beautiful houses. If Peter refuses, he'll go to Pluto, who will certainly allow the reconstruction of hell. At the end of the encounter, the frustrated apostle returns to the dismal state of Saint Peter's informing the architect that he will remain outside the gates until it is complete.

In *Simia*, Bramante comes off as an entertaining if villainous creature willing to strip his own patron of his purse. The notion of tearing down heaven and hell to rebuild them is a reference to Bramante's reputation as an architect quick to destroy before asking questions. Nicknamed "Ruinante" (the Destroyer), Bramante's designs often involved drastic solutions.[16] His initial idea for Saint Peter's was to reorient it so that those entering would first pass the ancient obelisk on the south believed to contain the ashes of Julius's namesake. (The obelisk was later placed at the entrance to the church under Sixtus V, not by moving Saint Peter's but by moving the obelisk.) The pope resisted. Bramante, according to the papal humanist Egidio of Viterbo, appealed to Julius's pride:

The result would be extremely beneficial if this most august church of Julius the pope would have the monument of Julius Caesar (as the populace believes) at … the very entrance to the church … so that all who entered the church to perform devotions could not make their entrance without being thunderstruck at the sight of the immense new structure.[17]

Another rejected project entailed destroying a good part of the Vatican palace to create an enormous colonnaded piazza in front of Saint Peter's mirroring the form of the new church and recalling the courts of late imperial baths. This antique-inspired *forum Julii* reflects the dreams of Renaissance theorists and reveals the impact of Vitruvius's *De architectura* (*Ten Books on Architecture*). A new illustrated edition of the ancient text, published a few years later (1511) by the erudite scholar and architect Fra Giocondo, was even dedicated to the warrior pope.[18] Such lofty Bramantesque dreams would collapse under the weight of the mundane not only at Saint Peter's but also in Julius's plans for the secular city.

A Tool for Political Conquest: Streets "Straight and Wide"
An inscription dedicated to Julius by the *maestri di strade* highlights the political agenda of Julian urbanism.

To Julius II, Pontifex Maximus, who, having extended the dominion of the Holy Roman church and having liberated Italy, beautified the city of Rome which was more similar to an occupied city than a [well] regulated one, by opening up and measuring out streets in accordance with the dignity of the empire. Domenico Massimi and Geronimo Pichi. Maestri di Strade, 1512. (*A marble plaque on a façade in Via dei Banchi Nuovi*).[19]

In the text, the beautification of Rome is treated as one of a series of papal victories. The first conquest refers to the successful battles to enlarge the papal state; the second praises Julius for his expulsion of the barbarians from Italy; and the last defines his achievements as an urban planner. From a disordered city, he transformed Rome into a well-regulated *urbs* whose new streets were suitable for an imperial capital. The words of the inscription, as Tafuri and Horrigan have demonstrated, contain clear references to Livy and Suetonius that were meant to tie Julius to two great men of Rome's real and mythic past: Augustus and Camillus. Like Camillus who found a devastated Rome and rallied the Romans to rebuild it, Julius resurrected Roman pride. Like Augustus who found a city of bricks and left a city of marble, Julius rebuilt Rome with dignity.[20]

Julius's original project for the secular city, as so many of his projects, was a fusion of the utopian and the practical. Two new straight streets, Via Giulia and its counterpart on the other side of the Tiber, the Via della Lungara, were to create a circuit connected by two bridges, the actual Ponte Sisto (1475) and the projected Ponte Giulia, each rising on the foundations of ancient Roman bridges (Fig. 5, nos. 17, 19, 22, 24). Uniting past and future

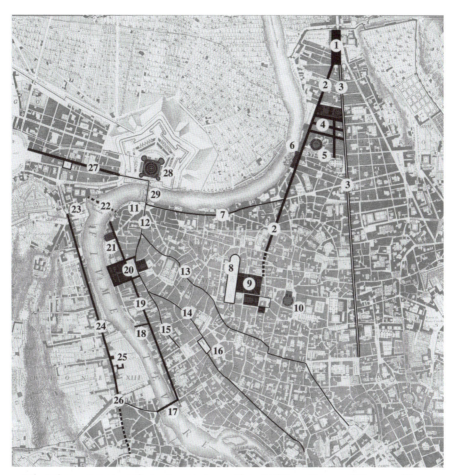

5. Selected monuments and streets superimposed on Nolli's 1748 map of Rome. 1. Piazza del Popolo; 2. Via Leonina (Ripetta); 3. Via Lata (del Corso); 4. Hospital of San Giacomo with Leo's new streets (Via delle Colonnette, Via delle Frezza, Via dei Pontifici, and Via Lombarda); 5. Mausoleum of Augustus; 6. Port of Ripetta; 7. Via Sistina (Sixtus IV); 8. Piazza Navona; 9. Medici complex including the Medici palace, the Sapienza, San Luigi dei Francesi, and the palace of Alfonsina Orsini; 10. Pantheon; 11. Piazza di Ponte; 12. Canale dei Ponte (also called Via dei Banchi); 13. Via Papalis; 14. Via Pellegrinorum; 15. Via di Monserrato; 16. Campo dei Fiori; 17. Ponte Sisto; 18. Via Sant'Eligio with church of Sant'Eligio; 19. Via Giulia; 20. Palazzo dei Tribunali with its piazza and the Chancery Palace (today Sforza Cesarini); 21. San Giovanni dei Fiorentini; 22. Ponte Giulio; 23. Porta Santo Spirito; 24. Via della Longara (today della Lungara); 25. Chigi villa and stables; 26. Porta Settimana; 27. Via Alessandrino; 28. Castel Sant'Angelo; 29. Ponte Sant'Angelo. Photo: Author.

actually and symbolically, the overall conception alluded not only to Rome's imperial past but to Julius's della Rovere lineage. Sixtus's bridge had been built to alleviate dangerous congestion on the Ponte Sant' Angelo (where two hundred pilgrims lost their lives in the Jubilee of 1450). The second della Rovere bridge would also have provided an alternative route for pilgrims, merchants, and, to suit the change in times, papal soldiers as well. Metaphorically the project expressed Julius's imperial pretensions and did homage to his papal uncle; practically it linked the Vatican, Trastevere, and the new Julian part of town into a seamless union.

Yet Julius's plan may have been grander still. A key function of his uncle's bridge was to facilitate the movement of goods between Trastevere and newly set-up markets at Campo dei Fiori and Piazza Navona. With the still-fresh memory of importing large quantities of grain at the outset of his reign to feed a starving population, Julius knew that rapid food distribution was key to controlling the city. To provision the voracious urban markets, he needed to expedite the flow of staples from the main port of Ripa in Trastevere. If Andrea Fulvio, writing in 1527, is correct, Julius wanted to extend Via della Lungara from Saint Peter's to the Tiber port, creating a street of utopian length.[21] Not until Sixtus V at the end of the century would any pope have the resources to execute such a project. In the event, Via della Lungara never reached beyond Porta Settimiana on the south and the site of the future Porta Santo Spirito on the north (Fig. 5, nos. 23 and 26).

While from his seat in heaven or hell, Julius might have viewed Via Giulia as a severed limb of a once organic plan – without the Pons Julii, it remained and remains peripheral to the city as a whole – it was his single most important contribution to the creation of a dignified secular city. Designed by Bramante, it was one of the new straight and wide streets – "rectae et latae" – as Egidio referred to them. In 1565, it was described as "the most beautiful [street] in Rome."[22] The first new street to cut through the secular city since the fall of the Roman Empire, Via Giulia has been praised as "a turning point in Renaissance urbanism"[23] for its breadth and the laserlike geometry of its kilometer-long path. Julius accomplished what earlier popes would not have dared: a surgical cut straight through the city of the Romans.[24] Today, lined with elegant palaces, Via Giulia appears as a Renaissance perspective stage-set expanded to three-dimensions. Decorous and tranquil, it belies its controversial past.

Via Giulia: Justice, Julius, and the "Città degli Romani"
The vision, scale, and location of Julius's two new streets reflect his political and economic agenda and reveal the mechanics of the pope's social

planning. When Julius donned the purple robe, the once-powerful *Urbs* was in shambles. The papal coffers were empty; famine and plague were rampant; crime and violence were endemic. The pope himself was accosted in 1504 by one of the many roving bands of starving men. Duels between feuding baronial families provided "civic" entertainment, and their standing personal armies threatened to turn vendetta into all-out war. Contesting papal rule, barons controlled sections of the city from their fortified enclaves (*monti*). In 1504, for example, a papal envoy was murdered while attempting to arrest a fugitive hidden in the Orsini *monte*. The Popolo Romano, on the other hand, while rarely a source of violence, held desperately to the concept of self-rule, attempting to govern the city from the Campidoglio. Thus, both barons and civic nobility threatened the growing power of the papacy and threw roadblocks at Julius's plan to mold Rome into a modern political state.[25]

Julius acted with formidable energy, attacking barons and Popolo Romano with equal vigor. He enraged the barons by denying them the cardinalate (and thus the papacy) and appointing a new Swiss Guard to replace them in their centuries-old role as papal protectors. He dampened the power of the civic government by stripping the commune of tax revenues, interfering in its legal jurisdiction over its own citizens, and assuming further control over the *maestri di strade* and thus all building.[26]

The embodiment of Julius's use of urban renewal as a political tool was Via Giulia. Conceived as a showcase of papal power, it was to be the locus of a new, daringly consolidated system of ecclesiastical justice that would challenge the Capitoline court, the seat of civic justice. It would also eviscerate a family *monte*, making clear on a large scale that private control must bend to the public good.

The need for a new administrative and legal center, as Butters and Pagliara have demonstrated, was obvious to those navigating the labyrinth of papal or civil courts.[27] The justice system was erratic. Subject to graft and endless, expensive appeals, it had "a nose of wax, that could be twisted this way and that, in keeping with private interests."[28] At times even the powerful could not control its terrible path.

On Friday our Lord,...sent the head of the police to arrest a very wealthy Roman gentleman,...: he was brought to the castle [Castel Sant'Angelo], and that very night his head was cut off, and was placed on the bridge, with four torches, where it remained all day Saturday. No one really knows why this was done; some say that the culprit had taken another Roman's wife....The following morning, when the Colonna lords came for him, they found him headless; all were amazed by such haste.[29]

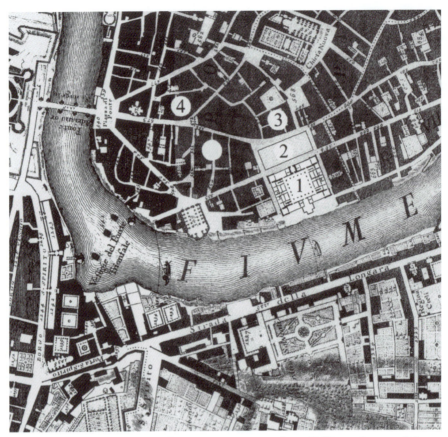

6. Via Giulia and surrounding areas superimposed on Nolli's 1748 map of Rome.
1. Bramante's plan for palazzo dei Tribunali; 2. Piazza dei Tribunali; 3. Chancery Palace
(Palazzo Sforza Cesarini); 4. Banchi area. Photo: Author.

Many of today's elegant urban spaces, such as the Ponte Sant' Angelo,
presented gory tableaux meant to act as deterrents to crime. Quartered
bodies or hanging corpses often decorated the Capitoline as reminders of
the consequences of breaking the law.[30]

The project's centerpiece, Bramante's colossal Hall of Justice (Palazzo dei
Tribunali), complete with four corner towers and a large central courtyard,
although never completed, began rising by 1508 (Fig. 6, no. 1; Fig. 7).[31] According to Vasari, it was

a very beautiful rusticated building; and it is a great loss that such an honored, useful,
and magnificent work, was not finished. Many other architects considered it the most
beautiful example ever seen of that type (*il più bello ordine*).[32]

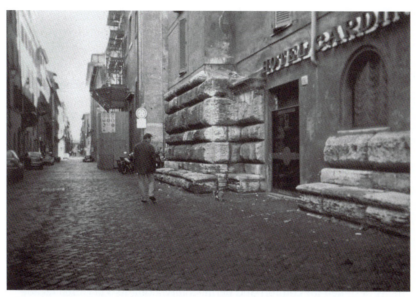

7. Via Giulia: detail of rustication of the Palazzo dei Tribunali. Photo: author.

Contained within the building was the newly designed church of San Biagio della Pagnotta that Vasari praised as "a Corinthian temple left incomplete, a very rare thing."[33] The ringing of a massive bell from a tall tower on its façade would have punctuated the daily legal process, competing for dominance with the bells of the Capitoline court.

United within its thick, rusticated walls were to be four major ecclesiastical courts that had previously been scattered about the city, some in semipermanent quarters.[34] Recalling Giuliano da Sangallo's earlier judicial project for the king of Naples, Bramante's Tribunali was enormous – easily accommodating courtrooms, living quarters for the justices and their familiars, space for clerks and other service employees, a prison, and a church. Its façade stretched about 328 feet along Via Giulia.

Although the image of the Tribunali recalls a medieval fortress with its formidable walls, towers, and battlements, for the papal humanists ancient Rome was a more obvious and appropriate reference. Egidio said it was built, like the Belvedere court, "cum Romanorum splendore."[35] The ground-floor blocks of travertine, which even in their fragmented present state are commanding (Fig. 7), recall the protective walls of the ancient *Urbs* or the rustication of Roman ruins thought to have been imperial palaces. Even the plan is inspired by antiquity. The giant courtyard with a church directly opposite the entrance resembles Renaissance interpretations of the ancient Roman house such as that published in Fra Giocondo's new edition of Vitruvius. Significantly, in 1510, Albertini included it as one of the Seven Wonders of the New Rome.[36]

In Bramante's original project, the huge fortress would have aggressively presided over a large piazza, probably surrounded by a colonnade similar to his projects in Vigevano or at Saint Peter's. Street, square, and surrounding buildings would have created a true *forum justiziae*, especially if the one important ecclesiastical court probably not housed in the Hall of Justice, the Rota (the court serving foreigners in their appeals against the civic courts), occupied the palace across the piazza, as has been suggested (Fig. 6, nos. 2 and 3). The grand square, left incomplete, was literally swallowed up in later years. Its very existence long denied by scholars, it was resurrected only through the discovery of a rough sixteenth-century sketch and scattered archival documents.[37]

Despite the defensive character of the rusticated building, one finds elements designed for comfort and permeability along its Via Giulia façade. A long, Florentine-inspired stone bench invites one to stop and rest. An outdoor place where supplicants can sit, it calls to mind Alberti's references to benches where the elders can sun themselves while they wait. Shops that open onto the piazza are also at odds with the protective thickness of the travertine walls. The Tribunali's shops, however, were not for ordinary businesses. No unseemly butchers or even flower vendors would enter their ranks. Rather, notaries, essential to the smooth functioning of the law, would serve the public here and facilitate not only the justice system but commerce as well. Again to quote Vasari:

> The pope resolved to build under Bramante's direction a home in Via Giulia for all the offices and courthouses of Rome in order to facilitate transactions which up to this point had been quite inconvenient.[38]

Both Albertini and Fra Mariano stress the public utility of the building; it was done "for the comfort and utility of the public" and "the officials of the Roman court."[39]

In this context, the location of the new justice complex assumes special significance. By means of its ample piazza, the Tribunali would have connected to Banchi, the nerve center of the financial district (Fig. 6, no. 4). If the chaotic nature of the court system in Rome was bad for the dispensation of justice, it was disastrous for the economy. From a business point of view, the endemic legal problems were due to the competition between the ecclesiastical and secular courts. Jockeying between the two systems made life uncertain for Romans and especially difficult for the foreigner bankers on whom the papacy depended. The papal system, more lenient with foreigners, attempted to overturn secular rulings, creating an atmosphere of palpable animosity. Thus, even more than a bulwark against crime, the Hall of Justice was meant to produce a more effective system that would favor the economy. The *forum justiziae* was also *forum mercatorium.*

Whether one wants to see Julius's daring scheme as equivalent to throwing a punch at the Capitoline court, as some scholars would have it, or as a more subtle attempt to gut the secular court through the increased efficiency of the ecclesiastical system, as others claim, Julius clearly intended to unseat Justice from the Campidoglio.[40] The Popolo Romano understood the message in no uncertain terms. In 1511, as the pope lay dying, nobility and barons united in an extraordinary move of solidarity. The tension was aptly described by the Venetian ambassador Lippomano, "the pope is passing away ... The city is in turmoil; every one is armed."[41] Swarming into the city with hundreds of private militias and rallying the citizens to the Campidoglio, the two groups that had suffered most called for the return of the Republic of Rome and the glory days of the past. Barons and civic nobility demanded the restoration of ancient privileges to the aristocracy and powers of taxation and civic rule to the conservators, specifically singling out the unambiguous return to the Capitoline of legal jurisdiction over the citizens of Rome. The speech delivered by Pompeo Colonna is a devastating indictment of papal supremacy:

It was an insult ... that the property of the citizens should have become the spoils of the avarice of a few priests; that only the phantoms of ancient honours should have been left to the city; that senators and conservators only showed themselves in the pomp of processions as ridiculous masqueraders in gold brocade. ... If the holiness of popes in former days had made their rule endurable, what virtue or dignity remained to cover the infamy of slavery?[42]

The unexpected, indeed miraculous, recovery of the fiery pontiff took everyone by surprise. In a public relations move typical of this Machiavellian prince, Julius appropriated their demands, dispensing them as so much papal largesse. The celebrated Pax Romana of 1511, which in reality was a defeat for Julius, made it into history as another of the pope's achievements.[43] With this move, however, the papacy's desire to extend the City of God into the secular city was momentarily thwarted.

Via Giulia: The Social Consequences

Cutting streets through a city entails destruction as much as construction. Any building in its path must be demolished or amputated. The political and economic consequences for resisting could be severe. The rich documentation on Alexander VI's Via Alessandrina illustrates the combination of threat and rewards essential to creating streets. As cities do today to stimulate construction, Alexander IV conceded tax benefits and other privileges to those who built on the new street. The rights came with strict stipulations, however. Façades had to conform to uniform standards and be at least seven canne (15.63 meters) high. More draconian was the order to begin construction within five days and complete it within two months. Those not able or willing to do so had to sell or lease their property to someone who would. Failure to comply within the requisite period resulted in the forfeiture of the property to the Apostolic Camera without further recourse.[44] Julius himself imprisoned owners who rebelled against destroying buildings in the path of his new streets. According to one Venetian writer, the cardinal of Auch was made temporarily homeless when Julius forced him, over his fervent protests, to tear down the façade of his palace.[45] Such ruthlessness was naturally hateful to property owners, especially those of the upper classes, who often owned the rental properties destroyed.

The construction of Via Giulia was no exception. Contemporary letters vividly describe the upheaval.[46]

I found Rome in shambles.... The pope is building a street that runs behind Banchi and ends up at that ruined bridge [Pons Triumphalis] at Santo Spirito: at present he is demolishing the church of San Biagio ... [to build] ... a huge palace measuring a full 40 *canne.*

Another says:

between this edifice [the Tribunali] and the Chancery he is destroying all the workshops and houses and creating a large square.... A large part of the Compagnia dei Fiorentini has already been destroyed, so here more effort is being spent on demolition than on building.

The havoc had a price tag:

[Julius] wants to make a square in front of the Chancery and to demolish houses and shops with a value of over 40,000 ducats.

One cannot help recalling Bramante's nickname as we eavesdrop on these shocked and incredulous witnesses. The last letter also confirms (what some scholars had previously doubted) that the piazza was not only integral to the plan but actually begun.

The 40,000 ducats worth of confiscated property belonged to the Chapter of Saint Peter's, which, according to a later court case, had not been compensated for the loss. Believing that his intervention would stimulate an increase in property values and rents, the pope considered that the appreciated value of the chapter's remaining holdings was payment enough. Thus, Julius clearly intended Via Giulia to be a catalyst for social change. In a district characterized by small, wretched houses and *orti* (vegetable gardens) typical of undeveloped areas, the increasing value of land would in turn stimulate a rise in the socioeconomic level of the vicinity.[47]

The river was another deterrent to social change that Julius wished to overcome. Whereas river sites are desirable today, they rarely were in the early modern period. The hygienic conditions along the Tiber were dreadful even into the early sixteenth century. From the Middle Ages on, sections of the river banks were regularly used to dump garbage collected from the streets.[48] Flooding was a constant threat even after Via Giulia was begun. In 1530, when gentrification was in full force, a letter describes the elevated social status of the part of Via Giulia near Banchi and the terrifying collapse of a house not far from the Tribunali:

Your Excellence knows how many beautiful houses there were: one sees signs that few will remain. The city was thrown into terror when a large house belonging to Mons. Eusebio... collapsed with him and about 30 other people inside killing all the men and [also] the animals inside. The Tiber, having infiltrated the land under the house, caused the earth to rise and the house to collapse. And the way it fell was even more frightening, seeing that the house didn't sink on one side only, but all at once, as if it had fallen into a big hole.[49]

Schemes to control flooding continued until the nineteenth-century embankments solved the problem. According to two later (and it must be noted somewhat suspect) texts, Bramante conceived of a spectacular plan to control the Tiber and construct another navigable waterway through Rome. A canal with locks and gates would divert excess water, bringing it safely though the city roughly along Via del Corso and channeling it out to irrigate the fields. Part of the scheme included using the canal "for a delightful waterway for the convenient use of the populace."[50] The river itself was navigable for small craft during the Renaissance. Both Julius and Leo X used it to travel to the papal hunting lodge at Magliana.

That Julius saw his urban renewal extending from the river to the business district is clear from his intention to regularize several small streets – some new and some newly renovated – that were to move out from Via Giulia like tines of a fork. In 1509, for example, the Confraternity of the Goldsmiths (the *orefici*) lost their church to Julius's rectifying mania:

Rafaele Casali and Mario Millini [the *maestri di strade*], having been ordered by the pope to straighten the public streets of Rome, and for that purpose in certain places demolish houses and religious buildings, and since they wanted to make Via dell'Armata into a public street, they demolished our church that already was in a decrepit state.... [In its place] they gave us another [site for our church].[51]

The new site, granted in 1508, is on the present-day Via di S. Eligio, which runs down to the river from Via Giulia (Fig. 5, no. 18). The new church, Sant'Eligio degli Orefici, is an elegant Greek-cross plan attributed to Raphael, begun only in 1515 and never completed.[52] By selecting a site on a small street running to the river, the *orefici* revealed their expectation that Via Giulia would indeed stimulate change. As it turns out, they had to wait six years for the Via di Sant'Eligio to be straightened and given its final form. By that time, the pope in charge was, of course, not Julius, but Leo X.

Julius's attempt at social and economic engineering in Via Giulia can finally be read as a manifesto of urban priorities in the face of aristocratic opposition. Via Giulia and its ancillary streets were a direct attack on the medieval system of Roman urbanism, which was based on the power of private families. The Planca Incoronati, who dominated the area before 1508, rose to power in the fifteenth century to become one of the most important and richest members of the civic nobility. With surgical precision Via Giulia slices through their *monte*, which ran from Via di Monserrato to the Tiber. Julius's public street eradicated the enclosure typical of aristocratic *monti*, severing even the extensive personal garden behind the Planca's quattrocento palace. As if to express their disdain for the new street, the family built their stables along its course, isolating themselves from it and blocking their view of the disruptive thoroughfare.[53]

Via Giulia after Julius

As in so many other cases where he had the opportunity to reverse one of his predecessor's policies, Leo X diminished Julius's insult to the Planca Incoronati when he became pope in 1513. By bestowing on the Planca the rights to the parish church of San Nicola Incoronati, he restored virtual control over the area to the family. Whether intentional or not, a part of the street once meant to embody the grandeur of an imperial papacy resembled a Broadway for base populations – prostitutes, pimps, and petty crooks. A late-sixteenth-century letter from a group of gentlemen residing in Via Giulia requests the pope to "disinfect this [end of the] street," which despite the presence of many churches and honest and honorable families, is plagued by "filthy and loathsome types of women," as well as "reckless…and dishonest…individuals" who say and do abominable things. Prostitutes, it turns out, were willing to pay more than artisans. The interests of landlords, wanting to squeeze every penny out of their property, "is not to be compared to the honesty, ornament, and costume of the city."[54] In the area near Ponte Sisto, famous in the mid–sixteenth century as the center of has-been courtesans and prostitutes down on their luck, hovels rather than grand palaces lined Via Giulia's path.

Although Leo's main urbanistic interests lay elsewhere, his desire to help the Tuscan populations of Rome led him inevitably to Via Giulia. Despite the unintended degradation resulting from the restitution of Planca control, Leo's interventions in Via Giulia were designed to enhance the social character of the street. He continued Julius's plan to straighten and improve small streets, especially in the area known as the Castrum Senese. Long a center of Sienese economic activity, the Castrum included the church of Sant'Eligio, mentioned earlier, and the Sienese counted prominently in the membership of the goldsmith's confraternity.

Yet Leo's biggest intervention in Via Giulia was saved for his conationals, the Florentines. Under Julius in 1508, the Florentine community had received a shock. In the diary of the director of their confraternity we find the following account:

I remember how today, 17 August, the pope sent Bramante with the *maestri* [*di strade*] to tear down our confraternity and our oratory [to make way for Via Giulia] … and with strong words we made the *maestri* remain [to discuss it further].[55]

After several negotiations, the pope conceded a large area near the head of Via Giulia on which the Florentines could build a new, larger church to replace the demolished oratory. Some scholars believe Julius's hidden agenda was to trick the confraternity into paying for a decorous piazza at the end of his street. The pope, however, was also aware that fighting the most powerful foreign group in Rome, despite his general dislike and ill treatment of them, would be futile and costly. Whatever the truth, a piazza at that end of Via Giulia was essential to resolving the difficult connection between the new street and the remains of the ancient Pons Triumphalis on which Julius hoped to build his new bridge (Fig. 5, no. 22).[56]

Neither the piazza nor the bridge materialized. Despite the grant of land, San Giovanni dei Fiorentini was barely commenced. Only around 1518, stimulated by Leo's economic and legal support, architects such as Raphael and Jacopo Sansovino began submitting designs for the new building. By the time of Leo's death in 1521, however, the church had barely been begun. Undoubtedly the cost of building on such difficult terrain had taken its toll. Nonetheless, Leo bestowed a crucial gift to the community. He gave San Giovanni the legal status of parish church for the Florentine nation, making it the de facto Florentine center of Rome. Thus, Via Giulia abandoned its politically charged association with papal Justice to become a symbol of Florentine economic ascendancy and of Leo's new policy of *Renovatio Etruriae* (which underlined positive associations between Florence and Rome).[57]

Under Leo the southern end of Via Giulia assumed the character of an elegant palace street. Its palaces, however, were not those of the socially established upper classes but the residences of painters, architects, goldsmiths, and other artisans, including the architect and entrepreneur Giuliano Leno who was responsible for organizing the daily work at Saint Peter's and the Tribunali.[58] As such Via Giulia became emblematic of the Renaissance artist's successful struggle for social acceptability. Before his untimely death in 1520, Raphael had purchased a large plot on which to build a remarkable palace – a showplace to display his ability to fuse elegant design with practical functions. The palace would have had two separate quarters, each with its own court and one with an *all'antica* fountain. Raphael's own workshop was neatly contained within his quarters in a tour de force of exquisite design.[59] In the end, neither Julius nor Leo succeeded in forcing Via Giulia into the ranks of Rome's elegant streets. Symptomatic of the street's low status, the funeral procession of Agostino Chigi, intimate of both Julius and Leo, avoided what should have been the most exceptional thoroughfare in town.[60]

The Country Life: Via della Lungara and Agostino Chigi's Villa Suburbana

While the utopian dream of directly connecting the Vatican to the port at Ripa was never realized, Via della Lungara as constructed formed a perfect foil to its counterpart across the river. If Via Giulia served law, business, and commerce, then Via della Lungara was dedicated primarily to the culture of the villa.

Originally a narrow street used by Roman pilgrims making their way to the Vatican, Via della Lungara was called Via Santa in the fourteenth-century statutes and designated as one of the streets where dumping garbage was prohibited (undoubtedly to stem regular dumping). Subject to frequent flooding, from its starting point in the ancient Roman Porta Settimiana as far as San Jacopo, Via Santa was often under water. With the advice of Bramante, Julius moved the section from San Jacopo to the Vatican walls away from the river and enlarged it. From a meandering, wet, refuse-strewn path, it became a "wide and straight" street of elegant palaces. By 1580, the Farnese, Riario, Massimo, and Salviati had palaces with extensive gardens along its uninterrupted path.[61] The property that epitomized Julius's ideal was, however, the exquisite suburban villa constructed by his intimate and banker, Agostino Chigi. A brilliant businessman who cornered the market in alum (an essential element used in dying cloth), Chigi became the richest man in Europe. Without Chigi's financial backing, Julius could not have executed his political, economic, or urban agenda. Without Julius, Chigi would not have amassed the wealth and power that, despite his merchant status, made him feared and respected.[62]

Probably as early as 1505, Chigi began planning his small but luxurious villa, known today as the Villa Farnesina[63] (Fig. 5, no. 25; Fig. 8). Called a *Viridario* and *Villa Suburbana* by the humanist poets Egidio Gallo and Blosio Palladio, Carandolet described it in 1512 as a "*maison de plaisance*...the most beautiful and rich thing...that I ever saw." The Frenchman also marveled at the money purportedly spent "more than 23,000 ducats."[64]

A true *rus in urbe* (country seat in the city) in the Albertian sense, the villa combined the delights of the country without losing the convenience of the city. Surrounded by gardens and perforated by loggias on two sides, the building opened on a path leading to the river, which as Gallo says, beckons one to "rest in the shade of the river...[and]...at the setting of the violent sun [two beautiful porticoes] invite drinking and sumptuous banquets." The grotto especially impressed him as did an artificial pond cleverly fed by the Tiber abounding with various species of fish. Palladio describes topiary hedges, a wood of laurel, fruit trees in bloom, trellises laden with vines, and scented trees and flowers.[65]

Despite the loggias and gardens, the house served the dual role of pleasure retreat and urban palace. Although not abandoning his house and office in Banchi, Chigi signed numerous bank contracts within the villa's walls. At his death, its strongroom contained 900,000 ducats of valuables. Upstairs the plan (with a large *sala* and rooms for business) also reflects the urban character of the building – a palace on the Tiber as it has been called.[66] In his last testament, Chigi confirmed its status as primary family residence because it, not the city palace, was entailed to the male line.

Stipulating that it was never to fall into other than Chigi hands as long as the family lived, Chigi's will, as the name Villa Farnesina indicates, was overturned before the century was out.[67]

An unusual fusion of unostentatious size, simple exterior materials, and lavish interiors, the palace reflects Chigi's personality – restrained and flamboyant, simple and sumptuous. The exterior, once painted with images of gods and goddesses, was made of simple *pepperino* stone, stucco, and terra-cotta. The interior by contrast was famed for its multicolored marbles. A letter to Isabella d'Este describes the building in July 1511 as incomplete, but "very rich in adornments of various types, but the marbles exceed all else so beautiful and richly colored are they."[68] Its murals by Raphael, Sebastiano del Piombo, Peruzzi, and Il Sodoma contain astrological references to Agostino's date of birth, allusions to triumph, and images recalling the works of emperors and Hellenistic kings, meant, as Rowland has compellingly demonstrated, to enhance the personal myth of Chigi's elevated status. Like an exhausted bird who bursts into magnificent song hoping to convince a predator of untapped strength, Chigi relied on ostentatious display to convince court aristocrats that he belonged in their ranks. Parading around Rome on a Turkish horse given to him by the sultan who called him a "great Christian merchant" or tricking merchants into believing he had flour bags filled with gold, Chigi was a showman as well as a brilliant investor.[69]

Like its grander cousin the Belvedere Court, Chigi's villa and gardens were used for relaxation, courtly tournaments, horse training, poetry readings, and theatrical presentations. Legendary feasts were described by numerous sources. Julius II, Leo X, and foreign dignitaries such as Federigo Gonzaga dined on delicacies including exotic fish or the tongues of rare parrots, a bird so expensive that merely possessing one signified wealth. On one occasion Agostino spent the enormous sum of 250 ducats on two eels and one sturgeon! Chigi's most extravagant banquets took place within the now destroyed Tiber loggia where he once astounded everyone by jettisoning gold and silverware into the river. The magnificent gesture was all theater. After the departure of the guests, the precious service was retrieved by servants from carefully laid nets.[70]

In the early stages of construction, Julius baited Chigi, wondering aloud whether Agostino's palace would equal that of the Riario rising opposite it. Responding with the now-famous remark that his stables would be more magnificent than Riario's palace, Agostino purchased more land and had Raphael design a stable that gained palatial status (Fig. 8, no. 2). In the 1520s,

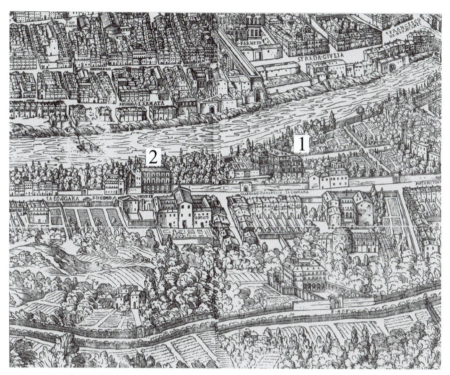

8. Agostino Chigi's villa (1) with river loggia and Raphael's stables (2) superimposed on the Maggi-Maupin-Losi 1625 map of Rome. Photo: Author.

the French pilgrim Jacques Le Saige described it as one of his few noneccle-siastical stops in Rome:

We went to see a stable where one saw 34 horses and there was still room for 18 more. Above the said stable is a room just as large with a beautiful stone vault; providing views of the streets; the riches of this merchant are out of this world.[71]

Executed from 1512 to 1514, the stable was articulated in the latest *all'antica* fashion with superimposed orders of paired pilasters of canonical propor-tions, and pilaster bases inspired by the Forum of Nerva. With elegant balustrades, recessed columns, and room for numerous horses, drawings of its plan, elevation, and details circulated in later Renaissance drawings. Riario's palace never achieved such posthumous fame.[72]

A famous moment in the life of the stable recounted in contemporary documents reveals Agostino's sense of humor and much about life in the papal Rome of Leo X. After a sumptuous meal in a hall hung with Flemish tapestries and tables covered with silver and other ornaments, Leo teasingly accused Chigi of trying to surpass the pope in magnificence. Laughingly, Chigi pulled back the curtains to demonstrate his Christian humility: they were eating, he noted, in a lowly stable.[73]

Thus, Chigi's villa exemplifies an unusual element of Roman urbanism, the creation of villa culture within the city in the vast rural space within the Aurelian walls.

THE CITY AS URBAN THEATER: ROME UNDER LEO X

Vision, Viewers, and Honor: Via Leonina and Piazza del Popolo

Like Julius II and Alexander VI before him, Leo X (Plate 15) cut a new, straight street, the Via Leonina (present-day Via Ripetta), into the fabric of the city for both personal and practical reasons. At the outset of Leo's reign, the old Roman Via Flaminia (called Via Lata in Leo's day and Via del Corso today) linked the main northern gate, the Porta del Popolo, to the Campidoglio – by the Renaissance no longer in the core of the *abitato*. Leo's new street dramatically cut the distance from the gate to the new heart of the city, the Campus Martius. Designed to facilitate movement from the north into the *abitato* and on to the Vatican, it also expedited the flow of goods from the Tiber port at Ripetta. At the intersection of Via Lata and Via Leonina, Leo envisioned an impressive new piazza, an unencumbered area before the gate for tourists and pilgrims seeing the city for the first time (Fig. 5, nos. 1–3; Fig. 9). For kings, ambassadors, and foreign dignitaries entering the city in ceremonial display, the piazza and Leo's new thoroughfare served as a grand *prospettiva* of suitable elegance.[74]

The visual impact was clearly paramount. Indeed, upon seeing the work in progress, Leo criticized the lack of decorum that he perceived:

The view of the hospital erected by us [San Giacomo in Augusta, today "degli Incurabili"] is obscured and the Via Lata is too narrow and the piazza and street named Leonina... do not present to those who see it, that visual beauty and dignified aspect that we wanted. Thus, it is not worthy of our name, doesn't satisfy the public or private good, and is not pleasing to the eye of those who view it.

Suspecting that his original design had been tampered with, he ordered the *maestri*

to lay out the piazza, the Via Leonina, and Via Lata with that amplitude and straightness that will redound to the perpetual glory and honor of the pope and to the agreeable satisfaction of everyone.... [It should be] of such beauty and breadth, and

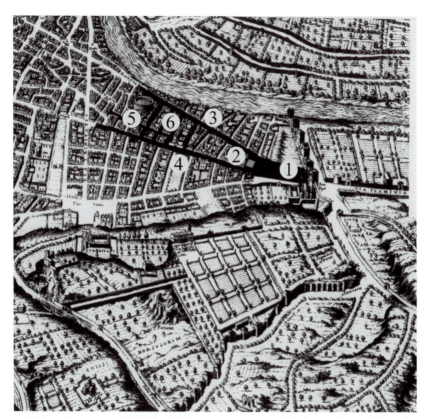

9. Du Perac's 1577 map of Rome with Leo's new streets and Raphael's Piazza del Popolo. Visible are the rectangular piazza (1), the bivium and the hypothetical footprint of the "Mausoleum of Nero" (2), Via Leonina (3), and Via Lata (4). The three new cross streets connecting Via Leonina with Via Lata (6) are visible as is the new Via Lombarda (5), running roughly from the Hospital of San Giacomo to San Carlo al Corso. Photo: Author.

made with the careful deliberation due the majesty of our city, that it could be said with pride, this was done by Leo X.[75]

In these few words, Leo expressed, in a way no earlier pope had, not only his aesthetic concerns but the importance of vision and the role of the spectator in urban design. Although his call for "large and straight" streets with "dignity and decorum" mirrors that of his predecessors, his emphasis on sight is new: the street and square must please the viewer and enhance the effect of important buildings. As a good Florentine and son of Lorenzo il Magnifico, Leo was acutely conscious of the importance of siting as an aesthetic criterion.

The new street and piazza were planned and executed sometime between 1518 and 1519 by Raphael and Antonio da Sangallo the Younger. Better known today as a painter and draftsman, Raphael was the most important architect of his day, assuming – after Bramante's death – the elevated position of architect of Saint Peter's. By 1516, Antonio da Sangallo was his main assistant, draftsman, and engineer. In keeping with Leo's taste for ornate, grand architecture, Raphael nearly doubled the size of Bramante's Saint Peter's, greatly enriched its decorative motifs, and began building it in marble rather than travertine.[76] The new design was extraordinarily expensive – confirming Leo's reputation as a spendthrift and contributing to his constant financial difficulties. Like so many grandiose papal projects, however, it, too, was to remain largely on paper.

The design for the Piazza del Popolo and Via Leonina met with only slightly more success. A bold, innovative project, it also was not completed as the pope had wished. Essential features, however, of Raphael's (and Antonio's) vision still define the way it looks today. To create a dignified stage for processions and overcome the impression that Via Leonina was a mere fork off the primary Via Lata, they cleared a large rectangular piazza in front of the gate. Both streets now began at the bottom of the piazza, equalizing their status. The piazza also eliminated the unfortunate side effect of most V-shaped street plans: the unattractively sharp point where the streets converge (Fig. 9). With the point sheared off, they were left with a broad façade, which in 1519 they faced in travertine. At the corner of Via Leonina and the piazza, a large stone plaque carrying Leo's coat of arms guaranteed (or so he thought) the perpetual memory of his generosity.[77] The resulting form, for which there is no good English translation, is often called a *bivium*. By transforming the lowly fork into an aesthetic object, Raphael made a major contribution to the urban design of Rome and beyond. The *bivium* introduced a new dynamism into the city that would be exploited to the fullest in the baroque. What developed from this and other papal-inspired areas within the city was the birth of a new planning device called the trident. A radiating street plan of three (rather than two) streets, it was more flexible than the ancient grid and would transform urban planning throughout Europe and even in the United States, where star-shaped boulevards criss-cross Washington, D.C. Because some scholars believe that Raphael intended a third street (the present-day Via del Babuino built only under Paul III), they consider him the creator of the Roman Renaissance trident. Others, however, vigorously contest such a conclusion.[78] For our purposes, it is enough that in executing the monumental and formal *bivium* at Piazza del Popolo, Raphael, Antonio da Sangallo, and Leo X illustrated the tangible reality of such a scheme and its enormous functional and aesthetic advantages.

Determined to create a piazza worthy of the "majesty of our city," Raphael and Antonio planned a fitting monument to decorate its center and honor the pope. The recently excavated obelisk from the Mausoleum of Augustus was meant to rise on a base of four elephants surmounted by sphinxes carrying a large inscription – no doubt dedicated to Leo. Although never executed, the project represented a significant innovation with respect to the designs of Julius and Alexander by creating a focal point that could be seen from either street. The placement of a tall, visual goal at the terminus of a street generated a dramatic energy for the spectator. Later in the century, Sixtus V would capitalize on this idea by using obelisks to animate and unify his city plan.

While the obelisk would have greatly dignified the Piazza del Popolo, a letter of 1519 from the Venetian ambassador reveals that it was not Leo's first choice for the ancient monument: "Raphael of Urbino, painter and genteel and talented architect, offered to move it [the obelisk] to Piazza San Pietro for 90,000 ducats."[79] It also indicates the expense of transporting such an object. The obelisk from Augustus's mausoleum never made it to Piazza del Popolo. After languishing for years in the middle of Via Leonina (where it blocked traffic), it eventually ended up at Santa Maria Maggiore under Sixtus V.

Another ancient monument associated with Leo's piazza sparked a controversy that may have delayed completion of the project. Opposite the gate was a large, towerlike structure believed by many to have been the mausoleum of Nero (Fig. 9). Visible even in schematic views of the fifteenth century, the large mass was in a ruinous state, stripped of all its marble sheathing. Its association with the ancient past, however, led to an unusual decision not to demolish it. Most unhappy about the decision were those who had stood to gain financially from knocking it down. In the battle between preservation and growth (not unfamiliar to modern cities), both pope and architect insisted on preservation. Günther has even suggested that behind-the-scene machinations to demolish the monument partly stimulated Leo's testy second papal brief in which he made clear to everyone that he wanted Raphael and Antonio's design executed. Like the Augustan obelisk, the "mausoleum" never played a major role in the later history of the piazza. When Paul III began the third arm of the trident, he tore it down as an unsightly heap of rubble.[80]

That the ideal of restoring the glory of the ancient *Urbs* was a priority for Leo cannot be in doubt. In making wide, straight streets, he was trying, like popes before him, to revive forms from the past. The Venetian Michiel gives us a picture of Leo's future plans for this section of the city:

> The pope rode on horseback to see it [Via Leonina]. And he liked it and said that he wanted to do the same for the Flaminia [Via Lata] that goes from Piazza del Popolo to the Capitoline, that is, enlarge, straighten and pave it as it was in antiquity.[81]

Yet in the paradoxical world of early modern Rome, destroying ancient Rome went hand in hand with reviving it. Ancient monuments disappeared to feed the machine of new construction. Leo's Brief (*motu proprio*) appointing Raphael inspector-in-chief of antiquities states what was long-standing practice – that the main stone "quarries" of modern Rome were the ruins of Ancient Rome:

> We know that the Roman ruins provide ... [building materials] abundantly, and that all sorts of stone are found by almost anybody who starts to build in or around Rome.[82]

In their passionate "Letter to Leo X," Raphael and Castiglione lament this willful destruction of Rome, pleading with him to save what is left:

> Why should we complain about the Goths, [and] Vandals ... if those who ... should be defending these poor relics of Rome have been the very same who [want] ... to destroy and extinguish them? How many popes ... permitted the ruin and disintegration of ancient temples, statues, arches and other glorious buildings? ... How much lime has been made from statues and other ancient ornaments? ... I would dare to say that all this new Rome, that one sees today, however beautiful and adorned with palaces, churches, and other buildings, ... is [all] built of lime made from ancient marbles![83]

While preservation was certainly a part of Raphael's job, it is evident from the rest of Leo's brief that keeping Saint Peter's rising was his main concern:

> It is of the utmost importance for the work on ... [Saint Peter's], that the stones and marble, of which a great quantity are needed, be easily obtained in the neighborhood. [Therefore all stones excavated in Rome must be brought to Raphael's attention] ... so that you can purchase them if they are useful for the work on the temple.[84]

Stimulating a Building Boom: From Workers' Houses to Princely Palaces

Most sixteenth-century papal planning initiatives sought to alleviate overcrowding in the *abitato* caused by years of sustained growth. Via Leonina was no exception. The area between Via Leonina and Via Lata was sub-divided into three new cross streets and a diagonal street running from Via delle Colonnette (called merely cross street number 1 in the documents) to Via dei Pontefici (cross street number 3) and beyond (Fig. 5, nos. 2–4; Fig. 9, nos. 5 and 6). The new streets facilitated speculation by religious institutions, wealthy individuals, and even artists and artisans such as Antonio da Sangallo. Typical of early modern Italian cities, convents, the major landholders in the area, were the prime developers. Conceding long leases at low rents to those who would build houses, the friars of Sant'Agostino and San Giacomo in Augusta fostered working-class developments in the newly subdivided area. Slavs and other ethnic groups had long been drawn to this inexpensive outlying *rione*. Communities of northern stonemasons and craftsmen, attracted by the burst of building activity under Julius and Leo, swarmed into the area resulting in the name Via dei Lombardi for the new diagonal street.[85]

If the census of 1526–27 is any indication, the above-normal population of the *rione* means that Leo's efforts must be judged a success. As elsewhere in the city, however, the 1527 Sack of Rome devastated the population and transformed the character of the zone. Maps of Rome, such as that of Bufalini (1551), label it "Ortaccio," indicating an overgrown and unsightly area with a prevalence of unsavory occupations.[86]

To pay for the widening, paving, and straightening of preexisting streets or the laying out of new ones, a tax, called a *gettito* (derived from the Italian word for "tearing down," because it often paid for clearing the street of buildings), was levied on the inhabitants of the street, for in theory at least, they stood to gain most from its improvement. The fun-loving pope might have enjoyed knowing that his dignified new street was largely financed by ladies of the night. Benignly tolerated by Leo as essential to a city of clerics, prostitutes and courtesans favored this area as Michiel records:

A street in Rome that went from Campo Marzio to [Piazza del] Popolo was paved and straightened with money collected from courtesans; the pretext for the tax imposed on them, was to facilitate movement on Saturdays to devotions at Santa Maria del Popolo. And although the street cost 500 ducats, it is said that 5000 were collected, without complaint from the courtesans, who, in competition with each other, paid more than they were taxed to increase their reputation. And in any case their clients (li cortigiani) ended up paying.[87]

While the development of worker's housing in outlying areas was important to stimulate growth beyond the densely packed *abitato*, palace construction was the sine qua non of a beautiful city. As a Florentine, Leo knew that the embellishment of a city depended on the magnificence of individual building projects. In a decree of 1514, he stabilized the price of building materials.[88] Understanding the chilling effect of inheritance laws on cardinals' desire to build, Leo broadened and extended Sixtus's earlier law allowing the heirs of churchmen to inherit palaces. He also reiterated and strengthened Sixtus's bull allowing those desiring to build a large, decorous palace to expropriate their neighbor's property. The decrees had their intended effect. Rome swelled with grand cardinals' palaces such as the impressive *domus* of Cardinal Alessandro Farnese.[89] To set an example, Leo planned an enormous Medici palace to replace his smaller cardinal's palace near Piazza Navona.

Renovatio Etruscae: Rome and the Medici Dynasty

It is no coincidence that Via Leonina, which led to the markets of Piazza Navona, also created a path to the new dynastic center of the Medici in Rome. Clustering round the eastern flank of Domitian's stadium several projected Medicean buildings were to rise: a giant Medici palace; the newly invigorated Sapienza (the University of Rome), which Leo was transforming into an international center; the palace of Alphonsina Orsini, widow of Piero de' Medici; and the pro-Medici French national church of San Luigi dei Francesi (Fig. 5, nos. 8 and 9; Fig. 10).[90]

Of all these enterprises, Leo's grandiose palace (c. 264 × 278 feet), was the most extraordinary. Never built, we know it through drawings. The earliest, a huge finished drawing by Giuliano da Sangallo (Fig. 10, no. 2), is dated 1 July 1513 (about 4 months after Leo became pope). In 1514–15 Giuliano's nephew, Antonio, was sketching new designs. With theatrical flare, both projects appropriated the entire Piazza Navona, believed in the Renaissance to have been an ancient circus, as their vestibule.

The palace-circus combination had undeniably imperial connotations. The Palatine palace had a circus at its feet. So did Constantine's palace in Constantinople, sketched and commented on by Antonio da Sangallo himself. Yet in the end, the palace was more show than substance; either project would have entailed significant demolition of private property to complete. It is unlikely that Leo, despite his new legislation on expropriation and his blatant use of funds from the Camera Apostolica for personal projects, would have had the economic or political clout to force such wholesale destruction near Piazza Navona.[91]

Still bristling from the arrogance of Julius's imperious papacy, the Popolo Romano was in no mood to tolerate another belligerent pope. Despite the regal scale of his palace, Leo's rhetoric emphasized reconciliation, not

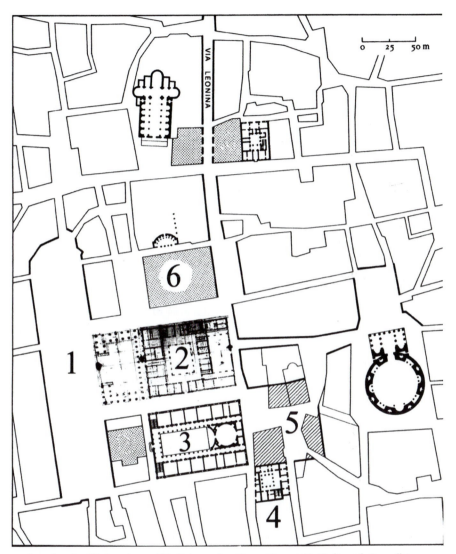

10. Area showing Via Leonina and Medici complex: Piazza Navona (1), Giuliano da Sangallo's project for a new Medici palace (2), the Sapienza (University) (3), Palace of Alfonsina Orsini (4), Piazza of the Dogana (5), site of S. Luigi dei Francesi (6). Plan from Tafuri, *Ricerche del Rinascimento*, modified by author.

conquest. His was not the bellicose *renovatio imperii* of Julius, but a *renovatio etruscae*, emphasizing the relationship of Etruscan and Roman civilization and the return of a new Golden Age. Peace would reign; art, literature, and music would flourish.

In 1513, as evidence of their faith in the rebirth of Rome under the Medici pope, the civic government held an extraordinary event on the Capitoline. Having approved Leo's request that Giuliano and Lorenzo de' Medici be granted Roman citizenship, the Popolo Romano treated its citizens (or at least the elite ones) to a festival of legendary proportions. For two days the audience was entertained with plays, music, and recitations. A temporary theater, constructed, according to contemporary descriptions, as a "true simulacrum of the ancient palaces that were built with much art and inestimable expense for Emperors and the highest classes of Rome when Rome was more properous," housed the festivities.[92] After washing their hands in scented water, the guests opened folded napkins releasing tame birds into the air. Of the twenty-five courses, many were *rivestiti* – skinned and cooked birds and wild game redressed in their feathers and furs and served as if alive. Small sugar sculptures, artificial mountains with scented springs, and incense were part of the lavish display. In the end, the guests could eat no more: "Things started to be thrown around, and one saw goats, rabbits, suckling pigs, capons, pheasant, and partridges flying through the air, so that the whole interior of the theater was full of them."[93] Meat, a rare and expensive treat for most Romans, became the main ingredient of an undignified food fight.

A leader of the 1511 revolt against Julius, Marc Antonio Altieri, a dyed-in-the-wool republican, made clear how much had changed: the pope, he maintained, has created a new Rome that is "liberated from worry and misery."[94] Thus, regardless of the imperial overtones that could have been read into Leo's grand, dynastic palace, the Roman civic nobility viewed him as friend, not overlord, at the outset of his reign.

The Street as Urban Theater: Ephemera into Stone

Festivities like that on the Capitoline, although exceptional in quality, were part of the urban ritual life without which no early modern city can be understood. In Rome especially, the processions, races, and festivals that enlivened the streets conveyed political messages or were vehicles to solidify or contest the social hierarchy. Even ordinary events, such as reading out a papal or civic decree, could transform a street corner into an epicenter of debate and lively interaction. Certain corners, like that where the battered ancient statue called *Pasquino* rested, became foci for expressing discontent. Satirical writings, called pasquinades, decorated the mutilated statue, providing an anonymous site for skewering cardinals, princes, and, above all, the pope.[95] Events such as the bullfights favored by Alexander VI or Julius

II, where men and bulls were killed or maimed, were gory reminders of the violence of Renaissance cities.[96] Others like Carnevale marked age-old festivals where masquerading (otherwise a punishable offence) was permitted and races of horses, nude prostitutes, Jews, and men of all ages provided entertainment and reconfirmed the social order.

Even courtesans had their urban rituals attended by pious and impious alike. Eating, drinking, and dancing in public, they paraded around Rome dressed in perfumed clothes, rare furs, precious Venetian lace, and exquisite jewels accompanied usually by an entourage of pages, servants, and rich churchmen or nobles. In Delicado's sixteenth-century novel about a famous Spanish courtesan, *La Lozana andaluza*, a guide, Rampin, escorts the newly arrived Lozana around Rome answering questions and describing the customs and social geography of the city.

LOZANA: And who is that lady from Andorra who is wearing a hat, and moves her hips well, and is accompanied by two young servant girls?
RAMPIN:...She is one of the dear courtesans from around here. Look what a multitude of them go by there! They seem like a swarm of bees, and the courtiers follow them.[97]

Of the political entrances so common in Rome and elsewhere, that of the ambassadors of the king of Portugal stood out in a city known for extravagant display. They astounded the city with Hanno, an elephant. Not seen in Rome since the empire, the elephant was a gift to Leo X, who housed Hanno in the Belvedere court to the delight of the Romans. The procession began, significantly, at Piazza del Popolo. With a Moor seated on his head, a Saracen leading him on foot, and a leopard perched on his back, the elephant arrived in full display surrounded by rare animals (gifts for cardinals). The enormous animal was covered with gold brocade carrying a howdah of silver with a golden tabernacle holding the Corpus Domini. What most struck eyewitnesses of the procession, however, was the size and intelligence of Hanno:

a beautiful elephant of about 6 years old, which is as large as three oxen, who understands two languages like a human being, that is Portugese and Indian, [and] cries like a woman....From speaking and beyond, [he] acts like a human being.[98]

Entertaining the crowd by filling his trunk with water and spraying the onlookers, at the entrance to Castel Sant'Angelo, the pachyderm knelt, bowed its head, and trumpeted his obedience to the pope as Leo watched from the loggia above. Hanno's death a few years later saddened all Rome. Raphael memorialized him in a portrait (now lost); a court humanist penned his epitaph.

Of the religious processions, none was more important than the *Possesso* – the ceremony expressing the ritual assumption of control of the papal lands by the newly elected pope. It followed a fairly standard trajectory from the Vatican to San Giovanni in Laterano.[99] Under both Julius II and Leo X, it became a simulacrum of an ancient triumph with temporary *apparati* and triumphal arches decorating its path. Both popes adopted the same means, but their respective messages could not have been more different. Leo celebrated not war and military victory, but peace, justice, and *liberalitas*. A splendid arch set up by Agostino Chigi exemplifies the new message. Supported on eight columns and displaying Leo's and Agostino's personal devices, it was decorated with paintings of allegorical figures such as Virtue triumphing over Vice. Real people dressed as Mercury, Apollo, two Moors, and a nymph decorated its niches. An inscription in gold heralded Leo's pacific reign:

> Once Venus reigned, once Mars held sway;
> Now Minerva will have her day.[100]

In contrast to the carnal reign of Alexander or the war-torn tenure of Julius, Leo, like Minerva, would foster art and science.

Given Leo's taste for urban display and Raphael's preference for richly complex architectural design, it is not surprising that the festive style of parades influenced permanent architecture. Convinced they could garner his favor through decorating the city, Leo's courtiers transformed their houses into enduring reminders of processions, races, and carnival festivities celebrating the Medicean myth of the revival of the arts. On Via Alessandrina (Fig. 5, no. 27), the favored, new route for processions beginning or ending in the Borgo, new palaces spread out beneath the pope's gaze from his newly decorated Vatican logge – a living street frozen into a permanent stage set.[101] Men such as Leo's personal physician Jacopo da Brescia or his chamberlain and keeper of the cherished Hanno, Giovan Battista Branconio dell'Aquila, hired Raphael to turn ephemera into stone.

Raphael designed the façades not only as mnemonic references to Leo's rule but also as backdrops to real processions. From the participants' point of view, Jacopo da Brescia's façade appeared longer through Raphael's clever use of perspective. In a brilliant move, the architect accentuated the shortest side of the façade – a corner sliced flat by a *bivium* – to theatrical ends. Despite the small area, its angled location made the *bivium* façade the most prominent from the parade's perspective, appearing momentarily in full face to the oncoming crowd. Raphael decorated it with a tall aedicular frame at whose center was an oversized Medici coat of arms hanging from a lion's head. An allusion to the real arches lining the processional route, it was also an obvious homage to Leo whose name in Italian (*leone*), of course, means lion.

As Burroughs has elegantly elucidated, the festive tone of Raphael's decoration was actually a critique of Bramante's interpretation of the past.[102] Although owing its basic type, rusticated base surmounted by architectural orders and aedicular windows, to Bramante's highly innovative Palazzo Caprini (also on Via Alessandrina and later Raphael's house), Jacopo's palace displayed a richness and complexity that was missing in Bramante's more sober prototype. The contrast in style – intended also as a contrast between Julius and Leo – is even more evident in Raphael's Palazzo Branconio dell'Aquila (Plate 39). Destroyed in the seventeenth century and known only through drawings and engravings, it was located in a prominent position near piazza San Pietro.

In the Branconio dell'Aquila, Raphael breaks with the Caprini model. Whether intending social commentary (i.e., eliminating the overtones of social stratification implicit in using the rusticated base only for the lower class below) or testing the limits of decorum as he had in using classical orders on Chigi's stables, Raphael employs engaged columns, normally reserved for the socially elevated *piano nobile*, for the ground-floor shops. The small palace, contemporary with his reconstruction of ancient Rome and his exceptionally erudite Villa Madama, is imbued with a sophisticated antiquarian atmosphere that he, Leo, and his patron and personal friend, Giovan Battista, shared. The remarkable number of antique-inspired medallions, as Burroughs suggested, refer undoubtably to dell'Aquila's collection of ancient coins and medals. The façade's centrally placed Medici coat of arms, statues, and painted representations of ancient stories likely made allusions to patron and pope. Spun across the façade are *all'antica* swags, ribbons, and lion heads related once again to the triumphant character of the *possesso's* march. Yet the underlying inspiration for this exceptional façade, as Pagliara brilliantly demonstrated, was the curved façade of Trajan's markets.[103] Transformed beyond recognition by Raphael's fertile imagination, the markets mutate in a series of drawings into a new design that is totally original and still Trajanic. In its virtuoso display of architecture, painting, and sculpture, the façade does homage to its patron, decorates and memorializes Leonine Rome, and serves as Raphael's *exemplum* of the artist's creative powers.

The Borgo palaces reflect another trend in Leonine Rome: they were built neither by nobles nor cardinals but by an educated middle class associated with the papal curia. In large part due to technical innovations introduced by Bramante and Giovanni da Udine – the substitution of plaster casting and stucco for expensive marble and stone – antique designs became possible for a sophisticated but not obscenely wealthy class. The rustication and the engaged columns of Palazzo Caprini were cast with a concrete-like substance – an invention praised by Vasari. On Palazzo Branconio dell'Aquila, Giovanni's new *all'antica* stucco (still visible in Raphael's Villa Madama) took the place of marble carving.

By the close of his pontificate, however, the city that had embraced this extravagant pope with such enthusiasm at the outset of his reign, came to revile him and his family. Although different in style, his goal was essentially that of Julius: increase the power of the papacy at the expense of the Popolo Romano. Even more disturbing was the combination of his desire for strong papal government with an insidious intention to enrich his family. The pope who loved such pomp died having emptied the papal coffers. His funeral procession was miserable by all accounts; his tomb insignificant. His final fate in a satirical poem was that of Julius's; he, too, was forbidden entrance to heaven. In a pasquinade chastising him for dissipating papal funds, an interlocutor discovers him in hell. Admitting that he squandered the money for Saint Peter's, left the church unfinished and the papal jewels in hock, Leo reveals how he ended in Pluto's domain:

Saint Peter, in a great temper, threw me out of the role of pastor saying: Go, you are unworthy of grace having left my church uncovered, where they defecate in every corner; To enrich your relatives, it remains deserted.[104]

Despite Leo's vilification after his death, his urbanistic innovations would bear remarkable fruit in the scenographic seventeenth-century city. Concern for the viewer, the creation of visual focal points at the end of straight streets, the *bivium* and the trident, the architectural style of theatrical display, and the incorporation of the movement of the spectator into design would become the commonplaces of baroque urban design.

Conclusion

The successes and failures of initiatives to transform Raphael's Rome would have been apparent even to the casual visitor. She, for let's make her somewhat like our Andalusian Lozana escorted through the streets, could not fail to see that Rome, first and foremost, was not a single city. The sacred city and its secular counterpart were separated by space, political goals, and economic realities. Small and sometimes overlapping areas controlled by private groups created mini-cities, dividing urban space into irregular and contrasting patterns: the fortified *monti* of Rome's barons; the vast undeveloped areas owned by convents; the bustling streets and piazzas devoted to single trades or populations. Bankers, elegant courtesans, Jews, food vendors, artisans, artists, cheap prostitutes, rich cardinals, and thieves – all created an urban kaleidoscope that popes, barons, and civic governments fought to control. Foreign enclaves – German, Sienese, Slav, Florentine, Lombard, and Spanish – carved the city up into zones whose power rose or fell with the national sympathies of the popes.

What would have made the biggest impression, however, as she moved around dense, narrow, curving medieval streets, were the new papal thoroughfares that cut straight trajectories through privately controlled areas, destroying what was in their paths to open up new avenues for circulation, profit, and display. Despite the authoritarian impetus behind their construction, the new streets provided all social groups with advantages: the poor profited from the rapid distribution of staples from the Tiber ports; monasteries and private individuals built speculative housing that freed the working classes from the overcrowded *abitato* and made their purses heavier; the rich constructed palaces, financed elegant churches, or conducted their businesses with greater ease. Whether benefit or curse, the two *borghi* – the rough and tumble Trastevere and the courtly Vatican – became more integrated into the urban core on the other side of the Tiber.

If permanent buildings and straight streets changed the face of the city, imagery gave it meaning and memory. Visual markers forced our visitor to interpret the urban spaces she maneuvered. Coats of arms, immured into every surface, advertised the urban virtues of patrons. Inscriptions, from the permanent marble plaques of popes to the temporary leaflets that gave voice (witty and often subversive) to the mute and mutilated Pasquino, assigned praise or blame. Ephemeral events – the races of Carnevale, papal and religious processions, the gruesome theater of executions – transformed ordinary spaces into highly charged symbols of the world order.

Finally, if her guide were educated, she would see that Rome in the early sixteenth century was achieving the humanist dream. The enormous ancient ruins that inspired all visitors to the Eternal City – from pious pilgrims to the nostalgic Petrarch, from antiquarians to artists – were meeting their match in modern buildings. The scale and *all'antica* design of Saint Peter's, the Belvedere, the palace of the Tribunali, and the projects for the Medici palace; the exuberance of the feasts in Agostino Chigi's garden of delights; the abilities of artists like Raphael, Michelangelo, and Bramante – all were returning Rome to her rightful place as the imperial city.

4 The Vatican Stanze

Ingrid D. Rowland

In 1507, more than three years into his pontificate, Pope Julius II (r. 1503–13) suddenly moved out of the traditional papal suite in the Vatican Palace to the rooms directly above it, tired, he said, of living among the frescoes commissioned by his hated predecessor, Alexander VI Borgia. It is easy to see how Julius might have become irked with Pinturicchio's life-sized fresco of Pope Alexander knelt in pious prayer as a resurrected Christ bursts forth from the tomb for his own especial benefit; Alexander's strong, fleshy face proclaims all his shrewd sensuality, as his satin robes and jeweled gloves glisten with three-dimensional ornaments in gilded stucco. It is also easy to see how Julius, already a great patron and collector of art, must have thought that he could commission something just as good on his own terms.

To decorate his new apartments, Julius revived a plan that had enabled his uncle, Pope Sixtus IV, to fresco the vast interior of the Sistine Chapel within the space of two years: he hired a team of artists to work on different parts of the suite simultaneously, confident that the pressure of competition would make them all do their best work, and as quickly as possible. Among the painters he assembled was a young man from Urbino, Raphael Sanzio, a distant relative of the pope's architect and confidante, Donato Bramante, who had recommended Raphael for the position. Like Bramante himself, Raphael soon revealed an aesthetic sensibility so in tune with the pope's that Julius fired the rest of his team of artists, sacrificing speedy completion of the apartments' decoration for the promise of uniformity and overall quality. He would not live to see the finished frescoes – nor, for that matter, would Raphael – but he must have recognized that they would proclaim the meaning of his papacy long after his death. This they have done with rare eloquence.

When Julius died, Raphael had completed not quite two rooms in a suite of three smaller chambers and one spacious hall, now called the Sala di

Costantino. The papacy, and the initiative for designing the papal suite, passed to Pope Leo X (r. 1513–21), who adjusted the themes of the frescoes to fit his own pontificate. At the same time, Raphael's reputation had grown to the point where his commissions greatly outnumbered his ability to fulfill them, despite the help of his large, meticulously organized workshop; the last of the three rooms that comprise the Stanze Vaticane was executed by Raphael's assistants, and both artist and pope had died well before Raphael's workshop put the finishing touches on the Sala di Costantino for Pope Clement VII.

The three Stanze Vaticane, as the papal apartments are called today, formed the center section of a more extensive suite. It began with a Bramante-built entrance loggia that faced the city of Rome, and continued into a small assembly hall that gave in turn onto the much larger Sala di Costantino. The pope's bedroom was tucked into a space between the Sala di Costantino and the room now known as the Stanza di Eliodoro. This little bedchamber has never been put on public display because its furnishings are so badly damaged (and because it makes such a handy storeroom for the well-trafficked Stanze and their gift shop). Two more rooms of the same size followed, the Stanza della Segnatura and, finally, the Stanza dell'Incendio, which opened into the fabric of the large defensive tower built into the Vatican Palace by Pope Alexander VI; here the papal suite ended in a large dining room, whose late nineteenth-century frescoes now honor the pontificate of the aggressive, ill-fated Pius IX (r. 1848–72) in a style whose imitation of Raphael is sheer wishful thinking; it resembles the original as little as Pius himself resembled Julius II.

The current names for these rooms are mostly based on the subjects of the frescoes on their walls: the Sala di Costantino shows scenes from the life of the Emperor Constantine, the Stanza di Eliodoro takes its name from the fresco depicting *The Expulsion of Heliodorus*, the Stanza dell'Incendio from the fresco *Fire in the Borgo*. The Stanza della Segnatura, on the other hand, the "Signing Room," takes its name from the activity that once took place within it; here the pope once put his signature to the bulls and other documents generated in massive numbers by the papal bureaucracy. The Stanza may have served this purpose already under Julius's successor Leo X, but Pope Julius himself probably put the room to a different use. John Shearman was the first to suggest on the strength of contemporary descriptions of the papal apartments that the Stanza della Segnatura housed Julius's private library of three hundred books, stored in wooden cabinets that were destroyed in the 1527 Sack of Rome.[1] Two floors below, in four rooms outfitted by his uncle Sixtus IV, the official Vatican Library, the Biblioteca Apostolica Vaticana, housed several thousand volumes, in Greek, Latin, Hebrew, and various vernaculars, both manuscripts and printed books.[2] Julius's private collection was restricted to Latin and Italian works; he is said to have told Michelangelo "I'm no scholar," and he was certainly not the sort of person to pore over the grammar of ancient authors or to discuss fine points of style.[3] Julius was, however, a wide reader and a man of refined, pioneering tastes, and ever since his election as cardinal in 1471 he had taken a special interest in the Vatican Library. The private library he installed in the heart of his apartments was not only meant for show; he made sure that it was used, by his friends as well as his staff.

Raphael began work on the papal suite in 1508, assigned to the Stanza della Segnatura. Painters like Sodoma, Baldassare Peruzzi, Timoteo Viti, and Lorenzo Lotto were painting in the rooms to either side of him, all of them newly discovered talents eager to prove themselves in this exalted setting. The subjects of the frescoes must have been planned beforehand according to a scheme for which the pope took ultimate responsibility. Julius already had long experience as a cardinal in negotiating with artists to invent themes and create designs that would call explicit attention to himself as patron without damaging his reputation for judicious sponsorship or curtailing the artists' own initiative. As an example of papal patronage, he looked above all to his own uncle, Sixtus IV, who had not only drawn up a detailed general plan for the walls of the Sistine chapel, but had also gone so far as to supply the captions for each of the frescoes. Despite his interventions, Sixtus also knew when to stand back. A more overbearing patron like Isabella d'Este, duchess of Mantua, drew up such detailed instructions for each figure in the paintings she commissioned that she stifled the imagination of artists as regularly as she sparked it.

Julius seems to have given artists comparative freedom, not for lack of interest – his surprise visits to the Sistine Chapel to ask Michelangelo whether he had finished yet are legendary – but because he seems to have known how to delegate responsibility. Certainly, both art and artists were better for his implicit trust, perhaps no more dramatically than in the case of the Sistine Chapel ceiling, where Julius asked for twelve Apostles and instead received the history of the Church traced forward from the creation of the universe. For the intricate details of the Stanza della Segnatura, the pope may have given significant responsibility for their actual design to the artists themselves; this certainly seems to be the case for Raphael, whose drawings for some of the Stanze frescoes show major changes as he thought through the rooms' design.

Both Julius and Raphael must also have used the varied talents of the pope's private librarian, Tommaso Inghirami, whose considerable abilities as a scholar were eclipsed in his own day by his achievements as an actor and orator (see Raphael's portrait of him, Plate 13).[4] The thirty-eight-year-old Inghirami's presence in the little Stanza could not have gone unnoticed; he was immensely fat, with a booming voice that could be heard, if need be, from one end of Saint Peter's basilica to the other. With a scholar's memory for stories and an actor's delight in retelling them, he loved to talk, and he loved the company of handsome young men, as Raphael certainly was in 1508. Inghirami's duties as librarian must have included reading aloud to Pope Julius, which would make the Stanza della Segnatura a louder, livelier place than the idea of a private library might normally imply. Raphael's first two frescoes for the Stanza della Segnatura reflect that liveliness, but they also reflect the lofty purpose that Julius ascribed to his papacy. The pope may have told Michelangelo that he was not a scholar, and unlike Inghirami he hated to speak in public, but he was nonetheless a man in love with ideas. So, to their mutual good fortune, was the young painter from Urbino. Before Raphael had finished the second wall of the Stanza della Segnatura, Julius had awarded him the entire commission.

THE STANZA DELLA SEGNATURA (1508–11)

The decorations of the Stanza della Segnatura are organized precisely along the lines of a contemporary library, with one wall devoted to Theology, one to Philosophy (including natural philosophy, as science was then called), one to Poetry, and one to Law. In essence, the frescoes give human form and human personalities to the authors whose books were stored in the wooden cabinets beneath them; they create a living library in pictures as Tommaso Inghirami's readings may once have done in performance by using the sound of the human voice.[5] There was no more important place to begin an account of the Julian papacy, although there were two others just as important in their own way, both the object of equally concentrated attention at the same time that Raphael busied himself with the Stanze: Saint Peter's Basilica, whose Early Christian version had already been razed to make room for a new church designed by Bramante, and the Sistine Chapel, where Michelangelo had set to work painting the ceiling in 1508. These were public places, however, whereas the Stanze served as the pope's personal suite; their decoration accordingly expressed the meaning of his papacy in a more immediate, personal sense. Within this pontifical suite, the library of the Stanza della Segnatura literally stood at its very heart.

Theology: *La Disputa del Sacramento*

Raphael began by working on the wall devoted to theology. His fresco's traditional name, *Debate about the Sacrament* (*Disputa del Sacramento*) (Plate 19) is misleading; aside from a few argumentative characters in the left foreground, its orderly ranks of figures display the supernal calm of minds in total agreement with one another, and in fact the earliest name for the painting, *The Triumph of Theology*, expressed its prevailing mood of "the peace which passeth all understanding." Raphael's design is a triumph of another kind, of ingenuity: in graphic form, he lays out the basic articles of Christian faith while suggesting at the same time that his art can communicate only an approximate idea of that faith's true glory.

On a freestanding altar draped in gold brocade, a monstrance displays the communion host, the unleavened bread that is mystically transformed in the course of the Christian communion into the body and blood of the resurrected Christ. One alternative term for communion, the Eucharist, comes from the Greek word for "thanks"; another, Mass, comes from the Latin word for "sent," *missa*; its terminology alone shows that this ritual meal that lies at the heart of Christian religious celebration is a common thanks-offering through which God sends divine grace to the participants.

In Raphael's painted presentation of the Eucharist, the center of the host coincides with the vanishing point for the fresco's carefully constructed perspective; visually as well as conceptually, the painting's composition radiates out from this focal point where, in Christian theology and in the basic structure of Raphael's composition, divine meets human. The monstrance, therefore, is lifted above the motley crowd of men that mills around the altar; although there are many saints among them, they are all, first and foremost, human beings, and their movements are as variegated as life itself. Closest in to the altar, sitting on thrones, are the four fathers of the Western Church, identifiable as such by their carefully lettered haloes: Saint Gregory the Great in papal tiara, a portrait of the darkly handsome Julius himself; Saint Jerome in his red cardinal's cape, an elderly, frail Saint Ambrose in bishop's miter looking up to heaven, and his protégé Saint Augustine, also in bishop's vestments, dictating yet another of his many books to an angel-faced young secretary. The black-bearded Augustine seems to bear the features of the man whom Julius had newly appointed as prior general of the Augustinian order: Egidio da Viterbo, a famous preacher, a promoter

of Greek Neoplatonism and Hebrew Cabala, and one of the pope's closest associates. The frescoes of the Vatican Stanze and Michelangelo's
design for the Sistine Chapel show a deep debt to Egidio's ideas, to their
optimism, their openness to other traditions, their close adherence to
Plato, and their occasional eccentricity. The *Disputa's* emphasis on communion may itself derive from Egidio's persuasive preaching about that
sacrament.

The four Church Fathers attained their status by their prolific writings;
they sit surrounded by books; indeed, books figure almost as prominently
as people in the bottom register of the *Disputa*, and like the people, few
of them sit idly by; they are being pored over, discussed, passed around, or
written on the spot. The library of Julius II must have been an equally active
place, for the pope was notoriously restless, and Tommaso Inghirami was a
great conversationalist as well as a great public speaker. Among the crowd
of readers and onlookers, it is easy to pick out Dante's hatchet profile and
poet's laurels; his *Divine Comedy* has earned him the right to mingle among
the great theologians. Other characters can be identified by labeled haloes,
some can only be sorted out now by educated guessing, and this must have
been still more emphatically the case in the sixteenth century, when many
of the faces portrayed in the crowd had real counterparts passing through
the halls of the Apostolic Palace.

In front of Dante, Pope Sixtus IV, a major theologian in his own right,
appears as the saintly Pope Sixtus I – but it was in fact Sixtus IV who wrote
eloquently on the significance of Communion. It is not surprising, then, to
see the eyes of this stately man fixed on the host. In the crowd to the left
of the altar, the elderly, balding painter Fra Angelico wears a black friar's
robe as he stands among a throng of Dominicans. In the foreground, another balding man in laymen's clothing looks up from a book he has been
discussing with a handsome young friend and turns at the gesture of a
blonde youth who is more handsome still. The bald man has been identified plausibly as Raphael's distant uncle, Donato Bramante, and Raphael
has conveyed something of Bramante's prickly, nonconformist character
in this active, contorted figure. The ethereal youth is more elusive; he has
been described as an "angel without wings" or as the Florentine philosopher
Giovanni Pico della Mirandola; in any case, he is performing an angel's mission in directing "Bramante's" and our attention to the divine tableau above
our heads.

Behind the crowds, in the distant background to the left, a building is
under construction on a hill; this is usually taken as an allusion to the great
architectural project that Julius had initiated in 1506: the reconstruction

of Saint Peter's Basilica on a design by Donato Bramante. A low marble structure in the right background may refer to the same project by alluding to the tomb of Saint Peter, and to the fact that the saint's name was actually a nickname meaning "rock."

Directly above the host, in a billow of white clouds, four little angels brandish the four Gospels, the four books describing the life, work, death, and resurrection of Jesus on which the entire Christian tradition depends. Raphael announces, in essence, that these are the four most important books in the entire pontifical library; indeed, if there were no Gospels, there would be no Church and no pope, and hence no Vatican, no Julius II, and no Stanze by Raphael. In the Gospels, as in the host, divine meets human; however, in the specific vision of the early-sixteenth-century Church, the host was available to all faithful Christians, whereas the Bible was regarded as primarily accessible to the clergy who maintained the sole right to interpret its meaning. By 1517, Martin Luther would have contended, among many other theses, that the Bible ought to be read by all Christians, in a language they understood, forever upsetting the graceful hierarchy of Raphael's *Disputa*, where the Gospels float inaccessibly in the divine sphere above the host.

Above and around the Gospels, a bank of gray clouds describes a perfect arc, creating the airy apse to an outdoor church whose floor is depicted as white stone but whose upper reaches are built of people rather than masonry. Great figures from the Bible perch on the cloud bank, rapt in intense conversations, Christian saints intermingled with Hebrew patriarchs. Saints Peter and Paul sit at either end, the two patron saints and divine protectors of the city of Rome.

Above the saints, in a pale gold circle surrounded by cherubs, the dove of the Holy Spirit darts between their divine realm and realms still higher, the third person of the Holy Trinity into which Catholic theology divided God. A dialogue of Plato, the *Timaeus*, had already introduced the idea that a single god might also have three different manifestations in the fourth century before the Christian era; Plato, like Pythagoras two centuries before him, was fascinated with numerology. Christians such as Saint Augustine who espoused the idea of a Holy Trinity usually did so under the influence of Platonic philosophy, and it was no different in the Rome of Julius II, where the Augustinian Egidio da Viterbo had brought the new Christian Neoplatonism of the Florentine philosopher-physician Marsilio Ficino to bear on this ancient and difficult Christian doctrine. The word for "spirit" in Hebrew, Greek, and Latin was the word for "breath" or "wind" – the dove gave that barely tangible idea some tangible form.

In a direct line about the Holy Spirit, the second person of the Holy Trinity, Jesus as Christ (Greek for "the anointed one") sits enthroned between the Virgin Mary and Saint John the Baptist. This is the Jesus who is explicitly remembered in the eucharistic liturgy and embodied in the host: a God who took on human form, underwent the human horrors of betrayal, crucifixion, despair, and death, and only then returned to life. Catholic theology holds that the host at communion is literally transformed into the body and blood of Jesus and eaten as actual flesh by the faithful; the fifteenth-century mystic Saint Catherine of Siena speaks graphically of feeling the breaking bones and spurting blood in her mouth. Raphael's idea is far more restrained but no less remarkable: in a single figure, his Jesus, seated with unhealed wounds on a heavenly throne, tells the whole story of incarnation, passion, and resurrection to eternal life. This was the pattern that practicing Christians hoped would obtain eventually for their own lives: birth into suffering, death, and resurrection to eternal life on another, more perfect plane.

Above the resurrected Christ, a square-haloed God the Father, the first person of the Trinity, holds the globe of the universe in his hands. In Raphael's day, the universe was regarded as spherical, bounded on the outside by the crystalline sphere of the fixed stars. Inside, seven more spheres containing seven planets revolved around the earth. A young Polish astronomer named Nicolaus Copernicus had stopped in Rome in 1507, the year before Raphael arrived to paint the Stanza della Segnatura; by 1543, his book *On the Revolutions*, with its sun-centered universe, would prove as menacing to Catholic orthodoxy as the contentions of Martin Luther. The beauteous calm of the Stanza della Segnatura is the calm before a storm that would engulf early modern Europe.

Raphael, however, has already told his viewers that his own portrayal is no more than a provisional account of the universe: his God the Father stands beneath a shower of golden rays, each one packed with cherubim, all spilling forth from a source that originates beyond the space of the fresco itself. There is a higher reality than this painted image of God the Father in human form, as different in kind from God's reality as light is different from human flesh. If Raphael were to try to paint this higher reality, it would look more like these phenomenally fertile rays of light, each one burgeoning with new life, than it would look like an elderly man with a globe. They are all only images of a reality that defies imagery.

In presenting theology as a succession of transcendent realities, Raphael may most directly reflect the influence of Egidio da Viterbo, who was himself greatly taken with the Christian Neoplatonism of Marsilio Ficino. The fertile rays of light that pour forth from the highest heaven portray an idea that was given particular currency by another of Ficino's contemporaries: Giovanni Pico della Mirandola, who spoke, following the ancients, of the sun's fertilizing rays as "seminal principles," *spermatikoi logoi*; the contemporary Jewish writer Leone Ebreo would use the same image in his *Dialogues on Love* (published in 1535, but written more than a decade earlier) to describe the whole universe as the expression of God's love. Ultimately, however, the inspiration for Raphael's imagery must lie with the pope; for Michelangelo's exactly contemporary Sistine ceiling traces an equally magnificent history of the Church from the moment when God created the heaven and the earth and separated light from darkness to Noah's sacrifice after the Flood, the first liturgical ceremony of the new, postdiluvian world. Julius, the nephew of a famous theologian, had some ideas about theology himself.

Philosophy: *The School of Athens*

Raphael's second undertaking in the papal library was the wall opposite Theology, probably because these two walls were the easiest of the four to design; the other two, with their large windows, made complicated demands on Raphael's skill at composition. He devoted this second fresco to Philosophy, a discipline that also included science and mathematics as "natural philosophy." Its present name, *The School of Athens* (Plate 17), may be as old as the fresco itself, for the joint legacy of Greece and Rome was an idea of exceptional importance in these first years of the sixteenth century. On 1 January 1508, about a year before Raphael began work on this painting in 1509, a long-haired, eccentric professor from the University of Rome, Battista Casali, had presented an oration before the pope in which he explicitly called Rome a "new Athens."[6] On that occasion, Casali reminded Julius and the rest of the audience that the conquest of Constantinople by the Ottoman Turks had entrusted Rome with the responsibility of preserving not only Latin culture, but also the culture of the ancient Greeks, indeed of Greece as a whole. Ever since the second quarter of the fifteenth century, hordes of Greek refugees had made responsibility for the Greek legacy a physical and moral as well as an abstractly philosophical imperative. Although the conquest of Constantinople had happened more than half a century earlier, the Turkish threat to Italy itself had only increased in the meantime. The Ottomans were now closing in on Egypt and would finally take Cairo in 1517, intercepting its trade routes as they had overtaken the trade routes of the Byzantine world. At the same time, Spain and Portugal were engaging in an endless series of battles in North Africa with the Moors. Turkish pirates regularly raided Italian shores, and would continue to do so well into the seventeenth century. When Raphael presented his vision of the *School of Athens* for Pope Julius, it made a brave statement of stable conviction in a highly unstable world.

The School itself has come together in a huge hall whose design and proportions are reminiscent of Roman baths, where philosophers did actually meet in ancient Roman times, and there ancient Roman schoolteachers often gave their lessons.[7] Like the Baths of Caracalla, Diocletian, and Trajan, all easily visible to Raphael and his contemporaries (if not always in the best state of repair), this School of Athens-in-Rome is decorated with colossal marble statues of gods and marble bas-reliefs. But Raphael's hall of philosophy is also designed specifically to reveal the Christian truth latent in ancient wisdom. As Pope Julius and his contemporaries firmly believed, only long experience of ancient wisdom had made it possible for the Apostles to grasp the meaning of the Christian gospel at the dawn of the Roman Empire and to use that empire's famous networks of communication to spread their message. As an integral part of God's plan, the creators of Julian Rome believed that ancient philosophy should merit not only their deep respect, but also their continued attention. The Vatican Library held thousands of manuscripts with ancient Greek and Latin texts, and the first registers of the Library show how eagerly their readers sought out the books they described as *vetustissimi* – extremely old. Many of these books can be seen, embodied as their authors, standing beneath the vault of the School of Athens.

The domed vault itself, pierced by a triple window, bears more than a casual resemblance to Donato Bramante's design for new Saint Peter's, not only because Bramante was the most important architect in the city (and Raphael's relative) but because the *School of Athens* is really an image of Rome under Julius II, a Christian kingdom. The triple window, echoed by the series of three large openings behind the dome, calls attention to the many subtle numerical elements in Raphael's design; and just as triads in Church architecture refer to the Holy Trinity, so do these triads in the pope's apartments. Only two of the statues along the walls are easily identifiable: Apollo on the left and Minerva on the right. Each of these ancient deities was explicitly compared to Christ in these same years by the influential theologian Egidio da Viterbo, and it is likely that Egidio himself, as the favorite preacher of Julius II, influenced Raphael's artistic choices in the Stanze Vaticane.[8] (We have already seen him tentatively identified as the Saint Augustine in the *Disputa*.) Through the strong Neoplatonic tradition that underpins Christian theology from the Gospel of John through Saint Paul and Saint Augustine, many of Apollo's associations as a young male god became associated with Christ: the imagery of sun, light, and music. Furthermore, like Apollo, Jesus was a healer. In the *School of Athens*, Apollo also stands on the side of the fresco that neighbors the wall devoted to poetry, where he will appear again. In both places, he stands as a reminder that in many ways Apollo stood as the ancient Greco-Roman precursor to the figure of Christ.

Minerva, who dominates the right half of the fresco, was born from the head of her father Jupiter, a foreshadowing, according to Egidio da Viterbo, of Christ's birth to the Virgin Mary. As the ancient goddess of reason and wisdom, she was also a precursor to the Virgin, especially in Mary's role as *Sedes Sapientiae*, "Throne of Wisdom"; in Rome, one important Marian church, Santa Maria sopra Minerva, stands on the remains of an ancient temple to Minerva. Julius was fervently devoted to the Virgin, and it would not be surprising in the least to find her here, just as she sits in the highest registers of the *Disputa* next to the resurrected Christ and John the Baptist.

Beneath the gleaming marble statues of the gods, three relief plaques in ancient style detail the three human impulses that, again in the theology of Egidio da Viterbo, can become virtues with discipline: beneath Apollo, a young man who has struck another represents Wrath, which can be tamed into becoming Courage; a Triton fondling a Nereid on the high seas represents Lust, the untamed side of the love of God. Under Minerva stands a relief plaque of Reason enthroned: Egidio da Viterbo claims that reason ennobled becomes Wisdom.[9]

The philosophers are arranged at various levels on a four-step staircase. At the top center, Plato and his onetime student Aristotle each carry books that identify not only who they are, but also what aspect of their many writings bears most directly on the fresco's larger point. Plato's *Timaeus*, labeled in Italian as "Timeo," is the first place in ancient literature where God is described as one being with three natures: a foreshadowing of the Trinity. Holding this proto-trinitarian work in one hand, Plato points meaningfully upward with one finger of the other, directing the viewer to look toward heaven and the dome of Raphael's great hall to find the three-in-one divinity to which the fresco, the Stanze, and the papacy itself are dedicated.

Aristotle holds his *Ethics*, labeled "Etica," and sweeps his hand out into the viewer's space; the insights indicated by Plato have their repercussion in right human behavior. Aristotle's elaborate treatise will be distilled by Jesus into two rules: love God and love your neighbor. By their own actions, Raphael's Plato and Aristotle embody these two basic principles.

Off to their left, snub-nosed, green-clad Socrates ticks off a point on his fingers to a handsome young soldier in dress armor, perhaps Alcibiades, who features so unforgettably as a drunken party-crasher in Plato's *Symposium*, and a short man who may be Xenophon, the Athenian general who also wrote a *Symposium* focused on Socrates. Still farther to the left, a large blue-clad man with a contented smirk and a Greek partygoer's wreath in his hair is probably Epicurus, the philosopher of pleasure, but his physical features are those of Tommaso Inghirami. Raphael himself appears on the opposite side of the fresco at about the same level, standing with another painter who has been variously identified as Sodoma, Timoteo Viti, or, most recently, Pinturicchio, all of whom had been painting in the Stanze Vaticane until Raphael obtained the entire commission.[10]

The other philosophers range beneath Apollo or Minerva, and their distribution seems to reflect yet another musing by Egidio da Viterbo, who cited Plato to remark that hearing and vision are the two senses that turn human thoughts toward God. In fact the lowest level of the left side of the *School of Athens* focuses on Pythagoras, the great musical and numerical theorist whose followers regarded him as a kind of human Apollo. As the great philosopher writes furiously in a book, a young man holds out a slate with a diagram of the "perfect" chord known by the Greeks as *diapason* ("through all") above a geometric representation of ten, the perfect number. The pose of these figures looks so much like contemporary representations of Saint Matthew and his inspiring angel that the sixteenth-century painter Giorgio Vasari, looking at a print of the fresco, actually identified them as the evangelist and his angelic muse.[11] The exact identities of the Arabic philosopher, the two very young men, and the marvelous older man squinting over Pythagoras's shoulder have been debated, and in a sense they each stand for the legions of philosophers and students who together have created the classical tradition.

On the side of the fresco devoted to literal visionaries, a group of astronomers gathers beneath Minerva, while a bald-headed Euclid crouches down to make a geometrical demonstration. This Euclid, like his balding twin in the *Disputa*, has been taken since the sixteenth century as a portrait of Bramante, an identification that ranges him close to his protégé Raphael. The astronomers include Ptolemy, viewed from the back, whose radiate crown (borrowed from the portraits of emperors on ancient Roman coins) reflects the sixteenth-century misconception that the Alexandrian scientist was a member of the Egyptian royal family (in fact, Ptolemaios, "warlike," was a fairly common name in the contentious Hellenistic world). The man holding the sphere of the fixed stars (like God the Father in the *Disputa*) has been identified both as Zoroaster and as a portrait of Raphael's friend Baldassare Castiglione.

Sprawled across the steps in the center of the *School of Athens*, a philosopher clad only in a blue rag pointedly ignores the eager conversations around him. He is Diogenes, the original cynic, a curmudgeon who lived in a storage jar and spent his life searching, with scant success, for an honest man. When Alexander the Great came to visit the philosopher and offered to give him whatever he wanted, Diogenes grumbled, "Stop blocking my sun." The late antique writer Boethius describes Diogenes reclining in the temple of wisdom, and so he is.

Slightly beneath Diogenes, with an expression no less sour, Heraclitus rests his chin in his hand and glowers at human folly. The spectacular musculature of his knees and the colors of his skin and clothing show that Raphael has not only slipped in a portrait of Michelangelo, then at work on the Sistine Chapel, but has boldly painted Michelangelo in his own style. (Similarly, the faces behind Plato, who looks a great deal like Leonardo da Vinci, are rendered with Leonardo's shadowy sfumato modeling.)

Thus, from the sublime heights of Platonic theology to the personal foibles of ancient philosophers and contemporary artists, Raphael's *School of Athens* presents a portrait of Rome in the time of Julius II. For all their oddities, the motley figures all make one thing clear: they are exactly where they want to be, and they all belong in this vision, catholic as the Church would never be again. For as Raphael worked away on the *School of Athens*, an Augustinian friar named Martin Luther made a visit to Rome that would soon change the history of the Church.

Poetry: *Parnassus*

Poetry was the next subject Raphael addressed, in 1511, with his *Parnassus*. Of all forms of literature, it was the one Raphael and his contemporaries, like the ancients before them, considered most divinely inspired. It took little stretch of the imagination to connect Raphael's presentation of Parnassus, the fabled mountain of Apollo and the Muses, with the Vatican Hill; the window that pierced the frescoed wall looked directly out onto it. Neither would Julius and his court have had any reservations about seeing Apollo as a Christ figure; Egidio da Viterbo had explicitly made this identification.[12] Most important, however, Raphael's design suggested that the cultural life of Julian Rome was itself a vibrant new development of, and progress beyond, the ancient tradition. Many of the figures in Raphael's fresco were portraits of contemporary poets, who mingle on Parnassus with the great poets of ancient Greece and Rome as if they had always been neighbors – and of course, on the shelves of the Vatican Library, they were.

At the painting's center, sitting beneath a grove of his sacred laurels (which are normally bushes rather than the trees of the painting) alongside the spring of Hippocrene, first brought to life by the stamping foot of the winged horse Pegasus, a rapturous Apollo plays a celestial tune – not on his lyre, but on its sixteenth-century equivalent, the *lira da braccio*.[13] The Nine Muses make up his entourage, of whom four are easily identified: in the left foreground Calliope (Epic) with the trumpet usually given to Fame, on the right Erato (Lyric) holding her lyre as she looks adoringly toward Apollo. The voluptuous dancer behind Calliope must be Terpsichore, the muse of dance; a tragic mask identifies Melpomene, Muse of Tragedy, to Apollo's right. Clio (History), Euterpe (Music), Polyhymnia (Sacred Poetry), Thalia (Comedy), and Urania (Astronomy) are harder to identify immediately.

The only other active musician on Apollo's holy mountain is blind Homer, singing *ta klea andrôn* "the glories of men" to a green-clad Virgil and stern, hawk-nosed Dante. The young man eagerly taking notes may be Ennius, the first Roman poet to write epic verse. The Muse who watches them, Fame's trumpet in hand, is surely Calliope, the patroness of epic poetry.

A conclave of lyric poets gathers to the fresco's lower left: a sultry blonde Sappho holds a scroll with her name, and Petrarch is recognizable by his round face and medieval dress. Their companions, both Greeks, are probably the Theban poetess Corinna and Alcaeus, Sappho's friend and colleague from ancient Lesbos.

The right side of the painting is peopled with Raphael's contemporaries. In the foreground "the one and only" Bernardo Accolti of Arezzo (L'Unico Aretino), his profile as distinctive as Dante's, converses with an old man who is usually identified as Pindar, the great sixth-century Theban poet whose odes celebrated the victors in the ancient Olympian, Pythian, Isthmian, and Nemean Games. Not far behind him, the copper-colored mantle and avuncular grin of Jacopo Sannazzaro beam like the sun of his native Naples. A black beard and robust physique identify Lodovico Ariosto, whereas that famous voluptuary Ovid is shown as a figure almost as chubby as Tommaso Inghirami. The elderly man facing right has been connected with the Ferrarese poet Antonio Tebaldeo, but he is in fact too old for the part; Tebaldeo was in his early forties. The pale youth with long hair may be the ancient Roman elegist Tibullus, a delicate soul who, like Keats, died young, leaving some exquisite poetry. We should probably be able to find great Roman poets like Horace, and perhaps one or two of the Greek tragedians, but the *Parnassus*, like the *Disputa* and the *School of Athens*, honors more contributors to a long tradition than Raphael can possibly portray. In the ancient world, too, there were at least eleven candidates for the Nine Muses!

Law: Justice

The fourth wall of the Stanza della Segnatura is devoted to what contemporary universities called "both kinds of law": the civil law of the secular state and the canon law of the Church. Raphael's designs focus on the moment when the completed texts of two great law codes (the word "code" derives from the Latin word for manuscript, *codex*), one of civil law and one of canon law, are handed over to the monarchs who commissioned them by the jurist who bore chief responsibility for their compilation. The English idea of a common law drawn up by the people is wholly alien to both traditions; they both depend instead on a monarch who assumes a divine right to rule. Julius II, however much he may have helped along his election by bribery, also regarded himself as the divinely ordained head of his theocratic state.

The greatest compilation of Roman law came late in the history of the empire, when its capital had moved to Byzantium with an important secondary capital in Ravenna. In the fresco to the left of the window, designed but not executed by Raphael, the Byzantine Emperor Justinian receives the civil code known as the Decretals from the jurist Trebonianus.[14] To the right of the window, the thirteenth-century pope Gregory IX (r. 1227–41) receives the code of canon law known as the Pandects from Raymond de Peñafort (Plate 20). Scenes of presentation like these are more common on the first pages of manuscripts than in monumental paintings; there were many examples, some quite beautiful, in the Vatican Library, and there must have been many in the pope's private collection. Like the other frescoes of the Stanza della Segnatura, the "Wall of Justice" is filled with contemporary portraits: Julius has posed for the image of Pope Gregory IX, and he is flanked by two future popes, plump Cardinal Giovanni de' Medici, who would succeed Julius as Pope Leo X, and the handsome Cardinal Alessandro Farnese, the future Pope Paul III. A third cardinal is the Tuscan Antonio del Monte.

Above the heads of these human lawmakers, in the wall's lunette, perch three personifications, statuesque female figures who represent the three essential components of justice as these are detailed in Plato's *Republic*: Strength (Fortitude), Temperance, and Prudence: all of these are feminine nouns in both Greek (*bia, sophrosyne, pronoia*) and Latin (*fortitudo, temperantia, prudentia*). Another Latin word for strength, however, was *robur*, the same word used for the oak tree whose Italian derivative, *rovere*, gave rise to the family name of Pope Julius II, della Rovere. Hence Raphael's Fortitude clutches a sapling of black oak, gently bending it with an apparent ease that shows just how strong she really is. Temperance carries a bridle to rein in excess. Prudence, whose name comes from pro-videntia, "foresight," has a double face to symbolize her long view of things, and a mirror that has the same significance. Appropriately, these divinities have been executed by Raphael's own divine hand, and the difference shows above all in the radiance of his colors, dominated by the red, white, and green whose association with these virtues and their sum, justice, has also determined the colors of the Italian flag.

The Ceiling and Floor
The ceiling of the Stanza della Segnatura ties its four faculties together by means of four personifications, each a stately woman seated on a throne set in the clouds. The thrones, the color of the clouds, and the attributes of the women are all subtly different. In between the personifications, four scenes in fictive mosaic develop the ideas of Theology, Philosophy, Poetry, and Law by interconnecting them. Theology, labeled as "knowledge of divine matters," *divinarum rerum notitia*, is enthroned on dawn-colored clouds, with a label taken from Virgil: the arms of Philosophy's throne are figures of the many-breasted Artemis of Ephesus, an evocative symbol of Nature for Renaissance artists and humanists; her label, *causarum cognitio*, is a paraphrase of Virgil's tag, "Felix qui potuit rerum cognoscere causas" ("Happy is he who is able to know the causes of things"). She carries two labeled books, one of *Natural* and one of *Moral* philosophy. Her dress is embroidered with symbols of the four elements, air, fire, water, and earth, and her clouds are the white clouds of daytime. Poetry, on pink sunset clouds, quotes Virgil's description of the Cumaean Sibyl to stress her origin in heavenly inspiration: *numine afflatur*, "she is inspired by divinity." Justice, carrying sword and balance, enthroned on black storm clouds, "grants each person the appropriate laws" (*ius suum unicuique tribuit*).

Between Theology and Justice, Adam and Eve commit the original sin; between Justice and Philosophy, Solomon executes his judgment; between Philosophy and Poetry, Astronomy holds out an armillary sphere as a model of the cosmos; between Poetry and Theology, Apollo wins a singing contest over the satyr Marsyas and condemns him to the terrible punishment of being flayed alive; here, at least, Apollo is no model of Christian charity, but is instead his beautiful, ruthless self. In antiquity, he was not only a healer but the bringer of plague.[15]

The floor of the Stanza della Segnatura is of a Roman type called "Cosmatesque," after a medieval family, the Cosmati, who specialized in this technique of four-color marble inlay. The marble itself comes from ancient Roman buildings and was quarried in the far-flung regions of the Roman Empire: green serpentine from the Peloponnese in Greece, deep maroon porphyry from Aswan in Egypt, "old yellow" (*giallo antico*) from North Africa, and luminous gray-white marble from Carrara, the only mines that were still easily accessible to Rome in the early sixteenth century. The pieces of Cosmatesque inlay are much smaller than the inlay of ancient Roman buildings, but tiny pieces were far easier to transport than big slabs. The roundels in the floor are cross-sections of ancient Roman columns, sliced as if they were salami (the cathedral in Ravenna also has cross-sectional slices of Corinthian column capitals, but this is unusual). The coat of arms of Pope Nicholas V shows that the design is older than that of the rest of the room, but Popes Julius II and Leo X have also added their arms to his.

THE STANZA DI ELIODORO (1512–14)

In 1511, with the entire commission for the papal apartment securely in hand, Raphael moved his operation from the Stanza della Segnatura to the adjacent room, just off the pope's bedchamber. Here he presented four examples of the Church in action, in keeping with the traditional contrast between the active and the contemplative Christian life. The pope's library, obviously enough, had been decorated as a contemplative space. The Stanza di Eliodoro, where the pontiff began his day, was dedicated instead to scenes of action. Raphael's experience with fresco in the first Stanza prompted him to make changes in his compositions for the second, opting now for fewer figures, each painted on a larger scale. He had also come into contact with a new painting style, for in August of 1511 the wealthy banker Agostino Chigi returned from a trip to Venice with a Venetian painter in tow. Sebastiano Luciani would soon be known as Sebastiano del Piombo, "Sebastian of the Lead," because of his job in the papal bureaucracy as a master of the pope's lead seals, but his real specialty was painting in oils so sumptuous that they glistened, especially in moonlit scenes, as Costanza Barbieri discusses in her contribution to this volume. Raphael would expend tremendous effort in trying to make the colored plaster of his frescoes in the Stanza di Eliodoro gleam with something of the sheen he saw in Sebastiano's oils, and because of his own phenomenal skill at fresco, he succeeded remarkably well.

The Expulsion of Heliodorus

Heliodorus, treasurer of the Hellenistic Syrian king Seleucus Philopator, was ordered by that monarch to confiscate the treasury of the temple in Jerusalem. The Second Book of Maccabees tells the story that as he and his entourage left the temple with their booty, Heliodorus was set upon by a mounted warrior and two youths armed with switches. Raphael's composition contrasts the violence of Heliodorus's punishment with the ethereal calm of the white-bearded chief priest, still at prayer in the Holy of Holies; for this holy man, external events cannot interrupt his communion with God. The temple itself is a remarkable structure, a series of domes supported on Corinthian columns, its floors inlaid with octagons of colored stone, ablaze with candlelight. Although he had never seen the golden stones of Jerusalem, Raphael had obviously heard of them and gave the temple's architecture a burnished glow.

On the fresco's extreme left side, Julius II enters on a litter borne aloft by Raphael and members of his workshop: Giulio Romano and, conspicuous in the front left, the tall engraver Marcantonio Raimondi. The pope had begun growing a beard in 1510, swearing that he would not shave it until he had expelled the French from the Italian peninsula. He finally shaved it in 1512; the *Expulsion of Heliodorus* (Plate 21) can thus be securely dated to 1511–12, and the choice to show this story in particular may have served as a warning to foreign powers, especially France, that the New Temple at Saint Peter's enjoyed the same divine protection as the Temple of Jerusalem – not to mention the vigilant protection of its fierce pope.

The Liberation of Saint Peter

The titular church of Cardinal Giuliano della Rovere had been that of San Pietro in Vincoli, Saint Peter in Chains. The chains that supposedly fettered Saint Peter in the dread Mamertine Prison of ancient Rome are still on view over the high altar of the ancient church, and they appear prominently in Raphael's painting of Peter's miraculous liberation from prison by an angel (Plate 22). A dramatic nocturnal setting allows Raphael to exploit the contrast between the silvery moonlight that plays over the soldiers' armor and the golden radiance of the angel who breaks Saint Peter's chains and leads him forth from prison. Only Piero della Francesca had done something so daring before, in his *Dream of Constantine* (1462) for the church of San

Francesco in Arezzo. The episode, like the *Expulsion of Heliodorus*, could easily allude to Pope Julius's efforts to rid Italy of foreign rulers; it may speak more broadly of Julius's sense that, as the successor of Saint Peter, he enjoyed the same protection. The central scene, with its iron bars crisscrossing our view of Peter and the angel, was much imitated by later artists, including Greek icon painters on the island of Crete, who would have seen the striking design in engravings.

The Mass of Bolsena

In 1263, in Bolsena, a small city north of Rome, a German priest was return-ing home from a pilgrimage. The wonders of Rome had not been enough to assuage his nagging doubts about the Eucharistic ritual; he could no longer quite believe that the Mass transformed the bread of the Host into the actual body and blood of Jesus. That day in Bolsena, the Host began to bleed, and this proof that it was real human flesh relieved the priest of every doubt. In the following year, a bull issued by Pope Urban IV established the feast of Corpus Domini ("The Lord's Body") to commemorate the miracle and reinforce its bearing on Church doctrine.

As a result, the bloodstained linen cloth that had been used in the miraculous service immediately became a venerated relic, the Sacred Corporal, so valuable that it was stolen from the church at Bolsena and spirited away to nearby (and more powerful) Orvieto, where it can be seen to this day. Julius II had stopped in Orvieto to pray before the Sacred Corporal in 1506, on the eve of his first military expedition against Bologna and other recalcitrant cities of the Papal States. In 1510, now with his peni-tential beard, he marched north again, to take on Ferrara, the French, and Venice, and spent the winter of 1510–11 headquartered in Bologna when he was not out leading the pontifical troops. By the time the *Mass of Bolsena* was underway, he had returned to Rome with the military results of his campaign "very indecisive," as one contemporary put it. His diplo-matic corps, however, would eventually obtain most of the pope's demands, and, by 1512, Julius would feel confident enough to shave his symbolic beard.

Raphael has given features of Julius II to the prelate who is being served communion by the doubting priest, and he has chosen to show the moment when doubt has been transformed into a shared profound faith. Like the High Priest in the *Expulsion of Heliodorus*, Julius is so deeply enraptured by his prayer that his attention has been entirely diverted from the events around him including the miracle itself. He has no need for such external signs of God's power. Not so the busy crowd of laypeople to the painting's lower left, or the cardinals and Swiss guards ranged to the right; they are engrossed in the unfolding event. The imposing man standing immediately behind Julius is his cousin Cardinal Raffaele Riario; as vice-chancellor of the Apostolic Chamber (chief financial officer of the Papal States) and cardinal protector of his Augustinian order, the largest in Christendom, Riario was a powerful political figure as well as an outstanding patron of art and architecture. Next to Riario is Cardinal Leonardo della Rovere, the pope's cousin, another of the era's most influential participants in Church politics. Beneath them kneel some of the Vatican's very first Swiss guards, mercenaries first hired by Julius to help on his military campaigns, and ever since an indispensable force at the Vatican. Their lush velvet uniforms are darker and heavier than the current outfits, which were designed by Michelangelo in the mid–sixteenth century at the behest of Pope Paul III.

The Repulse of Attila

Attila and his horde of Huns swept down on Europe in the fifth century, as the breakup of the Roman Empire led to conditions of instability all over the Roman world. From northern Europe, the Visigoths under Alaric attacked Rome in 410, sacking the city for the first time since the Gallic invasion eight hundred years before. In 456, it was the turn of Genseric and the Vandals. Attila never reached Rome; Roman legend said that he was deterred by a vision of Peter and Paul, the city's patron saints. Here a carefully detailed picture of the Roman countryside supplies all the most conspicuous landmarks: the Colosseum, an aqueduct, a basilica (possibly Saint John Lateran). Attila, the "Scourge of God," is announced by storms of wind and fire, but his tempests are no match for the flying saints, armed with fiery swords. Beneath Peter and Paul, Pope Leo I, Leo the Great, rides out to meet the enemy, accompanied by his cardinals. The fresco was conceived during the reign of Julius II, whose portrait should presumably have appeared as Pope Leo I, but by the time the fresco was finished, in 1513, another Pope Leo sat on Saint Peter's throne: Leo X, whose stout frame now burdens the pope's white mule. The repulse of Attila served as a warning to all prospective invaders of Italy; and for Pope Julius at least, the protection of Saints Peter and Paul worked its miracle. On 11 April 1512 (Raphael's twenty-ninth birthday), papal troops finally routed the French at Ravenna. Pope Julius shaved his beard in triumph. One of the cardinals shown accompanying Pope Leo the Great as he rides out against Attila, Cardinal Giovanni de' Medici, was present in person at the Battle of Ravenna, where he was captured and held for ransom – a year before his election as Pope Leo X.

THE STANZA DELL'INCENDIO (1514–17)

By 1514, under a new pope, Leo X, Raphael and his workshop had moved on to the next room in the papal suite, now named for the only fresco in the room that clearly bears the stamp of Raphael's design and execution. The rest of this Stanza was entrusted to his associates, for Raphael himself had embarked on a new project for the pope: designing a set of tapestries for the Sistine Chapel. In the early sixteenth century, tapestry was a far more valuable medium than fresco, because of its expensive materials and the intricacy of its workmanship; furthermore, the commission for the Sistine Chapel was a far more public project than the decoration of the pope's private apartments. It seems likely that Leo, clever and erudite, took an active part in planning the decorative scheme of this room; he was the son of Lorenzo de' Medici and prided himself on his family's history as patrons of the arts. Every one of the scenes in this chamber involves another Pope Leo, either Leo III, a contemporary of Charlemagne, or Leo IV, who first fortified the Vatican and its surrounding neighborhood against attackers, turning the area into a "Città Leonina" – a Leonine City.

Fire in the Borgo

By far the most accomplished fresco in the Stanza dell'Incendio, *Fire in the Borgo* (Plate 23) commemorates a miracle from the year 847, when the newly elected Pope Leo IV stopped a fire in the Borgo, the neighborhood around the Vatican, simply by making the sign of the Cross. This was the area that Leo was also enclosing within fortifications to create the Città Leonina; his protection was both spiritual and practical. Behind the pope, who stands in an elegant loggia in the painting's middle ground, we can see part of Old Saint Peter's with its painted façade; this is the ancient basilica, erected by Constantine, that Pope Julius II had declared structurally unsound and begun to demolish in 1506.

In the left foreground, as fire burns out of control, a striking trio walks away from a stately columned building: Aeneas, the Trojan hero, bearing his father Anchises on his back and leading his son Ascanius by the hand. Through imagery, the fire in the Borgo is being compared to the fires of Troy, and just as the destruction of old Troy led to the foundation of Rome, so, too, the destruction of old Saint Peter's was leading in these very years to the construction of a new church in a new Rome. The first architect of New Saint Peter's, Donato Bramante, died in 1514, just as Raphael began work on this Stanza. Leo X appointed Raphael as Bramante's replacement, together with the septuagenarian architect Fra Giocondo da Verona. Every element of *Fire in the Borgo* seems to reflect this important new appointment and Raphael's thoughts about how to proceed.

Pope Julius and Bramante had hoped to create a building whose classical beauty would rival the great buildings of ancient Rome, but whose Christian purpose would continue the comparably venerable tradition of the medieval basilicas. Bramante had devoted careful study to the different types of classical columns and their placement on ancient monuments. Raphael continued to develop the same interest, devoting special attention to what the ancient Roman architectural writer Vitruvius had said on the subject, but also studying Rome's surviving ancient monuments, many of which had been built long after Vitruvius wrote. The colonnade on the left of *Fire in the Borgo* shows a type of column capital first invented in imperial Rome and therefore unknown to Vitruvius: the Composite, a hybrid of Ionic volutes and Corinthian acanthus leaves that first appears on the Arch of Titus in the Roman Forum. Next to the column, a nude young man lets himself down the wall of the colonnaded building to escape the fire; taking a cue from Vitruvius, who likened Doric columns to the figures of a young man, Raphael ranges the beauty of this youth's body alongside a set of beautiful columns.

In the right foreground, statuesque women carry jars of water to quench the fire. Neither the poses of the women nor the shapes of the vases they carry are entirely practical for any emergency except an aesthetic one. The beauty of vases and women are explicitly compared in a dialogue attributed to Plato, the *Hippias Major*, and that same implicit comparison is evidently drawn in the fresco. The colonnade behind the women is Ionic, a type of column that Vitruvius compared to the form of a stately matron; in effect, this side of *Fire in the Borgo* also provides an extended musing on various kinds of beauty: in vases, women, and architecture. The loggia from which Pope Leo IV gives his powerful blessing illustrates yet another kind of colonnade: a combination of Tuscan capitals and Doric frieze above a rusticated base. This combination of rustication, Tuscan columns, and Doric frieze anchored Bramante's design for the ground floor exterior of New Saint Peter's. In *Fire in the Borgo*, Raphael provides a preview of how the completed basilica will look, or at least an exploration of its possible appearance, suggesting that one day its beauty will have as powerful an effect as Leo IV's gesture of benediction. Unfortunately, New Saint Peter's would never have the same capacity to put out fires of dissension. Three years after this painting was completed, in 1517, Martin Luther published his Ninety-Five Theses; in 1521, Pope Leo X excommunicated him in one of the last acts of his papacy. Ironically, too, Raphael's elegant painted discourse on beauty was largely executed by his assistants, whose skill, however great, could not compare with that of the master.[16]

The Battle of Ostia

In 846, Islamic raiders (generically called Saracens) attacked Rome, sacking and looting the basilicas of Saint Peter's and Saint Paul's outside the walls. In response, Pope Leo IV, elected the subsequent year, resolved to fortify the area of the Vatican, centering its defenses on the Castel Sant'Angelo, the former mausoleum of the ancient Emperor Hadrian. His military buildup paid off; in 849, papal troops repelled a second Saracen attack at Ostia ("Rivermouths"), the port of Rome. The Ostia shown in this fresco by Raphael's workshop is, however, the contemporary port, dominated by the castle erected by Julius II when he was bishop of Ostia, a gem of Renaissance military architecture notable both for curtain walls adapted to the new demands of gunpowder artillery and for its bath with hot and cold running water. Julius was not only one of the most active popes of all time, he was also one of the cleanest.

By the time of Leo X, the Saracen threat had been replaced by Corsicans and Ottoman Turks, who posed a real threat to the safety of the seas and the cities on the Italian coast. Not until the siege of Malta in 1565 and the Battle of Lepanto in 1570 would the Turkish threat recede from Italian shores – and even then, Europe was far from safe from Ottoman imperialism: the great Turkish siege of Vienna occurred in the late seventeenth century. The victorious soldiers in the Battle of Ostia do not look particularly fierce with their elaborate armor and studied poses, but they are drawn from the victorious Roman troops on the Column of Trajan, who were an invincible fighting force in their own day. The design of this fresco and its execution were probably entrusted to Raphael's pupil Giulio Romano, who made a complete sketch of the reliefs on Trajan's column at about the same time. He did this by using only his sharp eyes, for the telescope would not be invented until 1608, and binoculars followed much later.

The Coronation of Charlemagne

Both the papacy and the Holy Roman Empire laid claim to the authority, the rituals, and the physical trappings of the ancient Roman emperors. When Charlemagne asked Pope Leo III to crown him emperor in the year 800, he did so because he believed that the pope's blessing was the best way to invest his rule with the force of divine right. Later kings and Holy Roman Emperors were less eager to submit to the papacy, which used this authority to make additional claims – most importantly, the exclusive right to appoint bishops. The Vatican based its reasoning on two examples: the baptism of the Roman emperor Constantine by Pope Sylvester I in 327 and this coronation of Charlemagne in 800. By the time Raphael's workshop had embarked on these frescoes, Leo, a weak ruler, had an acute need to proclaim the historical basis for a power he could not hold by personal authority. The unrest that would lead Martin Luther to proclaim his Ninety-Five Theses in 1517 had already reached fever pitch; Leo's continuation of the Fifth Lateran Council would do little to assuage widespread doubts about the papacy's right – or fitness – to rule the Christian world.

The fresco's design, by Raphael's associate Gianfrancesco Penni, is ambitious but not entirely successful. The dramatic diagonals formed by the crossbows, the long table, and the rows of bishops in their miters are meant to create a deep perspective space, but instead they seem to zigzag improbably across the flat surface of the picture plane.

The Oath of Leo III

In the year 800, Pope Leo III used the state visit of Charlemagne to reinforce his own political position. In front of the newly crowned emperor and the College of Cardinals he made public act of penitence in Saint Peter's Basilica for all the misdeeds of which he had been falsely accused. Charlemagne can be identified by his gold chain. As always, the presence of a window in this wall presented a special problem, one that Raphael's young associate, whether Penni or the very young Perin del Vaga, solved less successfully than his master. As in the *Mass of Bolsena*, the central action occurs over the window, flanked by crowds on either side. But none of Raphael's students shared his ability to bind a composition together with an arresting architectural setting; the *Oath of Leo III* depicts the same crowds as the *Mass of Bolsena* but lacks that fresco's simple majesty.

Raphael had spent almost ten years decorating these three rooms in the papal suite. During that time, he transformed himself from an ambitious young painter to the most successful artist in Rome, not only a painter, but an architect and general designer with a large workshop and an international clientele. His only real rival, Michelangelo, had fled back to Florence after completing the Sistine Chapel ceiling for Pope Julius in 1512. The difference in painterly style between the clear Umbrian colors and elaborate compositions of the Stanza della Segnatura and the darker palette and simple, sculptural compositions of the late Stanze show how Raphael's rigorous self-criticism and constant rethinking continued to reshape his style. As his reputation grew, so did the demands on his talent. The Stanza della Segnatura shows the fierce concentration of a young man bent on succeeding; the Stanza dell'Incendio shows the delegated tasks of a successful man who can no longer fulfill all his commissions in person. The Stanza di Eliodoro stands somewhere in between, at the transition between the militant furor of Julius II and the cultured indolence of Leo X. And in the end, the effect of these two papal patrons on Raphael's work in the Stanze cannot be underestimated. It was Julius, after all, who compelled Michelangelo to paint the Sistine Chapel ceiling, whose triumphant success, at the same time as the painting of the Stanza della Segnatura, cannot be pure coincidence. And it is difficult to imagine Julius settling for anything less than Raphael's best work in any of the Stanze. The impatient prodding of that *papa terribile* has its own important place in the history of art.

5 One Artist, Two Sitters, One Role Raphael's Papal Portraits

Joanna Woods-Marsden

[Raphael] also made portraits from life like those of pope Julius II [and] pope Leo X...which are called divine.[1]

Lodovico Dolce

This essay considers the two portraits that Raphael painted of consecutive popes: Julius II (usually dated c. 1511–12) and Leo X (c. 1517–18). It explores how the individual with the highest rank and greatest powers in Christendom chose to figure the self visually during the period that we call the High Renaissance. The recently invented genre of portraiture allowed patrons in positions of power to create visual self-representations that, deliberately constructing their aspirations, could mediate between them and their audience. Which persona, the mask or role that an individual assumes in order to address the world, did each of these popes decide to adopt in his likeness? Such a query is particularly relevant to the papacy, in that the office incorporated two roles. On the one hand, as an institutional figure, the person of the pope was venerated as that of the living image of Christ.[2] On the other, the pontiff in his human dimension was the mortal who governed the church and the Papal States. Such a duality inevitably resulted in tensions between the pope's human condition and the sacred office he was called on to fill.[3] In this essay, I emphasize the mortal human by referring to Julius II and Leo X by their baptismal names of Giuliano and Giovanni, on the assumption that these were the masks with which they themselves most intimately identified.

The essay will further suggest the artistic context for Raphael's papal likenesses by briefly considering the portraits he painted before that of Julius II and between the latter and that of Leo X. The earliest portraits attributed to the artist exhibit the quattrocentesque forms that were employed by Perugino. It was not until Raphael's years in Florence that he formulated more personal conventions with which to express the relationship of the physical self to the picture plane and the psychic self to the viewer. His preferred formula presents the sitter as a tightly framed half-length, cut below the waist, and placed at a slight diagonal to the pictorial surface. One arm, located along the painting's lower margin, acts as a barrier between the sitter and the viewer, and the hands are brought together. With few exceptions, among which our two papal portraits, the sitters address their audience.[4]

The pendant portraits of the Florentine patricians Angelo Doni and his wife, Maddalena Strozzi, painted c. 1507–8, display these conventions (Plates 10 and 11).[5] The sitters face each other in complementary but subtly asymmetrical poses, the groom on the left, the heraldic dexter or place of honor. Unlike Leonardo da Vinci's *Portrait of Mona Lisa*, by which Raphael was profoundly influenced, he silhouetted the couple's heads and shoulders against the sky that overlooks a placid, Flemish-inspired landscape. Again unlike Leonardo's likeness, the sitters are richly attired in brilliant colors and sumptuous fabrics. Maddalena displays her nuptial jewels against orange-red watered silk and deep blue damask: a huge pearl hanging from a bejeweled pendant, a double row of gold ornaments, a gold chain belt, and rings. A strong gender distinction can be read in the vertical and horizontal grid that structures Raphael's presentation of Agnolo, compared with the voluptuous curves with which he described Maddalena's billowing sleeves, transparent veil, and bodice that emphasizes her breasts. The sinuous line that connects her jewels vertically is echoed in the continuous curve that Raphael imposed on the silhouette of her upper body that in effect eliminates her shoulders.

Raphael's first portrait in Rome depicts a sitter of a different ilk: the reigning spiritual leader of Christendom in the earliest autonomous painted portrait of an unaccompanied pope (Plate 14).[6] Raphael's sitter, Giuliano della Rovere (c. 1445–1513), chose to present the self in the nonliturgical winter garments of scarlet velvet *camauro* (cap) and *mozzetta* (short cape) both lined with ermine, over a rochet, a priest's liturgical robe, of pleated white linen. The artist depicts the pontiff at three-quarter length – that is, with more of his body showing than hitherto in Raphael's portrait oeuvre – in front of a green brocade hanging that acts as a cloth of honor.[7] Nephew of the first della Rovere pope, Sixtus IV (r. 1471–84), who nominated him to the cardinalate in 1471, Giuliano was elected pontiff in 1503. He assumed a papal identity as Julius II, a name similar to his own, with obvious reference to the greatest general of antiquity, Julius Caesar, with whom he equated the self after his liberation of Bologna in 1507. The name signified, it was conjectured at the time, the grandeur of Giuliano's future plans.[8] The pope was characterized by Guicciardini, on the one hand, as "notoriously very difficult by nature and formidable with everyone" and, on the other, as possessing integrity, "inestimable spirit, and resolution."[9] The reign of this choleric, indomitable, and impetuous individual was shadowed by war, in which he personally participated, to secure the independence of the Papal States and to rid Italy of foreign rulers.[10]

In 1970, Cecil Gould established that the National Gallery's version of the composition was Raphael's original painting.[11] The likeness is usually assumed to date between June 1511 and March 1512, when Giuliano – most unusually for the period – wore a beard. Such precision, however, may be overly positivistic in that the pope is also bearded in the *Expulsion of Heliodorus* and the *Mass of Bolsena*, usually dated c. 1512–13. Given that Giuliano's beard took on a pictorial life of its own after having been shaven, this portrait could as well have been painted in fall–winter 1512–13 as in winter 1511–12. The season is of course implied by the sitter's winter garments.

The seated pose that Raphael gave Giuliano, in which his thronelike chair, *sede camerale*, is canted obliquely to the picture plane, facing the light, became the prototype for subsequent papal likenesses. Papal precedents for the pose include Justus of Ghent's likeness from the mid-1470s of Sixtus IV seated obliquely in Federico da Montefeltro's *studiolo* in Urbino, from which Raphael further derived the Flemish three-quarter-length format.[12] The formula of canted chair may in turn have derived from the French artist Jean Fouquet's lost portrait from the mid-1440s depicting Eugenius IV with two members of his household; it hung in the sacristy of Santa Maria sopra Minerva in Rome and was therefore also known to Raphael.[13] A sixteenth-century engraved copy of Eugenius IV without his companions shows him half-length, at three-quarter view to the left, his chair invisible, his left arm placed horizontally on a flat surface, and hands clasped.[14] No independent Italian group portraits survive from the mid-quattrocento, and Fouquet's use of the half-length format in three-quarter view, with hands showing, was also unknown in Rome. The unfamiliarity and originality of the portrait must accordingly have stupefied its first viewers. As many have noted, another important precedent for Julius's oblique pose was the narrative fresco of *Gregory IX Approving the Decretals* that Raphael had just finished in the Stanza della Segnatura (Plate 20). In it, Giuliano, playing the role of Gregory IX, is shown full-length on a throne canted at an identical angle in the same direction.[15]

Raphael's apparently simple image is composed of a pyramid within a firmly structured grid of verticals and horizontals. The central axis, defined by the pope's head (which is also centered horizontally on the panel), the line of buttons on the *mozzetta*, and his right hand, is echoed in the shadow cast on the brocade cloth of honor by one of its folds.[16] The equilateral triangle created by the pope's *mozzetta* has his head at its apex and his right arm and hand at its base. Giuliano's diagonal location vis-à-vis the picture plane is emphasized, at lower right by his left hand grasping the chair's arm, and at upper left by one of the throne's prominent gold acorn finials, taken from the oak tree of the della Rovere arms, that, by enframing his head, identify his lineage.[17]

His scarlet *camauro* and *mozzetta* and white rochet as well as the saturated green curtain make this a painting of rich tonalities. The colors red and white, redolent of *imitatio imperii* and the Roman Empire, were also intrinsic to the Church, the red symbolizing the blood shed by Christ on the cross and the white marking its wearer's innocence and purity. Christ was, for instance, described as "white in sanctity and red in Passion."[18] As the living image of Christ on earth [*imago Christi*], the pope's pure white rochet thus signified the purity of his inner self. Just as his outer garments symbolized Christ's martyrdom and papal *potestas*, power, so the immaculate whiteness of his inner garment testified to his "clean" and "virginal" [*munda et virginea*] life.[19]

This charged symbolism may account for Renaissance preference for the use of nonliturgical garments in papal portraiture instead of the vestments of embroidered cope and tiara that were traditional earlier.[20] The latter, especially the tiara, were linked to the expression of territorial sovereignty rather than the Holy Father's personal probity and virginity.[21] For Giuliano, in addition, a famous portrait of his della Rovere predecessor, Sixtus IV, portrayed him in the same nonliturgical garments.[22] The symbolism of white, green and red as the theological virtues of Faith (white), Hope (green), and Charity (red) no doubt accounts for the choice of hue for the hanging behind. Similarly, the colors of the gems – glittering diamonds, emeralds, and rubies – in Giuliano's six conspicuous rings may have been a factor in his choice of which to wear in his likeness.[23]

Although Giuliano's beard caused much talk in papal Rome, it had ample historical justification, and he had many reasons for growing it. Traditionally, facial hair was a sign of mourning, and the pope, as temporal ruler, is believed to have vowed to remain penitentially unshaven until the French were driven from Italy.[24] Significantly, after a defeat of his soldiers,

Julius Caesar was reputed to have grown his beard as an expression of grief. In addition, a twelfth-century mosaic in Santa Maria in Trastevere showed Giuliano's namesake, the fourth-century Julius I, with a beard that was supposedly grown after a defeat by the same enemy: the Gauls.[25] An early sixteenth-century treatise on the beard further proclaimed it a sign of piety, gravity, and dignity.[26] The first pope, Saint Peter, for instance, was always depicted bearded, as was, typically, the high priest who prays for deliverance in the Temple of Jerusalem in Raphael's *Expulsion of Heliodorus*. Finally, there seems to be no doubt that in the Renaissance a beard constructed masculinity; the beard, in other words, made the man.[27] Appropriately for the pope who had just returned from a military campaign, facial hair was in addition often characterized as a weapon.[28]

The white cloth held by Giuliano would seem to be an attribute more appropriate to a woman, as seen in such portraits as Botticelli's unknown *Lady at a Window* (Victoria and Albert Museum, London) or Ghirlandaio's *Giovanna Tornabuoni* (Museo Thyssen-Bornemisza, Madrid).[29] Nonetheless, other men, such as Veronese's unknown gentleman displaying the magnificent lynx fur lining of his coat (Pitti Palace, Florence) also carry white cloths in their depictions; it seems inherently more likely that Giuliano habitually carried a *fazzoletto* with which to mop his brow than that he intended it to refer to the *mappa* of ancient Rome, an insignia of imperial authority, as has been claimed.[30] Such an overt reference to antiquity in his depiction does not accord with what we know of Giuliano's sensibilities and tastes.[31]

Raphael represented more of this sitter's body than he had hitherto or would hereafter. Nothing detracts from Giuliano's body, which forms the largest mass on the pictorial surface. And, indeed, the body of the vicar of Christ, successor to Saint Peter, was venerated as that of the living Christ on earth.[32] According to Grosseteste, the pope on election "assume[d] the person of Christ."[33] To become *persona Christi*, he had to divest himself of his own flesh. Innocent II's body, for instance, was, according to Saint Bernard, made of "the bones of [Christ's] bones and the flesh of his flesh."[34] Indeed, the person who was pope was so conflated with the office that, according to one fourteenth-century commentator, those who contemplated him with the eyes of faith saw "the image of Christ himself."[35]

But even if Giuliano, as an institutional figure, was "the image of Christ eternal and immutable," in his human dimension he was neither.[36] When this portrait was painted, he was either sixty-nine or seventy, which was very old by Renaissance standards, and had almost died in 1511. It seems inevitable that the aged sitter's consciousness of his own mortality lingered in his mind and may indeed underlie the commission of this portrait. At death, the individual who had embodied the person of Christ lost the *potestas* and *maiestas* with which the sacred office had endowed him. Not only was his corpse stripped of its power, but it was also often abandoned, naked, as proof that, dead, the pope "return[ed] to being a man."[37] "The pope," writes one historian, "did not have two bodies or substances, like a king, but only a natural body that is born and dies. What remains was Christ, the Roman church, the Apostolic See, but not the pope."[38]

The abandoned papal corpse might further be desecrated by the theft of his garments and goods in the "ritual pillage" that could take place at the death of a leader.[39] Such an event had occurred during Giuliano's grave illness in 1511, when he went into a deep coma.[40] Believing him to have expired, his household started to plunder the palace.[41] On his deathbed in February 1513 Giuliano spoke bluntly of the fate awaiting his own corpse, as recorded by Paride de' Grassi, papal master of ceremonies:

Having seen many popes who, once dead, were immediately abandoned by relatives and servants and...left lying there in a shameful way, downright naked with their private parts exposed, a thing which, for someone of authority – of majesty – as elevated as that of the papacy, was scandalous and degrading.[42]

In Raphael's image, however, far from being naked and exposed, the living incumbent is sacralized by the ritual uniform of his pontifical office, and his individual physiognomy would have been read as incarnating a saintly image, a "suprapersonality," as it were, that embodied the same power and majesty as Saint Peter himself, reinforced no doubt by the cloth of honor behind.[43] Indeed, when Giuliano died, he was rhetorically proclaimed to have been "adored as if he were a saint," and "as if his were the true body of Saint Peter."[44] Thus it is not perhaps as surprising as it may seem that Raphael's portrait of a living pope should have been recorded in an unprecedented location for this genre: on an *altar* in the della Rovere church of Santa Maria del Popolo in Rome in September 1513, seven months after his death.[45]

In 1474, Melozzo da Forlì had frescoed a portrait of the enthroned Sixtus IV with four nephews, located as if in the Vatican Library that the della Rovere pope had founded on the ground floor of the same wing as Raphael's Stanze (Fig. 11).[46] In it, the young Cardinal Giuliano stands before the seated Sixtus; in Raphael's likeness, the aged pope can be said to have taken over his uncle's throne. The seated pose was reserved for sovereigns, because, as Ripa said, "sitting is for princes wherein they display their authority."[47] For Vasari, the pose signified "taking possession over one's dominion."[48] Thus it may be said that an enthroned pope celebrated his power, both temporal and spiritual, whereas a kneeling one demonstrated his spiritual calling. Giuliano's seated pose has, nonetheless, been mistakenly characterized as "devotional" or "votive,"[49] perhaps due to its location in Santa Maria del Popolo, to which Giuliano gave it, along with the *Madonna di Loreto*,[50] just as he had previously given another likeness to the church of San Marcello in Rome.[51] Only a kneeling pose, however, similar to that given to the same sitter in the *Mass of Bolsena* or in the *Nativity* triptych he commissioned earlier in Savona, in which Saints Francis and Anthony present the kneeling Sixtus IV and Cardinal Giuliano to the holy family, could have justified a characterization of his demeanor here as "devotional."[52]

Michael Fried has called attention to the impermeability of a portrait's bottom framing edge and the edge's capacity to contain the represented sitter and bring the image to a stop.[53] This is one of the earliest likenesses in which there is no device, such as a parapet or chairarm, to terminate the composition at its lower margin. Instead, the pope's knees appear to continue outside the frame and into our space, stressing the ambiguity of the liminal area between the world of the painting and that of the viewer. The viewer's space seems to fuse with that of the painted pope. As John Shearman has argued, the relationship here between sitter and viewer is highly innovative.[54] On those occasions when the portrait was hung low on a wall, Raphael intended the viewer to imagine himself standing deferentially at the pope's right hand, looking down at him, as only a member of the inner papal *famiglia*, a household intimate such as, possibly, the young Federico Gonzaga, would have had occasion to do. Giuliano himself had been fashioned by Melozzo as similarly looking down at the seated Sixtus IV *within* his painted group portrait but the concept of such intimacy between a sitter of such high rank and a viewer of unknown origins – as, for instance, may have occurred in Santa Maria del Popolo – was completely unprecedented in portraiture at this date (Fig. 11).

In Melozzo's fresco, the first della Rovere pope can be read as communicating directly with his standing nephew, instead of, as has often been noted of this portrait, unlike all Raphael's earlier likenesses, avoiding eye contact. It seems not to have been remarked that in none of the autonomous papal portraits of these years can the sitter be said to meet the viewer's gaze. In the likenesses of Sixtus IV by Melozzo and Justus of Ghent, Leo X by Raphael, and Clement VII by Sebastiano del Piombo, the popes all decline to address

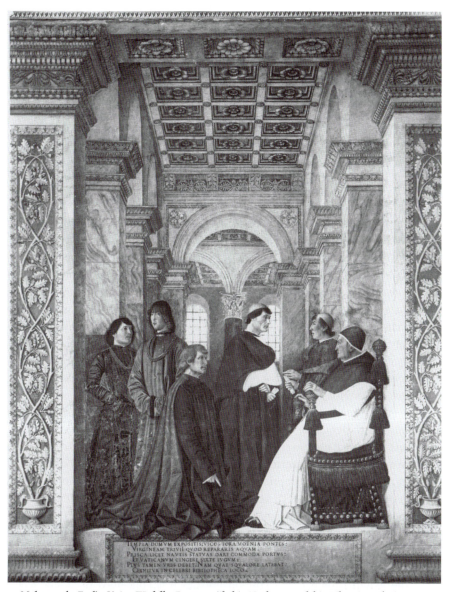

11. Melozzo da Forlì, *Sixtus IV della Rovere with his Nephews and his Librarian Platina.*
Detached fresco from the Vatican Library, Vatican, Pinacoteca. Photo: Scala/Art Resource,
NY.

the world.[55] While an image of the vicar of Christ was an appropriate object for the believer's gaze, the holders of that office, it seems, wished to be perceived as distinct from those scrutinizing them.

In contemporary metaphors of the body politic, the eye served as both watchman and judge. According to John of Salisbury, the eye, together with ears and tongue, served as a triumvirate of official power.[56] In addition, the eye since antiquity had been linked to divinity: juxtaposed by Horapollo with the term *devs*, the image of an eye still stood for *divvs* in a hieroglyph in the *Hypnerotomachia Poliphili*.[57] For Alberti, this powerful and divine eye was that of the all-seeing Christian God who "surveys all things...[and is an] ever-present witness to all our thoughts and deeds," as a result of which he "metes out moral judgments."[58] Like the eye of God, the gaze of the pontiff, God's regent on earth, may have been read as judgmental and all-seeing as well as powerful.

The eye is also an image of the soul. In discussing Byzantine painters' construction of a higher truth rooted in Neoplatonic distinctions between inward and outward, soul and body, Hans Belting argued that a "burning gaze testifie[d] to an inner life, the life of the soul, which is superior to that of the body."[59] The averted gaze in icons, he suggested, might therefore express freedom from mere corporeality. We may accordingly speculate that the vicar of Christ's gaze, symbol of his omniscient, judgmental power, might, when averted, have been understood as symbolizing his inner life, his concern for his soul rather than his body.

Furthermore, the pope's reciprocation of the viewer's look would have implied the equality of their respective statuses. A shared gaze is always one of mutual empowerment that affirms common humanity. Presentation of a pope with gaze averted accordingly precluded such a possibility as well as avoiding an inappropriate shared intimacy. Some combination of these arguments is required to account for this significant discrepancy between Raphael's other portraits and his papal imagery.

Comparison of this autonomous likeness with those frescoed by Raphael in the *Mass of Bolsena* or the *Approval of the Decretals*, where Giuliano was presented undertaking roles of central importance to the narrative, reveal the extent to which the London portrait was conceived of as an "icon." On the stage of the *Mass of Bolsena*, Giuliano as Julius acts the alert, deeply engaged, pious witness to the miracle of the Eucharist bleeding during Consecration of the Host. In the *Decretals*, Raphael constructed the pope as a regal and benevolent Gregory IX who, hand raised in the same gesture of blessing as that given to Sixtus IV by Justus of Ghent, approves a volume of canon law tended by the kneeling prelate (Plate 20).[60] In the independent panel, however, Raphael fashioned Giuliano outside of any narrative context, as if lost in thought, contemplating a world other than that immediately surrounding him. The pope's pose makes him appear both not to be posing and as if oblivious to being observed, whether by artist or viewer.

Raphael may well have drawn the pope from life as he sat waiting in his audience chamber for the next ambassador to make his entrance.[61] Under no circumstances, however, should it be imagined that Raphael figured the formidable Giuliano without the latter's knowledge or consent. On the contrary, this extraordinarily creative patron, known for his driving determination in all matters, must have been an active participant in the creation of his own likeness.[62] Such was the overwhelming force of this pope's uncompromising personality that Raphael's image cannot but represent him as he wished to be perceived. Giuliano, after all, had no self-interest in seeking a visual stereotype of the alarming *terribilità* that has fascinated historians ever since and that is often expected to inform his imagery.[63] Rather, he had himself depicted as physically passive, no matter how mentally active. Playing the role of Christ's surrogate with conviction and gravitas, this ever-restless man presents the self as if at rest, if not at peace.[64]

In the half-dozen years intervening between Raphael's two papal portraits, he produced a series of brilliantly inventive autonomous likenesses for some of the major cultural figures at the papal court. That of Tommaso Inghirami, prefect of the papal library, painted c. 1513–14 (Plate 13), displays the artist's extraordinary ingenuity in finding elegant formal solutions to awkward social dilemmas.[65] This image of the humanist at his desk about to undertake the cerebral action of composing a text is animated by the physical sway of his body sideways and the upward tilt of his head and glance. This is the first likeness into which Raphael introduced the concept of movement, and the seemingly natural turn that he gave to Inghirami, as though the writer were seeking inspiration from his muse, was a brilliant device with which to conceal the prefect's unfortunate walleye.[66] The painting also illustrates Raphael's continuing experimentation with the device of a diagonal across the picture plane as well as into space with which to animate his sitters. Just as Inghirami's head and hands are linked diagonally, so his body, enveloped in intense red against a plain, dark ground, is resolved into a diagonal oval turned on its axis.[67]

The theme of Raphael's famous likeness, c. 1515–16, of his close friend Baldassare Castiglione, author of *The Book of the Courtier*, is communication with his audience rather than that of solitary creation (Plate 16).[68] The viewer is both very close and on a level with Castiglione's eyes, implying that Raphael conceived of the diplomat as sitting at the same level as, and in intimate proximity to, himself as he sat painting – and hence to the viewer. The relationship of Castiglione's three-dimensional presence to the viewer is further enhanced by Raphael's typically tight framing of his body and deliberate cropping of his hands.[69] Here the ease and intimacy that obtained between the two friends is transmuted into that between the sitter and the viewer. Two years later, Castiglione would define this intimacy as that between husband and wife in a poem written in his wife's voice, in which he imagines her seated close to his likeness so that she and their baby son could commune with his painted alter ego during his absences from Mantua.[70]

In Castiglione's image, both color and movement are muted.[71] While sober in hue, as recommended in *The Courtier*, Castiglione's fashionable dress is nonetheless made up of sumptuous materials redolent of opulence and status as well as of touch: rich black velvet with sleeves of beaver fur in delicate shades of grey and brown. The relative absence of color in his attire highlights the brightest hue in the work: his deep blue eyes placed at the horizontal center of the canvas.

The rapid development of Raphael's art overall effected the forms of his portraits which, by the end of his life, had evolved from the contained forms of the early Renaissance to bold proto-baroque statements, infused with complexity, movement, and extreme contrasts of light. His last, and perhaps greatest, work in the genre, *Self-Portrait with a Friend* (Louvre, Paris), c. 1518–19, is dominated by dark, monochromatic tonalities, strong contrasts of light and shade, and dramatic action.[72] Cladding himself and his unknown companion in severe, albeit elegant, black silk over white linen, Raphael eschewed the warm browns and greys of Castiglione's likeness, with which this work, equally personal and equally communicative, should be linked.

The action and drama introduced into the portrait is directed toward a (perhaps specific) viewer on the other side of the frame. Raphael made his seated companion point theatrically out of the painting while turning in *contrapposto* to glance up at the creating artist, who stands behind him on the diagonal produced by his pointing arm. The gesture focuses attention away from the pictorial world to that of the seated painter at his easel, the self-portraitist's mirror, and, by extension, the viewer. The *contrapposto* posture and forceful action given to the artist's companion serve to energize the portrait with immense vitality. Although common in Raphael's contemporary narratives in the Stanze, the tapestry cartoons, and the *Trans-figuration*, such rhetorical gestures were unprecedented in contemporary portraiture. Indeed, the active drama, informality, and illusion of immediacy of this painting contrast sharply with the stasis, formality and ceremony of the nearly contemporary *Portrait of Leo X with Two Cardinals* (Plate 15).

The three lifesize protagonists of this majestic and monumental panel (155.2 × 118.9 cm) are attired in brilliant scarlets and luminous ivories – the same uniform with the same symbolism as in Julius II's portrait – in one of the most sumptuous color schemes in Renaissance portraiture.[73] In the center looms Giovanni de' Medici (1475–1521), son of Lorenzo the Magnificent, named a cardinal in 1489 by Innocent VIII Cibo, shortly after Giovanni's sister married into that family. In 1513, Giovanni succeeded Julius as the first Florentine pope in history.

He had many reasons for assuming a papal identity as Leo X. The Florentine lion, *Marzocco*, was traditionally paired with John the Baptist, his name saint, as guardians of his native city, and the ubiquitous representations of lions in Giovanni's artistic commissions were often referred to as *marzocchi*.[74] The king of beasts was known above all for two opposing virtues: ferocity and clemency.[75] Giovanni espoused the latter, especially the virtue of magnanimity.[76] The Battle of Ravenna, from which Giovanni miraculously escaped imprisonment, had taken place on the Feast of Saint Leo, and his choice of identity undoubtedly revealed a desire to appropriate the greatness of some of his leonine predecessors.[77] Investigating the implications of Giovanni's horoscope, Janet Cox-Rearick has argued that the rising sun in his ascendant Sagittarius led him to associate the self with the sign of Leo, zodiacal house of the sun, a combination that had a greater mystique of power than any other sign of the zodiac.[78] The name Leo further allowed him to be equated with Christ as the Lion of Judah, the prophetic beast of the Old Testament and the Book of Revelation, who alone could loosen the Seven Seals of the Apocalypse.[79] Characterized by Paride de Grassi as having a "tolerant and amiable disposition" and by Sanuto as disinclined to "tax himself too much," the personality of this easygoing, good-natured man, who favored the "dolce vita," could not have been more unlike that of his *terribile* predecessor.[80]

Located on the panel's central axis, Giovanni is accompanied not by nephews, as was Sixtus IV, but by two first cousins of his own generation with whom he had been educated.[81] To the left, on the heraldic dexter, Cardinal Giulio de' Medici, the future Clement VII, gazes toward the

papacy. Leo's closest advisor, he had served the pope since 1492, was elevated to the Cardinalate in 1513, and given the powerful position of vice-
chancellor of the Church in 1517.[82] Behind the pope stands cardinal Luigi
de' Rossi, named to the College of Cardinals as part of a mass promotion
in 1517. With hands placed protectively on either side of the throne's gold
finial in the form of a *palla* (ball) from the Medici arms, he seems to guard
the pope's exposed left side, just as cardinal Giulio's body, placed at right
angles to that of his cousin, protects Giovanni's dexter.[83] An illuminated
manuscript and a handbell lie on the scarlet-bedecked table in front. In the
background, a grey *pietra serena* interior – a unique feature for Raphael in
the genre – provides a dark foil for the protagonists.

It has been proposed that the figures of the two cardinals were added to
the portrait as an afterthought, on the grounds that underdrawings exist
only for the figure of the pope, not those of the two cardinals; that a layer
of green underlies the architecture, suggesting that the background might
have originally been a green curtain; and that Rossi's left hand was painted
over the already painted chairback.[84] Nonetheless, the notion that Raphael
originally planned a single portrait in the center of such a large panel, otherwise empty, is questionable in that it does not accord with his aesthetic
sensibilities. In the artist's contemporary portraits, as we saw, the protagonists are invariably tightly framed, and at times the frame even crops their
figures, as here. How the single figure of the pope would have related to
the scale of the panel can be seen in the unhappy relationship between
figure and frame in a partial copy of Raphael's portrait by Lodovico Buti.[85]
Moreover, a strong case can be made that the geometric structure of the
composition, defined by intersecting triangular and diagonal forms, successfully weave the three figures together.[86] My discussion is accordingly
based on the premise that the presence of the two cardinals was planned
from the beginning.

The *terminus post quem* for this panel is established by the presence of
Rossi, who was created a cardinal, along with thirty others, on 1 July 1517, and
the *terminus ante quem* is fixed by the work's presence at the banquet to
celebrate the marriage of Lorenzo de' Medici, duke of Urbino and ruler
of Florence, to Madeleine de la Tour d'Auvergne in September 1518 at
the Palazzo Medici in Florence.[87] Its presence signified a kind of papal benediction of the prestigious alliance, negotiated by the pope himself, in which the Medici succeeded in allying themselves to French royalty. More precisely, the heavy, fur-lined clothes worn by the pope, who
sweated continuously, implies that the painting took place during winter
1517–18.

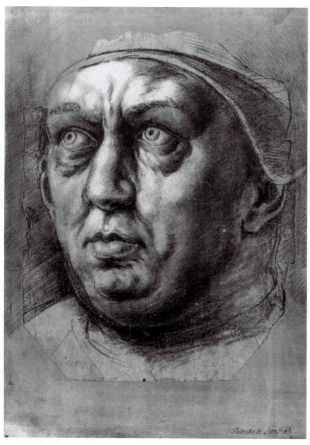

12. Head of Pope Leo X. Black and white chalk. Devonshire Collection, Chatsworth. Chatsworth Settlement Trustees; photo, Courtauld Institute of Art.

Raphael's portraits were consistently praised for their verisimilitude, and this work is a superb instance of the naturalism that his contemporaries claimed to admire so greatly.[88] At the same time, however, his sitters sought poetic and elegant likenesses that, while embellishing the truth, were nonetheless sufficiently recognizable to be convincing. Raphael conformed to cultural expectations by artfully refashioning the features that he ostensibly described. Just as he had smoothed the wrinkles from Julius II's brow and reduced the circumference of his bull neck, so a black chalk drawing at Chatsworth of Giovanni's features, probably by Giulio Romano (Fig. 12),[89] reveals the extent to which in the painting Raphael softened Giovanni's fleshy jowls and chin, the bags of loose skin under his eyes, his bulbous nose, and bulging eyeballs.[90]

Giovanni wears the same uniform of scarlet *camauro* (cap) and *mozzetta* (short cape) as his predecessor but added a rich fur-lined cassock of ivory satin damask over the white rochet. The sumptuous garment belies the impression of relative simplicity conveyed by the pope's decision to be painted without rings, an unexpected choice given the significance of precious gems for the culture. Along with the exquisite craftsmanship and precious materials of the bell and codex, the cassock reveals the pleasure that this pope derived from the huge sums he spent on the luxurious textiles and beautiful artifacts that signified Magnificence.

Canted diagonally to the left, at a similar angle to that of Julius II, the thronelike chair appears to be placed on a raised dais so that the pope, albeit seated, may dominate the stage that is the portrait. The seated pose and the table in front allowed Raphael to conceal some of Giovanni's physical defects: the heavy, obese body and huge head that were disproportionate to his short members and slender extremities, such as the small, feminine hands, of which he was very proud.[91] Needless to say, the pope's seated pose and his body were endowed with the same worldly and sacralizing significance as those outlined earlier for his predecessor: the enthroned pose implied sovereignty, whether sacred or profane, and an image of the vicar of Christ's body called for reverence emulating that accorded the person of Christ. Indeed, Shearman has shown how explicit was the analogy made between Giovanni and Christ, by citing from an oration given before the papal court at the beginning of his rule: "Weep not, O daughter of Zion, for behold the Lion of the Tribe of Judah.... The Lord has raised up for you a Savior, who will rescue you from all your enemies.... We put our trust in you, most blessed Leo, as the coming Savior."[92]

The exceptional background of Renaissance architecture recedes rapidly into the distance at a startling angle, creating a magnificent hall leading to an archway, a stage for the actors that is, of course, visual fiction and not depicted reality. In terms of the relationship between the figures and the setting, I read the protagonists as depicted in proportion to the architecture, which, I would argue, Raphael intended to be read as located far in the background.[93] Never before had Renaissance architectural forms been used so prominently in a portrait, other than the classicizing hall sheltering Sixtus IV and his nephews in Melozzo's fresco in the Vatican library two floors below, from which Raphael may well have drawn inspiration (Fig. 11).

The portrait's spatial construction is revolutionary. In Albertian perspective construction, the vanishing point establishes the location of the viewer, who stands directly opposite it. Here the entablature, so positioned as to emphasize the heads of Cardinal Giulio and the pope, recedes asymmetrically to the right, as does the other orthogonal created by the table and the pope's and Cardinal Luigi's arms.[94] The vanishing point where these two orthogonals meet can be seen to lie considerably to the right of the pictorial surface. In an unprecedented move, Raphael established the viewer's position not *in front* of the portrait but at a considerable distance to its right, as far away as necessary for him or her to meet Rossi's sideways glance. The viewer's position is identical, in reverse, to that established by Raphael for the wall on which the *Approval of the Decretals* was frescoed (Plate 20).[95] There, the vanishing point for the two side frescoes was located in the central window, implying that the *Decretals* was intended to be seen from a point considerably to the left of the scene.

The pontiff is accordingly fashioned as pointedly looking in the opposite direction from his audience. No more than in the earlier papal likeness does Raphael focus attention on the pope's reaction to the viewer. The vicar of Christ again declines to address his audience, perhaps because his gaze, as suggested for that of his predecessor, not only symbolized his omniscient, judgmental power, but also, when averted, his inner life, his soul. The same need to avoid the kind of inappropriate intimacy that could be attributed to an exchange of glances with the viewer may also have obtained here.

As in Raphael's likeness of Julius, no device terminates this composition at its lower edge, so that the pope's table juts palpably into our space. Here, too, the viewer's world may be said to fuse with that of the painted pope. Unlike Julius II's image, however, where no direct connection is made between sitter and viewer, this pictorial world is linked to that of the papal court by the gaze of cardinal Luigi, who was given the task of mediating with the viewer. We should not, however, read his admonitory gaze as inviting the viewer-courtier to step through the liminal picture plane and stand in the available space at the pope's sinister.[96] A discrepancy surely exists between Giovanni's extremely reserved self-presentation and the presumption involved in any notion that the viewer is being invited to enjoy such intimate proximity to the body of Christ's representative on earth.

Rarely did Raphael employ so many attributes and their inclusion must have been at the pope's request. The artifacts belonging to Giovanni on the jutting table refer to his role as sacramental priest and spiritual head of the Church. The lavish, finely proportioned, silver and gold handbell is decorated with two registers of spiraling acanthus. On the bell's left side is Leo X's pontifical coat of arms, crowned by the Medici device of *broncone*, the stump of a laurel tree with a new shoot; on the right is the Medici emblem of a diamond ring with three ostrich feathers, symbolizing eternity.[97] This attribute can be identified as the sanctus bell that was rung at the moment of the elevation and consecration of the host, when the very substance of the wafer became the real body of Christ.[98] The elevation was normally conducted in silence, broken only by the server's bell that announced the presence of Christ in the Eucharist and invited the congregation to adore it. Giovanni's great passion was for music, and it may be assumed that the tone emitted by his personal bell was particularly pleasing.[99]

Giovanni suffered from such severe myopia as to be almost blind, and the magnifying lens with which, according to Raphael's painted fiction, he inspects the manuscript never left his hand, becoming, in effect, his attribute.[100] By placing the trecento Neapolitan codex, which survives as the Hamilton Bible, on an orthogonal, Raphael gave it considerable prominence. On folio 400v., the left page, the artist appropriated the book as a Medici commission by substituting the pope's family arms in the lower border for those of the Beaufort family in the actual manuscript.[101] On the folio the opening words of the Gospel according to Saint John are fully legible below miniatures of the Passion, indicating that the codex's function was to highlight that passage: *In principio erat verbum et verbum...*, "in the beginning was the Word and the Word...."[102] The rest of the sentence continues in blurred form on the opposite folio, but the whole of Christendom knew how the text continued:

was with God and the Word was God. The same was in the beginning with God.... In him was the life, and the life was the light of men. And the light shineth in the darkness, and the darkness apprehended it not.

John I:1–5

The light shining in the darkness was of course Christ on earth.

The passage continues:

There was a man sent from God, whose name was John [the Baptist]. The same came for witness, to bear witness of the light, that all men through him might believe. He was not the light, but came that he might bear witness of the light. There was the true light, even the light that lighteth every man, coming into the world.

John I:6–9

The Prologue to Saint John's gospel announces that the coming of the light that was Christ was witnessed by John the Baptist, with whom the pope baptized John equated himself. In his portrait Giovanni also bears witness to the light by presenting himself to his court and the world as studying the most profound exposition of the mystery of the Incarnation in an intensely familiar passage that was recited at the end of every mass.[103] John O'Malley has pointed to a new focus on the Incarnation at the Renaissance papal court. Preachers at court tended to identify Redemption with the

Incarnation, the moment when Christ's divine and human natures were united, and to link the two in their interpretations. A blurring of the distinction between these two mysteries characterizes the prevailing religious ideology as "incarnational theology."[104] Like his name saint, Giovanni is fashioned as bearing witness to the light of the Incarnation, "when the Word became flesh and dwelt among us," having already appropriated the passage by way of his family arms. Just as the bell signals the real presence of Christ in the Eucharist, so the manuscript, open to the liturgical passage recited after Transubstantiation, symbolizes the promise of Redemption through the Incarnation of Christ on earth.

Bright sunlight enters the image from the upper right, dramatically illuminating the pontiff and his attributes but leaving his two subordinates in light-suffused shadow. The light ostensibly comes from a window that is reflected in the throne's shining gold finial in the shape of a Medici *palla*.[105] As a symbol of majesty and eternity, the sphere was an ancient emblem of the macrocosm or the orb of the cosmos, and the creation of the world. A window reflected on a glossy spherical surface signified the concept of light for the Renaissance.[106] By reflecting a window light with a crossbar, the pope's *palla* reveals the divine light of Christ together with the cross of the Crucifixion.[107] Thus the Medicean orb is imbued with the light of truth, brought into the world by the son of God. "I am the light of the world [*lux mundi*], he that followeth me shall not walk in darkness, but shall have the light of life [*lumen vita*]," reads a later passage in John (8:12).[108]

As it happens, the rising sun in Sagittarius in Giovanni's horoscope allowed him to associate the self with solar imagery and Sol/Apollo as well as with the celestial Leo.[109] He was addressed by poets as the "sun" pope whose rays illumined the whole world, and his heraldic imagery often combined a radiant sun with the ubiquitous lion.[110] Thus, the shape of the *palla* that reflects the light of Christ also echoes that of the sun, the ruler of the pope's ascendant sign. Raphael may accordingly be said to have presented the pope not only himself bathed in a strong flow of light but also beside a family emblem that embodied his personal solar identity. We may speculate that Raphael's use of the light-reflecting emblem and the flow of pervasive light across the pope's person allowed Giovanni to conflate his celestial solar persona with the light of divinity. Recalling the words, "we put our trust in you, most blessed Leo, as the coming Savior," the visual rhetoric may be said to echo the verbal.[111] The painting implies that through the presence of the "sun" pope beside the finial holding God's light and Christ's cross – as through the presence originally of his name saint, the Baptist – all humankind, including the populations recently encountered in the New

World, will believe and walk in the light of truth rather than in the darkness of disbelief (John 3 :19).[112]

Significantly, unlike Julius II, Giovanni did not choose to present the self as a lone sitter. Although, as we have seen, there was an important quattrocento precedent for the presentation of a pope with two dependents in Fouquet's lost image of Eugenius IV, political circumstances at the papal court immediately preceding this work may have played a larger role in determining its iconography and may even have been instrumental in its formulation.[113]

In May 1517, five cardinals confessed to participating in a conspiracy, led by Cardinal Alfonso Petrucci, to poison the pope through the connivance of his doctor.[114] The discovery of the plot shocked papal Rome, became the talk of European courts, and frightened the pope and cardinals. The commission of the portrait may even have been stimulated by Giovanni's new awareness of the transience of life. The work was started after the leading conspirator-cardinal had been secretly executed in prison, two others had gone into exile, and two had paid huge fines.

The relationship of pope and cardinals was not supposed to lead to murderous conspiracies of the one against the other. On the contrary, according to John of Salisbury, the cardinals and the pope together made a body: the pontiff formed the head of the corpus and the cardinals its members, from which they could not detach themselves.[115] Innocent III was the first to use this corporeal metaphor, referring to the cardinals as "the members of our body."[116] In Hostensis's elaboration on the metaphor, the cardinals as body were to be so united to the papal head as to not require an oath of fealty or obedience: "[the pope] does not receive an oath from these cardinals because they are part of his viscera."[117] In the triple likeness in the wake of the assassination plot, the Medici cardinals as bodily members can be read as guarding the Medici head of the papal corpus.

Giovanni took advantage of the weakness of the College of Cardinals in the immediate aftermath of the failed plot by nominating thirty-one cardinals, the largest number ever created at one consistory. Although the College was officially limited to twenty-four or twenty-five cardinals, thirty-three were already in place in 1517, so that the pope's concession of thirty-one new scarlet hats almost doubled the number.[118] The horrified cardinals vehemently opposed the move but, constrained by fear, eventually gave their consent.[119] Giovanni's person may thus be read in the painting as safeguarded by Cardinal Luigi, one of the new nominees, and Cardinal Giulio, his longtime advisor, both of them intimate – almost fraternal – relatives, with whom he had been brought up and whose own self-interest was so closely linked to his that their loyalty was seen as unquestioned.[120] To-day, the relationship among the three protagonists may seem ambiguous, but to the informed contemporary their configuration must have resonated with memories of the immediate past.

"In its silence, everything seems to speak," wrote Vasari of another work by Raphael.[121] The significance of this portrait is multivalent: a theological affirmation of the mystery of the Incarnation, as expounded in the Last Gospel, merged with a political assertion of the authority, divine and secular, lodged in this particular regent of God on earth. The two themes of sacred and profane power are conjoined in the luminous Medici orb, symbol of the macrocosm, light, and, hypothetically, the pope's sun. The work would seem to refer to the bull, *Unam Sanctam*, that Giovanni endorsed at the Lateran Council in December 1516. The bull asserted the precedence of spiritual over secular power by setting forth the claim of papal supremacy over that of all rulers and nations.[122] The pope's subsequent doubling of the cardinals in 1517 further concentrated unchallenged power in his own person by marginalizing the College of Cardinals. In the words of Innocent III:

From [Peter] I received the miter of my priesthood and the crown of my royalty; he has established me vicar of Him upon whose habit it is written: 'king of kings and lord of lords, priest for eternity according to the order of Melchizedek.'[123]

Two very different individuals, one near death, the other having just escaped it, play the same role, as interpreted by the same visual artist. Paintings, including portraits, belong to the same fictional realm as verse, and should therefore be interpreted as *poesie*. As Sperone Speroni put it succinctly in 1543, portraits are none other than the "dreams and shadows of our being" – *sogni e ombre del nostro essere*.[124] The painting of a likeness may be further defined as an art of deception in which artists and sitters are accomplices in the creation of these *sogni e ombre*. Serving as mediator between the pontifical sitters and their public, Raphael may be seen as collaborating with them in the creation of self-memorializing visual identities corresponding to the personae that they wished to project in paint. Raphael's rapport with both pontiffs, albeit as servant rather than equal, enabled him to translate their dreams and illusions into representations so expressive that the images in turn must have clarified the sitters' own understanding of the works' content.

While each pontiff as an individual is subsumed into his vision of the common role, the distinction between the person of the pope in his human dimension, and the sacred office he filled, proved impossible to sustain, and elements of the secular became inextricably fused with the sacred. Albeit pious embodiments both of the concept of holiness, each office holder sought to give a strong dynastic thrust to his representation. That of Julius II makes reference back to his uncle, Sixtus IV; that of Leo X asserts the future of a Medicean papal dynasty. Finally, the portrayals seem to have been conceived as if to counter the perceptions that their contemporaries held of each sitter. If the hyperactive Julius II preferred to be beheld in decorous repose – espousing the contemplative life, as it were – the essentially passive Leo X opted for the active life and a performance as a new Lion of Judah whose solar rays would spread the light of Christ's Redemption across the world.

6 The Competition between Raphael and Michelangelo and Sebastiano's Role in It

Costanza Barbieri

The aim of this chapter is to look at Raphael's genius from a different perspective, that is, from the point of view of the competition engaged with Michelangelo and Sebastiano del Piombo. This competition caused significant developments in the artistic styles of both Raphael and Sebastiano, urging the painters to an extraordinary artistic confrontation. Rivalry was the immediate consequence of a great challenge involving not only the skill of the painter, but also technical innovations, new methods of design,[1] unprecedented effects of light and color, and, finally, an intense quest for original, new aesthetic ideals and artistic expressions. I wish to suggest that Michelangelo's and Sebastiano's alliance in the competitive scenario of Renaissance Rome has a twofold meaning: it was not only intended to support Sebastiano's paintings with Michelangelo's drawings but was primarily a response to Raphael's supposed primacy in color compared with Michelangelo's later quattrocento palette.[2] Whereas Vasari's historiography focused on the central role of Michelangelo's drawings for Sebastiano's success, I argue that if their goal was to challenge the painter of Urbino, Sebastiano's Venetian *colorito* should be given equal importance as Michelangelo's *disegno*.[3] Indeed, from the very beginning of Sebastiano's Roman activity, the fresco cycle at the Villa Farnesina (Plate 28, Fig. 13), a long-standing competition initiated the work of the Venetian painter into a *paragone* with that of Raphael, and it persisted until the last of Raphael's paintings, the *Transfiguration* (Plate 33), commissioned by Cardinal de' Medici in competition with Sebastiano's *Raising of Lazarus* (Fig. 14). Even though in between these two commissions we do not have other paintings so closely connected in terms of time, space, and patronage, contemporary sources prove that Raphael and Sebastiano – helped by Michelangelo – were constantly competing on the ground of excellence of painting, to obtain the primacy in their field, that is, the "principato della pittura."

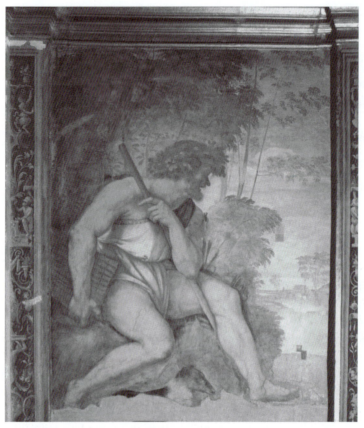

13. Sebastiano del Piombo, *Polyphemus*, Rome, Farnesina. Photo: Archivio Fotografico ICR, Rome. Courtesy of Accademia Nazionale dei Lincei.

Two perspectives shed light on the reasons and effects of this unique competition: the critical discussion of the sources, starting with Vasari as regards Michelangelo's peculiar position, and the analysis of the so-called "dark manner" that we can recognize, at about the same time, in the paintings of both Raphael and Sebastiano.[4]

THE CONTEXT OF MICHELANGELO'S AND SEBASTIANO'S ALLIANCE

Vasari's account of Sebastiano's Roman activity is focused on his alliance with Michelangelo: Vasari explained that Michelangelo became Sebastiano's mentor and principal supporter, providing his Venetian colleague with drawings.[5] The collaboration between the two artists represents a problem

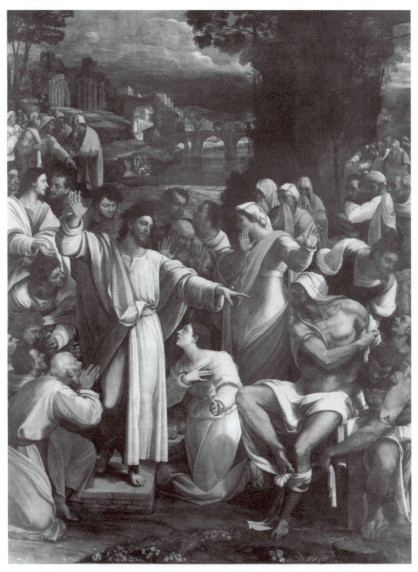

14. Sebastiano del Piombo, *Raising of Lazarus*, London, National Gallery. Photo: National Gallery.

of interpretation, however. Many scholars have viewed their respective contributions to the collaboration as unequal. Beginning with Vasari, the role of Michelangelo has been exalted, whereas that of Sebastiano has been characterized as a mere executor.[6] Other scholars have denied the subordination of Sebastiano, insisting that he, too, was a great and creative painter.[7] Vasari held that Sebastiano was often chosen as a surrogate for

Michelangelo, the latter being credited for the invention of Sebastiano's works as, for example, in the commission of the Borgherini chapel.[8] Vasari's characterization of Sebastiano's collaboration with Michelangelo as lacking autonomy has cast a misleading light on Sebastiano's creativity, and thus suggested an evaluation of the artist's skill that is incongruous with other aspects of his career. Indeed, even before Michelangelo, Sebastiano worked for eminent patrons such as Agostino Chigi, and after Raphael's death, he turned out to be the first painter in Rome.

Although biased by its Tuscan viewpoint, Vasari's text is nevertheless the only primary source for the partnership between Michelangelo and Sebastiano; therefore, it deserves careful examination. Vasari relates that the Viterbo *Pietà* (Fig. 15), the first collaborative work by Sebastiano and Michelangelo,[9] was also Sebastiano's first success in Rome:

A certain person from Viterbo, I know not who, much in favor with the Pope, commissioned Sebastiano to paint a dead Christ, with a Madonna who is weeping over Him, for a chapel he had caused to be built in S. Francesco at Viterbo. That work was held by all who saw it to be truly most beautiful, for the invention and the cartoon were by Michelangelo, although it was finished with great diligence by Sebastiano, who painted in it a dark landscape that was much extolled, and thereby Sebastiano acquired very great credit, and confirmed the opinions of those who favoured him.[10]

Sebastiano's *pala* of the *Pietà* (now at the Museo Civico, Viterbo) was painted around 1514 for the cleric Giovanni Botonti for his funerary chapel in San Francesco at Viterbo.[11] The painting is a perfect synthesis of Sebastiano's Venetian background, in the nocturnal landscape, and of his newly achieved Michelangelesque drawing style, in the figures of the dead Christ and the Virgin Mary. For these figures – according to Vasari – Michelangelo provided his friend Sebastiano with a cartoon that is now lost.

While recognizing Sebastiano's debt to Michelangelo's drawing, Vasari genuinely praises the Venetian painter's *colorito* as well: "He likewise painted some works in oils, for which, from his having learned from Giorgione a method of colouring of no little softness, he was held in vast account in Rome."[12] Soon after this encomium, Vasari describes without apparent motive the rivalry between Michelangelo and Raphael and the popularity of the latter:

While Sebastiano was executing these works in Rome, Raffaello da Urbino had risen into such credit as a painter, that his friends and adherents said that his pictures were more in accord with the rules of painting than those of Michelangelo, being pleasing in color, beautiful in invention, and charming in the expressions, with design in keeping with the rest; and that those of Buonarroti had none of those qualities,

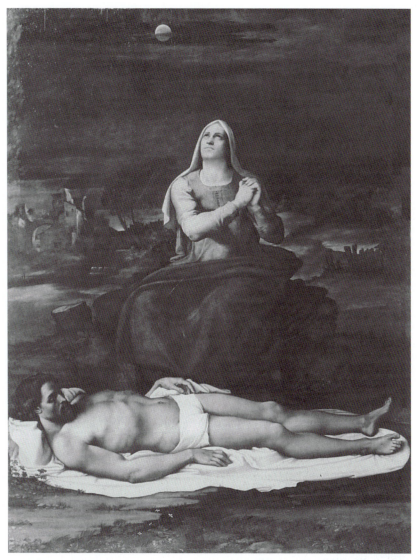

15. Sebastiano del Piombo, *Pietà*, Viterbo, Museo Civico. Photo: Archivio Fotografico ICCD, Rome.

with the exception of the design. And for such reasons these admirers judged that in the whole field of painting Raffaello was, if not more excellent that Michelangelo, at least his equal; but in colouring they would have it that he surpassed Buonarroti withouth a doubt. These humours, having spread among a number of craftsmen who preferred the grace of Raffaello to the profundity of Michelangelo, had so increased that many, for various reasons of interest, were more favourable in their judgment to Raffaello that to Michelangelo. But Sebastiano was in no way a follower of that faction, since, being a man of exquisite judgment, he knew the value of each of the two to perfection.The mind of Michelangelo, therefore, drew towards Sebastiano, whose colouring and grace pleased him much, and he took him under his protection, thinking that, if he were to assist Sebastiano in design, he would be able by this means, without working himself, to confound those who held such an opinion, remaining under cover of a third person as judge to decide which of them was the best.[13]

In the first edition of the *Vite*, written in 1550, the following sentence is missing: "But Sebastiano was in no way a follower of that faction, since, being a man of exquisite judgment, he knew the value of each of the two to perfection."[14] It was thus included as an addendum by Vasari eighteen years later. In his second edition, Vasari subtly, yet significantly, changes his picture of the dynamics among Michelangelo, Sebastiano and Raphael. By adding this sentence, he implies that Sebastiano is now playing an active role as an advocate of Michelangelo, in contrast to Raphael's supporters. On the other hand, the impression we have from the 1550 edition is that not only was Michelangelo promoting Sebastiano's paintings, but that he was using Sebastiano as a tool against Raphael's *colorito*, in an attempt to manipulate the opinions of the *conoscenti* and negate the primacy of Raphael's art. Thus, Vasari has altered his interpretation of Sebastiano from Michelangelo's passive tool to a willing participant in the debate. In this revised scenario Michelangelo gains an admirer, while his role as a envious conspirator against Raphael is remarkably subdued. To be sure, Michelangelo's manipulative behavior had to rely on a painter whose talent – as to the rules of painting – was comparable, if not superior, to that of Raphael, thus representing a real threat for the painter of Urbino.

In referring to Sebastiano's life, Vasari gives us another important piece of information concerning Michelangelo: that is, his isolation after completing the Sistine Ceiling, which is especially astonishing in comparison with the great favor obtained by Raphael during this same period. Apparently, courtiers, artists and literati judged Raphael's and Michelangelo's art *a paragone*, claiming that the former's works were "pleasing in color, beautiful in invention, and charming in the expressions, with design in keeping with the rest," while the only merit of the latter's art was *disegno*.

Dolce's interpretation is similar:

I am well aware that in Rome, while Raphael was still alive, the majority of lettered men on the one hand, and connoisseurs of art on the other, put him before Michelangelo as a painter; and those who inclined towards the latter were for the most part sculptors, who rested their claim solely on Michelangelo's draftsmanship and the overpowering grandeur of his figures – their opinion being that Raphael's delicate and restrained style showed too much ease, and consequently did not have as much contrivance to it. They were unaware that, whatever the art, the quality of ease is the main criterion of excellence, and also the hardest to attain. Art is the hiding of art's presence, and lastly the painter needs proficiency in other respects besides draftsmanship, all of them quite indispensable.[15]

These discussions probably took place after the completion of the Sistine Ceiling and of the first of Raphael's Stanze, and lasted for several years. Raphael, prince of painters, was reaching the climax of his social position, and his influence, authority, and friendship with Leo X were continually increasing. He could also rely on outstanding supporters, that is, poets and literati of the papal court. This milieu was highly important in defining artistic and literary taste,[16] and Raphael, the courtier-artist par excellence for both his artistic skill and humanistic competence, held a place "at the center of a world of knowledge and power."[17] During the second decade of the sixteenth century, Raphael was a central figure at the papal court, celebrated in countless poems and epigrams. A recently discovered poem by Girolamo Aleandro, dedicated to Raphael, honors the artist's ascendancy at the time of Leo X, exalting the artist's divine genius, "ingenii divina tui vis," a topos reflected in the literature and poetry of the time.[18] In fact, much before Michelangelo, it was Raphael who was celebrated as "divine." An epigram composed by the poet Tebaldeo in occasion of Raphael's death, for example, goes as far as equating Raphael to Christ. If the latter is the God of Nature, the former is the God of Art: "What wonder, if you, like Christ, perished in the fullness of your days? That one is the God of Nature, while you were the God of Art."[19]

Michelangelo's and Sebastiano's jealous awareness of the consideration in which Raphael was held – and of his "divinity" – is clear from their correspondence. In a letter to Michelangelo, dated 7 September 1520, Sebastiano tried to convince his associate to seek the commission for the decoration of the Sala di Costantino. Together, Sebastiano suggested, they "could accomplish the revenge of the one and the other all at once, and demonstrate to the malevolents that there were demigods other than Raphael from Urbino and his *garzoni*."[20]

Raphael's influence was firmly established by his close relationships with humanists and poets, such as Paolo Giovio, Andrea Navagero, Baldassar Castiglione, Ludovico Ariosto, Angelo Colocci, and others who favored him,[21] whereas Michelangelo had become isolated, which further explains how Raphael had surpassed him in public opinion. Also the artists who were established at the court, like Bramante, were arbiters in matters of taste, and many of them, according to Vasari, claimed that Raphael exceeded Michelangelo, especially in *grazia* and *colorito.*

On the other hand, in comparing Michelangelo to Raphael, Vasari admitted that the painter of Urbino, for his part, was well aware that in the representation of the human figure he could never attain the perfection of Michelangelo. Thus, according to Vasari, Raphael resolved to surpass Michelangelo in other aspects of the art of painting, namely, in color, composition, invention, light effects, landscapes – wherever he could highlight his pictorial talent.[22]

This was the field in which Raphael would have to compete with Sebastiano (and Michelangelo beside him) to maintain his preeminence in painting. Indeed, even though we do not have any document concerning Raphael's reaction to the challenge set by Michelangelo, we can imagine that he did not remain indifferent to the fact the Florentine wanted to confound those who held a high opinion of his work, by promoting and praising Sebastiano's paintings. Vasari asserts that "some works that Sebastiano had executed were being much extolled, and even exalted to infinite heights on account of the praise that Michelangelo bestowed on them, besides the fact that they were in themselves beautiful and worthy of praise."[23] Yet we can easily perceive the underlying meaning of Vasari's comment: Michelangelo intended to exalt the young painter from Venice to the detriment of Raphael. Nonetheless, Sebastiano possessed his personal merits: in praising the Viterbo *Pietà*, Vasari did not refer to the Michelangelesque figures as the most praiseworthy part of the painting, but instead, he recalled the night landscape that was much exalted, in which Sebastiano demonstrated his ability to represent the interplay of light and darkness through a wide range of grays, browns, greens, and blues. Vasari correctly pointed out the heart of the problem: the specific role of *colorito* as the characteristic that defined the work of the painter. Sebastiano's highly praised nocturnal landscape is the key in understanding contemporary discussions that Vasari defined as "ordine della pittura," that is, qualities specific to the nature of painting, as opposed to sculpture.

In criticizing Michelangelo's color and his highly saturated palette, which reflected the quattrocento tradition – when compared to Raphael's modern mode of coloring (*unione*) and to his skillful manipulation of other modes of coloring[24] – the public of artists and literati was showing a full awareness of new, updated ideals in painting. Around 1523 Paolo Giovio, one of the arbiters of artistic taste in Renaissance Rome and Vasari's mentor for the *Vite*,[25] affirmed that Raphael succeeded in color technique and oil painting, both techniques ignored by Michelangelo: "in softening and blending the harshness of colors which are too strong, Raphael, being a very fortunate artist, succeeded in the only skill Buonarroti lacked, that is, to unite well-drawn paintings with the ornament of luminous and lasting colors in oil."[26] On the other hand, Giovio stressed Michelangelo's ability to depict the three-dimensionality of the figures in the Sistine Ceiling: "he exalted so happily the light itself by means of a perfect contrast of shades, that even the most consummate artists had been induced, through the realism of the representation, to their surprise to perceive as solid figures that in fact are flat."[27]

Giovio's celebration of the two main artists of his time, by defining their essential characteristics, is crucial to cinquecento art theory. Raphael stands out especially as a refined colorist, while Michelangelo's ability resides primarily in his "rilievo."[28] By comparing and contrasting Raphael's and Michelangelo's styles, Giovio was also referring to a renowned Renaissance topic, that of the *paragone* between painting and sculpture.[29]

Color, and the more specific definition of *colorito* – which means expressive use of color, not just pigment per se – was exactly what defined painting as opposed to sculpture and characterized the former's ability to imitate nature in all its changeable appearances. In this context, the *paragone* between Raphael and Michelangelo became a comparison between coloristic values versus sculptural qualities. Of course, Michelangelo thought of himself primarily as a sculptor, as his famous response to Varchi on the supremacy of sculpture over painting testifies.[30] Because Michelangelo believed that sculpture was the first of the arts because the illusion of relief was the goal of painting, he excluded the depiction of coloristic values as a result.[31]

A sign of Michelangelo's frustration with the issues of oil painting and *colorito* is contained in a letter, dated 19 June 1529, which he received from Fra Giampietro da Caravaggio, prior of the church of San Martino in Bologna. After a verbal agreement concerning the execution of a design for an altarpiece in his church, the prior asked Michelangelo where he could find Sebastiano, whom he wanted to be involved in the commission as a colorist: "But if you could not color that [the painting], as you told me in person, I wish that your Sebastiano colored it, at the very least, of which Your Lord promised to inform me."[32] What was the reason behind Michelangelo's refusal to color the painting, if not his still burning defeat in *colorito, a paragone* with Raphael?[33] Later, in Florence, Michelangelo gave drawings to Pontormo to be painted, repeating the pattern of his collaboration with Sebastiano. He felt himself more at ease with fresco painting, as he demonstrated in his discussion with Sebastiano on the technique of the *Last Judgment.* Vasari reported:

Sebastiano, as has been related, was much beloved by Michelangelo. But it is also true that when the front wall of the Papal Chapel, where there is now the Last Judgment by the same Buonarroti, was to be painted, there did arise some disdain between them, for Fra Sebastiano had persuaded the Pope that he should make Michelangelo paint it in oils, whereas the latter would do it only in fresco. Now, Michelangelo, saying neither yea nor nay, the wall was prepared after the fashion of Fra Sebastiano, and Michelangelo stood thus for some months without setting his hand to the work. But at last, after being pressed, he said that he would do it only in fresco, and that painting in oils was an art for women, and for leisurely and idle people like Fra Sebastiano.[34]

In 1535 the debate on *colorito* was still alive, and Michelangelo remained extremely sensitive to it. Because he was not accustomed to compromise, however, he refused to use Sebastiano's oil technique, rupturing their long-standing friendship.[35]

Since Michelangelo pursued a career above all as a sculptor, believing that sculpture was "the lantern of painting," after the Sistine Ceiling he abandoned the competition in *colorito* and compelled Sebastiano to become directly involved in his place. Furthermore, at some point, Michelangelo may have felt that painting was not his primary art and that color was neither his principal concern nor his foremost skill. In fact, Michelangelo's coloring style derived from Cennini's technique of up-modeling, creating blocklike figures in a very hard-edged fashion, which was indeed appropriate for a sculptural style.[36] It is the case of Michelangelo's early tempera panels, such as the *Doni Tondo* and the National Gallery *Entombment.*

Interestingly, Michelangelo never used oil technique and, after his Roman experience, he even rarely committed himself to easel painting. Indeed his famous *Leda*, painted in 1530 for Alfonso d'Este and now lost, was, according to Vasari, a tempera panel.[37] Michelangelo was a great colorist in tempera and in fresco, but oil painting, with its effects of softness, transparency, and depth, was extraneous to his goals.

The comparison between Michelangelo and Raphael, and the discussion of their personal merits, were framed in a wider theoretical context, that is, the celebrated topic of the *paragone* between the arts. At the beginning of the sixteenth century, painting was considered "more worthy and more noble than sculpture," in Castiglione's words,[38] which confirmed Alberti's evaluation in *Della pittura.*[39] Indeed, Castiglione's statement on painting, expressed by Count Ludovico of Canossa in the *Courtier*, reflected his preference for Raphael's art over Michelangelo's.[40] Although on intimate terms with Raphael and not with Michelangelo, Castiglione was nevertheless a reliable witness to the artistic discussions in Rome.[41]

Entrusted by Michelangelo with the task of defeating Raphael's primacy on color, Sebastiano held a unique position in Rome. Thanks to his Venetian training, he possessed the necessary skills in oil painting and as a refined colorist. Additionally, he had the support of Michelangelo, who could offer an opportunity to overcome the limits of the two-dimensional image by creating a painting not only splendid in color, but also having the highest degree of *rilievo*, or three-dimensionality, which itself constituted a solution of the *paragone* problem.[42]

Sebastiano was the only painter who could rival Raphael in both *colorito* and, with the help of Michelangelo, *disegno*, achieving a perfect synthesis of sculptural qualities and coloristic values. Indeed, contemporary sources acclaimed Sebastiano's ability in synthesizing apparently opposite qualities. The poet Francesco Maria Molza, for example, in the *Stanze sopra il Ritratto della Signora Giulia Gonzaga*, celebrates Sebastiano for having unified the grandiosity of sculpture, accomplished by Michelangelo, with the *colorito* and *vaghezza* of painting, that is, the beauty of color, exemplified by Raphael. According to Molza, Sebastiano's colors are like sculpture in the same imposing monumentality and three-dimensional effects, yet they keep all their appealing characteristics:

> You, that with admirable care
> equate your art to the hammer,
> and the grandness once only possessed by sculpture
> you give to colors without making them less pretty,
> so that now painting may go proud,
> for you alone, to such a height,
> once you disclosed its wonderful secret,
> through your competence now, thoughtfully and contentedly,
> you set out this highminded enterprise.[43]

From this adulatory poem it seems that Sebastiano's goal, as perceived by his contemporaries, was to equate his painted images to sculpture by emphasizing relief, yet keeping at the same time all the freshness of colors. Moreover, the issues regarding the *paragone, colorito, disegno*, Michelangelo versus Raphael and so on, were very much on the minds of contemporary patrons and critics. Sebastiano's association with Michelangelo was possibly received by the artistic milieu as a project of stylistic syncretism. Interestingly, already in Venice, Vasari had praised Sebastiano's San Giovanni Crisostomo Altarpiece for the *gran rilievo* of its colors.[44]

Francesco Maria Molza's poem on Sebastiano's paintings was well known, because it was cited by Benedetto Varchi in his *Due lezzioni*. Varchi points out another of Sebastiano's victories in the *paragone* competition: the Venetian painted on marble to obtain for his paintings the durability of sculpture.[45]

A second poem by Gandolfo Porrino, a poet and friend of Sebastiano, also quoted by Varchi, praises Sebastiano's colors for their capacity to rival the monumentality of sculpture:

> And with that art, with which you alone
> honor our century and make it illustrious and beautiful,
> with a new mode you equate your colors
> to the hammer's and the anvil's strengths.[46]

The literary metaphor of a sculpted painting, or a painted sculpture, is well suited to represent Sebastiano's mastery of the excellence of both arts, gracefulness of painting and monumentality of sculpture, thus equating, or even exceeding, both Michelangelo and Raphael. In the context of the *paragone* debate, we can better understand Sebastiano's role and achievements in High Renaissance Rome and look at his paintings as continuous challenges to what Raphael was achieving at the same time and, very often, for the same patrons.

THE *PARAGONE* BETWEEN RAPHAEL AND SEBASTIANO

The first confrontation between Raphael and Sebastiano coincided with the first of Sebastiano's works in Rome: the decoration of the Loggia della Galatea at the Villa Farnesina, commissioned by Agostino Chigi. As soon as Sebastiano arrived in Rome, in 1511, brought by his patron from his native Venice, he was trusted with the decoration of the lunettes of the Loggia, representing eight scenes from Ovid's *Metamorphoses*.[47] When in Venice, Agostino could have looked at the decoration of the façades of Venetian palaces – like the Fondaco dei Tedeschi or Cà Soranzo at San Polo, painted by Giorgione in a completely different style from the central Italian one – with curiosity and admiration. The decision to bring Sebastiano, Giorgione's pupil, with him to Rome, could have stemmed from Chigi's fascination with Giorgione's frescoes.[48]

Thus, in Agostino's service, Sebastiano – the representative of the Venetian style – became directly involved in the competition with Raphael, as Michelangelo before him: his subsequent work, the *Polyphemus* (Fig. 13), was juxtaposed with Raphael's *Galatea* (Plate 28) in the decoration of the walls of the same room, probably between 1512 and 1513.[49]

We know little about the intended program of the entire loggia, the reason why at a certain point Raphael was preferred over Sebastiano (or were the painters since the beginning asked to work *a paragone*?), and why the loggia remained incomplete.[50] Current opinion among scholars is that Sebastiano painted his *Polyphemus* first, and then Raphael his *Galatea*.[51] In any case, Sebastiano could have shared some of Michelangelo's feelings of resentment for Raphael. Conversely, Raphael could have recognized the appeal of Sebastiano's vivid colors, newly imported from Venice. Moreover, the Venetian's frescoes at the Farnesina testify to his instantaneous appreciation of the Sistine Ceiling, as soon as he arrived in Rome. Michael Hirst, for instance, has identified the model for the *Polyphemus* in the *ignudo* above and to the right of Joel.[52]

It is worth recalling that Fabio Chigi, in his biography of Agostino, explains that the Sienese banker had such a close relationship with Raphael that he never became the patron of Michelangelo because of the rivalry between the two artists.[53] Perhaps Sebastiano – already passed to Michelangelo's camp – decided to bring his relationship with Chigi to an end with his work at the Farnesina, given Agostino's friendship with and loyalty to Raphael.

When Agostino decided to engage both Raphael and Sebastiano to paint on the same wall, however, he created the first, most enduring, and significant competition between two artists, thus orienting the artistic development and the artistic discussion in Renaissance Rome. Was this a conscious decision on Chigi's part or was this suggested by one of the many poets and literati that he counted among his friends?[54] It is difficult to believe that Chigi replaced Sebastiano with Raphael because he was disappointed with the former. On the contrary, not only was Sebastiano celebrated as a *faelix pictor* by Blosio Palladio in the poem *Suburbanum Augustini Chisii*, written in 1512, just after the completion of the lunettes,[55] but he also received other important commissions by the Chigi family, as, for example, the two altarpieces for the chapels in Santa Maria della Pace and Santa Maria del Popolo.[56] Rather, Chigi may have decided to stage a confrontation between Sebastiano's and Raphael's compositions, creating a scenario for their competition that was to be repeated a few years later by Cardinal Giulio de' Medici. Indeed, Vasari reported that Sebastiano, in the Farnesina frescoes, at the desire of Agostino, "spurred by rivalry with Baldassare

[Peruzzi] of Siena and then with Raphael, strove his utmost to surpass himself."[57] On the other hand, it seems that Agostino Chigi – through the competition with Sebastiano – found the most effective way of obtaining a painting by Raphael with Raphael's authorship.

If Sebastiano's *Polyphemus* came first, then his coherent program achieved by means of both the lunettes and in the main fresco – an open loggia, a transparent structure invaded by the blue sky – was somehow neglected by Raphael's fresco. The *Galatea* was conceived instead as a *quadro riportato* with an architectural frame – now almost completely lost – that isolated the painting from the rest of the decoration, enhancing its archaelogical and classical appearance.[58] On the other hand, if it is true that Raphael nullified Sebastiano's project with his striking *invenzione*, he looked at Sebastiano's color technique with interest close to emulation. According to Aldo Angelini, the conservator who studied the fresco techniques in the loggia della Farnesina, Sebastiano's vivid colors, obtained with an al-most watercolor technique, consisting in thin layers of pure colors mixed with whitewash, are different in tone from those more subdued ones of Peruzzi's and Raphael's frescoes.[59] Indeed, Sebastiano's color technique de-rives from the different tradition of the Venetian school. We may recall, for example, the very brightly colored figures of the Fondaco dei Tedeschi, painted by Giorgione and recorded by Vasari as "heads and parts of figures, very well painted, and most vivacious in colouring."[60] Vasari did not miss the novelty of Sebastiano's technique, a sign of the amazement that the frescoes aroused: "Sebastiano painted some poetical compositions in the manner that he had brought from Venice, which was very different from that one which was followed in Rome by the able painters of that day."[61]

According to Marcia Hall, Sebastiano's *Polyphemus* at the Farnesina, where "the preparation of the wall followed the Venetian method, resulting in a purplish-gray tint to the intonaco," was to inspire Raphael's *School of Athens* for the unifying effects that this technique could offer, in pulling the tones together into a harmonious balance.[62] The imminent restoration of the log-gia della Galatea will shed some light on this issue, adding important infor-mation concerning the stylistic development of Raphael's use of color.

A few years after the Farnesina, the competition between Raphael and Sebas-tiano (with Michelangelo behind the scenes) became sharper: their works seem to reflect similar fields of interests, as if carried out with reciprocal attention.[63] At the same time, for example, Sebastiano demonstrated with success his experimental oil painting technique on wall in the Borgherini chapel in San Pietro in Montorio – contemporary to the same experiments by Raphael and his pupils in the Sala di Costantino.[64]

For Sebastiano, however, easel painting was probably the most effective way to show off his ability in color techniques. Indeed, in addition to Michelangelo's and Vasari's comments, another keen art critic of the period, Paolo Giovio, provides us with an important means of understanding Sebastiano's soft coloring: his masterful glazes. In his *Fragmentum trium dialogorum*, Giovio pays homage to Sebastiano's "soft and fluid brush-strokes, veiled by very bland hues."[65] The same concept is expressed again by Giovio in his *Raphaelis Urbinatis Vita*, written around 1523–7, in which Sebastiano is mentioned among the best artists of his time, especially in portraiture: "Who surpasses everybody else in portraiture without comparison is the Venetian Sebastiano, who distinguishes himself extraordinarily in giving life to the paintings with an astonishing lightness of brush-strokes, veiling them with a tenuous layer of color."[66]

Interestingly, Giovio's technical observations concerning Sebastiano's glazing method are confirmed by the 1950 restoration report on the Viterbo *Pietà*, made by Cesare Brandi at the Istituto Centrale del Restauro of Rome.[67]

According to Brandi, Sebastiano's technique is unique in the uneven, plastic granulation of the ground coat, painted in dull and light gray, and in the transparent and liquid glazes. This preparation of a grayish base is similar to the method used in preparing the plaster in Venetian fresco technique. Thus, by relying on a ground coat containing a grayish tint, Sebastiano could use unblended tones to exalt the brilliance of pure colors.[68]

The use of pure hues was typical of the glazing method of oil painting in cinquecento Venice. Indeed, according to Lorenzo Lazzarini's technical analysis of Venetian paintings, Giorgione's artistic innovation – followed by Sebastiano and Titian – consists precisely in superimposing layers of pure colors: "the various zones of his works are no longer painted in the correct final colors from the start ... but instead are achieved by building up areas of color over color."[69] Unfortunately, in the *Pietà*, a large part of the color effects of the landscape, still visible in the 1950s and recorded by Brandi, are now irredeemably lost: "splendid clouds ... their magical iridescent reflections, unforgettable moonbeam ... so dark, transparent, and rich in colour."[70] The painting suffered injuries from both time and human contact.[71] Yet we can still form an idea of Sebastiano's glazing technique by examining the delicate handling of Christ's livid flesh with its soft transitions between color planes and delicate passages of light and dark – a masterwork of chiaroscuro[72] and a perfect example of the Venetian "method of coloring of no little softness" described by Vasari.

At the same time, Raphael was perfecting his glazing technique: his *Baldassare Castiglione*, for example, reveals a painting technique consisting of thin layers of superimposing colors to obtain the final hue, a method similar to the Venetian paintings analyzed by Lazzarini.[73]

The most significant innovation in Raphael's and Sebastiano's works, however, which had extraordinary effects on future developments, was their experiments with contrasts of light and darkness, especially in representing a night scene with artificial lights, which allows for a greater relief and dramatic outcomes by means of dark shadows.[74] At this time, according to Vasari, Michelangelo extolled Sebastiano's *colorito* as the finest in Rome; in the meantime Raphael – sensitive to any new experiments and technical innovations with light and color – changed his mode from *unione* (Stanza della Segnatura) to chiaroscuro (Stanza d'Eliodoro).[75]

The decisive moment in which experiments with the so-called dark manner seem to explode appears to be securely connected to the execution of Raphael's second Stanza.[76] In particular, the night scene of the *Liberation of Saint Peter* (Plate 22), dated around 1514, shows a specific interest in the variety of light from natural to supernatural phenomena: in the shining angel freeing Saint Peter, which contrasts with the darkness of the night, in the moon in the cloudy sky, the torches, and the light reflected on the soldiers' cuirasses. The other frescoes for the Stanza d'Eliodoro present the same special effects of light. The temple in the *Expulsion of Heliodorus* (Plate 21) presents golden barrel vaults and golden mosaic domes, which are again an opportunity to show a complex play of light reflections. Similarly, the *Repulse of Attila* offers a broad range of light effects, from fires and columns of smoke in the landscape to the contrast between the dark clouds and the dawn light coming from the left.[77]

Not coincidentally Sebastiano – around the same time[78] – painted the first nocturne for an altarpiece in the history of painting, the Viterbo *Pietà* (Fig. 15), an impressive night landscape illuminated by the full moon, with the figures of the mourning Virgin and the dead Christ based on the cartoon provided by Michelangelo. Sebastiano's painting presents a nocturnal scene where the darkness contrasts with the distant fires, while the shadows and the fire light reflected on the farms at the left, coupled with the glow of the moon, create a double light source, with a further play of light and shadow. That the burst of light in the background represents a fire and not a sunset, as previously suggested, is evident from an engraving by Mario Cartaro (Fig. 16), a Viterbese printmaker and merchant.[79] Although Cartaro simplified the landscape, added haloes to Christ and the Virgin Mary, and inserted the Cross behind them, which derives from Michelangelo's *Pietà* for Vittoria Colonna, he copied the original composition of the Viterbo *Pietà* almost slavishly.[80]

The original appearance of the painting, therefore, was much more a result of intense contrasts of glowing light and darkness. These details of the background are not of secondary importance because they reveal their affinity with Giorgione's oeuvre, in particular with Marcantonio Raimondi's print *Il Morbetto* (Plate 38), possibly a pastiche from Giorgionesque paintings, where a similar light blazes on the burning castle in the far right. Landscapes and nocturnes seem to have been combined in Giorgione's paintings. For example, Michiel describes a painting of Saint Jerome, seated naked in a moonlit desert,[81] and Isabella d'Este, in a letter written in 1510 to her secretary, Taddeo Albano, asks for "una pictura de una nocte, molto bella e singolare...de Zorzo da Castelfrancho pictore."[82] A lost Giorgione painting, for example, the *Self-Portrait as Orpheus*,[83] presents a moonlight reflected by the clouds very similar to that of the Viterbo *Pietà*.[84] It seems likely that in Venice the artists demonstrated their skill in painting nocturnes; moreover, it appears that patrons created a demand for this theme.

It was because of this astonishing nocturnal landscape – considered by Cesare Brandi the finest aspect of the painting[85] – that Sebastiano obtained his reputation in Rome, as recorded by Vasari.[86] Was the representation of nocturnes and related effects the major goal in painting and a challenge for the painters' skills and creativity in the 1520s?

Again, Giovio offers a precious source of information that sheds light upon the taste of the time: interestingly, when referring to the subject of the Stanza d'Eliodoro, he describes only the night scene of the *Liberation of Saint Peter*, misunderstanding the subject as a *Resurrection of Christ*. "In the other (Stanza), the sentinels of Christ's sepulchre glow with an indefinite light in the shadow of the night."[87] It is a telling mistake, because Raphael had been effectively entrusted with the commission for a nocturne representing the *Resurrection of Christ* for Agostino Chigi's funerary chapel in Santa Maria della Pace. Although it was never carried out (due to the painter's death), the altarpiece is known through several drawings. Raphael had planned a nocturnal *Resurrection* with dramatic *tenebroso* effects.[88] Giovio's confusion testifies, however, that the representation of nocturnal scenes and related night effects such as artificial lights was a contemporary preoccupation, confirming both patrons' and painters' fascination with nocturnes, the latest trend in painting. Raphael's never-accomplished *pala* for the Chigi chapel likely became famous before its execution, for it was expected to ensure spectacular results; because of the oil medium, the interplay of light and darkness would have been even more impressive than in the fresco of the *Liberation of Saint Peter*. In this context, Sellaio's report to Michelangelo that Sebastiano was to succeed Raphael in the Chigi commission is highly significant. Sebastiano was, by then, the acclaimed master of night scenes and their theatrical lighting effects, considered second to none, at least after the death of Raphael.[89]

In the early cinquecento, thanks to the newly achieved subtle effects of oil painting, the nocturne theme represented challenges and potentialities previously inconceivable. To High Renaissance painters the night scene could offer a new emphasis on tonal painting, dramatic outcomes by using different sources of light, new possibilities with painting local colors, the exploitation of sfumato, a more effective chiaroscuro, and a unifying dark tonality.[90] These potentialities were all the more consistent with Sebastiano's Venetian background, with his attention to tactile values and interest in special glazing techniques.

Marcantoni's print *Il Morbetto* is said to be a source of inspiration for Raphael's nocturnes;[91] however, we cannot exclude that Raphael had a more vivid example of Giorgionesque *tenebroso* landscape in Sebastiano's *Pietà* itself, the chronology of which is still uncertain, presumably around 1514.[92] If we accept the hypothesis that Sebastiano's *Pietà* predates, or was at least contemporary with Raphael's *Liberation of Saint Peter*, then we can assume that the idea of these Roman nightscapes came from Venice. Sebastiano's *virtuoso* depiction of natural scenery overwhelmed by darkness was firmly based on Giorgione's experiments with the effects of light in a dark setting, and rooted in the Venetian tradition of Giovanni Bellini's landscapes. On the other hand, this tradition was influenced by the taste of Venetian collectors for northern landscape paintings, often nocturnes. Indeed, it was in Venice that, according to Gombrich, the term "landscape" was first used.[93]

When Sebastiano brought from Venice his innovative night landscape, possibly with the taste for it, Raphael was able to create, at the same time, his own nocturnes – perhaps inspired by the Venetian – in the Stanza d'Eliodoro. We cannot reject the possibility that the *Pietà* served as inspiring model for Raphael: indeed, when working on the *Resurrection of Lazarus*, Sebastiano was extremely jealous of his invention, fearing that Raphael could steal his ideas for the *Transfiguration*.[94] Did this jealousy reflect a pattern already in place?

The painter's skill in representing landscapes and nocturnes became a celebrated topic in the art historical literature on the *paragone*, above all

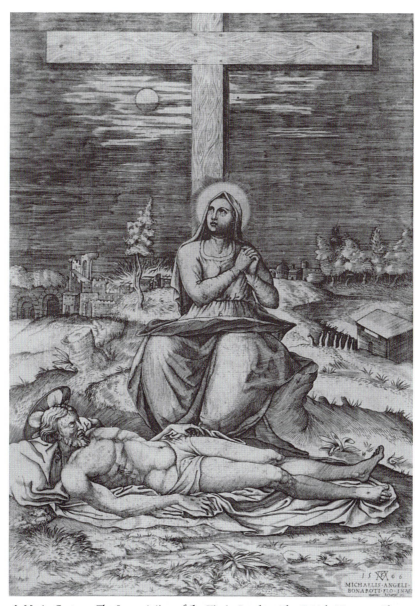

16. Mario Cartaro, *The Lamentation of the Virgin*, London, The British Museum. Photo: Department of Prints and Drawings, The British Museum, London.

in passages intended to demonstrate richness of expression and virtuosity of painting technique.[95] Baldassare Castiglione, in his *Book of the Courtier*, affirms the supremacy of painting by stating that the sculptor cannot

render...the dark of night, or a storm at sea, or lightning and thunderbolts, or the burning of a city, or the birth of rosy dawn with its rays of gold and red. In short, he cannot do sky, sea, land, mountains, woods, meadows, gardens, rivers, cities, or houses – all of which the painter can do.[96]

Not only do we find many of these characteristics in the Viterbo *Pietà* and in the Stanza d'Eliodoro,[97] but also in the last of Raphael's and Sebastiano's paintings executed *a paragone*: the *Transfiguration* (Plate 33) and the *Raising of Lazarus* (Fig. 14). The two altarpieces represent the culmination of their rivalry, both intended to be magnificent in relation to their setting, to their huge scale – never seen before in Rome[98] – and to their innovative compositions and theatrical effects.

Probably around the end of 1516, Cardinal Giulio de' Medici commissioned from Raphael and Sebastiano the two altarpieces for his archiepiscopal church at Narbonne, Saint Just.[99] Unfortunately, we do not have the documents relating to this commission; therefore, not only is the chronology uncertain, but also the very sequence and development of the events are unknown. Were both the paintings originally planned or did the commission to Sebastiano follow that to Raphael?

Hirst acutely suggested that it was Michelangelo who persuaded Cardinal Giulio to order a second altarpiece and recommended Sebastiano for the execution,[100] convincing the patron that his protégé, to whom he would have provided drawings and *cartoni*,[101] was even more accomplished than Raphael. If this was the case, that is, if Michelangelo forced the events of an already acute competition, with the ultimate purpose of challenging the favor held by Raphael, then the story is even more complex and rather unique. Scholars have agreed on the fact that first Raphael received the commission for the *Transfiguration*, and Sebastiano was subsequently involved. However, was the second altarpiece designed from the beginning or was it a later decision? Raphael was highly disappointed with Sebastiano's participation, as documented in a letter to Michelangelo by Leonardo Sellaio.[102] Was he originally granted the commission for both paintings? Conversely, if only one painting was intended, did the cardinal pay such a high price just to set up this formidable competition and please Michelangelo? To be sure, this was the first time, to my knowledge, that two artists were involved in a public competition in which the artistic results were more important than the commission itself, to the point that the paintings were eventually juxtaposed to permit to the *intendenti* a close view, a meticulous examination, and an objective judgment.

What seems extraordinary about Cardinal Giulio's patronage is that its primary intent was universally acknowledged to be a contest to obtain pre-eminence in the field of painting, instead of a traditional ecclesiastical commission. The risk was great, and it was perceived as such by the two artists. Indeed, in a letter of 19 January 1517 addressed to Michelangelo, Leonardo Sellaio affirmed that "Raphael turned the world upside down to prevent Sebastiano from painting it, because he does not want any comparison."[103]

Raphael was offended by the competition and tried hard to stop it. In the meantime, he did not begin work on his altarpiece, whereas Sebastiano was quickly completing his own, fearing that Raphael could copy his composition and steal his inventions, done with the help of Michelangelo. According to Michael Hirst, Michelangelo was of only partial assistance, his *invenzioni* probably limited to the figures in the foreground, that is the Christ, the Lazarus with his assistant – for which three drawings still survive – and perhaps the Magdalen and the Saint Peter.[104]

In 1518 Sebastiano was almost done, presumably way ahead of Raphael, who was now plotting to have Sebastiano's painting sent to France to be framed to avoid any comparison in Rome.[105] Raphael's anxious behavior testifies to his apprehension of the *paragone* and proves that Michelangelo achieved his end: in the Roman scene Raphael was not any longer the undisputed "prince of painters."

The competition became an event, and all Rome went to see the first painting to be completed, that is the *Raising of Lazarus*, which was shown in the Vatican Palace by 11 December 1519. "Everybody remained filled with wonder," Sellaio wrote to Michelangelo about Sebastiano's nearly finished *Raising of Lazarus*.[106] The comparison between the two finished paintings took place only after Raphael's death on 12 April 1520. Sebastiano wrote to Michelangelo that he brought his *pala* to the Vatican Palace, and he was not embarrassed by the *paragone* with Raphael.[107] Indeed, Vasari reported that "these altarpieces, when finished, were publicly exhibited together in the Consistory, and were vastly extolled, both the one and the other."[108] As to the victor, that was a dead heat; Michelangelo, however, was probably satisfied with that.

The similarities between the two paintings are striking; it has been suggested that Raphael changed his project for the lower part of the *Transfiguration* after Sebastiano's *Lazarus*, probably informed of the overall appearance of his rival's painting by the cardinal, who visited Sebastiano's studio repeatedly.[109] Indeed, according to Sydney Freedberg, Raphael added the repertory of *affetti* in the lower part of the painting after the *Lazarus's* "copiousness and variety (to use the Albertian terms) of actors and dramatic incidents; its multiplicity of postures, gestures, and expressions of physiognomy; its luxurious chiaroscuro and salience of colors."[110] At the same time, as has been observed, the *Lazarus* is also a tribute to Raphael's *Spasimo di Sicilia*[111] (Prado, Madrid) and to the tapestry cartoons, as for example, *Christ Gives the Key to Saint Peter* and *Saint Paul at Lystra* (Victoria and Albert Museum, London), whose classicism, monumental force, and spatial organization probably inspired Sebastiano's painting, especially the figure of Paul in the left-hand side, a possible source for Christ's position in the *Lazarus*. These similarities show again the many exchanges between the two artists, their reciprocal attention and experiments in analogous directions, as, for example, in developing a sophisticated use of color.[112] However, if both of them looked for similar results in terms of brightness and variety of colors to obtain a superb orchestration of the ensemble, the means through which they arrived to the goal are different.[113] Raphael's dark background and blackish shadows, quasi pre-Caravaggesque – a device to enhance the intensity of colors – were highly criticized by Sebastiano, thus showing that their dark manner evolved in different ways. In a letter dated 1518, he wrote to Michelangelo about two paintings by Raphael, that is, the *Saint Michael* and *Holy Family of Francis I* (Louvre, Paris)[114]:

I deeply regret that you were not in Rome to see two paintings by the prince of the Synagogue, that are now gone in France, of which I believe you cannot imagine more adverse things to your opinion than what you would have seen depicted there. I will not tell you other than they seem figures exposed to smoke, or figures in iron which shine, all bright and all dark, and drawn in such manner that Leonardo [Sellaio] will tell you about.[115]

In these paintings Raphael – defined by Sebastiano in an apparently offensive way "prince of the Synagogue" – was experimenting with the so-called chiaroscuro mode,[116] which he further developed in his *Transfiguration*, where he sought strong contrasts of light and dark, black shadows and dramatic light effects. Vasari also recalled the excessively dark effects of Raphael's late technique, inherited by his pupils, in criticizing the *Transfiguration*: "And if he had not employed in this work printers' smoke-black, the nature of which is to become ever darker with time, to the injury of the other colours with which it is mixed, I believe that the painting would still be as fresh as when he painted it."[117]

Sebastiano's chiaroscuro aimed for a warmer and less artificial appearance, by basing its soft interplay of light and dark on glazing techniques, also in

the use of characteristic Venetian pigments, such as the realgar, thus retaining its Venetian imprint, which is further evident in the tumultuous sky
and in the monumental landscape, described as halfway between Giorgione
and Poussin.[118]

After Raphael's death, Michelangelo was no longer motivated to support
his Venetian friend against the painter from Urbino and so stopped providing Sebastiano consistently with drawings. He had, however, achieved his
goal of making Raphael come off the pedestal of his splendid isolation by
the challenges of another painter. Even though Vasari, in retrospect, thought
of Sebastiano's challenge to compete with the great Raphael in executing
the altarpieces for Cardinal de' Medici as an act of brazenness – and, in fact,
Vasari could not even bring himself to write about it without adding the
qualifier "almost" in comparison to Raphael – at the time it was a reality,
and Raphael considered it a motivation to work harder and to explore innovative solutions. That he did so is precisely because such an exchange
between the Florentine and the Venetian brought about the seemingly impossible synthesis of two very different approaches. Sebastiano's syncretic
style, which influenced and stimulated Raphael himself, became the hallmark for subsequent generations of painters.

Yet if Sebastiano's role was so important in the competition, especially
regarding color, why was he considered, then and even until the present
day, Michelangelo's paintbrush? As Marcia Hall has pointed out,

Sebastiano has been a neglected figure on the Roman scene. His competition with
Raphael to produce the most impressive altarpiece for Cardinal Giulio de' Medici's
church in Narbonne is virtually his only work given wide attention…and his
role in that is denigrated by many who recognize him only as the executant of
Michelangelo's design. Actually, even when he was provided with drawings by
Michelangelo…he was no humble and obedient servant of Buonarroti….He
changed the drawing substantially and invented his own technique for executing
the *Flagellation* in oil on the wall….The coloring and technique of this work differ
from Michelangelo's frescoes in ways that reflect the taste for the "dark manner."[119]

Vasari is certainly responsible for discrediting Sebastiano by emphasizing
his dependence on Michelangelo and describing his proverbial laziness.[120]
Sebastiano's obliterated fame as a colorist, his forgotten primacy in painting,
was, however, also the result of a major change that occurred in the middle
of the sixteenth century, that is, the overwhelming importance acquired by
disegno over *colore*, theorized by Benedetto Varchi, and which would have
consecrated Michelangelo, a sculptor temporarily defeated by painters, in
the highest position in the artistic Pantheon, changing the results of the
paragone debate.[121] Varchi coined the term *arte del disegno* to express the

concept or essence of art. Indeed, according to him, the arts are unified via *disegno*. Although painting was considered "more worthy and more noble than sculpture"[122] at the end of the quattrocento and at the beginning of the cinquecento, the scene changed completely in the 1540s. The superiority of *disegno* was rarely discussed in the late sixteenth century, and, tellingly, no one dared to reverse Vasari's (and Varchi's) priorities by replacing *disegno* with *colore*.[123] By then Varchi's hierarchy was established, equating *disegno* with sculpture and giving *colore* a minor role.[124]

In light of Varchi's theory of art, a more balanced view of Michelangelo's and Sebastiano's collaboration was definitively lost. By Varchi's time, *disegno* and not *colore* held the premier position in the realm of art theory, according to the Roman and Tuscan exegesis of art. In this theoretical framework, Sebastiano, as *colore*, was relegated to a secondary role in comparison with the leading position of Michelangelo and draughtmanship, and Michelangelo became the acclaimed genius of sixteenth-century art, eclipsing even Raphael.

7 Raphael's Workshop and the Development of a Managerial Style

Bette Talvacchia

This chapter explores the question of Raphael's strategies in the development and deployment of his workshop and how the shop functioned to generate a product identifiable as Raphael's. Another path of inquiry considers what the artists who were formed within this bottega learned from their collaboration with the master. My main approach is to frame the issues in terms of broad questions such as the structure of the shop and its working procedures, ignoring on this occasion the sorts of valuable information that can be gleaned from the careful scrutiny of stylistic matters. If the fact of collaboration is by definition part of workshop practice, the joint effort of its members is most open to scrutiny at the stage when drawings were prepared in anticipation of the final product. Thus much research has gone into the study of drawings associated with workshop commissions, and our understanding of the process has largely been formed by the results of these studies.[1] In contrast, I intend my contribution to focus not on the issue of identification of individual hands, but on how the master conceived a way to employ those hands. Raphael's assumption of the role of a manager not only allowed his simultaneous engagement of several large-scale commissions, but also pushed him to conceptualize the works in a manner that took into account the talents of his numerous assistants and was fed by the particular ingredients that each collaborator could add to the overall effect.

My contention is that Raphael turned the necessity of collaboration into an impetus for innovation, both in terms of the way his shop functioned, as well as the style of the finished product. I want to explore the possibility that the need to employ many hands sparked the gradual evolution of a creative process of production. It provided Raphael with ideas for novel stylistic explorations as well as inventive managerial tactics. Furthermore, the demand for Raphael's output forced him, and his patrons, increasingly to privilege the underlying idea of the work as coming directly from the master's con-ception (*concetto*), with less emphasis on the execution, in which the inter-vention of collaborators would likely come into play.

In attempts to glean information about the less tangible aspects of how the workshop functioned, documentary evidence can be sifted for interesting implications, even when it is less precise than we would hope about the underlying structure of the operation. An amusing reference is found in Giorgio Vasari's biography of Raphael, where the author spins a story about how one client got the famous artist, in the throes of a love affair, to complete a demanding project:

Raffaello was a very amorous person, delighting much in women, and ever ready to serve them; which was the reason that, in the pursuit of his carnal pleasures, he found his friends more complacent and indulgent towards him than perchance was right. Wherefore, when his dear friend Agostino Chigi commissioned him to paint the first loggia in his palace, Raffaello was not able to give much attention to his work, on account of the love that he had for his mistress; at which Agostino fell into such despair, that he so contrived by means of others, by himself, and in other ways, as to bring it about, although only with difficulty, that this lady should come to live continually with Raffaello in that part of the house where he was working; and in this manner the work was brought to completion.[2]

The anecdote makes a humorous point about the obsessive nature of Raphael's amorous activity, and it has been often and salaciously repeated without much critical assessment. The irony is that the painting of the loggia in the Villa Farnesina (Plate 29) is regularly attributed largely to Raphael's shop, and it is argued that the master did but little of the work. The story of Chigi's ploy to keep Raphael at work on the site conflicts with the premise that the master was never expected to be around and that the painting of the frescoes fell to assistants in his absence. Yet there must be some basis for justification of the legend and for setting it specifically in the context of Chigi's household. At least we may imagine that Raphael was absorbed in a distracting love affair during the preparation of Chigi's commission, which propelled the clever patron to an extraordinary accommodation. To ring true, it also implies that the master could be counted on to be regularly on the scene of important projects, even if his assistants were responsible for much of the actual execution. Critics' often-unstated assumption that the master provided preliminary sketches and then walked away from the painting is not supported by the implications of Vasari's story. Even if the basic labor was delegated to assistants, Raphael would be in command, through routine physical presence as well as projected ideas.

Vasari, at least, is consistent in his scenario. He follows the passage just cited with the information that "for this work he [Raphael] made all the cartoons, and he coloured many of the figures in fresco with his own hand."[3] Because the visual evidence of the Farnesina frescoes and connected drawings show, without a doubt, workshop participation, the textual reference can be taken to balance the evidence that remains and to indicate common assumptions in the sixteenth century. These suppositions indicate that even when assistants and collaborators were carrying out a project, the master had a controlling hand in the preliminary work, might contribute to the cartoons, did a certain amount of the actual painting, and could be continuously found on the site of activity as the work progressed.

In addition to the judicial use of clues extrapolated from sound documentation, in order to gain an idea of workshop practices under Raphael's management, it is also crucial to attend to the results of technical investigations performed on the works themselves. By interrogating technical information with historical queries, illuminating areas of investigation open up. For our purposes, the question of the division of labor among Raphael's collaborators is a case in point. Technical examination of drawings, for example, can create parameters for the interpretation of evidence provided by the "blueprints" for the projects, that is, the many types of preparatory drawings that have survived the centuries. Put more succinctly, what I am suggesting is a fusion of drawing connoisseurship with methods of historical analysis that include textual and technical evidence, an amalgamation that is strangely infrequent within art historical practices, notwithstanding the obvious need for it.[4]

Notable exceptions to the neglect of information from the physical state of the works of art themselves were the sessions that composed the Princeton Raphael Symposium, held in 1983. It was conceived as a forum for a dialogue between conservators and historians, to build a bridge between the two specializations that would lead, in the words of one of the organizers, to the formulation of a "history of technique."[5] Among the contributions, Joyce Plesters discussed the results of technical studies of the Tapestry Cartoons, which were completed by Raphael and his workshop in 1516 and are now displayed in the Victoria and Albert Museum (Plate 24; *Miraculous Draught of Fishes*). In addition to extensive analyses of the surfaces and their state of preservation, comments are made about the paint execution, notably that large areas consist of "a single layer of paint applied directly to the paper."[6] This concurs with earlier observations made by John Shearman to the effect that although several hands are in evidence in the drawings, Raphael's share is present "in equally extensive measure in each Cartoon," and responsible for "the most prominent or expressively most essential parts."[7]

In her concluding remarks about the technical study of the Tapestry Cartoons, Plesters addresses the problem of the way in which such examination can clarify the "extent of participation of Raphael's assistants." She admits that this consideration was not given high priority in the restoration and conservation process that had taken place, but allows that the analyses attest to a high degree of uniformity in the material aspects of the drawings:

> From this limited technical study of the Cartoons the impression gained is that the degree of consistency of technique and materials throughout serves to emphasize a unity of conception and a conformity of execution which rather lessens the importance of the contribution of individual hands in relation to the series as a whole.[8]

I would like to apply this statement, taken from the "technical history" of the Tapestry Cartoons, as a very sensible guide for general study of Raphael's workshop. The "unity of conception and the conformity of execution" were established by Raphael for his commissions, and imposed upon his assistants and collaborators, with consideration of their own talents and level of understanding. I do not see the attribution of individual contributions as a goal sufficient in itself, asked, as it so often is, to stand alone. If the whole reason behind forming and training a cadre of assistants was to hone the process of joint effort to so fine a point that differences were eradicated in the interest of a coherent result, what does it gain us to undo the seams and simply leave them unraveled? Comprehension of the particular elements should ultimately serve to fathom the final product. In the instance of the Tapestry Cartoons, the significance of the commission precluded that Raphael would leave to chance the clarity of his imprint:

> Raphael worked up the cartoons to a level beyond what was strictly necessary for the weavers. This is true not only of the detail he applied to them, and the extent of his *chiaroscuro*, but also to the thickness of his paint and the range of colours used.[9]

The standard practice was to provide a much more summary indication of colors in more transparent washes with less detail and finish, yet Raphael left nothing for the weavers to second-guess or elaborate. The artist's departure from convention in the preparation of the Cartoons has led to the speculation that the patron may have intended acquisition of the drawings at the project's end.[10] Beyond that, the eventual placement of the tapestries in the Sistine Chapel would put them in direct comparison to the series of venerable fifteenth-century frescoes, not to mention Michelangelo's stupendous ceiling, only recently completed. Older theories that Raphael left the preparation of the Tapestry Cartoons solely or in large part to his shop is backed neither by the context of the high-profile project nor by the stunning visual results. When employing the assistance of his workshop to expedite a commission of such consequence, Raphael would want to utilize the strengths of his helpers while emphasizing his own virtuosity in the ideation of the work and its final appearance. In this particular commission, Raphael would have a lot invested in a final product that represented his sophisticated *concetti* and impressive compositional skills, despite its translation into a medium that was completely manufactured by another shop.

The vivid presence of the marine creatures that spill from the laden boat in the *Miraculous Draught of Fishes* (Plate 24), along with the birds that add such visual interest to the foreground, have consistently been seen as the contribution of Giovanni da Udine. This hypothesis has been supported by the recent technical studies that indicate different pigments and treatments in the areas of these details. This is in harmony with the picture that emerges of Raphael's collaborative strategy, which tended to incorporate and feature the skills of an assistant such as Giovanni da Udine, who was unusually accomplished in still-life genre.

All of this suggests that the question of hands can at times be illuminated by considerations of process. As John Shearman has eloquently reminded us, speaking of hands is really a reference to creative minds.[11] Sometimes our inquiries have neglected to contemplate sufficiently the imaginations that collectively fostered the work. Nor have we always established what might be called a "workshop identity" behind the product: the combination of Raphael's ideas, control, and application with the skills, understanding, and participation of his assistants, many of whom came and went at various intervals, as determining factors. I am constructing the nature of Raphael's shop as dynamic rather than static, with the purposeful choice of participants in any given commission, rather than as an unchanging group of assistants on whom rigidly determined schemes were imposed.[12]

How long did it take Raphael to form his particular version of a bottega in Rome, and how long to formulate a "workshop identity" for his expanding *équipe*? We tend to take the existence of Raphael's Roman workshop for granted, miraculously in place as he began work in the Stanze; but let us consider the historical facts. Prior to his relocation in Rome, Raphael's immediately preceding Florentine projects had been confined largely to easel paintings (Plates 5 and 6: *Small Cowper Madonna* and *La Belle Jardinière*), and it is evident that his decision to transfer to the papal city had a lot to do with the chance to insinuate himself within a campaign of monumental fresco painting. When he turned up at the Vatican, the decoration of the pope's apartment was already in progress, with several established masters on the scene, including Perugino, who was painting the ceiling of the eventual Stanza dell'Incendio. Julius II had set up a situation that mirrored the patronage practices of his uncle, Sixtus IV, in the Sistine Chapel about thirty years earlier. Sixtus's commission arranged for a precise division of labor that was based on the collaboration of several prominent artists, with one, most likely Perugino, assigned to be the general overseer.[13]

It seems that in the first instance Raphael was fit into this structure as a team player in collaboration with Sodoma, who was at work on the ceiling of what we call the Stanza della Segnatura. Although we do not know the details, it is clear that Raphael quickly supplanted Sodoma – indeed all of the artists who had been commissioned to work in the Stanze – and took over responsibility for the entire project (Plate 17, *School of Athens*; Plate 19, *Disputa*; Plate 21, *Expulsion of Heliodorus*; Plate 22, *Liberation of Saint Peter*; Plate 23, *Fire in the Borgo*). Strikingly, this was not an appointment as the general manager of a group of equals, but as the independent master and creator of the entire series of paintings, with aides working under his direct command. The results achieved in the *Disputa* and the *School of Athens* were enough to convince the pope to entrust the entire project to the young artist. If Julius's decisive response to Raphael's brilliant transformation of programmatic concepts into visually compelling scenes is easy to imagine, it is less apparent how Raphael could have so quickly set up a functioning system to get all the physical work done. If simple *garzoni* for the menial tasks could be quickly found and effectively employed and were presumably already on the site at the command of whoever was in charge, how long did it take to turn the available assistants into pupils? Obviously this could not be done overnight, but transpired over several years.

Indeed, the very concept of having pupils rather than apprentices might well have begun with Raphael's organization in the Vatican Stanze. Increasingly, emphasis was placed on a teacher-pupil rapport, instead of presuming a simple, practical relationship of the apprentice trained to mimic his master's style. The students learned not so much Raphael's style, but the means that the master himself had employed to achieve it, most significantly including drawing from life and study of the antique. These approaches were, of course, taken by the most advanced artists of the day, but Raphael systematically made them the basis of his workshop's style, having his assistants gradually create their own manner of executing his ideas, rather than training them to copy his designs by rote.

The Loggia painted in 1518–19 for Leo X (Plate 31) is a project for which the employment of many assistants was incorporated into the very conception of the project. I think it is a mistake to assume that this was a disappointing compromise on Raphael's part, who was pushed to despair by an excess of commissions. Pressed he certainly was; but in typical fashion, Raphael transformed pressure into innovation. Accepting the need to give over much of the preparation and execution of the decoration to his assistants, Raphael conceived a project closely suited to their abilities and created, literally, "section leaders," to perform jointly the usually singular role of the master. Taking the partitions of the bays as a point of departure, he designated discrete areas of fresco and stucco. Responsibility for painting was assigned to Giulio Romano, a pupil who manifested increasing *fantasia* with figures and narrative compositions, while the reliefs were overseen by Giovanni da Udine, the artist who studied and mastered the technique *all'antica* of sculpting in stucco. Each of his two "lieutenants" in turn coordinated their own group of assistants, all individually contributing to form a work that is balanced in its organization, but varied in its numerous components. Given the situation, Raphael did not try to disguise the several elements, but rather determined that they would give the work its distinctive character.[14]

The Loggia is a product par excellence of innovative workshop management, which calculated a project in terms of the participants' skills, interests, and predispositions, set into motion by the guiding ideas of the master. One of Raphael's concepts for the Loggia decoration was undoubtedly the calibrated mixing of *all'antica* forms with content that did not pertain to pagan culture, including religious and contemporary genre scenes. In this last category, an unexpected visual treat is offered to the viewer. We are shown an image of a group of artists at work, which by analogy can be understood as a projection of the workshop busy at the task whose results we are now observing (Fig. 17). This relief is not only an entertaining genre composition, it displays a self-conscious pride in the artist's profession. More surprisingly, the scene implies a belief in the observer's intrinsic interest in the gestation of the decoration, and its worth in being recorded. Surely it was a point of pride for these artists to be associated with Raphael's bottega and to have participated with a certain level of autonomy in bringing the work to life.

Perhaps this approach of managing a group of artists who were given some scope in their means of expression began as an expedient when Raphael abruptly displaced his older colleagues as absolute creative controller of the Stanze. He pragmatically employed several of them to continue work in various capacities until he put together a functioning bottega, as attested by the survival of the decorative parts of Sodoma's ceiling and decorative elements by Lotto in the Stanza della Segnatura. Our understanding of this aspect of Raphael's immediately astute managerial practices has recently been given an important clarification by Arnold Nesselrath's discussion of *Tribonian Presenting the Pandects to the Emperor Justinian* from the "Jurisprudence wall" in the Segnatura.[15] He convincingly attributes the fresco to Lorenzo Lotto, pointing out the artist's idiosyncratic technique that superimposed layers of color – a practice more suited to Lotto's bravura oil-painting effects – and brackets the work within the known dates of Lotto's Roman sojourn, 1509–11. The presence of Lotto's work in the fresco, devised along the lines of a compositional study by Raphael, attests to the collaboration of a fully independent master under the younger artist's direction from the start of Raphael's management of the decorative campaign for the Stanze. This is how the project progressed without interruption as Raphael began to gestate a functioning workshop with his own trainees. Such a procedure would also be an acknowledgment of the cooperation that was in effect at the start of Raphael's work in the Stanze, which was originally projected as a joint effort, even if this approach was subsequently modified radically.

Raphael's later incorporation of solid and pronounced artistic personalities in the execution of his commissions, strong artists such as Giovanni da Udine, Baldassare Peruzzi, Polidoro da Caravaggio, and Perino del Vaga, gives proof that he learned an important lesson from the arrangement he found in place when he arrived at the Vatican, and methodically built on this throughout his mature career. Collaboration must have been consistently relied on to a certain extent from his first moments in Rome, even while Raphael consolidated his position into one of absolute power and gradually formed his own group of newly constituted assistants and pupils.

It is fundamental to be clear with our terminology when discussing Raphael's workshop, so that we can appreciate the complexity of its structure. There was a considerable range in the makeup of Raphael's bottega. The evidence indicates that it would have consisted of menial, quite young workers to grind the colors and sweep up; slightly older apprentices who were in the stage of actively learning and participating in the rudimentary stages of preparation; the more advanced assistants who might more accurately be termed "pupils" acquiring skills as they were trained to aid in projects. I imagine this last category to be akin to our graduate students,

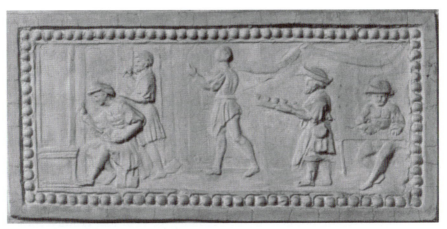

17. Stucco work showing the School of Raphael at Work, Loggia of Leo X, Vatican Palace.
Photo: Scala/Art Resource NY.

who take some steps into professional practices while still engaged in study
and student exercises.

The unit established by Raphael to complete the Stanze (where painting continued for the full extent of Raphael's career in Rome) certainly
took time to form and develop. It had to have behaved differently from the
botteghe that were purely commercial enterprises, by virtue of its functioning within the papal court. It operated solely on a bespoke basis, and that
on the most exalted level, so that it is undoubtedly more accurate to speak
of an *équipe*, or a team, rather than a shop in the commercial sense. The
team notably included freelance collaborators, applying their skills under
Raphael's direction toward the completion of his commissions and to the
execution of his ideas. The overwhelming effectiveness of Raphael's organization and the success of his double-pronged method of teaching as well as
involving independently trained artists on various projects are made clear
by a list of enterprises that were carried out while work continued in the
Stanze. Clearly the organization was up and smoothly running by around
1514, during the early phases of the Stanza dell'Incendio.[16] For by 1515, the
Tapestry Cartoons were underway, at the same time that the *Stufetta* of
Cardinal Bibbiena was being decorated (completed 1516). The initial commission for the Sala di Costantino was received around 1517, while work was
launched on the loggia of the Villa Chigi during 1517–18 (Loggia of Psyche,
Plate 29). This was overlapped by Leo X's Loggia (1518–19), as well as the
extensive undertaking to construct and decorate the Villa Madama starting

from 1518, and further plans for the Chigi Chapel dating from the last year of Raphael's life. Obviously this roster includes only the large-scale decorative programs, and not the easel paintings, altarpieces, or projects and responsibilities that Raphael took on in other media and areas. It is a breathtaking series of accomplishments.

As we know, parts of the multicelled organization created to handle the extraordinary workload developed into another sort of formation, mentioned earlier as a distinctive teacher-pupil rapport with some of the assistants.[17] This was in essence an academy of private instruction, even if its goal was the practical completion of given commissions. Raphael's arrangement had great influence as a model for the institutionalized variety of academies that took form later in the sixteenth century.

Let us return, however, to the beginning years of that century. During his initial phase in Rome, Raphael would have been ready to learn a lesson from the arrangement he found of collaboration, of pooling talents and manpower under the patronage of Julius II. In assembling a group of independent masters to carry out a complex campaign of fresco painting, Pope Julius followed the practice of the one predecessor whom he emulated, his uncle Pope Sixtus IV (r. 1471–84). In fact the master with whom Raphael was previously associated, Perugino, had taken part in this sort of teamwork under Sixtus, working on the frescoes in the Sistine Chapel. Indeed the name of Perugino has been put forward as the overall manager of the *équipe*. It is interesting that in these large-scale papal commissions for the walls of the Sistine Chapel, and subsequently for the Stanze, the collaborative structure was imposed by the patron, not evolved by the artists. Raphael, perhaps influenced as much by Julius's marshaling of forces as by Perugino's studio praxis, would make aspects of both approaches his own. The combination resulted in posing a fundamental contrast to the usual method of workshops such as Perugino's.

The procedure in Perugino's bottega, typical of quattrocento practice, yielded more of an "assembly-line" product, with the models strictly copied from the master and then plugged into prescribed formations.[18] In that enterprise, Perugino's style and figure-type were set, and not much modified over time. Perugino did not seek out and respond to individualistic contributions of the artists under his direction, but trained a small army of them to follow his established patterns without variation. A recent discussion of some of the technical aspects of how drawings were used in Perugino's shop speaks of a "tradition of design reproduction," giving a clear indication that assistants had no point of entry into the evolution of the master's work.[19] This blockage of extraneous input, which was so effective in maintaining a standard and establishing Perugino's recognition, ultimately led to his downfall. Ignoring the exciting innovations of contemporaries such as Leonardo and Michelangelo, Perugino did not allow new elements to enter his production by default, that is, through the input of assistants or collaborators. With a style increasingly marked as retrograde, Perugino lost the interest and esteem of his Florentine patrons, as his art began to repeat poses and motifs from his own earlier works.[20]

Raphael happened to be in Florence, working hard at establishing himself, when all this happened; or in David Alan Brown's words: "Raphael's advent in Florence coincided with one of the most extraordinary cultural mishaps of the epoch, namely, the sudden irreversible decline in Perugino's reputation."[21] The lesson would have had a forceful impact on the young Raphael, sharpened by a cautionary edge. Given Raphael's penetrating intelligence, and his ambition, I am sure that he pondered and was deeply affected by the fate of Perugino. The decline was epitomized by the altarpiece of the *Assumption* that Perugino carried out for the Santissima Annunziata (Fig. 18), which was unveiled to universal disparagement, particularly vociferous on the part of younger artists. Even Paolo Giovio referred to Perugino's plight as a cautionary example, noting that "the withering of his fantasy forced him always to return to those mawkish faces that he established in his early years, to the point that his spirit could hardly bear the shame of it."[22]

Stylistic obsolescence would never be a trap into which Raphael would fall. To avoid it, Raphael continually studied the styles of the best modern masters, incorporating what he valued into his own work. He constantly tested his skills by producing abundant variations around any given composition, inventing freely as he sought variation. Finally, Raphael immersed himself in deep consideration of antique art, which was then brought to bear as a corrective and an ideal through which to filter study from live models. These were the processes that he passed on to his students, which replaced the strict reproduction of the master's designs in the production of paintings and frescoes. I have argued that this is what distinguished Raphael's behavior as the head of a workshop; it is clear that his methods would be crucial to the formation of the artists he accepted as pupils. Thus, another way of assessing the innovative approaches that Raphael developed as a manager is to consider the results they had on the professional comportment of his students. One artist completely trained by Raphael who internalized his master's modes of operation as well as his professional profile was Giulio Romano. Mirroring the outlines of Raphael's Roman career, Giulio eventually led a workshop of his own, established himself as a court artist, attended to multifarious tasks for his patron, and lived as a gentleman. He was also a collector of ancient art and grounded his art on *all'antica* style.

Through the biography of Giulio Romano, we have some idea of how long it took before promising pupils were discovered and trained, and could be expected to play a satisfactory part in the completion of work in Raphael's Roman bottega. In his *Vita* of Giulio, Giorgio Vasari mentions the frescoes in the Stanza dell'Incendio as the site of the very young artist's first major intervention in the Stanze project. The room was completed in 1517, nine years after Raphael began his work in the papal apartments (Plate 23, *Fire in the Borgo*). Vasari singles out for comment the fictive bronze figures painted in the dado, which might indicate their significance in Giulio's professional development. The hypothesis is given support by the fact that Giulio eventually handed drawings for these figures over to Marcantonio Raimondi to serve as a basis for a set of prints. This has always struck me as a sentimental choice, Giulio's documentation of one of his first autonomous designs in a setting of great importance. This would also makes sense in terms of practice. If Giulio painted extensively in the Stanza dell'Incendio as Vasari states, the execution of the main parts of the frescoes would have been tied to the master's designs; but at that point of his training, Giulio could well have been given more latitude in the ideation and preparation, as well as in the painting, of the ancillary areas of the dado.

In assigning his assistants a more substantial role in the labor-intensive procedure of turning out hundreds of preparatory drawings for frescoes, Raphael initiated them into a rigorous working method, which they perpetuated as independent masters. The process devised by Raphael was to execute preliminary, rough compositional sketches, proceed with further consideration of the groupings and individual figures through studies from life (often *garzoni* in appropriate poses), and then combine the compositional arrangement with the figural studies to form *modelli*. Giulio Romano implemented the practice as head of his own workshop, in an approach that has been signally described as "a dialectic procedure of preparation."[23] The only variation was introduced later when Giulio, in a feat of virtuosity as well as practicality, regularly compressed two of the time-consuming phases. For most of his work in Mantua he moved directly from the generating sketch to a *modello*, which could then be transformed into a full-scale cartoon by his assistants.[24]

In addition to building on Raphael's stylistic legacy and working techniques, Giulio Romano certainly replicated his master's organizational principles when it came time to set up his own team of assistants and collaborators. Like Raphael, Giulio worked primarily in a court setting; after

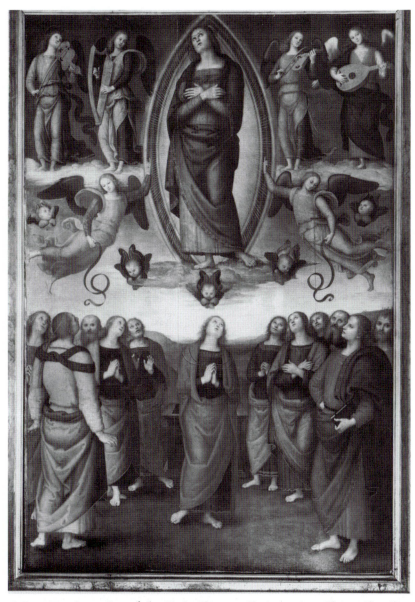

18. Perugino, *Assumption of the Virgin*, Florence, SS. Annunziata. Photo: Alinari/Art Resource, NY.

leaving the Vatican, he was employed by the Gonzaga of Mantua. Unlike his master, however, Giulio was compelled to stay in constant touch with a patron who frequently moved from one of his holdings to another. This generated an extensive correspondence, documenting much of the daily progress on the many projects underway, which would otherwise have been communicated verbally. Following the letters makes clear that the work was carried out sequentially, with the cartoons prepared bit by bit, as the designs were completed for individual sections of the rooms.

At one point during the painting of the Sala di Troia in the Ducal Palace (Fig. 19, View of the Sala di Troia), Giulio wrote to the duke that his two assistants, Rinaldo [Mantovano] and Fermo [Ghisi], are both home ill. He will deal with this setback, he says, by using the time to finish the drawings for the rest of the vault. He follows this with a heartfelt lament. It seems that in executing the painting of the ceiling, he gave a section to one assistant, Figurino, who made a mess of it:

> I gave another bit of it to Figurino, who has departed from me in such a way that I do not want to have students ever again.[25]

I think we can understand from this complaint that Giulio followed the work closely, cared deeply about the quality of the results, and in this case would have felt compelled to fix the offending passage. It is also worth noting that Giulio used the term student, *allievo*, for the disappointingly incompetent assistant, perpetuating the practice of forming an explicit student-teacher relationship between master and assistant that was a legacy from Raphael's teaching.

Another point I want to highlight from Giulio's missives to his patron is that he prepared cartoons for the most important room in the complex (the Sala di Troia), because his assistants fell behind in their work. When the situation warranted, the master might well take over tasks that were ordinarily assigned to his helpers.[26]

Progress reports from court overseers also regularly comment on the painting campaigns, with observations such as, "Fermo has finished his façade and will begin tomorrow to execute the cartoon from the drawing that Messer Julio gave him."[27] Once again we hear that drawings were created by the master to be supplied in succession to the assistants, who would then work up each cartoon to the appropriate scale and specific location. Just as in Raphael's practice, Giulio supplied drawings to numerous assistants and kept his eye on many projects at once, to the point where other court personnel marveled, saying that Giulio has "a head full of ideas," but that unfortunately,

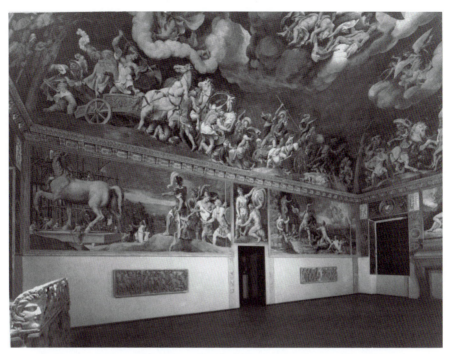

19. Giulio Romano, Montua, Palazzo Ducale, Sala di Troia. Photo: private collection.

Messer Julio has so much to do in designing and giving work to so many men, all of whom make their living off of him, that to tell the truth, he doesn't have the time to keep after them, and can only give everything a quick look once a day.[28]

The master was too busy to be able to stay on with his helpers and encourage them to expedite the work, but he made daily rounds to check quickly on the results. The practice that can be discerned from the letters is remarkably like the concise description that Vasari has left us regarding Raphael's manner of organization:

He never ceased to carry on the series of pictures that he had begun in the Papal apartments and halls; wherein he always kept men who pursued the work from his own designs, while he himself, continually supervising everything, lent to so vast an enterprise the aid of the best efforts of which he was capable.[29]

A further element can be gleaned from the letters with regard to the pressure put on the master designer. Although he was held responsible for creating the paintings and getting the large fresco cycles completed, at times he was dependent on other court personnel for the details of the program. One letter, a veritable litany of grumbles, ends with Giulio promising to hound his literary adviser to give him the particulars for what should go on the walls now that he has completed the ceiling.[30] This predicament echoes the situation, much more calmly stated twenty-two years earlier, when Pietro Bembo interrupted his letter to Cardinal Bibbiena to say that Raphael has just walked into the room and asks to be sent the other *istorie* for the *stufetta* so that he may proceed with the painting. Still writing on Raphael's behalf, Bembo continues that if Bibbiena will send the texts (*la scrittura delle historie*), he will provide the painters with the drawings during the coming week (*quelle che gli mandaste saranno fornite di dipignere questa settimana*).[31]

Without doubt Giulio Romano learned his workshop organization and systems for the production of monumental fresco cycles from his master and did not deviate from them for the length of his career. Just as obviously, he was not able to reproduce the high level of results or nurture strong creative personalities within the bounds of his *équipe*. For if Raphael was a brilliant artist, he was also an inspired manager, who could project a unified artistic goal by a very directed use of the skills and special competencies of his collaborators and assistants. It must also be said that Raphael was particularly fortunate in having had access to an extensive pool of artists with singular skills and personalities in the burgeoning cultural life of Rome that thrived in the first two decades of the sixteenth century, just to mention in passing Giovanni da Udine, Baldassare Peruzzi, Polidoro del Caravaggio, and Perino del Vaga.

Raphael's own practice was to learn from those around him, to analyze technical and stylistic innovations and to digest those elements that were useful to his own aims and visual vocabulary. The difference that I am trying to clarify is crucial: whereas all masters held the products of their shops under creative control, Raphael consistently expanded his visual vocabulary and stylistic means so that his own output was constantly evolving. To accomplish this he not only sifted through the offerings of contemporary art, he actively engaged collaborators and responded to their particular qualities and skills. He elicited individual elements from collaborators and then very aptly featured them in a specific commission. This also had an effect on the teaching of his students and close assistants, who eventually elaborated on his style. I see the "mannerism" of the following generation as, in part, a process of embellishment, which added more adjectives to Raphael's visual language, rather than engaging in polemics with it.

The part of Raphael's formal vocabulary that was based on classical models provided the common language from which all of his assistants, students, and collaborators drew (literally) when they worked as part of his *équipe*.

The physical creation of the works under such varied groupings of collaborators gave increasing importance to the master's intellectual processes as a controlling factor. The *concetto* and *invenzione* were increasingly privileged as the originating forces at the core of the work, and their inventor as the "prime mover." Perhaps Raphael himself came to a keener appreciation of the force of the distinction between conceiving the project and executing it in his capacity as architect of Saint Peter's, a post that he assumed in 1514. Finding himself inserted into the flow of an enormous building enterprise, with an established history and functioning *cantiere*, the nature of Raphael's input was well defined. He had to come up with designs that would push the construction ahead and assign the tasks to execute the plans, without ever having to plaster a wall or cut a slab of stone. This must have been grist to Raphael's mental machinations as he sought ways to fulfill the commissions for which he had little time but a prodigious inventive capacity.

Raphael's superabundance of ideas surged out beyond the routine demarcations of a master artist's domain. If his appointment to Saint Peter's followed a traditional crossing of boundaries between artists and architects that had a venerable precedent in Giotto's career, Raphael's designation as "overseer of marbles and stones" opened new possibilities. This most likely arose from a pragmatic decision to allow Raphael control over the use of ancient marble in connection with supplying the needs of the emerging structure of Saint Peter's.[32] However, Raphael's intensified submersion into the issue of conserving ancient artifacts seems to have sparked new interests and projects. By the time the artist collaborated with Baldassare Castiglione on the *Letter to Leo X* around 1519, he was deeply involved in the systematic study of ancient ruins and made a plea for their preservation.[33] Raphael evolved these activities in affiliation with another range of collaborators, beyond the group of his bottega. In the realm of practice, Raphael employed artists all over Italy in the task of drawing ruins, one imagines in order to have as large a database as possible of ancient remains.[34]

In terms of an intellectual basis for his own projects, Raphael formed partnerships with expert architects, antiquarians, and literati to expand the range of his pursuits. According to the wishes of Leo X, Raphael met daily with the pontiff and Fra Giovanni Giocondo, and together they discussed the building of Saint Peter's. Raphael himself mentioned this in a letter to an uncle, elaborating that the pope wished Raphael to form a rapport with the elderly architect, who had worked for a time alongside Bramante, in order to learn his secrets and so become "perfettissimo in quest'arte."[35]

Some of Fra Giocondo's most learned professional "secrets" must have come from his profound knowledge of Vitruvius, whose architectural

treatise Giocondo had published a few years earlier, in an exacting scholarly edition, whose emendations in some instances have held to the present
day.[36] This edition served as the basis for an Italian translation, which was
commissioned by Raphael himself, in connection with his architectural formation around the knowledge of Vitruvius, and its dissemination through
an impressive circle of humanists in Rome. Marco Fabio Calvo, responsible for the translation, was a guest in Raphael's home as he worked on
the project. Calvo, an authoritative antiquarian, further collaborated with
Raphael on the mission of compiling plans of the ancient sites in Rome,
eventually resulting in the publication *Antiquaria Urbis Romae*. In the early
phases of this project, Raphael studied the ancient sites with another highly
accomplished scholar, Andrea Fulvio, making the rounds of Roman ruins together. The artist sketched the remains that the antiquarian selected
and on which he expounded. Thus, in association with Fra Giocondo, Andrea Fulvio, and Fabio Calvi, Raphael perfected his study of architecture
and archaeology and worked closely with them on his ventures into these
fields.

Raphael's perceptive expansion of collaborative arrangements allowed for
diversification of creative achievements, and this was a business practice as
well as a gain of prestige. Status and commerce were mutually beneficial;
joint authorship on a volume recording the ancient *urbs* would translate
into potentially lucrative sales. Raphael had already developed a practice of
selling single sheets engraved with his designs, thanks to a structured organization that oversaw both the production and distribution of the prints.
Marcantonio Raimondi was the artist who seems to have worked most
closely with Raphael, and the print shop enterprise also included Marco
da Ravenna, Agostino Veneziano, and Ugo da Carpi. An associate known
by the name of Baviera apparently took up the function that we would
identify as a print dealer, representing the financial interests of Raphael
and keeping charge of the plates. According to Vasari, Raphael channeled
the income from one group of prints to provide for a lover, entrusting the
matter to Baviera's care.[37] This would imply retaining control over at least
some of the engraved plates themselves. Ownership must have been split,
because Marcantonio ultimately had possession of a good number, which
Antonio Salamanca then took over in the 1530s, recutting and reusing them
as a basis for his own commercial enterprise as a print dealer.

Having benefited from the remuneration – in fame and finance – derived
from the sale of single sheet prints, there are signs that Raphael was ready to
expand further into the area of printed editions. One author has suggested

that a number of prints linked by subjects from Virgil's *Aeneid* were part of a project to prepare an illustrated edition under the master artist's aegis, "a putative Raphael of Urbino press."[38] Such a scheme would have found a ready place within Raphael's practice of combining ancient culture with modern techniques and technology.[39] It would have also been custom-tailored to suit his modus operandi, anchored in the workshop approach of division of labor into various well-defined components as a means of production.

Finally, I think that this is what distinguished Raphael's workshop from all the others that preceded and influenced those to follow. In the pursuit of new areas of interest, Raphael reached both above and below his own skills, collaborating with colleagues who were experts in areas he was not and availing himself of the assistance of an *équipe* that was trained to think through and respond to the *concetti* of the master. In this system Raphael likewise reacted to and took advantage of the strengths of assistants skillfully deployed. These strategies allowed not only many major, complex decorative projects and painting commissions to be engaged at once, but also stimulated expansion into a very broad area of production, including architecture, printmaking, and archaeological recuperation and publication. All of these creative efforts were generated from the master artist's ideas, his *concetti*, and were produced by the ability of carefully chosen collaborators and assistants to pool their own skills in the service of Raphael's goals. In the case of artists who can be called Raphael's students, their self-reliance and flexibility were the results of his teaching the principles of an *all'antica* style buttressed by close study of the live model. Thus, the constant evolution of Raphael's art depended in part on the increasing importance of and reliance on drawings as a means to convey the *concetto*, not as templates for copying. *Disegno* was the vehicle for an unbroken cycle of learning and teaching, as Raphael recorded his ideas and presented them in drawings, then passed them on to students and collaborators for development and execution. This in a way takes us back to our point of departure. Raphael's success in producing highly valued and recognized art is a testament to his great skill as both a master and a teacher of drawing. By the same token, it was precisely his innovative uses of drawing and his emphasis on teaching that permitted Raphael's evolution as an inspired manager of complex projects in diverse media.

8 Raphael's Multiples

Patricia Emison

The conjunction of Marcantonio and Raphael in Rome in the second decade of the sixteenth century changed the course of the careers of both. The young Marcantonio had a taste for the off-color, the humorous, the obscure, and the awkwardly *all'antica*. Like Ripanda, his fellow Bolognese, his work had an antiquarian air, and like Sodoma, a slightly simpering one. In Rome he learned how to model anatomic structure; he discovered pictorial space. His figures seemed less twisted and more natural; they moved rather than posed. His backgrounds were sometimes simpler, never the flattening parallel hatching he had learned from niello technique. His subjects became majestical as he acquired compositional finesse.

As for Raphael, he became more antique Roman. His stylistic origins had not been so different from Marcantonio's: the courts of Urbino and of Bologna had their similarities in artistic taste. He had begun to develop a sense of monumentality and of ponderation in Florence (1504–8), studying Michelangelo's *David* and Donatello's *Saint George*, for example. But he was still "Raphael of the Madonnas"; he had no claim to epic qualities. Even the windfall of the commission in the Stanza della Segnatura kept him on the level of group portraiture, sidling toward epic-level *istoria*, it is true, but not yet there, and highly reliant on Bramante's architectural ideas for the grandest of the wall schemes, that of the *School of Athens* (Plate 17). His achieving narrative grandeur and even suspense in the Stanza d'Eliodoro (Plates 21 and 22) was due in part to his formal experiments with engraving.

As far as we know, Raphael was not interested in printmaking until after he moved to Rome, probably late in 1508.[1] Dürer had only recently sojourned in Venice (1505–7), and his prints – woodcuts and engravings – must have been increasingly available throughout the major centers of Italy. Both Lodovico Dolce (1557) and Giorgio Vasari (1568) record that Raphael admired the prints of Dürer; indeed, Dolce tells us that Raphael tacked up

Dürer's prints around his studio. Shortly after Raphael's death, his pupil Timoteo Viti arranged an exchange of work, primarily if not exclusively prints, at the request of Dürer, so the interest was mutual.

Marcantonio, who was very close to Raphael in age, had arrived in Rome in 1510 or after,[2] and it may well be that Raphael was as happy to find Marcantonio as vice versa. The painter may have wanted to distribute his art and achieve European recognition as he saw his German counterpart doing. He was ambitious, he lacked the advantage of Florentine birth, and he was younger than Leonardo or Michelangelo. Printmaking could help him. So Raphael fostered Marcantonio even as Marcantonio spread the name of "Raphael, Inventor," far and wide. The relationship was mutually beneficial. According to Vasari, Raphael set Marcantonio up with a German agent ("the Bavarian") to oversee the operation, and when in 1511 Raphael painted one of his grandest compositions, the *Expulsion of Heliodorus from the Temple* (Plate 21), with Julius II anachronistically present, he painted not only himself as one of the porters of the pope, but Marcantonio as well.[3] Marcantonio, moreover, came first.

Marcantonio is the only person neither painter nor sculptor nor architect who was accorded a biography, and a woodcut portrait, in Vasari's *Lives*, albeit solely in the expanded edition of 1568.[4] Yet in many ways the twentieth-century view of Marcantonio was less reliant on Vasari's account than on Adam von Bartsch's. Writing in the opening years of the nineteenth century, Bartsch catalogued the *peintre-graveurs* of the fifteenth through the seventeenth centuries, that is, the engravers and etchers who used their own designs. Nevertheless, he included very extensive treatment of Marcantonio (vol. XIV). Marcantonio's drawings, about which there has been speculation since,[5] were unknown to Bartsch. He inferred designers for Marcantonio: not only Raphael, but Francia, Giulio Romano, Baccio Bandinelli, Dürer, occasionally Mantegna, and, once in a while, "Un anonym." Sometimes Bartsch expended his own authority, sometimes he employed the phrase "some think that" (*quelques-uns croient*), or even more skeptically, "on pretend." When an engraving was obviously after Michelangelo, Bartsch would suppose that Raphael had drawn after Michelangelo and given his drawing to the engraver, or would say noncommittally, "after the Sistine vault." By far the dominant formula, however, was "after a drawing by Raphael." Raphael's reputation was near its apogee during Bartsch's time. So it was as Raphael's amanuensis that Marcantonio was integrated among the *peintre-graveurs* and awarded the palm as the best of the Italians.

Bartsch's contemporary, Quatremère de Quincy, also believed in the close association of drawing and engraving in Raphael's time, the former being "organs of improvised sentiment" – or as he even more memorably put it, "vèritable contre-èpreuve de la pensèe," the latter providing a regularizing and perfecting effect.[7] To nineteenth-century writers, Marcantonio offered the perfect compromise between classicism and romanticism: his works gave, as de Quincy once again put it so felicitously, "de la consistance et de la prècision aux idèes" and, in particular, gave consistency to those casual, nonpreparatory ideas with which Raphael amused himself in idle moments. It is a conception of Marcantonio that has lasted to our own days, except that it was reinforced with a conviction that no one since had been able to make engravings so felicitous as these.[8] The market value of Marcantonios in the nineteenth century was not without a rationale.

The role of engraving as an intermediary between the sketch and the masterpiece – not the chronological intermediary but an ontological one – was clear to nineteenth-century writers, but to twentieth-century writers the historical role of engraving was more cut and dried: its significance derived from its inauguration of the exactly repeatable pictorial statement, the mechanization of the visible world;[9] or from its closeness to the hand of a great draughtsman; or from its role in connecting old art with the production of new art.[10] These theories were not only incompatible; they were also wrong-headed, for like photography and cinematography in the twentieth century, engraving in the sixteenth century was at once fundamentally and radically distinct from established artistic practice and very much integrated with it. Its existence precipitated a mutation in the mainstream evolution. Engraving was neither autograph nor particularly scientific in conception or practice, but it did provide an important check to the unchallenged authority of the lordly and/or ecclesiastical patron and a simultaneous boost to an intercity de facto collaborative of artists. Like the printed book (and not unlike the Internet), the printed image made possible the distribution and mutual reinforcement of ideas marginal to the mainstream that might previously have withered.[11] In short, the world became a more interesting place.

Bartsch's primary rationale for including Marcantonio among the more authentic *peintre-graveurs* was one of functionality. He set out to catalogue the most desirable engravers, the ones sought after by collectors, and Marcantonio, even if he used the designs of others, qualified spectacularly. Marcantonios counted among the most valuable of prints throughout the nineteenth century; Rembrandts began to compete in price only at the end of the eighteenth.[12] They were reproduced photographically, to great acclaim, in 1863;[13] Bartsch's revised and much expanded catalogue raisonnè appeared just as Raphael was being more exhaustively studied, too.[14] But

Marcantonio was no shadow Raphael. His works outclassicized Raphael himself; Raphael was either devout or epic, but Marcantonio felt more pagan; he contained the seed of neo-classicism, but devoid of the prudery signaled by loincloths.

Marcantonio encapsulated several aspects of the history of art that could not otherwise be found together, and these aspects appealed, in varying degrees and kinds, to the nineteenth-century intellectuals who were founding the history of the Renaissance, whether Michelet, Burckhardt, or Symonds, who knew their Raphael and hence their Renaissance at least partly through Marcantonio. Marcantonio, perhaps more readily than Raphael, could appear as devout or as antique or as decadent as were the versions of the Renaissance being promulgated. So, indirectly, nineteenth-century historians of the Renaissance acted as publicists for Raimondi, as he had for Raphael four centuries before. Conversely, as long as this novecento-expanded double of Raphael is our Marcantonio, the Renaissance of Burckhardt continues to look familiar to us.

Whereas Vasari related a biography for Marcantonio, Bartsch constructed an oeuvre, an implausibly large and uneven oeuvre: 648 entries, many of which include subheadings for copies or variants, in the volume dedicated to Marcantonio and his two principal "students," Agostino de' Musi (Veneziano) and Marco Dente (da Ravenna). In a longer career, Dürer produced slightly more than one hundred engravings and etchings, plus approximately three hundred and fifty woodcuts, most of them cut by others, although of course in his case painting took much of his time. Another factor to be considered is who did the printing: Dürer, as the master of a shop, no doubt had help; and according to Vasari, Baviera was transferred from grinding colors for Raphael to printing for Marcantonio. It is hard to say what counts as an average career, and these two printmakers were both vastly more productive than the dabblers around them. Still what Bartsch assigned to Marcantonio is not the oeuvre of an individual but of an industry.

Bartsch introduced the category of deceptive copy, and the shadowy followers of Marcantonio in general, for purposes of cataloguing. They belonged with Marcantonio because the identification of impressions made this arrangement expedient – not because Bartsch was arguing that Marcantonio was prodigiously productive, and reproductive. But that which Bartsch tenuously placed under the umbrella of Marcantonio has tended (with the notable exception of Delaborde), over the decades and centuries, to get more and more firmly attached to the name. Recently, the deceptive copies have been explained as Marcantonio's own repetitions of plates lost in the Sack of Rome, or of plates controlled by Raphael's agent, il Baviera.[15] As our vision of the Renaissance has become less Burckhartian and more directed toward its consumerism, in reflection of our own less classicizing, more blatantly consummeristic ways, so, too, our interest in Marcantonio has shifted toward questions of the original market that little troubled our nineteenth-century predecessors.

Vasari tells us that Marcantonio, newly arrived in Rome, engraved *Lucretia* (Plate 34) after a drawing by Raphael. This being shown to Raphael, the painter set him to work, first on the *Judgment of Paris* (B. 245) (Plate 35), and later on the *Massacre of the Innocents* (B. 18/20) (Plate 36), the *Quos Ego* (B. 352) (Plate 37), the *Rape of Helen* (B. 209), and the *Santa Felicità* (B. 117), all of which amazed Rome, lifted Marcantonio to fame exceeding that of the northern engravers, and made the vendors rich. Late in 1515, when Raphael bought a house, Marcantonio acted as his witness.[16] Vasari lists other prints made by the team, praises them for displaying the invention and grace of Raphael combined with the diligence and skill of Marcantonio, and concludes by saying that Raphael sent some engravings to Dürer who praised Marcantonio highly and sent back engravings of his own, as well as his portrait, in what medium is not clear.

According to Vasari, it was the merchants who got rich from engravings in the time of Raphael. He seems relieved that the artists retained their dignity and achieved pure fame unsullied by venal considerations. Engraving is an art of *disegno*, and it is as such that Vasari harnesses it to his cause. The small saints Marcantonio engraved were a help, he says, to "i poveri pittori" who lacked *disegno*. These works, we might otherwise suppose, had served a purely devotional function.

Vasari begins the practice of overattributing designs to Raphael, such as the *Saint Jerome* (B. 102). There is in fact little in the "Life" that we could not reconstruct for ourselves on the basis of the prints, and much that must be corrected. What is of most interest in Vasari's account is the emphasis he puts on the money made from printmaking. Because we have little documentary evidence about how many prints were sold or at what prices, or even how long plates were printed, even this anecdotal evidence is to be taken seriously. None of Vasari's own paintings were engraved (although he was, of course, involved in woodcut production), and elsewhere in the *Lives* he has harsh words for those who make art solely for commercial motives. The engravings of his own time he evidently considered particularly debased, and he was not alone in decrying their effect. Giovanni Battista Armenini, for instance, treated engravings as a sort of ersatz drawing, accusing lazy artists of lifting their inventions from the engravings of Raphael and Parmigianino, so that "I was forced to condemn them in my mind as vile and sluggardly." Engravings themselves he associated with a harsh style (*la maniera cruda*).[17]

Diligence, which Vasari accords to Marcantonio, was not high on his list of praises; on the contrary, excessive diligence was a characteristic complaint of his. He lived in awe of Michelangelo, who despised engraving, but he found engravings useful for his history,[18] and his "Life" of Marcantonio expresses some genuine respect.

According to Vasari, Marcantonio engraved the *Martyrdom of Saint Lawrence* in thanks to Baccio Bandinelli for getting him out of prison after his scandalous *I modi*, his advocates having been Bandinelli and Cardinal Giulio de'Medici (after 1523, Clement VII, and both before and after, Bandinelli's patron). The *Martyrdom* is his largest engraving, and Bandinelli, although he was there to carve his copy of the *Laocoön* for the cardinal, commissioned in September 1520 and worked on intermittently through 1525, was yet relatively unknown in Rome. Apparently the engraving served its purpose of ingratiation well: Aretino and Giulio Romano left Rome and Marcantonio stayed, presumably at least until the Sack of Rome. Vasari says he had to pay a large ransom to the Spaniards and left the city ruined. He is referred to in the past tense in 1534 in a play by Pietro Aretino. Malvasia (1678) added the glamorous rumor, common in Bologna, that Marcantonio died in a duel, after doublecrossing a Roman patron by reengraving the *Massacre of Innocents* – although this did not stop Malvasia from also reporting, along with Filippo Baldinucci (1681), that Raimondi retreated to Bologna, where he died soon after the Sack. Also according to Baldinucci, Marcantonio had a wife who was well known as an engraver.

However, because Marcantonio dated prints only early in his career and his plates were no doubt printed after his death, his later whereabouts and the time of his death are matters for speculation. He could have died anytime between the mid-twenties and 1534, and judging from the works themselves, the latter end is not likely. His was the Rome of the Stanze and the Sistine Ceiling, but not the *Last Judgment*. The most mannerist work in his "shop" is the *Massacre of Innocents* by Marco Dente after Bandinelli (B. 21), and Dente is supposed to have died in the Sack. It has been conjectured that by 1524, Baviera was working with Caraglio and that the first sequel to *I modi*, that by Caraglio and Perino del Vaga, dates to 1527, Caraglio's part predating the Sack.[19] For in the Sack, according to Vasari, Caraglio lost everything, and his plates fell into evil hands who afterward printed them "tutto per cavar danari."[20] If Caraglio replaced Marcantonio in Baviera's enterprise, Marcantonio may have been finished as an engraver as early as

1524.[21] The lack of a secure death date for Marcantonio has been one of the factors in the elastic definition of his oeuvre. If we entertain the possibility of his having died not long after Raphael, perhaps even before the Sack, then his role as the bellwether of reproductive printmaking, the man whose career marks the endpoint of A. M. Hind's great opus on early Italian printmaking, fades somewhat.

It is significant that Marcantonio features so prominently in Vasari's opus, for by 1568 he had long been dead, unlike some of the confréres featured in the same "Life." Like Dolce, Vasari may not have minded associating Raphael with this lesser and problematic business, a business which had fundamentally changed meanwhile, after having been in the hands of Nicholas Beatrizet (1540s–50s) and Antonio Salamanca (active c. 1519–c. 1554), the latter an entrepreneur solely, the former entrepreneur cum engraver. Both, like Baviera, were foreigners, and Salamanca may have taken over Baviera's business, and been taken over in turn, or at least some of his plates, by Lafrery (active c. 1544–77).[22] The quantity, size, and scope of engravings had all grown, but not necessarily the quality or reputation of the works, a parallel to the book-printing industry. Later printmakers often borrowed the name of Raphael to enhance the value of their prints, but with no real connection to the master. Prints and fresco are the two media with which Vasari echoes Pliny's nostalgia for the good old days when these simple things were prized, and luxuriousness was not an issue. Accordingly, in Vasari's version *I modi* are assigned unequivocably to Giulio Romano, and moreover, in this instance Vasari is likely to be right. Probably he had talked to Giulio Romano about Marcantonio and other printmakers when he visited Mantua in 1541. So Vasari, in giving Marcantonio the prominence he did, dealt with the difficult problem of an art relatively absent in Florence and tried to rehabilitate it by digging into the past when it had been an integral part of a major artist's production.

And with Raphael, that it surely was. Just to take a few examples from Vasari's short list of the initial collaboration – the *Lucretia*, the *Massacre*, the *Judgment of Paris*, and the *Quos Ego* – a Raphael without those works included in his oeuvre has a different artistic center, more charming, graceful, and ingratiating, less vigorous, less indebted to the antique, and less learned. It is as though the painter Raphael achieved a sixteenth-century version of Masolino, and the inventor Raphael revived Masaccio. In terms of the politics of the Roman art world during the flourishing of patronage, Raphael used engraving to try to erase the stylistic difference between himself and Michelangelo, the difference examined at length in Dolce's *Aretino* and characterized there as analogous to that between Petrarch and Dante.[23]

Vasari accused Raphael of modeling his own style with a view to success, rather than, by implication, his own true *maniera*, but Raphael did more than this. It was not only his personal style he was self-conscious and deliberate about (that for which Vasari criticized him), not only his manners and gentlemanly aspirations (for which Michelangelo derided him), but the intersection of the two. He acted strategically not only to maximize his reputation but to mold it, to anticipate his critics and to make his art meet the developing checklist of incipient contemporary connoisseurs.

Michelangelo became the artist known for his limited range, Raphael for his unlimited one. In this he was protoacademic; it is no accident that Bandinelli, who inherited his interest in printmaking, founded an academy, and no accident that Agostino engraved its session in the Belvedere in 1531.[24] Leonardo, another artist who at least dabbled in engraving, did so in some sort of academic setting in Milan; likewise Serlio and Palladio used prints, in their case woodcuts, to establish a practice of reference to a published norm. Printmaking has sometimes been associated with mannerism because it enabled artists to shortcut their study of nature, but the case is not so simple, because printmaking – particularly after it was in the hands of publishers and had become big business – also provided accessible textbooks of design and composition and helped to regularize the practice and criticism of art and architecture.

Raphael also developed, in his role as designer for engraving, a sure sense of that realm between the private and the public that was engraving's peculiar domain. The *Massacre of Innocents, Judgment of Paris, Quos Ego*, and *Lucretia* are collectors' subjects rather than patrons' subjects. They make a spectacle of the artist's personal evolution rather than either teaching or delighting the viewer. Nonpleasing, nondidactic subject matter had intrigued humanists such as Guarino from early on, because in a Christian culture they had no purpose; they required a more classicizing definition of culture. Raphael's nondevotional engravings matched the interests of his Roman humanist associates, the members of that Tivoli expedition, for instance, as Mantegna had worked at least in the memory of his Lake Garda companions. Both for artist and intended viewer, these works were recreational; that is, they belonged outside the bounds of what an artist was meant to be doing to be of service to the powers around him. After the Sack of Rome and the Council of Trent, these conditions no longer existed, and printmaking became that more diffuse phenomenon, intended for popular consumption, that Vasari deplored.

Whether the collaboration continued at the same pitch as during those first couple of years is a valid question, although the art historical literature has always been happy to make that leap. But the flow of very Raphaelesque work is but a trickle after the first flush of mutual excitement. Scholars have long puzzled over why Raphael's *Parnassus* and Marcantonio's are so obviously disparate. Vasari says that Marcantonio was working from a *piccolo disegno*, and he probably was. The implication that Marcantonio was often left to his own devices, working from scraps that fell to him, no Raphael bending over the plate with him, or at least checking proofs, is, however, not one the literature has cared to entertain. Instead, despite the lack of any discernible pattern, the engraved *Parnassus* has been explained as reflecting lost preparatory drawings, the supposition being that Raphael had alternative ideas he did not care to discard altogether. Indeed, so great is the trust in the closeness of the two, that either fidelity or discrepancies between the works of the two are taken to support that tenet of close collaboration.

Two of the first collaborations between the Umbrian and the Emilian were *Lucretia* (Plate 34) and the *Massacre of Innocents* (Plate 36), both pictures of beautiful women in distress. Raphael had drawn scores of beautiful women in repose or in graceful and attractive movement. He had depicted sorrowing women. But the *Lucretia* is a project that exceeds those bounds. The Lucretia is heroic. Her pose is taken, with much modification, from the *Laocoön*, still the sensation of aficionados in Rome after its unearthing in 1506. Raphael's figure is statuesque. One foot is even raised to ensure the uneven distribution of weight across the body, as in so many statues both ancient and Renaissance. Her eyes are closed and her head is turned, as though she could not bear to look at what the viewer sees in all clarity: the moment is as terrible as the famous one in which Timanthes showed Agamemnon with his face averted, during the sacrifice of his daughter Iphigenia. She is modest, she is the soul of decorousness, and yet one breast is exposed, a pictorial license granted both by ancient precedent and by a tradition of depiction of the nursing Madonna. She is decorous, and yet the drapery and its lighting both accentuate her genital area, as in no other figure by Raphael. Thereby she is more than a suicide; she is also the victim of rape.

The narrative demands both her suicide and some explanation of it. Raphael gives both in a single scene, whereas Botticelli for instance, who had depicted this unusual scene for a *cassone*, took three and still managed to avoid both moments of crisis, the rape and the suicide.[25] Raphael's figure is also bigger than the diminutive Lucretias of Botticelli's panel, in which the central scene shows her corpse inspiring male heroism. Raphael chose the woman's heroic moment instead, and gave Lucretia, a figure from Roman history (c. 510 B.C.), a tag in Greek, and moreover, one not equivalent to the dying sentiment attributed to her by Livy. In place of "never shall Lucretia provide a precedent for unchaste women to escape what they deserve,"[26] we get the more general and typical heroic resolve, "better to die than to live in dishonor." All this promises the active role of Raphael, and moreover, a Raphael in contact with curial humanists actively reviving Greek tragedy.[27] Not so, however, the setting, a pastiche from Lucas van Leyden and the antique.

The *Lucretia* was a success, often copied and also imitated, and understandably so, for it marked out new artistic territory, not only for Raphael but for everybody. Heroic women had been seen in art before, but not many, and Judith for instance was the picture of cold-blooded calm, as were personifications of the virtues. An emotional, noble woman engaged in a heroic action had not been done before, although Raphael himself had provided premonitions thereof in his *Saint Catherine*, his Sappho on *Parnassus* (c. 1509–11), and his *Cardinal Virtues* (c. 1511), also in the Segnatura. With the *Lucretia*, it is as though a Muse had pushed Apollo aside and taken center place. And it is probably no coincidence that after a period in the quattrocento during which consorts, wives, and mistresses were notably inconspicuous, those of rulers and artists alike, quite the opposite came to prevail, possibly as the politics of marriages became more intricate and consequential among the upper classes. Beginning with Isotta Malatesta, Lucretia Borgia, Caterina Sforza, and culminating in the more respectable Elizabetta Gonzaga and Isabella d'Este, women are more often the subject of portraiture, of book dedications, and, more often, participants in dialogues. As a print subject, the *Lucretia* may have functioned as a canny choice, a tactful yet meaningful gift to a woman. It need not have been exclusively geared toward female viewers, though, because it claimed a more general validity as a subject of literary, historical, and even archaeological interest. The attempts to follow up on this success – the *Cleopatras* by Marcantonio after the antique and after Bandinelli, the *Dido*, Jacopo Francia's more nude *Lucretia*, the racy loves of the gods by Giulio Romano and by Perino del Vaga and Rosso – fell short, by being merely archeological or solely titillating. The more successful reprises were by Raphael himself: the *Massacre of the Innocents*, the foremost mother in the *Expulsion of Heliodorus*, the twisted kneeling figure near Marcantonio, picked up on by Titian as a source for Ariadne in the *Bacchus and Ariadne* for Duke Alfonso of Ferrara, the five sisters of the Lucretia who heroically fight the fire in the *Fire in the Borgo* (Plate 23) and finally *Galatea* (Plate 28) and *Psyche* (Plate 29) at the Farnesina.

The *Massacre of the Innocents* (Plate 36) was probably conceived about the same time as the *Expulsion of Heliodorus* (c. 1512), with its clinging, frightened mothers and children, and was still clearly in Raphael's mind when he painted the Sistine *Madonna* with its striding centerpiece and similarly alarmed child.[28] Again, nothing like it had ever been done. Side, frontal, and back views of nude warriors were arranged with choreographed precision amid mothers and babes with arms folded, arms raised, arms extended to the sides. A vignette on the left of a seated mother and dead child recalls both Madonna and Child compositions and Pietàs and conveys the deepest sorrow without relying on movement, with the face hidden. Raphael takes the stuff of beauty and love and creates a scene of imminent horror. It is his skill in creating a narrative instant that allows him to avoid hideousness without falling into bland excess of beauty either. It is a lesson he may have learned partly on the basis of Birago's engraving after Leonardo's *Last Supper* in Milan (H. 9), partly from the narrative exigencies of his own *Judgment of Solomon* in the Segnatura ceiling. If in the *Lucretia* he competed most clearly with the sculptor Michelangelo, here he pits himself against one of the greatest Italian prints yet made, the *Battle of the Nudes* by Pollaiuolo, and clearly wins, because that print of perhaps fifty years earlier was relatively planar, included only male figures, and had no expressive content beyond what murderous grimaces can convey. As in the *Lucretia*, the background of the *Massacre* has been lifted from other sources and pasted onto the figural composition.[29]

Like Lucretia, the mothers are victims, but ones whose vigor and determination (although not their opportunity) matches that of their oppressors. Raphael has taken the motif of mother and child further from its customary, comfortable presentation than anyone would until Bronzino's *Allegory* (National Gallery, London) at midcentury. This choreography of male violence against women, women sexualized by their flying hair, their exposed legs and arms, their open mouths, not to mention by the presence of naked men, is set against the backdrop of the Tiber. There are actually three bridges in the engraving: the flat structure on which the action takes place, and two arched bridges beyond, the closer (recognizably the Ponte Fabricius, itself associated, not inappropriately for the subject, with the Jewish ghetto, and datable to 62 B.C. by its inscription, so conceivably trod on by Romans who later served in Palestine),[30] and another that is probably the Ponte Rotto downstream rather than the Ponte Sisto upstream. The bridge on which the action rakes place then stands sequentially in the place of the Ponte Sisto, although the distances have collapsed.

The Ponte Sisto was then the center of the booming prostitution trade in Rome (and, indeed, mentioned as such in the play by Aretino that helps us to date Raimondi's death). The Ponte Sisto must have witnessed scenes that to an artist's eye might look something like Raphael's vignettes of a struggle for dominance by men over abnormally plucky women. This is not to say that the mothers of Bethlehem are meant to be identified with prostitutes. It is worth pondering, however, that this singular challenge to the prominence of Michelangelo markedly both vilified and sexualized the hitherto heroic nude, which was the signature theme of his rival. Moreover, that bridge was built by Pope Sixtus IV, likewise builder of the Sistine Chapel.

Perhaps Raphael was actually struck by the coincidence of Sistine patronage, and perhaps he was quite deliberately antagonistic in showing the brutal Roman soldiers in so strikingly Michelangelesque a manner. If so, there was good cause for Michelangelo's long-borne grudge against his younger colleague.

The Bronzino *Allegory* was to be a collector's painting, and this was a collector's print. The subject was hardly unknown to Christian iconography before, but Raphael's treatment of it was a tour de force for him, a display of range, rather than a tool for the intensity required for devotional purposes. The subject had usually belonged in a narrative cycle, to fill in the end of the story of the Wise Men and Herod, as well as to commemorate the first martyrs. Here, just as in using a Greek epigram for a Roman scene, Raphael declared his independence of text, using the most common text of all as the path by which to shake off subservience to literary models. No adviser was needed here. Like Shakespeare borrowing a plot, Raphael demonstrated not his originality but his ingenuity. He made art out of a scene of brutality, but not out of loyalty to historical memory or to the sacred text. He made art out of that scene because it suited his purposes.

This was novel. Michelangelo in 1492 bought a piece of marble and carved it on his own initiative, sans commission, into the *Battle of the Centaurs*, and that had been novel. Leonardo filled sketchbooks with ideas, most of which he lacked the means to realize. Raphael outdid them both in finding a medium that could take any idea he had and spread it throughout a utopian community of artists, patrons, and humanists – exactly the people apt to think about art as liberal (that is, as intellectual rather than practical or instrumental). In his efforts to make an art that would not be seen merely as text visualized, culminating in his devotion to grotesque decoration, he never succeeded better than in this, a work more public than the Stanze, a work seen in relation to him rather than his patron, a work that referred both to the antique and to contemporary Rome, a work both pathetic and dynamic, in which the narrative moment is chosen for aesthetic reasons rather than informational ones. Someone who did not know the Gospels would never reconstruct the text on the basis of this image, as they could, for example, the story of the *Expulsion of Heliodorus* or of the *Fire in the Borgo*.

The point in Raphael's career that has more than once been located at the *Fire in the Borgo*, the so-called moment of mannerism, the visual allusion to Aeneas and Anchises in the midst of a medieval history for the sake of demonstrating his artistry (as noted by Vasari), was already evident in the *Massacre*, had Raphael's engravings been incorporated into his oeuvre by scholars as fully as he himself did. Instead, paradoxically, the project of seeing Marcantonio as closely linked to Raphael, so closely linked that only Raphael could have designed those backgrounds, be they ever so ad hoc, has also been the project that has kept the engravings from being integrated into Raphael's painting oeuvre because it suggested an earlier dating for the landmark engravings, a tendency reinforced by Vasari's account. The point is not that Raphael has invented mannerism at the same moment as the High Renaissance, but that Raphael has found a way of addressing a selective audience looking only for delight, and he did so as early as the *Massacre* rather than first in the *Fire in the Borgo*. This suited him particularly in the difficult years under the irascible Julius II. He had less need of engraving in the flusher times under the more genial Leo X. After 1513, Raphael's involvement in printmaking diminished, although not Marcantonio's.

Even Pollaiuolo with his *Battle of the Nudes* had not deviated so far from the responsibilities of a didactic art, for his was an allegory, as was Mantegna's *Battle of the Sea Monsters*.[31] Raphael's course was bold, a declaration of independence cloaked cleverly under a biblical subject. Particularly because it was not entirely autograph, not even the design, Raphael's use of the medium was decisive. It was this engraving on which Raphael's signature first appeared, "RAPHA[ELUS] URBI[NUS] INVEN[IT]," on top of Marcantonio's monogram. It was a decisive moment, for double credit had never been given and accepted before. Marcantonio had given it on the *Bather* after Michelangelo, but without happy outcome. The public declaration of nonautograph work was not just one more stab at claiming liberal arts status, nor certainly was it meant to herald the start of a new practice of printmaking. Instead it marked the beginning of changed social relations within the artistic community itself. Like an Oedipal son, Raphael has eliminated the authority that had held sway over him (the patron) and at the same time found someone over whom to have an unnatural sway (the engraver who had never been his apprentice).

The *Massacre of the Innocents* not only belongs in the oeuvre of a major painter, but constitutes a major and central work by that artist, the innovative qualities of which were suitable to further development in his ongoing work as painter. Mantegna would have painted the Camera degli Sposi whether or not he had dabbled in engraving nudes *all'antica*; Pollaiuolo sculpted *Hercules and Antaeus*, and his engraving was more or less a corollary of that, but Raphael without the *Lucretia* and especially the *Massacre* might not have gone on to paint the *Fire in the Borgo* or the *Sistine Madonna*. It is not so much that he discovered art for art's sake four centuries early as that he invented, at least for a passing moment, art for the artist's sake – that is, he was able in this other medium to practice at being an artist, not in the sense of drawing and redrawing from the model as he could already do, but developing a composition that pleased him before it pleased anyone else. This evidently meant devising a composition that placed him relative to his competition, meaning Michelangelo and antiquity above all. The Raphael who designed the *Lucretia* and the *Massacre* had already heard something like the arguments of Dolce's subsequent *Aretino*, in which he is dismissed as a mere Petrarch, merely the painter of pretty women, and wanted to prove himself more versatile than the artists he heard praised above himself, Michelangelo and Leonardo. In an age in which the development of collecting catalyzed the concomitant development of theory and criticism, Raphael anticipated and responded to his own anticipations of what his humanist cronies would say. The combination of Raphael's social success in Rome and the opportunity presented by Marcantonio, his personal courtier, put him in a position neither Michelangelo nor Leonardo ever discovered. He received feedback that was not as onerous as a patron's directives, yet he had both the incentive and the ready opportunity to heed it. He made himself great, as Vasari accused, but not just by imitating Michelangelo; rather like Ghiberti, he ingratiated himself by listening and regrouping. The *Lucretia* and the *Massacre* were stepping stones to developing the artistic conviction to move from large-scale group portraiture to the expressively and compositionally more complicated *istoria* for which he became renown.

The *Massacre* thus understood becomes one of the pivotal works in the history of Western art, rather than a sort of sixteenth-century postcard sold on the side to make a bit of extra money. Its cheapness relative to a painting of similar complexity is certainly crucial to the history of the economics of art, and to the social history of its distribution, but the importance of this engraving pertains both to material culture and to style history. It was as an engraver that Raphael overcame his limitations, rather than simply exploiting his known strengths there or exploring a subgenre in a less monumental medium.

In these two engravings he discovered how to make an art that was not limited to beauty and grace but that was not obviously derivative from the antique either. For him the harder part was the former; Michelangelo, who had tackled roughly the same problem, had to work harder on the latter. Raphael grew up as an outsider in a culture dedicated to antiquities, having grown up in a court exemplary on the counts of humanistic learning and the new architecture, but without much direct contact with ancient marbles. One of Marcantonio's roles in Raphael's life was as a catalyst in the appropriation of antiquity, for whereas that had played a major part in Marcantonio's oeuvre before he met Raphael, it had been conspicuously absent from Raphael's, with the exception of ginger quotations like the *Three Graces* (c. 1504) and the Apollo Belvedere in the Christ of the *Madonna del Cardellino* (c. 1506). Bolognese artists such as Jacopo Ripanda and Michelangelo Anselmi had a cavalier attitude toward antiquity; it was a treasure shop rather than a temple to them, and Marcantonio shared this sense of freedom.

The art historical literature has recognized the *Massacre* as important, but not for the right reasons. Either the preparatory drawings that survive have made it of interest or its date during the flourishing of Raphael's powers. It has attracted remarkably little attention in its own right, however, as an integral part of Raphael's oeuvre, or of what we might now call his partially virtual oeuvre. Among the consequences of the ghettoization of Raphael's engravings (all for the sake of enhancing the prestige of Marcantonios) has been the longstanding hegemony of painting: Raphael as painter must surely outweigh Raphael the designer of engravings. Raphael the painter became the forefather of French academic painting, and consequentially, Raphael's identity as an engraver almost completely submerged into Marcantonio's. Marcantonio rather than Raphael took the place of *le peintre-graveur*.

The *Judgment of Paris* (Plate 35) combined beauty and grace with art *all'antica*.[32] Raphael's conception is as bold as, and perhaps more unorthodox than, the Hellenized *Lucretia*. The central figure is one of the two losers, namely, Athena – already a provocative composition to sell to humanists. Moreover, she is seen nude full-length from the back, a pose Raphael could have seen in Dürer's *Four Witches* (B. 75) engraving but seldom elsewhere in a finished work of art, until this engraving provided a precedent. Equally unexpected is the sentiment expressed in the Latin inscription (SORDENT PRAE FORMA INGENIUM VIRTUS REGNA AURUM) that exalts beauty even over virtue – not a moral you could proclaim to everybody, although certainly one the Homeric episode supports. These two elements work oddly together. The catalogue of female beauty, one of the most frequently encountered of Renaissance topoi, routinely excludes any element of the back of the figure. Moreover, Athena, although she dominates the composition, has lost the contest of beauty to Venus. So the principal figure signifies something other than perfect beauty, while the inscription touts beauty as the ultimate value. It is as though Raphael is teasing his humanist friends, by pitting the elements of that familiar dualism, pleasure and learning, against one another. This engraving too must have been intended for Raphael's intimate circle, the friends whose taste he was anticipating as he decided what he wanted to do with his freedom as engraver. In this case, he went considerably beyond merely gratifying their expectations.

Raphael based his drawing directly on an antiquity visible in Rome, not a freestanding statue but a more pictorial relief of the same subject at the Villa Medici. Its theme is the very *charis*, the female charm, for which Raphael was famed, as Apelles had been. He took a fairly ruined, damaged, relatively unimpressive antiquity and made it clearer, more sensuous, more "academic," by offering front, side, and back views of the female nude. The threesome of goddesses in the *Judgment* established his independence from the antique statuary group of the Graces he had so admired earlier; his Graces in the Farnesina are indebted instead to his own *Judgment.* The central figure, Athena robing, is a full-length version of the prominent mother in the *Expulsion of Heliodorus*, the woman kneeling in front of Marcantonio himself as pallbearer, the figure reminiscent of the famed antique relief of the bed of Polykleitos, with its seated female nude in torsion, the same figure Titian took up in his *Bacchus and Ariadne* for Duke Alfonso, the series of bacchanals to which Raphael was supposed to contribute.

Athena stands more frontally and centrally than Venus. The routine assumption is that the engraved Athena postdates the frescoed mother with arms out, but this bears reexamining. The engraved version is more complete, the posture more primary to the whole composition and less artificial there. Unprecedented it may be, but the figure appears to have been studied from life, the movement natural, whereas in the *Heliodorus* it is a bit forced and less integrated compositionally. Vasari mentions the *Judgment* as the second of Raphael's engraving projects – a drawing he already had on hand, says Vasari, the engraving of which "astounded Rome." If we cast out the premise that Marcantonio's engraving is basically reproductive, it becomes entirely plausible that the engraved design, again the primary figures rather than the whole landscape and skyscape ensemble, served as a sort of petri dish in which to try out this bold idea, which was subsequently tamed for the purpose of reuse in the papal apartment. The river god too, then, reworked from antiquity in the engraving, is reworked again into the figure of Heliodorus struck down.

By comparison with that arcing figure of Athena, declaring that beauty is not as important as the art she doubly personifies, the winsome *Galatea* (Plate 28), let alone the anonymous mother in the *Expulsion of Heliodorus*, is a conventional trifle. Almost every Renaissance depiction of a young female bears the genetic trace of the type of the Virgin Mary, modest, beautiful, graceful – until this one. Here, Raphael's strange, yet partly orthodox, homage to Greek antiquity, to the love of wisdom and to Homer, breaks the Virgin Mary's hegemony over the imagery of women. She is not shown as modest or with the benefit of the conventions for beauty or grace. She is inexpressive, her presence somewhat detached and abstracted. If this were the *School of Athens*, she would play Plato to Venus's earth-bound Aristotle; her body indicates otherness, inaccessibility. She is shown in a way designed to enhance Raphael's standing relative to the antique and Michelangelo, as were the conspicuously relaxed male nudes, with their varied angles (from the back seated, standing, and reclining). Raphael put a figure very obviously his in the center of a work basically *all'antica*, demonstrating in so doing that he could depict a beautiful woman for the sake of the art involved rather than in mere homage to nature.

If Raphael was responsible for the figural designs of the *Lucretia*, the *Massacre*, and the *Judgment*, in something like the way described earlier, then his use of engraving was deliberate rather than the repository for extra drawings it has sometimes been made into. The consistent element of strong female protagonists has less to do with our contemporary filter in favor of feminist images than with Raphael's personal artistic dilemma – that his natural inclination was toward sweet female figures and he needed to move closer to the center of the imagery of his time, away from Perugino's bland beatitudes and into competition with Michelangelo's predominantly male imagery. The fact that his great predecessors in Italian printmaking, Pollaiuolo and Mantegna, were better known for masculine than for feminine figures may have been an incentive; their prints could offer the medicine he needed to achieve a less blandishing art. And if, relative to our predecessors in the study of Renaissance printmaking, we emphasize matters of market and money, this too is not accountable solely as a reflection of our own consummeristic age, but instead is a question easier to ask as the market for Marcantonios slows relative to what it was a century or more ago: for historians for whom the value of a Marcantonio was self-evident and even cardinal, the problem of its original value held little interest. For us, reared with the idea of Marcantonio as a quasi-hack, the fountainhead of bad printmaking, it constitutes a discovery to recognize, on one hand, how much monetary value Marcantonios once had, and, on the other hand, to step back from the confusing pile of engravings cata-logued as Marcantonios to the few most closely tied to Raphael and re-alize that they are indeed beautiful sheets, comparable with Dürers, and more than that, that Raphael without them is a significantly lesser and less comprehensible artist.

The most essential Raphael engravings, indispensable even in a short overview such as this one, number five. The two left are both Virgilian, and both imply a more complete design on the part of Raphael. Both should be dated in that same narrow corridor of time, 1512–14, like the previous exam-ple. *Il Morbetto* (*The Pest*) (Plate 38) is stylistically related to the *Liberation of Saint Peter* (c. 1512–13) (Plate 22) and the *Fire in the Borgo* (the Stanza begun in 1514, Plate 23). Raphael is named as inventor, Marcantonio mono-grammed the work; it has impeccable intellectual credentials, illustrating and quoting Book III of the *Aeneid*, in which a plague afflicts the followers of Aeneas while they stop in Crete, and he is warned in a dream to travel further in search of a place to found a new Troy. Yet the engraving, mod-est in size, goes strangely unmentioned in the sixteenth-century authors. It is the only one of the five discussed here that is not listed by Vasari, for instance. It was copied, but much less than the three preceding engravings.

A beautiful and unusual metal point drawing for the right background survives at Windsor, an evocative study of ruins by moonlight, its pale light shimmering across the bluish grey paper. The mood of the whole scene is grim, grimmer than any Christian subject, and oddly presided over by a bearded head atop a herm, which divides the composition into two. Raphael has inverted the bare fundamentals of a Pietà in the foreground figural group, in which a young man bends over a dead woman, and does so in pity, although felt for the babe who wants to nurse rather than for the already putrifying corpse – a motif of sufficient horror for Poussin to copy it into his *Plague at Ashdod* more than one hundred years later. Not only the Pietà, but scenes of Lazarus and of the Madonna and Child shadow the figural grouping like palimpsests, while above a trio of figures expresses their shock by raised hands and cocked heads in two cases, to be echoed not only in Raphael's own *Fire in the Borgo* but in Parmigianino's etched *Lamentation* some twenty years later; the third figure huddles and refuses to look, like the grieving Agamemnon in the painting by Timanthes so admired by Pliny and his followers. The shielded faces, the torch, the visitation to a sleeping figure in the night all echo the fresco of the *Liberation of Saint Peter*.

The mood is extraordinary, both in itself and for Raphael. This woman is so far from attractive and charming as to be physically repellent – nothing less than putrid. But a proto-academic interest in variety will not do as an explanation for this apparently so un-Raphaelesque Raphael. Even those who like to explain Raphael's penchant for paintings of the Madonna and Child as reflecting his closeness to his mother, who (according to Vasari and contrary to upper-class practice) nursed him, have failed to claim this pathetic scene as tinged with autobiography, although Raphael's mother died when he was still a child. A third possibility exists, and that involves Raphael's humanistic, curial circle in Rome. He managed, like Michelangelo at the table of Lorenzo de' Medici two decades earlier, to be accepted into the circle of courtiers rather than artists. He became friends with Baldassare Castiglione, whom he painted so memorably (Plate 16), perhaps not long before his marriage in 1516. Castiglione had written a poem in honor of his dead friend Ludovico Pico della Mirandola, on the unfortunate occasion of Pope Julius II's attack on his widow in 1510–11.[33] That poem described the startling nocturnal visitation by the dead friend to the sleeping Castiglione in a highly Virgilian mode, based on the scene here illustrated by Raphael. Raphael need not be making a covert reference to della Rovere aggression (aggression related, however, to the pope's machinations concerning Urbino now that his nephew had been given the duchy in the absence of a Montefeltro heir) for Castiglione to be responsible for Raphael's interest in this Virgilian passage. It is possible that Crete (or Troy) was a code between them for Urbino, the sometime-happy place that they had had to abandon for Rome. This is not to affirm that Castiglione was guiding the illiterate painter à la Alberti, but instead that the engraving was made as the product of friendship, for a limited circle, rather than with an eye on the Roman print market. The woman with raised hand and averted face in the *Fire in the Borgo* plausibly was reused from an idea developed first for this engraving. Raphael was interested in engraving during the period in which he was working hardest to prove himself. By 1516 Michelangelo and Leonardo had left Rome, and Raphael's goals were less exclusively artistic. Marcantonio was left much more on his own. But during the earlier, more artistically intensive period, engraving was a full partner with painting, just as the fresco of the *Expulsion of Heliodorus* showed Marcantonio and Raphael to be.

The *Quos Ego* (Plate 37), although unsigned and unmonogrammed like the *Lucretia*, belongs in the most Raphaelsque cluster of Marcantonio's work. It again shows Raphael's closeness to the humanistic circle, for it is an elaborate composition based on a type of ancient relief associated with Homeric epic.[34] It also has the look of a Renaissance frontispiece, although engraved frontispieces had not yet replaced woodcut ones. Perhaps the hope was that the *Quos Ego* could serve as frontispiece to an edition of the *Aeneid*; perhaps Pietro Bembo, the great advocate of Virgil's style and Raphael's associate, encouraged the project. What we know for sure is that the *Quos Ego* stands out in Marcantonio's oeuvre, and even in Raphael's, as a particularly elaborate effort *all'antica*. Like *Il Morbetto*, it was not done on the initiative of Raphael alone. In both cases the Latin inscription implies a situation more like the customary commission, that is, a project in which Raphael provided middle-level management rather than holding the reins himself. The *Judgment* and the *Lucretia*, both of which include inscriptions in languages Raphael did not know, must have involved collaboration, but also a large dose of autonomy in matters of design. Each case has its own peculiar characteristics; Raphael never became a regular producer of prints, as indeed neither had Pollaiuolo or Mantegna. It is peculiar how the early Italians dabbled in printmaking, whereas the northerners became professionals of one sort or another from the start. Even in the case of the *Quos Ego*, where we can well imagine Raphael was following directions, it was almost certainly a matter of friendly collaboration rather than of traditional patronage. And it was also reliably not a money-making venture, despite the obvious investment of time and effort. This was a labor of love, the sort of print that Vasari thought justified the medium.

The central storm scene shows Raphael as the peer of the ancients, the *Laocoön* in particular being the source for the figure of Neptune (as it had been for the *Lucretia*). Yet it also shows him as the peers of the moderns. Leonardo's interest in storm scenes and in horses, including a drawing of this same subject now at Windsor, Raphael would have known well. The invention is comparable to Michelangelo as well, both for the taut, muscular god and for compositional similarities to the Sistine *Deluge*. There may even be a reminiscence of Mantegna's engraving of the *Battle of the Sea Gods*, in which Neptune plays a role along with sea horses. The engraving also comments on and furthers Raphael's own work. This is the male pendant to the *Galatea*, with the wind putti reminiscent of the *Sistine Madonna*'s cloud *angellini*. The *Quos Ego* is both a summa of Raphael's artistic ambitions as developed in engraving and a valedictory. In the last five years of his life, he was overwhelmed with work and overwhelmed with success. He was busy trying to manage his thriving shop, with a burgeoning number of apprentices. He could not keep up with the commissions from even the most important people. He had architectural ambitions, and marital ones, which claimed his time. Engraving had been a means for him to achieve his personal artistic goals in a realm of little risk, a kind of laboratory; and to develop his public, not the maximized public but a select circle, fellow explorers in the brave new world of the printed page. Marcantonio made prints to make money, but Raphael not; Raphael was looking for currency valid among a select group of nonartists and nonpatrons, the humanists in the curia. Neither engraver nor designer anticipated that through prints Raphael would not die, but would stay actively in the minds of artists and collectors for centuries in a way that no artist ever had before him. Even in an age much preoccupied with immortality, few recognized the futurity implicit in the multiplied image. The combination of an encyclopedia of imagery dominated by Raphael and the beginning of academic artistic culture placed Raphael in a dominant position for hundreds of years, and engravings supported that role. As Delacroix remarked after seeing a worn impression of Raphael's *Judgment of Paris,* "One must not indeed think too much about his quality, for fear of throwing everything out of the window."[35]

Raphael certainly haunts other engravings by Marcantonio; he may actively have participated in designing some of them. His designs were sometimes engraved by others, but these five engravings belong as much to Raphael as they do to Marcantonio. Despite this, this essay is not meant to continue Bartsch's bias, subsequently exaggerated by others, toward reducing Marcantonio to the left hand of Raphael. Marcantonio deserves his own biography, a more adequate one than Vasari's potpourri of hearsay, and he deserves to have his own oeuvre credited to him, rather than nearly every Italian print of the first four decades of the sixteenth century.

Marcantonio was in the business of selling *disegno* to the largest possible market, but neither designer nor printmaker had copyright protection. The story of the market for prints in Medicean and Counter-Reformation Rome remains unplumbed in the dozens of versions of Raphaelesque and Marcantonio-like engravings catalogued by Bartsch as copies and condemned by that worthwhile act to an undeserved obscurity.

9 Raphael Drawings, *Pro-Contra*

Linda Wolk-Simon

The subject of drawing (*disegno*) is taken up by Castiglione in the pages of *The Courtier*, the imagined dialogues on the subject of the model aristocrat spoken by a group of interlocutors gathered in the rooms of the duchess of Urbino. Castiglione was a friend and intimate of Raphael, who is invoked in the pages of *The Courtier* and whose example was undoubtedly in the author's mind as he extolled the virtues of drawing and painting as disciplines worthy of noble pursuit. (In like fashion was the poet's evocation of the ideal courtier the paradigm that the ambitious Raphael strove to achieve.) Thus, when his mouthpiece, Count Ludovico da Canossa, announces in Book One, "I would discuss another matter which I consider to be of great importance and which I think must therefore in no way be neglected by our Courtier: and this is a knowledge of how to draw and an acquaintance with the art of painting," the reader may fairly infer that the primacy of drawing (*disegno*) as the foundation of artistic pursuit articulated in the ensuing speech reflects not only the attitude of Castiglione, but the very practice of Raphael himself.[1]

Material evidence confirms this supposition. Including a small corpus of architectural studies (a subject outside the scope of this discussion but one that is accompanied by its own complex issues of authorship and invention), Raphael's extant graphic oeuvre consists of roughly 460 sheets, some double-sided. It has been estimated that only a small percentage – less than 10 percent – of his original output, which must have numbered several thousand sheets, has survived.[2] The presumed quantity is impressive for a career that spanned barely twenty years. Also of note is the range of media and techniques, and of drawing type: metalpoint, pen and ink, brush and wash, chalk – both red and black – stylus underdrawing, and pouncing were variously employed by Raphael in the production of preliminary sketches (*concetti*), finished compositional studies, figure drawings exploring elements of pose or of drapery, *modelli*, cartoons, and, a category of the master's own invention, "auxilliary cartoons."[3]

As scholars have consistently noted, and as this recitation of the categories of drawing he produced confirms, Raphael was primarily a utilitarian draftsman. Although *disegno* was for him (as for the ideal painter evoked in *The Courtier*) the foundation of art, it was rarely an end in itself. Rather, drawings were the means to the end – the building blocks that allowed him to formulate and investigate systematically the solutions ultimately realized in the final design, be it a fresco, panel painting, altarpiece, tapestry, or print. It is significant that when Raphael sent Dürer a drawing as a gift in 1515, it was not a finished, autonomous "presentation drawing" made expressly for the occasion, but rather a *garzone* study employed if not initially made for the *Battle at Ostia* (Fig. 20).[4]

An inscription in Dürer's hand records the circumstances by which he came to own this prized drawing by the Italian master. Yet even in the face of this unique contemporary documentation – a sixteenth-century equivalent of a notarized signature – Raphael's authorship of the drawing, now universally accepted, has in the past been disputed. That such unequivocal corroborating testimony from his own lifetime can be dismissed indicates the subjective bent that much of the attribution debate has taken since the canon of Raphael drawings was first formulated in the mid–nineteenth century. Not surprisingly, notions of Raphael the draftsman have not remained static, as each new generation of scholars has offered different, often divergent assessments of the quantity and quality of drawings that the master produced. Like an accordion, his graphic oeuvre has expanded and contracted over time, often in concert with the revisions to his canon of paintings proposed at a given moment – a cyclical phenomenon that Cecil Gould descriptively likened to a pendulum effect.[5] To comprehend the current state of the question of drawings by Raphael and his workshop, a summary review of the critical literature is in order.

J. D. Passavant's pioneering study *Raphael von Urbino und sein Vater Giovanni Santi*, published in 1839, has been acclaimed as the first modern, scholarly monograph of an artist by virtue of its adherence to stylistic criteria rather than biographical narrative as the construct for analyzing its subject.[6] Consequently, Raphael has the longest modern historiography of any artist. From the outset, his drawings have been treated as an integral component of his oeuvre; thus, the critical literature on Raphael's draftsmanship also extends back over a century and a half. Passavant's study

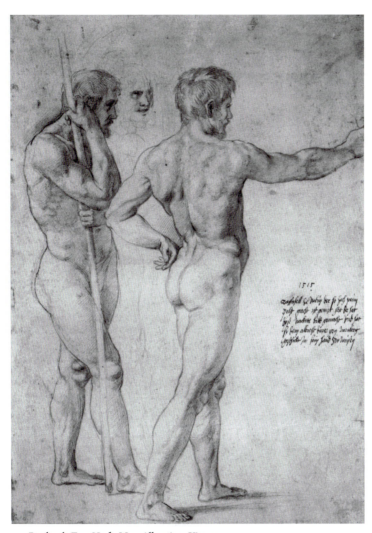

20. Raphael, *Two Nude Men*, Albertina, Vienna.

was novel not only in its methodology but in its effort at compiling a catalogue raisonné of works by Raphael. Even more remarkable for the time
was the author's recognition that drawings were as important as paintings
in constructing an artist's personality – a circumstance reflected by the fact
that included in *Raphael von Urbino* (and expanded in the 1860 French
edition but omitted from the 1872 English translation) is a catalogue of all
drawings by the master then known.[7]

Some twenty years after Passavant's publication the photographic reproduction of works of art came into widespread use; its efficacy in the study
of Raphael drawings was first evidenced in Sir Charles Robinson's *Critical
Account of Drawings by Michel Angelo and Raffaello in the University Galleries, Oxford.* Published in 1870, it has been described as "a pioneer work
in the detailed study of an artist's drawings."[8] Robinson's ambition to "arrive at definite conclusions as to the authenticity of the several specimens;
to determine, if possible, the approximate date, the intention and ultimate
destination of each drawing; and also, in the case of preparatory studies for
known works, to give some account of the finished productions" is no different from that of a present-day scholar engaged in compiling a catalogue
raisonné – a testimonial to his prescience and critical acumen.[9] Completing the first wave of modern criticism on Raphael is J. A. Crowe and G. B.
Cavalcaselle's *Raphael: His Life and Work,* which appeared in 1882 and
remained the standard monograph on the artist for a century. Drawings
were not considered separately, however, but literally and figuratively as
footnotes, entering into their discussion only in so far as they related to
paintings.

A new phase of scholarship in the study of Italian Renaissance painters
was launched in the early 1890s with Giovanni Morelli's self-avowed "scientific" connoisseurship.[10] Application of Morellian principles did much to
clarify the styles and hands of individual artists, but as far as the subject
of Raphael and his drawings was concerned, the approach proved both un-
sympathetic and counterproductive. Morelli, followed by Herman Dollmayr
and Franz Wickhoff,[11] liberally and with little substantiation removed drawings from Raphael's oeuvre and reassigned them to the likes of Peruzzi,
Giulio Romano, Perino del Vaga, and Giovanni Francesco Penni – artists
whose individual personalities were then nebulous and which these largely
unwarranted accretions only served to confuse further.[12] Even more reductive was the seldom-discussed work of the Danish scholar Vilhelm Wanscher, who credited Raphael with a graphic oeuvre comprising a mere eight
sheets.[13]

The first scholar to study Raphael's drawings as an autonomous body of
work rather than an appendage to his paintings was Oskar Fischel. The fruit
of Fischel's lifelong devotion to the subject is the magisterial eight-volume
series published between 1913 and 1941 (the last, posthumously), *Raphaels
Zeichnungen,* which catalogued 395 sheets.[14] It is a fitting testimonial to
Fischel's labors that many Raphael drawings retain and continue to be
cited by their eponymous "F" number, although inevitably joined in con-
cordances by references to more recent compilations. Fischel's work has

provided the foundation for all subsequent investigations of the subject of Raphael drawings and is unlikely to ever be fully eclipsed, even though his tendency to adduce retouching or later reworking as the explanation for elements of Raphael's drawings that he considered anomalous is no longer tenable.[15]

Like much art historical scholarship, the epicenter of the study of Raphael drawings shifted to Britain beginning in the 1940s. Most of the research was museum based, reflecting the exceptional concentration of Raphael drawings in three British collections – the Royal Collection housed at Windsor Castle, the Ashmolean Museum, and the British Museum – and was presented in permanent collection catalogues.[16] Through the efforts of A. E. Popham, Karl Parker, and Philip Pouncey and J. A. Gere, respectively, the rich holdings of these institutions were for the first time systematically submitted to the rigors of a modern, scholarly cataloguing process – a process that scrutinized not only the drawings of Raphael, but also copies after his inventions and works ascribed to his close followers, whose individual personalities as draftsmen (and, indeed, as painters) thus began to acquire definition.[17]

Another product of this period of "crystallization" in the study of Raphael drawings that built directly on the work of Fischel was Frederick Hartt's 1958 monograph on Giulio Romano, Raphael's principal pupil and collaborator, which included a catalogue of the artist's drawings.[18] The first (and until quite recently the only) monograph devoted to one of Raphael's followers, Hartt's study to some extent provided the first dose of a long-overdue antidote to Berenson's dismissive, collective condemnation of Raphael's pupils – "no wonder we have given over Giulio Romano, Pierino del Vaga, Giovan Franceschi [*sic*] Penni, Michelangelo [*sic*] Caravaggio, and their ignoble fellows over to oblivion. It is all they deserve."[19] Although this impressive tome succeeded in rescuing its subject from oblivion, the author's profile of the young Giulio was nonetheless judged too expansive. Giulio's proposed contributions to Raphael's late projects – and, by extension, his authorship of related drawings – were wrongly advanced at the expense of the master who, in Hartt's view, relinquished artistic control in many of the most important commissions of his later Roman period. Overzealous in awarding credit to Giulio, and succumbing to the temptation of "over-interpretation" in the effort to distinguish and separate individual hands,[20] Hartt in some respects seemed to revert to the by then discredited methodology of Morelli and his disciple Dollmayr.

An antidote of another kind was thus required. It was administered in Pouncey and Gere's masterful two-volume catalogue of drawings in the

British Museum, *Raphael and His Circle,* whose arguments were posited on the tripartite assumption that

it is more probable that stylistic innovations came from the still youthful master than from his followers; [that] there is no reason to suppose that Raphael, when barely out of his twenties, had already exhausted his prodigious capacity for development and his power of absorbing and transmuting current tendencies and initiating new ones; [and that] there is nothing in the underlying style of these late works which seems...inconsistent with the probable direction of Raphael's development so far as this can be inferred from his earlier, undisputed productions.[21]

Pouncey and Gere's catalogue located Raphael securely at center stage. His boundless capacity for *invenzione* and its implications for understanding his drawings was acknowledged, and his role as the head of an industrious, supremely organized and productive bottega whose talented members each possessed their own, distinctive styles was defined. In every entry, the grounds for proposing, endorsing, or dismissing an attribution were meticulously reasoned and carefully argued, often by recourse to a relevant painting, an archival document, or a related corpus of graphic works. So packed with information, much of it assembled for the first time, are these entries that they essentially function as "a series of small, independent monographs," as Konrad Oberhuber remarked in a lengthy review extolling the catalogue's fundamental contributions to the scholarship on Raphael and Raphael School drawings.[22] Some forty years after its publication, many scholars still find little ground for disagreement with the exegesis of Pouncey and Gere, whose catalogue remains an unsurpassed model of its kind.

Oberhuber was in a unique position to comment extensively and in great detail on the material covered by Pouncey and Gere because of his own immersion in the subject of Raphael drawings. (An addenda and corrigenda to their British Museum catalogue [pp. xvi–xvii] records insights on several drawings offered by Oberhuber after the volume had gone to press and was added primarily to register his opinions, which had significantly, if belatedly, influenced Pouncey and Gere's own thinking.) Like Fischel before him (whose unfinished work Oberhuber partially completed in a substantial ninth volume of the *Corpus*), he has made the study of Raphael, and particularly Raphael drawings, a focus of his life's work, publishing over the past four decades a steady stream of articles, reviews, and exhibition catalogues, as well as a monograph and a catalogue raisonné of drawings. Concentrating on the artist's later Roman period, Oberhuber from the outset has tenaciously maintained Raphael's primacy in the collaborative enterprises of his workshop, crediting him with the invention of compositions and, increasingly over time, with the execution of ever larger numbers of related drawings.

If his concept of Raphael the draftsman initially did not differ profoundly from that formulated independently by Pouncey and Gere, as his review of the British Museum catalogue makes clear, Oberhuber's thinking on the attribution question has undergone a dramatic metamorphosis over the years. Drawings that he once regarded as workshop products, often by the enigmatic Gianfrancesco Penni, "il Fattore," or as copies after lost designs, have of late been reassigned by Oberhuber to the master himself. In this construct – essentially an inversion of Hartt's, which diminished Raphael and elevated Giulio – Raphael has expanded from the center to encompass and indeed consume the periphery. As the current doyen of the study of Raphael drawings, Oberhuber's opinions have inevitably shaped recent debate on the subject among partisans and detractors alike, and they warrant review here.

The onset of Oberhuber's expansionist view of Raphael as a draftsman can be roughly traced to the Raphael year of 1983, the five-hundredth anniversary of the artist's birth, which generated numerous commemorative conferences, exhibitions, and publications. It began with a systematic questioning of the attribution of a group of drawings associated with Raphael's late fresco commissions – primarily the Vatican Logge and the Sala di Costantino – that scholars, notably Pouncey and Gere but also in some cases Oberhuber himself, had assigned to Penni. This was accompanied by a corollary proposal that some of the sheets in question were in fact by Raphael.[23] A logical progression from his earlier stated views on Raphael's graphic output – his willingness to see the master's hand in those disputed drawings occupying the problematic "gray area" of the attribution divide – Oberhuber's shifting opinion initially met with considerable support, including a typically measured and carefully formulated, if cautious and ultimately equivocal endorsement by Gere.[24]

Although chanting loudly, Oberhuber was not singing solo. A similar, though more circumscribed and restrained view was advanced at roughly the same time by John Shearman vis-à-vis two or three of these late drawings, whereas Sylvia Ferino Pagden, scrutinizing the other terminus of Raphael's activity, convincingly claimed for the artist a number of new or reattributed drawings from his early Umbrian and Florentine years.[25] All these investigations signaled the beginning of yet another phase in the study of Raphael drawings, one that endeavored to sharpen and refine (as well as expand) the contours delineating the graphic corpus of his early and late career. In focusing on those "gray areas" where Raphael intersected with Perugino at one end and with Giulio and Penni on the other, Oberhuber, Ferino Pagden, and other scholars writing on the occasion of the Raphael year of 1983 and its immediate aftermath sought to reassess and tackle the most vexing and longstanding problem in the connoisseurship of Raphael drawings.[26]

In this effort, exhibition catalogues provided the main channel for advancing new interpretations of Raphael as a draftsman. The British Museum, the Grand Palais in concert with the Louvre,[27] the Albertina, and the Palazzo Pitti in Europe, as well as the Pierpont Morgan Library in New York, all mounted major exhibitions of drawings in the mid-1980s commemorating the five-hundredth year of Raphael's birth. Several engaged in the Raphael-Perugino and Raphael-Giulio-Penni debates, manifesting a willingness to reconsider drawings that lay just beyond the margins of Raphael's accepted graphic corpus, particularly disputed sheets from the Umbrian and late Roman periods. (Some of those bore traditional attributions to Raphael but had been demoted by more recent criticism.)

As far as the late drawings were concerned, Oberhuber's contention that a number merited reevaluation was compelling. It also had far-reaching implications. A previously unrecognized aspect of Raphael's late style as a draftsman had been defined. Moreover, graphic evidence now existed documenting his creative involvement in late projects that, accordingly, could no longer be seen as strictly workshop productions. No more the master in absentia who had forsaken painting for architecture and personal advancement, as some critics had come to see him by the last years of his life, Raphael was restored to the role of active, "hands-on" head of his workshop, whose very mode of functioning and organization now needed to be reassessed.[28] Finally, Penni's convenient role as the "wastepaper basket artist" – the repository for Raphaelesque drawings that were too weak or inferior to be the work of Raphael or Giulio – of the Raphael School was no longer tenable, as his already vague personality as a draftsman began to be dismantled.[29] In the end, the picture of Raphael the draftsman that prevailed in 1983, while admitting some new attributions, did not differ fundamentally from that presented twenty years earlier by Oberhuber and Pouncey and Gere, but hindsight revealed this moment to be the fabled calm before the storm.[30] The revisionist undercurrent that was stirring in 1983 was about to explode into a tidal wave.

The Raphael year also engendered two substantial catalogue raisonnés of the artist's drawings: *The Drawings of Raphael* by Paul Joannides and *Raphael, die Zeichnungen*, by Oberhuber, Ferino Pagden, Eckhart Knab, and

Erwin Mitsch.[31] Joannides catalogued 460 sheets that he believed to be by Raphael. For Oberhuber et al. the tally was 619 drawings. The disparity can in part be accounted for by the exclusion of most architectural studies by Joannides and the inclusion of newly discovered drawings (among them some previously unknown versos[32]) by Oberhuber. Additionally, in the case of double-sided sheets, Joannides assigned a single catalogue number whereas Oberhuber et al. catalogued recto and verso separately. The remaining gap resulted from Oberhuber's transfer to the master of a number of drawings hitherto ascribed to his pupils Giulio and Penni. Because it surveyed his entire corpus of drawings rather than the holdings of a single collection, the 1983 catalogue by Oberhuber and his colleagues was the first systematic presentation of Raphael's newly burgeoning graphic oeuvre.[33]

Snapshots of the same subject taken from different vantage points, this pair of publications viewed in tandem revealed the beginnings of a rift that would subsequently come to polarize the field. Two distinct and essentially opposing schools of thought on the subject of Raphael drawings have emerged in their wake: the expansionist, revisionist approach championed by Oberhuber, which would see Raphael's graphic corpus vastly (and detractors would say, indiscriminately) enlarged; and the more restrictive, moderate view of Joannides, which in turn derives authority from the precedent of Pouncey and Gere and Parker, and – ironically – of Oberhuber in his preexpansionist mode.

The recent critical history of a drawing connected with the Vatican Logge decorations serves as a barometer of the broader debate. Executed in pen and ink with wash and squared for transfer, it is a *modello* for the fresco of *David and Bathsheba* in the eleventh bay (Fig. 21). In 1962, Pouncey and Gere ascribed it without hesitation to Penni, an opinion then endorsed and subsequently reiterated by Oberhuber.[34] In 1983, Gere and his then collaborator Nicholas Turner classified it under the rubric "school drawings" (a category synonymous with the aforementioned "gray area") without mentioning Penni's name in the entry.[35] Four years later, the drawing was catalogued as part of a group called "Raphael?" by Gere, who disclosed that Turner in 1983 "was inclined to demur and to wonder whether the drawing might not after all prove to be by Raphael himself," although that equivocal opinion was not recorded at the time. Gere acknowledged that Oberhuber's recently expressed expansionist views on the group of drawings connected with the Logge and other late Raphael workshop projects accounted for his own shift in opinion,[36] then proceeded to the observation that "once the possibililty of Raphael's authorship of one of the *modelli* is admitted, it becomes a theoretical possiblity for all the others."[37] Exercising qualitative

judgments of the sort that have been largely absent from recent pronounce-
ments, Gere stopped far short of admitting the whole group into Raphael's
graphic oeuvre. But the proverbial Pandora's Box had unquestionably been
opened.

One of the first scholars to endorse fully the expansionist view pro-
pounded by Oberhuber was Nicholas Turner. His unpublished pro-Raphael
stance of 1983, reported subsequently by Gere as noted earlier, was expressly articulated in two articles and a catalogue entry in which he argued
for Raphael's authorship of drawings variously ascribed to Penni and Giulio
Romano and, further afield, Battista Franco and Giacomo Cavedone. In some
cases resurrecting long-abandoned traditional attributions, Turner unilat-
erally pronounced in favor of Raphael, endorsing a historical view of his
draftsmanship that predated the more restrictive version forged by the modern critical tradition inaugurated by Passavant.[38] The same mind-set was
brought to bear on a group of stylistically homogenous red chalk drawings
that most scholars believed to be by Giulio, but of which Turner remarked,
"it is hard to resist the logical conclusion that they are by Raphael."[39]

Two substantial publications by Dominique Cordellier and Bernadette Py
that appeared in 1992 – a catalogue of the Louvre's holdings of Raphael
drawings and a related exhibition catalogue – significantly augmented the
number of drawings by or attributed to the master in that rich and histor-
ically important collection.[40] Most of the revised attributions pertained to
the contentious late drawings: in the past ascribed to Giulio, Penni, or more
cautiously and generically, the workshop, these were now given with varying degrees of conviction to Raphael, often on the authority of Oberhuber.
His published and verbal opinions are extensively cited, with dissenting
views rarely if ever ventured.[41] Cordellier and Py's *Raphaël, son atelier, ses
copistes* constitutes something of a milestone in the critical historiography
of Raphael drawings in being the first permanent collection catalogue to
sanction the enlarged conception of his draftsmanship.

In reformulating attributions, Cordellier and Py were inclined to upgrade
drawings from pupil to master. A different approach informs the exhibition
catalogue *Raphael and His Circle, Drawings from Windsor Castle* by Martin
Clayton, published in 1999.[42] Although Raphael's graphic oeuvre swells
slightly in these pages,[43] Clayton was more inclined to shift drawings later-
ally from one *garzone* in the workshop to another. Inspired by Oberhuber's
dismembering of Penni, he removed from his graphic oeuvre two drawings that had come to be regarded as signal works by "il Fattore," attributing them not to Raphael, as has been Oberhuber's wont, but to Perino del
Vaga.[44] Perino was also proposed, though without the cautionary "attributed

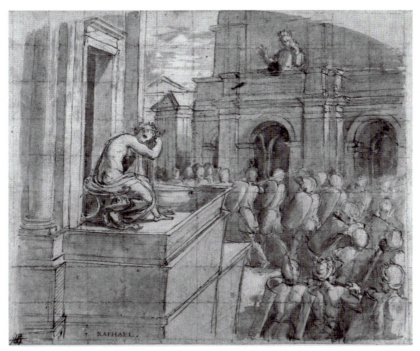

21. Raphael, Penni, or Perino del Vaga?, *David and Bathsheba*, The British Museum, London.

to," as the author of a third sheet that had not previously been associated in the literature with the Raphael school. Admitting that the latter, a study of a *Battle Scene*, bears little resemblance to Perino's readily recognizable graphic style, Clayton nonetheless decreed that "his authorship of the drawing seems indisputable."[45] Its perceived stylistic affinities with the two formerly-Penni-now-Perino drawings in Windsor were adduced as the very evidence supporting those new attributions[46] – a circular argument that avoided comparisons with characteristic sheets from Perino's established graphic oeuvre (other than to remark on dissimilarities) and was based solely on its own authority.[47] A number of its controversial new attributions have been challenged, but Clayton's catalogue in a number of instances offers convincing proposals on such matters as function and chronology. In this respect, *Raphael and His Circle, Drawings from Windsor Castle* stands apart from the field of purely revisionist literature whose content is foremost a recitation of new attributions, primarily to Raphael, for well-known and obscure drawings alike.

The most extravagant, and extreme, presentation of Raphael's "revised and expanded" graphic oeuvre is the 1999 exhibition catalogue *Roma e lo*

stile classico di Raffaello, 1515–1527 by Oberhuber and his pupil Achim
Gnann.[48] Although it endeavored to illustrate a rather straightforward
theme – the formation and dissemination of a "classical style" in Rome in
the twelve years preceding the horrific sack of the city by imperial troops in
1527 – the exhibition had a troubling "covert purpose," to appropriate Paul
Joannides's phrase, namely, "the radical enlargement of Raphael's oeuvre."[49]
Single-minded and zealous in their quest to recognize his hand where it had
not previously been detected, the authors assigned to Raphael a dazzling
number of stylistically heterogeneous drawings that had resided securely
in boxes designated Giulio Romano, Penni, and anonymous. In a seeming demonstration of the ineffable pendulum phenomenon, the process
could fairly be described as Dollmayr in reverse, with equally retrogressive
consequences. Oberhuber in 1999 had indulged in precisely the same
"over-interpretation in the discerning of hands" for which he had criticized
Frederick Hartt nearly forty years earlier. The dubious result was a troubling attributional "minefield," as Catherine Monbeig Goguel remarked in
a review in 1999.[50]

With Goguel's review, the alarm that many specialists had long felt was
finally sounded in print. One of the first published dissents opposing the expansionist trend that has dominated recent discussions of Raphael's draftsmanship, it condemned a flawed approach in which subjective judgment
and idiosyncratic personal opinion masquerade as critical methodology.[51]
Precisely analogous criticisms were registered by Joannides the following
year in another review that likewise took issue with both the myriad problematic attributions and the broader, likewise problematic revisionist school
of thought.[52] Formulating what may be called the cautionary "Parable of
the Stepping Stone,"[53] Joannides also called attention to a further disturbing phenomenon of the revisionist trend – the conferring of immutable
authority and canonical status on subjective attributions of precisely the
type that both he and Goguel decried. Accepted as dogma, these come to
provide the flimsy groundwork for advancing further, even more dubious
proposals – an indicator of just how perilous the current state of the study
of drawings by Raphael and his followers has become.[54]

Finally, a like-minded stance against the expansionist-revisionist trend
in Raphael drawings scholarship was recently taken by this writer, who
protested the willful dismembering of the autonomous and internally coherent personalities of Raphael, Giulio, and Penni as draftsmen. Defending
Giulio's graphic oeuvre against incursions by Raphael "attributionists," that
argument attempted to formulate an objective set of criteria for recognizing
his early drawings, and in so doing to distinguish them from Raphael's late

drawings.[55] By explicitly describing the hallmarks of Giulio's Roman-period drawings from ca. 1516 to ca. 1522, the late graphic manner of Raphael was implicitly defined as well. The point, in its most reductive distillation, was that (legitimate claimants to the "gray area" notwithstanding[56]) a drawing manifestly by Giulio (or Penni) could not be by Raphael. At once obvious and self-evident, this premise needed to be reiterated precisely because it has been conspicuously absent from the expansionist debate. No novel interpretations of either Raphael's or Giulio's drawing styles in the period ca. 1515–1520/22 were offered; rather, the views rigorously set forth by Oberhuber in his 1972 volume of Fischel's *Corpus*, but abandoned in his more recent discussions, were endorsed.

Far from presenting a compelling new construct of Raphael's draftsmanship, the expansionist campaign has been waged to the detriment of all parties. Late Raphael has become an unrecognizable, schizophrenic catchall, Penni has imploded, and Giulio, diminished but not entirely vanished, remains little more than a repository for the remaining detritus. Joannides' description of this vexatious state of affairs as a disaster, if intentionally hyperbolic, was not unwarranted.[57] Revisionism in the study of an artist's drawings is not in itself egregious – witness the richer and more nuanced understanding of Michelangelo as a draftsman that has been formulated in recent years, or the clarified personality of the enigmatic Jacone, whose graphic oeuvre and, consequently, artistic identity has been slowly reconstituted over the past quarter century.[58] But revisionism undertaken with declarative rhetoric as its principal arsenal and augmentation as its unwavering objective deserves to be challenged, as opponents of the approach have urged. In the case of Raphael and his followers Giulio Romano and Gianfrancesco Penni, the current picture is far murkier than the one that prevailed forty years ago, when Oberhuber, Pouncey, and Gere carefully constructed their group portraits, or even twenty years ago when Raphael's quincentenary was celebrated – an evolution that can hardly be considered progress. As the critical study of Raphael drawings enters the twenty-first century, it is to be hoped that the thesis-antithesis-synthesis principle of the swinging pendulum will obtain, and that the extreme "attributionist" views will be abandoned in a return to the rigors of moderation.

10 Classicism, Mannerism, and the Relieflike Style

Marcia B. Hall

Since the seventeenth century Raphael was seen to embody the classic style and to be the source of mannerism. He shared these responsibilities with Michelangelo in varying degrees, depending on the writer. Historians in the past generation have become uncomfortable with style labels, and particularly with period style labels. Although art historical textbooks still use these labels, many scholars in their writing avoid them. As the essays in this volume indicate, recent studies of Raphael have focused on a host of issues, such as patronage; the papal court and its revival of ancient Rome; Raphael's workshop and the division of labor within it; and the technical examination of his paintings to understand their construction and technique, or their condition. Much attention has been given in recent scholarship to political messages that the work of art may contain, or the political situation surrounding the work's creation. In the case of Raphael, an example would be Rolf Quednau's study of the Sala di Costantino.[1] Many of John Shearman's studies have contributed new contexts in which we now see Raphael's works. His book on the Tapestry Cartoons is an example.[2] His two studies analyzing the drawings and documents for the Stanze to show how the designs were developed and changed, and how they related to the function of the rooms and contemporary events are classics.[3] It is clear that interest has shifted in recent scholarship to the context of the particular work of art in the effort to account for its particularity; hence, there is little attention now given to the features that it may share with other works, both by the same artist and by his contemporaries.

In this situation the style labels left over from an earlier era, when aesthetic judgments ruled, can seem obsolete. When we regard each work as unique, it becomes difficult to step back and make generalizations that do not need endless qualification. Nonetheless, the constructs of classicism and mannerism have an important history and play an important role in our understanding of sixteenth-century art and of Raphael in particular. Mannerism is a label on which there is still little agreement, but it is the term most frequently used to identify the art produced in central Italy in the cinquecento after the death of Raphael. Little has been added to the discussion of the style since the lively debate of the 1960s died down. When asked to write a book on mannerism by Cambridge University Press in the mid-1990s, I discovered that the contextual studies of Rome made in the past generation allowed me now to see late Raphael and his followers' art in a new light. Earlier writers recognized that late Raphael, and then his successors, were often emulating sculpture in their paintings, but the full implications for the spirit and character of post-Raphaelesque art were never drawn. Now that we understand more fully the way antique culture was permeating life in Renaissance Rome, it is possible to appreciate these implications and to revise our understanding of the period 1520–1600 accordingly.

Although it is evident that there is much dissatisfaction abroad concerning the definition of the first two decades of the cinquecento as the High Renaissance and the period of the classic style, a new history has not yet been undertaken. There are hints, however, that it may be about to be redefined. Recent scholarship has focused on the tension that painters around 1500 felt between the requirements of art and the devotional function of the altarpiece.[4] Recognition that reform began to be a vital issue of concern with Savonarola in the last decade of the quattrocento suggests that the painters may have begun to rethink the questions of religion and art already at this time. Religious uncertainty produced not only programs to reform the institution of the Church, but parallel and simultaneous searching on the part of artists to find a satisfactory resolution of these tensions.[5] Raphael's altarpieces, in particular, can be interpreted as revealing a process in which he confronted the problem, culminating with the solution presented in his last painting, the *Transfiguration*, completed just before his death.[6] For the present moment, however, we are concerned with the understanding of the High Renaissance and the classic style, and mannerism as it has evolved from the sixteenth until the late twentieth century.

This essay provides historiographical background of the definitions of classicism and mannerism as applied to Raphael and his successors as these have come down to us. It describes the relieflike style, as identified by me in *After Raphael*,[7] and extends the exploration of its origins and its relationship to other aspects of mannerism begun there.

What was meant by the *classic* in Raphael's art in formal terms can be shown using the analyses of the two great scholars of the classic style, Heinrich Wölfflin and Sydney Freedberg.[8] For Wölfflin, the frescoes of the early Roman period in the Stanza della Segnatura and the Stanza d'Eliodoro represented the pinnacle of the style. To give the complete picture of what constituted the classic style, we need to integrate the study of its symbolism, or iconography, represented most importantly by Ernst Gombrich,[9] with these formalist analyses. These scholars shared a confidence that the period covered by the first two decades of the cinquecento in central Italy represented one of the moments of highest achievement in Western culture. Their willingness to make such value judgments sets them apart from writers today who take a more pluralistic stance and admit no absolutes. These scholars recognized certain qualities of ideality, harmony, unity, and seriousness that characterized this art and which they identified as the features of the classic style. The Stanza della Segnatura, and particularly the *Disputa* (Plate 19) can serve to exemplify Raphael's middle period and the essence of his classic style.

Gombrich explained how the program for the Stanza della Segnatura boldly demonstrated how each of the four disciplines represented on the walls attains truth, at the same time showing that all are paths to the same unified Truth. The ceiling lays out the program. In each of the quadrants is an allegory representing the discipline on the wall below. The scrolls they hold indicate the particular path of that discipline to knowledge of the truth. Thus, the philosophers in the *School of Athens* use rational thinking, the poets on *Parnassus* employ intuition, and *Jurisprudence* makes use of a honed sense of justice; only the theologians in the *Disputa* receive divine revelation. The whole intellectual enterprise is seen as striving toward that goal of finding a single Truth, approached through these several paths. The very grandeur, simplicity, and assurance of the conception are distinguishing marks of the classic style. The confidence to make such bold claims, untrammeled with provisos, to universality and wholeness was lacking in the periods that both preceded and succeeded.

Gombrich went on to identify the genre to which this kind of decoration belongs, and then to contrast Raphael's treatment with earlier examples. The genre is the Famous Men, who frequently peopled the walls of libraries, and were to be found in other locations as well. Most relevant to Raphael was Perugino's fresco campaign in the Cambio in Perugia at the turn of the century, which Raphael certainly knew.[10] There, as was typical of the genre, great men stand side by side, exemplifying the virtues whose personifications appear on the clouds above their heads, each labeled for easy identification. In Raphael's rethinking of this tradition in the Segnatura, he has indeed included the famous men one would expect to find, but they are shown participating in the search for truth. They interact with one another, and the scenes have been dramatized to turn them each into narrative events.

In the *Disputa*, the theologians are gathered to meditate on the meaning of the Eucharist. Formalists Wölfflin and Freedberg appreciated how, in departing from the tradition of the Famous Men, Raphael reinvented it by putting them in action, assigning each a different role: Jerome reading, Gregory meditating, Ambrose in visionary ecstasy, Augustine dictating – the successive stages of writing a theology. The auxiliary figures connect and articulate the flow through the composition. Nothing is left of the staccato isolation of individual figures that we see in quattrocento precedents. Nor do we find chatty, naturalistic asides, meant to persuade us of the actuality of what is depicted. The high seriousness of each figure invests the scene with a new solemnity. The stately rhythm that joins the figures conveys both the gravity and the harmony of their enterprise.

Raphael organized the scene around the vertical axis, which descends from God at the top of the lunette surrounded by angels, to Christ at the center of seated Apostles and patriarchs, from whom emanates the dove of the Holy Spirit, carried to the world below by angels holding the four books of the Gospel. At the center of the assembly of theologians is an altar bearing a monstrance and a host. A problem for many readers today is that these writers assumed an understanding of Christian theology that we no longer have. Ingrid Rowland, in response to this situation, shaped her analysis in this book to the modern reader by placing the fresco in the context of intellectual history. She refers to Renaissance texts that reveal theological meanings, the nuances of which – lost to us – would have been unconsciously absorbed by Pope Julius and his visitors when they were embodied in the frescoes.

What marks this as a work in the classic style at the level of composition is the focus Raphael gives with the same stroke to the form and to the content. The viewer's eye is led down the central axis by circles of gold of diminishing size to the host on the altar. The tiny circle surrounding the host is likewise the vanishing point of the perspective system, laid out in the pavement. The rationality of perspective converges with the revelation that descends from on high. The theologians in the earthly zone formulate rational language to translate the mystery revealed to them, and to us, in the vision of the presence of the Trinity in the sacramental host.

Raphael is not concerned, any more than was Michelangelo in his contemporaneous *Sistine* vault, with persuading us that this is a scene from daily life. Quite the contrary, the quotidian has been excluded in favor of representing a more elevated, idealized realm. We have entered here the world of contemplation, removed from the noise of ordinary life and its distractions. The tools at the command of the artists – composition, color, light, figure type, pose, gesture – have been put in the service of conveying a higher and more harmonious reality.

With his color Raphael chose to subdue the bright hues and sharp contrasts that animate quattrocento frescoes. Color plays an important role in the creation of the "chorded harmony of the whole design" of which Freedberg wrote, using the metaphor of music. Carefully selected tones blend the drapery of one figure with the adjacent one, fusing the group into "a chord of which the resonance is much more than the addition of its parts."[11] Heightened contrast demarcates the edge of another group. Just how carefully Raphael calculated these effects is shown by comparing with the frescoes in the next room. In the Eliodoro, where the subjects are historical events, Raphael intensified the contrasts and hardened the edges selectively for emphasis and dramatic effect (Plates 21–22).

Raphael massed light and shade to the same end, rather than illuminating each figure individually and equally, as his predecessors had done.[12] His figures have become broader, and they occupy more space; they are unified in contour but internally complex,[13] the lesson the young Raphael was striving to learn from Leonardo in Florence in such paintings as *La Belle Jardinière* and the *Canigiani Holy Family* (Plates 6, 9). His ponderations are stately, not the abrupt, jerky movements of his predecessors. The gestures his figures make create beautiful flowing lines; they are not the angular and jagged movements the quattrocento painters used to give animation to their compositions. Freedberg noted that the figures have a new magnitude and clarity of action, "a deliberation, a decorum, and even a stateliness that reflects, but even more ennobles, the ideal of behavior of the classicizing Roman court."[14] Imbedded in this last remark we may discern an oblique allusion to a famous contemporary book describing the appropriate behavior of a gentleman, Baldassare Castiglione's *The Courtier*, but Freedberg gives us no explicit reference.

Here, then, in capsule, is how the scholars of the classic style presented Raphael in his middle period. Like the classic style they described, their analysis excluded all that might distract from the purity, harmony, and unity of the image. Patronage, payment, politics – all the contextualizing factors that occupy art historians today were almost ignored. How this view of High Renaissance art had been arrived at is an interesting story in itself, and one we need to understand to appreciate the interpretation of Raphael's late period in which the scholars of the classic style, particularly Wölfflin, saw decline and the beginnings of mannerism.

The idea that the art of Raphael and Michelangelo achieved a perfection was already the premise of Giorgio Vasari's *Lives*.[15] Vasari placed Michelangelo at the absolute pinnacle of artistic accomplishment, but his scheme credited the artists at the beginning of the *terza età* (the cinquecento) with perfecting the technical means of art. From that point forward, artists had these means at their disposal and could explore artistic expression in their own personal styles.[16] If the word "classical" was not applied to the High Renaissance until romanticism, nevertheless the concept of the High Renaissance as having produced a style that was not only "of the highest rank" – the definition of classic – but also authoritative and worthy of imitation, arrived early on the scene. Giovanni Pietro Bellori, without using the terms, wrote about Raphael in the seventeenth century as though his style were both classic and embodying classicism.[17] Even at the end of the sixteenth century the Carracci were using the masters of the High Renaissance, above all Raphael, in their art and in their academy as authoritative models to be imitated.[18] The art of the Carracci, called "classicism" in retrospect, engendered the whole movement in the seicento that was later characterized as the alternative to the baroque, another term invented long after the fact.[19]

It was Johann Joachim Winckelmann who, in 1763 in his *Geschichte der Kunst des Altertums*, created the model of a systematic stylistic development that departed from Vasari's by postulating a final, necessary phase of decline.[20] Winckelmann analyzed Greek artistic development in terms of a five-stage organic process: (1) the archaic, (2) the high or sublime style of Phidias, (3) the beautiful style from Praxiteles to Lysipppus, (4) the imitative or eclectic style of the Romans, and 5) the decline or decadence. Winckelmann saw this pattern repeated in the Renaissance and so extended his analysis to that period: (1) archaic before Raphael, (2) a high style in Leonardo and mature Raphael, (3) a beautiful style in Correggio, (4) an eclectic style in the Carracci and their followers, and 5) a period of decadence commencing at the time of Maratta. These were the terms Winckelmann used; they did not include "classical" or "classicism," although the concept is certainly implied.

Those words in the stylistic sense were introduced in the nineteenth century, together with "baroque," by the romantics who needed terms to express the tension they found between reason and feeling.[21] These labels tell us as much about the time that invented the label as they do about the period that they intend to describe, as is frequently pointed out. Heinrich Wölfflin developed the concept of *classic style* to characterize the High Renaissance, and in *Principles of Art History*, he codified the contrast between

Renaissance classical and baroque.[22] His labels remain the most influential today, but here, too, the context in which he was writing profoundly affected his vision. The term "classic style" was introduced in the title of Wölfflin's book, *Die klassische Kunst*, published in 1899 and translated first in 1903 as *Classic Art*. Wölfflin identified in the style of Leonardo, Michelangelo, Raphael, Fra Bartolomeo, and Andrea del Sarto, features they have in common and that are distinct from the preceding early Renaissance. He reveals some of his criteria for distinguishing the classic style when he compares the early Raphael, who, he says, at this point in his development could hope at best to become "a second, perhaps better, Perugino," with the mature classical Raphael.

The Umbrian sentimentalist became the painter of great dramatic scenes; the youth who seemed shy of earthly reality became a painter of humanity, with a firm grip on physical appearances; Perugino's linear style became more and more painterly and the taste for calm beauty gave way to the need for bold massing – this is the Roman, adult master.[23]

He speaks of a charming and "chatty" style in the early Renaissance, which becomes "grave" in the classic style. Wölfflin was seeking to define what we sometimes call today the "period eye," the High Renaissance way of seeing the world. In *Principles of Art History* he called it a mode of perception,[24] which, he contended, changed with each period.

Wölfflin was, of course, influenced by the context in which he was living. We find it odd in the light of twentieth-century investigations of Renaissance Rome, which have exposed the pervasiveness of antique influence in every aspect of life, that Wölfflin denied that the classic style imitated antique Roman culture: "It was not an imitation of a foreign prototype – the Antique," he asserts. This curious statement is somewhat elucidated by what follows: "it is no spindly hot-house plant but one grown in the open fields in the full strength of vigorous life."[25] Wölfflin made it clear that for his contemporaries, centuries of copying plaster casts of antique statues as the means of learning how to be an artist had vitiated that tradition to the point where they could not imagine that it could inspire a new style. They stood at the opposite end of the trajectory of classicism, at the moment, four hundred years later, of its exhaustion.

Another anomaly of Wölfflin's analysis is that he could not encompass the late Raphael in his conception of the high style or the classic style. In his view, the Stanza d'Eliodoro was the pinnacle, unequalled by anything that succeeded it; it "furnished the pattern of monumental narrative for all time."[26] In the works after c. 1514 Raphael relied too heavily on the workshop, especially in the large-scale frescoes. The works that escaped his condemnation were in large measure oil paintings where workshop intervention was more limited. They include the *Saint Cecilia* (Plate 26), the portraits of Baldassare Castiglione (Plate 16) and Leo X (Plate 15), and the upper half of the *Transfiguration* (Plate 33). On the paintings he judged to be by the workshop he is unequivocal, however: "Strident in colour, ignoble in composition, theatrical in gesture, and above all, lacking in proportion, the products of Raphael's workshop must be accounted, for the greater part, among the most unpleasing pictures ever painted."[27]

What Wölfflin has done is to collapse Winckelmann's organic model of stylistic development and to see Raphael as a microcosm of the whole trajectory. His earliest style before Rome is still archaic, related to Perugino and the early Renaissance; there is a brief but glorious flowering of the high style, c. 1508–14, then his workshop carries it forward into inevitable decline. This accelerated development was necessary for Wölfflin because he discerned, unlike Winckelmann, a radical break between the sixteenth and seventeenth centuries. As he saw it, the seventeenth century was "neither a rise nor a decline from the Classic, but a totally different art."[28] He was able to account for the period that follows, c. 1520–1600, between the classic style and baroque (which interval he totally disregarded), as the period of decadence. It provided the necessary buffer zone so that a "totally different art" could be seen to emerge in the next century. The baroque is a twin peak along with the classic for Wölfflin. Interestingly, he does not mention Caravaggio or even the Carracci. The whole concept, dear to historians since Bellori, of the renewal of art in Annibale Carracci is disregarded by Wölfflin. Eventually scholars would enlarge Wölfflin's boundaries to incorporate all of Raphael in classicism, but not until considerable discussion of the interval 1520–1600 and the attempts to define mannerism had taken place.

Later scholars tempered Wölfflin's condemnation of Raphael's late style. Frederick Hartt admired mannerism and appears to have found it more interesting than the classic style. He found the origins of mannerism in the Stanza dell'Incendio, which he attributed to a very precocious Giulio Romano.[29] Although more recent scholarship has returned to Raphael credit for the design and even to some extent the execution of much that Hartt had taken away, Hartt recognized correctly that a new model was being followed in the *Fire in the Borgo* (Plate 23) and the *Battle of Ostia*. His attribution was wrong, but his analysis was frequently brilliant.

Hartt, refining Wölfflin, attributed to Raphael's principal pupil, Giulio Romano, responsibility for much of the workshop production beginning with the Stanza dell'Incendio. In the *Fire in the Borgo* Hartt recognized sculpture as a new model and the source as imperial Rome: "It is to Roman sacophagi, Roman historical reliefs, Roman triumphal arches that we must look for the sources of Giulio's peculiar style."[30] He eloquently described "statues set in lumbering motion," "statuesque inertia," "folds of cloth that seem like sheets of stone." Hartt noted with dismay and disbelief the departure from perspective in the *Battle of Ostia*. "Perspective, that hard-won symbol of spatial harmony, subsuming all visual phenomena under one embracing system, has here been ignored. A Renaissance artist has turned his back on the achievements of the Renaissance, and has revived medieval or even late classical modes of spatial formulation."[31] He recognized that the spatial organization, with its frieze of figures across the front, which appear to protrude outward toward the viewer, was new. "This is the principle active in Roman sacophagus relief, wherein forms pile upward and outward from a background which is at no point clear."[32] His analysis is admittedly ingenious, but like Wölfflin, his conception was too circumscribed, and he was incapable of enlarging his Raphael to admit this kind of innovation. Freedberg recognized that Raphael was exploring new directions in the Stanza dell'Incendio. What he found in the *Fire in the Borgo* was that Raphael was stretching the limits of the classic style, rupturing that unity of form and content that had distinguished the earlier Stanze. There is more frantic activity than the subject seems to call for, and the rendering of the figures in these expressive poses – carrying water, escaping the flames by climbing the wall, or fleeing with their families – seems more the subject than the miracle of quenching the fire being wrought by the pope.[33]

Hartt loved to legislate. He deduced from the paintings laws that governed Raphael's composition, and then he ruled that when violations were found it proved that Raphael could not have been the author. Scholars were skeptical of Hartt's conclusion that this must be the work of Giulio Romano,[34] and they eventually took back for Raphael much that Hartt and Wölfflin had taken away.[35] The debate has continued, often centered in the drawings, as Linda Wolk-Simon shows in her essay in this collection.

Freedberg never discussed Wölfflin, but his book is an extension and revision of *Classic Art* written at a distance of two generations. The new elements that had entered Raphael's style beginning in the Stanza dell'Incendio he believed contained the seeds of the mannerist style that would appear after the master's death. He called this a "faulted classicism," in the sense of a geological fissure.[36] He nevertheless encompassed all of Raphael in the classic style. That fissure was opened and exploited after Raphael's death, when his powerful example was removed. Unlike Wölfflin and Hartt,

Freedberg was able to appreciate the innovations of Raphael in his late works. He understood the painter to be "freer from control by a single, synthetic ideal of style." He spoke of "the phase of classical development succeeding maturity," avoiding reference to decline or decadence, but making use of the biological metaphor. In this phase of Raphael's development there is diversification of modes appropriate to particular thematic matter.[37]

What we can now see is that Raphael experimented in his final years with modes of composition that he derived from his study of classical antiquity, in particular of late antique relief sculpture. It was there that he derived permission to shift the focus to form, for there is more precedence, in fact, for aestheticism in this antique art than there is precedence for the classic style. It is from this concern with formal values at the expense of content – which Michelangelo shared with Raphael – that the painters of the next generation derived their permission to follow suit. As we shall see, another aspect of this assertion of the primacy of form over content has been found in Raphael's *Saint Cecilia* (Plate 26), which also became a model for the next generation in their search for a new beauty.

Hartt was only one of many commentators who have recognized that some of Raphael's late paintings came to resemble sculpture and that this became a significant aspect of style in the years following Raphael's death. Chief among these scholars is Craig Smyth, who traced the peculiar conventions of the figure that begin to dominate much of central Italian painting in the wake of Raphael to their source in late antique sarcophagus reliefs.[38] Study of the monumental mural cycles by Raphael's followers that became so important in this period reveals that the model of the Sala di Costantino, and particularly the *Battle of the Milvian Bridge* (Plate 32), lay behind not only the works of Raphael's direct descendents, Giulio Romano, Perino del Vaga, and Polidoro da Caravaggio, but also of that next generation who were formed in Florence but came to Rome: Salviati and Vasari in particular, and Bronzino, who visited Rome but whose career was in Florence.

Smyth recognized that the artists in their search for a new beauty created a new set of conventions for composing their figures. He pointed out, for example, the tendency to force the figures flat against the picture plane, an effect then reinforced with flat light. Figures often twist abruptly in two or three directions, and the limbs, given unusual prominence, enhance the twist. These compositions often lack a focal point. It was Smyth's brilliant insight to see that these conventions were imitated from late antique sculptural relief. This style I have therefore called the relieflike style. The style has a history of its own and was codified, rather than invented, by Raphael in his late career.

The new mode of composition developed by Michelangelo and Raphael was an alternative to the time-honored – and somewhat exhausted – system of linear perspective for organizing space that had been in use for almost a century. Certainly Mantegna deserves much credit for having first explored this avenue, and he was probably responsible for awakening interest in an antiquarian style in Rome when he painted the now lost frescoes in the Villa Belvedere in the late 1480s.[39] In Florence, perhaps as early as the late 1470s, Bertoldo had created a bronze relief of a battle (Florence, Museo Nazionale) in which he based his composition on a late antique sarcophagus,[40] rather than creating a pictorial relief utilizing single point perspective in the usual manner of Donatello, Ghiberti, and the other sculptors. Michelangelo would have been familiar with this piece because it was installed over a fireplace in the Medici Palace, where the young Michelangelo had been taken in by Lorenzo il Magnifico as a member of the household. His own marble relief of the *Battle of the Centaurs* (Florence, Museo Nazionale) pursues a similar experiment in nonpictorial relief. There is no space except that created by the figures, which are piled up to fill the field in the manner of antique relief. The space of the relief projects toward the viewer, rather than backward illusionistically. Michelangelo then continued his exploration of this alternative to linear perspective, this time for a painting, in his *Battle of Cascina* fresco, which he had to leave unfinished when he departed Florence for Rome. Our evidence for this composition is engravings, which no doubt exaggerate the hard-edged, sculptural appearance (compared with the artist's surviving sketches), but the relieflike composition and some of the conventions of twisting figures with prominent limbs cataloged by Smyth are already evident.[41] When he came to paint the Sistine vault, Michelangelo tried traditional linear perspective in his first narrative scene, the *Deluge*, and discovered that a composition using deep space was not legible from the floor. Thereafter, beginning with the other Noah scenes, he employed the relief model. The figures are held close to the picture plane, and they nearly fill the height of the field; there is only a rudimentary setting.

Some time after the Sistine was unveiled late in 1512, Raphael began experimenting with the relieflike mode in the Stanza dell'Incendio and simultaneously in the borders for the Sistine tapestries, which were conceived as fictive bas-reliefs.[42] We have seen that Hartt recognized the source of the new mode of composition in the Stanza dell'Incendio as Roman imperial relief sculpture, but it is also likely that Raphael was responding to Michelangelo's innovations in the Sistine vault. Raphael was always the painter who could assimilate influence and absorb it into his own stylistic language, as he had done with Leonardo in his Florentine period, and before that, with Perugino.

What may have been for Michelangelo a solution to a problem of legibility became in Raphael's hands a mode of composition that was not intended to replace linear perspective, but would offer an alternative. He expanded his style to include this kind of emulation of revered antique art. It could be said that he even surpassed antiquity in adapting it to painting. His patron Pope Leo was a true antiquarian. Such imitation of the antique is in keeping with the finding of recent scholarship on Rome, as already noted.

Raphael's culminating expression of the relieflike style was not even painted by him, but by his workshop after his death: the *Battle of the Milvian Bridge* and the scheme of the Sala di Costantino were, however, designed by Raphael, according to recent scholarship.[43] The adjacent fresco tells the story of Constantine's vision. Preparing for battle against the eastern emperor Maxentius, Constantine was assured that if he carried the Christian cross into battle, he would be victorious.

It was probably a combination of conditions that led the painter to design the *Battle of the Milvian Bridge* (Plate 32) in the relieflike mode. The room is long and narrow, and the *Battle* occupies the long wall. Given its extent, it would have been impossible to create a satisfactory illusion with perspective because the viewing distance – the length of the short walls – was not anywhere near sufficient. (For perspective to work the viewer needs to be able to stand at a distance of at least one and a half times the width of the picture viewed.[44] The viewing distance in the Sala di Costantino was only about half the width of the *Battle*.) There were, of course, many antique models of battles treated as a frieze, notably the whole class of battle sacophagi. But possibly the most cogent reason for Raphael to treat the scene as a frieze was that this was not a real battle at all. When Constantine proceeded onto the battlefield holding the cross, the army of Maxentius was swept away into the Tiber. A clash of equal forces rising to a crescendo at the center, as in Leonardo's *Battle of Anghiari*, was not the story to be told here. The processional movement of the composition from left to right, made possible by the relieflike style, suited the subject far better than traditional perspective. There could not have been a more appropriate choice for the fourth-century narrative than the late antique style that was regularly used to depict battles at the time this battle actually took place.

That match of style to story is among the most compelling reasons to attribute the conception to Raphael himself, even if in the execution Giulio Romano and the bottega (now under his and Francesco Penni's direction) exaggerated the exertions of the soldiers in the interest of creating arresting poses. The stylistic traits that we saw for the first time in the *Fire in the Borgo* are here evident everywhere. There is an urgency and a harsh insistence on effects of contrasts; the geometry is angular, no longer curvilinear; the identity of figures is stressed with hard edges and heightened chiaroscuro. We note again that the subject calls for urgency and stress, however, as the contemplative *Disputa* did not. This concern to match the style to the subject, which was a hallmark of the classic style, will continue to give way in the next generation, until we see the murderous King Saul appearing to dance as he poises to hurl a spear at David (Salviati), and we find a *Madonna and Child* so sensual that it might be mistaken for a *Venus and Cupid* (Parmigianino).[45]

This relieflike style is one direction that was embellished and extended after Raphael's death. Another was the development of physical beauty at the expense of emotional content, of which the Parmigianino just alluded to is an example. John Shearman saw this concern as central to the style of mannerism as he defined it. Raphael and Michelangelo were the inventors of this "new visual language" and "the inventors of the first vocabulary of the Mannerist style."[46] Works by Raphael like the *Saint Cecilia* (Plate 26) and the *Saint Michael* (Plate 27) are "incipiently Mannerist." His analysis of the Magdalen at the right of the *Saint Cecilia* altarpiece eloquently states his argument:

Tall of stature, impeccably composed in emotion and movement, she compels admiration, which is her function....Her clothing is brittle, formed upon the study of Hellenistic sculpture rather than real life, and metallic and a little unreal in color; the whole transformation freezes humanity out of her, but in compensation saturates her in beauty to a very high degree. Since it is beauty that is willed and artificial it is, and must be, beauty of a particular kind; like an exaggerated ideal, it is a departure from the universal.[47]

Such inventions as the cold, self-conscious beauty of Magdalen and the artificial grace of Saint Michael were the evident inspiration for Parmigianino, Primaticcio, Bronzino, and a host of artists gathered and discussed by Shearman. The relieflike style was not limited to large-scale decoration, but it served those projects particulary well. We might call this other kind of *maniera*, "the stylish style," using Shearman's term. There is much overlap between the two, and they both have their source in Raphael and Michelangelo. They have in common the preeminence of formal concerns over those of expression. In the language of the classic style, both sacrificed that unity of form and content that had characterized the period 1508–14.

Mannerism received intense examination in the 1960s, and the writers, like John Shearman, wished to show how it departed, unwittingly, from the classic style.[48] What Shearman, Smyth, and Freedberg have in common, despite their different emphases, is that they saw mannerism as intending continuity with High Renaissance classicism. Those artists felt they could improve on their models by emulating them. Freedberg understood the poignancy of their failure and the irony of the attempt. "To base one's forms on idealizations already made by others is to take them one step farther from the experience of nature and nearer to a realm of aesthetic abstraction. The very principles by which the Maniera artist professed his allegiance to the classical standards compelled him to betray them."[49]

Early-twentieth-century descriptions of mannerism saw it as a reaction and rebellion against classicism. For Walter Friedländer and Max Dvorak the artists were seeking a deeper spirituality.[50] The scholars who studied the style in the 1960s, although they debated certain issues, agreed that there was not evidence for an anticlassicism; rather, the artists were seeking to extend, and even surpass their great masters, Michelangelo and Raphael. Our understanding of the relationship of Raphael to the style of his successors continues to be refined and redefined, but there is never any doubt of his generative influence. As citizens of a world that recognizes many forms of artistic expression and credits them equally, we do not have to subscribe to the view that that brief moment of the classic style was superior to others or that what followed was inferior. Like Raphael's successors, we may find the simple statement, at which the classic style excelled, unconvincing and even impossible,[51] or we, like them, may yearn for a more ornamented beauty. Nevertheless, we can appreciate Raphael's extraordinary richness of invention and his ingenuity in constantly extending his style to meet new challenges without abandoning his sense of decorum, that is, the appropriateness of his style to his subject.

If it is possible to use the recent contextual studies to inform our understanding of style in the case of Raphael and the relieflike style, this may suggest that, in the future, when scholarship returns to concern with defining style, it will be able to use contextual studies to shed new light and see other such problems in a new perspective.

11 French Identity in the Realm of Raphael

Carl Goldstein

In spite of not being French, in spite of fundamental stylistic shifts and changes, Raphael lived on in the hearts and minds of French artists and art lovers over the course of three centuries and more. As much as he was adored by the English and Germans it was nothing compared with the French. This is an indisputable fact. It does not mean that his appeal was universal or that it was never contested. But even the periodic controversies revolving around his name only testify to his unique position in the history of French art: Raphael stood for French art as much as for Italian. This spell cast over the French could not have been anticipated and certainly was not inevitable. His stature as one of the great creative geniuses of Renaissance and European art history would not in itself account for it. More clearly involved, for one, was his position in the Renaissance tradition as that tradition was viewed from afar, and another, the determining conditions of French art history at the end of the Renaissance and later.

BACKGROUND AND ORIGINS

The beginnings were not particularly auspicious. The Renaissance master lured to the French court was not Raphael but Leonardo, who, according to legend, died in the arms of Francis I. Raphael had not been invited – Fra Bartolommeo, Cellini, and Michelangelo were among others who were. Although it is true that late in his life he painted works destined for French collections, the most famous the *Holy Family of Francis I*[1] commissioned by Pope Leo X as a gift to the French king, those sent were accorded places among no less esteemed works by other Renaissance masters: Leonardo, Michelangelo, Fra Bartolommeo, Andrea del Sarto, Pontormo, Titian, and others.[2] Nor was Raphael the clear favorite of French historians and critics.

That history was predominantly Italian and Vasarian, its Pantheon presided over by Michelangelo. Insofar as questions of history and criticism were discussed by French writers, they followed the lead of the Italians; references to Raphael in French texts before the mid–seventeenth century are vague and few and far between. It was no different among French artists. The dominant tendency in painting was "post-Raphaelesque," drawing principally on the Mannerist School of Fontainebleau; there are few if any traces of Raphaelesque classicism in sixteenth- or early-seventeenth-century French painting. So that in the one as the other, history and painting or theory and practice, a turn to Raphael involved not survival but revival and the reassertion of his classical style.

This was a process that did indeed begin in Rome, in theory and practice, in the early seventeenth century, gaining momentum from the 1620s on. The French artist Poussin, working in Rome, was one of its luminaries and a great exponent of the new classicism, which such of his friends as Remy Vuibert and Jacques Stella carried to Paris in the mid-1630s. At that time, they were joined by leading artists of the next generation who became founding members of the Royal Academy of Painting and Sculpture. This event, the creation of the academy in 1648, marks the beginning of a revolution in French taste grounded in the art of Raphael. The history of French art from this time on is the story of Raphaelism triumphant.

The earliest indication is a small book that was the first publication to emerge from the academy. Written by Abraham Bosse, its instructor in perspective and a major theorist of painting and engraving as well as author of books on perspective, it appeared in 1649: *Opinions on the Distinctions Between Different Styles of Painting, Drawing, and Engraving, and of the Relations Between Originals and Copies* (*Sentiments sur la distinction des diverses manières de peinture, dessin, et gravure, et des originaux d'avec leurs copies*).[3] This is a selective survey of painting from the Italian Renaissance through the early baroque conceived to change minds and reform taste. Mannerist art is dismissed, classic art extolled. Annibale Carracci is one of the classicists singled out for praise but neither he nor any of the others reached "perfection" – the distinction of the Vasarian Michelangelo, whom Bosse does not even mention! It is in the works of Raphael, he states, that good taste and the antique coalesce into incomparable perfection; these are the works that should serve as a beacon to French artists from this time – 1649 – on. Indeed, the aim of the academy, he affirms, is to produce "many Raphaels." The components of this perfection are then enumerated: marvelous compositions and arrangements of figures that are admirable in their poses and gestures and for their expressions, in short for works of such extraordinary power and unity that they cannot be improved on. They have, however, already been equalled. Here Bosse asserts a claim that was to echo through French art history and criticism: in Nicolas Poussin France has produced an artist whose works have reached the same high summit as Raphael's. Choosing Poussin as their model, painters confront a perfection no less singularly complete.[4] In a period intensely self-conscious of national identity, Raphael has been naturalized as a French artist.

Bosse's view was substantially confirmed by Fréart de Chambray in his *Idea of the Perfection of Painting* (*Idée de la perfection de la peinture*), 1662. He, too, extolled Raphael's perfection, bolstering his argument by confronting Raphael with Michelangelo, to the detriment of the latter: Raphael was the "good angel" of painting, Michelangelo the "bad." All the virtues catalogued by Vasari are as nothing as Michelangelo is exposed as a vulgar artist who flaunted accepted standards of decency; Raphael, by contrast, is the exemplar of grace, beauty, and decorum whose works should henceforth be regarded as models and guides – in every respect. This is where Fréart fell afoul of Bosse.[5] Raphael being "perfect," he must have carried out all the precepts of art to perfection. So logic dictated and so Fréart claimed. One of the precepts being perspective, with which French theorists were particularly preoccupied at this time, Fréart assumed that Raphael's *Judgment of Paris* (Plate 35),[6] as engraved by Marcantonio Raimondi, must have been carried out rigorously, according to the rules of one-point perspective. The paradox, however, as Bosse quickly pointed out, is that perfect as he was, Raphael was deficient when it came to this precept, his composition having been organized with several vanishing points rather than one. Bosse did not conclude, however, that Raphael was any less "perfect," only that henceforth artists be more careful in their application of the rules of perspective. Raphael's reputation remained intact.

Chambray was not alone in believing that Raphael's secrets might be discovered by means of a careful examination of his pictures. So it seemed, too, to the leaders of the academy, who subjected these works to the most careful scrutiny. This was done beginning in 1667, when a series of *conférences* or lecture-demonstrations was opened with an examination of Raphael's *Saint Michael* (Plate 27)[7]; a subsequent *conférence* was devoted to his *Holy Family of Francis I.*[8] It hardly seemed possible to find words adequate to express this relatively new-found admiration for an artist whose preeminence was already beyond dispute. Thus the *conférence* on the *Saint Michael* was opened with remarks about the admirable *contrapposto* of the figure and of the perfection of the drawing, with attention called to the flow of the contours of the arms and legs; no less extraordinary, the members were told, is the expression of divine grace radiated by the figure. The work was recommended, in sum, to all appreciative of the noble and sublime in art. Significantly, not everyone in the audience agreed. One of the artists present, after dutifully praising the work, suggested that it was not without its faults, the figure violating certain of the rules of anatomy. Nonsense was the reply. Raphael is so universal that it is inconceivable that he ever violated any of the rules, an assertion that was then "proven" to the satisfaction of the general membership. This point needs to be stressed: although Raphael was not the only artist honored with a *conférence*, great masterpieces by Titian and Veronese also having been brought out and examined at different times, he was the only one whose works were assumed by the leadership to be beyond criticism. (Titian, for example, was appreciated for his color and treatment of expression but roundly criticized for his drawing.) Of the masters discussed, Raphael eclipsed all others – except Poussin. Here again is that pairing that helps to explain Raphael's early hold on the French. It is summed up in remarks by Charles Le Brun on Poussin's *Israelites Gathering Manna in the Wilderness.*[9] Rehearsing the critical trope about an artist bringing together the different "parts" of painting, Le Brun argues that Poussin has joined the drawing of Raphael, to the color of Titian, composition of Veronese, and so forth, all necessary for true "perfection" – as though Raphael's works are somehow deficient. This was far, however, from Le Brun's mind. Raphael was to be no less a model to French artists than Poussin: Raphael and Poussin the two great exponents of classicism and exemplars of academic classicism.

The evidence for this linkage, it is to be noted, was abundant. For Poussin was not only another adherent of drawing and a great classic artist but one who clearly owed a considerable debt to Raphael. His figures, far from being generally Raphaelesque, were often based directly on prototypes in Raphael's paintings; his compositional arrangements were no less regularly inspired by Raphael's. In treating the Madonna and Child or Holy Family, for example, subjects especially closely associated with Raphael, Poussin borrows and modifies poses and arrangements found in such canonical works as the *Madonna di Foligno* (Plate 25) or *Holy Family of Francis I.*[10] His compositions are unmistakably Raphaelesque, with a comparable – or even more complete – unity achieved. Perhaps most Raphaelesque of all is Poussin's feeling for those types, poses, and arrangements suitable for conveying a sense of grandeur and nobility of spirit, a feeling that no doubt was instinctive and perhaps, as critics have from time to time claimed, distinctively French, but that obviously was strengthened through his study of Raphael's works. If at times Poussin's light was said to burn brighter, this was far from saying that Raphael's had gone out. That in the eyes of the academy it had not is proven by the place Raphael continued to occupy in its curriculum. As a guarantee of good faith and proof of dedication to their art, students sent to Rome for further study were expected to copy and recopy the great works of Raphael found there: the tapestries in the Vatican, the *Transfiguration* (Plate 33), *School of Athens* (Plate 17), and *Galatea* (Plate 28).[11] These copies in turn were given to beginning students in Paris to be copied, such copying considered foundational for their own development. Here we come to a key point whose importance for the French view of Raphael cannot be exaggerated: Raphael was known to French artists largely by means of reproductions and copies that they committed to memory during their early years of study and that continued to shape their understanding of the artist from that time on.

In the *Sentiments*, when discussing Raphael's greatness, Bosse refers not to actual paintings, to few of which he would have had access – and his readers even fewer – but to engravings by Marcantonio Raimondi, Cornelius Cort, and others.[12] Such were the engravings that served for Chambray's analysis, particularly *The Judgment of Paris* (Plate 35), engraved by Marcantonio after a composition by Raphael. Such engraved copies, as distinct from original drawings or paintings, were the means by which Raphael's inventions were disseminated throughout Europe, his reputation established, one, as earlier in the case of Dürer, far greater than could have been attained from one-of-a-kind originals. The *conférences* organized by the academy, in which originals were brought out and inspected, were the exceptions, the king's minister showing his support for the enterprise by arranging for the display of works from the royal collection. In the academy as elsewhere, the ordinary routine involved studying and copying not originals but engravings and drawings copied from the originals. Even those artists who eventually had the opportunity to stand in front of the originals in Rome saw them with eyes conditioned through the study of engravings. What this meant was that "Raphael" was to them, for one, largely an artist in black and white. It made no difference whether one work was a drawing, another a painting, in fresco or oil; mass and color were converted into line and tone, the line as such, which all the critics agreed was Raphael's singular achievement, made more regular and uniform.[13] The most popular engravings, moreover, were by Marcantonio after drawings by Raphael, *The Judgement of Paris, the Massacre of Innocents* (Plate 36),[14] and several others, engravings that are the same in all essentials. The same, for one, is a hieratic austerity, a nobility and pomp such as is associated with court culture, most of all that of Louis XIV and his successors. However receptive a classical and rational French "spirit" may have been, can it have been coincidental that Raphaelism took root in French soil during the Age of Absolutism and flourished so long as there was a king on the throne? To be sure, it did not share the fate of the king overthrown by the French Revolution, but by that time it had become an integral part of a professional tradition. To say it as clearly as possible, there is an obvious reason why Raphaelism reigned for so long in France: his art, as translated in the royalist academy, was central to the training of artists from the seventeenth century on, first in the academy itself and then in the Ecole des Beaux-Arts that took the place of the academy after the revolution; even those who in the end opposed the academy had been shaped by the Raphaelism with which they had been indoctrinated during their early training.[15]

That doctrine was most elaborately and systematically formulated in the early academy by its secretary, André Félibien, in an historical and critical work in the tradition of Vasari's *Lives*, the first such work, it is to be noted, to appear in France: *Discussions of the Lives and Works of the Most Excellent Ancient and Modern Painters* (*Entretiens sur les vies et sur les ouvrages des plus excellens peintres anciens et modernes*), published between 1666 and 1688. As Vasari, Félibien charts the progress of painting from ancient to modern times, crediting artists with their contributions to different areas or "parts": Titian for color, Correggio for the charm of his technique, Michelangelo for drawing and design – in which he was nevertheless surpassed by Raphael; learning from a variety of sources, Michelangelo among them, Raphael modified them to achieve perfection.[16] Such an "eclectic" procedure was acknowledged and endorsed, as noted, in the *conférences* of 1667 in a battle that had been waged earlier by Bosse and Chambray. By Félibien's time, a more vigorous attack on the Vasarian formulation had been led by Giovanni Bellori, who was associated with another academy, the Accademia di San Luca, and whose definitive statement appeared in his *Lives* of 1672 (*Le vite de pittori, scultori et architetti moderni*). Painting seems as though "descended from heaven," Bellori avers, "when the divine Raphael by his supreme drawing has raised its beauty to the summit of art, restoring to it all the graces of its ancient majesty and enriching it by the attributes that had once rendered it glorious among the Greeks and Romans."[17] The greatness of art since Raphael, whether by Annibale Carracci or Poussin, he goes on to argue, can be traced to its perfect conformity to the art of Raphael. This is the point of view that was taken up by Félibien, with the difference that to his mind the modern Raphael is Poussin alone. Félibien says in so many words that the works of Raphael and Poussin are sufficient for the production of further masterpieces, art apparently reducible to a single substance found in the works of these two greats; anything else is merely ancillary. The study – and copying – of this art at its source was facilitated by the founding of a branch of the French Academy in Rome in 1666. Ten years later, the French and Roman academies were amalgamated. (Bellori was made an honorary member of the French Academy in 1689.) Students arriving with a creed defined with reference to Raphael, found that system confirmed in the program of the Roman Accademia di San Luca. The art of the academy, which is to say the mainstream of French painting, would inevitably flow through Raphael.

THE BROAD MAINSTREAM

The above would hardly seem to apply to the rococo art of the eighteenth century. To think of that art is to call to mind the works of a Watteau or Fragonard that are not only different from Raphael's but would seem to have been conceived in opposition to their underlying principles. Moreover, it is well known that the original doctrine of the academy came under attack toward the end of the seventeenth century, particularly its almost exclusive attention to drawing and reverence for Poussin, a surrogate for Raphael. In the famous quarrel between *Poussinistes* and *Rubénistes*, an alternative was mooted, Rubens and color proposed as of at least equal importance as Poussin and drawing. Roger de Piles, the public standard-bearer of colorism, wrote in his *Idea of the Perfect Painter* (*Idée du peintre parfait*), 1699:

Many amateurs and connoisseurs of painting accept as an article of faith or trust in earlier authors, that all the perfection of painting resides in the works of Raphael....While Raphael was an ingenious composer and master draftsman, that he expressed the passions of the soul with an infinite grace and elegance, that he treated subjects with the greatest possible appropriateness and nobility, and that no other painter possessed as many parts of painting as he, it is nevertheless true that his grasp of color was not sufficient for rendering objects truly and vividly, that is imitating them perfectly.[18]

This notion of "simple truth" – as opposed to "ideal truth" – was to be the new cornerstone of painting; what matters is painting's directness and "naturalism," which depends primarily on color. Heir to a tradition tracing its origins to Giorgione and Titian, Rubens is the new champion for precisely the reasons he had hitherto been marginalized in the academy.

This is not to say, however, that Raphael was entirely displaced. For while his particular strength was said to be drawing, it was not on this alone that his reputation was based – as de Piles notes. If his too-great reliance on drawing leaves something to be desired, de Piles asserts, his high reputation is nevertheless justified on other grounds, on his handling of grace and of all those other things because of which he has been regarded as the first painter of the world ("premier peintre du monde"). In spite of his neglect of color, in other words, Raphael remains a remarkably complete artist. So de Piles reaffirmed in his notorious *Balance of Painting* (1708) assigning numerical values to the different "parts" of painting. Here Raphael is the only painter given a perfect 18 twice, for drawing and expression, for a total of 65 points – the same as Rubens. Poussin, by contrast, with a mere 53, comes in behind such artists as Domenichino (58) and Le Brun (56).[19] This is the change in academic doctrine, the reevaluation of Poussin, that was bound to have far reaching effects. Raphael's position was substantially unchanged, however, in theory and practice (Fig. 22). Students sent to Rome spent their time as before copying Raphael's masterpieces, and on the whole painting in the academy remained respectably Raphaelesque. With the exception of such truly exceptional artists as Watteau, painters gave Raphael his due while attempting at the same time to effect a synthesis of drawing and color. In this, at least, they bridged the seeming gap between the original doctrine of the academy and its modification at the beginning of the rococo.

A CRISIS

Overlooked in all these discussions and debates was one essential fact that eventually began to rankle: that an Italian artist had been placed at the head of the French school of painting. (The reputation of Poussin had had its ups and downs since the seventeenth century, the Poussin-Raphael linkage not as strong as it originally had been.) In a small book published in 1752, *Critical Reflections on the Different Schools of Painting* (*Réflections critiques sur les différentes écoles de peintures par M. le Marquis d'Argens*), the marquis d'Argens aimed to redress this imbalance and establish the essentially French, non-Italian roots of French painting, denying the importance for French art of artists of other national schools such as the Flemish as well; the greatest efforts and achievements of the French school stand apart from the others, he asserted, to which they are also superior. In question, then, was not only a break with the Italian school but also open rivalry with Raphael himself. France has produced an artist no less complete than Raphael, whom he has indeed surpassed. Who is this artist? Not that forerunner of Raphaelism in France, Poussin, but rather a completely homegrown

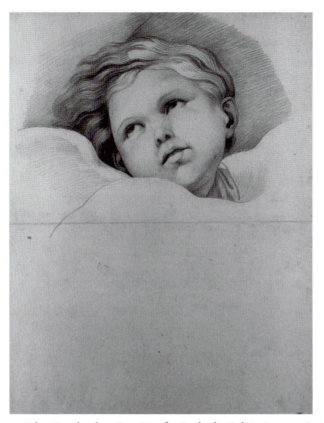

22. Edme Bouchardon, *Drawing after Raphael's "Galatea,"* c. 1725, Paris, Musée du Louvre, Cabinet des Dessins. Photo: Réunion des Musées Nationaux.

talent: Eustache Le Sueur. Never having visited Italy, Le Sueur could be considered all the more authentically and consistently French.

Admitting the impossibility of drawing a sharp line dividing the two, d'Argens argues both that Le Sueur compares favorably with Raphael and at times betters him.

The ideas of Raphael are simple, noble, natural: those of Le Sueur are as well.... Raphael's drawing is correct, varied according to the proprieties and always in the best taste; those of Le Sueur have the same qualities.... Raphael has demonstrated his genius in his grand compositions; those of Le Sueur are no less resounding, such as the painting of Saint Paul preaching at Ephesus.... Le Sueur had little knowledge of chiaroscuro; Raphael perhaps even less so.... Le Sueur's color is pale, Raphael's as well, and often less smooth.... Le Sueur, in striving for delicacy, at times makes his figures too light; Raphael, striving for correctness, can be dry and hard in his contours.... Le Sueur's landscapes are in the best taste; those of Raphael, in the

judgement of M. de Piles, very mediocre....Le Sueur did not only understand landscape better than Raphael, but...he often composed in a way that is more courtly
("galante") and picturesque ("pictoresque") than Raphael.

And d'Argens concludes:

Undoubtedly, this comparison will outrage many Italians. It could not be otherwise
since when one speaks of Le Sueur to them, they feign ignorance of both his works
and his name. We advise them, therefore, to come to Paris to see his works, as we have
always gone to Rome to see Raphael's. If they examine his works with an unprejudiced
eye, they will realize that we have in Paris a painter truly worthy of being compared
with Raphael.[20]

This sentiment was not d'Argens's alone, Le Sueur's reputation having for
some time been growing in Paris, surpassing even that of Poussin. In question here, however, is not whether Le Sueur's or Poussin's light burned
brighter or dimmer but of whether that of Raphael was in danger of going out altogether. For the claim, as noted, was that Le Sueur had not only
equalled but surpassed Raphael, a French artist to guide future generations
of French artists, rendering Raphael superfluous. Henceforth French painting would be exclusively and emphatically French. Let us examine this claim
in more detail.

The *Saint Paul Preaching at Ephesus* (Fig. 23) cited by d'Argens illustrates
a scene described in the Acts of the Apostles (19:1–20) in which Paul con-
verts the magicians of Ephesus, who then burn their evil books. Paul is
shown preaching in the center, in a symmetrical composition with corresponding figures on either side, gravitating toward this center with books
to be added to those scattered in the foreground. This onrush of figures is
carefully modulated, the movement itself suspended; there is no sense of
agitation or crowding, no confusion about which figure is where, in relation
to others or to the buildings to the side or in the background. Each figure
is an ample volume exactly placed in a space that it in turn controls. Put
succinctly, the closely felt relation between symmetrically arranged figures,
in a composition organized according to a sequence of zones or planes
parallel to the picture plane, is a hallmark of "classic" design and of French
classicism. It is characteristic more specifically of the classicism of the
French academy, of which Le Sueur was an original, founding member. The
Saint Paul was the culmination of a series of stylistic experiments dating
from the early 1640s and becoming increasingly classical with the foundation of the academy in 1648. "A resumé of the intentions of the new
academy," in the words of Alain Mérot, it is also, to borrow a phrase from
Mérot, "something of a neo-Raphaelite manifesto."[21] These words ask us to

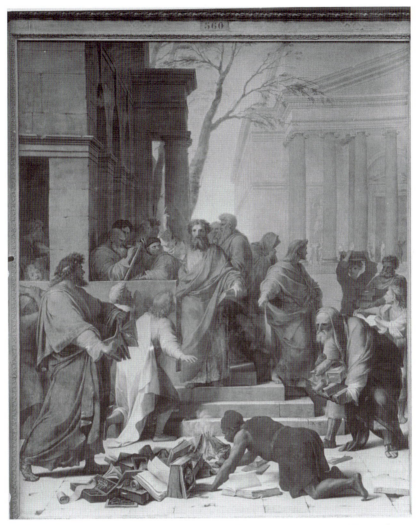

23. Eustache Le Sueur, *Saint Paul Preaching at Ephesus*, 1649, Paris, Notre Dame. Photo: Giraudon/Art Resource, NY.

consider Le Sueur in relation to Raphael, who was as we know the rallying point for the artists in the seventeenth-century academy. As Mérot notes too, the connection and direction of influence could not be more obvious. Le Sueur's figures in the *Saint Paul* are not only idealized in accordance with ancient sculptures but more specifically Raphael's types; figures and composition were modelled after Raphael's *Death of Ananias* and *School of Athens* (Plate 17).[22] The work must be counted in sum, as a demonstration of

the Raphaelism of the academy and as such as a marvel of "modern" painting, such painting envisaged in the academy as flowing through Raphael.
This is the problem with d'Argens's conceit: the centrality – rather than dis-
pensability – of Raphael is admirably exhibited by this work of Le Sueur,
who, as a result, is shown to have been as much indebted to the (Italian)
Raphael as had been Poussin or any other French classicist. To put Le Sueur
in his place would be to imply an unreal emphasis on the pupil over the
master. While it is true, as he states, that it would be possible to admire such
work in Paris, without going to Rome, Raphael, without whose example it
would have been inconceiveable, remains the unrivalled head of the French
school of painting.

D'Argens was indeed one of the few eighteenth-century French critics
who claimed otherwise. Before his book appeared, the Abbé Dubos had discussed Raphael in his popular *Critical Reflections on Poetry and Painting*
(*Réflexions critiques sur la poésie et sur la peinture*, 1719), lauding him much
as this had been done in the seventeenth-century academy.[23] During the period after d'Argens's book had appeared, Diderot did as well, recommending
Raphael's works for their grandiose and heroic subject matter; in the *Salons*,
the failings of a Hallé or Van Loo are made to appear all the greater in this
light, the achievement of a Deshay the more apparent, and so on.[24] How
much French artists – and the art public – still have to learn from Raphael
more than two hundred years after his death and more than a century
after he had first been placed at the head of the French school! That this
is evidence of his greatness cannot be in doubt. But something more was
obviously involved: a special orientation of consciousness, a mental disposition inculcated early in an artistic and more broadly aesthetic education.
This much was argued earlier, namely, Raphael's centrality to the program
of the academy. What is to be stressed here is that this program remained
substantially unchanged over the centuries. The same most notably was
its focus on drawing, specifically as conceived in the central Italian tradition. The drawing course, in turn, was intended to instill a vision of the
figure tracing its origins back to classical antiquity and especially vivid in
the works of the Italian masters. The end in view was of a narrative and
dramatic art calling up the emotions of life but in such ways as to be expressive of timeless moral values, these, too, as projected in the art of the
Italian masters. If Raphael was only one such master, he was the one in
whose works, it was more or less universally agreed, these means had been
carried out to perfection. Who better, then, to hold up as an example to
students? From the academy's point of view, had Raphael never existed, it
would have had to invent, and periodically reinvent, him.

THE NEW-OLD IDEAL

The neoclassicism of the end of the century being more obviously related to earlier classicisms, the high esteem in which Raphael was held by its artists will not come as a surprise. Less expected, however – indeed astonishing – is that to them he seems to have been a great discovery. As French artists moved on from the academy in Paris to Rome, they continued to study and copy Raphael's works as before – but with a new excitement. It was as though his works were only now being brought to light, after having been consigned to oblivion. After more than two centuries of exposure, Raphael's works were still capable of giving French artists an electric shock. Consider the words of the great and famous David:

Raphael divine man! It is you who has gradually lifted me toward the antique! It is you, sublime painter! It is you among the moderns who has most closely approached these inimitable models. It is you yourself that let me see that the antique is even superior to you! It is you, sensitive and beneficent painter, who has placed my chair before the sublime remains of antiquity. It is your learned and graceful paintings which have made me discover the beauties. Also, after an interval of three hundred years, given my enthusiasm for you, O worthy Raphael, recognize me as one of your pupils.[25]

David did indeed devote much time and energy to the study of ancient sculptures, perhaps with eyes, as he says, opened wide by Raphael, and he was no less a student of Raphael's own works. Key pictures such as the *Belisarius* and *Intervention of the Sabine Women*,[26] in the rendering of the figures, their types, and their poses, refer to Raphael's compositions, the last work specifically the *Massacre of Innocents* as engraved by Marcantonio (Plate 36). His works are, more importantly, in their restraint and dignity, in the Great Tradition and firmly in a tradition of Raphaelism tracing its origins back to the seventeenth-century French Academy. For all the differences between David and the artists of the early academy, for all the sincerity of his claims of a recent conversion, he was an exponent of a system of pictorial art with roots running deep in the history of French art and art training. As Davidian classicism, it was passed on to succeeding generations of artists, constantly reminded of the impossibility of looking too often or too closely at the works of Raphael.

That it was passed on needs to be stressed. For it was during this period that that bastion of Raphaelism, the academy, was suppressed. It was abolished by law during the Revolution, in 1793, on the recommendation of that same David. This act has led to no small confusion about David's aesthetic convictions, of whether or not he rejected the program of the academy and principles on which it was based – in this context, its Raphaelism. It should therefore be said at once that the displacement of those principles could not have been further from David's mind. David's opposition to the academy was the same as that of other members of his Club of Revolutionary Artists, namely, to its being a royal institution in which rank and privilege ultimately were enjoyed at the pleasure of the king and his ministers; an alternative was proposed, based on merit. That alternative was to be another organization, however, not fundamentally different from the academy but easily distinguishable from it by name. Such a new school was quickly organized and was called by different names until finding a home in the Ecole des Beaux-Arts that is with us still. Its original curriculum, as opposed to name and power base, were much as before, however, with drawing from casts, from works by the great masters, and from life in a program no less committed to Raphaelism than had been that of the Académie Royale.[27]

During the following years, the policies of Napoleon confirmed this commitment to Raphaelism. In striving for cultural as well as political and military hegemony in Europe, Napoleon had museums and churches looted, the greatest masterpieces of the tradition transferred to Paris. Seventeen of those by Raphael were collected from all over Italy, among them the *Saint Cecilia* from Bologna (Plate 26), *Coronation of the Virgin* from Perugia (Plate 2), the *Madonna di Foligno* (Plate 25), great treasures of the Palazzo Pitti in Florence such as the *Madonna della Sedia*, and the *Madonna dell'Impannata*, and most of all, the *Transfiguration* (Plate 33), regarded as his supreme achievement.[28] A Musée Napoleon was created in 1803 to house this booty, and, needless to say, Raphael's pictures received the most attention. (It is worth mentioning that David and his friend Quatremère de Quincy had opposed this entire policy on the grounds that works of art are best studied in the milieu in which they had been created and to which, in the event, they were returned after Napoleon's defeat.)

The Raphaelism of the "Ecole de David" of these years was, nevertheless, not precisely the same as that of the academic tradition. For the image of Raphael underwent still another transformation, resulting not from political upheaval but the rise of a new phenomenon: "primitivism." On the one hand, artists and critics began to focus attention on Italian art before Raphael and, on the other, on "Etruscan" or early Greek vase painting. Later classical works such as those of the Hellenistic and Roman periods were considered decadent and works by the later Italian masters as well. Classical painting of the type of David and the academy, moored in both late classical works and High Renaissance painting, was judged at best insincere and in need of "purification" by returning to the earliest works of ancient literature, namely, Homer and Ossian, and to sculpture of the time of Phidias and before. To be sure, David himself had felt that his early "Roman" style needed to be simplified in the direction of a so-called Greek mode and attempted to do so in his *Sabines*. The more radical of his students, however, felt that even this work was makeshift and pretentious. With not even David immune from criticism, how could Raphael continue to be venerated? To the minds of the "primitives," fervent Raphaelites for all their devotion to the new ideal, it was only a question of a change of perspectives on his work, with stress on his early production. Whereas the *Transfiguration* had always been regarded as Raphael's ultimate achievement, now that distinction was reserved for his early Madonnas and other early works. This is not to say that the great canonical works such as those in the Stanze were now despised. The schools continued to teach "Raphael" as before, and there are even works by the reformers that clearly were inspired by them. On the whole, however, what the artists of the School of David most pressed into service were Raphael's simpler and more austere works. This focus was further sharpened, it is worth mentioning, by a Catholic revival in France during the years around 1800. It is the "pious Raphael" who is singled out for praise in such books as Chateaubriand's *Genius of Christianity* (*Génie du Christianisme*), 1802, and Wackenroeder's influential *Effusions from the Heart of an Art-Loving Monk* (*Herzensergiessungen eines kunstliebenden Klosterbruders*), 1797. For the first, it is early Renaissance art that represents a triumph of faith; to Wackenroeder, for whom a true artist is a priest communing with God, the spirit emanating from Raphael's Madonnas can only have been divinely inspired.

The great example of the new Raphaelism is Ingres. David's star pupil, Ingres was raised, as one would have expected, on a diet of Greek and Roman paintings and sculptures and on the masterpieces of the later classical and Renaissance traditions. Even while in David's studio, however, he began distancing himself from his teacher in ways that were extreme even among the young radicals. That he had mastered the human figure, from observation and through the study of antique examples, is clear. But his figures are nevertheless unanatomical and unclassical, in the sense of the later classical tradition, the departures from anatomical and proportional correctness and late antique and Renaissance works undoubtedly justified on the basis of certain aspects of the classical tradition that had been inaccessible to artists up to the time of and including David, namely, of archaic and early classical works. Nowhere are these differences more striking than in his references to and revisions of works by Raphael, an artist whom he obviously adored.

Like Raphael he represented the Madonna – using Raphael's Madonnas as his direct sources. As one example among many, consider *The Vow of Louis XIII*, a painting showing Louis XIII placing France under the protection of the Virgin of the Assumption, commissioned in the early 1820s (Fig. 24). Here we see the king rendered in minute detail, his lace, velvet, and ermine robe palpably "real." The upper part, by contrast, is clearly grounded in a vision of an ideal, and it is specifically that of Raphael, on whose canonical *Sistine Madonna* and *Madonna di Foligno* (Plate 25)[29] it is based. For all his indebtedness to Raphael, however, Ingres's forms are harder, their rhythmic movement stronger. In the final analysis, his Madonna and child are as far removed from Raphael as from nature – while still being emphatically Raphaelesque. Here we circle back to the complexity of Raphaelism as a French phenomenon. To say that Raphael was honored above all other artists in France is not to claim that he was always the same "Raphael." From everything that has been said to this point, it should be clear that he was not. What is nevertheless so extraordinary is how profoundly artists were inspired by him – even if in different ways – and how persistently they remained in his orbit over so long a period of time. No matter how great the changes in French art over the centuries, its genealogical tree would always be rooted in Raphael. Or so it must by now seem.

It was in the early nineteenth century, too, that amateurs and art historians began to focus attention on Raphael as never before. In 1824, de Quincy, the friend and supporter of David and Davidian classicism, published an enormous book on the artist, running to 480 pages, *History of the Life and Works of Raphael* (*Histoire de la vie et des ouvrages de Raphaël*). It was followed by a more thorough study by Passavant in 1838, disinterring buried documents and forgotten pictures, enlarged and translated into French in 1860, *Raphael of Urbino and his Father Giovanni Santi...* (*Raphaël d'Urbin et son père Giovanni Santi... édition française refaite, corrigée et considérablement augmentée par l'auteur....*), and still another, twenty years later, in 1881, by Eugène Müntz, *Raphael, his Life, his Works and Times* (*Raphaël, sa vie, son oeuvre et son temps*). Bringing Raphael's art to life, this literature also had the perhaps unexpected effect of contributing toward a new and unprecedented interest in the artist himself. Whereas discussions of Raphael up until this time had been restricted to analyses of his works, now they extended to his life: the cult of Raphael became a cult not only of his art but also and as importantly of his personality.

That this was a rare personality Vasari had suggested. In his *Lives*, Vasari describes a Raphael – as also Michelangelo– with a new consciousness of his profession. He is half sinner, half saint, but a complete artist who

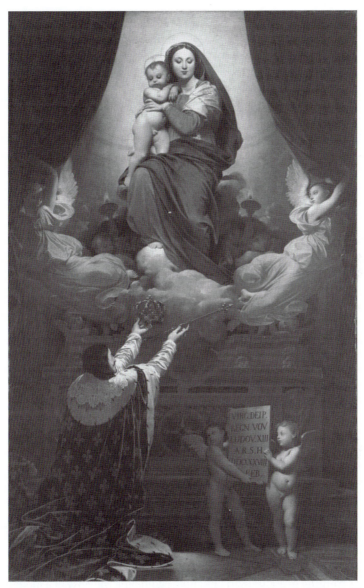

24. J. A. D. Ingres, *Vow of Louis XIII*, 1824, Montaubon, Cathedral. Photo: Giraudon/Art Resource, NY.

self-consciously dedicates his life to his art; his was a life, we are to understand, dominated by only one impulse and passion, a single-minded and all-embracing love of art, into which all of his experiences were channeled. To understand such an art it would seem necessary to study not only the art itself but also the personality that gave rise to it. So it seemed in more recent times to Ernst Kris and Otto Kurz, in a study examining biographies such as Vasari's and introduced with remarks on the "Riddle of the Artist." The riddle they explain is of the mystery surrounding the great artist, the magic associated with creative genius. It can be approached, they suggest, from two directions: one, the nature of the man capable of creating such great works, or two, how such a man was evaluated by his contemporaries. The justification for the first should be self-evident; the second or sociological approach is based on the assumption that the reception of the artist and his works are in the final analysis of no less importance.[30] Interestingly, from early in the nineteenth century on, French artists approached the "riddle" of Raphael from both these perspectives. To be sure, he was not the only early master singled out for such treatment at this time. But as Francis Haskell noted in a seminal study of the subject:

Raphael appears more frequently than any other painter, and in fact the vogue for treating episodes from his life (which played so important a role in the career of Ingres despite the fact that he never completed his intended series) was given a blessing by the most influential of the artist's nineteenth-century biographers and apologists, Quatremère de Quincy, whose own book on Raphael, first published in 1824, was often used as a source for artists in search of material.[31]

Ingres's series was to consist of pictures illustrating all of Raphael's life, from birth to death. In the event, those he completed are only of scenes of Raphael's public and private relationships with women: his betrothal to Cardinal Bibiena's niece (1813) and his love for the so-called Fornarina, the baker's daughter, first painted in a lost version of 1813 and repeated in later variants. These amorous escapades were clear favorites: Raphael and the Fornarina were repeated in works by Picot and by Coupin de la Couperie at the Salons of 1822 and 1824. Other episodes treated were Alexandre Evariste Fragonard's painting of about 1820 of Raphael adjusting the pose of a model for a painting of the Virgin and Child, Horace Vernet's related treatment of 1832 of Raphael in the Vatican drawing a woman and her child posed as the Madonna and Child, and various representations of Raphael in his studio, one by Mallet in 1814 that was especially telling, showing Cardinal Bibiena reading one of his comedies to the artist and his mistress, the clear intention being of stressing Raphael's intimate relationship with the

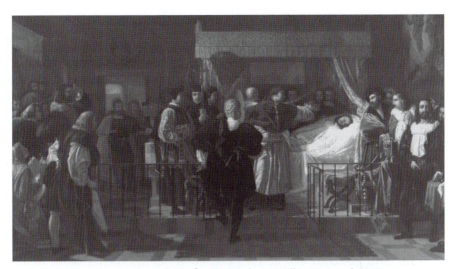

25. P.-N. Bergeret, *Homage to Raphael after His Death*, 1806, Allen Memorial Art Museum. Photo: Allen Memorial Art Museum, Oberlin College, Ohio, R. T. Miller, Jr. Fund, 1982.

great and powerful. The same point was made in paintings of Raphael's death that were especially popular, two examples: Nicolas-André Monsiau's death of Raphael exhibited in the Salon of 1804 and another such death by Pierre-Nolasque Bergeret shown in the Salon of 1806 (Fig. 25). Much evidently could be gained by French artists from an association with a master looming so large in the consciousness of the nineteenth-century French public.

The one nineteenth-century artist widely imagined as having thought otherwise was Ingres's rival, Delacroix. Was this exponent of romanticism not opposed to Ingres's neoclassicism? In a revival of the old Poussiniste-Rubéniste Quarrel of Drawing and Color, was he not committed to the second and thereby an enemy of the discipline of contour drawing associated with Raphael? The answer in a few words is that he was neither of the above, certainly not when put so baldly. It has repeatedly been demonstrated that while Delacroix was not as worshipful as Ingres, he was still a great admirer of the classical tradition and of Raphael.[32] This is not to say that he agreed wholeheartedly with the Academy or approved of Raphael's art uncritically. He had certain reservations about both, which he also saw differently at different times in his life. On balance, his opinion is summed up in these late observations (1852):

In Raphael, the execution, and I understand by that both line and color, is as it can be; not that I mean by that that it is bad; but that as it is, if we compare it to the wonders in that domain of Titian, Correggio, the Flemish painters, it falls into second place, and it had to be so; it could have been even much more so without distracting remarkably from the merits which place Raphael not only in the first rank, but above all artists, ancient and modern, in the areas in which he excels.[33]

The last, the areas in which he excels, are, Delacroix notes in another place, an "irresistible charm in his style, and a truly divine grace, which breathes throughout all his works and masks the defects and makes us excuse all his excesses."[34] An admirer of the Venetians and Rubens, of color, Delacroix nevertheless acknowledges Raphael's virtues, which he appreciates in much the same way as that earlier adherent to color, de Piles. Whatever the short-comings of Raphael in color and chiaroscuro, both assert, he remains ex-emplary for his drawing, grace, and composition. They may have preferred an art projecting a warmer feeling but gave Raphael credit where it seemed to them obvious that credit was due. It could hardly have been otherwise. For both Delacroix and de Piles maintained an unswerving belief in the superiority of the Grand Manner or Great Tradition and so could not but pay tribute to an artist to whose achievement and reputation the immense success and prestige of that Tradition were in no small measure owed; to denigrate or demote Raphael, to propose putting even a Titian or Rubens in his place, would have been to threaten the enabling structure of the entire art profession, particularly as that profession had been and continued to be represented by the academy. Other leading artists of the nineteenth-century academy, particularly Delaroche and Couture, were equally adherents to this tradition. If their works are not like Raphael's in all respects – least of all in spirit – or not as close to his as some produced earlier in the his-tory of the academy, they belong nonetheless to an unbroken sequence traceable to a curriculum grounded in the study of the antique and the masters of the Florentine Renaissance, Raphael foremost among them. One important difference, it should be noted, is that these last artists began a process of relative detachment from Raphael, tending to view him as only one of the great Renaissance masters. Aiming to reconcile the conflicting currents that had pitted an Ingres against a Delacroix, they advocated a more open and inclusive approach to the history of art. The most striking example is Delaroche's landmark *Artists of All Ages* painted between 1836 and 1841 for the hemicycle in the very seat of the academic tradition, the Ecole des Beaux-Arts.[35] The project, as the title suggests, called for paying tribute to the great artists of the past, which, in this temple, ordinarily would have meant the artists of the classical tradition presided over by Raphael. Raphael is indeed depicted together with Poussin – but in a group com-pleted by Leonardo and Michelangelo, this group in turn linked to others including Titian, Veronese, Mantegna, Dürer, Van Eyck, and so on, for a total of sixty-seven "greats." Of these, thirteen are French, Poussin and Le Sueur, of course, but also the landscapist Claude, the baroque sculptor Puget, and others, a veritable Pantheon of *French* artists. The gulf between the Italian and French traditions has finally been bridged.

CRISIS AND CHANGE

Signs of change nonetheless were in the air. In 1855, the brothers Goncourt publicly invoked the Raphael of the tradition. Here is that master of drawing, of a line "almost divine, of perfect beauty." But consider this rather astonishing entry in their *Journal* (1867), occasioned by the *Transfiguration*:

A most disagreable impression of wall paper by an oil painting. . . . In the entire work, no flash of brilliance, not the slightest instinct for feeling such as is found in the works of the least of the primitives who came before him, of Perugino, Pinturricchio. . . . In Raphael, the Resurrection is purely academic and pagan. . . . And yet this is a Christian image! I know of no other religious work painted in a style less conducive to spiritual striving. I know no other work meant to convey religious feelings that is more common or vulgar.[36]

The great Raphael, hitherto revered as a master of piety and grace, is now reviled for gross vulgarity. What an about-face! Its argument is based on the discovery of the "primitives" mentioned earlier, but that passion was at its height early in the century. What would have caused it to be revived at this late date? A clear answer is found in the Goncourt's contemptuous use of the word "academic." A term always associated with all that was deemed meritorious in the tradition has become a word of abuse. The decisive revolution that gave rise to modern art has begun.

It was at about midcentury that new tendencies began to appear, based on principles altogether different from those of the tradition and academy. If not all of precisely the same kind, they nevertheless originated with a new conception of art that was "realist" – as opposed to idealist – certain artists calling for a type of painting grounded in the "truth" of actual experiences. To be sure, there was no objective validity to this truth, which was rather a complex mix of objective and subjective elements. Yet the one thing on which all were agreed was that they would look neither to the tradition nor to the academy for guidelines as to what is beautiful and therefore worthy of being painted. In the present context, they adamantly refused to be guided by the example of Raphael or, one should say, the academy's "Raphael," a name they associated with academic pedantry.

The most striking example is the notorious *Luncheon on the Grass* (*Déjeuner sur l'herbe*, 1863) (Fig. 26) by the early modernist Manet. The basic facts about this work are well known, about how it was rejected by the jury for the Salon of 1863 and subsequently hung in the Salon des Refusés, about the scandal it caused when seen even among other provocative works. Equally well known is the fact that Manet's source of inspiration was Giorgione's *Fête champetre* in the Louvre – now agreed to be an early work by Titian – and that for his revision of Giorgione's idea he referred to that key image by Raphael, Marcantonio's engraving of the *Judgement of Paris* (Plate 35): the fashionably dressed men and nude woman in the foreground are based directly on the group of river gods in Raphael's composition. But while the shock of female nakedness reverberated through the exhibition, the real point of the work lay elsewhere – in figures originally Raphaelesque chosen neither for their beauty nor nobility; it was enough that they could be turned into ordinary people of the artist's own time. Borrowing from Raphael, Manet has created a work that is decidedly un-Raphaelesque – and definitely French. The suggestion is that a truly contemporary art must spring from the peculiar conditions of the time and place in which it is created. It is significant nevertheless that Manet felt it necessary to begin with Raphael even while waging war with the Italian tradition. By 1880 the impressionists had more or less won that war or, at the very least, made it unnecessary for artists to fight so hard a one again. The tradition of the academy was in full retreat, Raphael declared dispensable. In one respect, this was even acknowledged by the academy itself. For although its professors continued to send students to the Louvre to copy the masters, they did so with a complacency, suggesting that it hardly mattered which masters were to be studied – Titian or Rubens, Rembrandt, Leonardo, or Delacroix – all more or less equal for being artists of a broad tradition under attack. Indeed the one master generally avoided was Raphael, as though he had suddenly become too controversial; with the notable exception of Degas, the most traditional of the modernists, Raphael was now rarely copied, if at all.[37]

And so it was to the following generations of modern artists. Raphael was regarded as part of a collective patrimony mired in the past. To cite just one example, in their *Modern Painting* (*La peinture moderne*), 1925, Ozenfant and Jeanneret (Le Corbusier) list him among the masters of the past together with Mantegna, Michelangelo, Leonardo, Poussin, Le Brun,

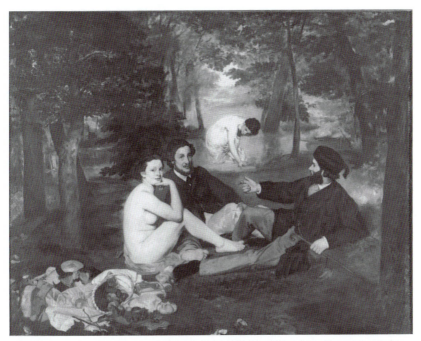

26. Edouard Manet, *Luncheon on the Grass*, 1863, Paris, Musée d'Orsay. Photo: Giraudon/Art Resource, NY.

and David, all traditional and therefore with nothing to offer artists whose preoccupation lay in another direction entirely: with the revolution of their own time, namely, the industrial transformation of the world. Their eyes conditioned by this revolution to see in a whole new and modern way (*l'optique moderne*), artists were discovering new worlds of color and form; art was opened up to approaches that were inconceivable so long as the tradition held sway, to Fauvism, Cubism, Purism, and so on.[38] Henceforth few artists would burn with the passion Raphael's works had aroused in a Poussin, a Le Sueur, a David, or an Ingres. The cult of Raphael has been replaced by the cult of the modern.

REFLECTIONS

To say that Raphael ceased to be the god of art in the nineteenth century is not to suggest that he had lost all of his former appeal to French artists. Degas, as noted, continued to consult his works as did more strict traditionalists and, from time to time, modernists such as Renoir and Redon. Later, on occasion, even Picasso drew inspiration from the tradition of Raphaelism.[39] This is a fact the importance of which should not be overlooked. It means that even after the Great Tradition had been overthrown and declared dead, its masterpieces – and the near mythical artists who had created them – continued to live on in the hearts and minds of artists and their public; Raphael's canonical works continued to be found compelling, that is, on purely artistic and poetic grounds. To be sure, this response has been limited to a handful of modern artists, a relatively sophisticated public, and, of course, art historians. It has been, therefore, of a fundamentally different kind from that of the centuries in which his reputation was at its zenith. During these three or so centuries, no artist of any nationality, French included, was so universally esteemed in France as Raphael, not Le Sueur, not even the great Poussin. His works were studied by one generation of artists after another, his "secrets" plumbed and assimilated. This was not, of course, coincidental but very clearly due to the fact that Raphael and Raphaelism were key to the program of an academy in which virtually every young artist was introduced – and indoctrinated – into the theory and practice of art from his earliest years of study; to remain close to Raphael, students were made to understand, was always to be on sure ground. So the academy taught and so we have seen its artists doing – but with significant differences and at times unexpected results.

What in the final analysis is so striking about French Raphaelism is how diverse it was, artists applying its lessons to different ends that went far beyond anything Raphael himself could have envisioned or that could have been anticipated from one period to the next. Nothing is more striking than the differences between seventeenth-century classicism, the rococo, and neoclassicism, and yet each in its own way traced its origins back to Raphael. No artist before and none since has been so fertile, not Poussin, not even Picasso. As a result, it would be tempting at this point to argue that this is proof that Raphael was the greatest artist in the history of European art. At the very least it can be said without fear of contradiction that he was the most prodigiously influential. From relatively inauspicious beginnings, he went on to inspire one generation of artists after another, first in Italy and then around Europe – the artists of France most of all. Their Raphaelism is a fitting monument to such an astonishing achievement.

1 2 Raphael's European Fame in the Seventeenth and Eighteenth Centuries

Giovanna Perini

Raphael is the major figurative model for classical and neoclassical art in terms of style, iconography, and composition, as much as for work method. From Roland Fréart de Chambray to Bellori, from Félibien and Scaramuccia to Lanzi, Mengs and Winckelmann (to name but a few), virtually no major historian nor theoretician within or even without the classicist coté avoids paying his respect (or at the very least some lip service) to the eternal name and art of Raphael.[1] His fame starts fading away at the beginning of the nineteenth century, in the very places where it had been most thriving – Italy, France, and Germany. Nevertheless, the new aesthetic creed of Romanticism, with its puristic emphasis on the religious and formal simplicity of pre-Raphaelite painting, only scratched the surface of his heritage, for official art academies throughout the Continent kept pointing to him as a model for their students, both in figurative terms and for his work method, just as they had been doing since their inceptions in the sixteenth century.[2] Suffice it to recall here a passage from Sir Joshua Reynolds's lofty *Discourse* of 1774 at the Royal Academy, where he discusses the notion of imitation, propounding his own eclectical approach, as well as referring to higher, better-established authorities:

It is from his having taken so many models that he [Raphael] became himself a model for all succeeding painters; always imitating and always original. If your ambition therefore be to equal Raffaelle, you must do as Raffaelle did, take many models, and not even *him* for your guide alone, to the exclusion of others.[3]

This is necessary because

He who confines himself to the imitation of an individual, as he never proposes to surpass, so he is not likely to equal the object of his imitation. He professes only to follow, and he that follows must necessarily be behind.[4]

Dissenting voices are hard to come by, inside or even outside Italy, France, and late-eighteenth-century Germany, where his name is most cherished and revered. Raphael's myth seems to thrive for nearly three centuries at a continental level, regardless of aesthetic penchants, stylistic inclinations, figurative creeds, or national traditions. Even fully baroque and rococo artists, historians, and theoreticians deem his art exemplary, for often enough what has been taken as more-or-less radical criticism on their part is in fact a misunderstanding on the part of readers and later critics. Paradoxically enough, if minor faults are occasionally singled out for discussion in Raphael's oeuvre, this is done by die-hard classicists.[5] Only in the eighteenth century is this widespread consensus at times openly challenged, but then individual criticism prevails on generally accepted authorities, giving vent to "scandalous" iconoclastic attitudes soon to be quenched.

It is most notably the case of Jonathan Richardson's *Account* of Italian artworks (1722) in which Raphael's Italian pictures often come under severe scrutiny, despite the author's well-known admiration for him.[6] Thus, although Richardson dutifully acknowledges the extreme beauty of the attitudes and airs of the various figures in Raphael's celebrated Bolognese altarpiece, *Saint Cecilia* (Plate 26), he hints that the protagonist is the least successful character, that the manner in general is "something dry and stiff," and that this is true also of the individual figures, for "elles ne sont point dessinées avec toute l'elegance possible." He has qualms also about the hues of the painting, which seem too dark or somber, although he finally admits that the picture gains brilliance, pleasantness, and some *je-ne-sais-quoi* if seen from a distance, matching Raphael's masterpieces like the *Transfiguration* (Plate 33).[7] Yet even the *Transfiguration* does not entirely escape his criticism, at least in terms of invention, for it allegedly joins two different and subsequent actions (Christ's Transfiguration and the miraculous healing of the possessed boy) in the same picture, giving more prominence to the less important one.[8] Also Falconet voiced more or less the same objections roughly half a century later, adding some further derogatory comments on individual parts of the picture, such as the three figures symmetrically kicking up in the air.[9]

The French edition of Richardson's book, published in Amsterdam in 1728, found audience – and answers – all over the Continent, and in France itself. Thus the French engraver Charles Nicholas Cochin, who was soon to reach an influential position in the French Academy and who traveled to Italy at the same time as Reynolds, in 1750, noted by contrast that the *Saint Cecilia* was of great beauty in fact. The heads are of admirable design and character. The figures are draped in the choicest manner, and their folds are beautifully executed. It is painted admirably well, although its colouring is a bit somber. It is one of the most excellent paintings of this great master.[10]

He seems to be responding pointedly, albeit indirectly, to Richardson's criticism, as his matching perplexity on the picture's coloring obliquely indicates. The Bolognese artist and historian Luigi Crespi, on the contrary, was very outspoken and direct in his reply to Richardson on this very matter:

In this picture there is no attitude nor position which may itself be hard, but each and every one is light, graceful and in beautiful motion....Is there a single outline anywhere which is not tender, smoothly soft, and which does not inadvertently and happily mingle in the ensuing hues? Is not everything smoothly soft, shading off well, well tuned, well unified?...If this picture is of a somewhat hard and dry manner, how can all the attitudes and airs of the heads be most beautiful and appropriate to each figure? And if they are most beautiful, how can they be somewhat dry nor perfectly outlined? And if they are dry and imperfectly outlined, how can this picture equal any other by the same master, and even his *Transfiguration*?...Where are you, Mr Watelet? Many years ago, while in Bologna and speaking to me of the particular beauty of this picture of Saint Cecilia, wouldn't you find the elegant design and draughtsmanship of this picture arresting?[11]

It is unfortunate that Crespi, while railing against foreigners' incompetence and lack of consistency in art criticism, apparently failed to realize that Richardson, a well-read man after all, was in fact expanding on a critique first levied by the Bolognese painter Annibale Carracci in a letter of 1580 to his cousin Ludovico, published by the equally Bolognese historian Carlo Cesare Malvasia in his famous *Felsina Pittrice* (1678):

And I swear to God that I would not exchange either one of these for Raphael's Saint Cecilia....[Who would deny] that the beautiful old man, the Saint Jerome [by Correggio], is at once grander and more tender than [Raphael's] Saint Paul, which once seemed a miracle to me, and now seems a wooden thing, so hard and sharp?[12]

Malvasia cannot be held responsible for Annibale's opinions, unless it is assumed that this letter is a forgery written by him (as was long believed),[13] no more than he can be said to share Simone Cantarini's dutifully reported contempt for Raphael, or Francesco Albani's Annibalesque criticism of the somewhat static, paratactical composition of the aforesaid *Saint Cecilia*.[14] (Interestingly enough, it is in the life of Albani that Passeri lists contemporary criticism on the limits of the greatest artists: "I have heard even professors of art say that Raphael from Urbino, who is in the first rank, is hard and sharp, that Titian lacks draughtsmanship, that Correggio is indecorous,

Paolo Veronese weak and too vague," wisely to conclude, "To please everyone is impossible, given that Nature itself, which is our universal parent, is
named imperfect, although she is our true teacher."[15]) Sometimes Malvasia
is still presented as a critic of Raphael's.[16] The erroneous attribution to him
of Annibale's feelings originates in the allegations of Maratta, Vittoria, and
Winckelmann[17] and has long seemed to find confirmation in his notorious,
deplorable slip of the pen to be found in the same life of the Carracci, where
he originally dubbed Raphael "a jugmaker from Urbino."[18]

As I have already explained in some detail elsewhere and as Anne
Summerscale has also well clarified,[19] this happens within a lengthy, fairly
topical tirade on the necessity for artists to rely on the advice of learned
men of letters to discuss and test their own inventions. Michelangelo's indecorous mistakes in the *Last Judgment* in the Vatican are contrasted with
the successful solutions to be seen in Zuccaro's frescoes in Caprarola and
in Raphael's *Stanze*. Difference in outcomes allegedly depends on the con-
ceited self-sufficiency of the former artist in opposition to the latter two's
wise reliance on distinguished advisors. According to Malvasia, visual evidence of this is the number and quality of rhetorical devices ornamenting
their pictures, which would be strange to painters, for artists were deemed
little more than mere craftsmen, artisans. Even Raphael and the Carracci
could not be mistaken for intellectuals.[20] To convey this idea, nourished by
his acquaintance with semi-illiterate geniuses like Reni,[21] Malvasia overdoes
it rhetorically, and instead of stating his case plainly, he connects abruptly
the name of one of the greatest artists of all times, possibly *the* greatest also
in his opinion (Raphael) to pottery decoration, a minor craft in which, at
Malvasia's time, Raphael was earnestly deemed to have been very active, by
Giulio Mancini among others.[22] This hastily conceived rhetorical firework,
however, blew up in Malvasia's face, resulting in a devastating effect on his
own reputation, thanks to the unfriendly attention drawn to it by his foe
Carlo Maratta, who used both the notorious hack Vincenzo Vittoria and
his very good friend Giovan Pietro Bellori to nail Malvasia for his unfortunate outburst. The fact that the Bolognese writer immediately suppressed
it, amending the text in most copies of his book just after its publication,
was not enough to save him, nor was Giampietro Cavazzoni Zanotti's later
defense particularly successful.[23] After all, Maratta, himself a man from the
Marches, was a protégé of the powerful Albani family from Urbino, just as
the German Winckelmann was to be in the following century. Besides their
different reasons to attack Malvasia (quite personal in the case of Maratta,
purely theoretical and methodological in the case of Winckelmann),[24]
they thus had ulterior motives to defend Urbino's most famous artist

from the debasing appreciation of his alleged craftsmanship as a pottery-painter.

The Urbino mansion of the Albani family hosted, amid several Baroccis, "a self-portrait by Raphael, truly wonderful, and it is the only work by Sanzio to be seen in Urbino,"[25] as Luigi Crespi pointed out in a letter to Bottari of June 1760, narrating his artistic pilgrimage to the native city of Raphael and Barocci. Urged by Bottari, Crespi later specified that "the self-portrait by Raphael in the Albani mansion in Urbino is painted on the wall, has a glass before it and a very high wing-like cornice."[26] This precious relic of Raphael's earliest production (as one would surmise, given its location and technique, which prevented mobility) has gone lost, nor can it be identified with a replica of the Uffizi portrait now on display in Raphael's home, because this is a nineteenth-century work in a different technique.[27] Crespi did visit the painter's house, but oddly enough he does not mention the still-extant fresco with the *Madonna and Child* preserved there, whose attribution has long been disputed between Giovanni Santi and his son Raphael.[28]

Thus the only tangible link between Raphael and his native city was his spurious activity as a pottery-painter, whose tradition, despite strong arguments to the contrary, lived on well into the eighteenth and nineteenth centuries, as Franz Christoph Scheyb in his art handbook for connoisseurs published in 1770 and Achim von Arnim in his fictional interpretation of Raphael's life and work entitled *Raphael und seine Nachbarinnen* and published in 1823, clearly prove.[29] Yet precisely in Germany Karl Heinrich von Heinecken in the late 1760s, followed by Johann Dominicus Fiorillo in the late 1790s, had been able to explain by what factual evidence this misunderstanding had come about and established itself.[30] Already at the beginning of the eighteenth century the Bolognese writer Pellegrino Antonio Orlandi, in his worldwide hit *Abcedario pittorico* (1704), had categorically refuted this, using the most sensible and objective terms:

And may I be allowed here to undeceive the many who assume that he painted so many dishes, urns, vases, when in his biographies written by so many authors there is no mention of this, so that it is appropriate to say that they are works of his disciples after his designs.[31]

While the moderately baroque Malvasia is still paying for his innocent slip of the pen despite Fiorillo's spirited defense of him against Winckelmann,[32] the classicist Bellori is generally considered one of Raphael's staunchest admirers, mostly thanks to a miscellaneous booklet published posthumously in 1695 by his friends Cardinal Albani and Carlo Maratta, his *Descrizzione delle immagini dipinte da Raffaelle d'Urbino nelle Camere del Palazzo*

Apostolico Vaticano.[33] This late work includes several parts written at different times, namely, a description of the frescoes in the Stanze followed by one of the frescoes in the Farnesina, together with an account of their restoration and of Annibale Carracci's Gallery in Palazzo Farnese, all carried out under Maratta's superintendence. Short essays on the problems of the alleged influence of Michelangelo on Raphael's stylistic development, in response to Roland Fréart de Chambray's assertions, on the comparison of the artistic gifts of Raphael and Apelles, on the monument to Raphael in the Pantheon, and the text of Bellori's lecture of 1677 at the Academy of Saint Luke, make up the rest of this rather patchy book. The *Descrizzione* itself very much reflects on one hand Bellori's position as keeper of the antiquities in Rome and its surroundings, held between 1670 and 1694, as well as his friendship with Maratta, and on the other hand, his commitment to the promotion of classicist poetics in accordance with the French cultural politics masterminded by his friends Colbert, Errard, and Le Brun.[34]

Admittedly, Bellori does not stoop to a mere popularization of Roland Fréart de Chambray's booklet of 1662 (*L'idée de la perfection de la Peinture*), which oozes anti-Vasarianism and anti-Michelangeloism virtually from every page.[35] While accepting the Frenchman's factual corrections to Vasari, Bellori refuses to share his steady abuse of Michelangelo. Even so, this was not enough to avert Luigi Crespi's later unfavorable reaction, expressed at length and in detail in three letters to Bottari, printed in the second tome of the latter's celebrated *Raccolta di lettere pittoriche* (1757).[36] Bottari was their obvious addressee because Bellori's book had been reprinted by him in 1751, together with Vasari's life of Raphael, thus merging Bottari's interest in Raphael's decorations in the Farnesina, just across Palazzo Corsini where he lived, with his preliminary work toward his new annotated edition of Vasari's book (1759–60).[37] Crespi, upon receiving a gift copy of the book, took exception to Bellori's analysis of Vasari's text and its alleged contradictions, showing how right Vasari had been in stressing Michelangelo's influence on Raphael and explaining the difference between copying and imitating former art in terms that are remarkably akin to Reynolds's later theory of borrowing.[38] Bottari must have been pleased with Crespi's staunch defense of his fellow national Vasari, although the assessment of Vasari's biography of Raphael is not the major issue at stake in Bellori's book.[39]

Regardless of its factual information and comments, its major asset is in fact a way of describing artworks quite different from the more literary and archaeological one adopted in his *Vite*, possibly at Poussin's request.[40] In the *Descrizzione* Bellori concentrates mostly on problems of style and on the expression of the passions, the *affetti* that were so important in academic teaching, as Le Brun in his *Conference* of 1668 had shown.[41] In particular, his description of the fresco with *Attila Meeting Pope Leo the Great* (or *The Repulse of Attila*) is striking. His dedicated defense of some details in Raphael's invention and composition, such as the static attitudes of the two Apostles hovering in the air and the presence of some anachronisms, clearly implies and therefore unwittingly gives away the fact that some specific contemporary adverse criticism of the picture was being refuted.[42] It is clear that this passage did not go unnoticed, as Winckelmann for one took it up again, almost literally, in his *Gedanken über die Nachahmung der Griechischen Werke in der Malerey und Bildhauerkunst* (1755), written right before coming to Italy.[43] Nevertheless, it is hard to establish where this criticism originated from. Maybe a hint is hidden in Bellori's own reply, where he mildly reproaches Algardi's opposite solutions, showing unbecoming and undignified rush and movement in the Apostles – a remark that he had not ventured to make in his biography of the sculptor.[44] It is fair to assume that in his invention Algardi was responding to the alleged shortcomings of his predecessor's. Therefore, it is possible that criticism came from artistic quarters close enough to the Bolognese sculptor's. This may indicate either Roman baroque artists in the circle of Pietro da Cortona or artists of Bolognese ascent, if the tone of Annibale's letter and of Albani's notes published by Malvasia and mentioned earlier on is borne in mind.

If this criticism came from Roman-Bolognese quarters, though, it would be clearer why Bellori almost tried to conceal it by glossing over it, while answering. It would in fact show how the forefather of the modern classicism that he was trying to peddle around in his writings was unpredictably criticized by some prominent modern artists of his same cotè. Interestingly enough, the analysis of what we know about Salvator Rosa's opinion on Raphael would seem to lend significant, albeit indirect, support to this interpretation. The most important biographical source on Rosa is probably Passeri's "Life," in which Passeri states that the Neapolitan painter greatly admired Paolo Veronese, "but he was not very conversant with Rafaele, for the school of Naples calls him hard, stony and dry, nor do they care for his nearness."[45] It sounds as if in Naples they pushed Annibale's views several steps further. On the other hand, this seems to be in conflict with Malvasia's account of Salvator Rosa's row with Simone Cantarini over Raphael's *Saint Cecilia*. According to the Bolognese writer, on a visit to Bologna Rosa had asked his colleague to see the picture, and Cantarini obliged by accompanying him but could not help criticizing it with scorn and bitterness. As Rosa tried to persuade him of its merits and invited him to use less abusive language when speaking of Raphael, a row started, which put an end to their mutual friendship.[46] In Malvasia's extant preliminary notes, where his source for the anecdote is identified as Giovanni Andrea Sirani, the two painters nearly came to blows, if they had not been stopped by onlookers.[47] It is almost unnecessary to stress how well informed, albeit unfriendly, Sirani could be as an oral source on Cantarini, given that both had worked in Reni's workshop.[48] On the other hand, it is also true that Cantarini's oeuvre challenges this account, for Raphael often seems to have been a source of inspiration for him.[49]

In fact, Malvasia's and Passeri's accounts of Rosa's attitude toward Raphael are less at odds than they may look at first sight. After all, Passeri does not say that Rosa did not like Raphael, nor does Malvasia state that he was enraptured by him. Passeri simply states that Rosa was not familiar with his work, given that it was not popular among Neapolitan artists. It is therefore conceivable that, when in Bologna, he was eager to see Raphael's local masterpiece and that he did find Cantarini's criticism too abusive, especially because it was coming from an artist brought up in a classicist context. Malvasia's book came out right before Passeri's demise, which may well be why Malvasia is less often attacked in it than Bellori.[50] Malvasia and Passeri, however, were also closer in intentions than they would seem at first sight. Although Passeri has always been considered both a reliable source and a classicist in the wake of Domenichino, his sympathy with Borromini should not be underestimated, for his reliability and open-mindedness would help cast a different light on one more anecdote on Salvator Rosa's attitude toward Raphael as it emerges from the *Carta del navegar pitoresco* (1660) by the Venetian Marco Boschini, a close ally of Malvasia in art theory. There the Neapolitan painter is introduced as a witness of Diego Velazquez's allegedly derogatory comments on Raphael, preliminary to his enraptured praise of Venetian painting: "To tell you the truth, for I like my freedom and earnestness, I am about to state that I do not like Raphael in the least."[51]

Nothing in Boschini's lines can suggest that either Rosa or himself would agree with Velazquez on Raphael. (Whether Velasquez actually said what Rosa reported to Boschini, is another matter, worth careful discussion.[52]) In fact, there is evidence enough to prove that Boschini, a faithful upholder of Venetian art, would follow the local art tradition favorable to Raphael inaugurated by Dolce in 1557.[53] Therefore, both Maratta and Bellori (who drafted his friend's life, reporting his ideas) were wrong in assuming that when the Venetian artist, dealer, and critic wrote those lines, "the poet Boschini, casting himself as a certain portrait painter, passed a final judgment [against Raphael]."[54] On the contrary, Boschini's page, just like Malvasia's on

Annibale, was simply instrumental in the diffusion of someone else's beliefs (in this case Velasquez's). Moreover, Boschini, like Malvasia, was no poet, no man of fiction, but of principles. (Nor was Velasquez a mere portrait painter.[55]) Truth is that neither Maratta nor Bellori were far-sighted enough, and they were both prone to mistaking effects for causes – as if life were to them an endless series of synechdoches. Besides, they were masters in the gentle art of slander and social hypocrisy, refined by their attendance at the papal court.

Quite apart from Bellori's unpublished life of Maratta, Boschini's passage did not go unnoticed in Rome. It seems to be the likeliest source for Passeri's paragraph on Rosa and Raphael quoted and commented on earlier,[56] given that Neapolitan painting could also be taken as a peculiar section of Spanish painting. But what was the prevailing attitude toward Raphael in Spain, if any? Palomino for one provides enough information to belie the essence of Velasquez's comment on Raphael as reported by Rosa and Boschini, while supplying the anecdote that may have originated it via a misunderstanding. It refers to Velasquez's youth in Spain, when he was little more than a student at Pacheco's workshop and started to make a name for himself thanks to *bodegones* (genre pieces), like tavern scenes and kitchen still lifes. Being an ambitious young man who wanted to be noticed, he did succeed in drawing attention to his works by adopting an original style, different from most genre painters. Indeed he would not underrate the examples of "Ticiano, Alberto [Dürer] and Rafael," whose fame had outlasted their lives, so he put all his creative powers and talent into the apparently menial tasks he was undertaking. "Some reproached him for not painting with delicacy and beauty more serious subjects, in which he might emulate Raphael of Urbino, and he replied politely by saying that he preferred to be the first in that sort of coarseness than second in delicacy."[57]

His witty answer, styled after Julius Caesar's famous saying that being first in a village in the Alps is a preferable position to being second in Rome, proves, if anything, that he was acutely aware of being active (and excelling) in a different, lower-rated field than Raphael's, but the sense of his reply could easily be misconstrued and subverted in Italy, especially by classicists like Bellori who rated Velasquez as little as a new Caravaggio. Thus his words could be made to sound disparaging of Raphael's work.

It is hardly worth pointing out how Maratta and Bellori's main source on Spanish matters was their friend Vincenzo Vittoria, a Spaniard from Xativa,[58] whose reliability is disputable. As for Velasquez and Raphael, what we know from Palomino is that Velasquez studied Raphael and Michelangelo carefully during his first Italian journey, obtaining from the Barberini special permissions to enter the Vatican at his convenience.[59] This is likely, for he had been trained by his father-in-law Francisco Pacheco, who greatly admired Raphael.[60] Besides, Velasquez had read a lot of Italian art literature,[61] in which praise was usually lavished on Raphael. During his second journey, he visited Bologna to see, among other works, Raphael's *Saint Cecilia*.[62] Admittedly, the accuracy of Palomino's account is open to question, because he states that there Velasquez also saw Michelangelo's statue of *Julius II* (destroyed during the riots of 1511).[63] Moreover Palomino makes every Spanish painter of note a pupil of Raphael's, including people like Alonso Sanchez Coello (born eleven years after Raphael's death) and Francisco Ribalta, who never went to Italy.[64] What is indisputable, however, is that during his second journey, on a mission to buy ancient statues and Old Masters and bring them back to Spain, Velasquez planned to buy some Raphaels for the Alcazar but failed.[65] The king himself, Philip IV, was more successful, for he secured at least three major Raphaels for his nation, namely, the so-called *Spasmo di Sicilia* (*Road to the Calvary*), the *Madonna del Pesce*, and the *Holy Family* nicknamed *La Perla* (the Pearl), which had been part of the Gonzaga collection in Mantua, before entering Charles I's in England.[66]

Oddly enough, Charles I Stuart had in turn discovered Raphael in Spain, during a state visit made in 1623. The pictures he saw were mostly copies, or school works,[67] but helped him make the decision to buy the original Tapestry Cartoons for the Vatican, at the time on sale in Genoa and now on display in the Victoria and Albert Museum (Plate 24).[68] They were bought as models for tapestries to be woven in England to decorate the Royal palaces, and won the respect of Oliver Cromwell, who prohibited their sale after the king's execution. As Johann Dominicus Fiorillo was quick to point out,[69] it was rather the Restoration king, Charles II Stuart, who planned to sell them to Louis XIV of France for his Gobelins workshops, although he was eventually prevented from doing so by his advisers. After the Glorious Revolution brought William of Orange to the British shores, the new king ordered Christopher Wren to design a space within Hampton Court for the display of the cartoons. This was opened in 1699, and it is not inappropriate to use this date to mark the actual beginning of the British school of painting, for both history painting and art theory start with Sir James Thornhill, Jonathan Richardson, and later William Hogarth, who spent their time on studying Raphael's cartoons – his major and most celebrated works in the country.[70]

There is nothing extraordinary in the special interest of the Dutch king of England in Raphael: both in the Netherlands and Flanders Raphael had always proved to be popular virtually from his own days. In 1545, for instance, the Guild of Saint Luke in Antwerp was presented with a silver cup portraying the four greatest painters of all times: Dürer, Raphael, Apelles, and Zeuxis.[71] Raphael's fame in the north was obviously fostered by a number of favorable circumstances, such as the traditional production of tapestries in the Flanders, where Raphael's cartoons were often rewoven; the thriving art market in Amsterdam, where works from all over the Continent, including some Raphaels, were constantly traded and auctioned; the influence of Italian art and art theory on local schools, individual painters and theoreticians, from mid-cinquecento onward, and so on.[72] As early as 1604 Karel van Mander praises Raphael for his *inventy* – that is, invention – but also in a way composition, ability at arranging things, and decoration in a picture, much like *ordinanty* and in connection with *verscheydenheden*, the descriptive ability that fosters variety.[73] In *Het gulden cabinet* (1661) the Flemish solicitor Cornelis de Bie lists "Raphael Urbien" among thirty-three Italian artists (mostly sixteenth- and seventeenth-century Venetian and Bolognese) whose works (paintings, drawings, and prints) were in the possession of his patron and friend, the collector Antoine van Leyen.[74]

Venetian painting was clearly the favorite of major Flemish artists such as Rubens and van Dyck. Even so, they did study, collect, and, in the case of Rubens, occasionally emulate Raphael, no matter what was said to the contrary by contemporaries such as Sandrart.[75] Rubens's studies after Raphael are especially evident in his emulative *Transfiguration* at the Musée des Beaux Arts in Nancy[76] but can be detected even in some of his portraiture, as Jacob Burckhardt and Michael Jaffé first proved.[77]

More unexpected, perhaps, is Rembrandt's involvement with Raphael, but this is proved both by some works in his collection attributed to the Italian painter and by his famous sketch after the portrait of Baldassare Castiglione, which he saw at the Amsterdam sale of van Uffel's estate in 1639. It became the source for his London *Self-Portrait* of 1640, which in turn became a model for his followers Ferdinand Bol, Govert Flinck, and Frans Mieris.[78]

An item in the March 1795 sale of Sir Joshua Reynolds's possessions at Christie's gives further pause for thought: "Rembrandt – *Raphael's Portrait*, half-length, coloured with great force and good effect."[79] In the *Morning Chronicle* an anonymous journalist was quick to point out that "the person who baptised it forgot how many years one of these great men lived before the other; besides, of Raphael it has no resemblance."[80] Rembrandt was no contemporary with Aristotle either, but this did not prevent him from portraying the latter next to a bust of Homer – nor has his Aristotle (New York, Metropolitan Museum) – much resemblance to the known iconography of the Greek philosopher. Whoever gave Reynolds's picture its title and attribution (whether it was Reynolds himself or somebody else in his circle) was making a statement in poetics and style. Indeed he was making the case for eclecticism, denying the opposition between design and color, idealism and realism, narration and description, Raphael and Rembrandt – in a word, northern and grand styles. Eclecticism (or, to use a term preferred at the time, emulation) was the operative creed for most of the greatest Western artists from the Renaissance to the end of the eighteenth century, including Raphael and Reynolds.[81] Oddly enough, however, in *The Idler* (1759) the young Reynolds had obliquely criticized Hogarth for mingling opposite styles such as the Italian and Dutch.[82] Ronald Paulson has surmised that Reynolds was referring specifically to the most overtly Raphaelesque picture by Hogarth, *Paul before Felix*, painted for Lincoln's Inn Fields.[83] Its composition deliberately echoes Raphael's cartoons already exploited by his father-in-law, James Thornhill, in his decoration of Saint Paul's dome.

As Frederick Antal has clearly shown in his seminal study on *Hogarth and His Place in European Art*, Hogarth's attitude toward Raphael is twofold.[84] On one hand he shares most of his contemporaries' genuine admiration for Raphael as a true visual authority, a great model for history painting, and he tries accordingly to adopt his compositional schemes and some of the motifs in his inventions (especially from the cartoons), adapting them to his own more ambitious works. On the other hand, given that Raphael is a veritable Old Master, he cannot often resist the temptation to use him as an indirect polemical target in spoofs like his engraving of *Paul before Felix Burlesqued* (1751), where his own painting for Lincoln's Inn Fields (which he had further Raphaelized through alterations removed by the unhappy restoration of 1970) is ridiculed in its invention, composition, and high style.[85]

As Ronald Paulson has pointedly noted, however, Hogarth did avoid alluding to Raphael in his polemical engraving *The Battle of Pictures* (1745), where Old Masters' paintings attack modern paintings by Hogarth. Indeed neither the *Saint Andrew* nor the *Feast of Gods* depicted there bear any resemblance to Raphael's lost picture in the Hall of the Palafrenieri in the Vatican or his extant fresco in the Farnesina.[86] On the contrary, in his famous print *Characters and Caricaturas* (1743) Hogarth had contrasted three heads drawn by Raphael (from the cartoons) to four heads drawn by Leonardo, Annibale Carracci, and Pier Leone Ghezzi, as sources and visual examples of the difference between a character and a caricature in history painting, as well as in fiction.[87] Most tellingly, at the beginning of the *Analysis of Beauty* (1753), Raphael is singled out as one of the Old Masters who would be aware of the great secret revealed in Hogarth's book, namely, the existence of the serpentine line of grace:

Raphael, from a straight and stiff manner, on a sudden changed his taste of lines at sight of Michael Angelo's works, and the antique statues; and so fond was he of the serpentine line, that he carried it into a ridiculous excess, particularly in his draperies: though his great observance of nature suffered him not long to continue in this mistake.[88]

The very terms used by Hogarth reveal that, despite all his proclaimed nationalism, his literary source was, if not French, at least Frenchified – if not de Piles, at least Richardson. And Richardson was one of Reynolds's most favored and revered readings in his formative years, much before his journey to Italy (1750–2), which was also inspired by Richardson's *Account*.[89]

As Reynolds's extant sketches show, when in Rome he would repeatedly study bits and pieces of Raphael's oeuvre in the Vatican Stanze (Figs. 30–32), trying to capture the essence of their innovative inventions through a careful selection of individual figures, expressions, or gestures recorded in a few, sketchy lines.[90]

Just like Roger de Piles before him,[91] he was very keenly aware that not every tourist or artist would readily understand the greatness of Raphael's Stanze, as an unused passage in his preparatory notes for his last discourse indicates:

how few would be struck with the grandeur of stile of M[ichael] A[ngelo] or R[affielle] without a previous preparation. The Keeper of the Vatican told me that it has frequently happend, that after he has attended a company and even artists through the Rooms, when he was about taking his leave has been asked why he has not shewn them what they came principally to see, the works of Raffiele, an[d] that he has then led them back to the rooms which they had passd before. I confess I was not myself struck with Raffielles works as I expected, but what my expectations were I can not tell. But I remained long enough in the Vatican to know that my disapointment was the child of ignorance.[92]

Some of his youthful, Richardsonian qualms on Raphael surface here and there in his manuscripts, when he recalls, "I was let in to the Capella Systina in the morning and remained there the whole day, a great part of which was spent in walking up and down with great self importance. In the hights of this paroxism, passing through, on my return, the rooms of Raffiel they appeared of an inferior order."[93]

When still in Rome, in a note jotted down in one of his sketchbooks, he had written, "in Raffiele nothing of the affectation of Painting, not dark (Guercino) nor light (Guido), no ridicolous affected contrasts, no affected masses of lights & shadows. He is the medium. In Annibale Carrach too wild. D[itt]o Michael Angelo. Domenicino too tame, Guido too effeminate."[94]

Nevertheless, his sketches do not reflect any interest in Raphael's use of light and shade, or in his coloring, or in his draftsmanship, or in his composition and style – which were best preserved in prints.[95] It is the essence of his invention for individual characters and attitudes that is recorded in a few sketchy lines, without any similarity to the standard academic renderings of contemporary Italian artists such as Carlo Giuseppe Ratti and Innocenzo Ansaldi, who were also among Mengs's most devoted followers in Italy (Figs. 29, 33).[96] Reynolds adopts an entirely British abstract notational system, possibly harking back to Hogarth's own as illustrated in the planches of his *Analysis of Beauty*.[97] His way of using Raphael's inventions in his own oeuvre, however, is in no way reminiscent of Hogarth's. This holds true even for his unique, youthful parody of the *School of Athens* now in Dublin, portraying a number of caricatured British tourists in their eighteenth-century clothes grouped according to the disposition of Raphael's figures in the context of a perfectly Gothic, Westminsteresque rephrasing of the original classical architectural setting.[98] In fact this is an exercise in the style of Thomas Patch and has nothing to do with Hogarth's more serious artistic ambitions.

Reynolds being even more ambitious than Hogarth, he did use Raphael's masterly groupings in some of his pictures according to the principles of imitation he had recommended in his *Discourses*. For instance, it is well known that the double portrait of *Miss Sarah and Elizabeth Crewe* is cast in the attitude of two figures from the *Parnassus* or that *Mrs. Lloyd* is after a Raphael drawing for *Adam Tempted*.[99] It is less known that both the portrait of *Miss Sarah Anne Child* and, more elaborately, that of *Lady Catherine Pelham-Clinton* derive from Raphael's *Galatea* (Plate 28).[100] More numerous examples might be made, at different degrees of removal from their original Raphaelesque models, some of which are not always obvious or renowned.[101] In any case, he did set a final standard for British painting until the end of the century, as even the works of his successor as president of the Royal Academy, the American Benjamin West, prove.[102]

In Reynolds, however, individual borrowings are much less important than the adoption of Raphael's work method, both in terms of invention (thanks to an eclectic approach and the use of a range of reusable visual patterns) and of execution (owing to the cooperation of a number of aids in the studio).[103] Thus, although his style is entirely different from Raphael's, he can be considered the most "Raphaelesque" of all British painters, and possibly of all his contemporaries. His judgment on Raphael ("Raffaelle's materials are generally borrowed, though the noble structure is his own")[104] would equally be applicable to himself. His attitude toward Raphael, in fact, is entirely different from his continental rival, Mengs's.[105] The latter inherits from Scannelli a veneration for the "holy trinity" of Raphael, Titian, and Correggio but assesses the merit of each artist according to a system that faintly echoes de Piles's "scales for painters," finding perfections and shortcomings in each of them.[106] Raphael is thus always a model for expression and composition, but not always for coloring and light and shade, nor even for draftsmanship, although his latest works are generally admirable, especially when it comes to draperies.[107] His harmony is also weak, when compared with Correggio's. Even so, "Raphael remains always the first."[108]

Although agreeing on individual parts of this analysis, Reynolds would indeed disagree on its conclusion. His final *Discourse* of 1790 in honor of Michelangelo is no easy concession to the rising tide of preromantic titanism fostered by the host of his former protégés and now rivals (Barry, Blake, Fuseli), but rather the confirmation of a long-held opinion, as the comparison between Raphael and Michelangelo drawn in his earlier discourse of 1772 shows.[109] His *Self-Portrait* in doctoral robes for the Royal Academy is nearly contemporary with it, and reinforces its message, by showing Reynolds proudly standing next to a bust of Michelangelo.[110]

Oddly enough, though, the real message of this painting has little to do with Michelangelo. It is in fact truly Raphaelesque and Hogarthian in that it combines Rembrandtesque invention and style to the monumental assertion of the intellectual supremacy of Italian art. Like Hogarth, here Reynolds does mix Italian and Dutch, but the two elements do not seem irreconcilably at odds with each other like in Hogarth's *Paul before Felix*. The reason is that, like Raphael, Reynolds has been able to make a new, original synthesis of antithetical ingredients, for he could master the inner principle of classical imitation – or eclecticism. Thus his official portrait – a visual manifesto of the first internationally acclaimed and most academic British painter – is a visual pun, a most serious and sophisticated double joke based on Raphael's lesson, in the best British tradition from Thornhill, Richardson, and Hogarth onward.

13 Restoring Raphael

Cathleen Sara Hoeniger[1]

Il restauro è lo specchio del gusto e della attitudine critica di ogni epoca;...
adesso...il restauro viene inteso come critica, come filologia in atto, come interpretazione dell'opera d'arte.

Cesare Brandi, *Carmine o della pittura*

Raphael's paintings, in fresco and on panel and canvas, have aged and
suffered damage over the centuries, as have other Renaissance works. An
early case of severe damage is related by Giorgio Vasari, who tells how the
Madonna del Cardellino (Florence, Uffizi) was broken literally into pieces
when the house of Lorenzo Nasi collapsed from a landslide in 1547 and that
the painting had to be recomposed from the fragments.[2] Because of the
prestige of Raphael's art, however, many of his paintings have undergone
more frequent or more substantial restorations than might otherwise have
been the case. Raphael's paintings were prominently situated in the Vatican
complex, in Italian churches, at courts, and in luxurious villas. A sequence of
wealthy patrons of the arts documented the condition of Raphael's paintings
with evident concern, and by the late eighteenth century, public museums
made the care of Raphael's art a high priority.

Although the intentions underlying the restoration of Raphael's paintings
from the late sixteenth century on have varied considerably, most often
restoration was a genuine response to the effects of age and deterioration.
Many other factors, however, nuanced the response to a painting's appearance. Raphael's *Saint Michael* (Plate 27) for instance, was hung by Louis XIV
above his throne at the Tuileries as an attribute of kingship.[3] The painting
had to look pristine because it had political symbolism. In the quite different
case of Raphael's frescoes in Rome, both in the Villa Farnesina and in the
Vatican Stanze, the approach taken to their first major restorations in about

1700 was determined in large part by the reverence the painter-restorer Carlo Maratti felt for Raphael's art.

The goal of prolonging the life of paintings by Raphael resulted in very different kinds and levels of treatment. In the case of a structurally unsound painting, halting deterioration often involved a major intervention to stabilize the painting's support, whether this was the *intonaco* plaster in a fresco or the wood of a panel-painting. In addition, restorers were quite routinely engaged in the cleaning and reintegration of the paint surface to clarify passages formerly obscured by discolored varnish films and old repaintings. As the observation of current conservation practice brings forcefully to our attention, the way a specific work by Raphael was restored in the past depended on the technical problems identified at that time and on the range of available practical solutions.

It is also important to stress that restoration was (and is) virtually inseparable from more theoretical and cultural attitudes toward art. Certainly the different ways each era conceived of its artistic heritage influenced painting restoration. Crucial philosophical discussions included how much human intervention into the past and its objects was acceptable, and whether preservation only or also recovery or even renovation would be expected.[4]

The ultimate goal of art conservation is understood today as achieving a balance between the past and the present in the work of art. Cesare Brandi's philosophical writings have been particularly influential in the development of this sophisticated theory of the role of the conservator. According to this view, the past in the work of art refers to the original whole and unified condition, now lost and irrecoverable; whereas the present is interpreted as the limited period of today, when the conservator must try to give the greatest possible unity and expression to the damaged work.[5] If one looks back through history, however, it was not always the restorer's intention to integrate sensitively the past and present. Historical views of how to salvage a painting for posterity were tied to the evaluative framework of the day and, therefore, were dependent on current rankings of relative artistic mastery and beauty, concepts of what was "pure" or "authentic" for a work of art, and so on.

But as well as purely aesthetic evaluations, the way that history was written and the way the past was viewed also influenced restoration. The understanding of the sweep of history during a particular era and the discussion of the impact of time and decay on works of art are broad arenas of intellectual thought that clearly would have affected preservation practices. Thus, during the Renaissance in Italy, when humanist historians largely annexed the immediate medieval past as "dark" and instead championed the more distant classical past, it was no coincidence that many patrons paid to have their gothic altarpieces rehoused in *all'antica* frames and their church chapels similarly renovated along classical lines.[6] Under the fifteenth-century popes in Rome, many ancient Roman buildings were renovated by removing contiguous medieval structures.[7]

By the seventeenth century, both classical and classical-revival styles were highly valued in Italy and France. However, selective emphasis on certain chosen aspects of the past occasioned an interpretive approach to history. Similarly, restoration often allowed for creative leeway. Most restorers continued to be trained as artists rather than as preservation specialists. Carlo Maratti studied to be a painter of the classicist style in Rome, inspired by Raphael's works, and his ability as a restorer was an extension of his artistic preparation.[8] When Maratti came to restore Raphael's frescoes in the Loggia of Psyche and the Vatican Stanze, some intelligent commentators valued the way he used his own understanding of Raphael to guide areas of reconstructive painting, although Maratti's repainting also received loud criticism.

Several of the Raphael restorations considered in this chapter were carried out in the eighteenth century, during the period of the birth of classical archaeology. Stimulated by momentous discoveries of classical sites, including Herculaneum (1711) and Pompeii (1748) with their remarkable wall paintings, historians began to write with greater awareness of the distance separating the ancient past from the present. Johann Winckelmann, whose *History of Art in Ancient Times* was published in 1764, believed the work of the restorer should fit with the precise research of the archaeologist, and restoration began to be seen as a means to reestablish the aesthetic of the ancient object.[9] In 1721, for example, the architect J. B. Fischer von Erlach proposed to reconstruct the ancient palace of Diocletian at Spalato (Split) on the Dalmatian coast. Bartolomeo Cavaceppi, who was in contact with Winckelmann, argued that the restorer should use the same materials as the original and that he must not touch or alter the original, although in practice Cavaceppi's own restorations transformed ancient sculptures.[10] A little later, during the first decades of the nineteenth century in Rome, the French architect and director of antique sites, Giuseppe Valadier, led restorations of archaeological monuments in which one style was not strongly valued over another.[11] There were concurrent attempts in the restoration of Raphael's paintings to adopt a more objective approach to documenting the condition, as well as to the restoration work itself.

Furthermore, as private and princely "cabinets" of artistic and natural rarities began to be transformed into national and state art museums, restoration was monitored by administrative bodies. Museum committees established regulations and eventually codes of ethics, and they supervised restorers closely, restricting the more individualistic aspects of traditional practice. Restorers worked more consistently with other experts. Both prominent artists, usually professors of painting at the local art colleges, and famous scientists scrutinized and guided restoration work within the institution.

Yet it is particularly interesting to discover that a number of Raphael restorations appear to be less effected by the trends of the day than one might otherwise expect. In the pages that follow, I contend that Raphael's enormous stature, as an artist held to be equal to or surpassing the greatest masters of classical Greece and Rome, served to elevate several Raphael restorations above contemporary circumstances. The value placed on his art usually ensured that only very talented restorers were allowed to touch his paintings. In addition, the restorations were often carefully watched by intellectuals and scientists, who provided commentary on the treatments. During an extended period of development in the practice and theory of restoration, from the late seventeenth through to the twentieth century, the restoration projects on Raphael's major works became the focus of informed theoretical discussion and regularly sparked pivotal controversy and debate.

CARLO MARATTI, GIOVAN PIETRO BELLORI, AND RAPHAEL'S LOGGIA OF PSYCHE

Carlo Maratti's restoration of Raphael's Loggia of Psyche frescoes in 1693–5 was framed by the commentary of his immensely learned and respected friend Giovan Pietro Bellori, who was the pope's official overseer of the antiquities of Rome. Bellori, who has been widely considered the most learned writer on art and architecture of the late seventeenth century, contended in his *Le vite de' pittori, scultori e architetti moderni* (printed in 1672) that Raphael's art was the ultimate, due to its humanistic and divinely inspired qualities.[12] Bellori also claimed that Raphael was the first Renaissance painter whose work truly rivaled that of the ancients: "the divine Raphael... [had] reached the peak of artistic beauty [in his paintings]... by achieving an ancient majesty... and grace... [reminiscent of the most glorious works] of the Greeks and Romans."[13] In his lengthy commentary on Raphael's Loggia of Psyche frescoes, published in 1695, Bellori argued that Raphael had achieved his goal of illustrating the Greek poetry of Apuleius with an appropriately ancient style of painting (Plate 29). Bellori compares

Raphael's group portrait of the three fraternal gods, *Jupiter, Neptune, and Pluto*, and his rendering of the *Marriage of Cupid and Psyche* to ancient portrayals of these deities and their stories, specifically the representation of the gods in a classical metal trophy on view in Rome. Bellori contends that Raphael has surpassed the ancients in the ability to characterize the gods physically according to their natures.[14]

When consulted about the imminent need to repair the loggia frescoes, Bellori promoted his close friend and protegé Carlo Maratti, whom he describes in the biography he wrote of Maratti as the "second Raphael."[15] Carlo Maratti had arrived in Rome from the Marches at a young age and was trained in the studio of Andrea Sacchi, with whom he became extremely close.[16] Maratti emulated Raphael's works from the start and later became a collector of Raphael's drawings. Both because he shared in the spirit of Raphael's art and because he was one of the most important and prolific classicist painters in late-seventeenth-century Rome, Maratti was seen as the ideal restorer for Raphael's frescoes.[17]

When Maratti began to work on the famous villa frescoes in 1693, he would have been well aware of current expectations. Seventeenth-century taste dictated that the works of Raphael be rejuvinated, and Maratti had been chosen to expertly imitate Raphael and even to create anew in the spirit of Raphael, as Bellori eloquently explained.[18] The fresco decorations of the loggia by Raphael and his close associates Giulio Romano, Giovanni Francesco Penni, and Giovanni da Udine, had suffered extensively due to their location in an open, north-facing loggia. It was not until 1649 that the loggia was closed in by glass.[19] The most fundamental problem was structural, at the level of the plaster support, and on the surface this caused areas of flaking paint. In addition, parts of the painting had faded and, more important, the tonal harmony of the whole was undermined by the darkening of Raphael's blue backgrounds to a blackish hue. Bellori detailed how Maratti had enhanced and completed passages in such a way that they blended harmoniously with the originals,[20] an approach to loss compensation that was used in Raphael restorations through until the early nineteenth century.

The restoration project was initiated with urgency in the early 1690s, when the loggia's owner, Ranuccio Farnese, duke of Parma, heard from his agent in Rome that repairs were desperately needed because in many places the *intonaco* was detaching from the loggia vault.[21] Maratti had to concentrate initially on this fundamental structural problem. To secure the plaster from falling, Maratti called on Giovanni Francesco Rossi, an experienced restorer of frescoes, with whom Maratti worked closely on several projects. Rossi had invented a useful technique by adapting a form of nail used in printing to the problem of detaching *intonaco*. As Bellori explains, 850 nails (called *grappe* or *chiodi*) were carefully inserted into the loosest areas of plaster, in places where the painting was also dark and therefore the nails could be most easily camouflaged:

Rossi...employed nails in the form of a capital letter "T"...[and] in order not to cover up the lighter areas of the paintings with the top part of the nail as much, he sometimes used a nail shaped more like an "L"....He made the holes with a drill...and then filled it with a gesso paste. He would then choose a nail of the appropriate length and insert it into the fresh gesso. He then covered the nail with plaster and then repainted in watercolors around the nails with the same colors that had been there before the intervention.[22]

After the *intonaco* on the vault had been secured by Rossi, Maratti turned to the less structural aspects of the project. Bellori describes how Maratti strove to restore the brightness and tonal harmony to Raphael's scenes by reinforcing faded areas of color and by going over figural outlines in order to better define the protagonists. Although most of the repainting from 1694–5 was removed in the cleaning of 1930 (as well, unfortunately, as some of Raphael's original), the recent conservation team (finished 1997) has discovered some areas where Maratti's repainting survives, including in the spandrel image of *Psyche Carried into the Heavens by Putti* (Fig. 27). Scientific testing of the blue strata of the mural suggests that Raphael painted the background initially in two layers: first a pale blue underlayer *affresco* of an enamel quality, probably smalt, and then a finishing layer of azurite *a secco*. The subsequent layer of intense blue enamel-like paint is also probably smalt, applied *a secco* and may be the remains of Maratti's repainting, although this is not absolutely certain.[23] Most significant is that the blue repainting for the background, probably by Maratti, is executed using *tratteggio* strokes, a technique of in-painting using a system of vertical hatchings executed in removable, water-soluble media. This sophisticated compensation method is usually held to be an invention of the 1940s during the period of Cesare Brandi's directorship of the Istituto Centrale del Restauro in Rome. Maratti's use of *tratteggio* more than two centuries earlier to integrate and lighten, only partially, areas of Raphael's frescoes reveals the sensitivity and tentativeness of Maratti's approach to works he respected above all others. Indeed, Bellori explained how Maratti, with considerable foresight, was aware that his work could never compete with Raphael's original and that his contribution would likely not be desired by later viewers. He lightly reinforced areas of color, as well as the outlines of figures, with only "a little lapis" and "*pastello*" (a water-soluble pastel stick), so that his contribution could, subsequently, be easily removed and then improved

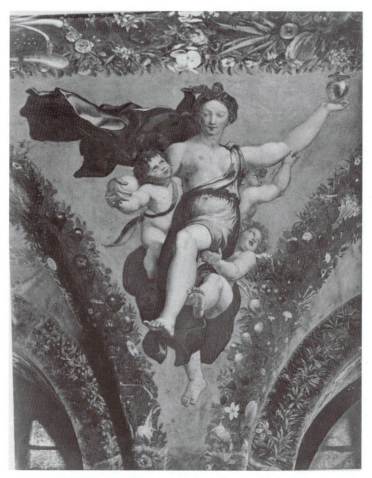

27. Raphael and assistants, *Psyche Carried into the Heavens by Putti (or The Assumption of Psyche)*, from the Loggia of Psyche, 1517–18, fresco, Rome, Villa Farnesina. Condition before cleaning of 1930, showing repainting by Carlo Maratti from 1694–5. Photo: Alinari/Art Resource NY; photographed by Adolph Braun de Dornach, 1887.

upon.[24] Diderot, in the *Encyclopédie* of 1751–2, quotes Maratti as having explained: "I will take and complete these images with pastel strokes, because if someone better than me comes afterwards, he will then be able to remove my work and add better retouching of his own."[25] "Reversibility" in painting conservation has been, very much, an ethical contribution of twentieth-century theory and practice. Nevertheless, a consciousness of reversibility emerges here in the work of Maratti and shows how unusually careful and thoughtful this compensation work was for its day.

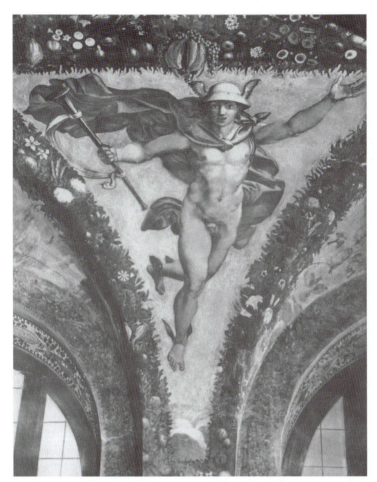

28. Raphael and assistants, *Mercury*, from the Loggia of Psyche, 1517–18, fresco, Rome, Villa Farnesina. Condition before cleaning of 1930, showing repainting by Carlo Maratti from 1694–5. Photo: Alinari/Art Resource NY; photographed by Adolph Braun de Dornach, 1887.

Maratti's cautiousness stems, however, not from a general, avant-garde restoration ethos, but rather from his reverence for Raphael per se. As suggested at the outset of this chapter, the fame of Raphael's art often occasioned extraordinary restoration practice and theory. In awe of Raphael's inimitable genius, Maratti stepped back, at least in part, from leaving his permanent mark on the coloring of the frescoes. In a similar way in 1754 in Paris, after Correggio's immensely famous *Leda* had been rashly mutilated to such an extent that the head of Leda was cut out and lost altogether, contemporary sources report how the most famous painters of the day, including Boucher, did not dare to attempt the task of recreating Leda's face for fear of having their art directly compared with that of Correggio.[26]

Yet the hesitancy of Maratti to leave his mark was downplayed by Bellori because his expectations, as I already mentioned, were quite different. Bellori stressed, instead, the importance of describing for posterity the exact locations of the repainting and he listed all the figures that Maratti had "adjusted".[27] Bellori's primary intention was to praise Maratti's superior ability as a Raphael restorer through use of precise examples. The surviving material evidence indicates that Maratti did much less than Bellori advertised, however. For instance, Bellori said that Maratti had completely renovated the figures of Bacchus and Hercules in the banquet scene; and yet recent technical analysis revealed that Bacchus and Hercules had not been totally repainted by Maratti and certainly not on new plaster. Rather, the intervention seems to have been confined to some retouching, for example in the shadow tones of the faces, where accents were added by Maratti in black pencil strokes and red ochre.[28] Similarly, in the case of the spandrel painting of *Mercury*, also discussed by Bellori as an area of exemplary intervention, recent evidence indicates that Maratti did not replaster and paint afresh, but only reinforced some of the outlines of the figure (Fig. 28).

Nevertheless, it would be anachronistic to expect from Maratti a mid-twentieth-century approach to compensation, in the consistent use of visible in-painting and only easily removable materials. Maratti disguised the locations of the 850 nails contributed to hold the *intonaco* in place by covering them with stucco and then camouflaging the areas with paints applied in watercolor. The disruption of Raphael's surface by visible structural additions would have been considered messy and disfiguring workmanship.

Moreover, as modern commentators have noticed, Maratti did not practice reversibility throughout the project but rather repainted and even painted totally afresh portions of decoration. For the sake of the successful overall impact of Raphael's work, Maratti invented areas of decoration for the parts of the loggia adjacent to the recently added windows. Maratti (and Bellori) evidently thought that the trompe l'oeil naturalistic decoration executed by Giovanni da Udine on the inside wall should be matched on the opposite glassed-in wall. Thus Bellori explains how Maratti's assistants continued the decoration of the lower part of the vault on the north side, extending the original festoons of fruit and flowers down to the level of the cornice and adding plain architectural forms on the underlying walls "out of respect for the vault."[29]

On the whole, however, Maratti's restoration of Raphael's Loggia of Psyche frescoes did stand apart, in spirit if not fully in practice, from the pervasive baroque tendency to allow artistic license and contemporary taste to refashion works of art. This was due in large part to the highly intellectual environment in which the project took place. Yet ironically, it seems to have been Bellori's commentary that sparked the controversy that followed Maratti's intervention, because the degree of repainting and overpainting was exaggerated by Bellori.[30] Bellori explained that the kind of complete restoration of the Raphaels to their original greatness that he would have favoured was not possible because of the "superstitions of some" who had rather the frescoes fall apart than that they be repainted by another hand. To defend the work, Bellori argued that the critics of Maratti contradict themselves because classical sculptural fragments are often reconstructed, and paintings should be similarly revived in honor of their now barely visible artistic potential.[31]

Those critical of Maratti, however, claimed the repainting was not in accord with the original work.[32] The most pronounced criticism came in 1756 from Luigi Crespi in a letter to the famous Venetian intellectual Francesco Algarotti. Based on a detailed reading of Bellori's commentary, Crespi's letter systematically criticized Maratti's work and completely rebutted Bellori's thesis that Raphael's frescoes had been revalorized through the sensitive restoration of Maratti. Bellori had exaggerated the learned and praiseworthy intentions behind Maratti's intervention, Crespi argued.[33] In response to Bellori's argument concerning sculpture, Crespi contended that ancient sculpture could be carefully restored in an acceptable way, as long as the parts (missing limbs, etc.) added to complete the statue were not attached in such a way that they transformed the overall perception of the work and thereby destroyed the original. The distinction is between repainting, which covers over the original work, and adding parts to a sculpture, which do not cover the original but only complete missing limbs, and so on.[34]

The final important intervention by Maratti was on the paintings in the Vatican Stanze, 1702–3. He was by then old and directed the restoration rather than taking part. Bellori records that some of the principal frescoes were in a poor state due in part to the large number of copyists who had climbed ladders and come too close to the originals. Maratti's preventative solution was to install an iron grill to isolate the painted walls from the public, who were also required to be silent when admiring the works of Raphael.[35]

The reverence for Raphael expressed by both Maratti and Bellori engendered an exceptional situation in which the restorer tried to limit severely his personal contribution to the appearance of the restored paintings, as I have already argued. In contrast, most of the restorations carried out during the baroque period in European courts and galleries imprinted the taste of the day onto historic works of art. Artistically trained restorers were commissioned to adapt paintings as fashions changed. Paintings were cut down, enlarged, reshaped, and repainted to accord with new styles of decoration.[36] The kind of respect for the original work shown by Maratti begins to emerge in restoration as a general practice only about a century later, and not in Italy but in Paris. In addition, the perhaps misguided but nevertheless intelligent criticism presented by Luigi Crespi in his letter of 1756 was just one symptom of a more rigorous impulse in restoration, which seems to arise at this time, concurrent with the development of the scientific encyclopedia in France.

THE TRANSFER TECHNIQUE AS APPLIED TO SEVERAL PANELS BY RAPHAEL IN PARIS, 1750–1850

The development of "modern" restoration-conservation can be traced from the late eighteenth century in Paris, as is well known.[37] From about 1740, and for a period of about a century, a large number of highly important Italian paintings were treated in Paris, many having been brought from Italy in the late eighteenth century as a result of the Napoleonic campaigns. During this period, the French realized the need to regulate and organize art restoration to a greater degree, eventually within the administrative structure of the Louvre Museum. Restoration as an artisanal practice began to be separated from creative artistic work and the principles and ethics of modern-day restoration and conservation slowly emerged.

The paintings of Raphael and their restoration figure prominently in these important French developments. A number of large works by Raphael were in the French royal collection by the late eighteenth century, as well as several by Andrea del Sarto. The *Saint Michael* (Plate 27) and the *Holy Family of François I* of 1517–18 (both Louvre, Paris) had been commissioned from Raphael by Lorenzo de' Medici and Pope Leo X, Lorenzo's uncle, as gifts for François I and his queen at Fountainbleau. Other important altarpieces by Raphael, including the *Madonna di Foligno* (Vatican, Pinacoteca) and the *Saint Cecilia* (Bologna), were brought to Paris during the Napoleonic period and subsequently returned to Italy (Plates 25 and 26). Three Raphael Madonnas were owned by the Duc d'Orléans. These paintings by Raphael ranked among the greatest art treasures of France during the seventeenth, eighteenth, and nineteenth centuries.

French art theorists celebrated Raphael as the most admirable Renaissance painter, from the early days of the French Academy in the mid–seventeenth century through into the neoclassical period.[38] The French followed, to varying degrees, the established model of the Italian humanist art theorists. Vasari and Lomazzo had described Raphael as the modern Apelles: excellent in all aspects essential to artistic perfection; and this is the stance adopted, eventually, by Bellori and by the French as well.[39] Thus, Roland de Fréart de Chambray in his *Idée* of 1662 instructs French artists to emulate Raphael.[40] More influential was André Félibien who argued, in a very similar manner to Bellori, that supreme beauty in art comes from first imitating nature, but then selecting the most perfect parts and thereby correcting and idealizing the forms. French artists should model themselves after artists who worked in this manner: the ancients, Raphael, and Poussin (the "French Raphael").[41] By the late seventeenth century, Roger de Piles swayed from exclusive reverence for Raphael because of his preference for Rubens's colorism. Nevertheless, de Piles ranked only Raphael as high as the perfect Rubens in his famous classification and scoring of the elements of artistic style, seeing Raphael as capable of embracing both design and color. Raphael's stature, though demoted somewhat under neoclassicism by those who prized only the antique, remained elevated and strongly entrenched in France. After all, already during Raphael's lifetime the French royal preference for Raphael had begun to be manifest in the collections in Paris, a taste that the treatises of the seventeenth and eighteenth centuries served to explain and reinforce. Under Napoleon, it was this very French taste that was reasserted within a quite different political arena through the aggressive acquisition and ostentatious display of numerous Raphaels in the Napoleonic museum.[42]

Because of the artistic value placed on Raphael's work, securing the most safe and advanced restoration methods became an urgent priority and attracted huge investments during the eighteenth and early nineteenth centuries in Paris. Although it has often been argued that it was the rise of scientific empiricism in chemistry and physics that propelled the advent of "modern" art conservation, the most important impulse toward reform in France c. 1800 came, it seems, from a reverence for the artistic masterpieces themselves. As I explore in the following pages, scientific innovation and experimentation did play a pronounced role in the influential Raphael restorations of this period. Nevertheless, the careful scrutiny of restoration practices that led to the regulation of the discipline along quite new and very structured lines, was primarily motivated by the concern to protect and preserve the immensely valued "original" paintings.[43]

Of all the Raphaels, his *Saint Michael* (Plate 27 and Fig. 29) and his *Holy Family of François I* were the most famous in the royal collection, and consequently, they were always on show and often transported from one royal location to another, as the king changed the seat of his court from season to season.[44] By 1749, a report commissioned from a group of royal painters and restorers describes the precarious condition of the *Saint Michael* and recommends, cautiously, the importance of further preventative measures. The report explains that Raphael's *Saint Michael* and his *Holy Family of François I* deserve the greatest attention of all the works of art owned by the king, but that they are difficult to manage because they are panel-paintings with attached frames.[45] As the king changes his location, they are moved, and "they suffer a lot due to these movements, as can be seen from how the paint surface is lifted up and is flaking off in many parts." The report expresses the fear that soon, due to the poor condition of the *Saint Michael* and the potentially threatened condition of the *Holy Family*, "we will be forced to have them transferred to canvas using the new secret practiced by Picault." It warns that Robert Picault's method of transfer is an "extreme procedure" and should only be undertaken as a last possible solution.[46]

Such cautious remarks, full of foresight, preceed by only two years the beginning of a sequence of radical transfers performed on the paintings by Raphael in the king's collection, initially by Robert Picault, and then by several other transfer experts including Jean-Louis Hacquin and his son François-Toussaint Hacquin. Undertaken in most cases because of the serious state of deterioration of the paint surfaces, the transfers were seen as the only way of preserving "all that remains of the pure Raphael original."[47] The transfers were preceded and followed by careful assessments by groups of experts and thus were undertaken with great seriousness. Experts recommended proceeding with transfer because heavily worm-eaten panels would no longer have been valid as supports, but would rather have contributed to the progressive destabilization of the paint layers. In short, as was the case in the 1690s in Rome when Maratti was commissioned to "repair" Raphael's Loggia of Psyche frescoes, substantial and innovative restoration procedures were motivated by severe states of deterioration, and learned discussion surrounded the restoration of these immensely valued works of art.

The French artisan and "chemist," Robert Picault, who claimed to have invented his unique method of transfer, although he had not, rose to fame in Paris with his momentous transfer of Andrea del Sarto's *Charity* in 1749–50.[48] The transferred *Charity* was received by the Académie des Beaux Arts,

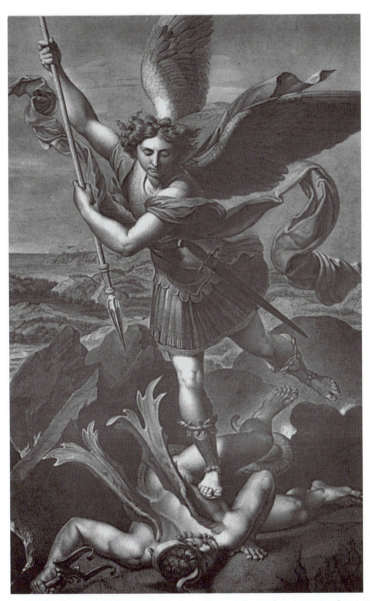

29. Raphael, *Saint Michael*, 1517–18, Paris, Louvre. From the engraving by A. Tardieu in Johann David Passavant, *Raphael of Urbino and His Father Giovanni Santi*, London and New York: Macmillan & Co., 1872, pl. 18.

and even by the king, with praise and pleasure and then exhibited in the Luxembourg galleries when they first opened to the public on October 15, 1750, with its "original," worm-eaten panel beside it.[49] (Actually, the heavily channelled panel, although reputed to be Andrea del Sarto's original, was from another source, only one indication of Picault's less than scrupulous behavior.)[50] Picault's transfer procedure was interpreted as a marvel that could immortalize art against the decay of nature by giving it new life ("lui redonner la vie").[51]

The considerable enthusiasm in Paris for Picault's method, despite its mystery and its ample risks, was generated at a time of remarkable scientific experimentation and writing. France was the world leader in science during the period 1750–1850 when many panel paintings by Raphael were transferred from panel to canvas. Moreover, the interest in the transfer technique seems to have been closely connected to a more widespread contemporary interest in the mechanical arts stimulated by the Enlightenment philosophers and scientists of Denis Diderot's circle. In an analogous way in Rome, techniques for detaching frescoes were practiced and refined by architects and engineers with creative abilities in the mechanical arts, and the extraordinary mechanical feats were watched with great contemporary enthusiasm.[52] Picault's reputation as a trustworthy and objectively rigorous artisan was definitely enhanced, if not created, by intellectuals, especially a Jesuit journalist Father Berthier, who was at the very same time writing a systematic evaluation of Diderot's *Encyclopédie*. Indeed, it is important to recognize how closely associated these major restorations in Paris were with the informed, French Enlightenment discussions about the arts and sciences in Diderot's encyclopedia.[53]

The massive *Encyclopédie*, or *Dictionnaire raisonné des sciences, des arts, et des métiers* (17 vols. text and 11 vols. plates; completed 1766) has been characterized as the "signet" of French Enlightenment thought.[54] It was Diderot's conviction that a dictionary should not be only a reference tool but should have "the character of changing the general way of thinking."[55] He explictly aimed to alter the hierarchical relationship between the liberal and the mechanical arts, celebrating the artisanal activities of the trades in great detail in many articles that he wrote himself.[56] Diderot advocates forcefully that it is time the respected professors of the liberal arts support and celebrate the artisans, finally giving them their due, and elevating them above "the contempt in which prejudice has for so long held them"; "it is for the patronage of kings to draw them from the poverty in which they still languish."[57]

Jesuit intellectuals who were reading the *Encyclopédie* wrote about the Raphael restorations in the pages of their journal, the *Mémoires de Trévoux*, in relation to wider arguments about the importance of newly innovative methods derived from the mechanical arts and applied sciences, that could be successfully used to save works of great artistic and cultural importance.[58] The presentation of Picault's methods by the Jesuit Father Berthier, editor of the *Mémoires de Trévoux*, in February 1751, is most important in this context. Father Berthier began his promotion of Picault by explaining that just as Apelles's exemplary painting on wood panel of "Venus rising from the waters" did not survive the inevitable processes of time, so too those of Raphael are vulnerable; but that Picault's technique, which "repairs the injuries of time," will give the works

longer life than painters themselves could give them: This is to say...that if the Saint Michael by Raphael has already survived for 230 or 240 years, once it has been transferred to a new support (new wood or canvas) it will survive...for three or four centuries.[59]

Berthier describes Picault's procedure, praising his great care and detailing how he labors at great length, appreciating the preciousness of each work. Picault manages to transfer entire compositions, not separate pieces, by softening the paint layers "as one would lift up a print in order to unglue it." The essential and most mysterious part of the ungluing is achieved by making a big fire of "liquors that are the secret."[60] The painting is then transferred to a new foundation, "coated with a strong substance that we call *maroufle*" that enables the creation of "an extraordinary bond,...an almost indissoluble ensemble" such that "paintings transported in this way have a second duration longer than the first."[61] Those who criticize Picault, Berthier points out, have not as yet achieved equivalent results. Moreover, as Berthier concludes, the painters of the French Academy, professors of the long-established Liberal Arts, have already agreed on the great usefulness of Picault's "art," and in this way "restored justice" to the genius artisan.[62]

It is true that some members of the academy had advised in November 1750 that Picault's procedure would enable the conservation of the original coloring in Raphael's famous *Saint Michael* by removing older repaintings. Nevertheless, there were other more cautious members who, after documenting the many losses already sustained, commented that such a transfer might result in even more surface paint losses and suggested that the painting be repaired without recourse to transfer.[63]

But as each month passed, the likelihood of transfer for the *Saint Michael* became more and more clear, and prior to treatment in January 1751, members of the Royal Commission on paintings conducted a careful assessment of the painting's condition. This document, which details the numerous repaintings on the *Saint Michael*, reflects the seriousness with which the transfer was undertaken. The Raphael is described as generally in deplorable condition, especially the lower portion, from the knee of Saint Michael down.[64] Increasingly, Picault's transfer method seems to have been considered the way to prolong the life of a painting otherwise barely salvagable.

In the restorer's memorandum concerning his eight months of work on the *Saint Michael*, submitted in late 1751, Picault describes his incredibly hard labor, day and night, and mentions how this work has jeopardized his health because of the sulphurous and nitrous substances that he was forced to inhale during the procedures. For the Raphael alone, Picault requested payment of 11,500 livres, eventually receiving a much-reduced but still very large sum of 7,000 livres.[65] The transferred *Saint Michael* was exhibited to public view on 18 October 1752, in the Luxembourg, and the members of the academy praised Picault saying that his treatment had "secured [the classic work] from the vicissitudes of time" and that the image had also "attained a new grace."[66] Since Giorgio Vasari, Raphael had been praised particularly for the *grazia*, or "grace" of his art, a stylistic term that implied his paintings were elegant and beautiful in the figures, coloring and arrangement, but also that his creative genius was divinely inspired. For the French painting masters to credit Picault with having given Raphael's *Saint Michael* new "grace" was the ultimate compliment.

Recent research on the degradation of Andrea del Sarto's *Charity* confirms that, as Robert Picault and his advocate Father Berthier had suggested, Picault did use chemical vapors, specifically nitric acid, to break down the adhesion between the paint layers and the ground. Unfortunately, these vapours enter into the chemical composition of the ground and also affect the chemistry of the paint layers. It was not possible for Picault to control the penetration of the vapor, and one persistent result are the grey stains in the sky of the much-damaged *Charity*. The new adhesive, ground layer, or "maroufle," applied by Picault as an alternative to the traditional gesso, did not prove to be at all sturdy. Chemical tests carried out in 1980–1 reveal that Picault's "maroufle" was made of calcium resinate, probably composed of a mixture of heated pine resin (colofonium) and white chalk, which darkens and which may not have stuck effectively over time.[67] Because of the poor adhesion of the "maroufle" as well as the fragmentation of the paint layers during transfer, many of the paintings treated by Picault had to be transfered again within only a few decades.[68]

Indeed, by 1766 the paint layers of the *Saint Michael* were described once more as flaking, and the necessity of another transfer was discussed. Robert Picault's reputation was no longer high, largely because of the belief that he had charged exhorbitant fees for what was actually a fairly straightforward chemical procedure of little cost in terms of the raw materials. Thus, although Picault offered to retransfer the painting free of charge, explaining that the basic problem was that he had not been able to completely remove the old ground, the royal administration at the Bâtiments decided to give this and many subsequent commissions to Jean-Louis Hacquin instead. The Bâtiments explained that they were more comfortable with Hacquin's methods because they were less secret, more easily understood, and much less expensive. Therefore, among many other paintings, Jean-Louis Hacquin restored Raphael's *Saint Michael* in 1777, as well as his *Saint John the Baptist, Saint Margaret,* and *Holy Family of François I.*[69]

Of course, Hacquin's methods of transfer were not secure and reliable either, and Hacquin also maintained some aura of mystery. The recent conservation of the *Holy Family of François I* has exposed the poor condition of the painting, due in large part to Hacquin's methods. The original color palette has been disturbed irreparably.[70] Writing in 1797, just twenty years after Hacquin's work, the ambitious dealer Jean-Baptiste Lebrun argued that the already apparent degradation of the *Saint Michael* and *Saint Margaret* was caused by Hacquin's glue ground, which had undermined the chemical stability of the paint layers (by increasing changes due to hygroscopy – sensitivity to humidity) and that the pressure applied during the transfer had resulted in the canvas weave being impressed onto the paint layers, depriving the paintings forever of their original panel characteristics.[71] Lebrun's criticisms betray the impact of new scientific knowledge in the assessment of restoration practices. As the eighteenth century came to a close, empirical research on the chemical and physical properties of artists' and restorers' materials gradually propelled restorers to adopt newly developed and tested methods under the scrutiny of scientists and artists alike.[72] The mystique of secretive entrepreneurs like Robert Picault, who worked in the spirit of an alchemist, guarding the miraculous elixir of life for aged artistic masterpieces, was no longer valued. Furthermore, Lebrun's observation that the transferred Raphaels no longer maintained the aesthetic features characteristic of works on panel because the canvas weave had become visible through the paint layers sounds hauntingly modern. Writing on the history of the transfer technique, Volker Schaible explains that full acceptance of the material nature of the original painted work, and the accompanying rejection of structural transformations, developed gradually during the late eighteenth and nineteenth centuries as a result of empirical research in attendant areas of the natural sciences and also due to museum policies that progressively defined the sphere of art preservation.[73]

THE *MADONNA DI FOLIGNO*

The direct participation of scientists in the assessment of a Raphael restoration is most clearly documented in the famous French report of 1801 concerning the *Madonna di Foligno* (Plate 25).[74] The first part of the report, written by two chemists, Louis-Bernard Guyton de Morveau and Claude-Louis Berthollet, is a description of the transfer method used by François-Toussaint Hacquin (son of Jean-Louis), and the second part by two painters, the famous François-André Vincent and Mr. Taunay, discusses the approach to retouching.[75] The altarpiece had been confiscated from Foligno (where it had been moved in 1565 perhaps because the Aracoeli was being remodelled in accordance with the strictures of the Counter-Reformation) by Napoleon's troops as a condition of the Treaty of Tolentino and brought to Paris in 1797.[76] In Paris, the condition was assessed as extremely dangerous. Not only was the panel rotten in parts and full of worm holes, but a large crack ran down the upper half.[77] Because the support had decayed so much, the ground and paint layers were destabilized. Extreme fluctuations in dryness and humidity due to wartime conditions and the transport of the altarpiece to Paris had contributed further to flaking paint. In addition, large areas of the image were obscured by previous repaintings and discolored varnish.

The report of 1801 is punctuated by the familiar rhetoric concerning the inevitable decay of paintings over time and the necessity of restoration to salvage masterpieces for posterity. Under Napoleon, numerous paintings by Raphael were collected in Paris for display beginning in 1803 as part of the Musée Napoléon.[78] In this context, it is tempting to interpret the argument that restoration methods were highly advanced in Paris, and that damaged treasures could be preserved there, as an attempt to justify the plunder. It is difficult to assess how genuine the language of the 1801 report actually is. Certainly, a new weight is given to the importance of careful procedure under museum surveillance. Such delicate procedures are only allowed when works are extremely degraded. Great care is required to ensure that works by the "immortal" Raphael are not artistically altered through restoration.[79] Therefore, the present commission has been appointed to scrutinize the mechanical procedure of the transfer of Raphael's *Madonna di Foligno* and also the subsequent cleaning and repainting.

Evidently, the chemists watched closely as Hacquin performed the transfer because they explain the procedure in detail. Instead of detaching the paint layers by breaking down the gesso ground and then removing them from the original wood support, as Picault had done, Hacquin worked from the back, gradually thinning down the panel. He destroyed the support to reveal the paint beneath the ground without causing undue stress to these fragile layers. The exposed and much damaged paint was then treated with mixtures of oil and glue to reduce the dryness and increase adhesion. After the paint had been flattened, it was applied to a new canvas covered with a new, and supposedly more durable, ground.

In the second part of the report concerning cleaning and repainting, the painters stress how precious the surface of Raphael's altarpiece is and that exceptional knowledge, experience, and "a great delicateness of the eye [are required] to fit the tones with the original."[80] The experienced specialist Roeser (also know as Roxin) had been chosen to carry out the repainting, with the object of recovering what the painters on the commission term Raphael's "pure" work. The concept of artistic purity, in this instance, was understood to include seamless compensation for loss. The restorer must struggle to ensure that his repainting blends in: "the most scrupulous care must be taken...to harmonize ["accorder"] the restoration work with that of the master...and to make the intervention disappear to the point that the eye...cannot distinguish the hand of the artist-restorer from that of the master."[81] The desire to return Raphael's paintings to their original aspect by repainting and blending in areas of loss came from a genuine belief that a painting had to be complete to be fully appreciated and that losses would mar, in a disrespectful way, the artistry of one of the greatest painters of all time.

Generally speaking, the approach to loss compensation did not shift markedly until the late nineteenth or early twentieth century, because such a change in approach required a totally different understanding of both the work of art and the restorer-conservator's role in its preservation. One of the first steps toward change came already in the late seventeenth century when the exceptional Maratti admitted not wanting to presume to compete with Raphael's hand. As I have presented, Maratti professed the need to practice removable, watercolor retouching for some of the areas of damage in the Loggia of Psyche in 1693–5, in reverence to Raphael. Then, by 1759, the Comte de Caylus, in one of his lectures to the French Academy, expressed the belief that restorations should be "visible."[82] In 1827, Christian Köstler (restorer in Heidelberg and later Berlin) wrote in his treatise *On the Restoration of Old Oil-Paintings* that the restorer must remain "invisible."[83] In Italy, Giovanni Battista Cavalcaselle, an artist by training and an experienced and articulate observer of paintings, spoke out strongly against the repainting approach of many artist-restorers. By 1879, he was using his government position to issue guidelines that prevented strong cleanings in which large losses were exposed. Cavalcaselle argued that the restorer's brush should only be used inside the confines of damage to lightly integrate the losses with the conserved parts of the original.[84] Nevertheless, it was not until the early twentieth century that visible in-painting was consistently employed. Furthermore, we do not see a fragmentary Raphael enthusiastically appreciated in its incomplete form until 1912, and even in major museum conservation projects as recently as the 1980s, there is a tendency to want to reintegrate loss quite fully in the case of Raphaels. By the 1980s, this tendency toward full reintegration is, of course, far more muted than previously, and it is justified in the self-aware conservation language of the late twentieth century.

Yet before considering a few case studies from the twentieth century, developments during the nineteenth century must be briefly acknowledged. I dwell only on one important step, which involves the increased understanding of the work of art in its complete material nature and the resulting efforts to preserve all of the original ingredients including damaged wood panel supports and "patina." Through the continuing impact of archaeology and of writings on ancient art, which posed the critical restoration problem of whether to prioritize the historical vicissitudes or the reconstructed original in the present, by the first decades of the nineteenth century, restoration had become a more logical, visible, and rationally presented operation. The role of the restorer had been constrained and circumcized during the eighteenth century and dissociated from that of the creative artist who attempted to make his mark by rejuvinating famous works. Instead, the notion of the restorer as the one who saves paintings from the inevitable decay caused by time and the environment, voiced in the French discussions of the transfer technique, led to a language of the restorer as healer and doctor of paintings. This medical metaphor, retained today in the terminology of a conservation project as a "treatment," enabled a conception of restoration as involving the entire body of the painting. In other words, a holistic philosophy of restoration that encompassed all aspects of the material nature of the work of art came about during the nineteenth century, as one major Raphael restoration, carried out by the famous Giuseppe Molteni, will show.[85]

GIUSEPPE MOLTENI AND RAPHAEL'S *MARRIAGE OF THE VIRGIN*, 1857–8

Raphael's elegant altarpiece of the *Marriage of the Virgin* of 1504 (Plate 4), painted for a family chapel in the Franciscan (Minori) church in Città di Castello, came to Lombardy and into the hands of the Milanese restorer Giuseppe Molteni through interesting circumstances. The altarpiece was given under duress to the Italian captain and "liberator" Giuseppe Lechi, when he arrived in Città di Castello in 1798 leading a campaign against the French. Raphael's altarpiece thus became part of the remarkable art collection of the Lechi brothers in Brescia until Giuseppe sold it in 1801, and it passed to the Ospedale Maggiore in Milan and then to the Brera by 1806.[86] These changes in location and ownership resulted in severe damage, however, particularly to the painting's panel support. Nevertheless, when Molteni was commissioned to repair Raphael's damaged *Sposalizio* in November 1857, he did not proceed to a transfer. Molteni considered the panel to be an integral part of Raphael's original. Such emphasis on the totality of the original materials is evident also in other facets of the restoration, particularly the cleaning of the varnish film which occasions a discussion of "patina."

It is telling to learn from Molteni's account of June 1858 how long he worked on the support in an effort to salvage it. When he received the altarpiece, the panel was significantly bowed and undulating, and there were three long cracks in the upper portion.[87] After identifying the cause of the warping as dessication, Molteni spent three months flattening the panel using various methods, including water baths.

An increasingly holistic approach is also reflected in his cleaning approach, whether we would be inclined today to agree with his views toward varnish removal or not. Molteni performed a partial cleaning, paying great attention to what he describes as the very thin, original patina, "the precious skin of the painting."[88] He explains that his goal was to equilibrate, or even out, the surface irregularities, which were the result of bad restorations in the past and which had created an aesthetic imbalance. Molteni emphasizes that a little of the patina has to be left and that it forms "a good varnish layer of Raphael's own, enabling recovery of the original, historic aspect of the altarpiece."[89]

Molteni's concern to restore the *Marriage of the Virgin* on its original, wood support, even though the damage to the panel would have led many to a transfer, reveals an inclination to preserve the original materials. It is this positivistic approach to conservation-restoration that became increasingly dominant during the course of the subsequent, twentieth century. The work of art began to be interpreted as a historical artifact or document in such a way that the complete material constitution of the original object became potentially of value and the sacrifice of authentic materials was taboo. In this instance, moreover, the retention by Molteni of the original support and ground has enabled late-twentieth-century conservators and art historians to examine Raphael's preparatory "underdrawing" using infrared reflectography.[90]

TWO ANGELS FROM THE CORONATION OF SAN NICOLA OF TOLENTINO ALTARPIECE: TWENTIETH-CENTURY APPROACHES TO CLEANING AND COMPENSATION

The following, very brief account of how two fragmentary angels from Raphael's early San Nicola of Tolentino Altarpiece were cleaned and inpainted at different moments during the twentieth century illustrates the positivistic approach of the period in the enthusiastic rediscovery and acceptance of incomplete works. At the same time, the enduring concern for the artistic integrity of paintings by Raphael also emerges in the compensation choices that are taken. Commissioned originally in 1500 for the Cappella Baronci of Sant'Agostino in Città di Castello, the Nicola of Tolentino Altarpiece was severely damaged in an earthquake of 1789. Two individual angels were, at this point, cut from the original *pala* and prepared for sale.[91] The *Angel* now in the Pinacoteca Tosio-Martinengo in Brescia was repainted to make it look as if it were a complete work, which involved providing a solid dark background for the figure and covering the angel's wings to create a self-sufficient portrait of a young man (Fig. 30). The painting was, nevertheless, recognized as an early Raphael by the intelligent collector Teodoro Lechi (the younger brother of Giuseppe Lechi). Teodoro Lechi corresponded closely with another Breschian count and collector, Paolo Tosio, who seems to have acquired the Raphael "portrait" on Lechi's recommendation in 1822 and from whom the panel passed in 1844 to the city of Brescia.[92] In 1894–5, the painting was transferred to canvas.[93] Later on, in 1912–13, the "portrait" was cleaned in a fascinating restoration carried out by Molteni's pupil, Luigi Cavenaghi.

Heir in part to the artist-restorer tradition of his prominent teacher, Luigi Cavenaghi worked on many important Renaissance paintings during his spectacular career in Italy before the First World War, including Giorgione's *Tempest.* His work for public galleries was momentous because he seems to

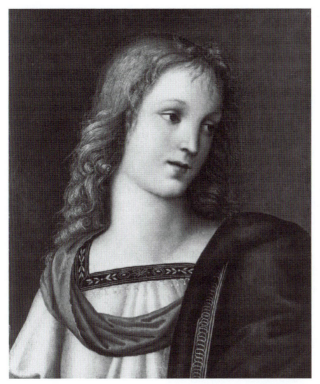

30. Raphael, *Angel*, fragment from the San Nicola of Tolentino Altarpiece, commissioned 1500, Pinacoteca Civica Tosio-Martinengo, Brescia. Condition before cleaning of 1912–13, showing post-1789 repainting to form a "Portrait of a Young Man." Photo: Alinari/Art Resource NY.

have been one of the first to remove voluntarily repaints by previous restorers, thereby laying bare original underlying layers on paintings such as the *Portrait of a Young Man* in the Borghese Gallery in Rome, then attributed to Perugino but now to Raphael.[94] For the panel in Brescia, Cavenaghi unveiled the fragmentary nature of the painting and the identity of the figure as an angel from the lost San Nicola of Tolentino *pala*, to the applause of the gallery director, Giulio Zappa.[95] The discovery of part of a much discussed, early *pala* by Raphael made the revelation particularly significant and encouraged the reconstruction of the altarpiece, encompassing other surviving fragments.[96] The cleaning laid bare a window on the left and the angel's wings, but also uncovered areas of loss. The losses were significant around the edges of the painting, although not in central areas such as the face. Cavenaghi chose to integrate the losses quite completely without disguising the painting's incomplete nature. Once again, the restoration of a Raphael seems to be more advanced than was generally the practice at this juncture in the early twentieth century. Cavenaghi's approach was more archaeological than most in fully freeing the painting of its later accretions.

More recently, in 1983, Cavenaghi's complete integrations have been removed and redone following late-twentieth-century techniques of visible in-painting. The method of *tratteggio* has been used in the picture to suggestively and only partially integrate the larger gaps, and thin watercolor washes have been employed to lightly blend in smaller losses to the paint surface (Plate 1).[97] The *tratteggio* method was conceived of by Cesare Brandi as a way of creating a visible dialogue between past and present on the surface of the painting. Although very difficult to execute well in practice, in theory *tratteggio* solved the problem of loss for mid- to late-twentieth-century conservators. Areas of loss could be bridged by colors and shapes that blended with the original, thereby enhancing the legibility of the design and subject without competing with the original artist's hand.[98] This incomplete hatching method is most effective for relatively small areas of loss, however. It is also most appropriate for use with paintings in fresco or egg tempera on panel because paintings executed in these quick-drying media are already made up of systems of hatched paint strokes.

When treating, in 1983, the second fragmentary *Angel* from the San Nicola of Tolentino *pala*, now at the Louvre, conservators, cognizant of the limitations of *tratteggio*, developed a method of in-painting more in harmony with the oil medium used by Raphael. A fuller reconstruction of the losses, using pointillist in-painting that is not as obviously visible as *tratteggio*, was held to be more urgent in the case of the Louvre *Angel* because a disfiguring system of losses ran down the center of the angel's face. Yet although in theory contemporary conservation specialists treat each damaged painting as a unique case, there may be some discrepancy in the way an almost full integration was selected for the Raphael *Angel*, at the same time that less complete compensation methods were considered necessary for several panels by earlier Italian masters at the Louvre.[99] It may be that the high stature of Raphael's art – an evaluation that has remained constant in art historical and restoration writings since before Raphael's untimely death – continues to impact on compensation choices by subtly persuading conservators to integrate losses in an unusually concealing manner, so as not to compromise the artistic communication of a Raphael.

Furthermore, contradictions in the holistic philosophy of conservation appear throughout the twentieth century because of the way in which "authenticity," "integrity," and "original" are understood. The material remains from the period of the painting's creation are usually prioritized above the testimony of later interpretations, both in conservation and in art history, particularly when later changes to the object obscure the original or are judged to be of lower quality.[100] As Cornelia Wagner has argued, however, a painting that is freed of all changes in an effort to recover the painter's original statement is not identical to the initial painting, because the removal of later materials, including varnishes, will have implications for the aesthetic of the image and often distort its integrity.[101] By the late twentieth century, conservators began to express an awareness that a full recovery of the original materials of an historic painting was never possible. In the coming decades, the implications of this realization will likely contribute to further important developments in conservation theory and practice. Already there is the potential for a more layered view of historic artworks and their existence through time. In the course of a painting's history, the sequence of changes brought about by time, the environment and human intervention, accumulate to form the restoration provenance, which is itself a stratification.

THE *CANIGIANI HOLY FAMILY*

More specifically, a painting by Raphael that has been restored several times, during different periods of restoration practice and historical thought, can be expected to display a sequence of alterations within its own restoration provenance due to the changing ways in which restoration has been approached from century to century. Perhaps the most striking example of such a transformation in Raphael's oeuvre is the *Canigiani Holy Family* (Plate 9). It was in the midst of the animated discussions concerning the methods of transferring panel paintings and whether practitioners such as Picault were mere technicians or deserved respect and generous remuneration that Raphael's influential *Canigiani Holy Family* underwent a restoration in the late eighteenth century that significantly alterred its appearance and also inflicted permanent damage. The restorer was François-Louis Colins, perhaps the most respected painting restorer in Paris of his day.[102] He was one of two restorers at the Bâtiments, working there alongside the Widow Godefroid on the paintings in the gallery of the King. Colins was given a royal pension from 1743 on and considered a highly skilled restorer to whom the most valued Old Master paintings would be brought.[103]

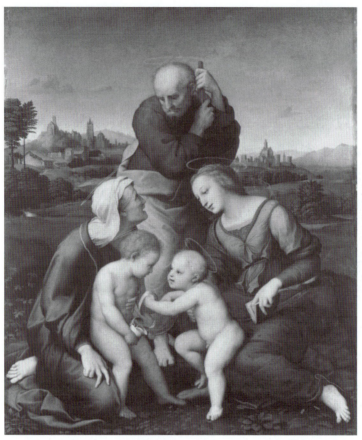

31. Raphael, *Canigiani Holy Family*, c. 1507–8, Alte Pinakothek, Munich. Condition following repainting c. 1755 and before cleaning of 1982. Photo: Bayerischen Staatsgemäldesammlungen, Alte Pinakothek, Munich.

At the center of painting restoration in Paris, Colins had been closely involved in the sensational transfers carried out by Picault, including Raphael's *Saint Michael* in 1751. After Picault completed the transfer of Andrea del Sarto's *Charity* to its new canvas in 1749, it was Colins who compensated through retouching for the myriad tiny losses to the painting's surface. Colins had also overseen the reconstruction of Correggio's famous *Leda* and *Io* (copy) in 1754, following the rash attack on the paintings by their royal owner, the unstable Louis d'Orleans, in about 1730. Colins acquired the cut-up canvas of the *Leda* from the estate of Charles Coypel, the royal painter, and he initiated the reconstruction with the help of the Widow Godefroid.[104] Subsequently, Colins was employed as inspector of the gallery

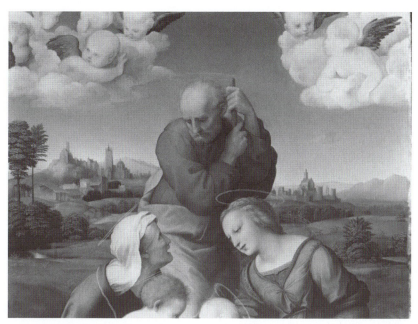

32. Raphael, *Canigiani Holy Family*, c. 1507–8, Alte Pinakothek, Munich, detail. Condition after cleaning of 1982. Photo: Bayerischen Staatsgemäldesammlungen, Alte Pinakothek, Munich.

of the Prince Electorate, Carl Phillipp von der Pfalz in Düsseldorf, for whom he compiled a catalogue of the collection in 1755. Under the patronage of the following Prince Electorate, Karl Theodor, Colins was commissioned to restore Raphael's *Canigiani Holy Family*.

How did it come to pass that such an experienced restorer, who had helped to salvage two famous Correggios following hostile mutilations, became involved in restoration work that has been described as destructive and even iconoclastic? Although the sources are not clear on the exact sequence of events and who was definitely responsible, it seems that the Prince Electorate's "Kammerdiener," Inspector Gregoire, found the clusters of angelic putti in the upper left and right corners of Raphael's painting offensive and therefore instructed Colins to scrape them away.[105] When that proved too onerous, Colins proceeded to overpaint, and thereby block out the child angels with the colors of the sky (Fig. 31). Writing in 1858, J. D. Passavant, director of the Frankfurt Museum, judged this liberal revision of Raphael's original "unforgivable."[106] It is, however, important to note that other commentators viewed the revised composition as perfectly classical in its pyramidal geometry. The formalist, Heinrich Wölfflin, in his extremely influential *Die klassische Kunst* of 1899, considered the compositional structure of the *Canigiani Holy Family* within a discussion of the development of harmonious groupings of figures in Raphael's exemplary Florentine Madonnas. Wölfflin described the repainted image as satisfying, strong, and archetypal, and illustrated the painting without any mention of restoration.[107] With influential formalists such as Wölfflin viewing the revised *Canigiani Holy Family* as exemplary, it is perhaps not surprising that the repainting was retained for a long time, despite the knowledge that Raphael had completed his *Holy Family* differently.

Colins's repainting was finally removed in 1982 by Hubertus von Sonnenburg in preparation for the quincentenary exhibitions of 1983 (Plate 9). The attempted erasure of the angel clusters, described by von Sonnenburg as "a brutal intervention...something similar to iconoclasm in the scratching off of the angels," was found to be limited primarily to the right section of clouds.[108] What is startling is the eighteenth-century restorer's insensitivity toward a Raphael, in great contrast to the earlier hesitancy and enormous care of Maratti. It may be that we do not have the full story and that someone other than Colins was responsible for the destructive erasure.

In the 1980s when von Sonnenburg took on the problem of the overpainted *Canigiani Holy Family*, the priority was to rediscover as much as remained of the original painting, an approach of enduring importance in the case of an artist of the stature of Raphael. Von Sonnenburg explained that Colins's overpainting did not constitute an important historical contribution but rather obscured the original.[109] By cleaning away the easily dissolvable eighteenth-century paint, von Sonnenburg exposed the evidence of the deliberate attempt to erase portions of the image, but also enabled the rediscovery of a large section of Raphael's painting not seen for hundreds of years (Fig. 32).[110] In step with late-twentieth-century approaches to integration, von Sonnenburg toned in the most disturbing areas of scratching with removable watercolor paints to reduce the distracting impact of the abbrasions without fully disguising the accretions of history.

CONCLUDING THOUGHTS

The extreme example of Raphael's *Canigiani Holy Family* reveals how changing cultural and restoration responses play themselves out on, and can remain embedded in, the fabric of an image.[111] The painting can become, in effect, an embodiment of its history through time, and for this reason the philosophical concept of the historicity (*historicité*) of the work of art is of relevance for contemporary conservation theory and practice.[112] As regards Raphael's paintings and their restoration history, this chapter has presented several important examples of how Raphael's works were treated at different periods and in varying ways, in response to shifting restoration practices and approaches, but also in relation to the ever-constant evaluation of Raphael's art as superior. Many surviving paintings by Raphael document – through their material structure and with the help of supporting archival and literary records – sequences of damage, decay, and rehabilitation. By examining the physical history of the paintings themselves, we gather concrete evidence of the critical fortune of Raphael from the fate of his art works. In this chapter, I have begun to place this material evidence of Raphael's *fortuna* in concert with the extensive literary and art historical discussions of Raphael's reputation through the centuries. The way that restorer-conservators often strayed from contemporary norms to enhance the aesthetic presentation of damaged paintings by Raphael provides particularly suggestive evidence of the artist's enduring stature.

Notes

INTRODUCTION

1. For artistic conditions in Florence between the expulsion of the Medici and the collapse of Borgia's seige, see Marcia B. Hall, "Savonarola's Preaching and the Patronage of Art," in *Christianity and the Renaissance. Image and Religious Imagination in the Quattrocento*, ed. Timothy Verdon and John Henderson (Syracuse: Syracuse University Press, 1990), 493–522.
2. On this and Bramante's other projects for Julius, see Linda Pellecchia's essay, this volume.
3. See my essay in this volume for discussion of this point.
4. Raphael included in the lower zone of the *Transfiguration* the episode of the apostles' attempted healing of the possessed boy, contrasted with the miracle above, an unprecedented iconographic combination. He treated the two zones differently in terms of coloring, chiaroscuro, and brushstroke. For further discussion, see Marcia B. Hall, *Color and Meaning: Practice and Theory in Renaissance Painting* (New York: Cambridge University Press, 1992), 131–6; and Hall, *Rome (Artistic Centers of the Italian Renaissance)* (New York: Cambridge University Press, 2005).
5. For analysis of the use of color and light in the Segnatura and the *Expulsion of Heliodorus*, see Janis Bell, "Color and Chiaroscuro," in *Raphael's "School of Athens,"* ed. Marcia B. Hall, *Masterpieces of Western Art* (New York: Cambridge University Press, 1997), 85–113.
6. The letter is dated 24 November 1647. See *Correspondance de Nicholas Poussin publiée d'après les originaux*, ed. Charles Jouanny, *Archive de l'art français* (Paris, 1911), 370–5; translation in Anthony Blunt, *Nicholas Poussin* (The A. W. Mellon Lectures in the Fine Arts), 2 vols. (1967), 367–70.
7. Panofsky, in an enormously influential book of 1925, dubbed linear perspective "the symbolic form" of the Renaissance (*Perspective as Symbolic Form*, 1925); translated by Christopher S. Wood (New York: Zone Books, 1991). Only recently have challenges begun to be raised, most usefully by James Elkins, *The Poetics of Perspective*. (Ithaca: Cornell University Press, 1994).
8. On the rediscovery of the Domus Aurea, see Nicole Dacos, *La découverte de la Domus Aurea et la formation des grotesques à la Renaissance*. Studies of the Warburg Institute, no. 31 (London: Warburg Institute, 1969).
9. Discussed in Hall, *After Raphael: Painting in Central Italy in the Sixteenth Century* (New York: Cambridge University Press, 1999), 162–4.
10. Hybrid modes of color are discussed in Hall, *Color and Meaning*, 158–9, 169–80.

11. Oscar Fischel, *Raphael*, trans. Bernard Rackham (London: Paul, 1948), 80.

12. Vasari related in the life of Perugino that when his altarpiece for Santissima Annunziata was unveiled in Florence in 1507, it was severely criticized because he had reused figures. Perugino was astonished and answered, "I have used the figures that you have at other times praised, and which have given you infinite pleasure; if now they do not please you, and you do not praise them, what can I do?" Vasari/de Vere, 4: 44.

13. Arnold Nesselrath ("Lorenzo Lotto in the Stanza della Segnatura," *Burlington Magazine* 142 [1999]: 4–12) has suggested that 1514 is when the workshop was formed. Thus it should be no surprise that it did not quite function smoothly at first when he designed the scenes in the Stanza dell'Incendio.

14. Vasari/de Vere 6:156, in the Life of Giulio Romano.

15. On Cardinal Alessandro Farnese's commission, see Clare Robertson, *'Il Gran Cardinale'. Alessandro Farnese, Patron of the Arts* (London: Yale University Press, 1992) 157–68.

16. See my discussion in *After Raphael* on the Sala dei Cento Giorni, 154–6; as well as 159–62, "Working Practices and Art Writing." It was reported to Vasari after he had returned to Florence that the Cento Giorni "had turned out more beautiful than expected, given the short time allotted to you" and that the patron was on the whole pleased.

17. On the competitions among sixteenth-century artists, see Rona Goffen, *Renaissance Rivals: Michelangelo, Leonardo, Raphael, Titian* (New Haven: Yale University Press, 2002).

18. The myth that Michelangelo worked solo, promoted by Michelangelo himself, has been disproved by William Wallace. See "Michelangelo's Assistants in the Sistine Chapel," *Gazette des Beaux-Arts* 110 (December 1987): 203–16. Reprinted in *The Sistine Chapel*, vol. 2 of *Michelangelo. Selected Scholarship in English*, ed. William E. Wallace, 5 vol. (New York: Garland, 1995).

19. William Wallace has analyzed Michelangelo's correspondence in several articles. See his "'Nothing Else Happened': Michelangelo between Rome and Florence," in *Michelangelo's Last Judgment*, ed. Marcia B. Hall (New York: Cambridge University Press, 2005).

20. *The Autobiography of Benvenuto Cellini*, ed. and abridged by Charles Hope and Alessandro Nova (Phaidon: Oxford, 1993), 95. Noted by David Franklin, *Rosso in Italy* (London: Yale University Press, 1994) 125.

21. Reported by Giovanni Battista Armenini, *De' veri precetti della pittura*, book 1, chap. 8 (1586; English trans. and ed. Edward J. Olszewski, *On the True Precepts of the Art of Painting*. Renaissance Sources in Translation. New York: Burt Franklin, 1977), 138.

22. For all too long the engravings have been treated separately from the rest of Raphael's oeuvre without regard for what they can tell us about his total development.

23. John W. O'Malley, *Praise and Blame in Renaissance Rome: Rhetoric, Doctrine, and Reform in the Sacred Orators of the Papal Court, c.1450–1521* (Durham, NC: Duke University Press, 1979); John F. D'Amico, *Renaissance Humanism in Papal Rome: Humanists and Churchmen on the Eve of the Reformation*, Johns Hopkins University Studies in Historical and Political Science, ser. 101, 1 (Baltimore: Johns Hopkins University Press, 1983); Peter Partner, *Renaissance Rome, 1500–1559. A Portrait of a Society* (Berkeley: University of California Press, 1976); Charles L. Stinger, *The Renaissance in Rome* (Bloomington: Indiana University Press, 1985); Ingrid D. Rowland, *The Culture of the High Renaissance: Ancients and Moderns in Sixteenth-Century Rome* (New York: Cambridge University Press, 1998).

CHAPTER 1. YOUNG RAPHAEL AND THE PRACTICE OF PAINTING IN RENAISSANCE ITALY

I thank Marcia Hall for inviting me to write this essay and Arthur Iorio, Anne Barriault, and Paul Barolsky for their constructive criticisms of the text.

1. See Giorgio Vasari, *The Lives of the Painters, Sculptors and Architects*, 2 vols., trans. Gaston du C. de Vere (New York: Alfred A. Knopf, 1996), 1: 710–48 (hereafter Vasari/de

Vere) or Giorgio Vasari, *The Lives of the Artists*, trans. George Bull (Harmondsworth: Penguin Books, 1977), 284–324 (hereafter Vasari/Bull). For the Italian, see Giorgio Vasari, *Le vite de' più eccellenti pittori, scultori ed architettori*, 9 vols., ed. Gaetano Milanesi (Florence, 1878–85; reprint ed. Florence: G. C. Sansoni Editore, 1981), 4: 315–89 (hereafter Vasari/Milanesi).

2. See Vasari/de Vere, 710–11. For the artistic family and genealogies in the *Lives*, see Paul Barolsky, *Giotto's Father and the Family in Vasari's Lives* (University Park: Pennsylvania State University Press, 1992), especially xvii–xix and 74–8. Also see the discussion of Vasari's "Life of Raphael" in Patricia Lee Rubin, *Giorgio Vasari: Art and History* (New Haven and London: Yale University Press, 1995), chap. IX.

3. The literature on Raphael is extensive; however, several monographs are particularly useful for his early career: Roger Jones and Nicholas Penny, *Raphael* (New Haven: Yale University Press, 1983); Konrad Oberhuber, *Raphael: The Paintings* (Munich, London, New York: Prestel Verlag, 1999); Sylvia Ferino Pagden and M. Antonietta Zancan, *Raffaello: Catalogo Completo* (Florence: Cantini Editore, 1989); and Jürg Meyer zur Capellen, *Raphael in Florence* (London: Azimuth Editions, 1996) and *Raphael, A Critical Catalogue of His Paintings*, vol. 1, *The Beginnings in Umbria and Florence, ca. 1500–1508* (Landshut: Arcos, 2001). Among the fine collection of essays prompted by the 500th anniversary of the painter's birth is *Raphael before Rome*, ed. James Beck, *Studies in the History of Art*, vol. 17 (Washington, DC: National Gallery of Art, 1986) (hereafter cited as Beck, 1986). Journal articles will be cited as the relevant issues emerge in the essay.

4. That is, the Umbrian period from the late 1490s until ca. 1505, the Florentine of ca. 1504–8, and the Roman (1508–20). Scholars have supplemented and corrected Vasari's account through archival research and by using the visual evidence supplied by the extant paintings. The quantity of information documenting Raphael's youth compares with that surviving for other masters of this era such as Perugino, Leonardo, and Michelangelo, whose initial careers are equally problematic. For the documents on the artist, see Vincenzo Golzio, *Raffaello nei documenti, nelle testimonianze dei contemporanei e nella letteratura del suo secolo* (Vatican City: Pontificia Insigne Accademia Artistica dei Virtuosi al Pantheon, 1936). Golzio's work has been updated in John Shearman, *Raphael in Early Modern Source, 1483–1602*, 2 vols. (New Haven: Yale University Press, 2003), which was published after the completion of this essay.

5. For example, in his discussion of Raphael's *Coronation of the Virgin*, he remarks: "Executed with truly supreme diligence, one who had not a good knowledge of the two manners, would hold it as certain that it is by the hand of Pietro, whereas it is without doubt by the hand of Raffaello" (Vasari/de Vere, 711–12).

6. I am referring particularly to the discussions of artistic and behavioral dispositions and the interplay of individual agency with producers and consumers in Pierre Bourdieu's studies of nineteenth-century French literature and painting. See Pierre Bourdieu, *The Field of Cultural Production* (New York: Columbia University Press, 1993).

7. See Golzio, *Raffaello*, 3–4. For the relatively high economic status of Raphael's parents, see Ranieri Varese, *Giovanni Santi* (Fiesole: Nardino Editore, 1994), 20–5.

8. Apprentices were sometimes as young as ten (i.e., Paolo Uccello), and the sons of artists probably began to help in the workshop as soon as they showed aptitude. For the structure of apprenticeships, see, most recently, Carmen C. Bambach, *Drawing and Painting in the Italian Renaissance Workshop, Theory and Practice, 1300–1600* (New York: Cambridge University Press, 1999), chap. 1.

9. He is referred to as *Johannis de Urbino scolaris* in a document appointing him *scripto brevium* in 1511. Although some believe that this means Santi taught him painting, the context equally suggests the learning of his letters from his father. See Golzio, *Raffaello*, 22.

10. Magia di Ciarla died in 1491, and Santi married Bernardina di Pietro Parte in 1492. Tom Henry published the testament in "Nuovi documenti su Giovanni Santi," in *Giovanni Santi*, Atti del convegno internazionale di studi Urbino, Convento di Santa Chiara, 17–19 marzo 1995, ed. Ranieri Varese (Milan: Electa, 1999), 223–6. The will states that his widowed sister Santa would occupy the other house. The pregnant Bernardina also was to receive her dowry, some clothing, and jewelry; the amount of their unborn child's inheritance depended on its gender. Also see Varese, *Giovanni Santi*, 23–5. Perhaps owing to the itinerant nature of the craft, many fifteenth-century artists rented workshops. For example, Perugino leased spaces in Perugia and Florence (although the latter was rented from the Ghiberti), and several Perugian painters banded together to maintain a workshop in ca. 1500–10; see Sylvia Ferino Pagden, "The Early Raphael and His Contemporaries," in Beck, *Raphael before Rome*, 93–107.

11. The *Sibyls* were commissioned by Agostino Chigi in 1514. Santi may have met Luca Signorelli, who was Piero della Francesca's student, earlier in the 1470s. As a member of the Confraternity of the Corpus Domini in Urbino, he performed duties that ranged from hosting Piero della Francesca during a visit in 1469 to painting candlesticks (Varese, *Giovanni Santi*, 15–16, 24–5). For the Fano altarpieces by Santi and Perugino, see Varese, 242–4, and Pietro Scarpellini, *Pietro Perugino* (Milan: Electa, 1984), 46, 92–3. For Santi as a model of the courtier-painter for his son, see Paul Joannides, "Raphael and Giovanni Santi," in *Studi su Raffaellino*, ed. Micaela Sambuco Hamoud and Maria Letizia Strocchi, (Urbino: Edizioni Quattro Venti di Anna Veronesi, 1987), 55–61.

12. "pittore non molto eccellente" (Vasari/Milanesi, 4:316).

13. See Varese, *Giovanni Santi*, 24–5, 250–2, and 255–6, and for the Montefiorentino Chapel, plate 30. None of his portraits survive, although letters between the duchess and the Gonzaga (Marchese Francesco, Isabella d'Este, and Giovanni Gonzaga) confirm their existence. He apparently painted Isabella and her brother-in-law Ludovico Gonzaga because Mantegna's unflattering attempt did not please. (While painting the portraits at Mantua, Santi contacted the malaria that caused his death.) The *Annunciation* for Santa Maria Maddalena, Senigallia, is now in Urbino; he also painted a *Visitation* in Santa Maria, Fano, for Giovanna in 1488 (Varese, *Giovanni Santi*, 242–4, and plates 17 and 18).

14. For the 1474 "*Amore al tribunale della Pudicizia*" and the nuptial performance, the "Contest between Diana and Juno," known from a letter to Maddalena Gonzaga, Elisabetta's sister, see Varese, *Giovanni Santi*, 186–90, and the preface in Giovanni Santi, *La vita e le gesta di Federico di Montefeltro, Duca D'Urbino*, ed. L. M. Tocci, 2 vols. (Città del Vaticano: Biblioteca Apostolica Vaticana, 1985), 1:xi–xi, ivii–xviii.

15. The English translations of Santi's words are from Creighton E. Gilbert, *Italian Art, 1400–1500, Sources and Documents* (Evanston, IL: Northwestern University Press, 1992), 97. Santi also argues for the superiority of the Italian painters over Netherlandish artists (except for Jan van Eyck and Rogier van der Weyden) and chastises rulers who do not support the arts, which flattered the Montefeltro and Gonzaga who did. Although the chronicle was for "persons of humble condition and deprived of culture" (Santi, *La vita*, 55), members of the court were a more likely audience. For analysis of this part of the Cronaca and quattrocento art theory, see Lise Bek, "Giovanni Santi's 'Disputa de la pictura' – a polemical treatise," *Analecta Romana Instituti Danici* V (1969): 75–102.

16. Vasari's claims were based on the knowledge of Giulio Romano and Perugian artists, and he states in the *Lives* that Perugino was Raphael's teacher not once, but at least four times (see Rubin, *Giorgio Vasari*, 380–4).

17. Agostino Chigi called Perugino the finest painter in Europe in a letter of 1502; see Roger Jones and Nicholas Penny, *Raphael* (New Haven: Yale University Press), 4, and Gyde

Shepherd, "A Monument to Pope Pius II: Pintoricchio and Raphael in the Piccolomini Library in Siena, 1494–1508," (Ph.D. diss., Harvard University, 1993), 21.

18. Ordered by Ludovico Sforza, the duke of Milan in 1496, the altarpiece for the Certosa di Pavia was mostly completed by 1500; it is now in the National Gallery, London. See Scarpellini, *Perugino*, 100–1, for documentation.

19. Also in the National Gallery, London. Measuring 280.7 × 165 cm, the panel is generally dated ca. 1503–4 based on the 1503 in the inscription on the stone frame still in the chapel; see Jones and Penny, *Raphael*, 13. For the quotation, see Vasari/de Vere, 1: 712.

20. He even copied the awkward leg and the flaccid anatomy of Jerome's bare foot typical of Perugino's versions, as in the *Madonna and Child with Saints* of 1500 (Perugia, Galleria Nazionale dell'Umbria), illustrated in Scarpellini, *Perugino*, 240, fig. 194 (who attributes the painting to Perugino and Eusebio di San Giorgio).

21. For Raphael's and Perugino's drawing techniques, see Bambach, *Drawing and Painting*, chap. 2; for his oil paintings, see Jones and Penny, *Raphael*, 16–17, and David Bomford, Janet Brough, and Ashok Roy, "Three Panels from Perugino's Certosa di Pavia altarpiece," *National Gallery Technical Bulletin* 4 (1980): 3–31. For Perugino as his teacher and the overlapping commissions that complicate the dating of these early works, see Oberhuber, *Raphael: The Paintings*, 17–19, and David Alan Brown, "Raphael, Leonardo, and Perugino: Fame and Fortune in Florence," in *Leonardo, Michelangelo, and Raphael in Renaissance Florence from 1500 to 1508*, ed. Serafina Hager (Washington, DC: Georgetown University Press, 1992), 29–53.

22. For the truce Pope Julius II effected between the warring clans of Perugia in 1506, see Christine Shaw, *Julius II, The Warrior Pope* (Oxford: Blackwell, 1993), 154–7, and chap. 5.

23. All three had completed additional projects for members of Sixtus IV's family. Perugino painted a polyptych for Cardinal Giuliano della Rovere's (later Pope Julius II) palace, now in the Albani Collection, Rome (Scarpellini, *Perugino*, fig. 78). Pinturicchio frescoed several funerary chapels for the family in Santa Maria del Popolo at Rome and then was favored by the Borgia pope Alexander VI, painting his apartments in the Vatican Palace and now lost frescoes in Castel Sant'Angelo (Enzo Carli, *Il Pintoricchio* [Milan: Electa Editrice, 1960], figs. 64–87). Perugino and Signorelli operated out of Florence and their hometowns of Perugia and Cortona in the 1480s and 1490s. Both executed projects in Siena and Sansepolcro, and Signorelli painted at Loreto and Città di Castello in the 1480s and 1490s. See Pietro Scarpellini, *Luca Signorelli* (Milan: Edizioni per il Club del Libro, 1964), 22–39.

24. At the start of 1501 he rented a workshop at Perugia to finish several altarpieces, including one for the Misericordia, and, in 1502, he signed contracts for a double-sided altarpiece in San Francesco al Monte (Perugia) and for a fresco of the *Crucifixion* in the Chigi family chapel at Siena; see Scarpellini, *Perugino*, 93–5, 112–13, for these commissions. His Florentine shop completed projects that had been ordered in the 1490s, such as the Vallombrosan Altarpiece.

25. Signorelli also executed several altarpieces, see Laurence Kanter and David Franklin, "Some Passion Scenes by Luca Signorelli after 1500," *Mitteilungen des Kunsthistorischen Institutes in Florenz* (1992), 171–91. Pinturicchio signed the Siena contract in June 1502 (Shepherd, "Monument," 18–19).

26. After his apprenticeship he probably produced Madonna and Child pictures, the bread-and-butter of most workshops and often assigned to assistants. A number of small Madonna and Child panels have been dated around the production of his Città di Castello altarpieces. Some of these, such as the panel in the Norton Simon Collection may actually predate those works. For illustrations, see Oberhuber, *Raphael: The Paintings*, 27–32, and Meyer zur Capellen, catalogue numbers 3–5, 10, and 11. A *Madonna and Child* at Matthiesen Fine Art Ltd., London, has recently been attributed to young

Raphael; see the gallery's catalogue *2001 : An Art Odyssey*, 46–61. (I would like to thank Janet Smith for calling my attention to this panel, Beverly Brown for information on the painting, and Gretchen Hirschauer for providing a reproduction.)

27. For the social ties between these families, see Enrico Mercati, *Andrea Baroni e gli altri committenti Tifernati di Raffaello, con documenti inediti* (Città di Castello, Petruzzi Editore, 1994); and most recently, Tom Henry, "Raphael's Altar-Piece Patrons in Città di Castello," *Burlington Magazine* 144 (2002): 268–78. It is tempting to speculate that Signorelli, who worked in Città di Castello in the 1490s, aided Raphael's receiving his first substantial commission in 1500, the Saint Nicholas of Tolentino Altarpiece for the Baronci Chapel in Sant'Agostino. Because it was jointly commissioned from Raphael and his father's assistant Evangelista di Pian di Meleto, the job may also have resulted from artistic or social connections at Urbino. The altarpiece exists in fragments, preparatory studies, and a partial copy by the eighteenth-century painter Costantini. For illustrations and a comprehensive historical and technical discussion, see Sylvie Béguin, "The Saint Nicholas of Tolentino Altarpiece," in Beck, *Raphael before Rome*, 15–28.

28. The lunette, central panel, and the *Pietà* from this altarpiece are now in the Metropolitan Museum, New York, and dated either ca. 1502–3 (Oberhuber, *Raphael: The Paintings*), or ca. 1504 (Jones and Penny, Meyer zur Capellen, *Raphael*). The predella panels of the *Agony in the Garden* and the *Carrying of the Cross* are in Boston and London, respectively.

29. See Francesco Federico Mancini, *Raffaello in Umbria: Cronologia e committenza, nuova studi e documenti* (Perugia: Volumnia Editrice, 1987). The Monteluce contract was renegotiated in 1516 and completed by Giulio Romano and Gian Francesco Penni in 1525; see Umberto Gnoli, "Raffaello e la 'Incoronazione' di Monteluce," *Bollettino d'Arte* (1917): 133–54; John Shearman, "The Chigi Chapel in S. Maria del Popolo," *Journal of the Warburg and Courtauld Institutes* 24 (1961): 129–60; and Jeryldene M. Wood, *Women, Art, and Spirituality: The Poor Clares of Early Modern Italy* (Cambridge: Cambridge University Press, 1996), 103–12, and n. 50. The *Coronation* and its predella (the *Annunciation, Adoration of the Magi*, and *Presentation*) are now in the Vatican Pinacoteca. The Baglioni Altarpiece also is dispersed, with the *Entombment* in the Villa Borghese, Rome, the predella in the Vatican Pinacoteca, and the lunette in the Galleria Nazionale dell'Umbria, Perugia. It is worth noting that Pope Julius visited the convent of Monteluce and said Mass at San Francesco al Prato during his visit in 1506 (Wood, 112; Shaw, 157; and Donal Cooper, "Raphael's Altar-Pieces in S. Francesco al Prato, Perugia: Patronage, Setting and Function," *Burlington Magazine* 143 [2001]: 561), but I have not been able to determine whether he went to Sant'Antonio. At Perugia he also painted the Ansidei Altarpiece for that family's chapel in the Servite church, San Fiorenzo, ca. 1506–7, and a fresco of the Trinity for the Camaldolite monks of San Severo in ca. 1505.

30. For the contract, see Gnoli, "Raffaello," 146–50.

31. See Wood, *Women, Art, and Spirituality*, 102–6, for this information, including the change of dedication from the Annunciation to the Assumption. The second contract in 1516 requested a drawing of the altarpiece for the nuns' approval; it seems likely that the previous one did as well.

32. Unfinished when he died in 1520, the work was completed by his assistants (see n. 28). The other is the Madonna del Baldacchino left unfinished when he departed for Rome in 1508. See Jones and Penny, *Raphael*, 47, fig. 56. The Monteluce contract indicates Raphael's employment of assistants on his larger Perugian works; however, no records disclose the location(s) or membership of his shop. As Ferino Padgen (1986, 194–5) has suggested, perhaps Raphael shared a workshop or entered into partnerships to complete projects, as he did with Evangelista for the Saint Nicholas of Tolentino

Altarpiece in 1500. When he received a number of Perugian commissions, he may have formed a *società* with one or several local artists, such as Berto di Giovanni or Eusebio di San Giorgio, who clearly knew his works.

33. Others include Signorelli's *Preaching of the Anti-Christ* at Orvieto and Pinturicchio's frescoes in the Bufalini Chapel (Santa Maria in Aracoeli, Rome) and Piccolomini Library. For illustrations, see Jones and Penny, *Raphael*, fig. 7, and 13–14; Scarpellini, *Signorelli*, fig. 49; and Carli, figs. 27–38.

34. For Perugino's work, now in the Musée des Beaux-Arts, Caen, see Scarpellini, *Perugino*, fig. 217.

35. For an illustration of the painting, see Scarpellini, *Signorelli*, fig. 34, and for the drawing Meyer zur Capellen, 107, fig. 2B/1.1. Gilbert was among the earliest to explore the connection with Signorelli, see Creighton E. Gilbert, "A Miracle by Raphael," *North Carolina Museum of Art Bulletin* 6 (1965), 3–35; and more recently, "Signorelli and Young Raphael," in Beck, *Raphael before Rome*, 109–24. For the Sant'Onofrio Altarpiece and Signorelli's processional standard with the Crucifixion and a Pentecost, which Raphael probably knew because it was painted for the Confraternity of the Holy Spirit at Urbino in ca. 1494, see Scarpellini, *Signorelli*, 120–2, and figs. 20 and 33.

36. The study for the *Meeting of Eleanora of Aragon and Ercole d'Este* (largely accepted as by Raphael) portrays a similar arrangement of figures; for the drawings, see Jones and Penny, *Raphael* 20; Meyer zur Capellen, fig. 6, and 26–9; Oberhuber, *Raphael*: The Paintings, 27–32; and Shepherd, "Monument," 29ff.

37. The rights to the chapel were acquired in 1461 by Guido di Carlo degli Oddi. His son Simone degli Oddi (d. 1498) married Leandra or Alessandra Baglioni (whose name appears in both forms in documents). Vasari mistakenly named Maddalena degli Oddi as the patron, see Vasari/de Vere, 1: 712. Who requested the iconography is unknown, but it conceivably stems from the chapel's dedication to the Madonna and the friars' devotion to Mary's Assumption. The *Coronation* is not documented, but 1503, the year of the Oddi return from exile, is usually proposed as the date of its commissioning. In the most recent study of the Oddi and Baglioni Chapels, Cooper (554–61) points out that women often commissioned art during family exiles, and clarifies the documentation, the confusion about the names of the patrons, and the original locations of the paintings. It is strange that the nuns of Monteluce did not refer to Raphael's picture rather than Ghirlandaio's panel as a model; perhaps it was ordered later and hence unfinished in December 1505. (That it was painted in the years when he should have been replicating Ghirlandaio's *Coronation* suggests he preferred the Oddi project, but whether for aesthetic or political reasons is unknown.)

38. For an illustration, see Scarpellini, *Perugino*, fig. 177.

39. See Frederick Hartt, "Leonardo and the Second Florentine Republic," *Journal of the Walters Art Gallery* 44 (1986): 95–116.

40. For information about the artists, architects, artisans, and public officials who attended the discussion, see Charles Seymour, *Michelangelo's David: A Search for Identity* (New York: W. W. Norton, 1974), 139–57.

41. For these workshops, see Patricia Lee Rubin and Alison Wright, *Renaissance Florence: The Art of the 1470s* (New Haven: Yale University Press, 1998), chaps. 2, 3, and 4.

42. For illustrations of Lorenzo's works, see Gigetta Dalli Regoli, *Lorenzo di Credi* (Pisa: Edizioni di Comunità, 1966). The same is true of the versions by Cosimo Rosselli and Piero di Cosimo; see Everett Fahy, *Some Followers of Domenico Ghirlandajo* (New York: Garland, 1976).

43. For illustrations of these works, see David Franklin, *Painting in Renaissance Florence, 1500–1550* (New Haven: Yale University Press, 2001), figs. 61 and 65, and his discussions of Fra Bartolomeo and Albertinelli (chap. 5) and Ridolfo Ghirlandaio (chap. 6).

44. See Seymour, as in n. 40, and Hartt, "Leonardo," 106–12.

45. For the Madonna del Baldacchino for the Dei Chapel in Santo Spirito, which he asked Ridolfo Ghirlandaio to complete, see Jones and Penny, *Raphael*, 47, and Franklin, *Painting*, 111–12. The letter from Giovanna della Rovere to Soderini stated that Raphael wanted to improve his painting by studying Florentine art (see Jones and Penny, *Raphael*, 5); some scholars reject the authenticity of the letter (see John Shearman, "On Raphael's Chronology, 1503–08," in *Ars Naturam Adiuvans: Festschrift für Mattias Winner* [Mainz: von Zebern, 1996]: 201).

46. The information about his clientele derives from Vasari's *Vita*, but much has been corroborated by additional family records such as letters and inventories. See Meyer zur Capellen, *Florence*, 38–43, and Andrée Hayum, "Michelangelo's Doni Tondo: Holy Family and Family Myth," *Studies in Iconography* 7–8 (1981–82), 209–51.

47. The *Madonna of the Meadow* was in the Taddei family collection until the seventeenth century; see Jones and Penny, *Raphael*, 33. Taddeo Taddei, who became a close friend of the painter, was also acquainted with Pietro Bembo (he is mentioned in a 1524 letter of Taddei's son; see Jones and Penny, *Raphael*, 250, n. 20). The *Madonna del Cardellino* was badly damaged when the Nasi home was destroyed by a landslide in 1548, as Vasari relates (Vasari/de Vere, 1: 713); also see Brown, "Raphael, Leonardo," 37–41, and Meyer zur Capellen, *Florence*, 38–42. For Madonnas as exemplars for mothers, see the advice of the Dominican Giovanni Dominici cited in Cristelle L. Baskins, *Cassone Painting, Humanism, and Gender in Early Modern Italy* (Cambridge: Cambridge University Press, 1998), 6–7, and Margaret L. King, *Women of the Renaissance* (Chicago: University of Chicago Press, 1991), 1–24.

48. The correspondence between the kneeling Baptist in the Taddei panel and Leonardo's John in the *Madonna of the Rocks* implies that Raphael may have had access to the elder master's drawings. For Florentine copies and versions of Leonardo's lost cartoon, see Hartt, "Leonardo," 100–3; Meyer zur Capellen, *Florence*, 61–73, and Franklin, *Painting*, 12–14.

49. For Michelangelo's letter about the Bruges Madonna, which Raphael thus may not have seen, see William E. Wallace, "Michelangelo in and out of Florence between 1500 and 1508," in *Leonardo, Michelangelo, and Raphael in Renaissance Florence from 1500 to 1508*, 76. Yet Raphael obviously studied Michelangelo's sculpture (who is himself looking at Leonardo's paintings), as shown by his drawings of *David* and the *Saint Matthew*, and his likely access to the Taddei and Doni tondi because of their shared patrons (see Meyer zur Capellen, *Florence*, 74–95). Signorelli's tondi for Florentine patrons such as the Medici may also have been seen by Raphael; see Scarpellini, *Signorelli*, figs. 27, 36, and 37.

50. We don't know who ordered this work; sometimes thought for a Sienese mentioned by Vasari, see Jones and Penny, *Raphael*, 33, and Meyer zur Capellen, *Florence*, 207–8. He does still adapt Christ's extended arm from Michelangelo's *Taddei Tondo*, a reference more obvious in the finished painting than in the extant cartoon (see Bambach, *Drawing and Painting*, 63–66, 100–5, for Raphael's transferring practices). The face of Christ resembles Michelangelo's youngsters, and the upward movement of the Baptist's head indirectly invokes the foreshortened head of the Virgin in the *Doni Tondo*.

51. "...the two [manners] might have belonged to different masters, one much more excellent than the other in painting"; see Vasari/de Vere, 1: 715.

52. For illustrations, see Scarpellini, *Perugino*, pl. 101.

53. This was a cliche that Vasari used for naturalistic figures and likenesses, for example, about Leonardo in the preface to Part Three "dette veramente alle sue figure il moto ed il fiato" (Vasari/Milanesi, 4: 11 and Vasari/de Vere, 1: 620).

54. For the term see, Baldassare Castiglinone, *The Book of the Courtier*, trans. Charles S. Singleton (New York: Anchor Books, 1959), 43.

55. The Ovidian and biblical deluges and the importance of family, suggested by these portraits and Michelangelo's *Doni Tondo*, are explored in Hayum, 220–3. Shearman, *Chronology*, 205, has suggested a later dating to ca. 1507–8; if correct, then Maddalena was either pregnant or had just given birth to their first child (born in 1508). Because he left Florence in 1508, Raphael may have asked the Master of the Serumido to paint the reverses, as he had requested Ridolfo Ghirlandaio to finish the Dei Altarpiece. That his adaptation of the *Mona Lisa* type struck a chord is borne out by other portraits of women in this period. Today assigned titles prompted by their appearance, the unidentified women of *La gravida* and *La muta* may have been residents of either Florence or Urbino. For the latter, see Jones and Penny, *Raphael*, 29–31, and Meyer zur Capellen, 294–302.

56. For documentation of his trips and the records about the quarrel over the estate dating 1499–1505/10, see Golzio, *Raffaello*, 5–18, and John Shearman, "Raphael at the Court of Urbino," *Burlington Magazine* 112 (1970): 72–77, and Jones and Penny, *Raphael*, 4–5. His letters to his maternal uncle and his documented contact with his paternal uncle at Urbino, as well as his naming of a cousin Girolamo Vagnini to supervise his tomb in the Pantheon at his death in 1520, corroborate the continuity of kinship. For the testament, see Golzio, *Raffaello*, 116–18.

57. Guidobaldo had married Elisabetta Gonzaga of Mantua in 1488, but the couple were unable to have children. Francesco Maria, the son of the pope's brother Giovanni della Rovere and Guidobaldo's sister Giovanna da Montefeltro, was related by blood and marriage to both families. For a succinct summary of this court, see Jones and Penny, *Raphael*, 1–5; for the relations between Francesco Maria and Julius II, see Shaw, 183–7; and for Guidobaldo and Elisabetta, see Bernardino Baldi, *Della vita e de' fatti di Guidobaldo i da Montefeltro, Duca d'Urbino*, 2 vols. (Milan: G. Silvestri, 1821), and Maria Luisa Mariotti Masi, *Elisabetta Gonzaga, Duchessa d'Urbino nello splendore e negli intrighi del Rinascimento* (Milan: U. Mursia Editore, 1983).

58. Eleanora was the daughter of the duchess's brother Francesco Gonzaga and her friend Isabella d'Este. The betrothal was at Rome in May 1505; the wedding took place in 1509. See Shearman, *Urbino*, 76–7.

59. In the *Book of the Courtier*, Castiglione set his nostalgic recollection of the days following Julius II's 1506 visit at the ducal palace, and the neo-Petrarchan poet Pietro Bembo was one of that book's chief protagonists.

60. During the 1480s and 1490s construction and decoration at the ducal palace evidently continued under the boy's guardian Ottaviano Ubaldini and then under the new duke himself. The Venetian painter and printmaker Jacopo dei Barberi is among the few foreigners known to work at Urbino; see *Urbino e le Marche primo e dopo Raffaello*, ed. Maria Grazia Ciardi Duprè dal Poggetto and Paolo Dal Poggetto (Florence: Nuova Salani Editrice, 1983), 178–83.

61. See Bek, "Giovanni Santi's 'Disputa'," 88–94, for these terms, which are redolent of Alberti.

62. In addition to portraits, Costa painted two allegories, which, together with one by Perugino, hung with Mantegna's pictures in the *studiolo* of Isabella d'Este.

63. The dates range from ca. 1503–4 (before Giovanna della Rovere's letter) to 1508, when the painter went to Rome. Among the works attributed to Raphael's Urbino oeuvre are the *Three Graces* (Musée Condé, Chantilly); the *Dream of Scipio*, also called the *Vision of the Knight* (National Gallery, London); *Saint George and the Dragon* (National Gallery of Art, Washington, DC); *Saints Michael and George* (Musée du Louvre, Paris); and the Portraits of Guidobaldo da Montefeltro, Elisabetta Gonzaga, and Francesco Maria della Rovere (Uffizi, Florence), Emilia Pia (Baltimore Museum of Art, Baltimore), and Eleanora Gonzaga della Rovere (Museum of Fine Arts, Boston). Presumably lost

works include an *Agony in the Garden* for Guidobaldo da Montefeltro or Elisabetta Gonzaga and two pictures of the Madonna and Child for Guidobaldo da Montefeltro. See Jones and Penny, *Raphael*, 5–10, and *Urbino e le Marche*, 248–65, for illustrations.

64. Vasari/Bull, 288, and Jones and Penny, *Raphael*, 3–6, for the 1507 letter discussing the duchess's picture.

65. See Brown, "Raphael, Leonardo," 37. For its provenance and condition, Ross M. Merrill, "Examination and Treatment of the *Small Cowper Madonna* by Raphael at the National Gallery of Art," in Beck, *Raphael before Rome*.

66. For illustrations and discussion of these panels, see Jones and Penny, 5–8; for arguments about the English king Henry VII as the patron of the Washington *Saint George*, see John Shearman, "A Drawing for Raphael's 'Saint George'," *Burlington Magazine* 125 (1983), 15–23, and Helen S. Ettlinger, "The Question of St George's Garter," *Burlington Magazine* 125 (1983), 23 ff.

67. Illustrated in Jones and Penny, *Raphael*, fig. 4.

68. The style suggests a date of ca. 1504–5 and thus may commemorate the bestowal of an office or honor, his adoption, or his betrothal. For the attribution and dating to ca. 1504, see Jones and Penny, *Raphael*, 4, and Meyer zur Capellen, 284–6; for a later dating to 1507, based on Francesco Maria's wearing winter attire, see Shearman, *Chronology*, 205. His proposal is arguable because sitters were often portrayed in the clothing they chose, as when Titian painted the dress sent to him in Giulia da Varano's portrait.

69. See Jones and Penny, *Raphael*, 8 and 249, nn. 30–3, for this proposal. Panofsky had connected the pictures with a Sienese branch of the Borghese family whose later inventories of their Roman collection (but after one of 1613) list the paintings (see Jones and Penny, 249, n. 31). Edgar Wind (*Pagan Mysteries of the Renaissance*, rev. ed. [New York, W. W. Norton, 1968], 81–5) refuted Panofsky's interpretation, proposing the theme of "virtue reconciled with pleasure." The paintings have been described as a diptych on account of their equal measurements and identical provenance, but as scholars have noted, the differences in figure scale and the design of the landscapes preclude such a pairing. Wind suggested that the panels were joined back-to-back like a medal, Jones and Penny speculated that one might be a lid for the other, and Meyer zur Capellen (158–65) mentions a proposal for their resemblance to Sienese *biccherne* (painted book covers), which aligns with the tradition of a Sienese patron.

70. The reverses of Niccolò Fiorentino's medals for Giovanna degli Albizzi and Pico della Mirandola (see Stephen K. Scher, *The Currency of Fame: Portrait Medals of the Italian Renaissance* [New York: Harry N. Abrams, 1994], 136, 140–1) and the sculpture in the Piccolomini Library at Siena are mentioned as prototypes (see Wind, *Pagan Mysteries*, 36–52).

71. Pietro Bembo, *Gli Asolani*, trans. R. B. Gottfried (Bloomington: Indiana University Press, 1954); for Caesar and Scipio, see Castiglione, *The Book and the Courtier*, 68–9, 292–3.

72. See Santi, *La vita*, 1: 55–8.

73. Raphael may have known Memling's Saints John and Veronica owned by Pietro Bembo (the most recent study of these is Mariner Belozerskaya, *Source* 21 (winter 2002): 17–21). Many Florentine artists (e.g., Domenico Ghirlandaio, Piero di Cosimo, Lorenzo di Credi, and Fra Bartolommeo) used northern motifs in their works, and Perugino's landscapes such as the *Apollo and Marsyas* (Musée du Louvre, Paris) and the *Lamentation* (Galleria Palatina, Florence) owe debts to Netherlandish art. Raphael also could have seen northern prints in the workshop of Perugino; see Marcia Hall, *Color and Meaning: Practice and Theory in Renaissance Painting* (New York: Cambridge University Press, 1992), 85–91, and Jeryldene M. Wood, "Perugino and the Influence of Northern Art on Devotional Pictures in the Late Quattrocento," *Konsthistorisk Tidskrift* 58 (1989): 7–18.

74. See Cooper, "Raphael's Altar-Pieces," 560–1. The apostle was a converted publican whose renunciation of money would have been an appropriate Franciscan theme for the chapel.

75. For a full account of this text, see Alexander Nagel, *Michelangelo and the Reform of Art* (New York: Cambridge University Press, 2000), 117–22.

76. Vasari/Bull, 290.

77. The drawings demonstrate borrowings from Perugino (the Santa Chiara *Lamentation* and the *Pietà* for San Giusto), Signorelli (the Carrying of Christ on the fictive relief in the back of the *Pietà* at Orvieto and in the banner for Sansepolcro), and Mantegna (engraving of the Entombment), and his knowledge of Roman sarcophagi depicting the death of Meleager. He used the pose of Michelangelo's *Saint Matthew* for one of the bearer figures, and the twisting motion of the Madonna in the *Doni Tondo* to resolve his arrangement of the swooning Virgin and the Marys at the right, as well as seeming to know the Roman *Pietà* and the unfinished London *Entombment.* For a thorough explanation of the relationship of the drawings to the finished picture, see Nagel, 120–35; the classic study of John Pope-Hennessy, *Raphael,* The Wrightsman Lectures (New York: New York University Press, 1970); and Cooper, "Raphael's Altar-Pieces," 560–1.

78. As recounted in Alberti's treatise on painting (Leon Battista Alberti, *On Painting,* trans. Cecil Grayson [London: Penguin Books, 1991], 91), although the point of the anecdote was a selective process based on nature not works of art.

79. He describes Perugino's art as "over-precise, dry, and feeble in draftsmanship" (Vasari/de Vere, 1: 741).

80. Vasari/de Vere, 1: 740–3.

CHAPTER 2. RAPHAEL AND HIS PATRONS: FROM THE COURT OF URBINO TO THE CURIA AND ROME

1. "Qui in 4 dì son morti duo grandissimi huomini et primi nelli exercitii loro. Messer Aug[osti]no Chigi in mercantia et Raphaello da Urbino in pictura: sepeliti con grandissima pompa l'uno et l'altro." Volterra, Biblioteca Comunale Guarnacci, Archivio Maffei, MS. XLVII, 2/1, filza I, 14 April 1520. I am grateful to Caroline Elam and the late John Shearman, who discussed the letter with me. This document (found by the present author) has recently been published with a slightly different transcription in John Shearman, *Raphael in Early Modern Sources (1483–1602),* ed. Julian Kliemann, 2 vols. (New Haven and London: Yale University Press [in Association with the Bibliotheca Hertziana, Max-Planck-Institut für Kunstgeschichte], 2003), 1: 588, doc. 1520/27.

2. Document cited in n. 1. "Raphaello hebbe cento torce portate tucte da dipintori. Et ha lassato p[er] una sua sepultura ducati mille cinquecento doro larghi." Cf. Vasari/Milanesi, 4: 383, "perchè non fu nessuno artefice che dolendosi non pignasse, ed insieme alla sepoltura non l'accompagnasse."

3. Document cited in n. 1. "Pensate la pompa et sepoltura di Aug[ost]ino Chigi el quale ha lassato una roba incredibile."

4. For Chigi's life, see F. Dante in *Dizionario biografico degli italiani,* 62 vols. to date (Rome: Istituto della Enciclopedia Italiana, 1960–) (henceforth cited as *DBI*), 24 (1980): 735–43. Dante, op. cit., 743 for Chigi's funeral rites, "degni di un sovrano," which were attended by some five thousand people. Recent considerations of Chigi's patronage and collecting include Enzo Bentivoglio, *Raffaello e i Ghigi nella chiesa agostiniana di S. Maria del Popolo* (Rome: L'Agostiniana, 1984); Ingrid D. Rowland,"Render unto Caesar the Things Which are Caesar's: Humanism and the Arts in the Patronage of Agostino Chigi," *Renaissance Quarterly* 39 (1986): 673–730; Roberto

Bartalini, "Due episodi del mecenatismo di Agostino Chigi," *Prospettiva* 67 (1992): 17–
38; Ingrid D. Rowland, *The Culture of the High Renaissance: Ancients and Moderns
in Sixteenth-Century Rome* (Cambridge, New York, and Melbourne: Cambridge
University Press, 1998), 72–83 and passim. For older bibliography, see Rowland, op.
cit., 278, n. 11.

5. I plan in the future to prepare a more comprehensive study of Raphael's patrons.

6. Vasari/Milanesi, 4: 385. "Egli, in somma, non visse da pittore, ma da principe."

7. Alison Luchs, "A Note on Raphael's Perugian Patrons," *Burlington Magazine* 125 (1983):
29–31; Alessandro Cecchi, "Agnolo e Maddalena Doni committenti di Raffaello," in
Studi su Raffaello, ed. Micaela Sambucco Hamoud and Maria Letizia Strocchi, 2 vols.
(Urbino: Quattro Venti, 1987), 2: 429–39; Gabriella Zarri, "L'altra Cecilia: Elena Duglioli Dall'Olio (1472–1520)," in *Indagini per un dipinto: La Santa Cecilia di Raffaello*
(Bologna: Edizioni ALFA, 1983), 81–118; Gabriella Zarri, "Storia di una committenza," in
L'Estasi di Santa Cecilia di Raffaello da Urbino nella Pinacoteca Nazionale di Bologna,
exh. cat. (Bologna: Edizioni ALFA, 1983), 20–38; Claudia Conforti, "Baldassare Turini
da Pescia: Profilo di un committente di Giulio Romano architetto e pittore," *Quaderni
di Palazzo Te* 2 (1985): 35–43.

8. L. D. Ettlinger, "Raphael's Early Patrons," in *Raphael before Rome*, ed. James Beck (Washington, DC: National Gallery of Art, 1987), 85–90. While the article makes some important observations (see later, n. 70), it relies heavily on Vasari and, surprisingly, does
not take into account then-known documentary material on patrons.

9. The literature on art patronage in early modern Europe – particularly Italy – has grown
enormously in the past three decades. Useful general discussions include D. S. Chambers, *Patrons and Artists in the Italian Renaissance* (Columbia, S. C.: University of South
Carolina Press, 1971); Salvatore Settis, "Artisti e committenti fra Quattro e Cinquecento,"
in *Storia d'Italia* IV. *Intellettuali e potere*, ed. C. Vivanti (Turin: Einaudi, 1981), 701–61;
Werner L. Gundersheimer, "Patronage in the Renaissance: An Exploratory Approach,"
in *Patronage in the Renaissance*, ed. Guy Fitch Lytle and Stephen Orgel (Princeton:
Princeton University Press, 1981), 3–23; F. W. Kent with Patricia Simons, "Renaissance
Patronage: An Introductory Essay," in *Patronage, Art and Society in Renaissance Italy*,
ed. F. W. Kent, Patricia Simons, with J. C. Eade (Oxford: Clarendon Press, 1987), 1–21;
Bram Kempers, *Painting, Power and Patronage: The Rise of the Professional Artist in
Renaissance Italy*, trans. Beverly Jackson (London and New York: Penguin 1992; first
published in Dutch, 1987); Evelyn Welch, *Art and Society in Italy 1350–1500* (Oxford and New York: Oxford University Press), chap. 4, "Defining Relationships: Artists
and Patrons." See also Mary Hollingsworth, *Patronage in Renaissance Italy: From 1400
to the Early Sixteenth Century* (Baltimore: Johns Hopkins University Press, 1994) and
Hollingsworth, *Patronage in Sixteenth-Century Italy* (London: John Murray, 1996). For
"*clientelismo*" and "*mecenatismo*" see the introduction to Kent and Simons, op. cit., 2,
and the contributions to that collection by Ron Weissman and Gary Ianziti; Dale Kent,
Cosimo de' Medici and the Florentine Renaissance: The Patron's Oeuvre (New Haven and
London: Yale University Press, 2000), 8 and 392, n. 63; and the fine analysis by Tracy
E. Cooper, "*Mecenatismo* or *Clientelismo*? The Character of Renaissance Art Patronage,"
in *The Search for a Patron in the Middle Ages and the Renaissance*, ed. David G. Wilkins
and Rebecca L. Wilkins (Lewiston, NY: Edwin Melon Press, 1996), 19–32. Along with
Dale Kent and Cooper, I see a complex interaction between the two types of patronage.
Jill Burke's important new book *Changing Patrons: Social Identity and the Visual Arts in
Renaissance Florence* (University Park, PA: Pennsylvania State University Press, 2004)
appeared when this essay was in press and I am not able to address her conclusions
here.

10. For these topics, cf. the literature cited in the previous note. For Stephen Green-blatt's now-classic formulation "self-fashioning" (first proposed in his *Renaissance Self-Fashioning from More to Shakespeare* [Chicago and London: University of Chicago Press, 1980]) and the visual arts, see *Fashioning Identities in Renaissance Art*, ed. Mary Rogers (Aldershot, UK, and Brookfield, VT: Ashgate, 2000). For status signaling and the application of economic theory to art patronage in early modern Italy, see the abstracts of the session organized by Jonathan Nelson and Richard Zeckhauser for the College Art Association of America meeting in Philadelphia, 2002, titled "Conspicuous Commissions: Status Signaling through Art in Italy ca. 1300–1700," in *Abstracts 2002* (New York: College Art Association of America, 2002), 312–15. The organizers are preparing a publication stemming from this session. See also Arnold Esch, "Sul rapporto fra arte ed economia nel Rinascimento italiano," in *Arte, committenza ed economia e nelle corti del Rinascimento 1420–1530*, ed. Arnold Esch and Christoph Luitpold Frommel (Turin: Einaudi, 1995), 3–49.

11. Kent, *Cosimo de' Medici*. This provocative thesis makes sense to me in the case of major, elite patrons with many commissions to examine. It is more problematic for less active patrons who might only have commissioned a single work or works of modest ambition.

12. For a different position, which emphasizes the priority of artistic invention, cf. Sylvia Ferino Pagden, "Iconographic and Artistic Achievements: The Genesis of Three Works by Raphael," in *Raffaello a Roma: Il convegno del 1983*, ed. Christoph Luitpold Frommel and Matthias Winner (Rome: Edizione dell'Elefante, 1986), 14: "The view persists, however, that any shift in subject matter must reflect not the artist's concern to provide a satisfactory artistic solution to the problems presented by the terms of his patron's commission, but must instead have been dictated by the patron himself who wished to see something of his own interpretation of the subject he had chosen." In reality, the patronage process was a "two way street" – indeed, as discussed later – a complex "multi-lane highway" that often involved intermediaries. In my view, a balanced and preferable position is that of Caroline Elam, "Drawings as Documents: The Problem of the San Lorenzo Façade," in *Michelangelo Drawings*, ed. Craig Hugh Smyth (Washington, DC: National Gallery of Art, 1992), 111: "For the best architectural patronage does not consist in giving the artist unlimited funds and license to do what he wants, but rather in having a clear idea of the project and directing it with intelligence and understanding."

13. For example, on collaborative patronage among members of the Medici family, see John Paoletti, "Fraternal Piety and Family Power: The Artistic Patronage of Cosimo and Lorenzo de' Medici," in *Cosimo 'il Vecchio' de' Medici, 1389–1464. Essays in Commemoration of the 600th Anniversary of Cosimo de' Medici's Birth*, ed. Francis Ames-Lewis (Oxford: Clarendon Press, 1992), 195–219; John T. Paoletti, "'…ha fatto Piero con voluntà del padre….,' Piero de' Medici and Corporate Commissions of Art," in *Piero de' Medici "il Gottoso" (1416–1469)*, ed. Andreas Beyer and Bruce Boucher (Berlin: Akademie Verlag, 1993), 221–50; Kent, *Cosimo de' Medici*, passim. See also my discussions of Cardinal Giulio de' Medici's relationship to Pope Leo X in Sheryl E. Reiss, "Cardinal Giulio de' Medici as a Patron of Art 1513–1523" (Ph.D. diss., Princeton University, 1992), 616–18 and of Alfonsina Orsini's collaborative patronage with her son Lorenzo in "Widow, Mother, Patron of Art: Alfonsina Orsini de' Medici," in *Beyond Isabella: Secular Women Patrons of Art in Renaissance Italy*, ed. Sheryl E. Reiss and David G. Wilkins (Kirksville, MO: Truman State University Press, 2001), esp. 134–6.

14. For the important role played by agents, see Chiara Peroni, "Funzionari e mecenanti alla corte dei Medici nel Cinquecento" in *Ianiculum-Gianicolo: Storia, topografia,*

monumenti, leggende dall'antichità al rinascimento, ed. Eva Margareta Steinby (Rome: Institutum Romanum Finlandiae, 1996), 199–204; Bruce L. Edelstein, "Leone Leoni, Benvenuto Cellini, and Francesco Vinta, A Medici Agent in Milan," *The Sculpture Journal* 4 (2000): 35–45; Sheryl E. Reiss, "Giulio de' Medici and Mario Maffei: A Renaissance Friendship and the Villa Madama," in *Coming About…A Festschrift for John Shearman,* ed. Lars R. Jones and Louisa C. Matthew (Cambridge, Massachusetts: Harvard University Art Museums, 2001), 281–8. Melissa Bullard has illuminated the role of what she calls "shared agency" in Lorenzo the Magnificent's political and cultural patronage, demonstrating how the importance of Lorenzo's secretaries and other agents – who took on considerable responsibility in the implementation of his policies – has been lost in the monolithic characterization of the individual "hero-patron." Melissa Meriam Bullard, "Heroes and their Workshops: Medici Patronage and the Problem of Shared Agency," in *Patterns of Patronage in Renaissance Italy,* ed. Louise Rice, *Journal of Medieval and Renaissance Studies* 24 (1994): 179–98.

15. See esp. Michael Baxandall, *Painting and Experience in Fifteenth-Century Italy: A Primer in the Social History of Pictorial Style* (Oxford: Clarendon Press, 1972), pt. 2, "The Period Eye"; Hans Belting, *Das Bild und Sein Publikum im Mittelalter: Form und Funktion früher Bildtafeln der Passion* (Berlin: Mann, 1981); John Shearman, *Only Connect…Art and the Spectator in the Italian Renaissance* (Princeton: Princeton University Press, 1992). Recent work that has emphasized the importance of audience and reception includes Bernardine Barnes, *Michelangelo's* Last Judgment: *The Renaissance Response* (Berkeley and Los Angeles: University of California Press, 1998); Pamela M. Jones, "The Power of Images: Paintings and Viewers in Caravaggio's Italy," in *Saints and Sinners: Caravaggio and the Baroque Image,* ed. Franco Mormando, exh. cat. (Chestnut Hill and Chicago: Boston College, McMullen Museum of Art and University of Chicago Press, 1999), 28–48; Megan Holmes, "'Behold the Head of the Baptist': The Engaged Spectator and Filippo Lippi's Feast of Herod," in Jones and Matthew, *Coming About…,* 65–72.

16. Recent books and special issues of journals devoted to the art patronage of women in early modern Italy and Europe include *Women Patrons of Renaissance Art, 1300–1600,* ed. Jaynie Anderson, in *Renaissance Studies* 10 (1996), and "Addendum" 11 (1997): 160; *Women and Art in Early Modern Europe: Patrons, Collectors and Connoisseurs,* ed. Cynthia Lawrence (University Park, Penn.: Pennsylvania State University Press, 1997); Catherine King, *Renaissance Women Patrons: Wives and Widows in Italy ca. 1300–1550* (Manchester and New York: Manchester University Press, 1998); *Committenza artistica feminile,* ed. Sara F. Matthews-Grieco and Gabriella Zarri in *Quaderni storci* 104 (2000): 283–421; Reiss and Wilkins, *Beyond Isabella.* For additional bibliography including individual studies, see ibid., "Prologue," nn. 1–6.

17. For Michelangelo and Clement VII's long-distance interaction by letter (and drawings), see Elam, "Drawings as Documents," 111; Reiss, "Cardinal Giulio de' Medici," chaps. 1, 6, and 11 and passim; Michael Hirst, "'per lui il mondo ha così nobil opera': Michelangelo und Papst Clemens VII," in *Hochrenaissance im Vatikan: Kunst und Kultur im Rom der Päpste I 1503–1534,* exh. cat. (Bonn: Kunst-und- Ausstellungshalle, 1999), 429–31; William Wallace, "Clement VII and Michelangelo: An Anatomy of Patronage," in *The Pontificate of Clement VII: History, Politics, Culture,* ed. Kenneth Gouwens and Sheryl E. Reiss (Aldershot, UK: Ashgate, 2005), 189–98. On Federico Gonzaga and Titian, see Diane Bodart, *Tiziano e Federico II Gonzaga: Storia du un Rapporto di Committenza* (Rome: Bulzoni, 1998), and Lisa Zeitz, "*Tizian Teuere Freund." Tizian und Federico Gonzaga: Kunstpatronage im Mantua im 16 Jahrhunderts* (Petersberg: Michael Imhof, 2000).

18. Donal Cooper, "Raphael's Altar-Pieces in S. Francesco al Prato, Perugia: Patronage, Setting and Function," *Burlington Magazine* 144 (2001): 554–61; Tom Henry, "Raphael's Altar-Piece Patrons in Città di Castello," *Burlington Magazine* 143 (2002): 268–78. Important observations on patronage and dating are also found in John Shearman, "On Raphael's Chronology 1503–1508," in *Ars naturam adiuvans: Festschrift für Matthias Winner* (Mainz: Philipp von Zabern, 1996), 201–07.

19. I must emphasize that my remarks on Raphael's early patronage in this essay are preliminary in nature, in anticipation of the publication of the catalogue to the major exhibition entitled "Raphael: From Urbino to Rome," to be held at the National Gallery, London, 20 October 2004–16 January 2005.

20. For Raphael's youth, see Jeryldene Wood's contribution to this volume. See also Roger Jones and Nicholas Penny, *Raphael* (New Haven and London: Yale University Press, 1983), chap. 1; Sylvia Ferino Pagden, "The Early Raphael and His Umbrian Contemporaries," in *Raphael before Rome*, 93–107; and Jürg Meyer zur Capellen, *Raphael: A Critical Catalogue of His Paintings. Volume I: The Beginnings in Umbria and Florence ca. 1500–1508* (Landshut: Arcos, 2001), pt. 2, chap. 1. Cf. Paul Joannides ("Raphael and Giovanni Santi" in Hamoud and Strocchi, *Studi su Raffaello*, 55–61, esp. 55–6), who emphasizes Giovanni Santi's charm and skills as a courtier, which would have provided a model for his son. Like Raphael, he was often associated with female patrons at the court.

21. Cf. Jeryldene Wood's essay in this volume for more detailed discussion of this topic. The late John Shearman (personal communications) and Jürg Meyer zur Capellen (*Critical Catalogue*, 17 and 58, n. 12) reject Vasari's widely accepted claim (Vasari/Milansi, 4: 317) that Raphael was sent to study with Perugino, proposing, instead, that the young artist would have studied with his father until 1494 and then with a painter from the Giovanni Santi workshop such as Timoteo Viti or Evangelista di Pian di Meleto. Cf. Ferino Pagden, "Early Raphael," 93 and 105, nn. 6–8. Raphael moved around quite a bit before 1508 and was often working for patrons elsewhere than the apparent location of his bottega (or botteghe). Crowe and Cavalcaselle's suggestion (1: 124) that Raphael's workshop was in Perugia when he worked on the Città di Castello altarpieces has been tentatively accepted by Henry, "Città di Castello," 278. Donal Cooper will be publishing a notarial document of 12 January 1504 in which Raphael is described as "magistri Rafaelis Iohannis pictoris de Urbino habitatoris Perusii," in an article to be published in the *Burlington Magazine* in November 2004. I am grateful to Dr. Cooper for sharing this document with me. Cf. Shearman, *Early Modern Sources,* 2: 1642, with a slightly different transcription. Shearman, "Raphael's Chronology," 202–3 and *Early Modern Sources*, 1: 90, however, argues against a Perugian workshop in 1505 because of expenses for transport and tax payment in the contract for the *Monteluce Altarpiece*. The contract of 1505 says that Raphael could be found in "Perugia, Assisi, Gubbio, Rome, Siena, Florence, Urbino, Venice" or elsewhere (Vincenzo Golzio, *Raffaello nei documenti, nelle testimonianze dei contemporanei e nella letteratura del suo secolo* [1936; reprint, Westmead, England: Gregg, 1971], 11). Francesco Federico Mancini, *Raffaello in Umbria: Cronologia e committenza. Nuovi studi e documenti* (Perugia: Volumnia Editrice, 1987), 38–9, has suggested that this formulation, is, in fact, commonplace in Perugian documents of the period. See, for example, two of Perugino's contracts of 1495 and 1499 in Fiorenzo Canuti, *Il Perugino*, 2 vols. (Siena: Editrice d'Arte "La Diana, 1931), 2: 175, no. 220, and 187, no. 251. Shearman (*Early Modern Sources*, 1: 90) suggests that Mancini may be correct but notes that it "has yet to be shown that such lists are local notarial conventions."

22. For the court of Guidobaldo da Montefeltro and its exile from Urbino, see James Dennistoun, *Memoirs of the Dukes of Urbino*, 2nd ed., ed. Edward Hutton, 3 vols. (London

and New York: John Lane, 1909), 1: bk. 3 and passim; Cecil H. Clough, "La 'Familia' del Duca Guidobaldo da Montefeltro ed *Il Cortegiano*," in *'Familia' del principe e famiglia artistocratica*, ed. Cesare Mozzarelli, 2 vols. (Rome: Bulzoni, 1988), 2: 335–46. See also Jeryldene Wood's contribution to this volume.

23. These undocumented and badly damaged paintings were first mentioned in 1627. See G. Magherini Graziani, *L'arte a Città di Castello* (Città di Castello: S. Lapi, 1897), chap. 18, 219–34; Luitpold Dussler, *Raphael: A Critical Catalogue of His Pictures, Wall Paintings and Tapestries* (London and New York: Phaidon, 1971), 3; Alessandro Marabottini in *Raffaello giovane*, 67–70 (dated ca. 1501–02) and 195–7, cat. no. 8, with bibliography; Mancini, *Raffaello in Umbria*, 25; Enrico Mercati, *Andrea Baronci e gli altri committenti tifernati di Raffaello* (Città di Castello: Petruzzi, 1994), 11–12 (dated 1499); Meyer zur Capellen, *Critical Catalogue*, cat. no. 2 (with bibliography); Henry "Città di Castello," 268.

24. Dussler, *Critical Catalogue*, 1–3, 8–10, 10–11, respectively; Meyer zur Capellen, *Critical Catalogue*, cat. nos. 1, 7, and 9, with bibliography; Henry, "Città di Castello."

25. Henry, "Città di Castello," 268.

26. For the history of the picture and the discovery of a fourth fragment, see Sylvie Béguin, in *Raphael dans les collections françaises*, exh. cat., Paris, Grand Palais (Paris: Réunion des Musées Nationaux), cat. nos. 1–3, and Sylvie Béguin, "The Saint Nicholas of Tolentino Altarpiece, in *Raphael before Rome*, 15–28. For the contract and notice of completion in September 1501 (first published in Giovanni Magherini Graziani, "Documenti inediti relative al *'San Nicola da Tolentino'* e allo *'Spozalizio'* di Raffaello," in *Bolletino della R. Deputazione di Storia Patria per l'Umbria* 14 [1908]: 83–95, at 88–9), Golzio, *Raffaello nei documenti*, 7–8 and Shearman, *Early Modern Sources*, 1: 71–3, doc. 1500/2. Mercati, *Andrea Baronci* (13–15) unconvincingly questions the generally accepted association of the San Nicola Altarpiece with these documents. Henry ("Città di Castello," 270) accepts the traditional relationship between the painting and the documents.

27. "cum illis figuris quibus dicet idem Andreas, de bonis picturis et coloribus, ad usum boni pictoris et magistri." Golzio, *Raffaello nei documenti*, 7. For a slightly different transcription, see Shearman, *Early Modern Sources*, 1: 71.

28. For this patron, Mercati, *Andrea Baronci* (with lists of his political offices); Henry, "Città di Castello," 270.

29. Mercati, *Andrea Baronci*; Henry, "Città di Castello."

30. Henry ("Città di Castello," 271) suggests that he was also a banker.

31. For the real estate dealings, see Mercati, *Andrea Baronci*, 77 ff. For Clara Baronci's will, see Henry, "Città di Castello," 273 and appendix, doc. 1.

32. Henry, "Città di Castello," 271, for the correct inscription. Golzio, *Raffaello nei documenti*, 9 (following Magherini Graziani, *L'arte*, 236), partially mistranscribed it. Alessandro Marabottini (*Raffaello giovane*, 65) and John Shearman ("Raphael's Chronology," 201) have suggested that this should not be understood as the date of the painting itself, which they place about two years later. Meyer zur Capellen (*Critical Catalogue* 122) suggests 1502–3, but (120) does not completely rule out a later date for completion of the painting. Henry ("Città di Castello," 274) accepts the traditional dating.

33. The chapel was sometimes referred to as the Cappella del Crocifisso. See, for example, Clara Baronci's will (cf. n. 31), which was drawn up "apud altare Crucifixi."

34. Henry, "Città di Castello," 276, and appendix, doc. 3. For the Brera *Sposalizio*, see also Carlo Bertelli et al., *Lo Sposalizio della Vergine di Raffaello* (Bergamo: Fiber, 1983).

35. For the cult of the Virgin's Holy Ring in Umbria and the relationship of the two altarpieces, see Jörg Traeger, *Renaissance und Religion: Die Kunst des Glaubens im Zeitalter Raphaels* (Munich: C. H. Beck, 1997). For the problematic underpinnings of this

book's historical and intellectual approach, however, see the cogent review by Alexander Nagel, *Art Bulletin* 82 (2000): 773–7. See also Jeryldene Wood's discussion of the iconography of the *Sposalizio*, in this volume.

36. The letter, one of two first published in Magherini Graziani, "Documenti inediti," 91–3, concerns the attempts of Duke Guidobaldo II of Urbino to obtain the picture. Abridged in Golzio, *Raffaello nei documenti*, 168, with the specific information concerning Ser Filippo eliminated. See now Shearman, *Early Modern Sources*, 2: 1223–4, doc. 1571/2.

37. For these offices, including prior on a number of occasions, see Mercati, *Andrea Baronci*, 33 and passim; Henry, "Città di Castello," 275.

38. The contract for Perugino's Corciano Altarpiece, which specifies that it should be "prout tabula Mag.ae Alexandrae Simonis de Oddis, quae est in Ecclesia S. Francesci de Perusia," is published in Canuti, *Il Perugino*, 2: 258–9, no. 430. Vasari/Milanesi, (4: 317) gives the patronage of the *Coronation* to "madonna Maddalenna degli Oddi." The patronage was clarified in Luchs, "Perugian Patrons" and has been further explained in Cooper "Raphael's Altar-Pieces," 554–5. For the painting, see Dussler, *Critical Catalogue*, 10; Meyer zur Capellen, *Critical Catalogue*, cat. no. 8. Cf. also Jeryldene Wood's essay in this volume.

39. For Perugia in this period, see the useful overview by James Banker, "The Social History of Perugia in the Time of Perugino," in *Pietro Perugino: Master of the Italian Renaissance*, ed. Joseph Antenucci Bercherer, exh. cat., Grand Rapids Museum of Art (New York: Rizzoli, 1997), 37–51. On the Baglioni and their relations with the Oddi, see Jacob Burckhardt, *The Civilization of the Renaissance in Italy*, 2 vols. (New York: Harper and Row, 1958), 1: 45–6; Baleoneus Astur, *I Baglioni* (Prato: La Tipografia Pratese, 1964), esp. pt. 2; Christopher F. Black, "The Baglioni as Tyrants of Perugia, 1488–1540," *English Historical Review* 85 (1970): 245–81; Sarah Rubin Blanshei, "Population, Wealth, and Patronage in Medieval and Renaissance Perugia," *Journal of Interdisciplinary History* 9 (1979): 597–619; Christopher F. Black, *Early Modern Italy: A Social History* (London and New York: Routledge, 2001); 118, 126–8, and passim. In periods of exile, women left behind often took on great responsibility, including art patronage. See Black, op. cit., 118; Christine Shaw, *The Politics of Exile in Renaissance Italy* (Cambridge and New York: Cambridge University Press, 2000), 118 ff.; and Reiss, "Alfonsina Orsini," 144, n. 21.

40. Luchs ("Perugian Patrons," 29–30) suggests two possible scenarios: (1) Maddalena commissioned the chapel and altarpiece, which would have passed to Leandra, and (2) Maddalena was the patron of the chapel and Leandra commissioned the painting. See Cooper "Raphael's Altar-Pieces," 554, for the family's much earlier patronage of the chapel. For the theological relationship of the Assumption and Coronation of the Virgin (which share the same feast day, August 15), see John Shearman, The Chigi Chapel in S. Maria del Popolo," *Journal of the Warburg and Courtauld Institutes* 24 (1961): 158–60. Cf. Jeryldene Wood's discussion in this volume.

41. See, for example, the contributions of Katherine McIver and Carolyn Valone to Reiss and Wilkins, *Beyond Isabella*, with further bibliography on this topic.

42. Dussler, *Critical Catalogue*, 23–4; Meyer zur Capellen, *Critical Catalogue*, cat. no. 31. The location in San Francesco has recently been identified by Cooper, "Raphael's Altar-Pieces," as the Chapel of Saint Matthew, at the northeast corner of the crossing, opposite the Oddi chapel at the southeast. This refutes the placement in the south transept chapel proposed by Hubert Locher, *Rafael und das Altarbild der Renaissance: Die "Pala Baglioni" als Kunstwerk in sakralen Kontext* (Berlin: Akademie Verlag, 1994), 23–4.

43. Vasari/Milanesi, 4: 325 and 327. The note on the back of the drawing (Lille, Musée des Beaux Arts, inv. no. 458/459) to Domenico Alfani (to whom the *God the Father* that topped the *Entombment* has been attributed) reads "Ancora ve ricor[d]

che voi solecitat[e] madona le Atalante che me manda li denari." Shearman, *Early Modern Sources*, 1: 111–12, doc. 1507-08/1. Cooper, "Raphael's Altar-Pieces," 560, n. 60. For the drawing, a modello for Alfani's *Holy Family with a Pomegranate* of 1511 (Galleria Nazionale, Perugia), see Eckhart Knab et al., *Raphael: Die Zeichnungen* (Stuttgart: Urachaus, 1983), cat. no. 212; Paul Joannides, *The Drawings of Raphael with a Complete Catalogue* (Berkeley: University of California Press, 1983), cat. no. 175v. (illustrated). Paul Joannides, *Raphael and His Age: Drawings from the Palais de Beaux-Arts, Lille*, exh. cat., Cleveland Museum of Art (Paris: Réunion des Musées Nationaux, 2002), cat. no. 34. An inscription on the now-lost frame is said to have read: "Atalanta Baliona hoc divo Salvatori/donum donat et sacrum dedicat/Raphael Urbinas 1507." See Cooper, "Raphael's Altar-Pieces," 560, n. 64, for the manuscript source. On Atalanta Baglioni, see Astur, *I Baglioni*, 62–2, 124, 135–8.

44. Burckhardt, 1: 48. The tragic events were recorded by Francesco Materazzo in his "Cronaca della Città di Perugia dal 1492 al 1503," *Archivio Storico Italiano* 16, no. 2 (1851): 1–243, esp. 133–4 for Atalanta and Grifonetto. Translated as *Chronicles of the City of Perugia 1492–1503* (London: J. M. Dent, 1905). For a detailed summary based on the Materazzo *Cronaca*, see Alexander Nagel, *Michelangelo and the Reform of Art* (Cambridge and New York: Cambridge University Press, 2000), 116–22. See also Black, *Early Modern Italy*, 126–8, and cf. Jeryldene Wood's essay in this volume.

45. Cooper, "Raphael's Altar-Pieces," 558.

46. For the will, Cooper, "Raphael's Altar-Pieces," 560, nn. 62 and 67.

47. Dussler, *Critical Catalogue*, 14–16; Meyer zur Capellen, *Critical Catalogue*, cat. no. 17. For an eccentrically early dating of ca. 1501–2, see Konrad Oberhuber, "The Colonna Altarpiece in the Metropolitan Museum and the Problem of the Early Style of Raphael," *Metropolitan Museum Journal* 12 (1977): 55–92.

48. Vasari/Milanesi, 4: 324. Leo Steinberg (*The Sexuality of Christ in Renaissance Art and in Modern Oblivion*, 2d ed. [1983]; reprint, Chicago: University of Chicago Press, 1996, 225) does not address how the response to what he calls the "provocation" of a "visibly sexed Christ" may have varied with different viewers. For recent studies that do address the issue of gendered reception, see, for example, Richard Trexler, "Gendering Christ Crucified," in *Iconography at the Crossroads*, ed. Brendan Cassidy, Index of Christian Art Occasional Papers II (Princeton: Princeton University Press, 1990), 107–19; Jeryldene M. Wood, *Women, Art, and Spirituality: The Poor Clares of Early Modern Italy* (Cambridge and New York: Cambridge University Press, 1996); Jeffrey F. Hamburger, *The Visual and the Visionary: Art and Female Spirituality in Late Medieval Germany* (New York: Zone Books, 1998). For further observations on the (negative) gendered associations of paintings that appealed to women, cf. the discussions of Francisco de Hollanda's famous passage in which Michelangelo is said to have disparaged Flemish painting for appealing to "women, especially the very old and the very young, and also to monks and nuns," in Philip Sohm, "Gendered Style in Italian Art Criticism from Michelangelo to Malvasia," *Renaissance Quarterly* 48 (1995): 773–84, and Nagel, *Michelangelo and the Reform of Art*, 192. Both authors also discuss Michelangelo's gendering of oil painting (surely identified with Raphael), as "arte da donna." It is worth noting that the *bambini* or "holy dolls" representing the infant Jesus, which were presented to both nuns and secular women and girls were, most often, richly dressed, like the Christ Child in Raphael's painting. See Christiane Klapisch-Zuber, "Holy Dolls: Play and Piety in Florence in the Quattrocento," in *Women, Family, and Ritual in Renaissance Italy* (Chicago: University of Chicago Press, 1985), 310–29, esp. 312–13. Linda Wolk-Simon of the Metropolitan Museum of Art is currently preparing a study of the Colonna Altarpiece for a forthcoming number of the museum's *Bulletin*. I am grateful to Alfred Acres, Pamela Jones, Alexander Nagel, and Linda Wolk-Simon for discussing the topic of gendered reception of sacred art with me.

49. Mancini, *Raffaello in Umbria*, 13–30. On the convent of San Antonio in Perugia, see Giovanna Casagrande, "Terziane francescane regolari in Perugia nei secoli XIV e XV," *Analecta TOR* 17 (1984): 450–66. For Ilaria di Braccio Baglioni, see Casagrande 455–6, and op. cit. Casagrande, "Aspetti del Terz'Ordine francescano a Perugia nella seconda metà del secolo XIV e nel XV," in *Il movimento francescano della Penitenza nella società medievale*, ed. Mariano D'Altari (Rome: Istituto storico dei Cappucini, 1980), 378–9, n. 41. For Braccio Baglioni, who had many daughters (Ilaria was the firstborn) and only one son, see Astur, *I Baglioni*, 53 ff. and 91.

50. If Mancini's identification of the figure as Margaret is correct, it is possible that the inclusion was commemorative, as Ilaria died in 1503. It is worth considering that the commission and execution of the painting were separated by a couple of years. Certainly the case of the Monteluce Altarpiece suggests that Raphael did not always deliver his paintings promptly.

51. For which, see Fabrizio Mancinelli in *Raffaello in Vaticano*, cat. nos. 108–14; Shearman, "Raphael's Chronology;" Wood, *Women, Art, and Spirituality*, 104–8 and 188. Wood, ibid., 104, emphasizes the intended location. Cf. her contribution to this volume.

52. *Memoriale di Monteluce: Cronaca del monastero delle clarisse di Perugia, dal 1448 al 1838*, introduction by Ugolino Niccolini (Santa Maria degli Angeli: Porzincuola, 1983), 127. Cf. Shearman, "Raphael's Chronology," 203 and 206, n. 17, for the delivery of the altarpiece in more than one crate.

53. On Suor Battista, see *Memoriale*, xvi–xvii (with a family tree of the Alfani), 67–8, for some of her patronage activities; Wood, *Women and Spirituality*, 102–6; Shearman, "Raphael's Chronology," 202. For Battista's nephew, Alfano di Diamante Alfani and the Hermitage *Madonna*, see Mancini, *Raffaello in Umbria*, 46–8. See Mancini, op. cit., ibid., 48, for the relationship to the painter Domenico Alfani, who sometimes collaborated with Raphael.

54. *Memoriale*, 85: "Ma fece trovare el maestro, el megliore li fusse consigliato da più citadini et ancho da li nostri venerandi padri, li quali havevano vedute le opere suoi, lo quale se chiamava maestro Raphaello da Urbino." Cf. Shearman, *Early Modern Sources*, 1: 93–6, doc. 1505/4.

55. Golzio, *Raffaello nei documenti*, 11–13 and Shearman, *Early Modern Sources*, 1: 86–92, doc. 1505/2 for the contract. Henry, "Città di Castello," suggests that the price for the San Nicola Altarpiece was "commensurate with … [the] reputation and experience" of Raphael and his older collaborator.

56. Shearman, *Early Modern Sources*, 1:87 : "et le ditce figure promette fare dicto mastro Rafaiello in dicta cona de mano sua propria." On "sua mano" clauses in Renaissance contracts, see Michelle O'Malley, "Late Fifteenth- and Early Sixteenth-Century Painting Contracts and the Stipulated Use of the Painter's Hand," in *With and Without the Medici: Studies in Tuscan Art and Patronage 1434–1530*, ed. Eckart Marchand and Alison Wright (Aldershot, UK, and Brookfield, VT.: Ashgate, 1998): 155–78; 158–9 and 165–7 for the Monteluce *Coronation*.

57. *Memoriale*, 86. For Suor Illuminata's bequest for "cose de chiesia," see Wood, *Women and Spirituality*, 104 and 242, n. 51. For the pious motivations of women patrons, particularly widows, see also Carolyn Valone, "Matrons and Motives: Why Women Built in Early Modern Rome," in Reiss and Wilkins, *Beyond Isabella*, 317–35.

58. Golzio, *Raffaello nei documenti*, 48–9 and Shearman, *Early Modern Sources*, 1: 253–7, doc. 1516/17, who notes (255) that the agreement does not follow the norms of a legally binding notarial document. The procurator was Alfano di Diamante Alfani, Suor Battista's nephew. Cf. n. 53 above.

59. Golzio, *Raffaello nei documenti*, 48–9 and Shearman, *Early Modern Sources*, 1: 253–4.

60. For which, see my subsequent discussion.

61. Dussler, *Critical Catalogue*, 68; Meyer zur Capellen, *Critical Catalogue*, cat. no. 16. The patronage has recently been associated with two successive *commendatarii* of the

Camaldolite monastery of Monte Acuto, the future bishop of Perugia, Trolio Baglioni and his successor as *commendatario,* Gabriello Gabrielli. See Mancini, *Raffaello in Umbria,* 54–6.

62. For the painting, cf. Jeryldene Wood's essay in this volume. The dating of 1505 or 1506 is based on a problematic inscription on the hem of the Virgin's robe. Golzio (*Raffaello nei documenti,* 10), says 1505, as does Meyer zur Capellen, *Critical Catalogue,* cat. no. 16. Shearman, *Early Modern Sources,* 1: 97–8, doc. 1505–6/1, leaves the question open, with a preference for 1506. Donal Cooper and Carol Plazzotta will have new suggestions for the patronage of this altarpiece in an article to be published in the *Burlington Magazine* in November 2004. On the Ansidei, see Pericle Ansidei, "La Famiglia Ansidei di Catrano," *Giornale araldico geneologico* 4 (1876): 109–19.

63. See Ansidei, "Gli Ansidei," 116, for the altar and its inscription; Mancini, *Raffaello in Umbria,* 57, for the donation. For the family's patronage in San Fiorenzo and for the setting of the altarpiece in the church, see also the forthcoming article by Cooper and Plazzotta cited in n. 62. I am most grateful to Dr. Cooper for discussing his findings with me prior to publication.

64. Golzio, *Raffaello nei documenti,* 16–18. The well-known letter of recommendation from Giovanna Feltria della Rovere to Piero Soderini (discussed later in this essay as a possible forgery) has been used to place Raphael in Urbino in the fall of 1504.

65. Pietro Bembo's letter of 6 May 1507, suggests that the painter had been in Urbino "molti mesi." See Golzio, *Raffaello nei documenti,* 16 and Shearman, *Early Modern Sources,* 1: 101–4, doc. 1507/1. For the ambience of the court, see the introduction to Baldesar Castiglione, *The Book of the Courtier,* trans. George Bull (Harmondsworth, UK, and New York: Penguin Books). See also *Urbino e le Marche,* esp. pt. I, sec. 3, and pt. II, secs. 6 and 7. For links between Castiglione's *Il cortegiano* and Raphael's Urbino paintings, David Alan Brown, "Saint George in Raphael's Washington Painting," in *Raphael before Rome,* 43–4. On Raphael and Castiglione, see also Lynn M. Louden, "Sprezzatura in Raphael and Castiglione," *Art Journal* 28 (1968): 43–9, 53; and Pierluigi De Vecchi, "Difficultà/facilità e sprezzatura nell'opera di Raffaello," in *Raffaello: Grazia e bellezza,* exh. cat., Paris, Musée National du Luxembourg (Milan: Skira, 2001), 29–39, esp. 31–3.

66. An overview of Raphael's activities at the Urbino court may be found in *Urbino e le Marche,* pt. II, secs. 6 and 7. Cf. also Jeryldene Wood's essay in this volume. For the silver *bacilli* "de desegno et fogia antiqua designati per Raphael," probably executed in 1506 for the Duchess Elisabetta, see Golzio, *Raffaello nei documenti,* 50 and Shearman, *Early Modern Sources,* 1: 260–2, doc. 1516/20, with a slightly different transcription from that of Golzio. The basins were apparently destroyed in 1516. For the association of small, secular subjects with the Urbino court, see Jones and Penny, *Raphael,* 5–8. For Raphael's Urbino portraits, see John Shearman, "Raphael at the Court of Urbino," *Burlington Magazine* 112 (1970): 72–8, and Shearman, "Raphael's Chronology," 203–5. Several of these portraits have been rejected unconvincingly by Meyer zur Capellen, *Critical Catalogue,* cat. nos. X–12 –X–14.

67. Vasari/Milanesi, 4: 322–3 "Fece al medesimo [Guidobaldo duca d'Urbino] un quadretto d'un Cristo che ora nell'orto." But see Bembo's letter (cf. n. 65) to the hermit Michele Fiorentino, which outlines the duchess's wish for "una imagine … per mano dun gran maestro della pittura" to present to the monk in gratitude for a rosary and "in memoria di lei." See Golzio, *Raffaello nei documenti,* 165–7 and Shearman, *Early Modern Sources,* 2: 1211–15, doc. nos. 1570/1–1570/6 for correspondence of 1570 concerning the later fortunes of the picture. Based on his reading of this correspondence Shearman (op. cit., 1: 103) has now argued for a separation of patron (Elisabetta) and donor (Eleonora, mother of Duke Guidobaldo) of the painting to the hermits.

68. Golzio, *Raffaello nei documenti*, 284 and Shearman, *Early Modern Sources*, 2: 936–7, doc. 1544/5, using a different edition of Serlio than Golzio (the duchess is misidentified as Isabella).

69. Golzio, *Raffaello nei documenti*, 171, citing the Anonimo Morelliano, who lists it in Bembo's Padua house and describes it as "in m[inia]ta." For Castiglione and the portrait of the duchess, see Shearman, "Raphael's Chronology," 203–5.

70. Vasari states repeatedly in his Raphael *Vita* that the artist worked in different "manners," attributing the stylistic shifts to his inner drive to learn and to change. No doubt this was very much at work, but as Ettlinger perceptively noted in 1986 ("Raphael's Early Patrons," 87): "The conventional style of the large altarpieces painted after Raphael had established close contacts with Florentine art in 1504 can only be due to the fact that the taste of his clients – all linked with churches in Città di Castello and Perugia – was conservative.... Taste was not determined by artists alone, and patrons obviously had their way." The Baglioni *Entombment*, of course, was not in the conservative mold of Raphael's other Umbrian altarpieces. For artists employing different modes of visual expression for different commissions or markets, see Leslie Korrick, "On the Meaning of Style: Nicolò Circignani in Counter-Reformation Rome," *Word and Image* 15 (1999): 170–89; Robert G. La France, "Bachiacca's Formula for Success," in *The Art Market in Italy, 1500–1600*, ed. Marcello Fantoni, Louisa Matthew, and Sara Matthews-Grieco (Modena: Franco Cosimo Panini, 2003), 237–52.

71. As noted in Jones and Penny, *Raphael*, 9.

72. For this fascinating woman – who deserves greater study – see Dennistoun, *Dukes of Urbino*, 1: 289, 2: 291, and Cecil H. Clough, "Daughters and Wives of the Montefeltro: Outstanding Bluestockings of the Quattrocento," *Renaissance Studies* 10 (1966): 48–9 and 52–4.

73. Clough, "Daughters and Wives," 52–3. Clough attributes to her patronage the church of Santa Maria delle Grazie outside Senigallia and Piero della Francesca's *Madonna di Senigallia* (now in Urbino). She has also been identified as a patron of Giovanni Santi's *Annunciation* for the church of Santa Maria Maddalena in Senigallia, which is now in the Casa di Raffaello, Urbino. See ibid., 53, and Ranieri Varese, *Giovanni Santi* (Fiesole: Nardni, 1994), 243–4. See also Jeryldene Wood's essay in this volume.

74. Biblioteca Apostolica Vaticana, Borg. Lat. 800 (henceforth BAV, Borg. Lat. 800). Golzio, *Raffaello nei documenti*, 18–19. Golzio presents the relevant passage as follows: "io scrissi laltro di alzio prete che me mandasse unatavoletta che era la coperta de la nostra donna dela prefetessa." As pointed out by Giovanni Morello, *Raffaello e la Roma dei Papa*, exh. cat., Biblioteca Apostolica Vaticana (Rome: Fratelli Palombi, 1986), 19, cat. no. 7, the word used in the letter is clearly "profetessa," and an alternate reading would be iconographic, that is, a painting of the Virgin as Seer ("nostra donna dela profetessa"). The problem with this interpretation (beyond its awkward phrasing) is that the next line asks for Raphael's uncle to send the cover as soon as possible "che io possa satisfare amadona." Most likely then, "profetessa" was an uncharacteristic slip of the pen by Raphael. See now the revised transcription of this letter in Shearman, *Early Modern Sources*, 1: 112–13, doc. 1508/1 with a discussion of the reading, 114–5.

75. For the intriguing identification of the *Small Cowper Madonna* (which has a probable Urbino provenance and shows the church of San Bernardino, burial place of the dukes of Urbino, in the background), with the painting mentioned in the letter, see Luisa Beccherucci, "Raffaello e la pittura," in *Raffaello: l'opera, le fonti, la fortuna*, 2 vols. (Novara: Istituto Geografico De Agostini, 1968), 1: 76, and *Urbino e le Marche*, 266–7, cat. no. 74. Other pictures that have been proposed include the *Madonna d'Orleans* in Chantilly and the *Holy Family with Lamb* in the Prado. For Giovanna as patron of the Louvre panels, see Shearman, "Court of Urbino," 77, n. 23, and Clough, "Daughters

and Wives," 54. Jones and Penny (*Raphael*, 7) suggest that Giovanna, whose father and brother belonged to the Order of the Garter and whose husband and son belonged to the Order of Saint Michael, might have been the recipient of the pair. For a summary of other proposals, *Urbino e le Marche*, cat. nos. 63 and 64; Sylvie Beguin, in *Raphael dans les collections françaises*, cat. nos. 4 and 5. Beguin argues that pictures were not painted simultaneously.

76. Golzio, *Raffaello nei documenti*, 9–10 and Shearman, *Early Modern Sources*, 2: 1457–1462, doc. F/5, with extensive bibliography.

77. See Golzio, *Raffaello nei documenti*, 9–10, for the *fortuna critica* of the letter. See also Milanesi, in Vasari/Milanesi, 4: 320, n. 1. The problems with the letter are both linguistic and factual. Clough, "Wives and Daughters," 53–4, accepts the authenticity of the letter, the problems of which he believes to be errors of transcription and printing. See also Francesco Caglioti, *Donatello e i Medici: Storia del* David e *della* Giuditta, 2 vols. (Florence: Leo S. Olschki, 2000), 1:337, n. 196. Shearman ("Raphael's Chronology," 201) and, especially, *Early Modern Sources*, 2: 1458–61, rejects the various attempts to correct the letter's inconsistencies. It must be said, however, that if it is indeed a settecento forgery, it is a brilliant one, too good to be true in fact, with much to tell us about the mechanics of the patronage that enabled Raphael's career. I am grateful to the late John Shearman, Nicholas Penny, and Caroline Elam for discussing the letter with me. Elam will express some doubt about whether the now-lost letter is indeed a forgery in a forthcoming piece on John Shearman to be published in the *Römisches Jahrbuch der Bibliotheca Hertziana*.

78. Cf. n. 74 for BAV, Borg. Lat. 800.

79. "Averia caro se fosse posibile d'avere una letera di recomandatione al gonfalonero di Fiore[n]za dal S. Prefetto.... me faria grande utilo per l'interesse de un certa stanza da lavorare, la quale t[oc]ha a sua S. de alocare." Shearman, *Early Modern Sources*, 1: 113. Golzio (*Raffaello nei documenti*, 19, n. 8) misidentifies the "Prefetto" as Giovanni della Rovere (late husband of Giovanna Feltria della Rovere) who died in 1501. The person from whom Raphael wishes the letter is actually Francesco Maria della Rovere. That Raphael was requesting a letter recommending him to Soderini in April of 1508 could shed further doubt on the letter of 1 October 1504. The "certa stanza" has been identified by Golzio (*Raffaello nei documenti*, 19, n. 10) as the Sala del Gran Consiglio, where Michelangleo and Leonardo had worked. John Shearman (*Early Modern Sources*, 1: 116–7) has argued that the "sua S." referred to in the letter is actually Julius II and that the room to be allocated is in the Vatican. Documents recently published by Caglioti (*Donatello e i Medici*, 1: 336 and 337, n. 194) concerning the gilding of the belt that once adorned Michelangelo's *David* and a Madonna for the Palazzo della Signoria name a certain "Raffaello di Giovanni dipintore." Although Caglioti states (op. cit., 337) that this painter could be none other than Raphael of Urbino, this is not at all certain. It seems likely that Raphael would have been identified in the documents as a non-Florentine and he never worked as a *mettiloro* (gilder). The late John Shearman (personal communication) has noted that Raphael is never referred to in this fashion in other documents. Cf. Shearman, *Early Modern Sources*, 118–20, doc. 1508/2, for his decision to suspend judgment on these payments until they are better understood.

80. For Taddeo Taddei and his family, see R. W. Lightbown, "Michelangelo's Great Tondo," *Apollo* 89 (1969): 27–30, and Alessandro Cecchi in *Raffaello a Firenze: Dipinti e disegni delle collezioni fiorentine*, exh. cat., Palazzo Pitti (Florence: Electa, 1984), 40–41. For Taddeo Taddei, Michelangelo made the *Taddei Tondo*, now in London (for which, see Lightbown, op. cit., and Roberta J. M. Olson, *The Florentine Tondo* [Oxford and New York: Oxford University Press, 2000], 161–5). On Michelangelo's relations with Taddei, see William E. Wallace, "Michelangelo: In and Out of Florence Between 1500 and 1508,"

in *Leonardo, Michelangelo and Raphael in Renaissance Florence from 1500 to 1508*, ed. Serafina Hager (Washington, DC: Georgetown University Press, 1992), 68 and esp. 84, n. 30. For Palazzo Taddei in the Via de' Ginori, see Leonardo Ginori Lisci, *I palazzi di Firenze nella storia e nell'arte*, 2 vols. (Florence: Giunti, 1972), 1: cat. no. 50.

81. Vasari/Milanesi, 4: 321, "[Raffaello] fu nella città molto onorato; e particularmente da Taddeo Taddei, il quale lo volle sempre in casa sua ed alla sua tavola." Raphael, in turn, wrote to his uncle of Taddeo, who was going to Urbino: "venendo là Tadeo Tadei fiorentino, el quale n'avemo ragionate più volte insieme, li facine honore senza asparagnio nisuno, e voi ancora li farete careze per mio amore, ché certo li so[n] ubligatissimo quanto che a omo che viva." Shearman, *Early Modern Sources*, 1: 112.

82. Vasari/Milanesi, 4: 321. "E Raffaello, che era la gentilezza stessa, per non esser vinto di cortesia, gli fece due quadri."

83. Filippo Baldinucci, *Opere di Filippo Baldinucci*, 14 vols. (Milan: Società tipografica de' classici italiani, 1808–12), 6: 230. Cf. Milanesi, in Vasari/Milanesi, 4: 321, n. 2. Baldinucci, op. cit., 229, implies that Raphael left the pictures to Taddei "in dono." On the Vienna painting, see Dussler, *Critical Catalogue*, 20; Meyer zur Capellen, *Critical Catalogue*, cat. no. 26.

84. Vasari/Milanesi, 4: 321. Ettlinger ("Early Patrons," 88) suggests the *Tempi Madonna* in Munich, but this seems to be based on a misreading of Dussler, *Critical Catalogue*, 21. The picture is certainly not Peruginesque.

85. For the longstanding ties of the Taddei to the Medici, see Cecchi in *Raffaello a Firenze*, 40. For an overview of the city's political life in these years, see H. C. Butters, *Governors and Government in Early Sixteenth-Century Florence 1502–1519* (Oxford: Clarendon Press, 1985), esp. chaps. 3–5. Butters (7) points out that by the end of the quattrocento, upwardly mobile families like the Taddei, Serristori, and Leoni were becoming de facto members of what he calls the patriciate, even if they were not considered *nobili*. In this period, of course, Florence did not have an aristocracy per se.

86. Vasari/Milanesi (4: 321) says that Raphael maintained an "amicizia grandissima" with Nasi and (326) that the heirs of Domenico Canigiani held their painting in "quella stima che merita un'opera di Raffaello da Urbino." For Nasi and Canigiani, see Cecchi, in *Raffaello a Firenze*, 39, 41, 43; see also 77. For the patronage of the Nasi and other Florentine families in the quattrocento, see now Burke, *Changing Patrons*. For Canigiani, see also F. Troncarelli, *DBI* 18 (1975): 89–90. Like Taddeo Taddei, Canigiani had strong and long-lasting ties to the Medici.

87. See Cecchi, in *Raffaello a Firenze*, 39–43 for the intricate family connections between the Nasi, Taddei, and Canigiani. See also Burke, *Changing Patrons*, 191–4.

88. For which Dussler, *Critical Catalogue*, 19 and 20; Meyer zur Capellen, *Critical Catalogue*, cat. nos. 27 and 30. For the *Madonna del Cardellino*, cf. *Raffaello a Firenze*, cat. no. 5, and for the *Canigiani Holy Family*, in particular its conservation, see Hubertus von Sonnenberg, *Raphael in der Alten Pinakothek* (Munich: Prestel-Verlag, 1983).

89. Vasari/Milanesi, 4: 321, "al quale [Nasi], avendo preso donna in que'giorni, dipinse un quadro." For the *Canigiani Holy Family* as a wedding picture, see Cecchi, *Raffaello a Firenze*, 43. New findings on the date of Nasi's marriage by Cecchi preclude Vasari's statement about the *Madonna del Cardellino*. I am grateful to Alessandro Cecchi for sharing this information with me in a personal communication. Canigiani's bride was Lucrezia di Girolamo Frescobaldi.

90. Shearman ("Raphael's Chronology," 203) placed the *Madonna del Cardellino* somewhat later than Nasi's marriage (then specified only as before February 1506), but rightly noted the "unquantifiable lapse between commission and delivery." Ettlinger ("Early Patrons," 88) suggests without explanation that the *Canigiani Holy Family* was probably intended for a chapel in Santo Spirito, but this seems unlikely given that

Vasari saw it in the family palazzo. Jacqueline Marie Musacchio believes that at least some of Raphael's Florentine Madonnas were associated with births. I am grateful to her for discussing them with me.

91. Ettlinger ("Early Patrons," 88–9) notes the domestic functions of such pictures and associates them with female and family life. Surprisingly, Rosi Gilday ("The Women Patrons of Neri di Bicci," in Reiss and Wilkins, *Beyond Isabella*, 62) has found that women patrons of the ubiquitous quattrocento painter bought primarily for church settings, whereas his male patrons – perhaps more than 50 percent of the time – bought for the home. But here issues of audience and use enter into considerations of patronage. As Roger Crum ("Controlling Women or Women Controlled? Suggestions for Gender Roles and Visual Culture in the Italian Renaissance Palace," Reiss and Wilkins, *Beyond Isabella*, 37–50) reminds us, even if men paid the bills for the *arredamento* of a palazzo (and are therefore the "documented" patrons), women often made the choices and took responsibility for the objects. Cf. also Jeryldene Wood's essay in this collection.

92. The *Large Cowper Madonna* in Washington was described in 1677 as in the Casa Niccolini in Florence (Francesco Bocchi and Giovanni Cinelli, *Le bellezze della città di Firenze* [Florence: Giorgio Gugliantini, 1677], 408) and the Berlin *Colonna Madonna* was noted in a Colonna inventory of 1783 as coming from the Casa Salviati in Florence.

93. This important question certainly needs to be explored for Raphael's activity, especially before Rome. Stephen Wolohojian ("The Warburg *Virgin and Child with Saints Jerome and Francis* in the Fogg Art Museum," in Jones and Matthew, *Coming About...*, 317) has noted that "Intimate religious works were an ideal way for the young artist to begin his career as they could be produced and reproduced at a reasonable cost without the need of established patronage." Raphael, of course, started out painting large altarpieces and if he and his shop did produce works "on spec," this practice would have supplemented, rather than substituted for, his efforts on commissioned works.

94. For the Doni, see Andrée Hayum, "Michelangelo's *Doni Tondo*: Holy Family and Family Myth," *Studies in Iconography* 7–8 (1981–82): 209–51, esp. 210–12; Cecchi in *Raffaello a Firenze*, 41–2; Cecchi, "Agnolo e Maddalena Doni" (as in n. 7).

95. On the paired portraits, cf. the contributions of Jeryldene Wood and Joanna Woods-Marsden to this volume.

96. Vasari/Milanesi, 7: 159, for the admonitory anecdote.

97. Dussler, *Critical Catalogue*, 26; *Raffaello a Firenze*, cat. no. 10; Meyer zur Capellen, *Critical Catalogue*, cat. no. 40. For the conservation campaign concluded in 1990, which revealed that Raphael completed much more of the painting than had been hitherto thought, see Marco Chiarini, Marco Ciatti, and Serena Padovani, *Raffaello a Pitti: 'La Madonna del baldacchino,'* exh. cat., Florence, Palazzo Pitti (Florence: Centro Di, 1991). For the Dei chapel in Santo Spirito, see David Franklin, *Rosso in Italy: The Italian Career of Rosso Fiorentino* (New Haven and London: Yale University Press, 1994), 85–6 and fig. 65 for the frame. For quattrocento patronage of chapels in Santo Spirito, see now Burke, *Changing Patrons*, chap. 3, with a discussion (80–2) of the departure from earlier traditions in the *Madonna del Baldacchino*.

98. On the Dei, originally a family of prominent Florentine goldsmiths, see Doris Carl, "Zur Goldschmeidefamilie Dei mit neuen Dokumenten zu Antonio Pollaiuolo und Andrea Verrocchio," *Mitteilungen des Kunsthistorischen Institutes in Florenz* 26 (1982): 129–66. For the lineage of Rinieri di Bernardo Dei, see 148, fig. 7; Cecchi, in *Raffaello a Firenze*, 43–4 and 119; Franklin, *Rosso in Italy*, 85–6. For the neighborhood ambitions of the Dei and motivations for the choice of Raphael, see Burke, *Changing Patrons*, 82.

99. An excerpt from this will was published in *Rivista d'Arte* 6 (1909): 151. See now Franklin, *Rosso in Italy*, 303, appendix D. Franklin (85 and 278, n. 6) has found an earlier will. See Franklin, 278, n. 8, for the archival collocations of the 1506 will and a copy.

100. For the palazzo, see Ludwig H. Heydenreich, "Über den Palazzo Guadagni in Florenz," in *Eberhard Hanfstaengel zum 75. Geburtstag* (Munich: Ruhmer, 1961): 43–51. See also Ginori Lisci, *Palazzi di Firenze*, 2: cat. no. 121, and Michael Lingohr, *Der Florentiner Palastbau der Hochrenaissance* (Worms: Wernersche Verlagsgesellschaft, 1997), passim.

101. Rinieri's first will, of 31 July 1505, ascribed the *jus patronatus* of the chapel to Rinieri's elder brother, Domenico. See Franklin, *Rosso in Italy*, 85–6 and 278, n. 6. Franklin, fig. 63, illustrates the quattrocento stained-glass window representing Saint Bernard, which is mentioned in Rinieri's will as "una fenestra vitrea supra dictum altare." This imagery, and the dedication of the chapel to the saint, suggest that Rinieri's father, Bernardo di Domenico Dei, may have been the chapel's founder.

102. As suggested by Alessandro Cecchi in *Raffaello a Firenze*, 119, and Giovanni Morello in *Raffaello e la Roma dei Papi*, 19–20, n. 9. For Pietro, who spent much of his life in France and who died in 1522, see *Raffaello a Firenze*, 119; Franklin, *Rosso in Italy*, 86. Carl ("Goldschmeidefamilie Dei," 148, fig. 7) also lists a legitimate son, Ruberto, but does not give birth or death dates for him.

103. *Raffaello a Firenze*, 119, and Franklin, *Rosso in Italy*, 86. The family stemma featured the crossed keys, another Petrine allusion granted to Bernardo Dei in the second half of the quattrocento.

104. "Per la tavola non ho fatto pregio, e non lo farò se io porò perché el serà meglio per me che la vada a stima." Shearman, *Early Modern Sources*, 112. For this practice, which was common in the quattrocento, see Hannelore Glasser, *Artists' Contracts of the Early Renaissance*, Garland Outstanding Dissertaions in the Fine Arts (New York and London: Garland, 1977), 41–2, and Deborah Krohn, "Taking Stock: Evaluation of Works of Art in Renaissance Italy," in *The Art Market in Italy, 1500–1600*, ed. Marcello Fantoni, Louisa Matthew, and Sara Matthews-Grieco (Modena: Franco Cosimo Panini, 2003), 203–11. I am grateful to Professor Krohn for sharing her manuscript with me prior to publication. This practice would eventually be used for appraising the *Raising of Lazarus*, by Raphael's rival Sebastiano del Piombo. See Reiss, "Cardinal Giulio de' Medici," 318–19.

105. "Fato le feste forse ve scrivirò quello che la tavola monta, ché io ho finito el cartone e fato Pascua serimo aciò." Shearman, *Early Modern Sources*, 113.

106. "…secondo me a ditto el patrone de ditta tavola, dice che me darà da fare per circha a trecenti ducati d'oro per qui e in Francia." Shearman, *Early Modern Sources*, 113.

107. The time frame for Raphael's tranfer to Rome is unclear. He was working on the cartoon of the Dei Altarpiece in April of 1508, but by 13 January 1509, he was paid for work in the Vatican and had clearly been in Rome for some time (Golzio, *Raffaello nei documenti*, 370 and Shearman, *Early Modern Sources*, 1: 122–3, doc. 1509/1). For the function of this room, see John Shearman, "The Vatican Stanze: Functions and Decorations," *Proceedings of the British Academy* 57 (1971), esp. 14–17. That the idea was proposed by several scholars in the late nineteenth century – most notably Franz Wickhoff – has often been overlooked since the publication of Shearman's article.

108. Franklin, *Rosso in Italy*, 85–92. Conforti, "Baldassare Turini," 39 and figs. 3, 4, for the *Madonna del Baldacchino* in Turini's funerary chapel in the Duomo of Pescia. For Turini, see also Claudia Conforti, "Baldassare Turini: funzionario mediceo e committente di architetura," in *Ianiculum-Gianicolo: Storia, topografia, monumenti, leggende dall'antichità al rinascimento*, ed. Eva Margareta Steinby (Rome: Institutum Romanum Finlandiae, 1996), 189–98.

109. Vasari/Milanesi, 4: 328–9. Julius was, apparently, none too fond of his ambitious sister-in-law Giovanna Feltria della Rovere, whom he once called "matta, et insolente." Clough, "Daughters and Wives," 49, n. 85.

110. For the special character (and sexual ambiguities) of the papal curia in this period, see John F. D'Amico, *Renaissance Humanism in Papal Rome: Humanists and Churchmen on the Eve of the Reformation* (Baltimore and London: Johns Hopkins University Press, 1983), esp. chap. 1. D'Amico (5–6) explains how marriage could hinder the career of those who wished to advance themselves in the curia and led to the prevalence of both prostitution and concubinage in Rome. This is not to say, however, that women related to popes, cardinals, and other churchmen did not attempt, through various means, to exert influence. See, for example, Natalie R. Tomas, *The Medici Women: Gender and Power in Renaissance Florence* (Aldershot, UK: Ashgate, 2003), chap. 5, "At the Papal Court" and Tomas, "All in the Family: the Medici Women and Pope Clement VII," forthcoming in Gouwens and Reiss, *Clement VII*, 41–53.

111. Cf. Bette Talvacchia's essay in this volume. See also Linda Wolk-Simon's contribution to this collection and her illuminating discussion in "Competition, Collaboration and Specialization in the Roman Art World, 1520–1527," in Gouwens and Reiss, *Clement VII*, 251–74. The question of Raphael's workshop before Rome is of considerable interest and remains to be thoroughly explored.

112. An overview of the patronage of Julius II and Leo, with an emphasis on the patrons' travels, is found in John Shearman, "Il mecenatismo di Giulio II e Leone X," in Esch and Frommel, *Arte, committenza ed economia*, 213–42. See also Hollingsworth, *Patronage in Sixteenth-Century Italy*, 8–20. In addition to studies of individual patrons from Raphael's Roman period such as those cited nn. 7 and 13, useful information is found in *Raffaello a Firenze*, 129–33, and Christa Gardner von Teuffel, "Raffaels römische Altarbilder: Aufstellung und Bestimmung," *Zeitschrift für Kunstgeschichte* 50 (1987): 1–45. I will return to the topic of Raphael's patrons in Rome at greater length in a future study.

113. For the Vatican Stanze, see Ingrid Rowland's essay in this collection.

114. "Eius extremum opus." See Shearman, *Early Modern Sources*, 1: 808.

115. For the *Portrait of Leo X and Two Cardinals*, see Joanna Woods-Marsden's contribution to this volume, with bibliography.

116. For Giulio de' Medici, a major patron of Michelangelo, Sebastiano del Piombo and others in the years he commissioned works from Raphael and his shop, cf. n. 13.

117. For Bibbiena, see G. Patrizi in *DBI* 41 (1992): 593–600.

118. For the identification of Alidosi, first proposed by Eugene Müntz, see Sylvia Ferino Pagden and M. Antonietta Zancan, *Raffaello: Catalogo completo dei dipinti* (Florence: Cantini, 1989), 89.

119. For Conti, see *DBI* 28 (1983): 470–5. Raphael's first Roman altarpiece was painted for the high altar of the Franciscan church of Santa Maria in Aracoeli, where the patron was buried. Sigismondo Conti is the only patron to appear undisguised as himself (or herself) in an altarpiece by Raphael.

120. For Goritz, see recently the brief biography in Julia Haig Gaisser, *Pierio Valeriano on the Ill Fortune of Learned Men: A Renaissance Humanist and His World* (Ann Arbor: University of Michigan Press, 1999), 295. See also Rowland, *Culture of the High Renaissance*, 189–92 and passim. Raphael's fresco was accompanied by a marble sculpture of the Virgin and Child with Saint Anne by Andrea Sansovino and the ensemble served as the focus of yearly rites on the Feast of Saint Anne, which culminated with poetry readings at the patron's *vigna*. For the multimedia ensemble, see Virginia Anne Bonito, "The St Anne altar in Sant'Agostino in Rome: A New Discovery," *Burlington Magazine* 122 (1980): 805–12, and Bonito, "The St Anne Altar in Sant'Agostino: Restoration and Interpretation," *Burlington Magazine* 124 (1982): 268–76. For the annual celebrations on 26 July, see Julia Haig Gaisser, "The Rise and Fall of Goritz's Feasts," *Renaissance Quarterly* 48 (1995): 41–57.

121. It is often said that this harmonious tondo, with its explicit Roman references, was given by Giovio to the church of the Olivetan monastery in Nocera dei Pagani, near Salerno, a bishopric he obtained after the Sack of Rome in the summer of 1527. This was first suggested by Anna Jameson in 1836 (introduction to *Collection of Pictures of W. G. Cosvelt, esq. of London, with an introduction by Mrs. Jameson* [London: J. Carpenter and Son, 1836] vii), was popularized by Passavant, and has often been repeated. For the recent tendency of scholars to name Giovio not merely as donor of the picture but as the patron, see A. Zezza, "Giovan Battista Castaldo e la chiesa di Santa Maria del Monte Albino: un tondo di Raffaello, un dipinto di Marco Pino e un busto di Leone Leoni a Nocera de' Pagani," *Prospettiva* 93–94 (1999): 29–41, at 39, n. 23. For a recent example, see Konrad Oberhuber, *Raphael: The Paintings* (Munich: Prestel, 1999), 110. For Giovio, the best modern study is T. C. Price Zimmermann, *Paolo Giovio: The Historian and the Crisis of Sixteenth-Century Italy* (Princeton: Princeton University Press, 1996). See also Zimmermann's biography in *DBI* 56 (2001): 430–40. For Giovio's move to Rome, Zimmermann, *Paolo Giovio*, 12–14, 295, n. 59, and Zimmermann in *DBI* 56 (2001): 430. The association of Giovio with the picture was questioned in Jack Wasserman, "The Genesis of Raphael's *Alba Madonna*," *Studies in the History of Art* 8 (1978): 35–7, as well as in the exhibition catalogue *Raffaello a Firenze*, 133, n. 35. Wasserman, op. cit., proposed Bernardino Orsini, bishop of Nocera from 1503 to 1511, as a possible patron. It is also worth considering the learned Domenico Jacobazzi (who served in that capacity from 1511 until 1517), as suggested in *Raffaello a Firenze*. Zezza (op. cit.), proposes Giovan Battista Castaldo, who rebuilt Santa Maria del Monte Albino as the donor of the painting, which she believes might have been painted for Julius II (an idea also proposed by Crowe and Cavalcaselle). Jones and Penny (*Raphael*, 88), suggest plausibly that the painting must originally have been intended for a domestic setting. The patronage of the *Alba Madonna* and the results of its recent cleaning will be discussed in the catalogue to the London exhibition "Raphael: From Urbino to Rome" (see n. 19).

122. For Inghirami, see Giovanni Batistini, "Raphael's Portrait of Fedra Inghirami," *Burlington Magazine* 138 (1996): 541–5 (at 541), and Rowland, *Culture of the High Renaissance*, 151–7 and passim. Batistini's research supports the autograph status of the Pitti version of the portrait and suggests that the Boston version is a seventeenth-century copy.

123. For the lost portrait of Tebaldeo, Golzio, *Raffaello nei documenti*, 43–4 and Shearman, *Early Modern Sources*, 1: 240–3, doc. 1516/8 and 277–8, doc. 1516/37.

124. For the letter of 3 April 1516, see Golzio, *Raffaello nei documenti*, 42 and Shearman, *Early Modern Sources,* 1: 238–40, doc. 1516/7. The double portrait was probably executed for Bembo, whom the artist had also known at the Montefeltro court and who owned the picture in 1538. For the picture in Bembo's possession, see Golzio, *Raffaello nei documenti*, 162 and Shearman, *Early Modern Sources*, 1: 906–7, doc. 1538/1.

125. For a summary of opinions, see S. Béguin in *Rapahël dans les collections françaises*, cat. no. 13, esp. 102. For Branconio dell'Aquila, proposed as the sitter by John Shearman in *Raffaello Architetto*, 107, see R. Zapperi in *DBI* 14 (1972): 7–8.

126. For Hanno the elephant, donated to Leo in 1514 by the king of Portugal, see Silvio A. Bedini, *The Pope's Elephant* (Nashville, TN: J. S. Sanders, 1998), with bibliography. For Raphael's memorial, Bedini, op. cit., 143 ff. On the Prado *Visitation*, see *Rafael en España*, 14 and 112–15. For Raphael's architecture in Rome, see Linda Pellecchia's contribution to this volume. See also the catalogue entries on specific buildings in *Raffaello Architetto.*

127. For the imbroglio and the patron's attitudes toward the quarreling "cervelli fantastichi dipintori," see Reiss, "Giulio de' Medici and Mario Maffei," cited earlier in n. 14.

128. See the correspondence concerning these pictures in Golzio, *Raffaello nei documenti,* 66–8 and Shearman, *Early Modern Sources,* 1: passim under the year 1518.

129. Giulio Romano's Louvre *Saint Margaret,* which Vasari (Vasari/Milanesi, 5: 525) says was designed by Raphael, was probably sent at the same time as a present for Marguerite of Valois, the king's sister.

130. Sebastiano del Piombo wrote to Michelangelo in July of that year saying that the figures in the two paintings (which he disparaged as Leonardesque in design and contrary to the sculptor's opinion), "pareno figure che siano state al fumo, o vero figure de ferro che luceno tutte chiare et tutte nere." *Il Carteggio de Michelangelo,* ed. P. Barocchi and R. Ristori, 5 vols. (Florence: S.P.E.S. Editore, 1965–83), 2: 32. Kathleen Weil Garris Posner suggested in 1974 (in *Leonardo and Central Italian Art: 1515–1550* [New York: New York University Press for the College Art Association of America], 56, n. 1) that this dark manner may have been intended to appeal to the tastes of the French king who had been "schooled" by Leonardo. Cf. also Reiss, "Cardinal Giulio de' Medici," 315 and 342, n. 31.

131. For Bindo Altoviti, see Corliano Belloni, *Un banchiere del Rinascimento: Bindo Altoviti* (Rome: Cremonese Editore, 1935) and A. Stella in *DBI* 2 (1960): 574–5. Around 1513 Bindo expanded his family's Roma palazzo near the site of San Giovanni dei Fiorentini, and he was a patron of many artists, including Vasari, Cellini, and Francesco Salviati. Michelangelo presented him with the cartoon for the Sistine *Drunkenness of Noah* and with a drawing of Venus, which was colored by Vasari. Bindo was the focus of an exhibition be held at the Isabella Stewart Gardner Museum in Boston and the Museo Nazionale del Bargello in Florence in 2003/04. See now the catalogue to this exhibition, *Raphael, Cellini, and a Renaissance Banker: The Patronage of Bindo Altoviti,* ed. Alan Chong, Donatella Pegazzano, and Dimitrios Zikos (Boston: Isabella Stewart Gardner Museum, 2003). Raphael's portrait is the subject of David Alan Brown's contribution, 93–114.

132. For basic bibliography on Chigi, see n. 4.

133. See n. 7 for bibliography on the Beata Elena Duglioli Dall'Olio, who was revered as a "second Cecilia," famed for living in a chaste marriage like her third-century onomastic saint. Vasari/Milanesi (4: 349) attributes the patronage to Lorenzo Pucci rather than to his nephew. Cf. Jones and Penny, *Raphael,* 146. Zarri, "Storia d'una committenza," discounts Lorenzo Pucci's involvement. See Golzio, *Raffaello nei documenti,* 29, for a document that attributes the patronage of both the chapel and its altarpiece to the Beata Elena, but Zarri ("L'altra Cecilia," 96–7, n. 53) has cautioned against its reliability. Cf. also Shearman, *Early Modern Sources,* 1: 196, doc. 1514/14 on the problematic nature of this document.

134. For the early history of the altarpiece and Basilicò's donation, see Gardner von Teuffel, "Raffaels römische Altarbilder," 19ff., and Maria Antonietta Spadaro, *Raffaello e lo Spasimo di Sicilia* (Palermo: Accademia Nazionale di Scienze Lettere e Arti, 1991), esp. 7–8.

135. For the Monteluce *Coronation,* see my discussion earlier and cf. Jeryldene Wood's contribution to this collection. For Cardinal Gregorio Cortesi's attempt to secure Raphael's talents for Modena, see Golzio, *Raffaello nei documenti,* 42. Shearman (*Early Modern Sources,* 1: 230, in his discussion of doc. 1515–25/1) questions the evidentiary value of the passage on Raphael.

136. The best account of the vicissitudes of the never-realized painting is John Shearman, "Alfonso d' Este's Camerino," in *'Il se rendit en Italie:' Études offertes à André Chastel* (Rome and Paris: Edizioni dell' Elefante and Flammarion, 1987), 209–30.

137. These included first Raphael's completion of his work on the Stanza dell'Incendio, then his architectural obligations (including at the Fabbrica of Saint Peter's), then

other works for the pontiff and the palatine cardinals (Bibbiena and Medici in particular). Indeed, on several occasions, Alfonso's agent Paolucci indicated that Raphael
was always excusing himself because of his work for the Cardinal de' Medici, saying
that he could work for the duke when the cardinal was out of town. See Golzio, *Raffaello nei documenti*, 106 and 95, respectively and Shearman, *Early Modern Sources*, 1:
554–5, doc. 1520/2 (as datable perhaps to 28 January 1520); and 1: 452, doc. 1519/32,
respectively.

138. The second reason stems from the duke's duplicity in having one of his artists
paint from a modello sent by Raphael. See Shearman, "Alfonso d' Este's Camerino,"
210–11.

139. Raphael's attempts to placate Alfonso by sending him cartoons (from the *Fire in the
Borgo* and for the Louvre *Saint Michael*) rather than the promised painting constitute an important and interesting episode in the history of changing attitudes in
the cinquecento toward such functional drawings. See Carmen C. Bambach, *Drawing
and Painting in the Italian Renaissance Workshop: Theory and Practice, 1300–1600*
(Cambridge and New York: Cambridge Univeristry Press, 1999), 256.

140. "Non ci stimar più che un vil plebeio." Shearman, *Early Modern Sources*, 1: 553, doc.
1520/1.

141. For the reidentification, see Michael P. Fritz, *Giulio Romano et Raphaël: la vice-reine
de Naples ou la renaissance d'une beauté mythique* (Paris: Mussot, 1997). For the eroti-
cizing of the portrait image, see Joanna Woods-Marsden, "Portrait of the Lady, 1430–
1520," in David Alan Brown et al., *Virtue and Beauty: Leonardo' Ginevra de' Benci and
Renaissance Portraits of Women*, exh. cat., Washington, DC, National Gallery of Art
(Princeton: Princeton University Press, 2001), 80–1. Surely the intended recipient in
part explains the erotic charge of the portrait.

142. Golzio, *Raffaello nei documenti*, 76–7 and Shearman, *Early Modern Sources*, 1: 379–80,
doc. 1518/76; 1: 392–3, doc. 1519/9.

143. Golzio, *Raffaello nei documenti*, 77 and Shearman, *Early Modern Sources*, 1: 438–9, doc.
1519/16. For the "sua mano" stipulation in the contract for the *Monteluce Coronation*,
see n. 56.

CHAPTER 3. THE CONTESTED CITY: URBAN FORM IN EARLY SIXTEENTH-CENTURY ROME

I thank my graduate students at the University of Delaware for a stimulating semester
in Fall 2001 discussing Renaissance Roman urbanism. I am also grateful to Sarah
McPhee for editorial suggestions. My thanks also to Jeff Klee for executing the modifications on Figs. 6, 8, 9, and 10 and to Jennifer Hitlian for those on Fig. 1. As always
my deepest gratitude goes to David M. Stone for his careful reading of the text and
constant support.

1. Robert Brentano, *Rome before Avignon: A Social History of Thirteenth-Century Rome*
(New York: Basic Books, 1974), 13.

2. The term *Popolo Romano* is an imprecise one that can refer to everything from all of
the Romans to those governing from the Campidoglio. On this term and its earlier
context, see Laurie Nussdorfer, *Civic Politics in the Rome of Urban VIII* (Princeton:
Princeton University Press, 1992), 64–9, 95–108.

3. For the history of this period, see Charles L. Stinger, *The Renaissance in Rome*
(Bloomington and Indianapolis: Indiana University Press, 1998); and Peter Partner,
Renaissance Rome 1500–1559 (Berkeley: University of California Press, 1979). For exemplary overviews of Roman urban planning, see James S. Ackerman, "The Planning
of Renaissance Rome, 1450–1580," in *Rome in the Renaissance. The City and the Myth*,

ed. P. A. Ramsey (Binghamton, NY: Center for Medieval and Early Renaissance Studies, 1982), 3–17; Christoph L. Frommel, "Papal Policy: The Planning of Rome during the Renaissance," *Journal of Interdisciplinary History* 17 (1986): 39–65; and Allan Ceen, *The Quartiere de' Banchi. Urban Planning in Rome in the First Half of the Cinquecento* (New York and London: Garland, 1986).

4. On planning under Nicholas, see Charles Burroughs, *From Signs to Design: Environmental Process and Reform in Early Renaissance Rome* (Cambridge: MIT Press, 1990); Manfredo Tafuri, "'Cives esse non licere': The Rome of Nicholas V and Leon Battista Alberti: Elements towards a Historical Revision," *Harvard Architectural Review* 6 (1987): 61–75; and Carroll William Westfall, *In This Most Perfect Paradise: Alberti, Nicholas V, and the Invention of Conscious Urban Planning in Rome: 1447–55* (University Park: Pennsylvania State University Press, 1974).

5. Author's translation. Cited in Egmont Lee, *Sixtus IV and Men of Letters* (Rome: Edizioni di Storia e Letteratura, 1978), 40.

6. As translated in J. Brian Horrigan, "Imperial and Urban Ideology in a Renaissance Inscription," *Comitatus* 9 (1978): 76–7.

7. See Horrigan, "Imperial", 74–5.

8. On Sixtus's pontificate and urban impact, see *Sisto IV: le arti a Roma nel primo Rinascimento (Atti del Convegno Internazionale di Studi)*, ed. Fabio Benzi (Rome: Edizioni dell'Associazione Culturale Shakespeare, 2000); Fabio Benzi, *Sisto IV Renovator Urbis. Architettura a Roma 1471–1484* (Rome: Officina Edizioni, 1990); L. D. Ettlinger, "Pollaiuolo's Tomb of Sixtus IV," *Journal of the Warburg and Courtauld Institutes* 16 (1953): 239–74; *Un pontificato ed una città: Sisto IV (1471–1484) (Atti del convegno, Roma, 3–7 Dicembre 1984)*, ed. Massimo Miglio et al. (Rome: Istituto Storico Italiano per il Medio Evo, 1986); Ludwig von Pastor, *The History of the Popes*, 40 vols. (London: Kegan Paul, Trench, Trübner, 1891–1953), 4: 197–523; and Roberto Weiss, *The Medals of Pope Sixtus IV (1471–1484)* (Roma: Edizioni di Storia e Letteratura, 1961).

9. *The 'Julius exclusus' of Erasmus*, trans. Paul Pascal, intro. and notes J. Kelley Sowards (Bloomington and London: Indiana University Press, 1968), 80–1.

10. Author's translation. Quoted from Sebastiano Tedallini's "Diario romano," in Massimo Miglio, "Sisto IV e Giulio II: il tema della Roma Moderna," in idem, *Scritture, Scrittori e Storia. Città e Corte a Roma nel Quattrocento* (Rome: Vecchiarelli, 1993), 129–36; see 135. For a characterization of Julius and the rhetoric of his court humanists, see Stinger, *Renaissance in Rome*, 235–46; and Ingrid D. Rowland, *The Culture of the High Renaissance* (Cambridge: Cambridge University Press, 1998), 141–92, with earlier bibliography. On Julius's pontificate in general, see Pastor, *History*, 6: 185–659; E. Rodocanachi, *Histoire de Rome. Le pontificat de Jules II, 1503–1513* (Paris: Hachette, 1928); and Loren Partridge and Randolph Starn, *A Renaissance Likeness: Art and Culture in Raphael's 'Julius II'* (Berkeley and Los Angeles: University of California Press, 1980).

11. For an overview in English of Bramante's work, see Arnaldo Bruschi, *Bramante* (London: Thames and Hudson, 1977).

12. See James S. Ackerman, "The Belvedere as a Classical Villa," *Journal of the Warburg and Courtauld Institutes* 14 (1951): 70–91, with illustrations of the present Belvedere and Perino del Vaga's fresco; and Bruschi, *Bramante*, 87–115.

13. On 6 April 1506, Julius entered a twenty-five-foot-deep ditch to lay the foundation stone, inscribed with his name. Twelve foundation medals resembling imperial examples were buried in the ditch. See Pastor, *History*, 6: 473–5; and Ferdinand Gregorovius, *History of the City of Rome in the Middle Ages*, trans. Annie Hamilton (London: George Bell & Sons, 1902), 8: 136.

14. Francesco Albertini, *Opusculum de mirabilibus novae et veteris urbis Romae*, in *Codice Topografico della città di Roma*, eds. Roberto Valentini and Giuseppe Zucchetti (Rome: Istituto Storico Italiano per il Medio Evo, 1953), 4: 457–546.

15. Author's translation. Andrea Guarna da Salerno, *Simia*, ed. Dardo Battaglini (Milan: Ariel, 1943), 58 and 60.

16. James S. Ackerman, "Notes on Bramante's Bad Reputation," in *Studi bramanteschi, Atti del convegno internazionale* (Rome: De Luca, 1974), 339–50.

17. Egidio da Viterbo, as translated in Rowland, *Culture*, 173.

18. Vitruvius, *De architectura*, ed. Fra Giocondo (Venice: Giovanni Tacuino, 1511). The dedicatory preface has Julius surpassing all sovereigns, living and dead, for his taste in decorating the city with "enormous and most magnificent" buildings.

19. As translated (with minor modifications) in Horrigan, "Imperial," 73–4.

20. On the meaning and context of the inscription, see Horrigan, "Imperial", 78–82; and Manfredo Tafuri, "Via Giulia: storia di una struttura urbana," in *Via Giulia: una utopia urbanistica del 500*, ed. Luigi Salerno et al. (Rome: A. Staderini, 1973), 65–152, see 67. For the political content of Julius's urban designs outside Rome, see Richard Tuttle, "Julius II and Bramante in Bologna," in *Le arti a Bologna e in Emilia dal XVI al XVII secolo*, Atti del XXIV Congresso Internazionale di Storia dell'Arte, 1979 ed. Andrea Emiliani (Bologna: CLUEB, 1982), 3–12.

21. Andrea Fulvio, *De urbis antiquitates* (Rome: Marcello Silber, 1527), 1:45. Cited in Tafuri, "Via Giulia," 67.

22. Egidio da Viterbo, cited in Tafuri, "Via Giulia," 67, n. 8. Annibal Caro, *Lettere Familiari*, ed. A. Greco (Florence: Felice Le Monnier, 1961) 3: 223–4.

23. Kurt W. Forster, "From 'Rocca' to 'Civitas': Urban Planning at Sabbioneta," *L'Arte* 5 (1969): 5–40; see 39, n. 36.

24. Nicholas and Alexander VI limited their new streets to the Borgo. Sixtus IV straightened a preexisting street, the Tor di Nona, in the Campus Martius. It was renamed Via Sistina for a short time.

25. My account of Julius's political agenda in his urban projects owes much to the seminal discussions by Luigi Spezzaferro, "La politica urbanistica dei papi e le origini di via Giulia," in Salerno, *Via Giulia*, 15–64; see esp. 46–7; and Tafuri, "Via Giulia," 65–76. See also, Manfredo Tafuri, "'Roma instaurata.' Strategie urbane e politiche pontificie nella Roma del primo '500," in *Raffaello architetto*, ed. Christoph L. Frommel et al. (Milan: Electa Editrice, 1984), 59–106, see 67–76. For conditions in Rome when Julius became pope, see Rodocanachi, *Histoire*, 30–49.

26. Julius's most controversial acts were the creation of a new coin, the *giulio*, and the control of food distribution and prices. Rodocanachi, *Histoire*, 32–3; Spezzaferro, "Politica urbanistica," 45–7; and Partner, *Renaissance Rome*, 72. For a report by the Venetian ambassador on the riots resulting from Julius's actions, see Clara Gennaro, "La 'Pax Romana' del 1511," *Archivio della Società Romana di Storia Patria*, 3 ser., 21 (1967): 2–60; see 37, 39, and n. 66. For the economic and social background of Rome, see the indispensable Jean Delumeau, *Vie économique et sociale de Rome dans la seconde moitié du XVIe siècle*, 2 vols. (Paris, E. de Boccard, 1957–9).

27. My account is based on the fascinating research of Suzanne Butters and Pier Nicola Pagliara, "The Palazzo dei Tribunali and Via Giulia in Rome," *Zodiac* 14 (1995): 14–29.

28. Baptista Fiera, *De Iusticia Pingenda. On the Painting of Justice (1515)*, trans. and ed. James Wardrop (London: Lion and Unicorn Press, 1957). As translated in Butters and Pagliara, "Palazzo," 26, n. 7.

29. As translated in Butters and Pagliara, "Palazzo," 19. Original source not given; readers are referred to a future publication.

30. On public executions, see Richard Joseph Ingersoll, "The Ritual Use of Public Space in Renaissance Rome" (Ph.D. diss., University of California, Berkeley, 1985), 408–48. See also the remarkable new book by Rose Marie San Juan, *Rome: A City Out of Print* (Minneapolis and London: University of Minnesota Press, 2001).

31. On the Palazzo dei Tribunali, see Butters and Pagliara, "Palazzo," 14–29; Arnoldo Bruschi, *Bramante architetto* (Bari: Laterza, 1969), 949–53; Bruschi, *Bramante*, 169–73; Arnoldo Bruschi, "Bramante e la funzionalità. Il palazzo dei Tribunali: 'turres et loca fortissima pro commoditate et utilitate publica,'" *Palladio* n.s. 7 (1994), 145–56; and Christoph L. Frommel, *Der Römische Palastbau der Hochrenaissance*, 3 vols. (Tübingen: Wasmuth, 1973), 2: 331–2. Butters and Pagliara state documents indicate construction was underway in October 1508 and proceeded at a sharp pace for a few years. The exorbitant sum of 200,000 scudi had been spent by Julius's death with little to show for it. The expense and difficulty of building on unstable terrain, according to Butters and Pagliara, probably explain the demise of the project more than politics. For opposing views on why the Tribunali was never finished nor revived in later years, see Butters and Pagliara, "Palazzo," 26–7; and Tafuri, "Il palazzo dei Tribunali," in Salerno, *Via Giulia*, 314–22.

32. Giorgio Vasari, *Le vite de più eccellenti pittori, scultori, ed architettori*, ed. Gaetano Milanesi, 9 vols. (Florence: Sansoni, 1878–85; reprint, 1906), 4: 160.

33. Vasari, *Le vite*, 4: 160.

34. On the court system in both Rome and the Vatican, see Pio Pecchiai, *Roma nel cinquecento* (Bologna: Lincinio Cappelli, 1948), 169–205. For the functions of the spaces within the Tribunali, see Bruschi, *Bramante architetto*, 950–1.

35. Egidio da Viterbo, quoted in Tafuri, "Via Giulia," 66.

36. For the influence of ancient rusticated buildings in the Renaissance see Andreas Tönnesmann, "'Palatium Nervae.' Ein antikes Vorbild für Florentiner Rustikafassaden," *Römisches Jahrbuch für Kunstgeschichte* 21 (1984): 61–70. On Vitruvius and the Tribunali, see Bruschi, "Bramante," 149–50. Francesco Albertini, *Septem mirabilia orbis et urbis Romae et Florentinae civitatis* (Rome,1510), facsimile ed. (Florence: Gonnelli, 1951), n.p.

37. Frommel, *Römische Palastbau*, 2: 330; and Butters and Pagliara, "Palazzo," 20 and 23.

38. Vasari, *Le vite*, 4: 159. Foreign notaries, for example, caused problems when they departed with their archives; see Butters and Pagliara, "Palazzo," 26

39. Albertini, *Opusculum*, 515; and Fra Mariano da Firenze, *Itinerarium urbis Romae*, ed. E. Bulletti (Rome: Pontificio istituto di archeologia cristiana, 1931), 68, quoted in Bruschi, "Bramante," 147.

40. For the opposing positions, see Spezzaferro, "Politica urbanistica," 57–60; and Butters and Pagliara, "Palazzo," 23. For the duties of each court, see Bruschi, "Bramante," 148.

41. As translated in Pastor, *History*, 6: 369. See also Gennaro, "La 'Pax Romana,'" 19–24. Such disorder was typical of the interregnum called the Vacant See.

42. As translated in Gregorovius, 8: 83.

43. On the concessions forced on Julius, see Gennaro, "La 'Pax Romana,'" 24–5; and Spezzaferro, "Politica urbanistica," 61–2.

44. On Via Alessandrina, see Giulia Petrucci, "L'apertura della via Alessandrina; idee e progetti, realizzazione, 'derivazioni' cinquecentesche," in *Urbanistica per I giubilei. Roma, Via Alessandrina. una strada "tra due fondali" nell'Italia delle corti (1492–1499)*, eds. Enrico Guidoni and Giulia Petrucci (Rome: Edizioni Kappa, 1997) 27–58.

45. Bruschi, *Bramante architetto*, 635.

46. The letters excerpted in the following pages are as translated in Butters and Pagliara, "Palazzo," 19 and 23.

47. See Butters and Pagliara, "Palazzo," 19; and Tafuri, "Via Giulia," 69. The modest houses rented by the chapter were the standard units for working classes.

48. In 1505, Julius constructed an enclosure – placed surprisingly at the level of the Farnese palace – to collect garbage before it was dumped into the Tiber. Pecchiai, *Roma*, 455.

49. Author's translation. Quoted in Tafuri, "Via Giulia," 68, n. 11.

50. Author's translation. Quoted in Bruschi, *Bramante architetto*, 632–3. See also Tafuri, "Via Giulia," 68, n. 11. The description of the scheme, first mentioned in 1663, has been greeted with skepticism by most scholars. Bruschi, however, believes there may be some truth to it.

51. Author's translation. Quoted in Tafuri, "Via Giulia," 69.

52. On the church of S. Eligio, which some scholars believe is Bramantesque, see Manfredo Tafuri, "S. Eligio degli Orefici," in Salerno, *Via Giulia*, 431–7; and Simonetta Valtieri, "Sant' Eligio degli Orefici," in Frommel, *Raffaello architetto*, 143–56.

53. On Julius's attitude toward family *monti* and the Planca Incoronati, see Luigi Spezzaferro, "Il monte dei Planca Incoronati," in Salerno, *Via Giulia*, 369–71; and Tafuri, "Via Giulia," 72–3.

54. Referred to by Tafuri, "Via Giulia," 72–3; and Spezzaferro, "Il monte," 371; see Caro, *Lettere Familiari*, 3 : 223–4 for the full text.

55. Author's translation. Quoted in Irene Fosi, "Il consolato fiorentino a Roma e il progetto per la chiesa nazionale," *Studi Romani* 37 (1989): 50–70; see 64–6.

56. Tafuri ("Via Giulia," 70–1), saw a trick, but Fosi ("Il consolato," 66 and n. 60) discovered numerous merchants seeking compensation. For reconstructions of the bridge and piazza, see Bruschi, "Bramante," 146, and Tafuri, "Via Giulia," 69–73.

57. Fosi, "Il consolato," 67–70; Tafuri, "Via Giulia," 78; and Spezzaferro, "Politica urbanistica," 62. On San Giovanni dei Fiorentini, see Tafuri and Spezzaferro, "San Giovanni dei Fiorentini," in Salerno, *Via Giulia*, 201–58; and S. Benedetti, "S. Giovanni dei Fiorentini a Roma (1508–1559): da celebrazione mondana a significazione cristiana," in *Firenze e la Toscana dei Medici nell'Europa del '500* (Florence: L. S. Olschki, 1983), 2 : 959–76.

58. For a list of property owners, see Christoph L. Frommel, *Die Farnesina und Peruzzis Architektonisches Frühwerk*, Excursus I: Via della Lungara und Via Giulia (Berlin: Walter De Gruyter, 1961), 163–170; esp. 163–4 and fig. 29.

59. Manfredo Tafuri, "Progetto di casa in via Giulia. 1519–1520," in Frommel, *Raffaello architetto*. 235–40.

60. Spezzaferro, "Politica urbanistica," 64.

61. On Via Santa, see Umberto Gnoli, *Topografia e toponomastico di Roma Medievale e Moderna* (Rome: Staderini, 1939), 273; and Rodolfo Lanciani, *Storia degli Scavi di Roma*, 6 vols. (Rome: Quasar, 1989–), 1 : 212. On Via della Lungara (and a list of property owners from 1462–c. 1550), see Frommel, *Die Farnesina*, 163–70.

62. On Chigi, see Felix Gilbert, *The Pope, His Banker, and Venice* (Cambridge, MA, and London: Harvard University Press, 1980), 77–93; and Ingrid Rowland, "Render unto Caesar the Things Which Are Caesar's': Humanism and the Arts in the Patronage of Agostino Chigi," *Renaissance Quarterly* 39 (1986): 673–730.

63. The name Farnesina dates to its 1579 acquisition by the Farnese family. For the history of the villa, see Frommel, *Römische Palastbau*, 2 : 149–74; and Frommel, *Die Farnesina*.

64. Author's translation. Carandolet's letter quoted in Frommel, *Römische Palastbau*, 2 :151, doc. no. 19a.

65. Author's translation. Gallo and Palladio quoted in Isa Belli Barsali, "Il Peruzzi architetto di giardini," in *Baldassarre Peruzzi. pittura, scena e architettura nel cinquecento* (Rome: Istituto della Enciclopedia Italiana Treccani, 1987), 119–20. For extensive excerpts of

the Latin texts of Gallo and Palladio, see Frommel, *Römische Palastbau*, 2: 150–1, doc. nos. 16 and 17.

66. Frommel, *Römische Palastbau*, 2: 167; and Rowland, "Render," 679, 684.

67. Gilbert, *The Pope*, 95; and Frommel, *Die Farnesina*, 2–4.

68. Frommel, *Römische Palastbau*, 2: 150, doc. no. 12. In his *Voyage de Jacques Le Saige de Douai à Rome, Notre-Dame-de-Lorette, Venise, Jérusalem et autres saints lieux* (ed. H. R. Duthilloeul [Douai: Adam d'Aubers, 1851]) from the 1520s, Le Saige described the villa as exquisite with door jambs of red and greenish jasper! That the Frenchman, who was merely a pilgrim on his way to the Holy Land, visited the villa suggests it was on a foreign (or French) tourist route.

69. Rowland, "Render," 688–92 and nn. 37 and 57. See also Gregorovius, *History*, 8: 128.

70. On banqueting and theatrical activities in the villa, see Frommel, *Römische Palastbau*, 2: 150–3, for the relevant texts; and Frommel, *Die Farnesina*, 7–10 and 36–9. See also Rowland, "Render," 688.

71. Author's translation. *Le Saige*, 1851, 26.

72. On the stable, see Frommel, *Römische Palastbau*, 3: 69–70; and Roger Jones and Nicholas Penny, *Raphael* (New Haven and London: Yale University Press, 1983), 211. On Riario's palace, see Frommel, *Römische Palastbau*, 2: 281–91.

73. The main source for this account is Fabio Chigi's biography of his great-uncle, for which see Giuseppe Cugnoni, "Agostino Chigi il Magnifico," *Archivio della Società Romana di Storia Patria* 2 (1879): 46–83, 209–26, and 475–90; 3 (1880), 213–32, 291–305, and 422–48; and 4 (1881), 56–75 and 195–216. See also Frommel, *Römische Palastbau*, 2: 168–9 and doc. nos. 33 and 34 on 153.

74. This section is indebted to Ferdinando Bilancia and Salvatore Polito, "Via Ripetta," *Controspazio* 5 (1973): 18–47; and Hubertus Günther, "Die Strassenplanung unter den Medici-Päpsten in Rom (1513–1534)," *Jahrbuch des Zentralinstituts für Kunstgeschichte* 1 (1985), 237–94 (abbreviated English version, idem, "Urban Planning in Rome under the Medici Popes," in *The Renaissance from Brunelleschi to Michelangelo. The Representation of Architecture*, ed. Henry A. Millon and Vittorio Magnago Lampugnani [Milan: Bompiani, 1994], 545–9); idem, "La nascita di Roma moderna. Urbanistica del Rinascimento a Roma," in *D'une ville à l'autre: structures matérielles et organisation de l'espace dans les villes européennes (XIIIe–XVIe siècles), Actes du Colloque 1986*, ed. Jean-Claude Maire Vigueur (Rome: École Française de Rome, 1989), 381–406; and Frommel, *Römische Palastbau*, 1: 19.

75. One of the problems was that powerful members of the Camera Apostolica had earlier been granted the land on which the pope now wanted to make his piazza and had convinced the *maestri* to respect their property. For the brief (*motu proprio*), see Angelo Mercati, "Raffaello da Urbino e Antonio da Sangallo 'maestri delle strade' di Roma sotto Leone X," *Rendiconti della Pontificia Accademia di Archeologia* 1 (1923): 121–5; and Günther, "Strassenplanung," 284–5, with the full transcription. The *motu proprio* has been dated between 1517 and 1520 by Mercati and to 1520 by Günther.

76. On Raphael as an architect, see Frommel, *Raffaello architetto*; and Jones and Penny, *Raphael*. See also the classic articles by John Shearman, "Raphael … 'Fa il Bramante'," in *Studies in Renaissance and Baroque Art Presented to Anthony Blunt* (London: Phaidon, 1967): 12–17; idem, "Raphael as Architect," *Journal of the Royal Society of Arts* 116 (1968): 388–409. On his work at Saint Peter's and his collaboration with Antonio, see Christoph L. Frommel, "St. Peter's: The Early History," in *Renaissance from Brunelleschi to Michelangelo*, 399–423; and idem, "San Pietro. Storia della sua costruzione," in Frommel, *Raffaello architetto*, 241–55.

77. For the documents, see Frommel, *Römische Palastbau*, 1: 19; and Günther, "Strassenplanung," 251. For a reconstruction of the original configuration, see Günther, "Strassenplanung," 251 and fig. 7.

78. On the debate, see Hubertus Günther,"Das Trivium vor Ponte S. Angelo. Ein Beitrag zur Urbanistik der Renaissance in Rom," *Römisches Jahrbuch für Kunstgeschichte* 21 (1984): 165–252; Richard Ingersoll, "Piazza del Ponte and the Military Origins of Panopticism," in *Streets: Critical Perspectives on Public Space*, ed. Zeynep Çelik et al. (Los Angeles: University of California Press, 1984), 177–88; Manfredo Tafuri, "Strategie di sviluppo urbano nell'Italia del Rinascimento," in Vigueur, *D'une ville à l'autre*, 338–42; Bilancia and Polito, "Via Ripetta," 30 and 40–2; Frommel, *Römische Palastbau*, 1: 19; Günther, "Urban Planning," 545–9; and Ceen, *Quartiere de' Banchi*, 52–3 and 66–8.

79. Author's translation. Quoted in Manfredo Tafuri, "Obelisco di piazza del Popolo," in Frommel, *Raffaello architetto* 229.

80. On the controversy and Leo's second *motu proprio*, see Günther, "Das Trivium," 249–50. On the "mausoleum," see Günther, "Strassenplanung," 251–3; and idem, "Urban Planning," 546. On the taste for antiquities in ruin, see Howard Burns, "I Marmi Antichi," in Frommel, *Raffaello architetto*, 409–10.

81. Author's translation. Quoted in Frommel, *Römische Palastbau*, 1: 19, n. 38a.

82. As translated in Robert Klein and Henri Zerner, eds., *Italian Art 1500–1600* (Evanston, IL: Northwestern University Press, 1966), 44–5.

83. Author's translation. Quoted in Francesco P. Di Teodoro, ed., *Raffaello, Baldassar Castiglione e la Lettera a Leone X* (Bologna: Nuova Alfa Editoriale, 1994), 65–6.

84. Translation, Klein and Zerner, *Italian Art*, 45. The Church had numerous conflicts of interest regarding ancient sites. The Camera Apostolica received one-third the price of marble and travertine from any ancient excavations – the license being called the "priest's quarries" (cave de prete). See Emilio Re, "Maestri di Strada," *Archivio della Società Romana di Storia Patria* 43 (1920): 5–102; see 41–2.

85. For a complete account, see Bilancia and Polito, "Via Ripetta," 21–47. On the housing along Via Leonina, see Frommel, *Römische Palastbau*, 1: 20. On working- or middle-class housing, see Deborah Nelson Wilde, "Housing and Urban Development in Sixteenth Century Rome: The Properties of the Arciconfraternita della SS.ma Annunziata" (Ph.D. diss., New York University, 1989); and Henri Broise and Jean-Claude Maire Vigueur, "Strutture famigliari, spazio domestico e architettura civile a Roma alla fine del Medioevo," in *Momenti di architettura, Storia dell'arte italiana* 12 (Turin: Einaudi Editore, 1983), 99–162.

86. On Armellini's 1527 census of Rome, see Domenico Gnoli, "Descriptio urbis o censimento della popolazione di Roma avanti il sacco borbonico," *Archivio della Società Romana di storia patria* 17 (1984): 375–520. On Bufalini, see Amato Pietro Frutaz, *Le piante di Roma*, 3 vols. (Rome: Istituto di Studi Romani, 1962). See also Günther, "Strassenplanung," 254.

87. Author's translation. Quoted in Frommel, *Römische Palastbau*, 1: 19, n. 38a.

88. Luigi Spezzaferro, "Place Farnèse: urbanisme et politique," in *Le Palais Farnèse*, 3 vols. (Rome: École française de Rome, 1981), 1: 85–123; see 95.

89. On this and other provisions of the 1516 bull, see Spezzaferro, "Place Farnèse," 95; and C. P. Scavizzi, "Le condizioni per lo sviluppo dell'attività edilizia a Roma nel Sec. XVII: La legislazione," *Studi Romani* 17, no. 2 (1969): 160–71; see 164–5.

90. Via Leonina was built in the main between 1518 and 1519. By 1516, the intended inhabitant of the grand palace, Giuliano (Leo's brother), was dead. Thus the palace project preceded the execution of the street and was defunct by the time work on the street began, leading some scholars to doubt the connection between street and palace. For

the debate, see Spezzaferro, "Place Farnèse," 95; and Manfredo Tafuri, "Principi, città, architetti," in *Ricerca del Rinascimento* (Turin: Einaudi, 1992), 106 and n. 63.

91. On Leo's Roman palace, see Tafuri, "Principi," 97–103. Although Leo often used the Camera Apostolica's funds for personal projects, the palace seems too grand to have been built. Similar extravagant and unrealizable projects were also designed in Florence during Leo's reign. See Linda Pellecchia, "Designing the Via Laura Palace: Giuliano da Sangallo, the Medici, and Time," in Michael Mallett and Nicholas Mann, eds., *Lorenzo the Magnificent. Culture and Politics*, Warburg Institute Colloquia 3 (London: The Warburg Institute, 1996), 37–63; and Caroline Elam "Lorenzo's Architectural and Urban Politics," in Gian Carlo Garfagnini, ed., *Lorenzo il Magnifico e il suo mondo*, Istituto Nazionale di Studi sul Rinascimento, Atti di Convegni 19 (Florence: Olschki, 1994), 357–84.

92. Author's translation. From Paolo Palliolo, "Narrazione delli spectacoli celebrati in Campidoglio,"in Fabrizio Cruciani, *Il teatro del Campidoglio e le Feste Romane del 1513* (Milan: Edizione il Polifilo, 1968), 21–68, see 27.

93. Bonner Mitchell, *Rome in the High Renaissance. The Age of Leo X* (Norman: University of Oklahoma Press, 1973), 69–70.

94. Cruciani, *Il teatro*, xxxv.

95. On the pasquinades under Leo, see P. Romano, *Pasquino nel cinquecento (Il pontificato di Leone X)* (Rome: Tipografia Agostiniana,1936); and Domenico Gnoli, "Pasquino satirico"; and idem, "La gazzarra delle pasquinate per la morte di Leon X e l'elezione di Adriano VI," in *La Roma di Leon X*, ed. Aldo Gnoli (Milan: Ulrico Hoepli, 1938), 300–29.

96. The annual animal combat in *Testaccio*, associated with Carnevale, carried ancient overtones of tribute and military valor. Contestants who refused to participate lost their right to hold public office. See Pio Paschini, *Roma nel Rinascimento, Storia di Roma*, vol. 12 (Bologna: Cappelli Editore, 1940), 219–21 and 449–51; and Ingersoll, "Ritual Use," 290–2.

97. Bruno M. Damiani, *Francesco Delicado* (New York: Twayne, 1974), 50. See also Francesco Delicado, *Portrait of Lozana the Lusty Andalusian Woman*, trans. Bruno Damiani (Potomac, MD: Scripta Humanistica, 1987). Rome was famous for its great number of prostitutes (accounts range from 6,800 to 30,000), from elegant courtesans to streetwalkers. On courtesans, Lynn Lawner, *Lives of the Courtesans: Portraits of the Renaissance* (New York: Rizzoli, 1987) and Domenico Gnoli, "La Lozana andalusa e le cortigiane nella Roma di Leon X," in *La Roma*, 185–216.

98. Author's translation. Quoted in Cesare D'Onofrio, *Gli obelischi di Roma* (Rome: Romana Società Editrice, 1992), 94–6. See also Mitchell, *Rome*, 76–7; and Domenico Gnoli, "I Cosmalia," in *La Roma*, 108–24, esp. 112–14. On Leo's elephant, see also Silvio A. Bedini, *The Pope's Elephant* (Nashville: J.S. Sanders & Company, 1998).

99. There were variations over time. See Ceen, *Quartiere de' Banchi*; Ingersoll, "Ritual Use"; and Irene Fosi, "Court and City in the Ceremony of the *Possesso* in the Sixteenth Century," in *Court and Politics in Papal Rome, 1492–1700*, ed. Gianvittorio Signorotto and Maria Antonietta Visceglia (Cambridge: Cambridge University Press, 2002), 31–53.

100. Author's translation. Quoted in Mitchell, *Rome*, 61. For English descriptions of Leo's *Possesso*, see Gregorovius, *History*, 8: 180–8.

101. On Palazzo Brescia, which was moved from its original site in 1938, see Christoph L. Frommel, "Palazzo Jacopo da Brescia," in Frommel, *Raffaello architetto*, 157–64; and Frommel, *Römische Palastbau*, 13–22. On Palazzo Branconio dell'Aquila, see Pier Nicola Pagliara, "Palazzo Branconio," in Frommel, *Raffaello architetto*, 197–216. For a sophisticated new analysis of these façades, see Burroughs, *The Italian Renaissance Palace*

Façade. Structures of Authority, Surfaces of Sense (Cambridge: Cambridge University Press, 2002), 151–66. On Raphael's experience with theatrical designs, see Frommel, "Scenografia teatrale," in Frommel, *Raffaello architetto*, 225–9.

102. My account here is indebted to Burroughs, *Italian Renaissance*, 160–5.
103. Pagliara, "Palazzo" 198–99.
104. Author's translation. Cited in Gnoli, *La Roma*, 347. On Leo's funeral and tomb, see Pastor, *History*, 8: 68–9.

CHAPTER 4. THE VATICAN STANZE

1. John Shearman, "The Vatican Stanze: Functions and Decoration," *Proceedings of the British Academy* 57 (1971): 367–472.
2. Leonard E. Boyle, "The Vatican Library," in *Rome Reborn: The Vatican Library and Renaissance Culture*, ed. Anthony Grafton (Yale University Press, 1993), xi–xv.
3. A catalogue of the private library was published by Léon Dorez, "La Bibliothèque privée de Jules II," *Révue des Bibliothèques* 6 (1896): 97–124. The story about Julius claiming not to be a scholar comes from Ascanio Condivi's biography of Michelangelo; see Christine Shaw, *Julius II: The Warrior Pope* (Oxford: Blackwell, 1993), 203, but also I. D. Rowland, *The Culture of the High Renaissance: Ancients and Moderns in Sixteenth-Century Rome* (Cambridge and New York: Cambridge, 1998), 158.
4. Rowland, *The Culture of the High Renaissance*, 151–7.
5. For a detailed analysis of this room, see Christiane Joost-Gaugier, *Raphael's Stanza della Segnatura: Meaning, and Invention* (Cambridge and New York: Cambridge University Press, 2002).
6. The text of Casali's oration is published by John O'Malley, "The Vatican Library and the School of Athens: A Text of Battista Casali, 1508," *Journal of Medieval and Renaissance Studies* 7 (1977): 271–87.
7. Raphael's younger contemporary Giovanni Battista da Sangallo insisted that a Roman bath must have "spacious hall with seats for philosophers and schoolmasters and all the other people who delight in study": [le exedre spatiose ancora abbino le sedie in elle quale: li filosafi: e lli rectori: e lli altri e' quali si dilettano delli studii].
8. See I. D. Rowland, "The Intellectual Background of the School of Athens," in *Raphael's "School of Athens,"* ed. Marcia Hall (Cambridge and New York: Cambridge, 1997), 130–70.
9. Egidio makes this claim in his *Sententiae ad Mentem Platonis*, written between 1506 and 1513 and never published. The passage can be found at 75v of the Vatican copy of this work, Biblioteca Apostolica Vaticana, MS Vat. Lat. 6325: referring to "cupiditas, ira, ratio."
10. Sabine Poeschel, *Alexander Maximus: Das Bildprogramm des Appartamento Borgia in Vatikan* (Weimar: Verlag und Datenbank für Geisteswissenschaften, 1999), 260–3. My thanks to Marcia Hall for this reference.
11. See Marcia Hall, introduction to *Raphael's "School of Athens"* (Cambridge and New York: Cambridge University Press, 1997), 22–5. My thanks to Marcia Hall for this reference.
12. See, for example, the *Sententiae ad Mentem Platonis*, Biblioteca Apostolica Vaticana, MS Vat. Lat. 6325, 117v–18r:

At Iuppiter [118r] atque Apollo (si non graeci homines, quos fabulae mentiae sunt Deos, sed aeternae ante orbem conditum personae, quas veritas unum ostendit, esse Deum cogitentur) et iandem prorsus habent impartibilem naturam, et sunt atque dicuntur idem Deus, unus inquam, non specie dumtaxat, sed indivisibili ac plane impartibili unitate, atque ideo idem ipse Dei filius, cum homo esse cepisset, Ego inquit, et Pater unum sumus.

"But Jupiter and Apollo (if not thought to be Greek men who are Gods in false myths, but eternal persons already before the creation of the world, which truth shows to be one, and God) also have the same indivisible nature, are and are called the same God, one I say, not in species, but in indivisible and plainly inseparable unity, and for that reason the same Son of God, when he began to be human said, 'The Father and I are one.'"

13. The *lira da braccio* was identified as such by Emanuele Winternitz, "Archeologia musicale del Rincascimento nel Parnaso di Raffaello," *Rendiconti della Pontificia Accademia di Archeologia* 27 (1951): 358–88.
14. See Arnold Nesselrath, "Lorenzo Lotto in the Stanza della Segnatura," *Burlington Magazine* 142, no. 1 (2000): 4–12.
15. Ernst Gombrich, "Raphael's *Stanza della Segnatura* and the nature of its symbolism," in idem, *Symbolic Images: Studies in the Art of the Renaissance* (London: Phaidon, 1972), 85–101, esp. 94–97. My thanks to Marcia Hall for this reference.
16. Arnold Nesselrath, "La Stanza dell'Incendio," in *Raffaello nell'Appartamento di Giulio II e Leone X* (Milan: Electa, 1993), 334–7.

CHAPTER 5. ONE ARTIST, TWO SITTERS, ONE ROLE: RAPHAEL'S PAPAL PORTRAITS

I am extremely grateful to the following experts in the fields of theology and papal politics for their generosity: Patrick Geary, Kenneth Gouwens, John W. O'Malley, and David S. Peterson. I also wish to thank John Shearman warmly for discussing Raphael's portraits with me, Nicholas Penny and Caroline Elam for discussing a drawing, and Alfred Acres for an important reference. Carolyn Malone, John O'Malley and David S. Peterson generously agreed to critique a draft, much to its benefit. The essay, written in summer 2002, is part of a larger project on papal portraiture. It greets the arrival into this world of Oisín Thornley Woods, Darragh Kennedy Woods, and Clíodhna Rua Woods.

1. "Fece ancora ritratti dal naturale come quello di papa Giulio secondo, di papa Leone decimo...che sono tenuti divini." Lodovico Dolce, *Dialogo della pittura intitolato l'Aretino*, 1547. In Paola Barocchi, *Trattati d'arte del cinquecento fra manierismo e controriforma*, 3 vols. (Bari: Laterza, 1960), I: 197.
2. Agostino Paravicini-Bagliani, *The Pope's Body*, trans. David S. Peterson (Chicago: Chicago University Press, 2000), 58–74, 235–41.
3. Ibid.
4. See Pier Luigi de Vecchi, *Raffaello: La Pittura* (Florence: Giunti Martello, 1981), 58–63.
5. Alessandro Cecchi, in *Raffaello a Firenze. Dipinti e disegni delle collezioni fiorentine* (Florence: Electa, 1984) 105–18, cats. 8 and 9; Joanna Woods-Marsden, "Portrait of the Lady, 1430–1520," in *Virtue and Beauty: Leonardo's Ginevra de' Benci and Renaissance Portraits of Women* (Washington, DC: National Gallery of Art, 2001), 63–87, 79; Jurg Meyer zur Capellen, *Raphael: A Critical Catalogue of His Paintings. I. The Beginnings in Umbria and Florence, c. 1500–1508* (Landshut: Arcos, 2001, 296–7), cat. 45.
6. The earliest autonomous sculpted images of a living pope were those created by Arnolfo di Cambio for Boniface VIII, c. 1300. Nancy Rash, "Boniface VIII and Honorific Portraiture: Observations on the Half-Length Image in the Vatican," *Gesta* 26 (1987): 47–58.
7. The most recent discussions of the portrait are by Konrad Oberhuber, "Raphael and the State Portrait. I: The Portrait of Julius II," *Burlington Magazine* 113 (1971): 124–30; Loren Partridge and Randolph Starn, *A Renaissance Likeness: Art and Culture in Raphael's Julius II* (Berkeley and Los Angeles: California University Press, 1980);

reviewed by Rolf Quednau, *Burlington Magazine* 123 (1981): 551–3; Ettore Allegri, in Cecchi, *Raffaello a Firenze*, 144–50, cat. 12 (the version in the Uffizi). See also Valentino Martinelli, "I ritratti papali di Raffaello," in *Studi su Raffaello*, ed. M. Sambucco Hamoud and M. L. Strocchi (Urbino: QuattroVenti, 1987), 517–31; Valerio Guazzoni, "La tradizione della ritrattistica papale nel Rinascimento e il Leone X di Raffaello," in Alfio Del Serra et al., *Raffaello e il ritratto di papa Leone X* (Milan: Silvana, 1996), 89–133, 103–7.

8. "...per significare la grandezza de' suoi concetti." Francesco Guicciardini, *Storia d'Italia*, ed. Alessandro Gherardi (Florence: Sansoni, 1919), II:90. The medal of Julius II with the inscription IVLIVS CAESAR PONT.II on the obverse is believed to have been created to celebrate the pope's triumphal entry into Rome in March 1507, and another of his medals bears the inscription VIRTVTI AVGVSTAE on the reverse. George Francis Hill, *Corpus of Italian Renaissance Medals before Cellini* (London: British Museum, 1930), I, nos. 874 and 875; Roberto Weiss, "The Medals of Pope Julius II (1503–13)," *Journal of the Warburg and Courtauld Institutes* 28 (1965): 163–82, 179, 180, 180 n. 163.

The triumphal arch through which Julius paraded in Rome further bore the inscription *Veni, Vidi, Vici*. Partridge and Starn, *Renaissance Likeness*, 63. See also Partridge and Starn, 47, for references to Giuliano as "Caesar reborn" after his election.

9. "...era notissimo essere di natura molto difficile e formidabile a ciascuno.... Principe d'animo e di costanza inestimabile." Guicciardini, *Storia*, II: 91; III: 40. Translated in Francesco Guicciardini, *The History of Italy*, ed. Sydney Alexander (New York: Macmillan, 1969), 172, 272–3; Alessandro Luzio, "Isabella d'Este di fronte a Giulio II negli ultimi tre anni del suo pontificato," *Archivio Storico Lombardo* 17 (1912): 245–334, 266, 273; Christine Shaw, *Julius II: The Warrior Pope* (Oxford: Blackwell, 1993), 171–2, 188; eadem, "A Pope and his Nipote: Sixtus IV and Giuliano della Rovere," *Atti e Memorie della Società Savonese di Storia Patria* 24 (1988): 233–50.

10. Niccolò Machiavelli, *Il Principe*, ch. 25. In Niccolò Machiavelli, *Opere*, ed. Corrado Vivanti (Turin: Einaudi, 1997), I: 188.

11. Cecil Gould, *Raphael's portrait of Pope Julius II: The re-emergence of the original* (London: National Gallery, 1970); idem, *National Gallery Catalogues. The Sixteenth-Century Italian Schools* (London: National Gallery, 1975), 208–10, cat. 27. His grounds were the work's provenance and changes made to the composition. Traces of yellow papal crossed keys and white tiaras, arranged in a diagonal pattern, were painted against a pale blue fabric; the left acorn finial of the chair back was moved further to the left; and originally the pope's head was midway between the two acorns. I thank Caroline Elam and Jill Dunkerton for confirming that the color of the fabric was blue, not pink as stated by Gould. For a differing view of the autograph status of the work, see James Beck, "The Portrait of Julius II in London's National Gallery: The Goose That Turned into a Gander," *Artibus et Historiae* 17 (1996): 69–95. For the other versions of the composition, see Allegri in Cecchi, *Raffaello a Firenze*.

12. See Nicole Reynaud and Claudie Ressort, "Les portraits d'hommes illustres du studiolo d'Urbino au Louvre par Juste de Gand et Pedro Berruguete," *Revue du Louvre* 41 (1992): 82–113, 96–7, pls. 28–32. For a color illustration, see Lorne Campbell, *Renaissance Portraits. European Portrait-Painting in the 14th, 15th and 16th Centuries* (New Haven and London: Yale University Press, 1990), fig. 68.

13. "...fe' a Roma [un ritratto di] papa Eugenio e due altri de' suoi appresso di lui." Antonio Averlino detto il Filarete, *Trattato di Architettura*, ed. Anna Maria Finoli and Liliana Grassi, 2 vols. (Milan: Polifilo, 1972), I: 265; Nicole Reynaud, *Jean Fouquet* (Paris: Musées Nationaux, 1981), 9–12, cat. 2; Klaus Schwäger, "Über Jean Fouquet in Italien und sein verlorenes Porträt Papst Eugens IV," in *Argo. Festschrift für Kurt Badt*, ed. Martin Gosebruch and Lorenz Dittmann (Cologne: DuMont Schauberg, 1970), 206–34,

fig. 57. See Campbell, *Renaissance Portraits*, 190, caption to pl. 208, for discussion of the possible scales of possible copies.

14. Oberhuber, "Raphael and the State," 129–30. The engraving by Panvinio dates from 1568. Because the pope does not wear a *mozzetta* in the print, the original portrait was presumably painted in summer.

15. A classical prototype was the full-length emperor in the *Liberalitas Augusti* relief on the Arch of Constantine. Partridge and Starn, *Renaissance Likeness*, 10, pl. 7.

16. I do not follow Oberhuber, "Raphael and the State," 127, or John Shearman, "The Vatican Stanze: Functions and Decorations," *Proceedings of the British Academy* 57 (1971): 369–424, 373, in reading Julius as seated in the corner of a room.

17. Partridge and Starn, *Renaissance Likeness*, 56. The oak tree further symbolized the cardinal virtue of Fortitude. Acorn finials also appear on the throne sustaining Julius II as Gregory IX in the *Approval of the Decretals*.

18. Paravicini-Bagliani, *Pope's Body*, 87, citing Rupert of Deutz.

19. Paravicini-Bagliani, *Pope's Body*, 79–81.

20. Justus of Ghent's portrait of Sixtus IV is an exception. In his half-length marble bust by Arnolfo in Saint Peter's, Boniface VIII was presented in full regalia of pluvial and tiara, right hand raised in blessing, left holding the papal keys. See Rash, "Boniface VIII."

21. Paolo Prodi, *The Papal Prince. One Body and Two Souls: The Papal Monarchy in Early Modern Europe*, trans. Susan Haskins (Cambridge: Cambridge University Press, 1982), 46. On his medals Julius was usually presented in cope and orfrey, and on a medal by Caradosso he is bare-headed. Weiss, "Medals of Pope Julius II," 174, pl. 30d.

22. See n. 46.

23. Julius loved jewels. See John Shearman, *Raphael's Cartoons in the Collection of Her Majesty the Queen and the Tapestries for the Sistine Chapel* (London: Phaidon, 1972), 13; Luzio (n. 9), 1912, 327, n. 2. Giuliano told Paride de' Grassi that he wanted to be buried wearing two rings; those put on his fingers were valued at 1,200 ducats. Alessandro Luzio, "Federico Gonzaga, ostaggio alla corte di Giulio II," *Archivio della Reale Società Romana di Storia Patria* 9 (1886): 509–82, 556; Partridge and Starn, *Renaissance Likeness*, 60–1. The ring on the fourth finger of the pope's right hand could conceivably be the Fisherman's Ring, *Anulus Piscatoris*, used for sealing letters and briefs. George F. Kunz, *Rings for the Finger* (Philadelphia: Lippincott, 1917), 262–5.

24. Mark J. Tucker, "Raphael and the Beard of Julius II," *Art Bulletin* 59 (1977): 524–33, 526–7; Partridge and Starn, 44–6.

25. Partridge and Starn, *Renaissance Likeness*, 44, 62–3. Julius promoted the cult of his early Christian namesake by offering a plenary indulgence to those visiting Santa Maria in Trastevere, where the relics of Julius I were discovered in 1505. Partridge and Starn, 62; *Bibliotheca Sanctorum* (Rome: Città Nuova, 1965), VI: 1234–5.

26. G. Piero Valeriano, *Pro sacerdotum barbis* (Rome: Calvo, 1531), trans. Johan Valerian, *A Treatise which is Intitled in Latin Pro Sacerdotum Barbis* (London, 1533); André Chastel, *The Sack of Rome, 1527*, trans. Beth Archer (Princeton: Princeton University Press, 1977), 187–8.

27. Will Fisher, "The Renaissance Beard: Masculinity in Early Modern England," *Renaissance Quarterly* 54 (2001): 155–87.

28. Ibid., 172–3.

29. See David Alan Brown, ed., *Virtue and Beauty: Leonardo's Ginevra de' Benci and Renaissance Portraits of Women* (Washington, DC: National Gallery of Art, 2001), cats. 25 and 30.

30. R. Levi Pisetzky, *Storia del Costume in Italia*, 5 vols. (Milan: Istituto Editoriale Italiano, 1966) III: 165 (who uses the term *fazzoletto*). For the Veronese portrait, see *Veronese e Verona: mostra nel museo di Castelvecchio*, ed. S. Marinelli (Verona: Valdonega, 1988),

207, cat. 9. In Roman ivories the consul and/or emperor holds a cloth with which to open the games at the beginning of the Roman new year (Partridge and Starn, *Renaissance Likeness*, 55–6, pl. 26).

31. See E. H. Gombrich, "Hypnerotomachiana," *Journal of the Warburg and Courtauld Institutes* 14 (1951): 119–25, 120–1.

32. See n. 2.

33. Paravicini-Bagliani, *Pope's Body*, 92

34. Ibid., 59.

35. Ibid., 66, citing Alvarus Pelagius. Cipriano Benet associated the miracle of Transubstantiation with the presence of divinity in Julius when dedicating a treatise on the Eucharist to him. Partridge and Starn, *Renaissance Likeness*, 32.

36. Paravicini-Bagliani, *Pope's Body*, 233, quoting Peter John Olivi.

37. Ibid., 130, 224, 238.

38. Ibid., 130, citing R. Elze, "*Sic transit gloria mundi*: la morte del papa nel medioevo," *Annali dell'Istituto storico italo-germanico in Trento* 3 (1977): 23–41, 24ff.

39. Carlo Ginzburg, "Ritual Pillages: A Preface to Research in Progress," in *Microhistory and the Lost Peoples of Europe*, ed. Edward Muir and Guido Ruggiero (Baltimore: Johns Hopkins University Press, 1991), 20–41, 32. The "rite of passage" is perceived as a phenomenon "through which the survivors, and perhaps the dead person himself, were first separated and then reintegrated, respectively, into the society of the living and the world of the dead" (31).

40. Paravicini-Bagliani, *Pope's Body*, 133.

41. Luzio, "Federico Gonzaga," 526–7; Guicciardini, *History of Italy* 230–1; Shaw, *Julius II*, 172, 327, n. 21 and 22.

42. "...videsse multos pontifices in obitu eorum a propriis affinibus et suis necessariis derelictos sic fuisse, ut indecenter, nudi etiam, detectis pudibundis, jacuerint, quod profecto in dedecus tantae majestatis cessit." "Das Pontificat des Papstes Julius II. nach dem Tagebuche des Grossceremoniars Paris de Grassis," in *Beiträge zur politischen, kirchlichen und Cultur-Geschichte des sechs letzten Jahrhunderte*, ed. J. J. J. von Döllinger, 3 vol. (Vienna, 1862–82; reprint, Frankfurt: Minerva, 1967), III: 428; trans. in Paravicini-Bagliani, *Pope's Body*, 127. When Giuliano died in February 1513, only the presence of Alberto Pio of Carpi, who refused to leave the corpse, prevented it from being abandoned like that of a beggar (*meschino*). Luzio, "Federico Gonzaga," 555 n. 2.

43. Paravicini-Bagliani, *Pope's Body*, 72, 232.

44. Partridge and Starn, *Renaissance Likeness*, 68 (without footnotes, so their source cannot be given).

45. "Il papa Julio si fè retrar e lo dete in Santa Maria in Populo...e fu posto su l'altar e starà cussì 8 ziorni." [Sept. 1513] *Diarii di Marino Sanuto*, ed. F. Stefani, G. Berchet, and N. Barozzi, 58 vols. (Venezia: Visentini, 1879–1903), XVII, col. 60; Vincenzio Golzio, *Raffaello nei documenti* (Vatican City: 1936), 174. Gould, *Raphael's portrait*, 1, assumes that Sanuto's reference must have been retrospective. Partridge and Starn, Renaissance Likeness; 79, justify the seven-month delay by the fact that the portrait appeared on the octave of the Nativity of the Virgin, to whom Giuliano was particularly devoted. The earliest independent likeness of a living pope to be located within a church was Arnolfo's waist-length portrait bust of Boniface VIII in Saint Peter's. Rash, "Boniface VIII," 49.

46. See Isabelle Frank, "Melozzo da Forlì and the Rome of Sixtus IV (1471–84)" (Ph.D diss., Harvard University, 1991), chap. 2. For a color illustration, see Del Serra, *Raffaello e il ritratto*, 96, pl. 81.

47. Cesare Ripa, *Iconologia* (Rome, 1764–67) I: 101; Joanna Woods-Marsden, "Per una tipologia del ritratto di stato nel Rinascimento italiano," in *Il ritratto e la memoria: materiali 3*

(Rome: Bulzoni, 1994), 31–62, 44–7. Partridge and Starn, *Renaissance Likeness*, 9, point to the tradition of statues of seated popes on city gates and cathedral façades as symbolic of temporal power, a contemporary example being Michelangelo's bronze sculpture of the seated Julius for the façade of S. Petronio, Bologna.

48. Paola Barocchi, *Scritti d'arte del cinquecento* (Milan: Ricciardi, 1971–77), II: 2710.

49. Partridge and Starn, *Renaissance Likeness*, 98, 101; Konrad Oberhuber, *Raphael. The Paintings* (Milan: Electa, 1999), 126; Rab Hatfield, review of Partridge and Starn, *Renaissance Likeness*, *Renaissance Quarterly* 34 (1981): 586.

50. It was previously incorrectly assumed that the two Raphael paintings in Santa Maria del Popolo formed pendants, despite the difference in their dates (the *Madonna* is believed to date c. 1509) and measurements: Julius' portrait measures 108 × 80 centimeters while the *Madonna di Loreto* measures 120 × 90 centimeters. Luitpold Dussler, *Raphael: A Critical Catalogue of His Pictures, Wall-Paintings and Tapestries* (London: Phaidon, 1971), 27–8; Sylvie Béguin and Cecil Gould in *La Madone de Lorette. Musée Condé, Chantilly* (Paris: Musées Nationaux, 1979), 5–14. A reconstruction of them as a diptych, in which the *Madonna di Loreto* was shrunk to the same scale as the portrait, demonstrates the impossibility of such a pairing. Julius indicates by neither gaze nor gesture his consciousness of the presence of Virgin and Child. Marielene Putscher, *Raphaels sixtinische Madonna* (Tübingen: Hoper, 1955), pl. XV.

51. This gift was made in December 1511.

52. The triptych was painted c. 1490 by Giovanni Mazone for the della Rovere chapel in San Francesco, Savona. Michel Laclotte and Élisabeth Mognetti, *Avignon, Musée du Petit Palais: Peinture Italienne* (Paris: Musées Nationaux, 1976), cat. 172.

53. Michael Fried, "The Beholder in Courbet: His Early Self-Portraits and Their Place in His Art," *Glyph* 4 (1978): 85–123, 93.

54. John Shearman, *Only Connect...Art and the Spectator in the Italian Renaissance* (Princeton: Princeton, 1992), 127. For a differing suggestion, see Barnaby Nygren, "Cognitive Psychology and the Reception of Raphael's Pope Julius II," *Source* 21, no. 2 (2002): 22–9.

55. An exception is Jan van Scorel's 1523 portrait of Adrian VI. Godefridus J. Hoogewerff, *Jan van Scorel, peintre de la renaissance hollandaise* (The Hague: Nijhoff, 1923), 37–8, pl. 8.

56. Sergei Lobanov-Rostovsky, "Taming the Basilisk," in *The Body in Parts: Fantasies of Corporeality in Early Modern Europe*, ed. D. Hillman and C. Mazzio (New York and London: Routledge, 1997), 195–217, 201, 213, n. 22; Jacques Le Goff, "Head or Heart? The Political Use of Body Metaphors in the Middle Ages," in *Fragments for a History of the Human Body. Part 3*, ed. Michel Feher, in *Zone* 5 (1989): 13–26, 17.

57. Horapollo, *Hieroglyphica* (Paris: Jacobu Kerver, 1551), 222; Gombrich, "Hypnerotomachiana," 120–1.

58. Leon Battista Alberti, *De re aedificatoria*, trans. and ed. G. Orlandi (Milan: Polifilo, 1966), 695–7; Leon Battista Alberti, *Dinner Pieces*, trans. David Marsh (Binghamton, NY: Medieval and Renaissance Texts, 1987), 213; Renée Neu Watkins, "L. B. Alberti's emblem, the winged eye, and his name, Leo," *Mitteilungen des Kunsthistorischen Institutes in Florenz* 9 (1960): 257.

59. Hans Belting, *Likeness and Presence: A History of the Image before the Era of Art*, trans. Edmund Jephcott (Chicago and London: Chicago University Press, 1994), 264.

60. Martinelli, "I ritratti," 520, equates the benign expression Raphael gave to Gregory IX with that of Pollaiuolo's statue of Innocent VIII.

61. A disputed red chalk drawing at Chatsworth of the head of Julius II, however, corresponds exactly in size, outline, and lighting with that in the portrait, but was probably not that drawing. It is regarded as authentic by Oberhuber, "Raphael and the State," 128;

Dussler, *Raphael*, 30; Paul Joannides, *The Drawings of Raphael* (Los Angeles: California University Press, 1983), 78, cat. 23; Oskar Fischel, *Raphael*, trans. Bernard Rackham (London: Kegan Paul, 1948), 93. It is dismissed as a copy, possibly based on a tracing, by J. A. Gere and Nicholas Turner (*Drawings by Raphael* [London: British Museum, 1983], 171–2, cat. 140) who also cite Popham's negative opinion; and attributed to a Raphael follower by Michael Jaffé (*The Devonshire Collection of Italian Drawings. Roman and Neapolitan Schools* [London: Phaidon, 1994]), II: 199, cat. 330. There is general consensus that the so-called cartoon of the portrait of Julius II in the Galleria Corsini, Florence, has nothing to do with Raphael. For an exception, see Maria Grazia Ciardi Duprè Dal Poggetto and Paolo Dal Poggetto, *Urbino e le Marche prima e dopo Raffaello* (Florence: Nuova Salani, 1983), 270, cat. 77.

62. See Harry Berger, Jr., "Fictions of the Pose: Facing the Gaze of early Modern Portraiture," *Representations* 46 (1994): 87–120.

63. J. A. Crowe and G. B. Cavalcaselle, *Raphael: His Life and Works* (London: John Murray, 1885), II: 102. For the term *terribilità* as it applies to a person, see David Summers, *Michelangelo and the Language of Art* (Princeton: Princeton University Press, 1981), 239–40.

64. Giuliano himself said that he could not stay still. Shaw, *Julius II*, 315, 338, n. 112. In the late Middle Ages, it was held that the ruler, in public, should express serenity, equilibrium and decorum. Paravicini-Bagliani, *Pope's Body*, 195.

65. Dussler, *Raphael*, 34.

66. "Inghirami's pen is poised in anticipation of divine afflatus." David Rosand, "The Portrait, the Courtier, and Death," in *Castiglione: The Ideal and the Real in Renaissance Culture*, ed. Robert W. Hanning and David Rosand (New Haven and London: Yale University Press, 1983), 91–129, 129, n. 18. See also the excellent discussion in Shearman, who characterizes the work as "describing the course of thought," *Only Connect*, 130–1.

67. S. J. Freedberg, *Painting of the High Renaissance in Rome and Florence*, rev. ed. (Cambridge: Harvard University Press, 1985), I: 178–9.

68. Shearman, *Only Connect*, 135–7; Rosand, "The Portrait," 92–5.

69. John Shearman, "Le portrait de Baldassare Castiglione par Raphael," *Revue du Louvre* 29 (1979): 261–72, 262–4.

70. Shearman, *Only Connect*, 1992, 135–6.

71. The muted tones may have been influenced by the presence of Leonardo, together with the unfinished *Mona Lisa*, in Rome in these years.

72. See Joanna Woods-Marsden, *Renaissance Self-Portraiture: The Visual Construction of Identity and the Social status of the Artist* (New Haven and London: Yale University Press, 1998), pl. 87, 124–32; Freedberg, *Painting*, I: 343–4; Roger Jones and Nicholas Penny, *Raphael* (New Haven and London: Yale University Press, 1983), 171.

73. Vasari greatly admired the painting. Giorgio Vasari, *Le opere di Giorgio Vasari*, ed. G. Milanesi. 9 vols. (Florence: Sansoni, 1906) IV: 352. For a differing interpretation of the color ("strident cacophony of too-close reds that speaks...of divisive tension among these men"), see Marcia B. Hall, *Color and Meaning: Practice and Theory in Renaissance Painting* (Cambridge: Cambridge University Press, 1992), 132.

As well as the references cited below, see Arnold Nesselrath, in *Hochrenaissance im Vatikan: Kunst und Kultur in Rom der Papste I. 1503–1534* (Bonn: Kunst- und Austellungshalle der Bundesrepublik Deutschland, 1998), 441, cat. 22; Guazzoni, "La tradizione," 110–21; T. J. Clark, *Image of the People: Gustave Courbet and the 1848 Revolution* (Princeton: Princeton University Press, 1973), 15. See, most recently, the literal reading by Nelson Minnich, "Raphael's Portrait Leo X with Cardinals Giulio de' Medici and Luigi de' Rossi: A Religious Interpretation," *Renaissance Quarterly* 56 (2003): 1005–52, with whose conclusions I disagree.

74. Bernice F. Davidson, *Raphael's Bible: A Study of the Vatican Loggie* (University Park, PA: College Art Association, 1985), 9, 20 (whose excellent study in part stimulated the interpretation offered here); William Roscoe, *Vita e Pontificato di Leone X*, trans. Luigi Bossi (Milan: Sonzogno, 1812), IV: 15–16; Karla Langedijk, *The Portraits of the Medici* (Florence: SPES, 1981), I: 51.

75. Peter Meller, "Physiognomical Theory in Renaissance Heroic Portraits," in *The Renaissance and Mannerism. Studies in Western Art. Acts of the Twentieth International Congress of the History of Art* (Princeton: Princeton University Press, 1963), 53–69, 63, and n. 37; Langedijk, *Portraits of the Medici*, I: 51; Guy de Terverant, *Attributs et Symboles dans l'art profane, 1400–1600* (Geneva: Droz, 1997), 289–94.

76. Giovanni's Roman mother supposedly had a dream during pregnancy that she had given birth in the Florence Cathedral to a meek [*mansueto*] lion. Meller, "Physiognomical," 66 n. 41; Adrian Randolph, "Il Marzocco: Lionizing the Florentine State," in *Coming About...A Festschrift for John Shearman* (Cambridge: Harvard University Art Museums, 2001), 11–18, 16.

77. John White and John Shearman, "Raphael's Tapestries and Their Cartoons," *Art Bulletin* 40 (1958): 193–221, 212; Shearman, *Raphael's Cartoons*, 16–20, draws parallels between Leo X and the personalities and achievements of Leo I, Leo II, Leo III, and Leo IX.

78. The pope was much preoccupied with fate and greatly interested in astrology. Davidson, *Raphael's Bible*, 21; Janet Cox-Rearick, *Dynasty and Destiny in Medici Art: Pontormo, Leo X, and the Two Cosimos* (Princeton: Princeton University Press, 1988), 178. The most important element of a natal horoscope in the Renaissance was the ascendant sign that arose on the eastern horizon at the moment of birth – in Giovanni's case Sagittarius. The planetary ruler of the ascendant sign – which for Leo was Jupiter – was considered by Marsilio Ficino to be the most auspicious of the entire horoscope. Cox-Rearick, 178–80, 184, 195–98, 185 n. 23. Needless to say, the pope's published horoscopes were inconsistent with his baptismal record. Cox-Rearick, 180 n. 5.

79. Shearman, *Raphael's Cartoons*, 1972, 17, 82–3. Other contributing factors may have been the lion's connection with Rome, as the city's zodiacal ruler, and with the Vatican, known as the città leonina. Cox-Rearick, *Dynasty*, 186.

80. "...non voria fatica si'l podesse far di manco....Il papa non voria nì guera, nì faticha." Davidson, *Raphael's Bible*, 9, 9 n. 11 (where the phrase is translated as reluctant to "put himself out"), citing Stefani, *I diarii di Marino Sanuto*, vol. 24, col. 90; John W. O'Malley, *Praise and Blame in Renaissance Rome: Rhetoric, Doctrine and Reform in the Sacred Orators at the Papal Court c. 1450–1521* (Durham, NC: Duke University Press, 1979), 31; Shearman, *Raphael's Cartoons*, 1–20; Carlo Falconi, *Leone X Giovanni de' Medici* (Milan: Rusconi, 1987), 450–76. Sanuto also claimed that the pope told his brother Giuliano "godianci il papato, poiché Dio ce l'ha dato" (let us enjoy the papacy since God gave it to us). Ibid.

81. Guazzoni, "La tradizione," 110.

82. The appointment occurred upon cardinal Raffaele Riario's dismissal from the office following the conspiracy against Leo X, which is discussed later.

83. The pope's affection for his cousin is revealed at the latter's death in 1519 in a letter from Castiglione to Isabella d'Este cited in Francesco P. Di Teodoro, *Ritratto di Leone X di Raffaello Sanzio* (Milan: Tea, 1998), 28. For more on cardinal Luigi, see Minnich, "Raphael's Portrait," 1015 nn. 34–37.

84. Antonio Natali, "Leone come Giulio? Tracce per un'indagine sull'invenzione del ritratto di Leone X con due cardinali," in Del Serra, *Raffaello e il ritratto*, 51–66; Alfio Del Serra, "Nota di restauro," in Del Serra, *Raffaello e il ritratto*, 67–88; Di Teodoro, *Ritratto*, 69.

85. Langedijk, *Portraits of the Medici*, 1401–2, cat. 103,6; Del Serra, *Raffaello e il ritratto*, 64, pl. 43. The copy was made in 1585. A number of sixteenth-century copies of the whole painting survive. Allegri in Cecchi, *Raffaello a Firenze*, 189–96, cat. 17, 190, 193, 196, 198 n. 14, 198 n. 18, 198 n. 41. Federico Gonzaga of Mantua and Alessandro de' Medici of Florence are documented as requesting the original painting as a gift. Golzio, *Raffaello*, 151–4.

86. Freedberg, *Painting*, I: 342.

87. "…el duca la fece mectere sopra alla tavola, dove mangiava la Duchessa et li altri signori in mezo, che veramente rallegrava ogni cosa." Letter from Lorenzo de' Medici's mother, Alfonsina Orsini, to her secretary in Rome. John Shearman, *Raphael in Early Modern Sources 1483–1602*, 2 vols. (New Haven and London: Yale University Press, 2003), I: 366–8. The portrait subsequently hung over a door in the Medici Palace in Florence. Vasari/Milanesi, *Le opere*, V: 41.

88. Federico Zuccari, for instance, repeated the topos that Baldassarre Turini was so deceived by the painting that he presented the painted pope with some bulls, along with inkstand and pens, for his signature. G. G. Bottari, *Raccolta di lettere sulla pittura, scultura ed architettura scritte dai più celebri personaggi*, 7 vols. (Rome: Eredi Barbiellini, 1754–73), VI: 131.

89. Gere and Turner, *Drawings by Raphael*, 226–9, cat. 183, succinctly sum up the controversy over the drawing's attribution: "The arguments for and against Raphael and Giulio [Romano] are nicely balanced. The quality of the drawing as a portrait is fully worthy of Raphael and is somewhat unexpected in Giulio; but it must be admitted that the way in which the lips and nose are formalized, and the overemphatic contrasts of light and shade, make it difficult to deny the correctness of the attribution to Giulio." Michael Jaffé (*Old Master Drawings from Chatsworth* [London: British Museum, 1993], cat. 70) also attributes the drawing to Giulio, whereas Shearman, *Raphael's Cartoons*, 61 n. 88, and Joannides, *Drawings of Raphael*, 246, cat. 455, attribute it to Raphael. Langedijk, *Portraits of the Medici*, I: 51, suggests that the artist adapted certain traits of the pope's features to hint at the features of a lion. For Julius's neck in profile portraits on medals, see Weiss, "Medals of Pope Julius II," pls. 30–3.

90. For a differing view, see Freedberg, *Painting*, I: 341.

91. For contemporary accounts of the pope's singular appearance, see Vittorio Cian, "Su l'iconografia di Leone X," in *Scritti varii di erudizione e di critica in onore di Rodolfo Renier* (Turin: Fratelli Bocca, 1912), 559–76. For the images, see Langedijk, *Portraits of the Medici*, 1400–53, cat. 103.

92. Shearman, *Raphael's Cartoons*, 15–17, 76, 82–83; Davidson, *Raphael's Bible*, 19. The speaker in 1513 was Bishop Begnius.

93. Davidson, *Raphael's Bible*, 12; Antonio Natali, in *L'officina della Maniera* (Venice: Marsilio, 1996), 194, cat. 57. Many, if not most, scholars read the architecture as immediately behind the figures, suggesting that there is barely room for cardinal Giulio to stand between the table and the out-of-scale cornice behind.

94. Freedberg, *Painting*, I: 342.

95. Jones and Penny, *Raphael*, pl. 88.

96. I no longer agree with my comments in Woods-Marsden, *Renaissance Self-Portraiture*, 1998, 126.

97. The emblem was often glossed with the motto SEMPER. Frances Ames-Lewis, "Early Medicean Devices," *Journal of the Warburg and Courtauld Institutes* 42 (1979): 122–43, 129; Di Teodoro, *Ritratto*, 51; Del Serra, *Raffaello e il ritratto*, pl. 54.

98. Davidson, *Raphael's Bible*, 13, 14 n. 27; Di Teodoro, *Ritratto*, 51–60; Joseph Braun, *Das christliche Altargerät in seinem Sein und in seiner Entwicklung* (Munich: Hueber, 1932),

574; Joseph A. Jungmann, *The Mass of the Roman Rite: Its Origins and Development* (*Missa Sollemnia*), 2 vols. (Westminster, MD: Christian Classics, 1986), II: 131 n. 22, 216–17; Benedetta Montevecchi and Sandra Vasco Rocca, eds., *Suppellettile ecclesiastica* (Florence, Centro Di, 1988), I: 285; Anselm Lange, *Europäische Tischglocken* (Kornwestheim: Minner Verlag, 1981), 102, illustrates Raphael's depiction of Leo's bell, along with other sixteenth-century ones (96, 99, 100, 101, 103); Herbert Thurton, "Bells," in *The Catholic Encyclopedia* (New York: Appleton, 1907), II: 418–22.

99. Davidson, *Raphael's Bible*, 14. See ibid., 13 n. 23, for other bells in portraits of ecclesiastics, such as that by Sebastiano del Piombo of Cardinal Bandinello Saulli and attendants, dated 1516 in Washington. *The Approval of the Decretals* makes a more convincing visual source for this work than Sebastiano's painting, as originally suggested by Freedberg, *Painting*, I: 341, and often repeated since.

100. The pope even took his lens hunting. Giuseppe Boffito, "L'occhiale e il cannocchiale del papa Leone X," *Atti del Reale Accademia delle Scienze di Torino* 62 (1927): 558–9.

101. The manuscript is today in the Kupferstichkabinett of the Staatlichen Museen Berlin. *Zimelien: Abendländische Handschriften des Mittelalters aus dem Sammlungen der Stiftung Preussischer Kulturbesitz Berlin* (Wiesbaden: Verlag Reichert, 1975), 68–9, cat. 48; Max-Eugen Kemper, *Hoch Renaissance im Vatikan: Kunst und Kultur in Rom der Papste. I. 1503–1534* (Bonn: Kunst- und Austellungshalle der Bundesrepublik Deutschland GmbH, 1998), 444, cat. 23; Di Teodoro, *Ritratto*, 61–3; Davidson, *Raphael's Bible*, 12–13. It seems unnecessary to posit that the depicted manuscript represents a copy of the Hamilton Bible in order to account for the different coat of arms.

102. Davidson, *Raphael's Bible*, 12–13; Del Serra, *Raffaello e il ritratto*, 117 and 118, figs. 94 and 95. For bibliography on the Gospel according to Saint John, see Davidson, *Raphael's Bible*, 13 n. 21.

103. Jungmann, *The Mass*, II: 447–51. Minnich ("Raphael's Portrait," 1024) cites Marsilio Ficino's paraphrase of this verse for Leo X: "There was a man of Florence sent by God whose name is John, born of the heroic stock of the Medici. This man has come for testimony that he might bear witness about the greatest authority among us of his father, the magnanimous Lorenzo" (giving reference to Marsilio Ficino, *Opera Omnia*, 4 vols. [Reprint, Turin, 1959] II, 2, 897).

104. O'Malley, *Praise and Blame*, 1979, 138–46.

105. The balls of the Medici insignia also had a classical interpretation as *mala Medica*, the citrous fruit that was equated with the apples growing in the mythical garden of the Hesperides. Susan R. McKillop, "L'ampliamento dello stemma Mediceo e il suo contesto politico," *Archivio Storico Italiano* 110, no. 552 (1992): 641–713, 641–53, whom I thank for sharing her article with me.

106. Jan Bialostocki, "The Eye and the Window: Realism and Symbolism in the Art of Albrecht Dürer," in *Festschrift für Gert von der Osten* (Cologne: Dumont Schauberg, 1970), 159–76, 170ff. I do not follow Davidson (*Raphael's Bible*) in her identification of the reflection in the finial as a "mystical window."

107. See color detail in Del Serra, *Raffaello e il ritratto* pl. 55.

108. See Fabio Barry, "Lux and Lumen: The Symbolism of Real and Represented Light in the Baroque Dome," *Kritische Berichte: Zeitschrift für Kunst- und Kulturwissenschaften* 30, no. 4 (2002): 22–37.

109. Davidson, *Raphael's Bible*, 15; Cox-Rearick, *Dynasty*, 184, 186; de Terverant, *Attributs*, 294.

110. Cox-Rearick, *Dynasty*, 28, 184, 198. A medal by Gambello with the reverse inscription of VIRTVTE TVA LVX MEA IN TE, "your light lies in virtue, my light in you," shows Christ/Apollo holding a sun that sheds its rays on a lion with its paw on a Medici *palla*. The analogy between Christ and Apollo was ancient. Langedijk, *Portraits of*

the Medici, I: 50; II: 1432, 103, 63; Hill, *Corpus,* 451; Cox-Rearick, *Dynasty,* 184, 186; Davidson, *Raphael's Bible,* 23 n. 75.

111. See n. 92.

112. Hans Peter L'Orange and Hjalmar Tarp, *Il Tempietto Longobardo di Cividale* (Roma: Bretschneider, 1979), 115ff; Charles L. Stinger, *The Renaissance in Rome* (Bloomington: Indiana University Press, 1985), 299.

113. For the Fouquet, see n. 13.

114. They were cardinals Bandinello Sauli, Francesco Soderini, Adriano Castellesi, and Raffaelle Riario. The pope was to be poisoned through an ulcer on his buttock. Pio Delicati and Mariano Armellini, *Il diario di Leone X di Paride de' Grassi* (Rome: Pace, 1884), 46–56; Ludwig Pastor, *History of the Popes,* ed. F. R. Kerr, 14 vols. (Saint Louis, MO: Herder, 1923), VII: 177–208; Alessandro Ferrajoli, *La congiura dei cardinali contro Leone X* (Rome: Biblioteca Valicelliana, 1919); Giovanni Battista Picotti, "La congiura dei cardinali contro Leone X," *Rivista Storica Italiana* 40 (1923): 249–67; Guicciardini, *History of Italy,* 294–8; Falconi, *Leone X,* 334–44.

115. Paravicini-Bagliani, *Pope's Body,* 63. The head was of course the principal member that the other members had to obey. Le Goff, "Head or Heart," 13, 23.

116. Paravicini-Bagliani, *Pope's Body,* 64.

117. Ibid., 64. See also Stinger, *Renaissance in Rome,* 158–66, on the issue of papal primacy in the fifteenth and sixteenth centuries. He shows how Renaissance popes were sustained in their absolutist views of ecclesiastic authority by a massive literature defending papal monarchy.

118. Massimo Firpo, "The Cardinal," in *Renaissance Characters,* ed. Eugenio Garin, trans. L. C. Cochrane (Chicago: Chicago University Press, 1991), 76.

119. Pastor, *History,* VII: 200.

120. See William Roscoe, *The Life and Pontificate of Leo X* (London: Bohn, 1846), II: 77, for the extra precautions that the pope took in the aftermath of the conspiracy.

121. "Ogni cosa nel suo silenzio par che favella." Vasari/Milanesi, *Le opere,* IV: 361.

122. Davidson, *Raphael's Bible,* 18.

123. Paravicini-Bagliani, *Pope's Body,* 60.

124. "...non essendo altro che sogni e ombre del nostro essere." *Dialoghi di M. S. Speroni* (Venice, 1543), 25v–26, cited in Jodi Cranston, *The Poetics of Portraiture in the Italian Renaissance* (Cambridge and New York: Cambridge University Press, 2000), 115, 223 nn. 70 and 71.

CHAPTER 6. THE COMPETITION BETWEEN RAPHAEL AND MICHELANGELO AND SEBASTIANO'S ROLE IN IT

I am profoundly and forever grateful to Rona Goffen and Marcia Hall for their insights, comments, and suggestions regarding my work. Without their help, this work would not have been possible. My gratitude to Sarah McHam and Tod Marder, who helped me in various ways to improve my arguments. I am also indebted to Adriana Greci-Green, Stephanie Leone, Shilpa Prasad, Beryl Smith, and Aileen Wang who read and corrected my manuscript.

1. See, for example, John Shearman, "Raffaello e la bottega," in *Raffaello in Vaticano,* exh. cat., Città del Vaticano, Braccio di Carlo Magno, 16.10.1984–16.1.1985 (Milan: Electa, 1984), 258–63, 258: "Raphael was the first artist who involved assistants in the process of creating preparatory drawings. Neither Leonardo nor Michelangelo did implicate garzoni in what they considered their exclusive duty." Also Sebastiano's partnership with Michelangelo – the latter providing drawings, the former *colore* – was unprecedented in the history of art. For recent analysis of Raphael's drawings,

see Konrad Oberhuber, "Lo stile classico di Raffaello e la sua evoluzione a Roma fino al 1527," in *Roma e lo stile classico di Raffaello*, ed. Konrad Oberhuber (Milan: Electa, 1999), 17–28; Paul Joannides, *The Drawings of Raphael, with a Complete Catalogue* (Oxford: Phaidon, 1983). The issues of rivalry and competition among High Renaissance artists have been extensively analysed for the first time by Rona Goffen, *Renaissance Rivals. Michelangelo, Leonardo, Raphael, Titian* (New Haven: Yale University Press, 2002).

2. I refer here extensively to the issues I discussed in *Sebastiano del Piombo and Michelangelo in Rome: Problems of Style and Meaning of the Viterbo Pietà* (Ph.D. diss., Rutgers University, 1999), esp. 37–103.

3. On the importance of Sebastiano in the Roman scenario in relation to Raphael, in its duplicity as a venetian colorist and as Michelangelo's surrogate for *disegno*, see Sydney J. Freedberg, *Raphael, Michelangelo, and others: Raphael and His Contemporaries in Rome* (Poughkeepsie: Vassar College, 1983), who (p. 4) defined Sebastiano "the possessor of the most formidable talent in painting in Rome other than Raphael himself." For the importance of Sebastiano's work "a paragone" to Raphael's, see Marcia B. Hall, *Color and Meaning. Practice and Theory in Renaissance Painting* (Cambridge: Cambridge University Press, 1992), 137–42. For valuable observations on Michelangelo's reaction to Raphael's success and on his association with Sebastiano, see Robert S. Liebert, "Raphael, Michelangelo, Sebastiano: High Renaissance Rivalry," in *Source* 3 (1984): 60–68. However, his conclusions about the end of Michelangelo's and Sebastiano's friendship are not convincing.

4. On the "dark manner," experimented with both by Raphael and Sebastiano, see Hall, *Color and Meaning,* 131–6.

5. For the English translation, see Giorgio Vasari, *Lives of the Painters, Sculptors and Architects*, trans. Gaston de Vere and with an introduction and note by David Ekserdjian, 2 vols. (New York-Toronto: Alfred A. Knopf, 1996), 2: 140–52 (hereafter Vasari/de Vere). See also Giorgio Vasari, *Le vite de' più eccellenti pittori, scultori e architettori: nelle redazioni del 1550 e del 1568*, ed. Paola Barocchi and Rosanna Bettarini, 6 vols. (Florence: Sansoni-SPES, 1966–87), 5: 85–103, esp. 88 (hereafter Vasari/Barocchi).

For recent monographs on Sebastiano del Piombo, see Mauro Lucco and Carlo Volpe, *L'opera completa di Sebastiano del Piombo,* (Milan: Rizzoli, 1980), and Michael Hirst, *Sebastiano del Piombo* (Oxford: Clarendon Press, 1981).

5. Lucco, *L'opera,* 87. Hirst, *Sebastiano del Piombo,* 46–7, 99–100.

6. After Vasari, the concept of Sebastiano as Michelangelo's brush was revived in early modern scholarship by Giovan Battista Cavalcaselle and James A. Crowe, in *Tiziano, la sua vita, i suoi tempi,* 2 vols. (Florence: Le Monnier, 1877–78), 2: 51. See, more recently, Cecil Gould's considerations of Sebastiano as Michelangelo's pawn: Cecil Gould, *The Raising of Lazarus by Sebastiano del Piombo* (London: National Gallery, Trustees, 1967), 11–12.

7. See, in particular, Rodolfo Pallucchini, *Sebastian Viniziano –Fra Sebastiano del Piombo* (Milan: Mondadori, 1944), and Lucco, *L'opera.* According to Hirst (*Sebastiano del Piombo,* 148–51), the problem of Michelangelo's drawings mistakenly attributed to Sebastiano is an obstacle to the understanding of Sebastiano's oeuvre.

8. "Pier Francesco Borgherini…had taken over a chapel in San Pietro in Montorio…allotted it at the suggestion of Michelangelo to Sebastiano, because Borgherini thought that Michelangelo would execute the design of the whole work, as indeed he did." Vasari/de Vere, 2: 142. Vasari/Barocchi, 5: 89.

9. For the analysis of Sebastiano's and Michelangelo's *Pietà*, an oil on panel now in the Museo Civico in Viterbo, see Barbieri, *Sebastiano*, and the most recent *Notturno*

Sublime. Sebastiano e Michelangelo nella Pietà di Viterbo, ed. Costanza Barbieri, exh. cat., Viterbo, Museo Civico, 30.5–25.7, 2004 (Rome: Viviani Editore, 2004). In this occasion, the painting has been analyzed through infrared reflectography and has revealed a magnificent Michelangelesque underdrawing, thus confirming Vasari's account concerning the *cartone* Michelangelo offered to Sebastiano. In addition to that, the scientific analyses revealed other interesting, unpublished drawings on the back of the Viterbo panel, see *Notturno Sublime*, 2004, 97–105, 153–9.

10. Vasari/de Vere, 2: 142. Vasari/Barocchi, 5: 89.

11. As hypothesized by Hirst (*Sebastiano del Piombo*, 43–4), a plausible date *ante quem* for the painting is 1516, when the patron Giovanni Botonti donated sacred fittings for the new altar built in the church of San Francesco at Viterbo. This implies that the painting was already in loco. The document was found and published by Giuseppe Signorelli, *Memorie francescane in Viterbo* (Viterbo, 1928), 37. See also Barbieri, *Sebastiano*, 107–9, and *Notturno Sublime*, 2004, 153–9 for the hypothesis of an earlier chronology.

12. Vasari/de Vere, 2: 141. Vasari/Barocchi, 5: 87.

13. Vasari/de Vere, 2: 142. In this passage, the word "giudice" of Vasari's original version – maintained in de Vere's translation – has been interpreted as a mistake for "giudicare" by Paola Barocchi and Rosanna Bettarini (5: 88), who followed the 1550 edition: "Battere coloro che avevano sì fatta openione, ed egli, sotto ombra di terzo, giudic[ar]e quale di loro fusse meglio." In my opinion, however, both versions are close to the intended meaning, whereas Milanesi [Giorgio Vasari, *Le vite de' più eccellenti pittori, scultori et architetti*, 1568, ed. Gaetano Milanesi, 9 vols. (Florence: Sansoni, 1878–85), 5: 567], who expunged the word "giudice," has a text that makes no sense: "Battere coloro che avevano si fatta openione, ed egli, sotto ombra di terzo, quale di loro fusse meglio."

14. Vasari/de Vere, 2: 142. For Vasari's edition of 1550, the most recent and updated text is *Le Vite de' più eccellenti Architetti, Pittori et Scultori Italiani, da Cimabue, insino a Tempi Nostri*, ed. Luciano Bellosi and Aldo Rossi, 2 vols. (Turin: Einaudi, 1991), 2: 840.

15. Mark Roskill, *Dolce's "Aretino" and Venetian Art Theory of the Cinquecento* (New York: New York University Press, 1968), 90–1.

16. See the keen analysis by Clark Hulse, *The Rule of Art. Literature and Painting in the Renaissance* (Chicago and London: University of Chicago Press, 1990) 83–90: "Courtiership…as the intermediate identity-form of both poets and painters, the arena in which they are able to play out the Albertian script and display their visual and literary knowledge…. The consummate artist of the new model is Raphael."

17. Ibid., 83. See also, on the same topic, the relevant contributions by Patricia Rubin, "Il contributo di Raffaello allo sviluppo della pala d'altare rinascimentale," *Arte Cristiana* 78 (1990): 169–82.

18. Giovanna Perini, "Raffaello e l'Antico: alcune precisazioni," *Bollettino d'Arte* 89–90 (1995): 111–44, presents for the first time Girolamo Aleandro's poem, dedicated to Raphael. The manuscript was found by Perini in the Biblioteca Universitaria di Bologna (ms. 400). It is a short Latin poem, titled "Divo Leone X Pont. Max. Raphaeli Urbinati Veterem urbem Pinguenti." The author discusses extensively Raphael's primacy at the time of Leo X and its reflection in literature and poetry.

19. Ibid., 116: "Quid mirum, si qua Christus tu luce peristi?/ Naturae ille deus, tu deus artis erat."

20. Paola Barocchi and Renzo Ristori, eds., *Il Carteggio di Michelangelo*, 5 vols. (Florence: Sansoni, 1965–83), 2: 242: "Et con mezo vostro far le vendette vostre et mie a un trato, et dar ad intendere a le persone maligne che 'l c'è altri semidei che Rafael da Urbino con e' soi garzoni."

21. Minor poets were also in the same circle, like Marc'Antonio Casanova and Evangelista Maddaleni Capodiferro (ibid., 111–17). On Colocci and Raphael, see Ingrid D. Rowland, "Raphael, Angelo Colocci, and the Genesis of theArchitectural Orders," *Art Bulletin* 76 1994): 86–112.

22. Vasari/de Vere, 2: 742: "(Raphael) reflected, like a man of supreme judgment, that painting does not consist only in representing the nude human form, but has a wider field; that one can enumerate among the perfect painters those who express historical inventions…, fine judgement in their fancies…, compositions of scenes…distributed with beautiful invention an order…with a bizarre variety of perspectives, buildings and landscapes…; with an endless number of other things, such as…trees, grottoes, rocks, fires, skies turbid or serene, clouds, rain, lightning, clear weather, night, the light of the moon, the splendour of the sun." Vasari/Barocchi, 4: 206.

23. Vasari/de Vere, 2: 142. Vasari/Barocchi, 5: 88–9. Cf. the 1550 edition: "Furono questi umori nutriti gran tempo così, in molte cose che fece Sebastiano, come quadri e ritratti, e si alzavano l'opere sue in infinito, per le lodi date da Michelagnolo. Alle quali opere, oltra l'essere di bellezza, di disegno e di colorito, facevano grandissima credenza le parole dette da Michelagnolo ne' capi della corte." (Vasari/Bellosi, 2: 840).

24. On Raphael's revolutionary modes of coloring and on general innovations in color technique, see Hall, *Color and Meaning*, 92–115 and 131–6. See also, by the same author, "From Modeling Techniques to Color Modes," in *Color and Technique in Renaissance Paintings, Italy and the North*, ed. Marcia B. Hall (Locust Valley, NY: Augustin, 1987), 1–29. Useful information also in Janis Bell, "Color and Chiaroscuro," in Marcia B. Hall, ed., *Raphael's School of Athens*, (Cambridge: Cambridge University Press, 1997), 85–113.

25. Stated by Vasari in his own life: Vasari/Barocchi, 6: 389–90.

26. Paolo Giovio, *Raphaelis Urbinatis Vita*, in *Scritti d'arte del Cinquecento*, ed. Paola Barocchi, 9 vols. (Naples: Ricciardi, 1971–3, reprint, Turin: Einaudi, 1977–9), 1: 15: "in mitiganda commiscendaque vividiorum pigmentorum austeritate iocundissimum artifex ante alia id praestanter contendit, quod unum in Buonarota defuerat, scilicet ut picturis erudite delineatis etiam colorum oleo commistorum lucidus ac inviolabilis ornatus accederet" (translation provided by author). Giovio's *Lives* were written around 1523–7 (ibid., XXXV).

27. Ibid., 1: 10–11: "In Vaticano Xistini sacelli cameram a Iulio secundo ingenti pecunia accitus, immenso opere brevi perfecto, absolutae artis testimonium deposuit, Quum resupinus, uti necesse erat, pingeret, aliqua in abscessus et sinus refugiente sensim lumine condidit…in aliquibus autem…lucem ipsam experimentibus umbris adeo feliciter protulit, ut repraesentata corporm veritate, ingeniosi etiam artifices, quae piana essent, veluti solida mirarentur" (translation provided by author).

28. Cf. Barocchi's comment, ibid., 1: 3–4: "Gli scritti figurativi di Paolo Giovio… meritavano una riedizione, segnando il fortunato punto d'incontro d'una eccezionale esperienza, sociale e letteraria, coi problemi artistici, tutti nuovi, delle opere di Leonardo, Raffaello, Michelangelo, il Dosso, Sebastiano del Piombo."

29. On the general issues concerning the *paragone* debate between painting and sculpture, see Moshe Barasch, *Theories of Art from Plato to Winckelmann* (New York: New York University Press, 1985), 164–74. See also the important study by Claire J. Farago, *Leonardo da Vinci's Paragone. A Critical Interpretation with a New Edition of the Text in the Codex Urbinas* (Leiden: Brill, 1992).

30. Michelangelo, "Lettera a Benedetto Varchi," in Barocchi, *Raphaelis Urbinatis*, 3: 522 (as in n. 26): "Io dico che la pittura mi par più tenuta buona quanto più va verso il rilievo, et il rilievo più tenuto cattivo quanto più va verso la pittura; e però a me soleva

parere che la scultura fussi la lanterna della pittura, e che da l'una a l'altra fussi quella differenza che è dal sole alla luna."

31. For an interesting analysis of Michelangelo's complex behavior concerning the *paragone*, see David Summers, *Michelangelo and the Language of Art* (Princeton, NJ: Princeton University Press, 1981), 269–70.

32. Barocchi and Ristori, *Il Carteggio*, 3: 272 : "Ma se quella non puotesse collorire, comme essa mi disse a boccha, almeno vorebe che Sebastiano vostro lo colorisse, dil che Vostra Signoria mi promisi advisarci."

33. In the letter (ibid.), there is no indication of "the great artist's other commitments [which] prevent his furnishing the work," as suggested by Hirst, *Sebastiano del Piombo*, 42. The problem with "colorire," I believe, was of a different kind for Michelangelo, who felt himself not at ease with oil coloring. For Michelangelo's use of tempera and hatred of oil, see also Rona Goffen, *Titian's Women* (New Haven and London: Yale University Press, 1997) 229, 231–9.

34. Vasari/de Vere, 2: 151. Vasari/Barocchi, 5: 101–2.

35. It is interesting to note how Vasari reported, with extreme delicacy, Michelangelo's problems with colors. In describing the *Last Judgment*, Vasari states that Michelangelo succeeded in the representation of the human figures, disregarding the beauty of color. Perhaps it is not without reason – Vasari observes – that painters use beautiful colors, *capricci*, and other delicacies (Vasari/Barocchi, 6: 69). A veiled criticism of Michelangelo's color?

36. On Michelangelo's color technique, see Hall, "From Modeling," 14–15, and Hall, *Color and Meaning*, 95, 123–9. On the same argument, see also *Il Tondo Doni di Michelangelo e il suo Restauro*, ed. Luciano Berti et al. (Florence: Uffizi, Centro Studi e Ricerche, Centro Di, 1985): 77–9. Cf. Leonardo's *colorito* and sfumato, for which see John Shearman, "Leonardo's Colour and Chiaroscuro," *Zeitschrift für Kunstgeschichte* 25 (1962): 13–47; Kathleen Weil-Garris Posner, "Raphael's *Transfiguration* and the Legacy of Leonardo," *Art Quarterly* 35 (1972): 343–74; Alexander Nagel, "Leonardo and sfumato," *Anthropology and Aesthetics* 24 (1993): 7–20; John Moffitt, "Leo's 'sfumato' and Apelles's 'atramentum,'" *Paragone Arte* 40, NS, no. 16 (473), (July 1989), 88–94.

37. Vasari/Barocchi, 6: 63. The *Leda* is known through several copies; the engraving by Nicholas Beatrizet and the two paintings, one in the National Gallery, London, and the other in the Museo Correr, Venice, are probably those closest to the original. See Cecil Gould, *Catalogue of the Sixteenth-Century Italian Schools* (London: National Gallery, the Trustees, 1975; reprint, 1987), 150–1. For Michelangelo's *Leda*, his use of tempera and hatred of oil, and falling out with Sebastiano, see now Goffen, *Titian's Women*, 229, 231–9.

38. Baldassare Castiglione, *The Book of the Courtier*, trans. Charles S. Singleton (New York: Doubleday, 1959), bk. I, chap. LII, 80.

39. In his *Della pittura*, bk. II, Alberti states that "painting and sculpture are cognate arts, nurtured by the same genius. But I shall always prefer the genius of the painter, as it attempts by far the most difficult task.... I have always regarde it as a mark of an excellent and superior mind in any person whom I saw take great delight in painting." English translation from Leon Battista Alberti, *On Painting and on Sculpture*, ed. Cecil Grayson (London: Phaidon, 1972), 65.

40. Castiglione *The Book*, 79. It is highly meaningful that Michelangelo is referred to as a sculptor, not a painter.

41. Castiglione had been in Rome several times, but between 1513 and 1516 he lived in the papal city uninterruptedly, in close association with Bembo, Tebaldeo, Fregoso, and Raphael. See Robert W. Hanning and David Rosand, eds., *Castiglione. The Ideal*

and the Real in Renaissance Culture (New Haven and London: Yale University Press, 1983), XX–XI.

42. Sebastiano was already familiar with *paragone*; in Venice Giorgione was experimenting with the possibilities of the representation of many points of view in the two-dimensional image. See, for example, Pino's account of the multiple views at first glance invented by Giorgione, to "the perpetual confusion of sculptors" (Mary Pardo, "Paolo Pino's Dialogo di Pittura: A Translation with Commentary" [Ph.D. diss., University of Pittsburgh, 1984], 367). On Sebastiano's interaction with Venetian sculptors, see also Barbieri, *Sebastiano*, 11–18.

43. Francesco Maria Molza, *Stanze sopra il Ritratto della Signora Giulia Gonzaga*, st. XV, in Pier Antonio Serassi, ed., *Delle poesie volgari e latine di Francesco Maria Molza* (Bergamo, 1747), 1: 139: "Tu, che lo stile con mirabil cura/ pareggi col martello, e la grandezza/ che sola possedea già la scultura/ ai colori doni e non minor vaghezza,/ sì che superba gir può la pittura,/ sola per te salita a tanta altezza,/ col senno, onde n'apristi il bel segreto,/ muovi pensoso a l'alta impresa e lieto" (translation provided by author). The same poem is quoted by Varchi, *Due Lezzioni*, in Barocchi, *Raphaelis Urbinatis*, 3 : 532. The portrait of *Giulia Gonzaga* has not been identified with certainty: see Hirst, *Sebastiano del Piombo*, 115–19, and Lucco, *Le opere*, 121, who suggests the *Portrait of a Lady*, Longford Castle, Salisbury, earl of Radnor.

44. Vasari/Barocchi, 5: 86.

45. Varchi, *Due lezzioni*, in Barocchi, *Raphaelis Urbinatis*, 3 : 532. On Sebastiano's interests in finding new surfaces for painting, for example, slate instead of panel or canvas, intended to challenge sculpture in terms of durability, see Marco Chiarini, "Pittura su pietra," *Antichità viva* IX (1970): 29–37; see also Barbieri, *Sebastiano*, 15–19.

46. "E con quell'arte, di che solo onori/ il secol nostro e lo fai chiaro e bello,/ con nuovo uso agguagliando i tuoi colori/ alle forze d'incude e di martello" (translation provided by author). Gandolfo Porrino, the secretary of Giulia Gonzaga, was, according to Vasari, on intimate terms with Sebastiano (Vasari/Barocchi, 5: 100). Porrino's poem, published by Serassi together with Molza's and mistakenly ascribed to him (st. XLII, p. 148), was also quoted by Varchi in his *Due Lezzioni* (Barocchi, *Raphaelis Urbinatis*, 3 : 533). Varchi's interpretation of the two poems by Molza and Porrino seems to me equivocal: in reporting the sculptor's criticism on the frailty of painting, he states that the painters advocate the use of marble as a support, in order to obtain eternal works. Then he quotes the poems to prove this fact. Molza and Porrino were clearly using the comparison between the brush and the hammer as a metaphor to stress Sebastiano's achievements in both the use of color and the effects of *rilievo*, however, not to illustrate the new painting technique with oil on marble.

47. Lucco, *Le opere*, 99–100; Hirst, *Sebastiano del Piombo*, 33–6.

48. For Chigi's activity in Venice, see Felix Gilbert, *The Pope, His Banker, and Venice* (Cambridge, MA and London: Harvard University Press, 1980).

49. Although Vasari stated that Raphael painted his *Galatea* before Sebastiano's *Polyphemus* (Vasari/Barocchi, 5: 87), scholars agree on the fact that it was presumably Sebastiano who began the wall decoration after having completed the lunettes, also in the light of technical analysis. See Sydney J. Freedberg, *Painting in Italy 1500–1600*, Pelican History of Art, rev. ed. (Harmondsworth, England: Penguin Books, 1975; first edition New Haven and London, 1971), 68; Alma Maria Mignosi Tantillo, "Restauri alla Farnesina," *Bollettino d'Arte*, 57 (1972): 33–42, esp. 40; Lucco, *Le opere*, 100–1; and Hirst, *Sebastiano del Piombo*, 34.

50. See the hypothesis advanced by Hirst, *Sebastiano del Piombo*, 34, in relation to a heavy flooding of the Villa in 1514, that could have caused the patron to renounce the decoration of the garden loggia.

51. See n. 49.

52. Hirst, *Sebastiano del Piombo*, 36. See also Pallucchini, *Sebastian Viniziano*, 33.

53. Giuseppe Cugnoni, *Agostino Chigi il Magnifico* (Rome: Società Romana di Storia Patria, 1878), 29. See also Ingrid D. Rowland, ed., *The Correspondence of Agostino Chigi (1466–1520) in Cod. Chigi R.V.c.* (Città del Vaticano: Biblioteca Apostolica Vaticana, 2001), 20–1.

54. For the discussion of the artistic tastes of Agostino Chigi, see Rowland, *Correspondence*, 20.

55. Hirst, *Sebastiano del Piombo*, 34, n. 8.

56. Michael Hirst, "The Chigi Chapel in S. Maria della Pace," *Journal of the Warburg and Courtauld Institutes* XXIV (1961): 161–85. The altarpiece was never carried out. For Sebastiano's altarpiece in Santa Maria del Popolo, see Lucco, *Le opere*, 120–1 and Hirst, *Sebastiano del Piombo*, 87–9.

57. Vasari/de Vere, 2: 141. Vasari/Barocchi, 5: 87.

58. See Tantillo, "Restauri," who advanced evidence for the hypothesis concerning the priority of Sebastiano's painting (39) and the contrast between his *Polyphemus* and Raphael's *Galatea*, framed with the intention to separate the subject from the rest of the decoration (35). The latter's intervention – almost an intrusion, according to Tantillo (40–1) – changed and made inconsistent Sebastiano's project of decoration.

59. A. Angelini, "La Loggia della Galatea alla Villa Farnesina a Roma: l'incontro delle scuole Toscana, Umbra e Romana (1511–1514)," in *Tecnica e Stile: esempi di pittura murale del Rinascimento italiano*, ed. Eve Borsook and Fiorella Superbi Gioffredi (Milan: Silvana Editoriale d'Arte, 1986), 95–100. Curiously, the title of this article, based on Sebastiano's Venetian technique compared with Raphael's, has no reference to the Venetian school. According to Angelini (95–6), Raphael's and Peruzzi's colors, compared with Sebastiano's lively *cangianti*, look almost naïve. Angelini noticed that Sebastiano, in the *Polyphemus*, used for the first time in Rome the so called '*pastellone*,' that is, plaster with brick powder added. This mixture created colored ground color, with a surface as smooth as marble, very much suited for the 'incarnati.' Also Tantillo, "Restauri," 36–9, recorded a reddish plaster for the incarnati.

60. Vasari/De Vere, 1: 643. Vasari/Barocchi, 4: 45.

61. Vasari/De Vere, 2: 141. Vasari/Barocchi, 5: 87.

62. See Hall, *Color and Meaning*, 102: "The preparation of the wall [for the *Polyphemus*] followed the Venetian method, resulting in a purplish-gray tint to the intonaco. Raphael's wall for the *Galatea* adjacent had been prepared in the same way, apparently because Sebastiano was originally supposed to paint it as well, so that Raphael could not have avoided learning of the technique." According to Angelini ("La Loggia," 101), it was at the time of the Stanza d'Eliodoro that Raphael took advantage of a new color technique, possibly inspired by the Venetian.

63. See, for example, Charles Davis, "A Note for Sebastiano del Piombo Portraitist," in *Mitteilungen des Kunsthistorisches Institutes in Florenz* XXVI/3 (1982): 383–8, who analyzed the similarities between Raphael's and Sebastiano's group portraits.

64. For the Borgherini chapel, see Lucco, *Le opere*, 108–10, and Hirst, *Sebastiano del Piombo*, 49–65. For Sebastiano's oil painting, see Hall, 1992, 104. For Raphael's presence in the Sala di Costantino, see Jones and Penny, *Raphael*, 243.

65. Paolo Giovio, "Fragmentum trium dialogorum," in Barocchi, *Raphaelis Urbinatis*, 1: 22 (as in n. 26): "In humanis vultibus, quos egregie Sebastianus exprimit, suaves et liquidos tractos blandissimis coloribus convelatos intuemur."

66. Paolo Giovio, "Raphaelis Urbinatis Vita," in Barocchi, *Raphaelis Urbinatis*, 1: 16–17: "Ante alios autem Sebastianus Venetus oris similitudinis incomparabili felicitate repraesentat, qui et singulari cum laude picturas mira tenuitate linearum excitare ac

amoeno subinde colorum transitu adumbrare didicit" (translation provided by author).

67. Cesare Brandi, "The Restoration of *The Pietà* of Sebastiano del Piombo," *Museum* 3 (1950): 207–19, esp. 208.

68. Ibid.: "This great painting, which has always been so admired, requires for its restoration the use of a very delicate technique, owing to the fact that it was almost entirely overlaid with glazes.... On the ground coat the painter spread a thick layer of oil ... this layer was not uniform but made up of dull and light grey.... On this rough layer have been superimposed layers which are so liquid and transparent that they resemble water-colour.... The old dark varnish, which stood out particularly against the white colours (the small flowers in the foreground, the waterfall, the shroud of the Christ) had been expressly chosen in order to veil the brilliance of the pure colour while maintaining for it the freshness of an unblended tone. Had it not been the artist's intention to make use of the roughness of the thick colour and of the brush-marks, he would not have painted with such a heavy hand a picture of which the first paint layer was smooth. It was precisely this smooth surface which was to give way to a kind of uneven, plastic granulation.... The secret of the unforgettable moonbeam ... simply lies in these splendid glazes, which the previous restorers had darkened but not removed." On Sebastiano's technique see the recent analysis by Bruno Marocchini, "La Pietà di Viterbo: la tecnica di esecuzione" in *Notturno Sublime* (2004), 89–95, which basically confirms Brandi's observations.

69. Lorenzo Lazzarini, "The Use of Color by Venetian Painters, 1480–1580: Materials and Technique," in Hall "From Modeling," 115–136. In the same article, Lazzarini states that Sebastiano, like Titian, continued Giorgione's technical innovation of painting with overlying colors. On Giorgione's and Sebastiano's painting technique and underdrawing see also Jayne Anderson, *Giorgione. The painter of poetic brevity* (Paris-New York: Flammarion, 1997), 83–12.

70. Brandi, "Restoration," 208.

71. Maria Grazia Franceschini, "Il restauro ottocentesco della *Pietà* di Sebastiano del Piombo (da un carteggio conservato nell'Archivio di Stato di Viterbo)," *Biblioteca e Società* 7–8 (1985–6): 40–2. In 1839, a french painter, Montessuy, damaged the *Pietà* by tracing its design and using oil to brighten up colors. It was then sent to Rome and restored by G. Camuccini, Ispettore delle Pitture Pubbliche of Rome. See also Anna Maria Corbo, "Sulla *Pietà* e *Flagellazione* di Sebastiano del Piombo," in *Lunario Romano. Rinascimento nel Lazio* IX (1979): 129–36.

72. For chiaroscuro, related to Sebastiano's virtuoso performance of Christ's flesh – a particularly soft coloring that any Renaissance viewer would have understood as the Venetian imprint – I simply mean the interaction of light, shade, and color, not as separate departments, but, as clarified by John Shearman ("Leonardo's Colour," 13) in discussing Leonardo's color, as simply one medium.

73. See Roger Jones and Nicholas Penny, *Raffaello* (Milan: Jaca Book, 1983), 159, 162; for Lazzarini's analysis see n. 69 to this chapter.

74. For Raphael, see Jones and Penny, *Raphael*, 128–9.

75. For Raphael's modal thinking, that is, a color mode that matches the content with the appropriate color style, see Hall, *Color and Meaning*, 102–4.

76. Marcia Hall ("From Modeling," 18) has already indicated the differences between the Stanza della Segnatura and the Stanza d'Eliodoro, with its blackish shadows. On Raphael's dark tonality of his late works, see Weil-Garris, "Raphael's *Transfiguration*", 349. For the chronology of Raphael's Stanza d'Eliodoro, see S. Ferino Pagden, "Raphael's Heliodorus Vault and Michelangelo's Sistine Ceiling: An Old Controversy and a New Drawing," *Burlington Magazine* 132 (1990): 201–3.

77. Cf. with Jones and Penny, *Raphael*, 125. See Vasari's enthusiastic description of Raphael's *Liberation of Saint Peter.* "Questa è la più divina e da tutti tenuta la più rara" (Vasari/Barocchi, 4: 179–80).

78. For the chronology of the *Pietà* see n. 11. Stylistic and historical data invite one to anticipate the execution of the *Pietà* to 1514, more or less during – if even not before – Raphael's *Liberation of Saint Peter.*

79. In 1566 Cartaro copied the Viterbo *Pietà* with few variations, crediting the invention of the composition to Michelangelo. For the biography of Cartaro, see Vincenzo Federici, "Di Mario Cartaro Incisore Viterbese nel Sec. XVI," *Archivio della Reale Società Romana di Storia Patria* 21 (1898): 535–52. See Cartaro's biography by Fabia Borroni in the *Dizionario biografico degli italiani* (Rome: Istituto della Enciclopedia Italiana, 1977), 20: 796–9, who did not recognize the derivation from Sebastiano's *Pietà*. See, most recently, Evelina Borea, "Roma 1565–1578: intorno a Cornelis Cort," in *Fiamminghi a Roma. 1508–1568*. Atti del Convegno Internazionale, ed. Nicole Dacos, Supplement to *Bollettino d'Arte* 100 (1997): 215–30, esp. 218, who correctly identified Sebastiano's authorship, and Emilia Talamo, "Mario Cartaro e l'incisione della *Pietà*," in *Notturno Sublime*, 2004, 39–41.

80. In the engraving, the flames appear to be consuming several buildings, reducing their walls to ashes and revealing their frames. Indeed, black profiles of burned frames are still visible along the skyline in the painting, together with a reddish color. Moreover, in Cartaro's engraving, Mary appears with tearful eyes. Mary has no tears in Sebastiano's painting, but they were originally present since Vasari recorded them in describing the *Pietà*: "un Cristo morto con Nostra Donna che lo piagne" (Vasari/Barocchi, 5: 89).

81. (Marcantonio Michiel), *The Anonimo. Notes on Pictures and Works of Art in Italy Made by an Anonymous Writer in the Sixteenth Century*, ed. George C. Williamson, trans. Piero Mussi (New York: Blom, 1969): 162. The landscape *all'antica* as a motif deriving from classic models such as *Pastorale* or *Idillio*, especially in Giorgione's paintings, is stressed by Goetz Pochat, *Figur und Landschaft* (Berlin-New York: De Gruyter, 1973), 375–7. See, more recently, David Rosand, "Giorgione, Venice and the Pastoral Vision," in Robert C. Cafritz, Lawrence Gowing, David Rosand, *Places of Delight. The Pastoral Landscape*, exh. cat., Washington, DC, The Phillips Collection, November 6, 1988–January 22, 1989 (London: Weidenfeld and Nicolson, 1988), 21–81.

82. For a recent discussion of the problem concerning the identification of this painting, see Anderson, *Giorgione*, 294–5.

83. The painting is known through the copy by David Teniers the Younger (now at Austin, University of Texas, Jack S. Blanton Museum of Art). See Anderson, *Giorgione*, 317.

84. For the analysis of the landscape of the *Pietà*, see Freedberg, *Painting in Italy*, 67: "The conception is emphatically a sculptor's, of a figure's group that is massive and aggressively substantial....But despite the action on him of Rome and Michelangelo, Sebastiano is not only residually Venetian, but above all a painter, and he has given the sculptor's theme a context of landscape, moonlit, tragic, and romantical, that vibrates with *Giorgionismo*.... As it appears they meant this work to do, Michelangelo and Sebastiano made an effective challenge in it to the highest classical accomplishment to date of Raphael." More recently Hirst (*Sebastiano del Piombo*, 48), crediting the invention of the landscape and its Giorgionesque features to Sebastiano, yet making him a passive executor of Michelangelo's *invenzione*, stressed the inconsistency of the final effect of the *Pietà*: "In the Viterbo panel there is a marked disjunction between figures and setting in terms of tone. The two forms are brightly lit, plastic units; they come close to pictorial divorce from

the dark *tenebroso* landscape lit fitfully by the moon." However, the impression of a "pictorial divorce" may be generated by a recent selective cleaning of the *Pietà*: the two figures, where the hues are light and stronger, have been cleaned, while the landscape, with its frail dark colors, has remained untouched. I wish to thank Lorenza D'Alessandro, restorer, for her kind suggestions after a close scrutiny of the painting.

85. Brandi, "Restoration," 203: "The landscape likewise was darkened with a sort of 'beverone' (wash). That explains why the group of the Virgin and the Christ seems to stand out and dominate the painting, whereas the landscape was the finest part of the painting."

86. Vasari/Barocchi, 5: 89: "Sebastiano...vi fece un paese tenebroso molto lodato." Michael Hirst (*Sebastiano del Piombo*, 48) pronounces the panel the first nocturnal altarpiece: "It seems to have been the first Roman altar-piece of its period carried out as a nocturne."

87. Paolo Giovio, *Raphaelis Urbinatis Vita*, in Barocchi, *Raphaelis Urbinatis*, 1: 14: "Pinxit in Vaticano...cubicula duo ad praescriptum Iulii Pontificis:..., in altero ad Christi sepulchrum armati custodes in ipsa noctis umbra dubia quadam luce refulgent" (translation provided by author).

88. Hirst, "The Chigi Chapel," 171–4: "An altarpiece conceived in highly dramatic language, which must date from about the period when Raphael was completing the second Stanza....Whether Raphael had a night scene in mind we cannot say. But when we recall that all four scenes...show a particular preoccupation on the artist's part with varying effects of *tenebroso*, we see that the Chigi chapel altarpiece would have provided him with another striking opportunity in this direction. None of the drawings provides us with conclusive evidence, though there is, in the group of chalk studies, an especial richness of *chiaroscuro* and a marked play of light over the forms. But we should not...neglect one piece of evidence in the form of another *Resurrection*, painted in 1519 or 1520, also commissioned by Agostino Chigi. This is the altarpiece painted by Girolamo Genga, in S. Caterina da Siena in Rome....The subject [deriving from Raphael's composition] is 'di notte.'"

89. For Sellaio's letter to Michelangelo, see Barocchi and Ristori, *Il Cartegio*, 2: 266: "15.12.1520: Bastiano...à preso una tavola alla Pace, sotto le fighure di Rafaello."

90. For Renaissance painters' fascination with Apelle's *atramentum*, see Weil-Garris, "Raphael's *Transfiguration*," 354–5, and, by the same author, *Leonardo and Central Italian Art, 1515–1550* (New York: New York University Press, 1974), 12–18.

91. Jones and Penny, *Raphael*, 129. For the controversial attribution to Giorgione of the lost original, see the recent catalogue entry by Konrad Oberhuber in *Le siècle de Titien. L'âge d'or de la peinture à Venise* (Paris: Réunion des Museés Nationaux, 1993), 521.

92. For the chronology of the Viterbo *Pietà*, see n. 11.

93. On the Venetian taste for Flemish paintings, see Ernst H. Gombrich, "The Renaissance Theory of Art and the Rise of Landscape," in his *Norm and Form. Studies in the Art of the Renaissance*, 2d ed. (London and New York: Phaidon, 1971), 109–21: "It is in Venice, not in Antwerp, that the term 'a landscape' is first applied to any individual painting....Marc'Antonio Michiel uses the expression 'a landscape' quite freely in his notes. As early as 1521 he noted *molte tavolette di paesi* in the collection of cardinal Grimani...by the hand of Albert of Holland. We do not know if they were pure landscapes – probably they were not – but for the Italian connoisseur they were interesting as landscapes only."

94. See Sebastiano's letter to Michelangelo, dated 2 July 1518, in Barocchi and Ristori, *Il Carteggio*, 2: 32: "L'o intertenuta tanto, ché non voglio che Rafaello veda la mia, insino lui non ha fornita la sua."

95. See, for instance, Vasari in Barocchi, *Raphaelis Urbinatis*, 3: 495–6; Ludovico Dolce in Roskill, *Dolce's "Aretino,"* 154–5, and, with particular emphasis on night landscapes – a particular legacy of Venetian art – Cristoforo Sorte, *Osservationi nella pittura* (Venice: Girolamo Zenaro, 1580), cc. 11r–12r.

96. Castiglione *The Book*, 80 as in n. 38. The character discussing the advantages of painting over sculpture is Ludovico da Canossa. For the analysis of this paragraph, inspired to the accomplishments of the Venetian painters, especially Giorgione, see Andrew J. Martin, "Giorgione e Baldassar Castiglione. Proposte per l'interpretazione di un passo fondamentale del *Cortegiano*," *Venezia Cinquecento* 3 (1993): 57–66. For a different opinion, see Weil-Garris (1974, 13), who identified in Raphael's *Transfiguration* the model to which Castiglione refers in the *Courtier*. "He mentions some of the very elements that characterize the poetry of the *Transfiguration*, with its 'oscura notte.'" Contrary to this, Jones and Penny (1983, 129) trace the origin of this kind of subject to Venetian oil painting. See also Hall, "From Modeling," 42 n. 27. It seems to me that the *Transfiguration* (1517–20) dates too late to have been referred to by Castiglione's account. The *Book of the Courtier* was already circulating in the second decade of the sixteenth century: Castiglione wrote in 1515 the prologue to the first redaction, and a second redaction was sent to Sadoleto in 1518; see Robert W. Hanning and David Rosand, "Chronology," in Hanning and Rosand, *Castiglione*, xxi.

97. As noted by Jones and Penny (*Raphael*, 128–9) in relation to Raphael's second Stanza.

98. Correctly pointed out by Michael Hirst, *Sebastiano del Piombo*, 69, n. 18.

99. Vasari/de Vere, 2: 143–4. Vasari/Barocchi, 5: 91. According to Christa Gardned Von Teuffel ("Sebastiano del Piombo, Raphael, and Narbonne: New Evidence," *Burlington Magazine* 126 [1984]: 764–6), the *Raising of Lazarus* was a monumental altarpiece and not a lateral for a chapel with Raphael's *Transfiguration*. See also Hirst, *Sebastiano del Piombo*, 67 n. 9, and Lucco, 1980, 110–11. For a recent discussion of this grand competition see Goffen, *Renaissance Rivals*, 46–55.

100. Hirst, *Sebastiano del Piombo*, 66–7.

101. Vasari/de Vere, 2: 144: "[*The Resurrection of Lazarus*] was counterfeited and painted with supreme diligence under the direction of Michelangelo, and in some part from his design." Vasari/Barocchi, 5: 91.

102. Barocchi and Ristori, *Il Carteggio*, 1: 243: "Ora mi pare che Rafaello metta sotosopra el mondo perché lui non la facia, per non venire a paraghoni." The letter is dated 19 January 1517.

103. Ibid.

104. Hirst, *Sebastiano del Piombo*, 69, 71.

105. Letter by Domenico Terranova to Michelangelo: Barocchi and Ristori, 1965–83, 2: 38: "Raphaello ... opera quanto può con monsignore reverendissimo che tale lavoro si finisca d'innorare in Francia, per fare dispecto a Bastiano."

106. Letter of 1 May 1519, in Barocchi and Ristori, *Il Carteggio*, 2: 187: "Ogn'uomo resta balordo." See also Hirst, *Sebastiano del Piombo*, 68–9; Lucco, *Le opere*, 110.

107. Sebastiano to Michelangelo, 12 April 1520, in Barocchi and Ristori, *Il Carteggio*, 2: 227: "Ho portato la mia tavola un'altra volta a Palazo con quella che ha facto Rafaello et non ho avuto vergogna."

108. Vasari/De Vere, 2: 144. Vasari/Barocchi, 5: 91.

109. Hirst, *Sebastiano del Piombo*, 68. The changes from the first to the final version of the *Transfiguration* are analyzed by K. Oberhuber, "Vorzeichnungen zu Raffaels *Transfiguration*," in *Jahrbuch der Berliner Museen* IV (1962): 116.

110. Freedberg, *Raphael, Michelangelo*, 14–15. Freedberg explained that the affinities between the two paintings may be explained by "the notable process of intersection we have observed between these two chief painters."

111. Ibid., 11–13, 16–17; Hall, *Color and Meaning,* 133.

112. Hall, *Color and Meaning,* 133–4: "His (Sebastiano's) dialogue with Raphael, discussed by scholars in terms of composition and tenor of speech, was as importantly, perhaps more importantly, carried on in color."

113. According to Hirst's analysis of the color technique of the *Transfiguration,* in relation to the *Raising of Lazarus,* Raphael's figures "may be cut by shadows, but they do not fuse with it," as Sebastiano's (Hirst, *Sebastiano del Piombo,* 73).

114. The paintings, largely executed by Giulio Romano, are dated 1518, and, according to Hall ("From Modeling," 14, 19), painted in the chiaroscuro mode.

115. Barocchi and Ristori, *Il Carteggio,* 2: 32: "Duolmi ne l'animo non sette stato in Roma a veder dua quadri che son iti in Franza, del principe de la Sinagoga, che credo non vi possete imaginar cossa più contraria ala opinion vostra de quello haveresti visto in simel opera. Io non vi dirò altro che pareno figure che siano state al fumo, o vero figure de ferro che luceno, tutte chiare e tutte nere, et desegnate al modo ve dirà Leonardo" (translation provided by author). See Weil-Garris's discussion of Sebastiano's criticism to Raphael ("Raphael's *Transfiguration,* 352): "For the Venetian, the idea of 'smoke' (fumo) may also have carried the association with Leonardo's *sfumato* darkness that it does for us today, and the letter may reflect the Venetian's awareness of the source of the darkness he criticized in Raphael." However, although Weil-Garris equated Raphael's smoky figures to Leonardo's sfumato, the intended meaning of Sebastiano's "figure che siano state al fumo" is, literally, blackened with smoke, with no Leonardesque consequence.

116. Hall, "From Modeling," 14: "The chiaroscuro mode strives for dramatic effect through contrast of light and shade....Beside Sebastiano del Piombo and il Sodoma, Giulio Romano exploited it....Raphael himself provided the archetype with his masterful creation of a night scene in this mode, the *Liberation of Saint Peter* in the Stanza d'Eliodoro." In my understanding, however, Sebastiano's chiaroscuro is characterized by a major emphasis on *velature.*

117. Vasari/Barocchi, 4: 207. Vasari/de Vere, 2: 744.

118. Hirst, *Sebastiano del Piombo,* 74. For the use of realgar, idem, 73. For the Venetian origin of Sebastiano's dark manner, see Hall, "From Modeling," 27 n. 42: "I cannot subscribe to the view, advocated by Weil-Garris Posner (1974) that he owed his chiaroscuro style to Leonardo's precedent, unless it might be through his master, Giorgione. Nor do I agree with some earlier writers who connect Sebastiano's color with Michelangelo. His dependence upon Michelangelo does not extend to color, in my view, and his use of the chiaroscuro modality predates his arrival to Rome. He used a black background in his *Saint Louis of Toulouse* in the Accademia."

119. Hall, Color and Meaning, 137–8.

120. See n. 6.

121. Leatrice Mendelsohn, *Varchi's "Due Lezzioni": Paragone and Cinquecento Art Theory* (Ph.D. diss., New York University, 1978), 246–247: "sculpture had acquired a more positive platonic connotation...from earliest classical times it was thought that sculpture could not only represent, but could possess the essence of the god....In the fifteen-forties, the climate was ripe for renewing sculpture's early positive association with divinity. Aided with the example of Michelangelo, the sculptor was again identified with the poet, and his work seen not as mere fabrication of nature, but as an invocation of divine power. If 'defining' was the same as expressing 'essences,' then sculpture was an art of 'definition,' while painting as a representation of particulars or 'accidents' was merely descriptive."

122. Castiglione *The Book,* 106–7.

123. Hall, *Color and Meaning,* 2: "The Venetian critics of the mid-sixteenth century understandably rejected Vasari's position, but not by asserting the primacy of color. Dolce

held that both *colore* and *disegno* were essential – he would not permit Titian to
be praised 'because he tints well'....Many of the other writers in the late sixteenth
century also dissented on Vasari's views in various ways; significantly, however, no
one reversed Vasari's priorities and insisted on the superiority of *colore* to *disegno*."
Even Dolce, from the Venetian camp, although claiming the equal importance of *colore*, criticized the use of color *per se*: "that diversity of colors, which most painters
nowadays affect in their work...please the eyes of the ignorant and are also outside
the bound of probability....Some painters do not know how to imitate the different
nuances of cloth, but put the colours on fully saturated as they stand, so that in
their works there is nothing to praise but the colours" (Roskill, *Dolce's* "Aretino," 208).
On the *paragone* debate concerning *disegno* versus *colorito*, and Michelangelo versus
Titian, especially in relation to Titian's *Danae*, see now Goffen, *Titian's Women*, 224–5,
229, 234–5, 240–1.

124. Mendelsohn, *Varchi's "Due Lezzioni*," 271: "Painting's edge is only in respect to the
depiction of 'minutiae' and colors which are accidents, it does not supersede sculpture
either in regard to 'substantive things' (*cose sostanziali*), or 'in making things as similar
to reality as possible' (*più somiglianti al vivo che possono*), because sculpture is less
deceptive, and closer to truth."

CHAPTER 7. RAPHAEL'S WORKSHOP AND THE DEVELOPMENT OF A MANAGERIAL STYLE

A version of this essay was presented as a paper at the Renaissance Society of America's
conference in March 2002. I am grateful to Marcia Hall for inviting me to participate
in her session, "The Legacy of Raphael," and for the many comments and observations
made in response to my presentation at that meeting. Further research and the writing
of this essay were supported by the Metropolitan Museum of Art during my residences
there as an Andrew W. Mellon Fellow. In particular, I would like to thank Dr. George
Goldner, with whose Department of Drawings and Prints I was associated during my
stay at the Met.

1. From the vast literature, I cite a few representative studies, all with extensive bibliogra-
phies. For discussions of the drawings of Raphael's shop in the context of a specific
commission, see John Shearman, *Raphael's Cartoons in the Collection of Her Majesty
the Queen and the Tapestries for the Sistine Chapel* (London: Phaidon Press, 1972). For
catalogues of the works of the various artists involved, see Martin Clayton, *Raphael
and His Circle* (London: Merrell Holberton, 1999); J. A. Gere, *Drawings by Raphael and
His Circle* (New York: Pierpont Morgan Library, 1987); Philip Pouncey and J. A. Gere,
*Italian Drawings in the Department of Prints and Drawings in the British Museum;
Raphael and his Circle*, 2 vols. (London: Trustees of the British Museum, 1962); *Autour
de Raphaël: dessins et peintures du Musée du Louvre* (Paris: Musée du Louvre, 1983–4).
2. Giorgio Vasari, *Lives of the Painters, Sculptors and Architects*, trans. Gaston Du C. de
Vere (New York: Knopf, 1996), I: 737–8.
3. Ibid.
4. For its fusion of research from technical, formal, and historical bases, the work of
Arnold Nesselrath in the Vatican Stanze should be singled out as exemplary. Some of
his findings will be discussed later in the essay.
5. Marcia Hall, ed., *The Princeton Raphael Symposium* (Princeton: Princeton University
Press, 1990), xv.
6. Ibid., 116.
7. Shearman, *Raphael's Cartoons*, 115.
8. Ibid., 124.
9. Ibid., 63.

10. Thomas P. Campbell, *Tapestries in the Renaissance: Art and Magnificence* (New York: Metropolitan Museum of Art and New Haven: Yale University Press, 2002), 192, for both the differences between Raphael's cartoons and the conventional preparatory drawings, as well as the hypothesis about reuse of the elaborate drawings.

11. Shearman, *Raphael's Cartoons*, 112.

12. This point can be seen as an expansion of, or perhaps as a corollary to, the observation that John Shearman made in his essay on the Raphael shop about the elasticity of its arrangement, noting that "Il gruppo degli aiuti si allargò e si contrasse secondo i lavori in corso, e sembra che ci sia stata una grande varietà di affiliazioni più o meno casuali." See "Raffaello e la bottega," in *Raffaello in Vaticano* (Milan: Electa, 1984), 258.

13. See L. D. Ettlinger, *The Sistine Chapel before Michelangelo* (Oxford: Clarendon Press, 1965), 30–1; Roberto Salvini also suggests that Perugino was the primary artist, *La Capella Sistina in Vaticano*, vol. 1 (Milan: Rizzoli, 1965), 31. For earlier documentation, Paolo Giovio recorded that Perugino received the most recognition in the Sistine, saying that Sixtus "gli dette la palma quando gli artisti gareggiarono aspramente nel decorare la sua cappella privata." Paola Barocchi, ed., *Scritti d'arte del cinquecento*, vol. 1 (Milan and Naples: Riccardo Ricciardi, 1971), 19.

14. For clarifying thoughts along similar lines, see the comments by Marcia Hall in her section on Raphael's "Working Practices," in *After Raphael* (Cambridge and New York: Cambridge University Press, 1999), 49–50. Among other ideas is the suggestion that Raphael may have anticipated the stylistic diversity in the Loggia and considered it appropriate, in part encouraged by the segmented architectural form of the bays (50).

15. Arnold Nesselrath, "Lorenzo Lotto in the Stanza della Segnatura," *Burlington Magazine* 142 (1999): 4–12.

16. I am in agreement with the assessment made by Nesselrath, who also proposes a date of c. 1514 for the workshop's formation; ibid., 12.

17. Vasari specifically used the word "school" on several occasions when speaking of Raphael and his assistants. For example, in the *Vita* of Giovanni da Udine, Vasari states that due to an introduction from Baldassare Castiglione, Giovanni was "accomodato nella scuola de' giovani di Raffaello," and later that "niun de' giovani di quella scuola il superava." Giorgio Vasari, *Le vite de' più eccellenti pittori scultori ed architettori*, ed. Gaetano Milanesi, (Florence: Sansoni, 1906), 6: 550.

18. Jones and Penny, *Raphael*, 4.

19. Carmen Bambach, *Drawing and Painting in the Italian Renaissance Workshop* (Cambridge and New York: Cambridge University Press, 1999), 15. In a later discussion Bambach notes that "Raphael continued to invent his designs" through the practices of compositional sketches and life studies (314).

20. This incident is cited in Hall's introduction to this volume.

21. David Alan Brown, "Raphael, Leonardo, and Perugino: Fame and Fortune in Florence," in *Leonardo, Michelangelo, and Raphael in Renaissance Florence from 1500 to 1508*, ed. Serafina Hager (Washington, DC: Georgetown University Press, 1992), 41.

22. Paolo Giovio, taken from the "Fragmentum trium dialogorum," in *Scritti d'arte del cinquecento*, ed. Paola Barocchi (Milano-Napoli: R. Ricciardi:, 1971) 1: 20. I have translated the passage from Barocchi's Italian version, "l'inaridirsi della sua fantasia lo costrinse a tornare sempre a quei volti leziosi in cui si era fissato da giovane, tanto che il suo animo reggeva a stento alla vergogna" (20). She describes the fragment as "una esemplificazione figurativa dei pericoli connessi all'età degli artisti" (19). The citation from Giovio is also discussed by Brown, "Raphael," 43.

23. See the essay by Janet Cox-Rearick in the exhibition catalogue *Giulio Romano Master Designer* (New York: Hunter College, City University of New York, 1999), esp. 19–20.

24. Ibid., 20.

25. "Ne ho dato un altro pezzo a Figurino quale s'è del tutto partito da me, in modo ch'io non voglio mai più far allievo alcuno" (23 May 1538). *Giulio Romano: repertorio di fonti documentarie*, ed. Daniela Ferrari (Rome: Ministero per i beni culturali e ambientali, 1992), 2: 776.

26. "Circa alla sala io ho fatti li cartoni acciò li depintori non stiano in tempo a farli loro" (13 June 1538), ibid., 777.

27. (2 June 1538), ibid., 772.

28. "Messer Iulio ha tanto che far, a dir il vero, in disignar e dare daffare a tanti homeni che tutti vivano dil suo pane, ch'el non ha tempo de poterli solicitar, salvo che dargli una ochiatta al giorno" (23 May 1538), ibid., 764.

29. Vasari/de Vere, 733.

30. (13 June 1538), Ferrari, *Repertorio*, 777. I have also discussed this letter in my article, "Homer, Greek Heroes and Hellenism in Giulio Romano's Hall of Troy," *Journal of the Warburg and Courtauld Institutes* 51 (1988): 235–42.

31. Shearman, *Early Modern Sources*, 1516/18, vol. 1, 24. The letter dates from 19 April 1516.

32. The papal brief of 27 August 1515 gave Raphael authority to acquire marble from ruins in Rome for the Fabbrica di S Pietro, "ad impedire che le iscrizioni antiche siano distrutte dagli scarpellini." Ibid., 1515/8, 209.

33. In the view of one scholar, "L'idea della difesa dell'antico, quale noi la concepiamo, come funzione pubblica, nacque proprio in Raffaello." See Piero Buscaroli, in *Raffaello. Il pianto di Roma, lettera a Leone X* (Torino: Fògola Editore, 1984), 12–13. For the three versions of the *Letter to Leo X*, with discussion and bibliography, see Shearman, *Early Modern Sources*, 500–45.

34. Vasari says that Raphael kept designers "all over Italy, at Pozzuolo and even in Greece," presumably to commission drawings of ruins. Vasari/de Vere, 736.

35. See the letter published by Shearman, *Early Modern Sources*, 1514/6, vol. 1, 1180ff.

36. Fra Giocondo's edition of Vitruvius was published in Venice, 1511, by Giovanni Taccino. See Ingrid Rowland, "Vitruvius in Print and Vernacular Translation: Fra Giocondo, Bramante, Raphael and Cesare Ceseriano," in *Paper Palaces: The Rise of the Renaissance Architectural Treatise*, ed. Vaughan Hart (New Haven and London: Yale University Press, 1998), 105–21.

37. Vasari/Milanesi, 4: 354–5.

38. See Carla Lord, "Raphael, Marcantonio and Virgil," *Source* 3 (1984): 81–2.

39. Ibid., 81, for the apt formulation: Raphael "guided his associates in applying ancient motifs to a new technology."

CHAPTER 8. RAPHAEL'S MULTIPLES

1. My thanks for a Faculty Development Grant from the University of New Hampshire, which helped me to visit the British Museum, the Albertina, and the Szépművészeti Múzeum, Budapest, and my thanks for my kind reception at each and also at the Museum of Fine Arts, Boston. A shorter version of this paper was given at the Renaissance Society of America meeting in Arizona in 2002, under the title "Disegno for Sale." The following were not available to the author at the time of writing in 2002, but are recommended to readers: Corinna Höper, *Raffael und die Folgen, Das Kunstwerk in Zeitaltern seiner graphischen Reproduzierbarkeit* (Stuttgart: Hatje Cantz Verlag, 2001); Lisa Pon, *Raphael, Dürer, and Marcantonio Raimondi, Copying and the Italian Renaissance Print* (New Haven: Yale University Press, 2004); Christopher Witcombe, *Copyright in the Renaissance: prints and the privilegio in sixteenth-century Venice and Rome* (Leiden: Brill,

2004) and Ben Thomas, "The Dissemination of *Disegno*: Baccio Bandinelli and Anton Francesco Doni," *Print Quarterly*, forthcoming.

2. The basic bibliography includes Innis Shoemaker, *The Engravings of Marcantonio Raimondi*, exh. cat. (Lawrence, KS: Spencer Museum of Art, 1981); Gianvittorio Dillon, "Il vero Marcantonio," in *Studi su Raffaello*, ed. Micaela Sambucco Hamoud and Maria Strocchi, Atti del Congresso Internazionale di Studi 1984 (Urbino: QuattroVenti, 1987), I: 551–61; *Raphael Invenit: Stampe da Raffaello nelle Collezioni dell'Istituto Nazionale per la Grafica*, ed. Grazia Bernini Pezzini (Rome: Edizioni Quasar, 1985); *Bologna e l'umanesimo, 1490–1510*, ed. Marzia Faietti and Konrad Oberhuber (Bologna: Nuova Alfa Editoriale, 1988), esp. 43–236; *Roma e lo stile classico di Raffaello, 1515–1527*, ed. Konrad Oberhuber, exh. cat., Palazzo Te and Albertina (Milan: Electa, 1999); Stefania Massari, *Giulio Romano pinxit et delineavit* (Rome: Fratelli Palombi, 1993); *Illustrated Bartsch*, vols. 26–27; as well as the still important Henri Delaborde, *Marc-Antoine Raimondi,...étude historique et critique* (Paris: Librairie de l'Art, c. 1888).

3. B. 487, *The Climbers*, after Michelangelo's *Battle of Cascina* cartoon in Florence, is dated 1510.

4. Matthias Winner ("Allusio auf die Reliquie der Veronika in Raffaels Eliodor," in *The Holy Face and the Paradox of Representation*, Villa Spelman Colloquia, vol. 6 [Bologna: Nuova Alfa, 1998], 301–17) finds this so incredible that he suggests the portrait is instead of the functionary Pietro de Folariis and the reference to the relic of the vera icon. Vasari identified the figures in the fresco and used a less bearded version for the woodcut portrait in the *Vite*. See Wolfram Prinz (*Vasaris Sammlung von Künstlerbildnissen*, Beiheft zu Band XII, *Mitteilungen des Kunsthistorischen Institutes in Florenz* 115 [1966]: 133–4, where, interestingly, a comparison to Dürer's appearance is also invoked.

5. In 1550, the following notice appeared in the "Life of Raphael," "avendo veduto Raffaello lo andare nelle stampe d'Alberto Durero, volonteroso ancor egli di mostrare quel che in tale arte poteva, fece studiare Marco Antonio Bolognese in questa pratica infinitamente; il quale riusctanto eccellente, che fece stampare le prime cose sue: la carta degli Innocenti, un Cenacolo, il Nettuno e la Santa Felicita quando bolle nell'olio. Fece poi Marco Antonio per Raffaello un numero di stampe, le quali Rafaello don ò poi al Baviera suo garzone, ch'aveva cura d'una sua donna," Vasari (IV: 190) proceeding on to mention Marco da Ravenna and Ugo da Carpi. This notice was retained in the 1568 "Life of Raphael."

6. For example, *The Drawing Collection, Stanford University Museum of Art*, ed. Lorenz Eitner, Betsy Fryberger, and Carol Osborne (Stanford: Stanford University Museum of Art, 1993), 10–13, no. 17. See also Faietti and Oberhuber, *Bologna e l'umanesimo*, op. cit.

7. Q. de Quincy, *Histoire de la vie et des ouvrages de Raphael* (Paris: Le Clere et cie, 1833), 152.

8. Konrad Oberhuber ("Raffaello e l'incisione," in *Raffaello in Vaticano* [Milan: Electa, 1984], 333–42, inter alia) argues for a distinction based on the belief that Marcantonio and his colleagues had closer access to drawings, especially preparatory ones, whereas the reproductive engravers, properly speaking, worked from finished paintings. Cf. Johann D. Passavant (1787–1861), *Raphael d'Urbin et son pére, Giovanni Santi* (Paris: Renouard, 1860, first printed 1839), I: 343: "Les gravures de Marc-Antoine ont le mèrite de nous rendre presque le souffle du maitre, qui en dirigea l'execution."

9. Walter Ivins, *Prints and Visual Communication* (Cambridge: Harvard University Press, 1953); Walter Benjamin, "The Work of Art in the Age of Mechanical Reproduction," in *Illuminations*, trans. Harry Zohn (1936; reprint, New York: Pimlico, 1968), 217–51.

10. Inter alia, Hubert Damisch, *The Judgment of Paris*, trans. John Goodman (Chicago: University of Chicago Press, 1996).

11. This same phenomenon is sometimes measured as a turn from classicism to mannerism, for the eccentric could be validated once validation represented less of an investment. At the same time, certain localized cultural phenomena may have withered as the exportable and printable ones flourished and as great reputations engulfed lesser ones.

12. See Antony Griffiths, *Landmarks in Print Collecting: Connoisseurs and Donors at the British Museum since 1753* (London: British Museum Press, 1996), 48, 51, 122, 165, 269, 280, 301. William Ottley, (*An Inquiry into the Origin and Early History of Engraving* [London: J. M'Creery, 1816]) speaks of Marcantonio's engravings as "many of them of very high price and great rarity." See also Clay Dean, Teresa Fairbanks, and Lisa Pon, *Changing Impressions: Marcantonio Raimondi and Sixteenth-Century Print Connoisseurship*, exh. cat. (New Haven: Yale University Art Gallery, 1999).

13. See Charles Blanc, "L'oeuvre de Marc-Antoine reproduit par la photographie," *Gazette des Beaux-Arts* XV (1863): 268–75. On Raphael's special importance for the French artistic tradition, see, inter alia, *Raphael dans les collections françaises*, exh. cat. (Paris: Editions de la Rèunion Musèes Nationaux, 1983), esp. 323ff. on engravings.

14. J. D. Passavant's monograph appeared first in 1839; his addenda to Bartsch in 1860–1; in 1887, Delaborde's reduced catalogue raisonnè of 309 works.

15. Roger Jones and Nicholas Penny, *Raphael* (New Haven: Yale University Press, 1983), 88; David Landau and Peter Parshall, *The Renaissance Print, 1470–1550* (New Haven: Yale University Press, 1994), 132–42.

16. Vincenzo Golzio, *Raffaello nei documenti* (Città del Vaticano: S. a. arti grafiche Panetto & Petrelli, 1936), 40–1. Golzio suggests that the "Baverio Charocii de Parma pictori" who was also present might be "Il baviera."

17. Giovanni Battista Armenini, *On the True Precepts of the Art of Painting*, trans. Edward Olszewski (1586; reprint, S.I.: Burt Franklin, 1977), 74, 267 (preface and bk III, xiii).

18. David Landau, "Vasari, Prints, and Prejudice," *Oxford Art Journal* VI (1983): 3–10.

19. Eugene Carroll, *Rosso Fiorentino: Drawings, Prints, and Decorative Arts*, exh. cat. (Washington, DC: National Gallery of Art, 1987), 128–33.

20. Vasari, V: 17.

21. Such a hypothesis would entail rejecting the idea that the blank tablet replaces Marcantonio's monogram, which had never been a reliable hypothesis anyway.

22. Landau and Parshall, *The Renaissance Print*, 200, 302–5.

23. Raphael was characterized in terms of his *gratia* and *venusta* as early as the "Life" by Paolo Giovio, believed to predate the Sack of Rome in 1527.

24. See Kathleen Weil-Garris Brandt, "The Self-Created Bandinelli," in *World Art: Themes of Unity in Diversity*, ed. Irving Lavin, vol. II (University Park: Pennsylvania State University Press, 1989), 497–501; (incidentally, again labelled BRANDIN, as on the *Saint Lawrence*).

25. See *Botticelli's Witness: Changing Style in a Changing Florence*, exh. cat. (Boston: Isabella Stuart Gardner Museum, 1997), cat. 10.

26. Livy, *Early History of Rome*, trans. A. de Sèlincourt (Harmondsworth: Loeb, 1960), 99, I.59: "nec ulla deinde inpudica Lucretiae exemplo vivet."

27. Patricia Emison, "The Singularity of Raphael's *Lucretia*," *Art History* XIV (1991): 373–97. For a drawing recently claimed as preparatory, see Carmen Bambach, *Metropolitan Museum of Art Bulletin* (fall 1998): 18–19.

28. A drawing for the ceiling painting of the *Judgment of Solomon* was used for the *Massacre* (Vienna), but they need not be therefore identical in date.

29. On the print, see, recently, Robert Getscher, "The *Massacre of the Innocents*, an Early Work Engraved by Marcantonio," *Artibus et Historiae* XXXIX (1999): 95–112, and Patricia Emison, "Marcantonio's *Massacre of the Innocents*," *Print Quarterly* I (1984): 257–67.

30. The drawing long cited as the source for the background seems to have been in Spain when the engraving was made, although the resemblance implies that some other version of that drawing, in which the bridge is labelled "Ponte Giudeo," was used; see Getscher, "The *Massacre*," 108.

31. Patricia Emison, "The Word Made Naked in Pollaiuolo's *Battle of the Nudes*," *Art History* XIII (1990): 261–75; idem, "The Raucousness of Mantegna's Mythological Engravings," *Gazette des Beaux-Arts* (1994): 159–76.

32. Cf. Patricia Emison, "Grazia," *Renaissance Studies* V (1991): 427–60.

33. Patricia Emison, *Low and High Style in Italian Renaissance Art* (New York: Garland, 1997), 82–5.

34. Lawrence Nees, "Le *Quos Ego* de Marc-Antoine Raimondi: L'adaption d'une source antique par Raphael," *Nouvelles de l'Estampe* (1978): 18–29, dated c. 1516. Cf. Madeleine Viljoen, "Raphael and the Restorative Power of Prints," *Print Quarterly* XVIII (2001): 379–95.

35. Eugene Delacroix, *Journals*, trans. Walter Pach (1847; reprint, New York: Covici, Friede, 1937), 156.

CHAPTER 9. RAPHAEL DRAWINGS, *PRO-CONTRA*

I am grateful to Hugo Chapman, George Goldner, Paul Joannides, and Sheryl Reiss for carefully reading earlier drafts of this essay and suggesting numerous improvements.

1. Castiglione, *The Book of the Courtier*, trans. Charles S. Singleton (Garden City, New York: Doubleday, 1959), 77. Francis Ames-Lewis evokes this passage of *The Courtier* in the opening page of *The Draftsman Raphael* (New Haven and London: Yale University Press, 1986), 1.

2. Paul Joannides, *The Drawings of Raphael with a Complete Catalogue* (Oxford: Phaidon Press, 1983), 11.

3. Raphael's "auxiliary cartoons," studies of heads (and occasionally hands) made after the final, cartoon stage (usually from the cartoon, the outlines of which were transferred by means of pouncing) as a vehicle for exploring in greater depth and detail the figure's expressive aspects, were first characterized and discussed by Oskar Fischel, "Raphael's Auxiliary Cartoons," *Burlington Magazine* 71 (1937): 167–8.

4. Vienna, Albertina, inv. Bd V, 17575; red chalk over stylus; 403 × 281 mm; on Dürer's ownership of this sheet, the nature of its relation to the *Battle at Ostia*, and the question of its authorship, see the study by Arnold Nesselrath, "Raphael's Gift to Dürer," in *Essays in Memory of Jacob Bean (1923–1992)*, ed. Linda Wolk-Simon and William M. Griswold, Master Drawings vol. 31, no. 4 (New York: Ars Libri Ltd, 1993), 376–89; see also Joannides, *Drawings of Raphael*, no. 37. With the exception of Frederick Hartt, who was overzealous in reattributing Raphael's drawings to his pupil Giulio Romano (and whose contribution to the Raphael drawings debate is discussed later), and Erwin Panofsky, scholars have unanimously regarded this sheet as the work of the master, following the arguments set forth by John Shearman (review of *Giulio Romano*, by Frederick Hartt, *Burlington Magazine* 101 [1959]: 458).

5. Konrad Oberhuber, "Raphael versus Giulio Romano: The Swing Back," *Burlington Magazine* 124 [1982]: 479–86. The applicability of Gould's metaphor to shifting views on the subject of Raphael drawings was suggested by the present author, "He Says, She Says: Giulio Romano's Early Graphic Oeuvre and the Fine Art of Attribution," *Te: Quaderni di Palazzo Te*, no. 8 (2000): 21, 29, and is reiterated in this essay.

6. This point is made by J. A. Gere and Nicholas Turner, *Drawings by Raphael from the Royal Library, the Ashmolean, the British Museum, Chatsworth and other English Collections*, exh. cat. (London: The British Museum, 1983), 10.

7. Gere and Turner, *Drawings by Raphael*, 10. The following discussion of the early historiography of Raphael drawings is indebted to this source.
8. Ibid., 11.
9. J. C. Robinson, *A Critical Account of the Drawings by Michel Angelo and Raffaello in the University Galleries, Oxford* (Oxford: The Clarendon Press, 1870), ix.
10. Ivan Lermolieff (Giovanni Morelli original author), *Kunstkritische Studien über italienische Malerie. Die Galerien Borghese und Doria Panfili in Rom* (Leipzig: F. A. Brockhaus, 1890); *Die Galerien zu Berlin*, 1893.
11. Herman Dollmayr, "Die Zeichnungen zur Decke der Stanza d'Eliodoro," *Zeitschrift für Bildende Kunst*, n.s. 1 (1890): 292–9; idem, "Raffaels Werkstätte," *Jahrbuch der Kunsthistorischen Sammlungen in Wien* 16 (1895): 231–363; Franz Wickhoff, "Die italienischen Handzeichnungen der Albertina," *Jahrbuch der Kunsthistorischen Sammlungen des allerhöchsten Kaiserhauses* 12 (1891): 205–314; 13 (1892): 175–283.
12. Two later scholars of Raphael's drawings to be discussed in this essay, Philip Pouncey and John Gere, remarked that "Dollmayr's learning far outweighs his connoisseurship and his arguments, though ingenious, are often far-fetched and unconvincing"; Philip Pouncey and John Gere, *Italian Drawings in the Department of Prints and Drawings in the British Museum, Raphael and His Circle*, 2 vols. (London: Trustees of the British Museum, 1962), vii.
13. Vilhelm Wanscher, *Raffaello Santi da Urbino: His Life and Works* (London: E. Benn, 1926; translated from the 1919 Danish edition). I owe this reference to Paul Joannides.
14. Oskar Fischel, *Raphaels Zeichnungen*, 8 vols. (Berlin: G. Grote, 1913–41). A substantial ninth volume devoted to later Roman period drawings by Raphael and his workshop, edited and enlarged by Konrad Oberhuber, appeared in 1972; *Raphaels Zeichnungen, IX, Entwürfe zu Werken Raphaels und seiner Schule im Vatican 1511/12 bis 1520* (Berlin: G. Grote, 1972). A projected tenth volume on drawings connected with later panel paintings never materialized. Fischel's corpus was preceded by his earlier study, *Raphaels Zeichnungen: Versuch einer Kritik der bisher veröffentlichen Blätter* (Strasburg: Trübner, 1898), the Morellian bent of which is reflected in its "restrictive hypercriticism and centrifugal tendency to remove drawings arbitrarily from the master and to assign them, no less arbitrarily, to a number of associates and pupils" (Gere and Turner, 13). Fischel had renounced his Morellian approach by the time of the publication in 1913 of the first volume of the *Corpus*.
15. Two overviews of Raphael's drawings were published during the years that Fischel was producing the *Corpus* – Adolfo Venturi, *Choix de cinquante dessins de Raffaello Santi* (Paris and New York: Braun, 1927); and Ulrich Middledorf, *Raphael's Drawings* (New York: H. Bittner, 1945). These were followed twenty-five years later by two further surveys: Richard Cocke, *The Drawings of Raphael* (London: Feltham, Hamlyn, 1969); and Anna Forlani-Tempesti, "The Drawings," in *The Complete Work of Raphael*, ed. Mario Salmi (New York: Harrison House, 1969), 303–420, not elsewhere discussed in this essay.
16. Although not a public collection, the rich and then-undepleted holdings of the Devonshire Collection at Chatsworth deserve mention in this context. Its contents were long known and accessible to scholars, but a catalogue of the collection was only published many decades after those referred to here. The other major concentration of Raphael drawings in a public collection is in the Palais des Beaux-Arts, Lille, but it, too, was not the subject of a systematic scholarly catalogue until long after the British efforts of the mid-twentieth century. Barbara Brejon de Lavergnée, *Catalogue des Dessins Italiens. Collections du Palais des Beaux-Arts, Lille* (Paris and Lille: Réunion des musées nationaux, 1997); see also the recent exhibition catalogue by Paul Joannides, *Raphael and His Age: Drawings from the Palais des Beaux-Arts, Lille* (Cleveland, OH: Cleveland Museum of Art, 2002).

17. For a synopsis of the scholarly contributions of these scholars and the state of re-
    search on the question of drawings by Raphael and his pupils in the 1950s and 1960s,
    see Paul Joannides, "Raphael and His Circle," *Paragone/Arte* 51, 3d ser., no. 30, 601
    (March 2000): 5.

18. Frederick Hartt, *Giulio Romano* (New Haven: Yale University Press, 1958). This mono-
    graph was preceded by the author's article "Raphael and Giulio Romano, with notes on
    the Raphael School," *The Art Bulletin* 26 (1944): 67–94, in which his view of Giulio was
    already formulated. In the 1958 monograph, Hartt catalogued 371 sheets by Giulio, a
    number of which had been traditionally ascribed to Raphael, although he claimed not
    to reattribute to the pupil a single drawing that Fischel had given unequivocally to
    the master (285).

    Bernice Davidson's studies of the drawings of another of Raphael's major follow-
    ers, Perino del Vaga – the results of which appeared in a series of articles and an
    exhibition catalogue published between 1959 and 1966 – also belong to this moment.
    "Drawings by Perino del Vaga for the Palazzo Doria, Genoa," *The Art Bulletin* 41 (1959):
    317–26; "Early Drawings by Perino del Vaga," pts. 1 and 2, *Master Drawings*, vol. 1, no.
    3 (1963), 3–16; no. 4 (1963), 19–26; *Mostra di disegni di Perin del Vaga e la sua cerchia*,
    trans. Françoise Pouncey Chiarini, exh. cat. (Florence: Gabinetti disegni e stampe degli
    Uffizi, 1966). In contrast to Giulio, Perino's graphic style was never closely imitative
    of Raphael's, however, and so the study of his drawings did not involve removing or
    reassigning sheets from his graphic oeuvre. Finally, John Shearman and Michael Hirst
    likewise published important studies dealing with aspects of the question of drawings
    by Raphael and his workshop at this time. John Shearman, "The Chigi Chapel in S.
    Maria del Popolo," *Journal of the Warburg and Courtauld Institutes* 24 (1961): 129–60;
    idem, "Die Loggia der Psyche in der Villa Farnesina und die Probleme der letzen Phase
    von Raffaels graphischem Stil," *Jahrbuch der Kunsthistorischen Sammlungen in Wien*
    60 (1964): 59–100; Michael Hirst, "The Chigi Chapel in S. Maria della Pace," *Journal of
    the Warburg and Courtauld Institutes* 24 (1961): 161–85. Their respective studies of the
    two Chigi chapels integrated drawings with archival evidence to formulate substantial
    new contributions to the scholarship on Raphael's late Roman period and his patron
    Agostino Chigi. Shearman's probing analysis of the chalk drawings connected with the
    Psyche Loggia in the Villa Farnesina, painted for the same patron, arguably remains
    the fundamental discussion of this problematic aspect of Raphael's graphic oeuvre.

19. Bernard Berenson, *The Central Italian Painters of the Renaissance*, 2d ed. (New York
    and London: G. P. Putnam's Sons, 1909), 129.

20. Quoted from Konrad Oberhuber, review of *Raphael and His Circle*, by Pouncey and
    Gere, *Master Drawings* 1, no. 3 (1963): 49. See also John Shearman's 1959 review of
    Hartt's monograph, esp. 456, which likewise challlenged the expansionist view of
    Giulio.

21. Pouncey and Gere, *Raphael and His Circle* (London: Trustees of the British Museum,
    1962), v–vi.

22. Oberhuber's words still ring true and deserve to be quoted here: "The biographical no-
    tices contain new information in nearly every case, recording hitherto unknown works
    or offering new interpretations. The entries testify to the profound knowledge of the
    authors far beyond the immediate limits of the material they set out to catalogue.
    The indications of provenance, models of completeness and precision which carry us
    straight to the core of British collecting, reveal the extraordinary care with which draw-
    ings have been traced back to their former owners and the ingenuity which has been
    employed to disentangle complex situations or at least to offer likely hypotheses for
    their solution. In the body of the text not only are past scholarly opinions summarized
    and set forth along with the reasons for the proposed attribution and the relationship

to executed works, but also every work in any way tangentially related has been noted. Finally, the exact position of each drawing in the formative process of a work – as far as it can be reconstructed today – has been fixed. Each entry thus becomes a small independent monograph and yet the authors could never be accused of straying beyond the boundaries of purely factual interpretation as required in a catalogue. In order to do justice to the British Museum catalogue, one should treat [it] not so much as [a] catalogue to be consulted but as [a] book to be read from cover to cover." Oberhuber, review of Raphael and His Circle, 44.

23. Oberhuber verbalized this revisionist view in various lectures delivered during the celebration of the Raphael year and articulated it in print in Christoph Frommel, Stefano Ray, and Manfredo Tafuri, with the collaboration of Howard Burns and Arnold Nesselrath, *Raffaello architetto* (Milan: Electa, 1984), 429ff. The argument was vastly enlarged in his essay "Penni ou Raphaël," in *Raphaël: Autour des dessins du Louvre*, exh. cat. (Rome: Académie de France à Rome, 1992), 21–6. For the history of the question, see J. A. Gere, *Drawings by Raphael and His Circle*, exh. cat. (New York: The Pierpont Morgan Library, 1987), 15–16.

24. Gere, *Raphael and His Circle*, 15–19. Vowing to see the reattributed drawings "as if for the first time, without any preconceived ideas," he conceded that some were indeed worthy of Raphael, but went on to remark in conclusion that "having said as much, I have to admit that while arguments can be found in support of the attribution to Raphael … when each is considered individually, these drawings reveal disturbing contrasts of technique and style and, apparently, purpose, when considered as a group. These disjointed remarks on the Raphael-Penni problem … are provisional and inconclusive. All that one can safely suggest at this stage is that our current view of Penni's personality is to some extent a negative one, erring on the side of over-inclusiveness; and, correspondingly, that our view of Raphael's development in his last years may be unduly restrictive."

25. Sylvia Ferino Pagden, *Disegni umbri del Rinasimento da Perugino a Raffaello*, exh. cat. (Florence: Gabinetto disegni e stampe degli Uffizi, 1982); see also idem, "Raphael's Activity in Perugia as Reflected in a Drawing in the Ashmolean Museum, Oxford," *Mitteilungen des Kunsthistorischen Institutes in Florenz* 25, no. 2 (1981): 231–52; Marco Chiarini et al., *Raffaello a Firenze: dipinti e disegni delle collezioni fiorentine*, exh. cat. (Florence: Electa, Palazzo Pitti, 1984), 291, in which the oral opinion of John Shearman is cited.

26. The nature of the problem was articulated by Gere and Turner in the introduction to the catalogue of the British Museum's quincentenary exhibition: "There are two 'grey areas' where the connoisseurship of his drawings presents particular problems: at the start of his career when he was a pupil in Perugino's studio, and towards the end when he himself was at the head of a busy studio and dependent on the help of assistants" (Gere and Turner, *Drawings by Raphael*, 7).

27. *Raphaël dans les collections françaises*, exh. cat. (Paris: Réunion des Musées Nationaux, 1983); Roseline Bacou and Sylvie Béguin *Autour de Raphaël, dessins et peintures du Musée du Louvre*, exh. cat. (Paris: Musée du Louvre, 1983). In separating the work of Raphael from that of his followers and presenting the material in two separate venues, the Paris exhibitions did not allow the viewer to engage in the debate through direct visual comparisons.

28. Oberhuber's arguments favoring Raphael's authorship of the late drawings in question mirrored the contemporaneous debate about his participation in late paintings emanating from his workshop, particularly Cecil Gould's contention (which countered then prevailing opinion) that the master had a hand in the *Perla* and certain other late devotional paintings ("Raphael versus Giulio Romano, the Swing Back," passim). The

complex question of the organization of Raphael's worskhop, addressed in this volume
by Bette Talvacchia, has not been fully explored. A prolegomenon is John Shearman,
"The Organization of Raphael's Workshop," *The Art Institute of Chicago Centennial Lectures*, Museum Studies, vol. 10 (Chicago: Art Institute of Chicago, 1983), 41–57; see also
Linda Wolk-Simon, "Competition, Collaboration and Specialization in the Roman Art
World, 1520–1527," in *The Pontificate of Clement VII, History, Politics, Culture*, ed. Kenneth Gouwens and Sheryl Reiss (Aldershot: Ashgate Press, 2005), 251–74. Alessandro
Marabottini, "Raphael's Collaborators," in Salmi, ed., *The Complete Work of Raphael*,
199–302. More tangential though relevant is Nicole Dacos, *Le Logge di Raffaello: maestro e bottega di fronte all'antico* (Rome: Istituto Poligrafico dello Stato, 1977); 2nd ed.,
1986.

29. This dismantling of Penni's personality as a draftsman occurred in a piecemeal fashion
as Oberhuber reattributed specific drawings to Raphael both verbally and in print.
The argument was fully articulated in his essay "Penni ou Raphaël," 21–26. For an
alternative view arguing that the personality that had been assembled for Penni was
coherent (written before the publication of Oberhuber's essay), see Gere's discussion
of Penni in *Raphael and His Circle*, 15.

30. Joannides ("Raphael and His Circle," 7) systematically contrasts opinions expressed in
various collection-based exhibition catalogues of 1983–4 with opposite views voiced
a few years later about the same drawings.

31. Joannides, *Drawings of Raphael*; Eckhart Knab, Erwin Mitsch, and Konrad Oberhuber,
with the collaboration of Sylvia Ferino Pagden, *Raphael, die Zeichnungen* (Stuttgart:
Urachhaus, 1983); published in Italian as *Raffaello, I Disegni* (Florence: Nardini,
1983).

32. For the occasion of the Raphael year, a number of drawings were lifted from old
mounts to reveal previously unknown versos. This was one of the most fruitful contributions to the scholarship of Raphael drawings that occurred as the result of the
quincentenary.

33. A case in point is a red chalk drawing in the Louvre for the figure of Ganymede in
the *Marriage of Cupid and Psyche* ceiling fresco in the loggia of the Villa Farnesina.
Traditionally ascribed to Giulio Romano, whose authorship was upheld by Hartt in
his 1958 monograph, by Oberhuber in his 1972 volume of Fishel's corpus, and by
Joannides in his catalogue raisonné, it was given to Raphael by Oberhuber in his 1983
compendium (*Raphael, die Zeichnungen*, no. 563).

34. Pouncey and Gere, *Raphael and His Circle*, no. 66; Fischel-Oberhuber, *Raphaels
Zeichnungen*, no. 469.

35. Gere and Turner, *Drawings by Raphael*, cat. no. 194. Gere, Drawings by *Raphael and His
Circle*, 166, states that the attribution to Penni was maintained in the 1983 catalogue,
but in fact it is nowhere expressly stated and no author is proposed in the entry,
although he may then still have believed the earlier attribution. Most recently, Martin
Clayton (*Raphael and His Circle, Drawings from Windsor Castle*, exh. cat. [London: The
Queen's Gallery, 1999], 21) has attributed the drawing to Perino del Vaga, who most
scholars concur was the executant of the corresponding fresco.

36. Gere, *Raphael and His Circle*, 15, 18. Catherine Monbeig Goguel in a review in the
Burlington Magazine to be discussed later (vol. 141, [1999], 496) charges Gere with
opening the expansionist floodgate and Oberhuber with enthusiastically following in
his wake, although Gere himself credits Oberhuber with influencing his change of
heart.

37. Ibid., p. 18.

38. Nicholas Turner, "Three Raphaelesque Drawings in the Ashmolean Museum, Oxford,"
Drawing 10, no. 3 (September–October 1988): 49–53; idem, "Raphael at Chatsworth:

The Problem of His Late Drawings," *On Paper* 1, no. 2 (November–December 1996): 8–12; see also Nicholas Turner et al., *Catalogue of the Collections. The J. Paul Getty Museum. European Drawings*, vol. 3 (Los Angeles: Getty Museum, 1997), cat. no. 21, the *Sacrifice of Isaac*, catalogued as Giulio Romano (or Raphael?), henceforth cited as Turner et al., *Getty Museum*. Joannides, "Raphael and His Circle," 7, notes that Turner arrived at his revised attributions by "pursuing certain implications of Oberhuber's work." On the Getty drawing and related sheets, see further n. 39.

39. Turner et al., *Getty Museum*, under no. 21. Turner's conclusion was indeed found irresistible by Oberhuber and Gnann, who expressly ascribe the entire group to Raphael (*Roma e lo stile classico*, (Milan: Electa, 1999), cat. nos. 15–18; 93). Giulio's authorship of the *Sacrifice of Isaac* was reasserted in *Giulio Romano, Master Designer: An Exhibition of Drawings in Celebration of the Five Hundredth Anniversary of His Birth*, ed. and intro. essay by Janet Cox-Rearick, with contributions by Richard Aste et al., Bertha and Karl Leubsdorf Art Gallery (New York: Hunter College of the City of New York; Seattle: University of Washington Press, 1999), cat. no. 1; and Wolk-Simon, "He Says, She Says," 29, who endorses Giulio's authorship of the entire group of red chalk drawings. The case for Giulio was compellingly presented in a synthetic fashion by Sylvia Ferino Pagden, "Giulio Romano pittore e disegnatore a Roma," in *Giulio Romano*, exh. cat. by E. H. Gombrich et al. (Mantua: Electa, Palazzo Te, 1989), 65–95, 247–76.

40. Dominique Cordellier and Bernadette Py, *Musée du Louvre, Musée d'Orsay, Département des arts graphiques, Inventaire général des dessins italiens, V, Raphaël, son atelier, ses copiste*s (Paris: Réunion des Musées Nationaux, 1992); idem, *Raphaël: Autour des dessins du Louvre* (Paris: Réunion des Musees Nationaux, 1992). Six drawings that had been presented as the work of Raphael's pupils in the 1983 Raphael year catalogue *Autour de Raphaël* were upgraded to autograph status in the 1992 collection catalogue, while other sheets were newly catalogued as the master's work (see, e.g., cat. no. 251, a previously unpublished drawing with no critical history, here given to Raphael on the basis of Oberhuber's verbal communication). Oberhuber's opinion is repeatedly cited throughout both publications, and it is clear that his vision of Raphael's draftsmanship significantly shaped Cordellier and Py's presentation, as earlier noted by Joannides, "Raphael and His Circle," 7.

41. See, for example, cat. nos. 440–1, 570, 626, 920. A revealing case is cat no. 857, a study for a funeral monument for Francesco Gonzaga. Traditionally (and erroneously) ascribed to Peruzzi, it was first attributed to Raphael by Oberhuber in 1984 and repeatedly thereafter, although as Caroline Elam noted early in the debate, the viability of the attribution depends on an acceptance of Oberhuber's view of Raphael's late drawings (Caroline Elam, "Rome and Florence, the Raphael exhibitions: Architecture," *Burlington Magazine* 126 [1984]: 456–7).

42. Clayton, *Raphael and His Circle*.

43. Most notable, and controversial, in this regard is the red chalk study of the *Virgin and Child with Saint Elizabeth and the Infant Saint John* first attributed by Fischel to Giulio – an attribution "emphatically maintain[ed]" by Oberhuber and endorsed by Gere – which Clayton attributes to Raphael (*Raphael and His Circle*, cat. no. 34). However, as Joannides, "Raphael and His Circle," 15, reports, Clayton subsequently rescinded this suggestion. The critical history of the drawing's authorship is summarized by Gere, *Raphael and His Circle*, 203–4, from whom Oberhuber's opinion, expressed in the 1972 volume of Fischel's *Corpus*, is quoted.

44. Clayton, *Raphael and His Circle*, cat. nos. 48–9.

45. Ibid., cat. no. 47, p. 164.

46. Discussing the study of *Jonah* that he removed from Penni's oeuvre and ascribed to Perino, Clayton wrote that "the attribution of the drawing here to Perino del Vaga is

based on the similarity of its style to that of cat. 47, a new piece in the puzzle of the 'Penni group' drawings." Ibid., p. 168.

47. Precisely the same circular argument is used to bolster Clayton's new attribution to Perino of the *Jonah* drawing discussed in the previous note, which, he explains, is "based on the great similarity of its style to that of cat. 47," the *Battle Scene* (ibid.). Again he observes that the drawing exhibits a "manner not normally associated with Perino," yet proceeds to the conclusion that "an attribution to Perino seems unavoidable" (ibid., 170). Sharing the doubts earlier expressed by Joannides ("Raphael and His Circle," 12), this writer disagrees with these attributions.

48. Konrad Oberhuber and Achim Gnann, *Roma e lo stile classico di Raffaello*, exh. cat. (Mantua: Palazzo Te; Vienna: Graphische Sammlung Albertina, 1999).

49. Joannides, "Raphael and His Circle," 3.

50. Catherine Monbeig Goguel, "Mantua, Vienna and London: Drawings by Raphael and his Circle," review of *Roma e lo stile classico di Raffaello* by Konrad Oberhuber and Achim Gnann and *Raphael and His Circle* by Martin Clayton, *Burlington Magazine* 141 (1999): 495–99; see p. 497 for her reference to Oberhuber's creation of a "minefield of propositions which many will find troublesome."

51. Goguel criticized Oberhuber for "abandoning his own former hesitations and those of his predecessors, in several cases overturning his own earlier judgments. In this he follows an entirely personal line of reasoning, seeking to put forward his unique vision of a new Raphael. Unfortunately, his method is somewhat questionable as is the rigour with which it is applied" (Goguel, "Drawings by Raphael and his Circle," 496).

52. Joannides, "Raphael and His Circle," 3–42. The author's criticisms are closely aligned to Goguel's. Commenting on the slackening of the standards employed by Oberhuber to ascertain Raphael's authorship and his eager willingness to overturn his own earlier attributions – a phenomenon discerned by Goguel, whose remarks are quoted in the previous note – Joannides observed that "Not merely has Oberhuber leap-frogged others, he has leap-frogged himself" (7). A third catalogue, *Giulio Romano, Master Designer*, cited in n. 39, is also discussed (and in more favorable terms) in Joannides's lengthy piece, which is a far-ranging survey of the evolution of the Raphael drawings debate. An essay more than a conventional review, it should be read in conjunction with the present study.

53. Joannides, "Raphael and His Circle," 8: "The next stepping-stone in a swamp is not necessarily as reliable as the stone which preceded it. To accept a superior Penni as a substandard Raphael is to court disaster; to take the 'Raphael' thus created as a foundation for further attributions to Raphael is to embrace disaster. To elevate these additions to masterpiece rank by excited prose is to procreate disaster."

54. A demonstration of this phenomenon of uncritical acceptance of problematic attributions is Elena Parma et al., *Perino del Vaga tra Raffaello e Michelangelo*, exh. cat. (Mantua: Palazzo Te, 2001); see, e.g., cat. no. 2 (ascribed to Raphael on Oberhuber's authority although that attribution has been roundly challenged, including by Goguel in the review [cited in n. 50], p. 496, whose doubts were ignored by Parma); and cat. no. 24, where a drawing attributed to Perino by Clayton (see n. 35) is enlisted to support the artist's authorship of the catalogue number in question – a drawing long ago rejected as Perino's work by Bernice Davidson and dismissed again in subsequent reviews of the 2001 Perino exhibition and catalogue.

55. Wolk-Simon, "He Says, She Says," 20–33. Aspects of this article elaborated points made in Linda Wolk-Simon and Carmen Bambach, "Toward a Framework and Chronology for Giulio Romano's Early Pen Drawings," *Master Drawings* 37, no. 2 (1999): 165–80. Another "anti-attributionist" effort mounted at this time was the exhibition of drawings by Giulio Romano organized by Janet Cox-Rearick, *Giulio Romano, Master Designer,*

which presented sheets from Giulio's canonical graphic oeuvre – notably the red chalk *Sacrifice of Isaac* in the Getty Museum (discussed in n. 38) that have recently, and dubiously, been claimed for Raphael – with their traditional attributions to Giulio; see further the review by Linda Wolk-Simon, *Apollo* 151 (March 2000): 57–9.

56. Primarily the late chalk drawings and a relatively small number of pen drawings.

57. See his comments quoted here in notes 52 and 53.

58. See Michael Hirst, *Michelangelo and His Drawings* (New Haven: Yale University Press, 1988), among other recent publications by him on the subject. The reevaluation of Michelangelo as a draftsman began in the middle of the twentieth century with the investigations of Johannes Wilde. On Jacone, see the recent article by Charles Davis, "Michelangelo, Jacone and the Confraternity of the Virgin Annunciate called 'dell'Orciuolo,'" *Apollo* 155 (September 2002): 22–9, with earlier bibliography.

CHAPTER 10. CLASSICISM, MANNERISM, AND THE RELIEFLIKE STYLE

1. Rolf Quednau's exhaustive study appeared in 1979: *Die Sala di Costantino im Vatikanischen Palast. Zur Dekoration der beiden Medici-Päpste Leo X. und Clemens VII.* Studien zur Kunstgeschichte, no. 13 (Hildesheim: Olms, 1979). He presented a summary of the essential points in Italian at the Rome Raphael conference: "Aspects of Raphael's 'ultima maniera' in the light of the Sala di Costantino," in *Raffaello a Roma. Il convegno del 1983* (Rome: Edizioni dell'Elefante, 1986), 245–57.

2. John Shearman, *Raphael's Cartoons in the collection of Her Majesty the Queen and the Tapestries for the Sistine Chapel* (London: Phaidon, 1972).

3. Idem, "Raphael's Unexecuted Projects for the Stanze," in *Walter Friedlaender zum 90. Geburtstag* (Berlin: De Gruyter, 1965), 158–80; idem, "The Vatican Stanze: Functions and Decorations," *Proceedings of the British Academy* 57 (1971): 369–424.

4. See Alexander Nagel, *Michelangelo and the Reform of Art* (New York: Cambridge University Press, 2000) and Hans Belting, *Likeness and Presence. A History of the Image before Art* (Chicago: University of Chicago Press, 1994), esp. chap. 20.

5. Nagel for example, suggests (19): "In contrast to the progressivist view, which sees it [the High Renaissance] as a culminating period of harmony and classical perfection, this view of the period reveals a more anxious art of disjunction, compensation, projection, and desire – and as a result casts a sharper light on the new forms of artistic and historical self-awareness that mark the period as a whole. It helps to explain why what we call the High Renaissance was such a brief episode and was so quickly followed by the strange experiments of the art of the 1520s and after."

6. I have outlined the evolution of Raphael's Roman altarpieces in terms of his confrontation with the conflict between the requirements of art and the Church in "1503–34," in *Rome. Artistic Centers of the Italian Renaissance*, ed. Marcia B. Hall (New York: Cambridge University Press, 2005).

7. Marcia B. Hall, *After Raphael: Painting in Central Italy in the Sixteenth Century* (New York: Cambridge University Press, 1999).

8. Heinrich Wölfflin, *Classic Art*, trans. Linda and Peter Murray, (1899; reprint, London: Phaidon, 1948). Sydney J. Freedberg, *Painting of the High Renaissance in Rome and Florence*, 2 vols. (Cambridge: Harvard University Press, 1961).

9. E. H. Gombrich, "Raphael's Stanza della Segnatura and the Nature of its Symbolism," in *Symbolic Images. Studies in the art of the Renaissance* (London: Phaidon, 1972), 85–101.

10. Gombrich analyzed and reproduced the ceiling (pl. 63–71), identified the genre, made the comparison to Perugino, and reproduced his frescoes in the Cambio, pl. 79–80.

11. Freedberg, *Painting of the High Renaissance* 120.

12. The massing of light and shade is still more effective in the *School of Athens*, for which see my discussion in the introduction to this volume and the cartoon for that fresco (Plate 18).

13. Freedberg, *Painting of the High Renaissance*, 121. Freedberg compared them to Michelangelo's contemporary achievement in such a figure as the Delphic Sibyl on the Sistine vault.

14. Ibid., 120.

15. See Vasari's preface to *Terza età* of the 1568 edition, as well as his biography of Michelangelo.

16. See Svetlana Alpers, "Ekphrasis and Aesthetic Attitudes in Vasari's Lives," *Journal of the Warburg and Courtauld Institutes* 23 (1960): 190–215.

17. See G. P. Bellori, "Idea," a lecture used as the Introduction to his *Le Vite de'Pittori, Scultori et Archtetti moderni* (Rome, 1672), translated as appendix II in Erwin Panofsky, *Idea. A Concept in Art Theory*, trans. Joseph J. S. Peake (Columbia SC: University of South Carolina Press, 1968); and *Descrizzione delle imagini dipinte da Rafaelle d'Urbino nelle camere del Palazzo Apostolico Vaticano* (Rome, 1695). Part of it has been translated by Alice Sedgwick Wohl ("The Image of the Ancient Gymnasium of Athens, or Philosophy," in *Raphael's School of Athens*, ed. Marcia B. Hall [New York: Cambridge University Press, 1997], 48–56). For important new additions to the Bellori literature, see E. Borea and C. Gasparri, eds., *L'idea del Bello, Viaggio per Roma nel seicento con Giovan Pietro Bellori* (Rome: De Luca, 2000).

18. Carl Goldstein has examined the Carracci Academy and its use of earlier High Renaissance models: *Verbal Fact over Visual Fiction. A Study of the Carracci and the Criticism, Theory, and Practice of Art in Renaissance and Baroque, Italy* (Cambridge: Cambridge University Press, 1988), and "Rhetoric and Art History in the Italian Renaissance and Baroque," *Art Bulletin* 73 (1991): 641–52.

19. On classicism and the development of the concept, see R. Wellek, "The Term and Concept of Classicism in Literary History," in E. R. Wasserman, ed., *Aspects of the Eighteenth Century* (Baltimore; Johns Hopkins Press, 1965), 105–28; also Eugenio Battisti, "Classicism," in *Encyclopedia of World Art*.

20. See A. D. Potts, "Political Attitudes and the Rise of Historicism in Art theory," *Art History* 1, no. 2 (1978): 191–213. "The idea that the whole history of Post-Renaissance art could be encompassed within some general pattern of decline to which any artistic tradition was subject after its classic phase can be traced to Winckelman but not any earlier" (193).

21. Elizabeth Cropper and Charles Dempsey (*Nicholas Poussin. Friendship and the Love of Painting* [Princeton: Princeton University Press, 1996]) discuss the development of the concepts of "classic" and "baroque," and their use by the romantics; see esp. 24.

22. Heinrich Wölfflin, *Principles of Art History: The Problem of the Development of Style in Later Art* (German ed. 1915; trans, M. D. Hottinger, New York: Dover, n.d.)

23. Ibid., 73.

24. Wölfflin, *Principles of Art History*, 13.

25. Wölfflin, *Classic Art*, xvi.

26. Ibid., 101.

27. Ibid., 139.

28. Wölfflin, *Principles of Art History*, 14.

29. Hartt's monograph, *Giulio Romano* (2 vols. [New Haven: Yale University Press, 1958]), had been preceded by an article of interest to us: "Raphael and Giulio Romano," *Art Bulletin* 26 (1944): 67–94.

30. Frederick Hartt, "Raphael and Giulio Romano," 71.

31. Ibid., 72.

32. Ibid.

33. Freedberg (*Painting of the High Renaissance*, 305) saw a "disparity between form and content, in which the theme is not adequate to the charge of expression laid on it, and where the primacy of meaning tends to be assumed by form."

34. John Shearman wrote in his review of Hartt's book on Giulio Romano, published in 1958: "it seems to me the estimate of Raphael's range is altogether too retracted...as a result of this, many contrasts are drawn between master and pupil, where in reality no contrast exists, but continuity, and a false stature is given to the pupil on the basis of innovations which are not his." *Burlington Magazine* 101 (1959): 457.

35. When the *Fire in the Borgo* was cleaned in the late 1980s it was definitively determined that Raphael's hand was evident. See Arnold Nesselrath, "Art-historical Findings during the Restoration of the Stanza dell'Incendio," *Master Drawings* 30 (1992): 31–60.

36. Freedberg (*Painting of the High Renaissance*, 304): "In the *Fire* classical synthesis is compromised by separation in analysis of that which, in the previous history of the classical style, had existed in a fused and equal harmony: reason and emotion, ideal and real, order and accident, activity and stasis, and a host of other nominal antitheses. These factors are now used instead as if in effortful compensation of each other; but used in this way they do not produce the effect, so evident in the Eliodoro frescoes, of their resolution in synthetic equilibrium. It is at this point that a visible seam appears in the hitherto integral system of the classical style, and the structure of the style is, in our geological simile, as if faulted."

37. Freedberg, *Painting of the High Renaissance*, 352.

38. Craig Hugh Smyth, *Mannerism and Maniera*, with introduction by Elizabeth Cropper (1963; reprint, Vienna: IRSA, 1992). Originally published in *The Renaissance and Mannerism. Studies in Western Art: Acts of the Twentieth International Congress of the History of Art* (Princeton: Princeton University Press, 1963) vol. 2, 181–221.

39. Mantegna was called from Mantua to Rome to work on a chapel in the Villa Belvedere for Pope Innocent VIII. The frescoes in the chapel dedicated to John the Baptist, which were destroyed in the eighteenth century, were painted in 1488–89. Ronald Lightbown, *Mantegna. With a Complete Catalogue of the Paintings, Drawings, and Prints* (Oxford: Phaidon, 1986), chap. IX, 154–8.

40. James David Draper (*Bertoldo di Giovanni: Sculptor of the Medici Household. Critical Reappraisal and Catalogue Raisonné* [Columbia: University of Missouri Press, 1992]), dates it c. 1479. The sarcophagus, which Bertoldo studied with care, is in Pisa, Campo Santo, reproduced in Draper, fig. 83.

41. Smyth mentioned and reproduced the engraving of the *Battle of Cascina*, 68 and fig. 40.

42. John Shearman (*Raphael's Cartoons*) reproduced the borders of the tapestries.

43. Hartt asserted correctly that "the absolute coherency of the decorative system of the room as a whole necessitates a single creator" (77), but he went on after some analysis to declare "the Sala di Costantino as a whole cannot therefore have been based upon designs left by Raphael" (79). For discussion of the reattribution to Raphael of drawings for the Costantino, see Philipp P. Fehl, "Raphael as a Historian: Poetry and Historical Accuracy in the Sala di Costantino," *Artibus et Historiae* 14, no. 28 (1993): 9–76; and more recently, Linda Wolk-Simon, "He Says, She Says: Giulio Romano's Early Graphic Oeuvre and the Fine Art of Attribution," *Quaderni di Palazzo Te* 8 (2000): 19–33. For a full discussion of the relieflike style in the Sala di Costantino, see Hall, *After Raphael*, 42–8.

44. On the viewing distance required for a successful illusion with linear perspective, see Claire Farago's discussion of Leonardo's fresco of the *Battle of Anghiari* planned for

a very long field in the Sala di Consiglio in the Palazzo Vecchio: "Leonardo's *Battle of Anghiari*: A Study in the Exchange between Theory and Practice," *Art Bulletin* 76 (1994): 301–30.

45. Salviati's fresco is part of his decoration of the Ricci-Sacchetti Palace in Rome (1553–54), reproduced in Hall, *After Raphael*, fig. 107. Parmigianino's devotional picture, *Madonna of the Rose*, of 1529–30, today in Dresden, Gemäldegalerie, is also reproduced in ibid., fig. 80. An eighteenth-century legend, presumably apocryphal, tells how the subject of Parmigianino's picture was converted when the patron, the worldly Pietro Aretino, decided to make a gift of it to Clement VII and deemed a *Madonna and Child* more suitable to the pope. I suppose that Raphael would have found such a conversion a violation of his sense of decorum.

46. Smyth, *Mannerism*, 60.

47. Ibid., 58.

48. Freedberg, addressing the relationship of *maniera* to Raphael and the High Renaissance and how they differed, remarked that "even the most extreme instances we possess of *bella maniera* in Raphael or Michelangelo do not give the effect of instantly apparent artifice that emerges from a Salviati, a Jacopino del Conte, or a Bronzino. Between the time of the High Renaissance and that of the Maniera the conception of what makes Maniera *bella* evidently changed." Sydney J. Freedberg, "Observations on the Painting of the Maniera," *Art Bulletin* 47 (1965): 187–97. Quotation from 188.

49. Ibid.

50. Walter Friedländer, "The Anticlassical Style," in his *Mannerism and Anti-Mannerism in Italian Painting,* (New York: Columbia University Press, 1957), 3–43, translation of "Die Entstehung des antiklassischen Stiles in der italienischen Malerei um 1520" (1925). Max Dvorak, "Uber Greco und den Manierismus," in his *Kunstgeschichte als Geistesgeschichte* (Munich: R. Piper, 1928). An abbreviated translation by John Coolidge is cited here: *Magazine of Art* XLVI, no. 1 (1953): 18.

51. Freedberg ("Observations," 191): "Maniera painters are all too aware that there is no longer any virtue in the simple statement; indeed there are no longer any simple certitudes to state."

CHAPTER 11. FRENCH IDENTITY IN THE REALM OF RAPHAEL

1. Roger Jones and Nicolas Penny, illus., *Raphael* (New Haven: Yale University Press, 1983), pl. 201. Much of the material to be discussed in this chapter is brought together in two basic studies of this large topic: Jacques Thuillier, "Raphaël et la France: présence d'un peintre," in *Raphaël et l'art français*, ed. J. P. Cuzin, exh. cat. (Paris: Galeries Nationales du Grand Palais, 1984), 11–36; Martin Rosenberg, *Raphael and France: The Artist as Paradigm and Symbol* (University Park: Pennsylvannia State University Press, 1995). Unless otherwise indicated, all translations from the French are mine.

2. Janet Cox-Rearick, *The Collection of Francis I: Royal Treasures* (New York: Harry N. Abrams, 1996), esp. 96–8, 160–257.

3. Abraham Bosse, *Le peintre converty aux précises et universelles règles de son art; Sentiments sur la distinction des diverses manières de peinture, dessin et gravure*, ed. R.-A. Weigert (Paris: Hermann, 1964).

4. Bosse, *Sentiments*, 150.

5. See J. Thuillier, "Polémiques autour de Michelelange au XVII e siècle," *Dix-septième siècle* 13, nos. 36–7 (1957), 353–69; also my "Studies in Seventeenth Century French Art Theory and Ceiling Painting," *Art Bulletin* 47 (1965): 231–56.

6. Jones and Penny, *Raphael*, pl. 186.

7. Ibid., pl. 202.

8. *Les conférences de l'Académie Royale de Peinture et de Sculpture au XVIIe siècle*, ed. A. Mérot (Paris: Ecole Nationale Supérieure des Beaux-Arts, 1996), 60–7, 81–90.

9. Anthony Blunt, illus., *Nicolas Poussin* (New York: Pantheon Books, 1967), III, pl. 128.

10. Jones and Penny, *Raphael*, pls. 99, 201.

11. Ibid., pls. 87, 106, 264.

12. Bosse, *Sentiments*, 137.

13. For Raphael's engravers, see Marcia B. Hall, *After Raphael: Painting in Central Italy in the Sixteenth Century* (New York: Cambridge University Press, 1999), 50–3. See also my *Teaching Art: Academies and Schools from Vasari to Albers* (New York: Cambridge University Press, 1996), 82–7.

14. Jones and Penny, *Raphael*, pls. 97, 186.

15. Goldstein, *Teaching Art*, 40–5, 50–4.

16. André Félibien, *Entretiens sur les vies et sur les ouvrages des plus excellens peintres anciens et modernes* (Paris, 1666, reprint ed. 1690), 1, 217–18, 251.

17. Gio. Pietro Bellori, *Le vite de pittori, scultori et architetti moderni* (Rome, 1672), translation from Erwin Panofsky, *Idea: A Concept in Art Theory*, trans. Joseph J. S. Peake (New York: Harper and Row, 1968), 175.

18. Roger de Piles, *Abrégé de la vie des peintres* (Paris, 1699), 37–8, cited in Thuillier, "Raphaël et la France: présence d'un peintre," 21.

19. Roger de Piles, *Cours de peinture par principes* (Paris, 1708).

20. D'Argens, *Réflexions critiques sur les différentes écoles de peinture* (Paris, 1752), 37–49, cited in Thuillier, "Raphaël et la France: présence d'un peintre," 22–3.

21. Alain Mérot, *Eustache Le Sueur (1616–1655)* (Paris: Arthena, 1987), 236–40.

22. Jones and Penny, *Raphael*, pl. 87.

23. Abbé Dubos, *Réflexions critiques sur la poésie et sur la peinture*, 3 vols. (Paris: 1719).

24. Rosenberg, *Raphael and France*, 117.

25. D. Wildenstein and G. Wildenstein, *Documents complémentaires au catalogue de l'oeuvre de Louis David* (Paris: Fondation Wildenstein, 1973), 157, cited in Rosenberg, *Raphael and France*, 135.

26. Antoine Schnapper, illus., *David* (New York: Alpine Fine Arts Collection, 1982), figs. 27, 110.

27. See my *Teaching Art*, 58–61.

28. Jones and Penny, *Raphael*, pls. 99, 154, 188, 264.

29. Ibid., pls. 99, 140.

30. Ernst Kris and Otto Kurz, *Legend, Myth, and Magic in the Image of the Artist: A Historical Experiment* (London: Yale University Press, 1979), 1–3.

31. Francis Haskell, *Past and Present in Art and Taste: Selected Essays* (London: Yale University Press, 1987), 94; also Thuillier, "Raphaël et la France: présence d'un peintre," 24–7, 429–46.

32. See most recently, Dorothy Johnson, "Delacroix's Dialogue with the French Classical Tradition," in *The Cambridge Companion to Delacroix*, ed. Beth S. Wright (New York: Cambridge University Press, 2001), 108–29; Michèle Hannoosh, "Delacroix as Essayist: Writings on Art," in ibid., 154–69.

33. Cited in Hannoosh, "Delacroix as Essayist," 165.

34. *Oeuvres littéraires*, 2:9, cited in Rosenberg, *Raphael and France*, 179.

35. See Stephen Bann, *Paul Delaroche: History Painted* (Princeton: Princeton University Press, 1997), 200–27.

36. Edmond and Jules de Goncourt, *Journal*, ed. R. Ricatte (Paris, 1956), 8, 19–20, cited in Thuillier, "Raphaël et la France: présence d'un peintre," 30.

37. See the examples collected in J. P. Cuzin, et al., *Copier Créer de Turner à Picasso: 300 oeuvres inspirées par les maîtres du Louvre*, exhib. cat. (Paris: Réunion des musées nationaux, 1993), passim.

38. A. Ozenfant and Ch.-E. Jeanneret, *La peinture moderne* (Paris: Les éditions G. Crès, n.d. [1925]), e.g., 73.

39. For the last, see Cuzin, *Raphaël et l'art français*, no. 358.

CHAPTER 12. RAPHAEL'S EUROPEAN FAME IN THE SEVENTEENTH AND EIGHTEENTH CENTURIES

1. I have sketched out a profile of Raphael's fame in seventeenth-century Europe in my essay, "Una certa idea di Raffaello nel Seicento," in *L'idea del bello, viaggio per Roma nel seicento con Giovan Pietro Bellori*, ed. E. Borea and C. Gasparri (Rome: De Luca 2000), I: 153–61, to which reference will often be made hereafter. Here I focus on a limited number of more specific issues in connection with his fame in eighteenth-century Italy, England, and Germany. Martin Rosenberg's important book on *Raphael and France. The Artist as Paradigm and Symbol* (University Park: Pennsylvania State University Press, 1995) gives precious insight and information beyond its stated geographical limits and is often evoked here. It is also the obvious reason why next to nothing has been said here on France. As for Raphael as a style model, see most recently Philip Sohm, *Style in the Art Theory of Early Modern Italy* (Cambridge: Cambridge University Press, 2001), passim, esp. 27–45.

2. The literature on art academies and their teaching methods is vast. Suffice it to recall here B. Teyssèdre, *Roger de Piles et les débats sur le coloris au siècle de Louis XIV* (Paris: La Bibliothèque des Arts, 1957), passim and esp. 76–83, 90–2, 156, 186–7, 304, 321–3, 339, 347, 350, 360–1, 379, 384–6, 434, 464, 527–8, 542, 544–5, 557, 558, 566; A. W. A. Boschloo, E. J. Hendrikse, L. C. Smit, and G. J. van der Sman, eds., *Academies of Art between Renaissance and Romanticism* (special issue of the *Leids Kunsthistorisch Jaarboek*, Gravenhage, 1989); C. Goldstein, *Teaching Art. Academies and Schools from Vasari to Albers* (New York: Cambridge University Press, 1996), esp. 75–87; P. Duro, *The Academy and the Limits of Painting in Seventeenth Century France* (Cambridge: Cambridge University Press, 1997), esp. 45, 54, 71–6, 129–30, 137, 142, 174–5, 212, 221, 228. On Raphael and academic training in England, see B. Krismanski, "Benjamin Ralph's *School of Raphael* (1759): Praise for Hogarth and a Direct Source for Reynolds," in *British Journal for Eighteenth Century Studies* (2001): 15–32, esp. 16–30. It is not surprising that in Florence, Michelangelo's home, the impact of Raphael on the local academy is perhaps somewhat understated: cf. Z. Wazbinski, *L'accademia medicea del disegno a Firenze nel cinquecento – Idea e istituzione* (Florence: Olschki, 1987), I, passim; and K. E. Barzman, *The Florentine Academy and the Early Modern State. The Discipline of Disegno* (New York: Cambridge University Press, 2000), 78 and 214.

3. J. Reynolds, *Discourses on Art* (New Haven and London: Yale University Press, 1981), 104.

4. Ibid., 103.

5. For Velazquez, Salvator Rosa, Boschini, and Malvasia on one hand, Annibale Carracci, Francesco Albani, and Simone Cantarini on the other, see infra. On Raphael's fame, see P. Magnanimi and G. Morolli, eds., *Raffaello: elementi di un mito* (Florence: Centro Di, 1984).

6. For a detailed analysis of Richardson's attitude toward Raphael, see Rosenberg, *Raphael*, 80–9. See also C. Gibson Wood, *Jonathan Richardson Art Theorist of the English Enlightenment* (New Haven and London: Yale University Press, 2000), esp. 150–7 and most notably 220–5.

7. J. Richardson, *An Account of Some of the Statues, Bas-reliefs, Drawings and Pictures in Italy etc. with Remarks* (London: Knapton, 1722), 34. It should be emphasised, however, that Richardson's writings were mostly known in the French version of 1728 (*Traité*

de la Peinture et de la Sculpture [Amsterdam: Uytwerf, 1728]), to which continental authors respond, often using its very terms (e.g., see infra Crespi and Cochin). The passage on the Bolognese altarpiece is printed in the second volume, 43–5. Maybe also Lavater was somewhat affected by Richardson's analysis: see J. K. Lavater, *Essai sur la physiognomie* (La Haye: Van Karnebeck, 1781–1803), III, 206–7, where he finds Raphael more admirable for the variety and expressiveness of the attitudes of his characters than for the expression of their faces, as he states with specific reference to the head of the Bolognese *Saint Cecilia*.

8. Cf. Richardson, *An Account*, and id., *Traité*, III, 611–27.

9. E. Falconet, *Oeuvres complètes* (Paris: Dentu, 1808), I, 391–2. For further criticism, see Rosenberg, *Raphael*, 136–8.

10. C. Michel, *Le voyage d'Italie de Charles Nicholas Cochin (1758)* (Rome: Ecole Française de Rome, 1991), 283: "en effet d'une très-grande beauté; les têtes en sont d'un dessein et d'un caractere admirable; les figures sont drapées du plus beaux choix, et les plis bien exécutés. Il est admirablement bien peint, quoique la couleur en soit un peu bise. C'est un des plus excellens tableaux de ce grand maître." On Cochin's admiration for Raphael, see C. Michel, *Charles Nicolas Cochin et l'art des Lumières* (Rome: Ecole Française de Rome, 1993), esp. 411 and 427; more problematic is the view on Raphael given in writings by Cochin other than his *Voyage*: see idem 305 and 306, as well as Rosenberg, *Raphael*, 106–7.

11. Undated letter to Innocenzo Ansaldi published in G. Bottari and S. Ticozzi, *Raccolta di lettere sulla pittura, scultura e architettura scritte da' più celebri personaggi de' secoli XV, XVI e XVII* (Milan: Silvestri, 1822), VII, 63–4: "In questo quadro non si vede alcuna attitudine o positura la quale sia per se stessa dura, ma ciascheduna è leggiera, graziosa e ben mossa.... V'è egli un sol contorno di qualsisia parte che tenero non sia, impastato, e che insensibilmente e felicemente non perdasi nelle tinte che sieguono? Tutto non v'ha forse impastato, degradato, accordato tutto, tutto unito...?
...Se questo quadro è d'una maniera un poco dura e secca, come mai possono essere tutte le attitudini e le arie delle teste bellissime e proprie di cadauna figura? E se sono bellissime, come esser ponno un poco secche e non perfettamente disegnate? E se sono secche e non perfettamente disegnate, come mai può egli questo quadro andar del pari con qualunque altro di questo maestro, eziandio di quello della Trasfigurazione?...Dove siete, o Signor Watelet? Voi che, anni sono, essendo in Bologna e meco appunto parlando della singolar bellezza di questo quadro della santa Cecilia, non vi sapevate dar pace dell'elegante disegno di tal opera?" The first edition of this volume of the *Raccolta* was published in 1774 and edited by L. Crespi without Bottari's knowledge or permission. This letter is a different version of an unpublished one autographed by Crespi dated 7 April 1764, to be found in the collection of letters to Bottari preserved in the Biblioteca Corsiniana, Rome (ms. 2033, letter n. 45). Its text has been edited in grammar and spelling by Bottari but must have been eventually rejected for publication, given its polemical overtones.

12. *Malvasia's Life of the Carracci: Commentary and Translation*, trans. A. Summerscale (University Park: Pennsylvania State University Press, 2000), 96. The original Italian text is reprinted in G. Perini, *Gli scritti dei Carracci* (Bologna: Nuova Alfa, 1990), 150: "Io non baratteria nissuna di quelle [pitture di Correggio a Parma] con la Santa Cecilia...Quel bel vecchione di quel San Girolamo [di Correggio, nel *Giorno*] non è più grande e tenero insieme che quel che importa di quel San Pavolo, il quale prima mi pareva uno miracolo, e adesso mi pare una cosa di legno, tanto dura e tagliente?"

13. See Perini, *Gli scritti*, 71–7 (with earlier literature) and, most recently, J. Shearman, *Raphael in Early Modern Sources* (New Haven and London: Yale University Press, 2003), II, 1279–82. A perceptive commentary on this passage is in Sohm, *Style*, 29–30.

14. C. C. Malvasia, *Felsina Pittrice* (Bologna: Tipografie guidi dall'Ancoza, 1841), III, 163–4 and 378.

15. G. B. Passeri, *Die Künstlerbiographien,* ed. J. Hess (Worms: Wernersche Verlags-gesellschaft, 1995), 274: "Io ho sentito discorrere, et anche da Professori, che Raffaele da Urbino, che porta il primo vanto, è duro e tagliente, che Titiano è privo di di-segno, il Correggio scostumato, Paolo Veronese debole e troppo vago....Il dar gusto a ciascheduno è impossibile, perchè l'istessa natura, che è madre universale, ha titolo d'imperfetta, benchè sia la vera maestra." See also Sohm, *Style,* 31.

16. A. Emiliani, "La coscienza dell'artista moderno," in *Simone Cantarini detto il Pesarese, 1612–1648,* ed. A. Emiliani (Milan: Electa, 1997): 13–49, esp. 31–2, and idem, "La prospettiva storica di Giovan Pietro Bellori," in Borea and Gasparri eds., *L'idea,* I, 90.

17. On Maratta, see G. P. Bellori, *Le vite de' pittori, scultori e architetti moderni,* ed. E. Borea (Turin: Einaudi, 1976), 626–8 (this passage is translated and discussed in Sohm, *Style,* 28); V. Vittoria, *Osservazioni sopra il libro della Felsina Pittrice per difesa di Raffaello di Urbino, dei Carracci e della loro scuola* (Rome: Zenobi, 1703), reprinted as an ap-pendix to Malvasia, *Felsina,* III, esp. 8–14 and 30; J. J. Winckelmann, *Abhandlung von der Fähigkeit der Empfindung des schönen in der Kunst und dem Unterricht in derselben* (1763), excerpted in J. J. Winckelmann, *Il bello nell'arte. Scritti sull'arte antica* (Turin: Einaudi, 1973), 84.

18. Malvasia, *Felsina,* I, 337 n. 1 (1678 ed., I, 471).

19. Perini, "Una certa idea," 153–61, esp 157; Summerscale, *Malvasia's Life,* 273–4, n. 434; and Sohm, *Style,* 31–2.

20. See also Malvasia's preface to his *Felsina Pittrice,* I, n.p.: "Circa lo stile e la frase, tu già cominci a sentire qual sia: dimestica affatto e popolare. Scrivo a' Pittori, non a' Letterati" (and see also the different versions of this passage extant in Malvasia's manuscripts, as commented in G. Perini, "L'epistolario del Malvasia – Primi frammenti: le lettere all'Aprosio," in *Studi secenteschi* [1984]: 183–230, esp. 203–4).

21. See Malvasia's own remarks on the style of Reni's letters, in his *Felsina,* III, 55, and as commented in G. Perini, "Le lettere degli artisti da strumento di comunicazione, a documento a cimelio," in the proceedings of the conference *Documentary Culture: Florence and Rome from Grand Duke Ferdinand I to Pope Alexander VII,* ed. E. Cropper, G. Perini, and F. Solinas (Bologna: Nuova Alfa, 1992), 165–83, esp. 172–3.

22. G. Mancini, *Considerazioni sopra la pittura,* ed. L. Salerno (Rome: Accademia Nationale des Lincei, 1956–1957), I, 20. Incidentally it should be observed that Vittoria's *Osser-vazioni,* 30, although providing a likely explanation to the rise and lingering fortune of Raphael's spurious fame as a pottery painter, supplies the very historical and factual ground on which it was established.

23. The *Lettere familiari scritte ad un amico in difesa del Conte Carlo Cesare Malvasia autore della Felsina Pittrice* (Bologna: Pisarri, 1705) are reprinted as an appendix to Malvasia's *Felsina,* III, 33–66 (on Raphael, see 39, 41–4 and 63). On Zanotti as a writer on art and on his relation to his predecessor Malvasia, see G. Perini, "Letteratura artistica e società a Bologna al tempo di Giuseppe Maria Crespi," in *Giuseppe Maria Crespi, 1665–1747* (Bologna: Nuova Alfa, 1990), CXCIII–CCVI, and E. Grasman, *In de schaduw van Vasari – Vijf opstellen over kunstgeschiedschrijving in 18de-eeuws Italië,* s.l. (1992), 49–82 (Italian trans., *All'ombra del Vasari – Cinque saggi sulla storiografia dell'arte nell'Italia del Settecento* [Florence: Istituto Universitario Olandese di Storia dell'Arte, 2000], 67–103).

24. As for Maratta's personal motives, see G. Perini, "Paura di volare," in *Domenichino* (Milan: Electa, 1996), 57–119, esp. 109, n. 244. On Maratta and the Albani, see S.

Rudolph, "La direzione artistica di Carlo Maratti nella Roma di Clemente XI," in *Papa Albani e le arti a Urbino e a Roma, 1700–1721*, ed. G. Cucco (Venice: Marsilio, 2001), 59–61.

25. Bottari and Ticozzi, eds., *Raccolta*, IV, 428–9: "il ritratto, fatto da se stesso, di Raffaello, veramente maraviglioso, ed è l'unica cosa del Sanzio che si vegga in Urbino."

26. Ibid., 430: "Il ritratto di Raffaello in casa Albani a Urbino è dipinto sul muro, con cristallo dinanzi e cornicione di battente ben alto." This answers Bottari's letter of 9 July 1760, preserved in the Biblioteca Comunale dell'Archiginnasio, Bologna, ms. B 15, letter n. 77, where he seems to believe that the picture seen by Crespi is of the same type as the "Bindo Altoviti" portrait used by Vasari to illustrate his Life of Raphael, because it was long thought to be a self-portrait of the painter.

27. On the history of this lost picture (most probably an eighteenth-century Roman forgery), see G. Perini, "Un presunto autoritratto perduto di Raffaello a Palazzo Albani a Urbino," in the proceedings of the conference *Cultura nell'eta delle Legazioni*, ed. R. Varese and F. Cassola (Florence: Le Lettere, forthcoming).

28. Cf. P. de Vecchi, *L'opera completa di Raffello* (Milan: Rizzoli, 1966), 86, entry n. 6; L. Becherucci, "Raffaello e la pittura," in *Raffaello. La pittura i disegni*, ed. M. Salmi (Novara: De Agostini, 1998), 14; A. Marabottini, "Raffaello fino all'ottobre del 1504," in *Raffaello giovane e Città di Castello* (Rome: Oberon, 1983), 43–4; G. Cucco ed., *Casa Natale di Raffaello – Urbino* (Urbino: Accademie Raffaello, 1997), 48–9.

29. Köremons [Fr. Chr. Scheyb], *Natur und Kunst in Gemälden, Bildhauereyen, Gebäuden und Kupferstichen, zu Unterricht der Schüler und Vergnügen der Kenner* (Vienna: Gräffer, 1770), III, 316, and A. von Arnim, *Raffaello e le sue vicine* (Milan: SE, 2002), 19–30.

30. K. H. von Heinecken, *Nachrichten von Künstler und Kunstsachen* (Leipzig: Krauss, 1768–1769), III, 19, and J. D. Fiorillo, *Geschichte der Mahlerey in Rom*, in *Geschichte der zeichnenden Künste von ihrer Wiederauflebung bis auf die neuesten Zeiten* (Göttingen: Rosenbusch, 1798), I, (Italian version in S. A. Meyer, *La storia delle arti del disegno (1798–1820) di Johann Dominicus Fiorillo con un'antologia di scritti* [Bologna: Minerva, 2001], 169–71). See also the explanation later given by a learned nobleman from Urbino, Autaldo Antaldi (*Notizie di alumiarchitetti, alcuni pittori, scultori di Urbino, Pesero e de'luoghi circonvicini*, ed. by A. Cerboni Baiardi, [Ancona: Il lavoro editoriale, 1996] p. 38, *ad vocem* "Ciarla Raffaello"), although it is not entirely plausible.

31. P. A. Orlandi, *Abcedario pittorico*, ed. P. Guarienti (Venice: Pasquali, 1753), 441: "E qui siami lecito disingannare quei molti che suppongono aver egli dipinti tanti piatti, urne, vasi, quando nella vita di lui scritta da tanti autori non se ne ritrova fatta alcuna menzione, onde conviene dire essere opere delli discendenti da lui, lavorate con suoi disegni." Interestingly enough, Orlandi does not use the same (often backfiring) arguments put forth by Vittoria, for which see my n. 22.

32. Fiorillo, *Geschichte*, I, (Meyer, *La storia*, 170).

33. G. P. Bellori, *Descrizzione delle imagini dipinte da Rafaelle d'Urbino nelle camere del Palazzo Apostolico Vaticano* (Rome: Komarck, 1695). Part of it has been translated by Alice Sedgwick Wohl ("The Image of the Ancient Gymnasium of Athens, or Philosophy," in *Raphael's School of Athens*, ed. Marcia B. Hall [New York: Cambridge University Press, 1997], 48–56). On the publication of this volume, see G. Previtali, "Introduzione" to Bellori, *Le vite*, p. XXVIII, n. 1, reprinted with additions in Borea and Gasparri, eds., *L'idea*, I, 166 and 177 n. 42. On Bellori and Raphael, see Perini, "Una certa idea," esp. 157–9.

34. For Bellori's appointments, see *Cronologia* in Bellori, *Le Vite*, LXI–LXIV. For his relations with the French, see J. C. Boyer, "Bellori e i suoi amici francesi," in Borea and Gasparri, eds., *L'idea*, I, 51–4, and idem, "La publication des *Vite*: une affaire française?"

in the proceedings of the conference on Bellori held at the Villa Medici in June 2000 (forthcoming). For an alternate view, see also G. Perini, "Belloriana Methodus – A Scholar's *Bildungsgeschichte* in Seventeenth-Century Rome," in *Art History in the Age of Bellori*, ed. J. Bell and T. Willette (New York: Cambridge University Press, 2002), 55–74. For Maratta, see Rudolph, "La direzione artistica," 59 and eadem, "Carlo Maratti," in Borea and Gasparri, *L'idea*, III, 456–8.

35. R. Fréart de Chambray, *La perfezione della pittura*, ed. F. Fanizza, (Palermo: Aesthetica, 1990).

36. Bottari and Ticozzi, *Raccolta*, III, 406–76.

37. On Bottari's edition, see P. Barocchi, "Premessa al commento secolare delle Vite di Giorgio Vasari," in eadem, *Studi vasariani* (Turin: Einaudi, 1984), 3–34, esp. 4–8.

38. Cf. L. Crespi in Bottari and Ticozzi, *Raccolta*, III, 445–50 and Reynolds, *Discourses*, 94–107.

39. In Bottari and Ticozzi, *Raccolta*, III, 387–443. Crespi addresses two letters to Algarotti on the problem of the restoration of pictures, often referring unfavorably to the restorations carried out under Maratta's supervision and celebrated by Bellori in his *Descrizzione* (see esp. 390–2, 406–8, 443).

40. On Bellori's technique of ekphrasis, see G. Perini, "L'arte di descrivere: la tecnica dell'ecfrasi in Malvasia e Bellori," in *I Tatti Studies* (1989): 175–206; L. Faedo, "Percorsi secenteschi verso una storia della pittura antica: Bellori e il suo contesto," in Borea and Gasparri, *L'idea*, I, 113–20 (with earlier literature); and most recently Sohm, *Style*, 45–50, and M. Hansmann, "*Con modo nuovo li descrive*: Bellori's Method of Describing," in Bell and Willette, *Art History*, 224–38. On Poussin's verbal descriptions of paintings as opposed to Bellori's and on his alleged role as an advisor to Bellori on the format for descriptions of art works, see G. Perini, "Il Poussin di Bellori," in *Poussin et Rome*, ed. O. Bonfait, C. L. Frommel, M. Hochmann, and S. Schütze (Paris: Réunion des Musées Nationaux, 1996), 293–308, esp. 297–9.

41. See J. Montagu, *The Expression of the Passion. The Origin and Influence of Charles Le Brun's Conference sur l'expression generale et particuliere* (New Haven and London: Yale University Press, 1994), esp. 9–30, 68–84.

42. Bellori, *Descrizzione*, 36–8.

43. Winckelmann, *Il bello*, 32–3 (English version in H. B. Nisbet ed., *German Aesthetic and Literary Criticism: Winckelmann, Lessing, Hamann, Herder, Schiller, Goethe* [Cambridge: Cambridge University Press, 1985], 44).

44. Cf. Bellori, *Le Vite*, 410–11. On this passage see also M. G. Barberini, "Giovan Pietro Bellori e la scultura contemporanea," in Borea and Gasparri, *L'idea*, I, 121–9, esp. 126.

45. Passeri, *Die Künstlerbiographien*, 397: "ma con Rafaele non haveva molta domestichezza, perchè la scuola Napolitana lo chiama tosto, di pietra e secco, e non vogliono amicizia sua." See also Sohm, *Style*, 31.

46. Malvasia, *Felsina*, III, 378. See also Emiliani, "La coscienza," 21.

47. L. Marzocchi, ed., *Scritti originali del Conte Carlo Cesare Malvasia spettanti alla sua Felsina Pittrice* (Bologna: Nuova Alfa, s.d. [1983]), 179. This episode has been dated to 1645: see A. Colombi Ferretti, "Simone Cantarini," in *La scuola di Guido Reni*, ed. M. Pirondini and E. Negro (Modena: Artioli, 1992), 124, n. 38.

48. See most recently M. Pirondini, "Guido Reni: la bottega e la scuola," in Pirondini and Negro, *La scuola*, 14.

49. Colombi Ferretti, "Simone Cantarini," 117–18, and Emiliani, "La coscienza," 19, 29–32, 41, 45, and also idem, "Simone Cantarini: la coscienza dell'artista moderno," in *Simone Cantarini nelle Marche*, ed. A. Emiliani et al. (Venice: Marsilio, 1997), XXI–LI esp. XXVIII, XXXI, XXXIII–XXXV, XLV.

50. J. Hess, *Einleitung*, in Passeri, *Die Künstlerbiographien*, esp. X–XVI.

51. M. Boschini, *La carta del navegar pitoresco*, ed. A. Pallucchini (Venice and Rome: Istituto per la collaborazione culturale, 1966), 79: "Rafael (a dirve el vero,/ Piasendome esser libero e sinciero)/ Stago per dir che nol me piase niente," repeated in E. Harris, *Velazquez* (Ithaca: Cornell University Press, 1982), 28 and 150–1, and in A. Perez Sanchez, "Velazquez e la sua arte," in *Velazquez*, (Milan: Fabbri, 1990), 44. In a different essay the same author (A. Perez Sanchez, "Raffaello nelle fonti letterarie spagnole," in *Raffaello e l'Europa*, ed. M. Fagiolo and M. L. Madonna [Rome: Istituto della Enciclopedie Italiane, 1990], 657–76, esp. 672) seems to credit Velazquez's opinion as repeated by Boschini. His essay (together with A. Avila, "L'influenza di Raffaello nella cultura spagnola del cinquecento attraverso le stampe," and R. Lopez Torrijos, "L'influsso di Raffaello nella pittura spagnola del Cinquecento," idem, 677–9 and 701–13, respectively) is the basic reference for Raphael's fame in Spain. On Boschini's passage see also Sohm, *Style*, 28–9.

52. See infra, preceding discussion.

53. On Dolce, see P. Barocchi, *Trattati d'arte del cinquecento* (Bari: Latezza, 1960–2), I, 141–206, especially 144, 148–50 (comparison between Raphael and Michelangelo), 153, 161–3, 166, 178, 187–93, 204. On Boschini's opinion of Raphael, see Perini, "Una certa idea," 156. It should be noted that until the late seventeenth and early eighteenth centuries, and more precisely until de Piles, Raphael was often appreciated also as a colourist, especially in opposition to Michelangelo and the Florentines: see J. Bell, "The Critical Reception of Raphael's Coloring in the Sixteenth and Early Seventeenth Centuries," in *TEXT. Transactions of the Society for Textual Scholarship*, ed. D. C. Greetham and W. Speed Hill (Ann Arbor: AMS Press, 1996), 199–215. See also eadem, "Color and Chiaroscuro," in Hall ed., *Raphael's School of Athens*, 85–113.

54. Bellori, *Le vite*, 627: "il poeta Boschino, parlando in persona d'un pittore di ritratti, formò una definitiva conclusione." On the life of Maratta, preserved in a manuscript that remained unpublished until 1731, see Borea, "Nota al testo," in Bellori, *Le Vite*, LXVII and LXXXI. On Maratta and Raphael, see M. Mena Marques, "Carlo Maratti e Raffaello," in Fagiolo and Madonna, *Raffaello*, 541–59.

55. Portrait painting did not rank high in the academic hierarchy of genres, nor in Hogarth's opinion, for which see M. Kitson, "Hogarth's 'Apology for Painters'," *The Walpole Society* (1966–8): 46–111.

56. See n. 45.

57. A. Palomino, *Lives of the Eminent Spanish Painters and Sculptors* (Cambridge: Cambridge University Press, 1987), 141. Cfr. A. Palomino, *Vidas*, ed. N. Ayala Mallory (Madrid: Alianza Ed., 1986), 156: "Objentáronle algunos el no pintar con suavidad y hermosura asuntos de más seriedad, en que podía emular a Rafael de Urbino, y satisfizo galantemente diciendo: *Que más quería ser primero en aquella groseria, que segundo en la delicadeza.*"

58. On Vittoria see, beside Palomino, *Lives*, 380–2, S. Rudolph, "Vincenzo Vittoria fra pitture, poesie e polemiche," in *Labyrinthos* (1988–9): 223–66.

59. Palomino, *Lives*, 149.

60. Ibid., 117.

61. Ibid., 142–3.

62. Ibid., 157–8.

63. Ibid., 158.

64. On Coello, see ibid., 42; on Ribalta, ibid., 91.

65. Ibid., 156–63. Cf. Perez Sanchez, *Velazquez*, 36 and J. L. Colomer, "Roma 1630. La tunica de José y el estudio de las pasiones," in *Reales Sitios* (1999): 39–49, esp. 44.

66. F. H. Taylor, *Artisti, principi e mercanti. Storia del collezionismo da Ramsete a Napoleone* (Turin: Einaudi, 1954), 293–305, and J. Brown, *The Golden Age of Painting in Spain* (New

Haven and London: Yale University Press, 1991), 202–4 and 208. On the dispersion of the collection of Charles I, see H. Trevor Roper, *The Plunder of the Arts in the Seventeenth Century* (London: Thomes & Hudson, 1970), 53–9 and, more specifically, A. Mac Gregor, "The King's Goods and the Commonwealth Sale – Materials and Context," in ed. A. Mac Gregor, *The Late King's Goods: Collections, Possessions and Patronage of Charles I in the Light of the Commonwealth Sale Inventories* (London and Oxford: Alistair Mc Alpine & Oxford University Press, 1989), 13–52.

67. Perini, "Una certa idea," 154.

68. J. Shearman, *Raphael's Cartoons in the Collection of Her Majesty the Queen and the Tapestries for the Sistine Chapel* (London: Phaidon, 1972), 138–64, and S. Fermor, *The Raphael Tapestry Cartoons* (London: Scala Books, 1996), 20–3.

69. Fiorillo, *Geschichte*, I (Meyer, *La Storia*, 167).

70. See Perini, "Una certa idea," 154–5.

71. Z. Z. Filipczak, *Picturing Art in Antwerp, 1550–1700* (Princeton: Princeton University Press, 1987), 26.

72. See, e.g., Filipczak, *Picturing*, 32, 81, 127.

73. See W. Melion, *Shaping the Netherlandish Canon. Karel van Mander's Schilder-boeck* (Chicago and London: University of Chicago Press, 1991), 38–59, esp. 51–6 and 168–9.

74. C. De Bie, *Het Gulden Cabinet van de Edele vry Schielder Const* (Soest: Davaco Publishers, 1971), 198.

75. On Sandrart and Raphael, see Perini, "Una certa idea," 153 and 155, nn. 38 and 40. On the Dutch and Raphael, idem, 153–5, with bibliography.

76. C. Petry, "La Transfiguration ou les leçons d'une restauration," in *Rubens dall'Italia all'Europa*, ed. C. Limentani Virdis and F. Bottacin (Vicenza: Neri Pozza, 1992), 49–59, esp. 49 and 57–9.

77. J. Burckhardt, *Rubens* (Turin: Einaudi, 1967), 5–14, and M. Jaffé, *Rubens and Italy* (Oxford: Phaidon, 1977), 22–9 and 46–9. For further literature see Perini, "Una certa idea," 159, n. 11.

78. See Perini, "Una certa idea," 153.

79. [Anon.], "Sir Joshua Reynolds' Collection of Pictures," in *The Burlington Magazine* (1945): 264, n. 82.

80. Quoted in F. Broun, *Sir Joshua Reynolds' Collection of Paintings* (Ph.D. diss., Princeton University, 1987), III, 68.

81. See G. Perini, "'L'ottino universale' del divino Raffaello: alle radici di una prassi eclettica dell'imitazione," in *Accademia Raffaello – Atti e studi* (2002): 9–28.

82. See Paulson, *Hogarth – III – Art and Politics, 1750–1764* (Cambridge: The Lutterworth Press, 1993), 255–7. See later Reynolds, *Discourses*, 254–5.

83. Paulson, *Hogarth – III*. On the history of this picture and its engraved reproductions, see idem, *Hogarth – II – High Art and Low, 1732–1750* (Cambridge: The Lutterworth Press, 1991), 342–52, and *Hogarth – III*, 41–7.

84. F. Antal, *Hogarth and His Place in European Art* (London: Routledge and Kegan Paul, 1961).

85. Paulson, *Hogarth – III*, 41–4.

86. Paulson, *Hogarth – II*, 231–8, esp. 231.

87. Ibid., 206–8.

88. W. Hogarth, *The Analysis of Beauty*, ed. R. Paulson (New Haven and London: Yale University Press, 1997), 5.

89. On Richardson's importance for Reynolds, see C. R. Leslie and T. Taylor, *Life and Times of Sir Joshua Reynolds* (London: John Murray, 1865), I, 9–12.

90. For Reynolds's sketches after Raphael, see at least the following sketchbooks: British Museum, London: Dept. of Prints and Drawings, sketchbook 201 a 10, fols. 20v (*Holy*

Family under the oak-tree), 21v (*Madonna dell'impannata*), 55r (*Portrait of Leo X with his cardinals*: around 1750 all these pictures were at Pitti, Florence); Copland-Griffiths collection, UK: larger sketchbook: fol. 25r (after the drawing of the *Leo X Nativity* now in the Louvre; I am grateful to Sylvia Ferino for indicating the source to me); smaller sketchbook: fols. 11r (a figure from the *Fire in the Borgo*), 22r (the figure of Heliodorus), 25r (*Mansuetudo*, in the Sala di Costantino: published by N. Penny, in the exhibition catalogue *Reynolds* [London: Weidenfeld & Nicolson, 1986], 333, entry and fig. n. 158), 30r (a figure from the *Parnassus*), 31r (*Prudence*, in the Sala di Costantino); Metropolitan Museum of Art, New York, sketchbook n. 1811, fol. 45v (the head of Heliodorus from the fresco of his expulsion); Yale Center for British Art, New Haven, sketchbook B 1984.24, drawing n. 3 (the Angel from the *Liberation of Saint Peter*), and possibly 73 (unidentified source: Raphael's name in Reynolds's handwriting); idem, sketches B 1975.4. 1575–1578 (individual figures from the *Stanze*, in particular, from the *Disputa*, the *Parnassus*, and the *Sala di Costantino*). No sketches after Raphael are evident amid the ones in the sketchbooks at the Fogg Art Museum, Cambridge, Massachusetts, the British Museum (sketchbook 201 a 9), Sir John Soane's Museum, and the Pierpont Morgan Library. In the Herschel Album (on loan to the Royal Academy, London), the following sketches are after Raphael, but not necessarily by Reynolds (some of them have been identified independently by Paul Joannides): fol. 25r (this sheet has been published by Penny in *Reynolds*, 334–5, entry and fig. 160); 26r (from the *Repulse of Attila*), 27r (same source), 28r (from *The Battle of Constantine*), 43r (it is a sixteenth-century drawing with *Loth and His daughters fleeing from Sodoma*, from the *Logge*), 46r (from the *Expulsion of Heliodorus*, not by Reynolds); possibly 79r, n. 1; possibly 84r, n. 2; 93r, n. 1 (published in L. Herrmann, "The Drawings of Sir Joshua Reynolds in the Herschel Album," in *Burlington Magazine* [1968]: 650–8, fig. n. 2); possibly 95r, n. 2; 105r, n. 3 (published in Herrmann, "The Drawings," fig. n. 16); 109r, n. 1 (from a drawing or print); 114r, n. 3 (a variation on the *Colonna Madonna*, holding a bird instead of a book); 125r, n. 4 (*Mercury* in the Farnesina); possibly 126r, n. 1.

91. Quoted in T. Puttfarken, *Roger de Piles' Theory of Art* (New Haven and London: Yale University Press, 1985), 55; see also Michel, *Charles Nicolas Cochin*, 216, n. 47.

92. F. W. Hilles, *The Literary Career of Sir Joshua Reynolds* (Cambridge: Cambridge University Press, 1936), 246–7. This point is addressed also by Mengs (A. R. Mengs, *Pensieri sulla pittura*, ed. M. Cometa [Palermo: Aesthetica, 1996], 48): "La causa per cui le opere di Raffaello a prima vista non piacciono egualmente a tutti, si è che le sue bellezze sono bellezze della ragione, e non degli occhi: onde non sono sentite subito dalla vista, ma soltanto allorchè abbiano penetrato nell'intelletto; ed essendo molte persone di un senso intellettuale assai fiacco, esse non sentono niente affatto le bellezze di questo gran pittore." Practically, he repeats a point first made by Giovanni Boccaccio on Giotto; see Boccaccio, *Decameron* (Milan: Hoepli, 1942), 388 (V story of the VI day).

93. Hilles, *The Literary Career*, 226.

94. Copland Griffiths sketchbook, fol. 4r (my numbering, which follows the original sequence of text and sketches).

95. An extraordinary number of drawings attributed to Raphael and prints after his works are indeed recorded in the sales catalogues of Reynolds's collection; see, for instance, de Poggi (*A Catalogue of the First Part of the Cabinet of Ancient Drawings which Belonged to Sir Joshua Reynolds Deceased* [...] [London, 1794]), XIX (where a total of twenty-four drawings by him is given as on sale), p. 11, lots 226–7; p. 12, lots 239–40; p. 13, lots 253–4, 257–8, 264–5; p. 14, lots 293–5; p. 15, lots 304 and 319; 16, lots 334–8; p. 17, lots 356–7 and 371–2; and Phillips (*Unique Collection of Drawings and Prints. A Catalogue of all the Great and Valuable Collection of Ancient Drawings, Scarce Prints and Books of Prints which Belonged to Sir Joshua Reynolds Deceased* [...] [London, 1798]), p. 5, lot

26 (5 drawings); p. 6, lots 61, 65–6, 68 (prints); p. 7, lots 103, 110; p. 8, lots 113, 116, 119(?);
p. 11, lots 180, 184 (prints); p. 12, lots 216, 218; p. 15, lots 292 (prints); p. 17, lots 353 and
358; p. 19, lot 391 (prints); p. 20, lots 434–5 (prints); p. 21, lots 437–8 and 450 (prints),
451, 453–4 (described as drawings but must be prints); p. 22, lot 480 (drawing?); p. 24,
lot 510 (prints); p. 25, lots 518–20, 523–4, 536, 538–9 (prints); p. 26, lots 554 and 571;
p. 28, lot 612 (prints); p. 29, lots 617–19; p. 31, lots 678 and 687; p. 35, lot 775; p. 37,
lots 801–3 (prints); p. 38, lots 821, 824–5, 832, 842 (prints); p. 40, lots 874, 889, and
898; p. 41, lots 904, 910, 912, 914 (prints); p. 42, lots 918, 921–2, 924, 928, 936, 938,
941–2, 946 (prints); p. 43, lot 949 (prints); p. 46, lots 1004–5, 1011 (prints); p. 47, lots
1019–24, 1040 (prints); p. 48, lot 1067; p. 49, lot 1088; p. 50, lot 1109 (prints); p. 51,
lots 1109, 1124, 1133, 1136, 1138 (prints); p. 53, lots 1174–5; p. 55, lots 1211 and 1213–14
(prints); p. 56, lots 1216, 1220, 1222, 1224–5, 1227–8, 1230, 1234, 1238–40; p. 58, lot
1291; p. 60, lots 1307–13 (prints); p. 61, lots 1314, 1318, 1320, 1329 (prints); p. 62, lot 1341
(prints); p. 65, lots 1416–18 (prints); p. 67, lot 1446 (prints); p. 68, lot 1480; p. 70, lots
1511, 1514, 1520 (prints); p. 71, lot 1529 (prints); p. 72, lot 1557; p. 73, lot 1600; p. 75,
lot 1628 (prints); p. 76, lot 1642 (prints); p. 77, lots 1675, 1681; p. 78, lots 1686, 1695,
1696, 1702; p. 80, lots 1742, 1744, 1746–8 (prints); p. 81, lots 1752 (prints) and 1776,
1778 (drawings); p. 83, lots 1816 and 1818; p. 85, lots 1863, 1871 (prints); p. 86, lots 1878,
1884 (prints), 1888 (drawings); p. 87, lot 1920; p. 88, lots 1942, 1945 ("Madonna and
Child, large as life, a remarkable fine coloured drawing by Raphael"), and 1947; p. 89,
lot 1967 (print). Some of Raphael's drawings in Reynolds's collection were reproduced
in C. Rogers, *A Collection of Prints in Imitation of Drawings* (London: Joseph Kay,
1778), pl. I and XXVIa. For paintings attributed to Raphael in Reynolds's collection of
pictures, see [Anon.], "Sir Joshua Reynolds," p. 216, n. 57: "Raphael, The Head of the
Madona"; p. 267, n. 4: "Raphael, The Portrait of Baltazer Castiglione, after"; p. 268,
n. 64: "Raphael, The Virgin and Child with Saints – valuable as a juvenile specimen
of the innate merit and beauties of a surprising genius"; p. 270, n. 95: "Raphael –
The Madona, Infant Christ and Saint John. This picture sufficiently proves the great
superiority of Raphael's admired taste and elegance: the lovely sweetness and attention
expressed in the Madona, the admiration in the St John, the delicacy and beauty of
the infant Jesus sleeping all combine to render it unique."

96. On Ratti's studies after Raphael and his relation to Mengs, see R. Collu, "L'attività sto-
riografica di Carlo Giusepe Ratti," in *Atti e Memorie della Società Savonese di Storia
Patria* (1981): 185–204, esp. 196–8 and fig. 7 (*Head of Saint Peter*, from *The Freeing of
Saint Peter* in the Vatican), and eadem, *Carlo Giuseppe Ratti pittore e storiografo d'arte*
(Savona: Editrice Liguria, 1983), esp. 25, 36, 45, 89–90, 94–5, 103. For his copies after
Raphael (the *School of Athens* and the *Madonna della seggiola*), see idem, 40–2 and
202–3, entries nn. 25 and 28 and fig. 2; for drawings after Raphael, see idem, 207,
entry no. 45 and fig. 7. The oil painting featuring *Raphael and Bramante offering the
projects for the Vatican to Julius II* formerly in Palazzo Sansoni in Savona is lost (idem,
235, entry no. 102). As for Ansaldi's drawings (figs. 1 and 5), they are preserved in
the Fondo Ansaldi of the Museo Civico in Pescia, nos. 1844–136 and 1845–137. Given
that both the male figure from the *Transfiguration* and the female figure from the
Expulsion of Heliodorus are in reverse, it is apparent that they have been copied from
prints rather than from the actual works in Rome. In particular, the only known print
of the Heliodorus in reverse is the one by Maratta; as for the *Transfiguration*, the
prints in reverse are by Agostino Veneziano, Johannes Sadeler and van Westerhout:
see G. Bernini Pezzini, S. Massari, and S. Prosperi Valenti Rodinò, eds., *Raphael Invenit* (Rome: Quasar, 1985), 46 (entry I.1) and 304 for Heliodorus; 177–81 (entries
nn. X.2, X.6, and X.7), and 680–1 for the *Transfiguration*. (Stylistic reason rule out
Agostino Veneziano as a source; van Westerhout's version seems closer to the character

of the drawing than Sadeler's.) It should be noted that also Mengs's drawings after Raphael are taken from prints: see my n. 105. On Innocenzo Ansaldi, see G. Perini, "Mengs e Correggio: a proposito di un manoscritto fiorentino delle 'Memorie'," in *Il Settecento tedesco in Italia- Gli italiani e l'immagine della cultura tedesca nel XVIII secolo*, ed. G. Cantarutti, S. Ferrari, and P. M. Filippi (Bologna: Il Mulino, 2001), 467–96, passim, esp. 490, n. 84; P. Vitali, "Lettere d'arte del secolo XVIII. Luigi Crespi ad Innocenzio Ansaldi (1768–1776)," in *Accademia Clementina. Atti e Memorie* (2000): 47–71; idem, "Innocenzo Ansaldi critico ed artista del Settecento," in A. Labardi, ed., *Gli Ansaldi: una famiglia di storici e di chierici* (Pisa: ETS, 2003), 15–93; E. Pellegrini, "Genesi di una *Descrizione*," in *Descrizione delle sculture, pitture et architetture della città e sobborghi di Pescia nella Toscana*, ed. I. Ansaldi and L. Crespi (Pisa: ETS, 2001), 9–28.

97. See G. Perini, "Hogarth's Visual Mnemotechnics: Notes on Abstraction as an Aide-Memoire for Figurative Painters," in *Memory and Oblivion, Proceedings of the XXIX International Congress of the History of Art*, ed. W. Reinink and J. Stumpel (Dordrecht: Kluwer, 1999), 837–46. In fact Hogarth's sketch for the headpiece of *The Jacobite Journal* of 1747 (Windsor, Royal Library) is stylistically akin to most of Reynolds's sketches in his Italian sketchbooks (see A. P. Oppé, *English Drawings – Stuart and Georgian Periods in the Collection of His Majesty the King at Windsor Castle* [London: Phaidon, 1950], 63, entry no. 352 and pl. 62. On its disputed attribution, see Paulson, *Hogarth – II*, 447, n. 10).

98. D. Mannings, *Sir Joshua Reynolds – A Complete Catalogue of His Paintings* (New Haven and London: Yale University Press, 2000), I, 491–92, entry no. 1962, and II, 154, fig. 61.

99. For Reynolds's pictures, see Mannings, *Sir Joshua*, I, 153, entry no. 450, and p. 309, entry n. 1137, and II, p. 376, fig. 878, and p. 460, fig. 1171. For their sources, some had been noted first by Nathaniel Hone in his notorious *The Conjuror*, see, for instance, J. Newman, "*The Conjuror* Unmasked," in Penny, *Reynolds*, 344–54, with further examples; and idem, 275, entry n. 103. For the fortune of Mrs. Lloyd's portrait in Anglo-American literature, see E. Wharton, *The House of Mirth* (New York and London: Bantam Classics, 1986), 128–9. Incidentally, it should be noted that the two figures from the *Parnassus* used in the double portrait of the Crewe sisters are sketched out in the sheet marked B 1975.4.1575 at the Yale Center for British Art, New Haven (see my n. 90).

100. For Reynolds's pictures see Mannings, *Sir Joshua*, I, p. 131, entry no. 358, and p. 136, entry no. 380; and II, p. 429, fig. 1064; and p. 518, fig. 1354. J. Merz ("Reynolds' Borrowings," *Burlington Magazine* [1995]: 516–17) is grossly mistaken in assuming that *Galatea* is also the source for the portrait of *Colonel Tarleton*. Sound factual and documentary evidence earlier supplied by me ("On Reynolds's Art of Borrowing: Two More Italian Sources," *Burlington Magazine* [1994]: 26–9, taken up by J. Egerton, *National Gallery Catalogues – The British School* [New Haven and London: Yale University Press, 1998], 218–27, esp. 223–4) and basic methodological reasons later summarised in Perini, "Paura," 114, n. 405, disprove every line in his contribution.

101. E.g., the portrait of *Lady Cathcart and Her Daughter* (1755) loosely derives from Raphael's *Madonna del Granduca, Theory* from a figure in the vault of the Chigi Chapel as E. Gombrich has shown ("Reynolds's Theory and Practice of Imitation," *Burlington Magazine* [1942]: 40–5); in the portrait of *Lady Elizabeth Herbert and Her Son*, the latter derives from the little angel on the right in the *Virtues* in the Stanza della Segnatura, reversed; the portrait of *Master Wynn* finds an interesting precedent in the Christchild of the *Madonna with Child* in Baltimore; in the double portrait nicknamed *The Archers* the rear archer recalls the fleeing figure in the forefront of the *Expulsion of Heliodorus*, running next to the horseman (for which see Royal Academy of Arts,

London, Herschel Album, fol. 46r, mentioned in my n. 90). For all these pictures, see Mannings, *Sir Joshua Reynolds*, respectively I, p. 123, entry no. 324; p. 567, entry no. 2168; p. 253, entry no. 885; p. 485, entry no. 1946; p. 58, entry no. 41; and II, p. 163, fig. 97; p. 616, fig. 1704; p. 359, fig. 817; p. 445; fig. 1116; p. 401, fig. 961.

102. H. von Erffa and A. Staley, *The Paintings of Benjamin West* (New Haven and London: Yale University Press, 1986), esp. 19 and 44, as well as entries no. 513–14 (p. 446), 535 (p. 457), and 676 (p. 541). The *Moses and Aaron before Pharaoh* at Bob Jones University (entry no. 252, pp. 296–7) clearly derives both its composition and style from Hogarth's *Paul before Felix*, rather than from Raphael's Cartoons. On Raphael's reputation in America, see G. A. Hirschauer, "La fortuna di Raffaello in America nel XVIII e XIX secolo," in Fagiolo and Madonna, *Raffaello*, 799–817.

103. On Reynolds's reuse of visual patterns and on his studio, see M. Kirby Talley Jr., "'All Good Pictures Crack: Sir Joshua Reynolds's Practice and Studio," in Penny, *Reynolds*, 55–70, esp. 57–8 and 61–2. As for Raphael's studio practice, see most recently K. Oberhuber, "Lo stile classico di Raffaello e la sua evoluzione a Roma fino al 1527," in *Raffaello e lo stile classico di Raffaello*, ed. K. Oberhuber and A. Gnann (Milan: Electa, 1999), 17–29 (with earlier literature), and, for its derivation from Perugino's workshop, R. Hiller von Gaertringen, "On Perugino's Reuse of Cartoons," in *Le dessin sous-jacent et la technique dans la peinture. Perspectives*, ed. R. van Schoute and H. Verougstraete (Louvain: Collège Erasme, 1996), 223–30.

104. Reynolds, *Discourses*, 84.

105. On Mengs and Raphael, see S. Röttgen, "Mengs e Raffaello. Rendiconto di un rapporto programmato," in Fagiolo and Madonna eds., *Raffaello*, 619–53. On works by Mengs inspired by Raphael, see eadem, *Anton Raphael Mengs, 1728–1779. Das malerische und zeichnerische Werk* (Munich: Hirmer, 1999), 70–1, entry no. 38; pp. 72–3, entry nos. 39 and 40; pp. 74–5, n. 43; pp. 75–6, n. 44; pp. 77–8, n. 45; pp. 79–81, n. 46; pp. 112–17, n. 69; pp. 164–7, n. 108; pp. 187–8, n. 126; 188–9, nn. 127–8; 189–96, n. 129; pp. 433–4, nn. Z 42–Z 46 (from prints); pp. 442–3, n. z 61; p. 463, Z 114–5; pp. 474–87, n. Z 141.

106. On Scannelli and the other major Italian seventeenth-century art historians not discussed so far (such as Scaramuccia, Baldinucci, etc.) see Perini, "Una certa idea," 155–7.

107. Mengs, *Pensieri*, 46–8, 49–52, 54–62. Of course, see also idem, *Opere*, ed. G. N. D'Azara (Bassano: Remondini, 1783), esp. I, 136–74, and II, 205–305.

108. Mengs, *Pensieri*, 48: "Raffaello resta pertanto sempre il primo."

109. Reynolds, *Discourses*, 83–4.

110. Mannings, *Sir Joshua*, I, 51, entry no. 21, and II, 511, fig. 1330. Mannings's dating to "c. 1780, or slightly earlier" replaces an earlier, widely accepted 1773.

CHAPTER 13. RESTORING RAPHAEL

1. I acknowledge the assistance of my doctoral students – Andrea Bubenik, Kim Muir, and Krystina Stermole – and my colleagues David McTavish, John Osborne, and Hans-Christoph von Imhoff, in the research and completion of this chapter. Financial support was generously given by the Social Sciences and Humanities Research Council of Canada.

2. Giorgio Vasari, *Le vite…* (1568), ed. Gaetano Milanesi (1878–85), vol. 4 (1879), 321–2. *Raffaello a Firenze: dipinti e disegni delle collezioni fiorentine*, exh. cat., Florence, Palazzo Pitti, 1984 (Milan: Electa, 1984), 77–87.

3. "There it was protected by two shutters lined with green velvet, ornamented with gold"; G. B. Cavalcaselle and J. A. Crowe, *Raphael: His Life and Works*, 2 vols. (London:

John Murray, 1882, 1885), vol. 2, 396, note *. Also Andrew McClellan, *Inventing the Louvre: Art, Politics, and the Origins of the Modern Museum in Eighteenth-Century Paris* (Cambridge and New York: Cambridge University Press, 1994), 28.

4. Ségolène Bergeon, "Contribution à l'Histoire de la Restauration des Peintures en Italie au XVIIIe et au début du XIXe siècle: Fresques et Peintures de Chevalet," (Unpublished Thesis, L'École du Louvre, 1975), 2–3.

5. Cesare Brandi explained that the conservator must use his or her imagination and critical judgment to bring the potential unity of the fragments to the greatest possible validity for representation in the present, rather than naïvely attempting to bring back the irrecoverable wholeness of the past. Cesare Brandi, *Teoria del Restauro* (Turin: Einaudi, 1963; reprint, 1977); and N. S. Price, M. K. Talley, Jr., and A. M. Vaccaro, eds., *Historical and Philosophical Issues in the Conservation of Cultural Heritage* (Los Angeles: Getty Conservation Institute, 1996), 231–5.

6. *Maestri e botteghe: Pittura a Firenze alla fine del Quattrocento*, exh. cat., Florence, Palazzo Strozzi, 1992; and Cathleen Hoeniger, *The Renovation of Paintings in Tuscany, 1250–1500* (Cambridge and New York: Cambridge University Press, 1995).

7. Two examples are the destruction of medieval houses surrounding the Pantheon under Eugène IV and the isolation of the Arch of Titus from the Fortress Frangipani under Sixtus IV.

8. Anna Lo Bianco, "Capolavori da salvare: Restauri dei secoli scorsi," *Art Dossier* 6 (October 1986): 50–5, at 51.

9. Johann Winckelmann, *Geschichte der Kunst des Altertums* (Dresden: Waltherischen Hof-buchhandlung, 1764). Winckelmann had planned to write a treatise on restoration, but what remains are his numerous comments, often highly critical, on contemporary reconstructions of ancient remains. See Roger H. Marijnissen, *Dégradation, conservation et restauration de l'oeuvre d'art* (Brussels: Arcade, 1967), 42–3; Seymour Howard, *Antiquity Restored: Essays on the Afterlife of the Antique* (Vienna: IRSA Verlag, 1990), 162–71; Francis Haskell, *History and Its Images: Art and the Interpretation of the Past* (New Haven and London: Yale University Press, 1993), 218–24. For a more general discussion of approaches to the past, David Lowenthal, *The Past Is a Foreign Country* (Cambridge: Cambridge University Press, 1985).

10. Bartolomeo Cavaceppi, *Raccolta d'antiche statue, busti, bassirilievi ed altre sculture restaurate da B.C. scultore Romano* (Rome, 1786), 3 vols., as discussed by Michelangelo Cagiano de Azevedo, *Il gusto nel restauro delle opere d'arte antiche* (Rome: Olympus, 1948), 68–70.

11. Paolo Marconi, *Giuseppe Valadier* (Rome: Officina Edizioni, 1964); Bergeon, "Contribution," 9–10.

12. Giovan Pietro Bellori, *Le vite de' pittori, scultori e architetti moderni*, ed. Evelina Borea, intro. by Giovanni Previtali (Turin: Einaudi, 1976), 31. On Bellori, see E. Panofsky, *"Idea": Ein Beitrag zur Begriffsgeschichte der älteren Kunsttheorie* (Leipzig and Berlin: B. G. Teubner, 1924); Julius von Schlosser, *Die Kunstliteratur* (Vienna: A. Schroll & Co., 1924).

13. In Giovan Pietro Bellori, "Descrizzione delle Imagini Dipinte da Rafaëlle d'Urbino nelle Camere del Palazzo Apostolico Vaticano," in *Descrizzione delle Imagini Dipinte da Rafaëlle d'Urbino* (1695; reprint, Farnborough, England: Gregg International, 1968), 38–9. Also: "Onde la presente battaglia [the Battle of the Milvian Bridge] resta da paragonarsi solo alla fama di Polignoto, di Apelle, e degli altri Greci più celebri, di cui solo rimane il grido"; Bellori, *Descrizzione*, 59.

14. Giovan Pietro Bellori, "La favola di Amore e Psiche dipinta da Rafaëlle d'Urbino nella loggia dette de' Chigi, oggi del Sereniss. Signor Duca di Parma, in Roma alla Lungara," in *Descrizzione delle imagine dipinte da Rafaelle* (Roma, 1695), op. cit., p. 74;

see also 78–9 on the *Marriage of Cupid and Psyche*. Bellori also wrote a Latin treatise on Raphael's rendering of the story by Apuleius, published together with thirty-two engravings after Raphael by Nicolas Dorigny: *Psyches et Amoris nuptiae in fabula a Raphaele Sanctio Urbinate…Romae in Farnesianis hortis expressa a Nicolae Dorigny ad similitudinem delineata et aeri incisa at a Io: Pietro Bellori notis illustrata* (Roma, 1693).

15. Giovanni Previtali, "Introduction," in Bellori, *Le vite*, xxviii. Maratti's biography is the only one Bellori wrote of a living artist; in Bellori, *Le Vite*, 569–654. See also Stella Rudolph, "Carlo Maratti," in *L'Idea del Bello: Viaggio per Roma nel Seicento con Giovan Pietro Bellori*, exh. cat., Rome, Palazzo delle Esposizioni, 2 vols. (Rome: Edizioni De Luca, 2000), vol. 2, 456–79.

16. Ann Sutherland Harris, *Andrea Sacchi: complete edition of the paintings with a critical catalogue* (Oxford: Phaidon, 1977).

17. Bellori writes about how Maratti followed above all else "la guida di Rafaello"; in Bellori, *Le vite*, 573–654, esp. 625–33. See also Lo Bianco, "Capolavori," 51.

18. Bergeon, "Contribution," 101.

19. Rosalia Varoli and Gabriella Serangeli, "A conservative intervention planned for frescoes by Raphael in the Loggia of Psyche. 1) Preliminary historic-artistic investigation. 2) Problems and experiences relating to the intervention," in *Restauro degli affreschi: Esperienze, metodologie e criteri di conservazione*, Brescia, 5–9 July, 1993, (Emilia Romagna: Irecoop, 1993), 107–16, at 108. See also Rosalia Varoli-Piazza, "La 'Considerazione' della Loggia di Psiche attraverso i restauri da Maratti a Hermanin," in *Raffaello e L'Europa*, Atti del IV Corso Internazionale di Alta Cultura, eds. M. Fagiolo and M. L. Madonna (Rome: Ist. Poligrafico dello Stato, 1990), 567–80.

20. Bellori, *Vita del signor Carlo Maratti*, in *Le vite*, 649: "nella loggia dipinta da Rafaelle alla Longara, la quale…è stata da lui restituita alla sua prima bellezza e compimento delle lunette ed ornamenti, quasi venga ora dalle mani del maestro."

21. Bellori, "Della riparazione," in *Descrizzione*, 81.

22. Ibid., 81–2. This very full description of Rossi's technique is actually provided by Bellori in his discussion of Maratti's restoration of the frescoes by the Carracci in the Palazzo Farnese across the river; however, following this discussion of the work on the Carracci frescoes, Bellori turns to consider the Raphaels in the loggia of the Farnesina and refers to Rossi's technique again, though far more briefly (83).

23. R. Varoli-Piazza et al., "La Loggia di Psyché à la Farnesina: anciennes restaurations et études interdisciplinaires en vue d'une intervention de conservation," in *Les Anciennes Restauration en Peinture Murale*, Journées d'études de la S.F.I.I.C., Dijon, 25–27 March 1993, 153–67; Varoli and Serangeli, "A conservative intervention," in *Restauro degli affreschi* (1993), 111–12.

24. "…operazione di meraviglia che avrebbe fatto tremare ogni piú ardito pennello, ove il signor Carlo con un poco di lapis e di pastello ha perfettamente ristorato i contorni ed il colore," *Vita del signor Carlo Maratti*, in Bellori, *Le vite*, 649. Also Bellori, *Le vite*, 616, where the pastel restoration method is described in relation to another image: "Pigliati dunque colori di pastelli di terre macinate a gomma, con essi dipinse il velo sovra 'l petto della Vergine,…in modo che rimane durabile; e quando si voglia torre con la sponga, ritorna il color di prima." Also Alessandro Conti, *Storia del restauro e della conservazione delle opere d'arte* (Milan: Electa, 1973; rev. ed. 1988), 107–11.

25. Varoli-Piazza, "Considerazione," 571 and n. 27; also Varoli and Serangeli, "A conservative intervention," in *Restauro degli affreschi* (1993), 110.

26. See C. P. Landon, *Vies et Oeuvres des Peintres les plus Célèbres de toutes les Écoles* (Paris: Treuth & Würtz, 1817), 35; Casimir Stryienski, *La Galerie du Régent, Philippe, duc d'Orléans* (Paris: Goupil & cie, 1913), 70–2. Also Conti, *Storia*, 135, 233–4.

27. Lo Bianco, "Capolavori," 51–2.
28. Varoli and Serangeli, "A conservative intervention," in *Restauro degli affreschi* (1993), 113.
29. This work was carried out by Maratti's assistants, Domenico Paradisi and Giuseppe Belletti. Bellori, *Descrizzione*, 85–6. Also Varoli and Serangeli, "A conservative intervention," in *Restauro degli affreschi* (1993), 109.
30. This point is also made by Andrea G. De Marchi, "Il restauro marattesco delle Stanze: aspetti tecnici e storico-critici," *Rivista dell'Istituto Nazionale d'Archeologia e Storia dell' Arte* 3, no. 13 (1990): 265–81, at 266.
31. Bellori, *Descrizzione*, 84–5.
32. Charles De Brosses, "Lettres Familieres sur l'Italie" (1739–40), republished as *Viaggio in Italia. Lettere familiari*, trans. B. Schacherl, 3 vols. (Rome: Parenti, 1957), 2, 193–4.
33. L. Crespi, "Lettere a Francesco Algarotti" (1756), in G. G. Bottari, *Raccolta di lettere sulla pittura, scultura ed architettura* (Rome, 1754–1773), ed. S. Ticozzi (Milan, 1822–1825; reprint, Hildesheim: G. Olms, 1976), 3, 387–417, 419–43. Conti, *Storia*, 99–100. Also Francesco Algarotti, "Saggio sopra la pittura" (1762), in *Saggi*, ed. G. da Pozzo (Bari: Gius. Laterza & Figli, 1963), 130–1 (on Raphael and Carlo Maratti).
34. Filippo Titi, *Descrizione delle pitture, sculture e architetture*, 2d ed. (Rome, 1763; reprint with intro. by F. Prinzi, Rome: Multigrafica Ed., 1978), 34–5.
35. Bellori, *Le vite*, 617. De Marchi, "Il restauro." Lo Bianco, "Capolavori," 52–3.
36. Cornelia Wagner, *Arbeitsweisen und Anschauungen in der Gemälderestaurierung um 1800* (Munich: Callwey, 1988), 22. One example is Andrea del Sarto's *Holy Family* in the Louvre.
37. Marijnissen, *Dégredation*, 34.
38. Martin Rosenberg, *Raphael and France: The Artist as Paradigm and Symbol* (University Park: Pennsylvania State University Press, 1995).
39. For Bellori's discussion of Raphael as the modern Apelles and as well rounded in his greatness, see Bellori, *Descrizzione*, 93–9.
40. Roland de Fréart de Chambray, *Idée de la perfection de la peinture* (Le Mans, 1662).
41. André Félibien, *Entretiens sur les vies et sur les ouvrages des plus excellens peintres anciens et modernes* (Paris, 1666).
42. Martin Rosenberg, "Raphael's *Transfiguration* and Napoleon's Cultural Politics," *Eighteenth-Century Studies* 19, no. 2 (1985–86): 180–205.
43. Volker Schaible stresses the importance of "ethical and aesthetical reflections" in motivating art policy changes that led to modern restoration approaches, in "Die Gemäldeübertragung: Studien zur Geschichte einer 'klassischen Restauriermethode'," *Maltechnik – Restauro* 2, no. 89 (1983): 96–129.
44. A document of c. 1530 records that the court painter, the Italian mannerist Francesco Primaticcio, had been paid to "wash and clean" (lavé et nettoyé) the two panels early on; Marijnissen, *Dégredation*, 30 and n. 23.
45. Typically, Italian Renaissance wood panel supports were prepared by the carpenter's shop with frames attached, and only subsequently gessoed and painted. The attached frame hampered and complicated the natural movement of the panels comprising the wood support, a movement caused by changes in temperature and humidity. When the wood support and frame were naturally warped from aging (loss of moisture in the wood cells) and climactic variations (humidity), the fact that the frame was permanently attached resulted in increased tension in the paint layers.
46. Conti quotes from the report of 1749 addressed to the director of the Bâtiments, *Storia*, 126–7.
47. Pierre Marot, "Recherches sur les origines de la transposition de la peinture en France," *Les Annales de l'Est* 4 (1950): 241–83, at 250.

48. On Picault describing himself as the inventor of the transfer method, see Anon., "Beaux Arts: Tableaux du Roi, placés dans le Palais du Luxembourg," *Mercure de France* (Decembre 1750): n. 1, 146–51, at 150–1; and Lépicié, Secretary of the Academy of Painting in Paris, in his catalogue of the king's pictures, *Catalogue raisonné des tableaux du Roy* (Paris: Imprimerie Nationale, 1752), vol. 1, 43–4; also Gilberte Émile-Mâle, "La première transposition au Louvre en 1750: La Charité d'Andrea del Sarto," *Revue du Louvre et des Musées de France* 3 (1982): 223–31, at 223, n. 1. On the development of transfer techniques in Italy prior to Picault, see Bergeon, "Contribution," 30–40. It is interesting to note that the experts in fresco detachment in Italy, such as Antonio Contri, also kept their methods secret; Bergeon, "Contribution," 43 and 46. However, as the critical anonymous author of a letter to the *Mercure de France* in 1755 pointed out, Picault had probably learned how to transfer paint layers from panel to an intensively prepared new canvas from one "Riario." Cavalier Francesco Maria Riario was an Italian nobleman interested in medicine, optics, physics, and painting restoration, who displayed his ability to transfer paintings on visits to Brussels (1741) and Paris (1756). On "Riario," see Anon., "Peinture: Lettre écrite de Bruxelles sur le secret de transporter les tableaux sur de nouveaux fonds, & de les reparer," *Mercure de France* (Janvier 1756): no. 2, 174–85, at 174–5; Anon. [Father Berthier], *Mémoires de Trévoux* (January 1751): 452 ff., and also 105–25, "Lettre au P. B. J. Sur les Tableaux exposes au Luxembourg"; Émile-Mâle, "Première," 225. For further discussion of the earliest transfer experts in Italy and elsewhere, see Licia Borrelli, "Restauro e restauratori dei dipinti in Francia dal 1750 al 1860," *Bollettino del Istituto Centrale del Restauro* 3–4 (1950): 71–84; Michelangelo Cagiano de Azevedo, "Una scuola napoletana di restauro nel 17 e 18 secolo," *Bollettino del Istituto Centrale del Restauro* 1 (1950): 44–5; D. Coekelberghs, "Précisions sur la vie et l'oeuvre du peintre-restaurateur bruxellois Frédéric Dumesnil (vers 1710–1791)," *Bulletin de l'I. R.P.A.* 9 (1969): 172–8.

49. Anon., "Beaux Arts," *Mercure de France* (Decembre 1750): 150–1, n. 1.

50. Émile-Mâle, "Première," 226.

51. Lépicié, *Catalogue raisonné des tableaux du roy*, tom. 1 (Paris, 1752), 43–44; see Émile-Mâle, "Première," 223.

52. Niccolo Zabaglia's celebrated transfer in 1700 of Domenichino's *Martyrdom of Saint Sebastian* was an engineering feat. See the account by Filippo Titi in his *Descrizione delle pitture, sculture e architetture* (Rome, 1763), 10. Bergeon, "Contribution," 35–7.

53. Diderot had been educated by the Jesuits (as were many of the *philosophes* of the Enlightenment), and he maintained close ties with Jesuit intellectuals in Paris. See Jacques Chouillet, *Diderot* (Paris: Societé d'Edition d'Enseignement Superieur, 1957), 277; and Charles Coulston Gillispie, "Denis Diderot," in the *Dictionary of Scientific Biography*, ed. Charles Coulston Gillispie, 18 vols. (New York: Charles Scribner's Sons, 1970–), vol. 4 (1971), 84–90, at 84.

54. Gillispie, "Denis Diderot," 86.

55. Arthur M. Wilson, *Diderot: The Testing Years, 1713–1759* (New York: Oxford University Press, 1957), 244.

56. Diderot's family background was among the prosperous artisans of provincial Langres, north of Dijon.

57. Gillispie, "Denis Diderot," 86–7.

58. Indeed, in the Janvier 1751 issue of the *Mémoires de Trévoux*, in which Picault's transfer of Andrea del Sarto's *Charity* is discussed in vol. 1 on p. 110, the publication of Diderot's encyclopedia by Le Breton in ten folio volumes with two volumes of plates is announced in vol. 2, on 302–27.

59. *Mémoires pour l'Histoire des Sciences & des beaux Arts* (known as the *Mémoires de Trévoux*, because it was published in Trévoux), Février 1751, Article XXVI, "Observations sur l'Art de conserver les Ouvrages de Peinture qui menacent ruine," 452–65, esp. 457.

60. Ibid., 458–9.

61. Ibid., 459.

62. Ibid., 464. The reflective realization, expressed frequently during the seventeenth, eighteenth, and nineteenth centuries, that precious and exemplary works of art were in danger due to the inevitable effects of degradation also led to the commissioning of copies. Wagner, *Arbeitsweisen*, 23; and Hubertus von Sonnenburg, *Raphael in der Alten Pinakothek*, exh. cat. Munich, Alten Pinakothek (Munich: Prestel Verlag, 1983), 78.

63. Marot, "Recherches," 250.

64. Conti, *Storia*, 127.

65. Ibid., 128.

66. Ibid., 128–9.

67. At one point Father Berthier refers to the new "maroufle" as a "resin." *Mémoires de Trévoux*, Fev. 1751, p. 121.

68. Émile-Mâle, "Première," 227, with technical analysis by Jean Petit; Gilberte Émile-Mâle, "Étude de la restauration de La Charité d'Andrea del Sarto," in *Le XVIe siècle florentin au Louvre*, dossier no. 25, Département des Peintures (Paris: Réunion des Musées Nationaux, 1982), 223–30; Gilberte Émile-Mâle and Nicole Delsaux, "Laboratoire et Service de Restauration: collaboration à propos de La Charité d'Andrea del Sarto," *7th Triennial Meeting*, ICOM, September 10–14, 1984, Copenhagen (preprints); Conti, *Storia*, 132–3.

69. Marot, "Recherches," 254; Conti, *Storia*, 140–3.

70. "Oeuvres transposées," in *Raphael dans les collections Françaises*, exh. cat. (Paris: Louvre, 1983), 433–4 and 441–3; Conti, *Storia*, 143.

71. Conti, *Storia*, 143–48; and Gilberte Emile-Mâle, "Jean-Baptiste Pierre Lebrun (1748–1813): Son rôle dans l'histoire de la restauration des tableaux du Louvre," *Mémoires de Paris et Ile-de-France* 8 (1956): 371–417, at p. 406.

72. The French chemist, Guyton de Morveau, who collaborated in 1801 as one of the scientific advisors on the condition and treatment report for Raphael's *Madonna di Foligno*, performed experiments on artists' materials and their permanence. For instance, as early as 1781 he tested various white pigments with H_2S to determine which blacken by air pollution.

73. Schaible, "Gemäldeübertragung."

74. "Rapport a l'Institut National sur la restauration du Tableau de Raphael connu sous le nom de La Vierge de Foligno, par les citoyens Guyton, Vincent, Taunay et Berthollet," in J. D. Passavant, *Raphael D'Urbin et son père Giovanni Santi*, 2 vols. (Paris: Renouard, 1860), vol. 1, 622–9; also in *Mémoires de l'Institut national des sciences et arts – Litterature et beaux-arts*, Tome 5, Paris, An. XII, 444–56.

75. On Berthollet, see Barbara W. Keyser, "Between Science and Craft: The Case of Berthollet and Dyeing," *Annals of Science* 47 (1990): 213–60.

76. Deoclecio Redig de Campos, "La *Madonna di Foligno* di Raffaello: Note sulla sua storia e i suoi restauri," *Miscellanea Bibliothecae Hertzianae: zu Ehren von Leo Bruhns, Franz Graf, Wolff Metternich, Ludwig Schudt*, Römische Forschungen der Bibliotheca Hertziana, Bd. 16 (Munich: Anton Schroll, 1961), 184–92, at 186–8.

77. See "Rapport" in Passavant, *Raphael*, and in Crowe and Cavalcaselle, *Raphael*, vol. 2, 166, n. 1.

78. M.-L. Blumer, "Catalogue des peintures transportées d'Italie en France de 1796 à 1814," *Bulletin de la Société de l'Histoire de l'Art Français*, 2 fasc. (1936), 244–348, at 305–8.

79. Passavant, *Raphael*, vol. 1, 629.

80. Ibid., 627.

81. Ibid., 627. The Brussels restorer Dumesnil explained this widespread approach to fully integrated retouching with great pride, claiming to be such a master that works left his studio looking as if they had just left the studio of the master, with "a freshness preferable to the best varnish"; see Marijnissen, *Dégredation*, 41–2.

82. On the Comte de Caylus, see Rosenberg, *Raphael and France*, 104–7.

83. *Über Restauration alter Oelgemälde*, 1827, Heft I, 49–50; Wagner, *Arbeitsweisen*, 24.

84. G. B. Cavalcaselle, "Sulla conservazione dei monumenti ed oggetti di belle arti e sulla riforma dell'insegnamento accademico," *Rivista dei Comuni Italiani* (Torino, 1863): 36–37. See the essays by Anna Chiara Tommasi, Bernardina Sani, and Valter Curzi in *Giovanni Battista Cavalcaselle: conoscitore e conservatore*, Atti del convegno, "Giovanni Battista Cavalcaselle 1819–1897," Legnago and Verona, Nov. 28–29, 1997, ed. A. C. Tommasi (Venice: Marsilio, 1998), 23–33, 35–51, and 53–63.

85. If there were more space, it would also be appropriate to include the important restoration by Palmaroli in 1827 on Raphael's *Sistine Madonna* in Dresden, which was very closely watched by the local experts and commented on; see 'Staatsmann von hohem Rang, Kunstfreund und selbst ausüben der Künstler,' "Über die Restauration der Madonna des heiligen Sixt von Raffael in der Dresdner Bildergalerie durch Palmaroli," *Berliner Kunstblatt* 2, Heft I, (Jan. 1829): 24–9; Moriz Stübel, "Gemälderestaurationen im 18. Jahrhundert," *Cicerone* 18, no. 4 (1926): 122–35; G. Rudloff-Hille, "Goethe und die Dresdner Galerie," *Beiträge und Berichte der Staatlichen Kunstsammlungen Dresden* (1972–1973): 37–63; Karl Heinz Weber, "Die Sixtinische Madonna: Bemerkungen zu Erhaltungszustand, maltechnischem Aufbau, konservatorischen Maßnahmen," *Maltechnik – Restauro* 4 (1984): 9–28; Wagner, *Arbeitsweisen*, 28.

86. Fausto Lechi, *I quadri delle collezioni Lechi in Brescia* (Florence: L. S. Olschki, 1968).

87. Giuseppe Molteni, "Relazione intorno alle operazioni fatte al quadro di Raffaello rappresentante lo Sposalizio di Maria Vergine," ms. Archivio Vecchio della Soprintendenza ai Beni Artistici e Storici, Milano, II, Parte 54[I], reprinted as Appendix in C. Bertelli, P. L. De Vecchi, A. Gallone, M. Milazzo, *Lo Sposalizio della Vergine di Raffaello* (Treviglio: Grafica Furia, 1983), 76–80.

88. Molteni in Bertelli et al., *Lo Sposalizio*, 79: "la preziosa epiderme de quadro."

89. Ibid., 78–80.

90. Bertelli et al., *Lo Sposalizio*, 7–51.

91. Bruno Passamani and Renata Stradiotti, *Raffaello e Brescia: Echi e presenze*, exh. cat. (Brescia: Grafo, 1986), 15.

92. Giulio Zappa, "Il Nuovo Angelo di Raffaello," *Bollettino d'Arte* 6 (1912): 332–7.

93. Passamani and Stradiotti, *Raffaello e Brescia*, 15.

94. For general discussions of Cavenaghi's work, see Conti, *Storia*, 315–28, and Alessandro Conti, "Vicende e cultura di restauro," in *Storia dell' Arte Italiana* (Milan: Einaudi), 10 vols., vol. 3 (1991), 39–112, at 95–7. For Cavenaghi's cleaning of the portrait in Rome, see E. Modigliani, "Il Ritratto del Perugino della Galleria Borghese," *L'Arte* (1912): 70–1.

95. See Zappa, "Nuovo Angelo," with before and after restoration photographs; also Passamani and Stradiotti, *Raffaello e Brescia*, 31–2.

96. Giulio Zappa's article in the *Bollettino d'Arte* of 1912 is followed by two associated articles, by Vittorio Spinazzola and Corrado Ricci, which also discuss fragments from the San Nicola *pala* and its reconstruction.

97. "Scheda tecnica di restauro," in Passamani and Stradiotti, *Rafaello e Brescia*, 31.

98. Ursula Schädler-Saub, "Theorie und Praxis der Restaurierung in Italien: Zur Entwicklung der Gemälderetusche von der Renaissance bis zur Gegenwart," *Maltechnik-Restauro* 92 (1986): 25–41, at 31.
99. I have discussed this in "The Restoration of the Early Italian 'Primitives' during the 20th Century: Valuing Art and Its Consequences," *Journal of the American Institute for Conservation* 38 (1999): 144–61, at 155. See also Ségolène Bergeon, *Science et patience ou la restauration des peintures* (Paris: Editions de la Réunion des musées nationaux, 1990), 230–1, 254.
100. Hoeniger, *Renovation.*
101. Wagner, *Arbeitsweisen*, 21.
102. He is sometimes called Collins, and also Collinze.
103. McClellan, *Inventing the Louvre*, 26–7. See the long poetic eulogy by M. Le Chevalier de Saint-Germain in honor of Colins's restoration of Correggio's *Io* (copy) in the *Mercure de France* (Avril 1756): vol. 2, 175–7: "C'est par ton art qu' Io respire...."
104. Cecil Gould, *The Paintings of Correggio* (Ithaca: Cornell University Press, 1976), 194–5; Cathleen Sara Hoeniger, "The Reception of Correggio's *Loves of Jupiter*," in *Coming About....A Festschrift for John Shearman*, ed. L. R. Jones and L. C. Matthew (Cambridge: Harvard University Art Museums, 2001), 191–7.
105. Passavant, *Raphael*, vol. 2, 52–3; Cavalcaselle and Crowe, *Raphael*, vol. 1, 294–7.
106. Passavant, *Raphael*, vol. 2, 52–3 and 69.
107. "...the original solution [for the Holy Family grouping, as seen in the *Canigiani Madonna,*] was a simple pyramid with the base formed by the two kneeling women holding the children between them, and the standing figure of St. Joseph as the apex. The *Canigiani Madonna* is a masterpiece of formal articulation, already far exceeding the capacities of a Perugino." Heinrich Wölfflin, *Die klassische Kunst* of 1899; trans. P. and L. Murray, *Classic Art: An Introduction to the Italian Renaissance* (1952; reprint, London: Phaidon, 1964), 85. Also Conti, *Storia*, 140.
108. Von Sonnenburg, *Raphael*, 40. See also Hubertus von Sonnenburg, in *The Princeton Raphael Symposium: Science in the Service of Art History*, ed. John Shearman and Marcia B. Hall (Princeton: Princeton University Press, 1990), 67.
109. Von Sonnenburg, *Raphael*, 39–41.
110. Ibid., 39–41.
111. See also Martin Kemp, "Looking at Leonardo's Last Supper," in *Appearance, Opinion, Change: Evaluating the Look of Paintings* (London: United Kingdom Institute for Conservation, 1990), 14–21; and Hoeniger in Jones and Matthew, *Coming About* (2001), where the importance of reception theory is discussed.
112. The most recent conservation campaign on the *Loggia of Psyche* in the Villa Farnesina in Rome (completed 1997) yields rich documentation of how present-day specialists approach a complexly layered physical structure, rich with cultural value and literary history.

Selected Bibliography

Ames-Lewis, Francis. *The Draftsman Raphael.* New Haven and London: Yale University Press, 1986.

Bambach, Carmen C. *Drawing and Painting in the Italian Renaissance Workshop, Theory and Practice, 1300–1600.* New York: Cambridge University Press, 1999.

Beck, James, ed. *Raphael before Rome.* Studies in the History of Art 17. Washington, DC: National Gallery of Art, 1986.

Bellori, Giovan Pietro. *Descrizzione delle imagini dipinte da Rafaelle d'Urbino nelle camere del Palazzo Apostolico Vaticano.* Rome: Giacomo Komarek, 1695.

Bonner, Mitchell. *Rome in the High Renaissance. The Age of Leo X.* Norman: University of Oklahoma Press, 1973.

Brown, David Alan. "Raphael, Leonardo, and Perugino: Fame and Fortune in Florence." In *Leonardo, Michelangelo, and Raphael in Renaissance Florence from 1500 to 1508.* Edited by Serafina Hager. Washington, DC: Georgetown University Press, 1992, 29–53.

Bruschi, Arnaldo. *Bramante architetto.* Bari: Laterza. 1969. English edition, London: Thames and Hudson, 1977.

Cecchi, Alessandro. "Agnolo e Maddalena Doni committenti di Raffaello." In *Studi su Raffaello.* Edited by Micaela Sambucco Hamoud and Maria Letizia Strocchi. 2 vols. Urbino: Quattro Venti, 1987, 2:429–39.

Clayton, Martin. *Raphael and His Circle: Drawings from Windsor Castle.* Exh. cat. London: The Queen's Gallery, 1999.

Cooper, Donal. "Raphael's Altar-Pieces in S. Francesco al Prato, Perugia: Patronage, Setting and Function." *Burlington Magazine* 143 (2001): 554–61.

Crowe, J. A., and G. B. Cavacaselle. *Raphael: His Life and Works.* London: John Murray, 1882.

Davidson, Bernice F. *Raphael's Bible: A Study of the Vatican Loggie.* University Park, PA: College Art Association, 1985.

Delaborde, Henri. *Marc-Antoine Raimondi:…étude historique et critique suivie d'un catalogue raisonnè des oeuvres du maitre.* Paris: Librarie de l'Art, 1887.

Del Serra, Alfio, et al. *Raffaello e il Ritratto di papa Leone X.* Milan: Silvana, 1996.

Dussler, Luitpold. *Raphael: A Critical Catalogue of his Pictures, Wall-Paintings, and Tapestries.* Translated by Sebastian Cruft. London: Phaidon, 1971 (German original, 1966).

Ettlinger, L. D. "Raphael's Early Patrons." In *Raphael before Rome.* Edited by James Beck. Studies in the History of Art 17. Washington, DC: National Gallery of Art, 1986.

Fehl, Philipp P. "Raphael as a Historian: Poetry and Historical Accuracy in the Sala di Costantino." *Artibus et Historiae* 14, no. 28 (1993): 9–76.

Ferino Pagden, Sylvia. "Iconographic and Artistic Achievements: The Genesis of Three Works by Raphael." In *Raffaello a Roma: Il convegno del 1983*. Rome: Edizioni dell'Elefante, 1986.

Ferino Pagden, Sylvia. "The Early Raphael and his Contemporaries." In *Raphael before Rome*. Edited by James Beck. Studies in the History of Art, 17. Washington, DC: National Gallery of Art, 1986.

Ferino Pagden, Sylvia, and M. Antonietta Zancan. *Raffaello Catalogo Completo*. Florence: Cantini Editore, 1989.

Fermor, Sharon. *The Raphael Tapestry Cartoons: Narrative, Decoration, Design*. London: Victoria and Albert Museum, 1996.

Fischel, Oscar. *Raphaels Zeichnungen*. 8 vols. Berlin, 1913–1941. Vol. 9, edited by Konrad Oberhuber, 1979.

Fischel, Oscar. *Raphael*. Translated by Bernard Rackham. 2 vols. London: Paul, 1948.

Freedberg, S. J. *Painting in Italy 1500–1600* (1971). Pelican History of Art. Rev. ed. Harmondsworth: Penguin Books, 1975.

Freedberg, Sydney J. *Painting of the High Renaissance in Rome and Florence*. 2 vols. Cambridge: Harvard University Press, 1961.

Frommel, Christoph L. *Der Römische Palastbau*. 3 vols. Tübingen: Wasmuth, 1973.

Frommel, Christoph L., Stefano Ray, and Manfredo Tafuri, eds. *Raffaello architetto*. Milan: Electa, 1984.

Frommel, Christoph L., and Matthias Winner, eds. *Raffaello a Roma: Il convegno del 1983*. Rome: Edizione dell'Elefante, 1986.

Gardner von Teuffel, Christa. "Raffaels römische Altarbilder: Aufstellung und Bestimmung." *Zeitschrift für Kunstgeschichte* 50 (1987): 1–45.

Gere, J. A. *Drawings by Raphael and His Circle*. Exh. cat. New York: Pierpoint Morgan Library, 1987.

Gere, J. A., and Nicholas Turner. *Drawings by Raphael*. London: British Museum, 1983.

Gnoli, Umberto. "Raffaello e la 'Incoronazione' di Monteluce." *Bollettino d'Arte* (1917): 133–54.

Goldstein, Carl. *Teaching Art: Academies and Schools from Vasari to Albers*. New York: Cambridge University Press, 1996.

Golzio, Vincenzo. *Raffaello nei documenti nelli testimonianze dei contemporanei e nella letteratura del suo secolo*. Vatican City: Pontificia Insigne Accademia Artistica dei Virtuosi al Pantheon, 1936; 2d ed., 1971.

Gombrich, Ernst. "Raphael's Stanza della Segnatura and the Nature of Its Symbolism." In *Symbolic Images: Studies in the Art of the Renaissance*. London: Phaidon, 1972, 85–101.

Gould, Cecil. "Raphael versus Giulio Romano: The Swing Back." *Burlington Magazine* 124 (1982): 479–86.

Gregori, Mina, ed. *Raffaello a Firenze. Dipinti e disegni delle collezioni fiorentine*. Florence: Electa, 1984.

Günther, Hubertus. "Urban Planning in Rome under the Medici Popes." In *The Renaissance from Brunelleschi to Michelangelo. The Representation of Architecture*. Edited by Henry A. Millon and Vittorio Magnago Lampugnani. Milan: Bompiani, 1994, 545–49.

Hall, Marcia B. *After Raphael: Painting in Central Italy in the Sixteenth Century*. New York: Cambridge University Press, 1999.

Hall, Marcia B., ed. *Raphael's School of Athens*. Masterpieces of Western Painting. New York: Cambridge University Press, 1997.

Hartt, Frederick. "Raphael and Giulio Romano." *Art Bulletin* 26 (1944): 67–94.

Henry, Tom. "Raphael's Altar-Piece Patrons in Città di Castello." *Burlington Magazine* 144 (2002): 268–78.

Indagini per un dipinto: La Santa Cecilia di Raffaello. Bologna: Edizioni ALFA, 1983.

Joannides, Paul. *The Drawings of Raphael, with a Complete Catalogue.* Oxford: Phaidon, 1983.

Joannides, Paul. "Raphael and Giovanni Santi." In *Studi su Raffaello.* Edited by Micaela Sambucco Hamoud and Maria Letizia Strocchi. 2 vols. Urbino: Quattro Venti, 1987, 55–61.

Jones, Roger, and Nicholas Penny. *Raphael.* New Haven: Yale University Press, 1983.

Joost-Gaugier, Christiane L. *Raphael's Stanza della Segnatura: Meaning and Invention.* New York: Cambridge University Press, 2002.

Klein, Robert, and Henri Zerner, eds. *Italian Art 1500–1600.* Evanston: Il: Northwestern University Press, 1966.

Knab, Eckhart, Erwin Mitsch, and Konrad Oberhuber, with the collaboration of Sylvia Ferino Pagden. *Raphael, die Zeichnungen.* Stuttgart: Urachaus, 1983.

Landau, David, and Peter Parshall. *The Renaissance Print 1470–1550.* New Haven: Yale University Press, 1994.

Lanzi, Luigi. *History of Painting in Italy.* Translated by Thomas Roscoe. London: G. Ball, 1847.

L'Estasi di Santa Cecilia di Raffaello da Urbino nella Pinacoteca Nazionale di Bologna. Exh. cat. Bologna: Edizioni ALFA, 1983.

Locher, Hubert. *Rafael und das Altarbild der Renaissance: Die "Pala Baglioni" als Kunstwerk in sakralen Kontext.* Berlin: Akademie Verlag, 1994.

Luchs, Alison. "A Note on Raphael's Perugian Patrons." *Burlington Magazine* 125 (1983): 29–31.

Mancini, Francesco Federico. *Raffaello in Umbria: Cronologia e committenza, nuova studi e documenti.* Perugia: Volumnia Editrice, 1987.

Mercati, Enrico. *Andrea Baroni e gli altri committenti Tifernati di Raffaello, con documenti inediti.* Città di Castello: Petruzzi Editore, 1994.

Meyer zur Capellan, Jürg. *Raphael in Florence.* London: Azimuth Editions, 1996.

Meyer zur Capellan, Jürg. *Raphael, a Critical Catalogue of His Paintings, Vol. 1: The Beginnings in Umbria and Florence, ca. 1500–1508.* Landshut: Arcos, 2001.

Morello, Giovanni. *Raffaello e la Roma dei Papa.* Exh. cat., Biblioteca Apostolica Vaticana. Rome: Fratelli Palombi, 1986.

Nagel, Alexander. *Michelangelo and the Reform of Art.* New York: Cambridge University Press, 2000.

Nesselrath, Arnold. "Lorenzo Lotto in the Stanza della Segnatura." *Burlington Magazine* 142 (1999): 4–12.

Oberhuber, Konrad. *Illustrated Bartsch.* Vols. 26–27. New York: Abaris, 1978.

Oberhuber, Konrad. "The Colonna Altarpiece in the Metropolitan Museum and the Problem of the Early Style of Raphael." *Metropolitan Museum Journal* 12 (1977): 55–92.

Oberhuber, Konrad. *Raphael: The Paintings.* Munich: Prestel Verlag, 1999.

Oberhuber, Konrad, and Achim Gnann. *Roma e lo stile classico di Raffaello.* Exh. cat., Palazzo Te, Mantua, and Graphische Sammlung, Vienna, 1999.

Onians, John. "On How to Listen to High Renaissance Art." *Art History* 7 (1984): 411–37.

Partner, Peter. *Renaissance Rome 1500–1559.* Berkeley: University of California Press, 1979.

Partridge, Loren, and Randolph Starn. *A Renaissance Likeness: Art and Culture in Raphael's Julius II.* Berkeley and Los Angeles: University of California Press, 1980.

Passavant, Johann David. *Raphael d'Urbin et son père, Giovanni Santi.* Paris: Renouard, 1860. Abridged English version of German (1839), New York: Macmillan, 1872.

Pastor, Ludwig Freiherr von. *History of the Popes. From the Close of the Middle Ages.* 5th ed. London: Kegan Paul, 1923–53.

Perini, Giovanna. "Una certa idea di Raffaello nel Seicento." In *L'idea del Bello, Viaggio per Roma nel Seicento con Giovan Pietro Bellori*. Edited by E. Borea and C. Gasparri. Rome: Edizioni de Luca, 2000, vol. I, 153–161.

Pope-Hennessy, John. *Raphael*. The Wrightsman Lectures. London: Phaidon, 1970.

Pouncey, Philip, and J. A. Gere. *Italian Drawings in the Department of Prints and Drawings in the British Museum: Raphael and His Circle*. London: Trustees of the British Museum, London, 1962.

Quatremère de Quincy. *Histoire de la vie et des ouvrages de Raphael*. Paris: Le Clere et cie, 1833.

Quednau, Rolf. "Aspects of Raphael's 'ultima maniera' in the light of the Sala di Costantino." In *Raffaello a Roma. Il convegno del 1983*, 245–57. Rome: Edizioni dell'Elefante, 1986.

Raffaello a Pitti: 'La Madonna del baldacchino.' Exh. cat., Florence, Palazzo Pitti. Florence: Centro Di, 1991.

Raffaello: Grazia e bellezza. Exh. cat., Paris, Musée National du Luxembourg. Milan: Skira, 2001.

Raffaello in Vaticano. Exh. cat. Milan: Electa, 1984.

Raffaello: l'opera, le fonti, la fortuna. 2 vols. Novara: Istituto Geografico De Agostini, 1968.

Raphael Invenit. Stampe da Raffaello nelle collezioni dell'Istituto Nazionale per la Grafica. Exh. cat. Essays by Grazia Bernini Pezzini, Stefania Massari, Simonetta Prosperi Valenti Rodinò. Rome: Edizioni Quasar, 1985.

Redig de Campos, Deoclecio. *Raffaello nelle Stanze*. Translated by John Guthrie. Milan: Martello, 1973 in reduced format.

Rodocanachi, Emmanuel. *Histoire de Rome. Le pontificat de Jules II, 1503–1513*. Paris: Hachette: 1928.

Rodocanachi, Emmanuel. *Histoire de Rome. Le pontificat de Leon X, 1513–1521*. Paris: Hachette, 1931.

Roscoe, William. *The Life and Pontificate of Leo the Tenth*. London: H. G. Bohn, 1846.

Rosenberg, Martin. *Raphael and France: The Artist as Paradigm and Symbol*. University Park: Pennsylvannia State University Press, 1995.

Rowland, Ingrid D. *The Culture of the High Renaissance*. New York: Cambridge University Press, 1998.

Rowland, Ingrid. "Render unto Caesar the Things Which Are Caesar's: Humanism and the Arts in the Patronage of Agostino Chigi." *Renaissance Quarterly* 39 (1986): 673–730.

Rubin, Patricia Lee. *Giorgio Vasari: Art and History*. New Haven: Yale University Press, 1995, esp. chapter on Raphael.

Santi, Giovanni. *La Vita e le Gesta di Federico di Montefeltro, Duca D'Urbino*. Edited by L. M. Tocci. 2 vols. Città del Vaticano: Biblioteca Apostolica Vaticana, 1985.

Scarpellini, Pietro. *Pietro Perugino*. Milan: Electa, 1984.

Shearman, John. "The Chigi Chapel in S. Maria in Popolo." *Journal of the Warburg and Courtauld Institutes* 21 (1961): 129–60.

Shearman, John. "Raphael's Unexecuted Projects for the Stanze." In *Walter Friedlaender zum 90. Geburtstag*. Berlin: De Gruyter, 1965, 158–80.

Shearman, John. "Raphael . . . 'Fa il Bramante'." In *Studies in Renaissance and Baroque Art presented to Anthony Blunt*. London: Phaidon, 1967, 12–17.

Shearman, John. "Raphael as Architect." *Journal of the Royal Society of Arts* 116 (1968): 388–409.

Shearman, John. "Raphael at the Court of Urbino." *Burlington Magazine* 112 (1970): 72–8.

Shearman, John. "The Vatican Stanze: Functions and decorations." *Proceedings of the British Academy* 57 (1971): 369–424.

Shearman, John. *Raphael's Cartoons in the Collection of Her Majesty the Queen and the Tapestries for the Sistine Chapel*. London: Phaidon, 1972.

Shearman, John. "Raphael, Rome, and the Codex Escurialensis." *Master Drawings* 15 (1977): 107–46.

Shearman, John. "Raffaello e la bottega." In *Raffaello in Vaticano.* Exh. cat. Milan: Electa, 1984, , 258–63.

Shearman, John. "The Expulsion of Heliodorus." In *Raffaello a Roma. Il convegno del 1983.* Rome: Edizioni dell'Elefante, 1986, 75–87.

Shearman, John. *Only Connect...Art and the Spectator in the Italian Renaissance.* A. W. Mellon Lectures in the Fine Arts, 1988 (National Gallery of Art, Washington). Princeton: Princeton University Press, 1992.

Shearman, John. "On Raphael's Chronology, 1503–08." In *Ars Naturam Adiuvans: Festschrift für Mattias Winner.* Mainz: von Zebern, 1996, 201–7.

Shearman, John. *Raphael in Early Modern Sources (1483–1602),* ed. Julian Kliemann, 2 vols. New Haven: Yale University Press [in association with the Biblioteca Hertziana, Max-Planck-Institut für Kunstgeschichte], 2003.

Shearman, John, and Marcia B. Hall, eds. *The Princeton Raphael Symposium: Science in the Service of Art History.* Princeton: Princeton University Press, 1990.

Stinger, Charles L. *The Renaissance in Rome.* Bloomington and Indianapolis: Indiana University Press, 1998.

Tafuri, Manfredo. "'Roma instaurata': Strategie urbane e politiche pontificie nella Roma del primo 500." In *Raffaello architetto.* Edited by Christoph L. Frommel et al. Milan: Electa, 1984, 59–106.

Talvacchia, Bette. *Taking Positions: Giulio Romano's "I modi" and Sexual Representation in Renaissance Prints.* Princeton: Princeton University Press, 1999.

Thuillier, Jacques. "Raphael et la France: présence d'un peintre." In *Raphaël et l'art français.* Edited by J. P. Cuzin. Exh. cat. Paris: Galeries Nationals du Grand Palais, 1983, 11–35.

Traeger, Jörg. *Renaissance und Religion: Die Kunst des Glaubens im Zeitalter Raphaels.* Munich: C. H. Beck, 1997.

Vasari, Giorgio. *Le vite de' più eccellenti pittori, scultori, ed architettori.* Edited by Gaetano Milanesi. 9 Vols. Vol. 4. Florence: Sansoni, 1906.

Vasari, Giorgio. *Le vite de' più eccellenti pittori, scultori ed architettori nelle redazioni del 1550 e 1568.* Edited by Rosanna Bettarini and Paola Barocchi. 6 vols. Florence: Sansoni; Studio per Edizioni Scelte, 1966–87.

Vasari, Giorgio. *The Lives of the Painters, Sculptors and Architects.* Translated by Gaston du C. de Vere. 10 vols. London: Philip Lee Warren, 1912–14.

Wölfflin, Heinrich. *Classic Art.* Translated by Linda Murray and Peter Murray. London: Phaidon, 1948.

Index